"Chumney...often comes to mind for her willingness and readiness to fight for causes she believes in. ..however, [others paint]..a deeper, fuller portrait of the former legislator and city councilwoman [and mayoral candidate]: They say she is smart, articulate, and community-oriented."

—Tri-State Defender, Wiley Henry, "Compassionate politics & service," Sept. 3, 2009

Chumney is "a successful attorney," "well-prepared," an "effective legislator," with a "wealth of ideas," and "would potentially be a strong mayor."

—Commercial Appeal editorial, Sept. 14, 2007

Carol Chumney is a "results-driven politician," with "personal and professional ethic[s]," "personally capable of swimming with all manner of sharks."

—Daily News, Andy Meek, "Can Carol Chumney Out-Shark 'King Willie' in Mayoral Race?" May 4, 2007.

Chumney's proposal to repeal a twelve year pension for elected and appointed city officials "demonstrates a degree of political courage that is in short supply in local government."

—Commercial Appeal editorial, April 18, 2004.

"Few state legislators are as effective in their service to all Tennesseans as Rep. Carol Chumney...Chumney's name will long be associated with a host of child and family issues throughout the state....She was chief architect of the legislation that dramatically changed Tennessee's child care laws...On a wide range of issues from domestic violence to women's health, Chumney has shown leadership and courage. She's been a valuable asset to her party in the legislature, but she's also had a bipartisan ability to bridge the gaps on important issues... Throughout her tenure in the legislature, lawmakers have looked to Chumney for leadership and for inspiration on children's issues.

—Tennessean editorial, "A champion for children," Oct. 28, 2003.

"Chumney was one of the most accomplished lawmakers in the Shelby County delegation during her 13-year tenure. She has been the chief advocate on Capitol Hill of meaningful reform of the state's corrupt, and sometimes deadly, system of tax-subsidized child care. She also has developed valuable expertise in such areas as early childhood education, metropolitan development and 'smart growth,' and public school funding and governance."

–Commercial Appeal editorial, Oct. 24, 2003.

"Representative Carol Chumney, chairwoman of the house family-affairs committee, introduced 10 separate [day care] reform bills…the pressure for change at last overwhelmed the religious, financial, and political opposition… Chumney, happy with her victory, is nevertheless cautious about the future."

–TIME Magazine, Andrew Goldstein, "It took three dead babies," July 3, 2000.

"An advocate of women's issues in particular, [Chumney]… successfully sponsored a variety of legislation – ranging from the famous 'potty parity' bill that increased the number of rest rooms for women in public arenas to a bill mandating a 48-hour stay in hospitals for new mothers."

–Memphis Flyer, Jackson Baker, "Defender of the City," July 17, 1997

"Chumney is [o]ne of the legislature's bright lights"…who "launched the drive for 'total quality management' now used by the state government; helped the Church Health Center in Midtown expand volunteer health care; was instrumental in state funding of Memphis Zoo improvements; gained funding for community revitalization groups; sponsored Tennessee's first stalking law, and led creation of a registration and monitoring program for sex offenders."

–Commercial Appeal editorial, Nov. 3, 1994

"the leading crusader for women's issues in the Tennessee General Assembly."

–Johnson City Press, Robert Houk,
"Lawmaker continues her crusade for women," Jan. 19, 1994

The ARENA

One Woman's Story

To: President Jimmy & First Lady Rosalynn Carter

Thank you for fighting for the truth!

Carol Chumney

CAROL J. CHUMNEY

LADY
JUSTICE PUBLISHING
Memphis, TN

Published in the United States by
Lady Justice Publishing, Memphis, TN.
www.carolchumney.com

Printed in the United States of America.

ISBN: 978-1-7353428-0-1 (paperback)
ISBN 978-1-7353428-2-5 (hardback)
ISBN: 978-1-7353428-1-8 (ebook)

Library of Congress Control Number: 2021914961

This work depicts actual events in the life of the author as truthfully as recollection permits and/or can be verified by research. The author and publisher take no responsibility for any errors or omissions. No liability is assumed for damages that may result from the use of information contained within. All persons within are actual individuals; there are no composite characters. The author has striven to be fair and is grateful for everything she has learned from all experiences set forth herein.

Cover Photo: Jack Kenner

Cover and Interior Design: Wordzworth

Thanks to Bill Thompson for professional content editing
recommendations and Rob Bignell for initial copy editing.
A special thanks to my sister, Mary Chumney Strench,
for generously donating her time for additional
and invaluable content and copy editing!

"It is not the critic who counts; not the man who points out how the strong man stumbles, or where the doer of deeds could have done them better. The credit belongs to the man who is actually in the arena, whose face is marred by dust and sweat and blood; who strives valiantly; who errs, who comes short again and again, because there is no effort without error and shortcoming; but who does actually strive to do the deeds; who knows great enthusiasms, the great devotions; who spends himself in a worthy cause; who at the best knows in the end the triumph of high achievement, and who at the worst, if he fails, at least fails while daring greatly, so that his place shall never be with those cold and timid souls who neither know victory nor defeat."

– THEODORE ROOSEVELT, CITIZEN IN THE REPUBLIC SPEECH, 4/23/1910.

Official City Council Photo of Carol Chumney 2003 by Keith Renard/Skipworth Photography

Contents

Acknowledgements   xi

Foreword   xiii

Part 1   **Dreams of Public Service**   **1**

Section 1   The Beginning of My Dream   2

Section 2   A Dream Come True   11

Part 2   **Early Years at the State House**   **23**

Section 3   Dubbed the "Woman with Balls"   24

Section 4   The Year of the Woman   33

Section 5   Standing Up Against Sexual Harassment   44

Section 6   Leading Crusader for Women   52

Section 7   Why Women's Suffrage Matters   62

Section 8   Breaking the Same Old *and* New Ground   76

Section 9   Defender of the City   90

Part 3   **Daycare Reform**   **99**

Section 10   The Only Woman Chair   100

Section 11   The Babies Died   108

Section 12   "I'm Sticking with My Bill"   118

Section 13   More Daycare Reform Battles   133

Section 14   The Death of Tax Reform   139

Part 4   **First Effort at Higher Office**   **145**

Section 15   Kicking off Race for County Mayor   146

Section 16   Why Does She Stay In?   152

Section 17   Focused and Deliberate   158

Section 18   Back to the State House   170

Part 5   **Memphis City Council**   **177**

Section 19   Taking Reform to City Hall   178

Section 20   "You're Just Stupid"   189

Section 21   Iraqi Delegation Banned from City Hall   208

Section 22   A Reformer   213

Section 23   Veritable Tribune of the People   222

Section 24   You're Looking Good Carol!   229

Section 25   The Incredible, Unshrinking Violet   236

Section 26   A Lightening Rod   248

Part 6   **Memphis Mayor's Race I**   **259**

Section 27   The City   260

Section 28   The Sex-Plot Thickens   278

Section 29   The People's Mayor   293

Section 30   It's a Man's World   305

Part 7   **Memphis Mayor's Race II**   **323**

Section 31   Cracks in the Glass Ceiling   324

Section 32   Winds of Change   339

Section 33   Flying Saucers?   349

Section 34   What Message for Young Girls?   365

Section 35   Will There Ever Be a Wonder Woman?   381

Part 8   **Election Security and Other Reform Efforts**   **389**

Section 36   It Will Take a Miracle   390

Section 37   On the Mountaintop   406

Section 38   Truths and Injustices   416

Section 39   Broken Promises   425

Section 40   Musical Chairs 1   433

Section 41   Musical Chairs 2   440

Section 42   Sexism in the City   449

Section 43   Musical Chairs 3   462

Section 44   Working to Save Democracy   469

Section 45   What's Ahead   477

Notes   **483**

About the Author   **573**

Acknowledgements

*A special thanks to Almighty God who has allowed
me to pursue my dreams. Also, to so many who have
helped me with my public service over the years,
including my parents Jim and Sara Chumney,
and sisters Mary Chumney Strench and Gail Elizabeth Stephens.*

Recognition by University of Memphis of James and Sara Chumney for having
three daughters who were Presidential Scholars- 1991- from left Univ. of Memphis
President Thomas G. Carpenter, Gail Chumney, Sara Chumney, Dr. James Chumney, Jr.
and Carol Chumney (sister Mary Chumney out of town) ©University of Memphis

Photo of Carol's parents, Jim and Sara Chumney

Photo of Carol with her mother, Sara, and sister, Mary, at her campaign headquarters for the victory celebration of her first election to the state house in 1990

Foreword

To Dare Greatly

This book is about my experiences in the political arena as a female politician in Memphis, Tennessee. Although a successful attorney in private practice, I devoted years of my life to public service. I won some elections, and I lost some. I dared greatly; reached for the stars with efforts to serve in higher office; and tried to go where no woman had gone before. Following my real passion and calling for public service required the sacrifice of money, family, and other opportunities.

What compelled me to public service? My desire to be an advocate for change, a voice for people, and to speak truth to power. A dream about a united city and nation for the betterment of all. A dream where a qualified woman who works hard has an equal opportunity to lead at the highest levels. A dream to use my God-given abilities to serve the people and lead.

On my law office wall is a poster with a quote about winning by the famous football coach Vince Lombardi. As he said, you have to give it your all, and "it's not whether you get knocked down, but whether you get back up." I have done both following my dream.

Eventually, I realized that two things had to happen for the doors to open to higher office for a woman here: (1) election reform; and (2) a cultural shift away from gender bias. So, I spent years submitting open records requests to the local election commission with other like-minded friends. We submitted a report to the U.S. Congress in 2017. Then we filed an election integrity civil rights lawsuit, taking the fight all the way to the U.S. Supreme Court. And I wrote this book, documented with thousands of endnotes, to expose gender bias and the glass ceiling, the need for reform, and to tell my story.

The book is divided into parts about my service as a Tennessee state legislator, nationally recognized child care reform, work as a Memphis city councilwoman, races for county and Memphis mayor, and election reform efforts. Although I served as a Democratic state legislator, the city council was a nonpartisan position, as well as the Memphis mayoral elections. I have included a great deal about my record, primarily to show my qualifications for the higher offices sought and denied.

Since I began writing this book in 2013, gains have been made by many women who are now big-city U.S. mayors, governors, and leaders of other countries. And, in 2020, Kamala Harris was elected the first female vice-president of the United States. I am glad. But Harris's position was afforded by the Biden selection *after* she lost the presidential nomination. All the women who ran for president in 2020 lost. Women in the current U.S. Congress still only comprise about 25% of the membership.[1] And, we've still never had a woman Mayor of Memphis, a female governor of Tennessee, or a woman President of the USA. So, while one barrier has been broken, many more remain.

With the extraordinarily close presidential elections in 2016 and 2020, candidates of both major parties and their supporters have raised concerns about election integrity. As an attorney, I have a responsibility to uphold the administration of justice. Justice requires the right to vote and the right to have your vote counted accurately. This book describes the election abuses found and the reforms sought by me and others to protect our democratic form of government.

Moreover, I wouldn't be able to vote today if women and men 100 years ago had not secured the just passage of the *19th Amendment* to the *U.S. Constitution*. But justice in the exercise of the vote requires a level playing field for women candidates.

I hope that my story as one woman in the arena will aid the cause for true election reform to preserve our democracy and bring more awareness necessary to open more doors for women everywhere.

PART ONE

Dreams of Public Service

1

———

The Beginning of My Dream

1

Even as a junior high school student, politics fascinated me. According to my mother, I was justice-minded even as a small child. My parents always encouraged me to follow my dreams, unequivocally saying that I could succeed as long as I worked hard and played by the rules. My gender was never mentioned by them as an obstacle for seeking political office.

My parents taught me values. Love of country is one. My dad, a dark-haired, handsome officer, served in the Air Force. I was born in San Antonio on Lackland Air Force Base.

After four years of military service and an M.A. degree in history earned in Trinity University's evening school during that period, my father left the service to pursue a Ph.D. in American history as a graduate student at Rice University. Three years later after he graduated, we moved to Lafayette, Louisiana, where he began his college teaching career at the University of Southwestern Louisiana and experienced the Arcadian culture for one year.

Months after my fourth birthday, we all moved to Memphis near my grandparents. It was a happy time. As a blonde-haired, blue-eyed, chubby, quiet child, I was very close to my mother. I played outside with my older sister, Mary, and my friend who lived next door, Jim, at our small rental home in Midtown Memphis near the historic Pink Palace museum. Our favorite television shows were *The Lone Ranger* and *Batman*. We danced around the room in glee when they aired.

My parents saved up. When I was five, they bought a modest red-brick home in a middle-class East Memphis area. The move exposed me to a melting pot neighborhood with a large Catholic and Jewish population. My sister and I walked to the local Catholic church for the city's summer camp program.

As a teenager, I babysat for Jewish families and even rabbis with strict household rules based upon their religion.

My parents raised us in the Methodist, and then later Episcopal, church. Christian faith was reinforced by my maternal grandmother, Helen Culbreath Hamer, who came to Memphis from her humble family farm home in rural Tennessee and secured a government job with the Corp of Engineers. Whenever her grandchildren spent the night, she quoted Bible verses frequently, said prayers, and always washed our feet with the humility of Jesus before tucking us in bed.

Several years before Dr. King was killed in Memphis, my mother served as a Methodist church volunteer with a juvenile delinquency program at the Bethlehem Center near Lemoyne Gardens' housing units. She made home visits to encourage the mothers and invited them to the counseling sessions held at the Center and bus trips to visit their child away at detention school. Knowledge of people living in poverty communities who needed help was thus provided to me as a preschooler as I listened to my mother's conversations. The memory still remains about visiting the Center one day with my mother and seeing the South Memphis neighborhood.

My family was of moderate means. My father was a college history professor at the University of Memphis, and my mother a full-time homemaker. As the middle child, I shared a room with my sister Mary, three years older. Mary, brown-haired, green eyes, very bright and independent, bumped heads with my mom regularly in typical teenage fashion. She ruled the roost in our room but also was a close confidant.

My sister, Gail (seven years younger), was very petite, blonde-haired and blue-eyed, and had her own room. We were also close. While having her own room was a plus, there were drawbacks. The house had no central air and my parents often only ran the window units at night to keep the electric bill down. So, Gail being further away from the units was often hot in the steamy Memphis summer months.

Court-ordered busing began during my elementary school years. I recall the turmoil even as a young child attending the public Shady Grove Elementary. The push for change was more intense in Memphis after the death of Dr. Martin Luther King Jr. When desegregation began, my mother served as my school's PTA president. She set an example of unity by starting the meetings with the Pledge of Allegiance. Shady Grove was nearly all white, with only a few African American students and teachers.

One day many of the children on the school playground sang chants in protest against busing and then ran across the street. I was one of the few students who stayed on the playground. Perhaps because of my parents' positive example, at that age, I knew racism was wrong. Even as a sign of the times, the walkout was quite a controversial event for children of such young ages.

After grade school, my parents, although with limited income, gave me the choice of attending St. Mary's Episcopal School, an elite private school for girls, or the academically well-respected public White Station Junior High and High School. The fact that I had a choice when many other parents simply yanked their kids out of the public schools after court-ordered busing was a tribute to my parents' character. Although early on I was identified as a "gifted child" in elementary school, and St. Mary's was a top school, it was a no-brainer to me—I wanted to attend the public school that my older sister, Mary, attended. Plus, I had heard how much homework the St. Mary's students were assigned and wanted time for extracurricular activities like basketball—and politics!

My junior high was vastly different from grade school. Many African American students rode buses from economically disadvantaged neighborhoods. Many white students fled the public schools as new private schools formed in response to the judicial ruling to desegregate the schools, fueled by the fears of parents who did not want their children to ride the bus to other unfamiliar neighborhoods. After the exodus of so many white students, our school was still one of the few in the city that remained fairly balanced, with about 60% white and 40% black students. The exposure to students from other parts of the city of all different economic backgrounds, religions, and races, helped prepare me for public service.

Although I lost the student government election for vice president in eighth grade, neither the elected president nor the vice president returned to school in the fall. So, even though we each lost our elections, Kent Roberson, an African American student, was sworn in as the junior high student government president, along with myself as vice president.

Our principal was Florence Leffler, who was later elected to the Memphis City Council in 1987. Who would think at the time that she and I both would each one day hold the position of Memphis city councilwoman, albeit in different years? She asked me to pen our Student Government Association (SGA) Constitution. I eagerly drafted my first legal document.

Kent and I became friends. It was a real sign of the changing times that in 1976 we worked together as teenagers at my family's home on SGA business one day. A few years earlier, we probably wouldn't even have attended the same school.

At White Station High School, I also became involved in student government. Although I ran, I was not elected as an officer. The elections were more like talent contests with skits and performances. My pitch was playing a song on the piano and handing out construction paper pianos bearing my name. Maybe I would have done better with a platform.

At least the students did not laugh at me like another girl who gave a speech beginning with Dr. King's famous words, "I have a dream." Perhaps it was because she was white and speaking to a diverse student body. But Dr. King's dream was to make justice a reality for all of God's children. Later, when my name wasn't called as a winner, I tried not to cry. At home, I did.

Yet, I still managed to find a way to learn about the political process. Pam Gaia, a petite Democratic state legislator, was a guest speaker to Astra, a girls' service club, during my high school senior year. Perhaps she saw something in me as the president of the club since she gave me her pass to attend the 1978 mid-term National Democratic Convention taking place in Memphis.

Gaia inspired me as one of the few female elected officials in Memphis. I was thrilled to attend the convention also as a reporter for the White Station High School *Scroll* newspaper. Jimmy Carter was the president. Although I was generally shy, when it came to politics it was a whole different story. At the convention by myself, I managed to interview delegates, secure a press pass from a veteran reporter, and get a photo with the president's son, Chip Carter. I even chatted with a Pulitzer prize-winning Associated Press reporter about politics in the press room while waiting for my mom to pick me up.

When I asked Chip Carter if he would run for President of the United States one day, he said, "No." When I asked him what profession he was interested in, he flashed that wide trademark Carter smile and wryly said, "Peanuts."

Another bemused reporter gave me a tip on how to gain entrance to the 1980 Democratic Convention as a reporter by getting a small magazine or publication to pay my way for a convention story. He added, "You're not a true journalist at the convention unless someone pays your way."

My love of public service, justice, and people brought out the very best in me. As editor-in-chief of the high school student newspaper, I wrote a full report on the convention. My news report to the *Scroll* ended by bidding the A.P. reporters goodbye, and wondering if I would meet them again when I got into the White House? I added that only the future knew whether it would be as a tourist, news reporter, or maybe even president!

Perhaps my interest in politics came from watching my mother debate my paternal grandfather regularly when we visited him and my grandmother, Mary Rose Chumney, at their home in Memphis. My grandfather, a retired postal employee, was a huge Richard Nixon fan, and my mother is more moderate politically. She married my dad at nineteen and therefore never finished college, which was typical of women of that generation.

She also was a beauty queen - tall with dark blonde hair and a beautiful smile - having been elected by the student body as Memphis State College Homecoming Queen. However, my mother was nothing like the stereotypical image of a beauty queen who never finished the last year of college. Although she encouraged students to vote for her, she was a candidate for the homecoming queen election not affiliated with a campus organization. She believed a girl running as an independent could be elected the college's Homecoming Queen. She was the first to win the popular vote as an independent candidate, which changed the usual pattern of a sorority girl holding the title.

And my mother never shied away from expressing her political opinion. She was a fine example for a budding young politician, like myself, to watch as she debated political issues with my grandfather all by herself (while my dad mostly listened). Years later, my cousin, who taught Native Americans on a reservation in Oklahoma, sent me my grandfather's autographed Richard Nixon books, which brought back fond memories of those spirited living room debates.

My father, although later a college professor, in 1953 articulated his life goal in the East High *Mustang* yearbook "To be Governor of Tennessee." And my mother's 1955 *Mustang* yearbook professed her dream "to be a successful lawyer and play a large part in Tennessee politics." At that time, my father's dream was accepted, while my mother's was unusual due to the traditional gender roles for her generation. Maybe my dream was in the family genes, as my mother's side of the family included a former governor of Mississippi, state legislators, a justice of the peace, a county constable, and sheriff over the past years. All were instrumental in bringing better facilities to the state and county.

In our family discussions, my father always made witty remarks. His passion was teaching. Many nights he led our conversation at dinner about current events. He knows just about everything you can about American history. And he and my mother taught me the important three C's: courage, character, and compassion. All were principles based upon the most important "C"—Jesus Christ.

My parents encouraged a strong work ethic. It was modeled upon my father. He had worked his way through college with two newspaper routes; attended the University at night for an M.A. degree while serving as an Air Force officer; and later served twenty-three years as a Navy Reserve Officer while he was a University of Memphis college professor.

An example of the family work ethic was my maternal grandfather, James Hamer. He began working with a local automotive parts company while in public high school. He continued forty years with the business now known worldwide as the Genuine Parts Corporation in relation with the NAPA affiliation. Grandfather's many long work hours, exceptional knowledge, and ability in the auto parts business helped build that corporation, and his personal success permitted a better standard of living appreciated by family members.

And I always worked. My booming business as a pre-teen helped me save up $100 (for 100 hours of babysitting) to buy my first three-speed bike. Other jobs included teaching piano, flipping hamburgers at a fast-food restaurant, and working in the credit office at a local department store in college. During the summer before college, I worked at both the hamburger joint and the department store—sometimes up to seventy hours a week to save for school expenses. My parents provided the basics, but it was clear that any entertainment expenses, car insurance, and a vehicle to drive would have to be earned on my own. The values learned in those formative years helped lay the foundation to follow my dream of public service.

2

My passion for politics never faded, even as I entered college at the University of Memphis. Although recruited by the military to attend the United States Military Academy, and with grades and test scores high enough to be accepted at most colleges in the country, my choice was Memphis State University (now the University of Memphis). The decision was due primarily to a full academic Cecil C. Humphreys Presidential Scholarship that included books, room, board, and tuition. Getting a scholarship was a must to have the independence of living in the dormitory, although my mother still insisted on picking up my laundry on campus every week. Also, I was not too keen on the idea of climbing glaciers at the Academy, as featured in the military recruiters' video.

The values my parents taught, such as quality public education, encouraged my political activism. Good grades, where your dad has a PhD, were required. But politics was an arena where I could forge my own path.

In addition to politics, my other interest was classical piano, and I studied with a professor until my junior year in college. The experience of playing for my high school graduation and accompanying other musicians in college performances was valuable in feeling comfortable on the stage. However, at some point in college, I had to choose—continue to devote hours a day to practicing piano or to student government as an officer. I left piano behind.

During my first year in college, I attended SGA meetings simply to watch. Later, I was appointed as a senator to fill a vacancy and then elected speaker of the senate. Finally, I broke my first glass ceiling to be elected the first woman Memphis State University SGA President in 1982.[2] Even then my populist roots were evident since my articulated focus was to represent the students. We wasted no time in surveying them about policy changes.

My involvement even led me to the State Capitol and election as Lt. Governor of the Tennessee Intercollegiate State Legislature (TISL), a mock state legislature composed of students from public and private colleges and universities across the state. After working hard to get the votes for the position, some students from Vanderbilt University caused a runoff after initially promising me support and then throwing it to another candidate. After the first vote, I gave up and then was surprised when they lobbied for me to win the runoff. It was one of my first lessons in politics—never give up.

My sister and I shared my paternal grandfather's hand me down 1968 Buick LeSabre, which comfortably fit eight people and was a gas guzzler. This car was perfect for the three-hour trek to the State Capitol by the student government officers to lobby a state legislative committee for changes in the law. We carefully planned our work, some at the famous Garibaldi's pizza parlor near the campus. We also took a reporter from the MSU *Helmsman* student newspaper and other student government senators to present proposed legislation to an actual legislative governmental affairs committee of the Tennessee General Assembly.

Unfortunately, halfway to Nashville, we had a flat tire. Then, more bad news- I didn't have the key to the trunk to get the spare. We flagged down a truck driver, who took us to the next exit where we found help. We pushed ahead to the State Capitol, arriving just as the legislative committee adjourned with legislators streaming down the Legislative Plaza halls. I wanted to grab them and beg them to return to the chambers so the trip would not be for naught. However, two of the legislators, Rep. Mike Kernell and Rep. Roy Herron, were kind enough to go to lunch with us all and talk about issues, and we felt like the trip was a success after all.

Our SGA had a productive year, operating a book co-op, convincing the State Board of Regents to reverse a policy charging graduate students higher fees for undergraduate classes, monitoring the university's standing committees, and registering voters. The student newspaper editorialized in favor (based on "sound principles") of my veto of a bill giving money to a program for some of the sororities and fraternities when the African American Pan-Hellenic fraternities were omitted.[3] And I took administrators on a walking tour to push for emergency telephones on campus in the wake of reports of an attempted rape.[4] We let off stress by playing basketball in our spare time.

The college campus abounded with opportunities to hear divergent views. On-campus speakers arranged by the SGA and other groups included Memphis Councilman J. O. Patterson, former U.S. Congresswoman Shirley Chisholm, Congressman Al Gore, candidates for Congress Bob Clement and Don Sundquist, and Ralph Nader. Even convicted Watergate burglar G. Gordon Liddy came to speak, albeit hosted solely by other student organizations after my veto of SGA funding.[5]

And President Jimmy Carter spoke in 1980. I was one of the few students recognized in the crowd for a question. Perhaps in light of the Watergate scandal, I asked him about whether integrity in a candidate's personal life matters, which he affirmed was paramount. I didn't realize that the talk was being broadcast over the radio until a friend later said he had heard my question while listening elsewhere.

I loved hearing the various politicians speak and debating the issues of the day with other college students. Imagine my surprise at the end of 1982 to be among the "big names on campus" identified by the student newspaper, along with All-American Tiger basketball player Keith Lee; Liddy; and the Memphis mayoral candidates J. O. Patterson, Mike Cody, Pat Vander Schaaf, and Dick Hackett.[6]

As president of the MSU SGA, I was invited by Governor Lamar Alexander to the Tennessee Governor's Mansion in 1983 with all student government presidents from across the state. I spoke up against his proposed 15% college tuition increase, which he defended.[7]

After the governor spoke, we were offered iced tea and cookies and to look around the mansion. The governor then stood on the back steps of the mansion, politely waiting for us to leave. I boldly stood right beside him on the steps and had a photo taken. Although the governor didn't speak a word to me on those steps, the photo published in the student newspaper looks like we were just hanging out together on the back steps of the Governor's Mansion.[8]

On those steps of the Governor's mansion, I thought, *who knows, maybe I'll be governor someday if I work hard and play by the rules.*

As the first woman elected TISL Lt. Governor, I drafted legislation and debated it in the actual house and senate chambers at the Tennessee State Capitol. At the time, I only hoped that one day one of the nameplates on the legislative seats would actually bear my name, and I would stand in the state house well as an elected state representative and present my own proposed laws.

Those early years truly helped prepare me for the real public service in elected office ahead. When I later walked across the stage in 2012 in full regalia as one of one hundred honored at the University of Memphis Centennial Celebration, I was surrounded by many others who had been involved in student government over the years.

We gladly posed and exchanged photos, fondly recalling the lively debates in the SGA offices. Yet, only a few of us had gone on actually to serve in public office. What was it that spurred us on where others lost interest or chose other career paths?

For me, it is the love of the people, wanting to make a difference and the belief that if I work hard and play by the rules, *I can.* As a young woman, this was my version of the American Dream.

2

A Dream Come True

1

Because the law is a good profession for someone who aspires to public service, I decided to attend law school. Even though offered a substantial partial scholarship to Vanderbilt Law School, I gratefully chose to be one of twelve to accept the full academic Herff Law Scholarship from the University of Memphis.

Law school days were long but also fun. We studied and partied, and I enjoyed getting to know students from other parts of the state and the country. Over the summers, I clerked at law firms in Memphis and in Dallas, where my older sister already was an attorney.

During law school, I was active in politics, even hosting a party for fellow law students at the Garibaldi's pizza parlor for Al Gore's U.S. Senate campaign. My father and I saw another trailblazer on campus when Geraldine Ferraro appeared with Jesse Jackson in 1984. I admired her courage to run for vice president of the United States.

In my last year in law school, I served as editor in chief of the law review. Perhaps that is why I was selected as a panelist for a *WMC-TV* news show, serving up questions to the Tennessee Attorney General Mike Cody. It was an excellent experience for an aspiring politician!

Upon graduation, I accepted a judicial clerkship with the U.S. Sixth Circuit Court of Appeals. Just before beginning the judicial clerkship, I spent two months clerking for a world-wide law firm based in Washington, D.C. On the weekends, I hung out with U.S. Sen. Al Gore's staff, knocked on doors for a local city council candidate, and even went sight-seeing with my father who was in town for two weeks while on active duty as a Navy Reserve intelligence officer. Imagine my surprise the last week at the firm when I learned that Vic Raiser, the National Democratic Committee finance chair, was a partner. I rushed downstairs to meet him. Later, he contributed to my first campaign for public office.

Back in Memphis, the judicial clerkship challenged me intellectually, and my horizons were broadened with travel to Cincinnati to hear the oral arguments. Among the brightest recent law graduates from several states, the judicial clerks socialized together and enjoyed a year of intense legal scholarship.

In my spare time, I coordinated a legal education seminar for the Memphis Federal Bar Association. A featured speaker was Republican U.S. Sen. Nancy Kassenbaum from Kansas (who later married Tennessee U.S. Sen. Howard Baker). I still found a way to experience politics—even within the Hatch Act's guidelines as a judicial clerk.

Meanwhile, I watched fascinated as Minerva Johnican, a politician who was African American, tried to break barriers to be elected the first woman Memphis mayor. She got on TV and dished it right back to the guys. Despite her best efforts, she came in second to County Clerk Dick Hackett, who avoided a runoff.

I always set my sights high, keeping with the belief instilled by my parents that if I work hard and play by the rules, I can accomplish anything. So, knowing no limits, I applied for a U.S. Supreme Court clerkship with Justice Rehnquist and was one of fifteen or twenty in the country afforded an interview in 1987. I flew to Washington, D.C., met with his law clerks, and then with the stern Justice in his chambers at the U.S. Supreme Court.

It was a rather heady experience and an honor since we were not aware of any other graduate from my law school ever selected to interview for a U.S. Supreme Court clerkship. In my interview, Rehnquist cross-examined me thoroughly about Memphis. Ultimately, despite my best efforts to the contrary, he sheepishly pried out of me that the city still was somewhat backward in some respects. When asked if I had any questions, perhaps naively or prophetically, I wondered whether the Justice felt frustrated in having to decide the law as opposed to making the law. I'm sure he got a kick out of that one.

Afterward, one of Rehnquist's judicial clerks gave me a tour of the U.S. Supreme Court building, including the gym. We walked out onto the basketball court. The tall thin clerk handed me a basketball, issuing a challenge. "When I applied for a judicial clerkship, I was offered the same chance to make a basket. Every interviewee who accepted the challenge and made the basket has been selected by the Justice to serve as a judicial clerk." This part of the interview process had not been explained to me before my arrival. In any event, I guess the law clerk didn't realize that I had played basketball in junior high and high school.

Although in high heels, pantyhose, and a business suit, not in the least taken aback, I accepted the challenge, went for a lay-up, and made it. When I received my rejection letter from the Justice, I called this clerk and jokingly asked, "What happened since, after all…I *did* make the basket?"

2

After a summer vacation backpacking through Australia with another judicial clerk, staying at youth hostels, snorkeling on the Great Barrier Reef, and visiting Ayers Rock in the outback, I turned down offers from the U.S. Department of Justice and other prestigious law firms from across the country. Instead, mindful of the maxim that all politics is local, I accepted an offer as an associate attorney with one of the largest and most well-established local Memphis law firms.

Frank Glankler, a weathered-looking thin man, was the patriarch of the firm. I admired his ethics and values. He stood for the highest standards in the legal profession. He was well respected not only for his ability but also for his honesty, forthrightness, and fortitude, having been a former decorated Marine. A colorful man, known for hard-drinking, dove-hunts, and raw language, he still embodied the principles of equal justice and integrity taught to me. It was never about the money with him—it was about character.

Years later, when I ran for Memphis mayor, he hosted a party for me at his upscale home on East Parkway and talked about my dedicated public service. I was honored that he truly understood me and appreciated the sacrifices involved. He always stood by me in all of my political endeavors and was a true gentleman in my mind.

With only a handful of women attorneys at the firm, it was a very masculine environment. After my first review, I was heart-broken, having received anonymous comments that I laughed too much and too loudly and needed to dress more like another tall and modelesque female partner attorney. However, I made some adjustments, and eventually they accepted that all women lawyers are not alike.

During the late 1980s, the social norms had not caught up entirely with women's infiltration in the legal field. On one occasion, a male partner took a client and me to the exclusive University Club for lunch. However, to his chagrin, it was the "men only" day, so instead, we were seated at a table specially set up outside for us by the tennis court. Similarly, the Petroleum Club at the top of our office building was an after-work watering hole, with one room designated for men only. One day, I walked by and saw a female partner eating lunch in that room. It was exhilarating and amusing to know that she bucked the rules.

I also volunteered as a camerawoman for the local access Shelby County Democratic Women's television show. Eventually, I became a host of the show thanks to Rep. Mike Kernell, who specifically asked for me to host when he appeared as a guest. That first show was awkward at best, shaking my head and using "ums" due to lack of television experience. Kernell handled my inexperience like a pro. The show was a great training ground, giving me needed exposure, including interviews with the local sheriff and other public figures.

We taped one show at the home of the organization's president, Joan Briggs, during a reception where Al Gore was the guest speaker. We interviewed Gore in Joan's bedroom, where it was quiet and to escape the crowd. The show was aired on cable—the bed not in camera view, of course!

National politics beckoned with the candidacy of Al Gore for president. I eagerly volunteered for his local steering committee, even riding the bus overnight to Iowa to go door to door and to attend a campaign debate. The youthful true believer who traveled across the country came face to face with the jaded when in Des Moines, I knocked on the door of an elderly man who had never voted in his entire life!

In 1988, my volunteer efforts continued at the National Democratic Convention in Atlanta. The Tennessee delegation and the California delegation were housed in the same hotel, which made for some exciting parties. Among those I met were handsome John F. Kennedy Jr. and movie star Rob Lowe. "John John" autographed my convention floor pass, and Lowe posed with me for a photograph. Needless to say, there was a lot of kidding back at the law firm over my photograph with Lowe when the scandal broke over his partying with some teens at the same hotel (and ribbings about whether I had a private meeting with him, too).

Al Gore was present at one party after his concession speech. While the press made fun of Gore for being too stiff, he was understandably a bit tipsy on this night. We posed for a photograph while he shared with me that he had his tie in his pocket. It was good to see him relaxed and having fun.

With an extremely early morning flight and due to heavy expected traffic, I checked out of the hotel and watched Bill Clinton's nomination of Dukakis while at the airport lobby. Even today, I marvel how he overcame the jeers over the length of his speech and applause when he said, "in conclusion."

Thereafter, I remained politically active, even serving as finance chair of the Shelby County Democratic Party. Maybe one day, my turn would come to run for public office.

3

While I always wanted to serve in public office, I felt like the door would never open for me. So, on my birthday in February 1990, at the ripe old age of twenty-nine, I decided to let go of those hopes and instead give my full attention to my law practice. Then, the unexpected happened. Only a few months later, State Rep. Pam Gaia, who had visited my high school years earlier, announced she was not seeking reelection. Instead, she would challenge U.S. Congressman Harold Ford Sr.[9] My friends in politics began to call to ask if I would seek the open seat.

Having done a 180 degree turn around earlier in the year on my dreams of public service, I first said "no." A major reason was my concern that the law firm would not allow my absence for several months of the legislative session each year in Nashville. I tested the waters with one senior partner who replied, "You are too young and should be a partner first."

Later, one of the few female partners at the forty-plus attorney firm took me aside and wisely encouraged me to ask another senior partner, because after all…it was my dream. So, I did. He said, "Will you win?" I said, "Yes." He got it approved, and I was off and running.

Getting elected wasn't easy. I worked at one of the top law firms in a major U.S. city. Even though the partners agreed to allow time off to campaign, the workload did not let up. Just before the primary election, a partner tapped me to second chair a two-week trial in another county about ownership of a lake. When I confided my frustration to another partner, even I was surprised with my rare burst of tears due to the pressure. He must have said something. Although I still attended the trial, the workload did lighten up a bit until after the election. Coincidentally, the opposing attorney on that case later became a colleague in the state legislature – Craig Fitzhugh.

The primary field was intense, including Paul Gurley, who was Memphis Mayor Dick Hackett's legislative and community affairs director, another well-respected female candidate, and two Democratic friends. One friend dropped out. Another, whom I had helped in his unsuccessful bid a year earlier in another legislative district, initially stayed in the race.

That friend and I were both summoned to state Sen. Steve Cohen's midtown home to discuss whether one of us would drop out since we had mutual supporters. Cohen, a liberal gadfly legislator, wanted to keep the district Democratic. Since I was not dropping out, the friend ultimately did. With that handled, Cohen backed me.

Gurley had no problem raising money due to his mayoral connection and established government career. As a youthful woman with lots of energy but less financial resources, my campaign strategy was to knock on doors and meet as many voters as possible before the August primary Election Day. Suffice it to say that Memphis gets rather hot in the summer. Going door to door for hours after work each evening and on the weekends took a lot of dedication. I hoped that my work would pay off and override Gurley's substantial financial advantage.

At one point, while knocking on doors, he rode by me in a convertible with a Memphis State Tiger mascot waving to people. Gurley was an announcer at the Tigers' basketball games. I worried if I should get a Tiger mascot, too, but my more experienced advisors told me to keep knocking on doors.

Supporters and family members campaigned for me by knocking on doors, making phone calls, and pressing the flesh. Mike Gatlin took a team of boy scouts leafleting many nights; John Freeman put up signs. My top advisors included Kernell, an expert on a political ground campaign, and Cohen, who worked to get support from mid-towners and Democratic political leaders.

Waiting on the other side of the primary for the general election was an intelligent, progressive Republican attorney, Kevin Pfannes, tall and thin, age thirty-five. He was a neighborhood leader, had run against Gaia two years earlier, and was already going door to door as well. An African American independent candidate was initially disqualified but ended up back on the general election ballot.

The primary campaign heated up. We raised the question of Gurley's conflict of interest due to his city job, with duties including lobbying the legislature. [10] While Gurley was respected by many, it was a legitimate issue.

Also at issue was Gurley's party affiliation, with Cohen saying, "If it walks like a Republican, if it talks like a Republican, if it looks like a Republican, it is a Republican."[11]Cohen noted Gurley's Republican affiliations through Mayor Hackett. [12]Gurley replied that he had supported some Democrats, such as Governor McWherter. However, his literature included endorsements from several prominent Republicans, such as Memphis Councilmen Jack Sammons and Oscar Edmonds.

The race was deemed the "most watchable legislative race" in the county.[13] My platform included letting the people vote on a constitutional resolution to allow charity bingo, protecting the environment, safer neighborhoods, and better public education. I pledged to work on consumer protection legislation, so auto repair shops would not fleece customers by making unauthorized expensive repairs.

The local powerbroker, U.S. Congressman Harold Ford Sr., was known for his get out the vote ability in the African American community. He was determined to beat Gaia. Ford Sr. was respected for constituent service. Many candidates coveted the Ford ballot as a sure vote-getter. I was on it.

However, his brother, state Sen. John Ford, a more flamboyant family member, had his own ballot that included one of my opponents. John Ford backed Jean Ray Bowers, a well-respected African American who was the project director for a nonprofit. The Democratic primary had 42% black voters, and there were three white candidates, which appeared to favor Bowers. [14]But there was also a sentiment that the Democrats needed to nominate a candidate who could win the general election in a majority white district.

Cohen and Kernell hosted a fundraiser on my behalf, which was attended by Lieutenant Governor Wilder. From the adjoining Fayette County, Wilder was an attorney, farmer, and powerful politician, having built a bipartisan coalition in the state senate. He was slow-speaking and shrewd.

Not only were Democrats getting behind me to keep the seat, but there was an interest in maintaining a female representative for the district. The local Women's Political Caucus ran an ad listing sixteen female candidates' names and encouraging women to vote. [15]At the time, in the county, there were no female judges for the circuit or chancery courts, only one female general sessions court judge, one woman of thirteen Shelby County commissioners, four women in the county's twenty-plus state legislative delegation, and no woman had served as district attorney general. [16]

My campaign centered on strong Democratic issues, such as removing the sales tax from food. I campaigned in public housing developments and poor neighborhoods. My slogans – "Carol is the Democrat in Tune" and "She'll Put the Job First" – played on the conflict of interest theme. When a low-income voter said he was glad I wanted to bring jobs, I realized and was happy that the slogan could be interpreted more than one way (and that also was part of my platform).

The campaign was intense, and as a first-time candidate, it was a learning experience as to puns and digs. As Governor McWherter always said, "If you can't take the heat, stay out of the kitchen."[17] I even ended up in a cartoon on the front cover of the *Memphis Flyer* newspaper in bed with several other candidates for the story "Strange Bedfellows: A between-the-sheets look at the odds and ends of this summer's campaign trail." [18]

With Mayor Hackett airing radio ads and campaigning at a poll on Election Day for Gurley, it was a hard-fought victory. After the primary victory, I was tired and ecstatic. Shortly thereafter, I rewarded myself with a double-scoop ice-cream cone. Unfortunately, while taking my first lick walking to the car, I tripped off a curb (in part due to my fallen arches).

In denial about my hurting foot, I went to a local drug store and walked around, and then home in pain. Finally, a young doctor at a medical clinic told me my foot was not broken, gave me a crutch, and said to stay off it a few days. Three days later, an orthopedic specialist pronounced it broken and put my leg in a walking cast striped with my campaign colors of red and white. My main concern was how to win the general election now that my door to door efforts would be slowed.

4

For the general election, a significant issue was whether to widen Sam Cooper Boulevard, an artery off the major interstate I-40 that dead-ends at Overton Park, and what to do with lots that had become vacant. Years earlier, a lawsuit by environmentalists stopped plans to extend Sam Cooper through the park and zoo. Also on the forefront were issues such as reproductive rights, term limits for state legislators, and the controversial proposed state income tax. I opposed the road expansion.

Harold Ford Sr. invited my team over after seeing my yard signs up and down the main street by his upscale home. Ford Sr. was controversial. He had been tried in the spring on bank fraud and conspiracy charges, which he claimed were racially and politically motivated. [19] The first trial had resulted in a hung jury along racial lines. [20]Later, a majority white jury selected from outside of the county acquitted him. [21]

After the primary, Hickman Ewing, the U.S. Attorney who later was a Whitewater investigator, had a grand jury look into the Ford, Sr. ballot because it was delivered so quickly to the voters by postal employees. When the press asked me about it, I simply stated the obvious, "It's nice to know we have such prompt mail service in our city." The investigation went nowhere.

My Republican opponent, Pfannes, also an attorney and commercial real estate broker, had moved to Memphis from Illinois six years earlier. He was aggressive, claiming that I was part of machine politics and that Sam Cooper Boulevard would be expanded if the voters elected me. But the press noted his difficulty in the Democratic-leaning district because we had similar positions on many issues, such as not extending the road. [22]

During the general election, Democratic Governor Ned McWherter traveled to Memphis to greet constituents at my headquarters. McWherter, a large man, looked like Dan Blocker who played Hoss Cartwright on *Bonanza*—another of my favorite childhood TV shows. He had served as speaker of the state house for many years and was popular. He joined the Tennessee Secretary of State Bryant Millsaps and about 350 other guests at my fundraiser. I've never seen a politician shake so many hands so fast, perhaps due to his imposing size in pushing through the crowd.

The governor predicted a low turnout for the general election and encouraged voters to turn out to elect me.[23] Gurley showed up with a contribution, and my other primary opponents endorsed me for the general election. Also, U.S. Sen. Al Gore and Tipper stopped by my campaign headquarters shortly before the November election.[24] For this campaign, the team stuck together.

During the campaign, I emphasized my homegrown roots and that Pfannes appeared to be interested only in transportation issues. We debated at a Midtown neighborhood forum, where he criticized McWherter and others' involvement in my campaign. On my side was the Democratic Party support, and on his side was the low turnout predictions due to the lackluster gubernatorial and other statewide races.

The campaign got dirty with Pfannes attacking me on several issues. I responded by keeping to the high road and answered every point in a mailer to the voters.

While the then conservative *Commercial Appeal* endorsed Pfannes without any mention of my qualifications, the *Memphis Business Journal* endorsed me due to my "larger view of the critical issues facing" the district and the city. [25]

Having campaigned extensively in the African American community, my name recognition increased. With support from black and white leaders, perhaps some voters were confused about my racial identity. My father told me that while getting his hair cut, he overheard a conversation by two white men on their way out of the barbershop about whom they were supporting in the election. One said, "I want to vote for Carol Chumney," *and then a long pause,* "....but she's black."

In fact, barber and beauty shops were prime venues for campaign stops. The famous North Memphis Morris Barber Shop, operated by Alma and Charlie Morris, was a required stop to obtain the coveted Kennedy Democratic Club endorsement. The shop, opened in the 1950s in a bustling African American community, was now like taking a step back in time.

Four days before the election, Pfannes unexpectedly began running television ads attacking me. My election was one of the first in Memphis, where the candidates spent thousands of dollars in television advertising for a state legislative race. [26] An ad centered on the issues of a state income tax and my opposition to state legislative term limits. At first, I decided not to air any ads in response. However, my consultant, Dr. John Bakke, recommended otherwise.

Getting a studio and filmographer on such short notice was difficult. And I was booked for a prayer breakfast the next morning sponsored by former mayoral candidate Otis Higgs and a local pastor, both African American community leaders.

Miraculously, we booked a studio, and one of the best videographers in the country, Marius Penczner, filmed the ad. He and Bakke wrote an ad responding to the accusations, shot nearly in the dark, and focused only on my face talking directly to the voters. It aired just in time.

Not to be outdone, Pfannes dropped a leaflet in voters' driveways that "Halloween's over but some people still haven't taken off their disguises," claiming that the powerbrokers controlled my campaign, including Harold Ford Sr. The leaflet had a photo of the Harold Ford ballot endorsement.

We did not know what to expect with the low voter turnout and all the last-minute dirty tricks on Election Day. I shook hands at the polls, along with family members and supporters. At one poll, a supporter seeing my campaign sign nodded "I am voting for her," apparently mistaking my mother, whom I favor, as the candidate because she had knocked on doors in that neighborhood.

Later in the day, a long-time friend, Oran Quintrell, picked me up from another poll. He broke the news that I might lose the election. I continued to campaign and hoped for the best.

Pfannes had worked the majority Republican precincts the hardest, and they turned out in droves. The poll trackers at two polls in the district reported to Bakke that I was losing as he went on air with a local news station to talk about the campaign. At my campaign headquarters, we anxiously waited for our poll watchers to arrive with each poll's results. Then we won!

In November 1990, after winning the tough August primary, breaking my foot, and still knocking on thousands of doors in a walking cast, as well as putting $10,000 of my own limited funds into the race, and with the help of many, I was finally elected as a state representative—a dream come true!

PART TWO

—

Early Years at the State House

3

Dubbed the "Woman with Balls"

1

Winning the election was one thing; doing the job of a state legislator was another altogether. I was one of thirteen women legislators in the state house of ninety-nine, and one of the youngest. But I took it in stride and hit the ground running. My motto was this might be my only term, so I would get as much done as possible in those two years.

After the election, the House Democratic Majority Leader's contest heated up between attorneys Rep. Bill Purcell from Nashville and Rep. Frank Buck from Dowelltown in rural East Tennessee. Imagine my surprise one Saturday at 6 a.m. to get a call from Buck saying he was parked outside my apartment complex and wanted to talk about the race. Apparently, there is truth to the saying that folks in the country are early risers!

Democrat Jimmy Naifeh, of Lebanese heritage and from the rural town of Covington (only a county away), was elected House Speaker, and long-serving Lt. Gov. John Wilder was re-elected to his position by the state senate. The Democrats controlled the governorship, state senate, and state house. West Tennessee never had more power, with Governor Ned McWherter also hailing from rural West Tennessee.

Of course, the Republicans weren't going to take things lying down and staged a filibuster on the day we took the oath of office. Excited to be elected, I had invited supporters for a reception in the Legislative Plaza, which I barely got to attend due to the session's late adjournment.

During a recess until the gubernatorial inauguration, I drafted bills to eliminate the sales tax from food and attended seminars on tax reform and education.[27] I also teamed up with an African American legislator in an adjoining district to blast a road proposal for an interchange that would displace citizens in a low-income neighborhood.[28] When we returned, the inauguration was toned down out of respect for the U.S. troops serving in the Persian Gulf War.

As the session resumed, I let my colleagues know my preference to be called "Representative" Chumney instead of the traditional "Lady" for female legislators.[29] Since the men were not addressed as "Lord," I didn't see any reason to abide by an antiquated custom. After all, we are in America, not England!

The legislature was a mix of rural, urban and suburban legislators. Speaker Jimmy Naifeh led the state house, leaving others to tend his family grocery store and other business ventures in his rural district. His office staff included the top assistant Rita Adams, a thin blonde with a strong Southern accent.

Every year most of the legislature, members of the executive branch, public officials from across the state, and the "third house" lobbying corps, trekked to Naifeh's hometown for an outdoor event named the Coon Supper. The fare included raccoon and venison. It was a must-do for anyone seriously interested in higher office in the state due to Naifeh's powerful position. Rita wore her "coon" earrings to work as a tribute to the annual event, said to be raccoon testicles encased in yellow shellac.

Back at the State Capitol, standing true to my pledge to oppose the Sam Cooper Boulevard extension, I met with Governor McWherter in his office to ask that he reconsider the plans.[30] The project would create a dead end on a major street in the low-income area known as Binghampton, jeopardizing several businesses in that struggling neighborhood that relied on the ongoing traffic.

Years later, in 2000, work commenced planning the redevelopment of the Binghampton neighborhood vacant land from the Sam Cooper Boulevard extension.[31] The people finally had won with the road extended as a parkway rather than an interstate highway. I was pleased to be a part of the long-awaited revitalization of the area.

Not only sponsoring bills, I also worked to defeat bills, such as one that would provide some exemptions for high school physical education requirements. Recalling my high school days of softball, basketball, and volleyball during P.E. and cognizant of the obesity problem in America, I sought the help of none other than the Terminator, Arnold Schwarzenegger. Schwarzenegger was the chairman of the President's Council on Fitness. At my request, he wrote a letter opposing the bill; the letter was placed on each legislator's desk.[32] The sponsor of the bill, sensing defeat, promptly removed the bill from that day's agenda.

Believing strongly in democracy, in April 1991, I kicked off four town hall meetings around the district to discuss my legislative package and discern the voters' opinions on the key issues before the Tennessee General Assembly.[33] Town hall meetings can be intense but are an important way to connect with constituents and have a reality check on the lobbying corps' spin.

My package included: requiring auto repair shops to make parts removed during vehicle repair available for inspection, reducing government waste, and requiring another individual besides the bus driver to check that disabled children were not left on buses.

In fact, I sponsored so many bills as a freshman that Paula Wade, a reporter with the *Commercial Appeal* (and former White Station High School classmate), wrote an entire column about how I was bucking the unwritten rule that a freshman legislator was to be seen and not heard and how I had passed more legislation than any other freshman lawmaker that year.[34] Rep. Karen Williams (R-Memphis), in the spirit of bipartisanship, commented on my hard work and preparation.[35] And reporter Paula Wade noted my lack of hesitation to "amend other people's bills or disagree with powerful people." [36]

Wade reported my vocal opposition to the governor's bill to provide state grant funds to private colleges, my amendment of the secretary of state's bill over his objection to allow overseas military voters to register for absentee voting via fax, and my lead sponsorship of bills on behalf of the Tennessee Supreme Court and Secretary of State. She also noted my passage of The Memphis Plan that allowed the Memphis Church Health Center to contract with a private health insurer to set up a basic health coverage program for the working poor, including janitors, cooks, and domestic workers. [37]

The Memphis Plan is a coordinated effort by Memphis hospitals and laboratories who agree to provide diagnostic care and services for free, with the Regional Medical Center to provide hospital services and Blue Cross Blue Shield to administer the program. With estimates of 100,000 working poor in the county, it was needed.[38] Senate sponsor Jim Kyle and I are credited with taking the idea of Dr. Scott Morris (who is also a Methodist minister) and navigating the administrative and legislative hurdles with him to get the law passed. [39]

Years later, I was gratified to read reports that the program had served about 40,000 patients in the Memphis metropolitan area who mostly worked for small businesses or were self-employed, reducing the average length of hospital stays nearly in half.[40] The Center is the largest privately funded faith-based health care organization, relying upon over 1,000 volunteers.[41]

Wade acknowledged in her article about me that "whisper campaigns" circulated that Sen. Steve Cohen would control my vote because of his support in my election.[42] And the annual roasting of politicians by the Memphis Gridiron show, hosted by the local press and media, portrayed me as the senator's "shoeshine girl."[43] Yet, Wade pronounced that those claims had proven false. [44] Instead, the mayor's lobbyist, Paul Gurley, who lost in the primary, lobbied me at the State Capitol. [45] I am glad she set my record straight!

Of course, I had been thrilled to have Sen. Cohen's support in the election. After the election, we worked together well on a great deal of legislation. However, at times he expected me to be at his beck and call in terms of carrying any piece of legislation he wanted in the state house. To gain the respect of my colleagues, I made a concerted effort to sponsor bills with other senators as well.

Cohen, who was passionate about his work, sometimes was angry that I would not sponsor a bill. While our districts had a considerable overlap, they were not identical. If I did not believe my constituents overall would favor the proposal, I declined. The double bind was either to be controlled by a powerful male or to pay the price for being my own woman and using my best judgment.

2

As a state legislator, I spent at least half of my time in Nashville at a salary of $16,500. It was truly a labor of love. My colleagues back at the law firm earned substantially more while building their client base. Most of the associates at the law firm sported brand new BMWs while I drove my economical Saturn coupe (made in Tennessee). When house parties were held to wine and dine the summer law clerk recruits during the summer months, I looked in awe at my colleagues' large homes. Instead, I rented an apartment and then a small townhouse. They had more time to develop friendships and family relation-ships since they were not constantly on the road. It was part of the price to pay for public service, something I gladly sacrificed.

For me, public service is noble. Born only a few weeks after President John F. Kennedy's inauguration, I had been taught his famous words, "Ask not what your country can do for you – but what you can do for your country." Public service is still honorable in my view, even though some have tainted the process, and many in the public have come to despise and be skeptical of those who offer their time, skills, and services in the political arena.

During session, I arrived at the law office on Monday morning, and then around 1 p.m. drove three hours to Nashville for the legislative committees and session, which often lasted until mid-evening. Taking my legal files in the car, I worked on my cases at night at my hotel in Nashville. Staying at the Capitol until after Thursday's session, I tried to leave in time to arrive at the Memphis law office before the end of that work-day. Friday and the weekend were spent catching up at the law firm.

When the session adjourned after about four months, the legislative work continued with local neighborhood meetings, events, and out of session com-mittee meetings. There were also the reelection campaigns every other summer and fall, as well as special legislative sessions. Needless to say, it took all of my time. But I didn't mind because it was my dream.

But it wasn't all work. Like the Coon Supper, another annual rite was a dinner where the women legislators each brought a male legislator as their "date." This was the brainchild of Speaker Pro Tempore Lois Deberry, a powerful long-serv-ing state legislator from Memphis, who rose to the state house's second highest leadership position. Deberry, an African American, was an amazing woman who over the years was accepted and respected by the "white boys," including governors, house speakers, members of Congress, and presidential candidates.

Rep. Lois Deberry told stories about the 1970s when she was one of the very few women serving in the state legislature, including one tale about her having to attend after-hours legislative receptions with male colleagues that featured topless female cocktail waitresses. She had a rare ability to read and understand people and forge compromises, yet also would hold out if she felt strongly about an issue. She served on the three-person subcommittee that routinely stopped legislation to restrict abortion rights. Perhaps to appease religious conservatives in her majority-black legislative district, Deberry pro-claimed that she was both pro-choice and pro-life.[46]

Being invited to the women's legislative dinner as a "date" was considered an honor. Many clients of the women lobbyists funded the event at a Nashville restaurant. At first, I asked Senator Cohen since he was one of my mentors. When he hedged, I discussed it with Sara Kyle, a commissioner on the Tennessee Public Service Commission with regulatory oversight over trucks, telephones, and cable television. She encouraged me to invite the governor.

Having not heard back from Senator Cohen, I took Kyle's advice and called the governor's office. When the dinner was fast approaching, and I still didn't have a confirmed "date," I made the mistake of triple-booking and asked my legislative office suitemate, freshman Rep. John Mark Windle. Needless to say, I did not know what to do when all three eligible bachelors finally called back and said, "yes." One of the hosts encouraged me to bring all three men to avoid embarrassment and political fall-out of canceling their "date."

The governor picked me up in a limousine and gave me a small teddy bear in remembrance of the event. When we arrived at the restaurant, Rep. Lois Deberry was furious that the governor was my "date." There was angst over his income tax proposal, and apparently, they were on the "outs." Deberry announced that there was not a table for us in the reserved room and we would have to sit in another room in the restaurant.

Not knowing what to do, I made the only strategic move possible and went to the ladies' room to powder my nose. In the ladies' room, I told a female lobbyist what had happened, fearing that my legislative career had just taken a nosedive. I had three "dates," including the governor, and Deberry was so angry that she would not seat us.

The lobbyist laughed. "Carol, don't you know what they are calling you?"

"No what?"

"They are calling you the woman with balls because you stood up to Lois."

After leaving the ladies' room, the restaurant staff miraculously set up a special table in the reserved room for me and my "dates." When toasts were made, the governor took quite a bit of heat for his income tax proposal, but he dished it right back. Cohen and Windle eventually arrived, and there was another surprise. Some of the female lobbyists were upset with Cohen. Regardless of his strong record on women's rights, they took the opportunity to thoroughly roast him, much to his chagrin. It certainly was an evening to remember!

Despite my "date" with the governor, my assertive advocacy took even him by surprise with the House Education Committee's adoption of my amendment to his education reform bill to provide additional funding to urban areas for teacher benefits and special education programs. [47] Adding nearly $80 million to the cost of his bill was a gutsy move for a freshman legislator, even though it was later stripped off the bill. [48]

While many of my bills passed, there were a few roadblocks. I quickly learned the enormous influence of the "third house" on Capitol Hill—the lobbying corps. One of my bills, sponsored at Cohen's request, required rape crisis centers to allow a friend or family member to be present when the police interviewed the victim. This sounded reasonable enough, but Rep. Joe Kent, who was a former police officer, and municipal lobbyists, opposed it with a vengeance contending that it would interfere with investigations. As the state senate is more of a horse-trading body than the state house, Cohen could pass most of his bills with no problem. He did not understand why I could not do the same. Not to be bullied by the lobbyists, I held my ground. But after many tense meetings and phone calls from opponents of the measure, the bill was rolled over to the next year's session, never to see the light of day again.

Governor McWherter was also having difficulty with his income tax and education reform bills, although there was support from some in the press and media. *The Memphis Business Journal* wondered why city and county officials did not weigh in. [49] Tennessee is one of a few states without a state income tax, relying primarily on sales tax and user fees to fund the government. Because there is no income tax, workers from the eight adjoining states who cross the border daily to work in Tennessee pay no income tax in the state. With Memphis adjoined by Mississippi and Arkansas, and the growing number of citizens in Shelby County moving over the border, the tax reform arguments resonated with progressive voters. However, there was strong opposition from many others. It was a volatile issue that dominated the news and some of my town hall meetings.

Many of my bills met with success. My Reduction of Waste in Government Act was transformed during the legislative session into a resolution requiring the state's Department of Finance & Administration to consider a performance incentive program for state employees and agencies to improve inefficiencies. [50] Administration officials visited Federal Express and Dobbs International in Memphis to learn about their quality improvement programs. [51] A supporter, Wayne Shannon, volunteered to work as a consultant to the state *per gratis* to devise its own quality improvement program. [52]

In the fall, my efforts to include funding for building and maintaining schools in the governor's education bill resulted in his administration's promise that it would become a component of the funding formula.[53] Memphis had many old school buildings that needed repair and maintenance, while other areas needed more classrooms.[54]

My overall work resulted in the *Tennessee Journal* mentioning me as bright, hardworking, and "atypically aggressive in sponsoring bills as a freshman."[55] I just wanted to get things done.

3

On the local front, the Memphis mayoral race was underway, with W.W. Herenton challenging Mayor Dick Hackett. Hackett had some negatives. One was the loan defaults and the bankruptcy related to developer Sidney Schlenker's efforts to develop an island (Mud Island) and build a huge pyramid-shaped arena on the Memphis riverfront. Millions of losses were estimated for the city, county, and Memphis State University.[56]

Herenton, an African American six-foot-six former boxer, had negatives as well, including his calling Memphis "a mean-spirited city."[57] He had recently resigned as school superintendent after an alleged affair with a teacher who claimed he had made promises and reneged.[58] Herenton denied her claims, except that there had been a relationship. Also, a damaging study of the school system alleging serious administrative irregularities and the resultant withholding of some school monies by local bodies preceded his resignation.[59]

Herenton had surprised U.S. Rep. Harold Ford Sr. and others by getting the majority of votes at the African American People's Convention organized by potential mayoral candidate Shep Wilbun.[60] This anointed him as the consensus African American candidate to challenge Hackett, with the goal to elect a black mayor for the first time in the city's history.[61] Ford Sr. held out for his own summit but ultimately decided not to run.[62] Even State Sen Cohen, called the Duke of Midtown, was mentioned as a possible mayoral candidate but declined saying that the city was not ready for a third candidate.[63]

A few weeks before the election, I was in Washington, D.C. for a conference and went by the congressional offices. Ford Sr. kept me in his office for over an hour talking about the municipal election. The congressman asked my opinion on who would win and then called one Memphis council candidate. I could hear him on the speakerphone. From what I could tell, the councilman had no idea it was a speakerphone or that I was listening.

Ford Sr. forecast the mayor's election to me weeks ahead, predicting a Herenton victory by one or two percent of the vote. He then went to Memphis and helped make it happen, campaigning round the clock for Herenton. Ford Sr. was a masterful campaigner and had a powerful political machine. I saw him standing in front of the bus stop downtown one day, with a swollen arm, shaking hands with every voter who went on or off the buses asking them to vote for Herenton.

Election eve was a cliffhanger when there was a delay in counting the absentee ballots. Ford Sr. went to investigate.[64] As I drove around the city, the radio announcer described the chaos at the election commission. Democratic Election Commissioner O. C. Pleasant Jr. and Ford Sr. had tense words. I wondered if there would be a riot.

Finally, the votes were counted. Herenton won by only 142 votes. Boosted by Martin Luther King III and Jesse Jackson Sr., with the latter calling Election Day the "resurrection" of African American people for the "cruci-fixion" of Dr. King, Herenton was elected as part of a "crusade" to become the first elected black mayor of Memphis.[65] Although Hackett had raised more than $713,000, he only spent $365,000, which upset some of his supporters due to the close margin.[66]

Even with the mayor's race decided, there would be more politics under-way before the end of the year as the presidential election heated up. I favored Bill Clinton, the governor of Arkansas, although conventional wisdom was that he was a long shot for the Democratic nomination. In December 1991, he appeared at a fundraiser at the Racquet Club in Memphis. The crowd was small because many expected New York Governor Mario Cuomo to announce for president that same day and win the nomination.

Clinton personally shook each of our hands. When we met, I handed him a postcard that featured the famous cartoon character Garfield, with his Cheshire cat smile, holding a red Christmas stocking. The card had the words "Get Stuffed." Smiling, I said, "This is what you should tell George Bush on the campaign trail."

Clinton moved on to shake other hands and gave a good speech. When he left, I stood by the exit door to say goodbye. Seeing me, he placed his hand over his heart, saying "Carol, I want you to know that I am going to keep your postcard right here next to my heart throughout the campaign." We both smiled. After the event, it was announced that Cuomo was not running, and Bill Clinton's campaign took off. It was a great way to end my first year in public office.

4

The Year of the Woman

1

As the 1992 New Year began, newly elected Councilman Myron Lowery, an articulate former television news anchor, hosted a prayer breakfast in Memphis. Senator Cohen, Rep. Mike Kernell, and I had jointly endorsed him, aiding in his third effort to win election to the Memphis City Council. Lowery, an African American, and Democrat, won the super-district in 1991, defeating a twenty-year white Republican incumbent.

Memphis Mayor Herenton strode into the Memphis Peabody Hotel ballroom that day with famous civil rights leaders Jesse Jackson Sr. and Benjamin Hooks in tow and received a standing ovation. Criminal Court Clerk Minerva Johnican called for unity, saying the city was more racially divided than when she had been elected to the Memphis City Council in 1983.[67]

While Memphis had broken one barrier with Herenton's election, there still has never been a female mayor of Memphis. When my turn came to speak, I boldly included on my New Year's Day "wish list" for Memphis that Herenton would appoint more women to his cabinet.[68] He had appointed all men, except the city attorney.[69]

A few days later, Herenton's inaugural events took place, and several celebrities and dignitaries attended due to his election's historic significance. The photo spread in the *Tri-State Defender* newspaper included civil rights leaders Rev. Billy Kyles and Rev. Jesse Jackson Sr. who were at the Lorraine Motel when Dr. King was murdered. Also present were musician Rufus Thomas, inaugural dinner co-host actor Kris Kristofferson, Isaac Hayes, Barry White, and U.S. Sen. Jim Sasser. Cohen invited me to attend, and we were photographed with Jackson. When the newspaper came out, Cohen called laughing hysterically and told me to buy a copy. There we were in our formal attire, identified in the photo as "State Senator Steve Cohen, Rev. Jesse Jackson, and *Mrs.* Steve Cohen." [70] Herenton, preferring to be called "Dr." Herenton, moved into City Hall and publicly thanked U.S. Rep. Harold Ford Sr. [71]

Back in Nashville, state tax reform was still the hot issue, along with ethics and Medicaid reform. The governor called for a special legislative session on taxes and education reform. Senator Cohen, Representative Kernell, and I hosted a joint town hall meeting at a Memphis public library to discuss the special session and budget cuts. [72] Also, I made some headway, along with the Tennessee Black Caucus and other constituent groups, in getting the governor's administration to review ways to improve the Midtown expressway interchange without taking 220 North Memphis homes, businesses, and churches. [73]

The legislative process was like a locomotive. Usually, the session started slowly with brief sessions on the legislative floor, short committee meetings, with a lot of constituents, and lobbyists for the private sector, public interest groups, or the administration stopping by the legislative offices. In addition, there were caucus meetings such as the political party caucuses, the black caucus, the rural West Tennessee Caucus, the Shelby County delegation caucus, and the women's legislative caucus.

Every night there were invitations to attend dinners and receptions, sometimes followed by later night ventures to local night clubs or watering holes. While some of this was fun, it was also work. If you wanted to get things done, you had to build relationships with your colleagues. And, if a constituent drove three hours from Memphis to attend the statewide accountants' reception, or the statewide attorneys' reception, or the municipal league reception, they expected to see their legislators at that reception.

While enjoying the legislature's social aspect, I found it very difficult to juggle my law work at night with the after session events at local restaurants and hotels. I rarely attended the "choir practice" at TGI Fridays, a weekly dinner paid for by lobbyists, or visited the "Kremlin," a suite on the 19th floor of the Crown Plaza Hotel where legislators hung out. [74] Some groups, like the black caucus, went bowling together to build comradery. Legislative sessions began early in the morning. I also tried to find time to work out at the local gym.

Reports from old-timers were that late-night lavish parties funded by lobbyists had calmed down since the 1980s due to a bingo corruption FBI investigation called "Operation Rocky Top." The Tennessee secretary of state had committed suicide, distraught after being subpoenaed to testify by a federal grand jury in Memphis. [75] And a state legislator had done the same after bribery charges were brought. [76]

Yet, pranks at the Legislative Plaza still abounded, which helped break the tension of often tedious late-night legislative sessions after the locomotive picked up steam and roared down the tracks in late spring or early summer. On occasion, a legislator taped a sign on the back of an unsuspecting colleague on the house floor with the words "Kick me" or another silly saying. Others shot paper wads or rubber bands. To his credit, Speaker Naifeh set out a new dress and conduct code in an effort to bring more decorum to the sometimes raucous proceedings on the state house floor.

Under the state constitution, legislators only have ninety days a year to get their work done in the legislative session, absent any specially called session. Usually, three days a week were in legislative session in the state house, with Tuesdays reserved solely for committee work. If the days ran out and the work wasn't finished, then one of the staff members would get a ladder, climb up, and stop the hands on the large clock on the wall at the back of the state house chamber to comply with the *Tennessee Constitution*, literally making time stand still.[77]

Rep. Frank Buck, chair of the House Judiciary Committee, was a colorful character. He always wore a leather vest over his good-sized belly and loved to play pranks on colleagues. He often told how a friend was played by undisclosed persons when a "suggestive" note was sent to a female legislator with his name forged.[78] The press came to ask the purported sender about the note and reports of sexual harassment on the state house floor.[79] Worried, he paused and then figured out it was a joke.[80]

Buck was also the butt of some jokes at the annual legislative talent show, another brainchild of Rep. Lois Deberry. The legislators sang, danced, and performed various skits, all to build relationships and relieve stress. At one show, Rep. Jere Hargrove imitated the famous TV host Johnny Carson's "Carnack" comedy routine. In a hat and cape, he held an envelope to his forehead. He said the envelope was hermetically sealed and had been kept in a mayonnaise jar on Funk & Wagnalls' porch. Hargrove announced the answer to the unknown question as "Invest." The participants tried to guess the question, which was "How does Rep. Frank Buck go skinny dipping?"[81]

2

With the presidential election primaries underway in 1992, Hillary Clinton appeared before about a thousand people at the Memphis Peabody Hotel.[82] I stood on the stage with her and other Democratic leaders, including Mayor Herenton.[83] Although we did not color coordinate in advance, Clinton and I both wore red and stood out in the mostly male crowd on the platform.

The Peabody is a luxurious hotel in Memphis, with a fountain in the lobby. The hotel keeps several ducks housed on its roof, which at set times of the day ride the elevators down to the lobby and then march to the fountain where they swim and are photographed by hotel patrons and visitors. After her speech, Hillary Clinton was named "an honorary keeper of the ducks" by the Peabody duck master and marched with them as they waddled back to the elevators to ride up to their roost.[84] So, the first female nominee of a major party for president of the United States has "duck keeper" among her long list of accomplishments.

Another woman had made national news in 1991 when Anita Hill testified to the U.S. Senate Judiciary Committee about allegations of sexual harassment by U.S. Supreme Court nominee Clarence Thomas. Before the all-male Judiciary Committee, the televised hearings prompted an outcry by women across the country and a slew of new female candidates. Gains were made in the U.S. Senate with the election of women such as Sen. Patty Murray, whose opponent mistakenly derided her as "just a mom in tennis shoes."

It wasn't much different at the Tennessee State Capitol, especially for some female secretaries. While as a young female lawmaker, I had my share of male legislative attention, they were, for the most part, respectful, with a few exceptions.

One of the legislative pranks went too far. At my desk on the state house floor one of the security officers passed a folded piece of paper from an anonymous legislative colleague. In the note was a condom.[85] I froze with shock, not knowing what to do, feeling embarrassed. After discarding the note and its contents, I decided to brush it off, although feeling extremely uncomfortable about the anonymous note and the implications.

On another day, a prank involved one male legislator stuffing a pair of women's pink panties in another male legislator's coat pocket without his knowledge.[86] When the legislator pulled the pink panties out of his pocket, he waved them over his head and ran down the center aisle on the house floor for all to see. It was shown on the local evening news over and over again.

A retired schoolteacher from Clarksville, Rep. Peggy Knight, wrote the House Speaker a blistering letter complaining that the incident was a "disgrace to the state" and sexist and noting that a class of school children were in the gallery when it happened.[87] I, as well as Rep. Beth Halteman (R-Nashville), addressed the press, observing that the prank obviously was done in jest but was not appropriate. [88]

Speaker Pro Tempore Lois Deberry said she did not see the "pink panties incident" and that "every time someone describes it to me, they describe it differently."[89] The legislator who waved the panties claimed that he had no idea they had been stuffed in his pocket by an anonymous colleague and thought it was his handkerchief.[90] Even Speaker Jimmy Naifeh admitted that though humor was often used to deal with the stressful last days of session, the pink panties prank went too far.

The women legislators were further aggravated because only one female was appointed to any of the three key conference committees to work out the serious issues on taxes, workers compensation reform, and redistricting between the house and the senate near the session's end.[91] Rep. Shirley Duer (R-Crossville) was quoted as saying, "Once again, women have been locked out of the system."[92] Also troubling was the disclosure that one of the Democratic caucus leaders had donated twice as much money from his large campaign account to the male legislators than to the female legislators with the same years of experience.[93]

On the positive side, Jackson Baker, a political columnist with the *Memphis Flyer*, dubbed 1992 as the Year of the Woman due to the emergence of Hillary Clinton as the "prototypical female candidate for president" and the candidacy of Carol Moseley Braun of Illinois for the U.S. Senate.[94] Also on the horizon was Blanche Lambert, who was challenging Arkansas U.S. Rep. Bill Alexander, having served as his legislative assistant. Needless to say, his overdraft practice at the House of Representatives' bank gave her an edge. I was excited to see women making some gains, although Baker told me it would be our only year—perhaps mischievously, just to see what I would say.

3

Despite the pranks, there was serious work to be done. Redistricting was still in the works. With what one reporter called "white flight" from the inner city, it was a fight for survival for some of the incumbent urban Shelby County legislators to retain district boundaries sufficient enough to have a chance at reelection.[95] My district boundaries would forfeit some of North Memphis, such as the public housing development Hurt Village, add a different public housing development (Dixie Homes), and pick up a mainly working-class neighborhood further east that was known as Nutbush. Reelection for me would require knocking on thousands of doors of new constituents once the legislature approved the plan.

The tax reform resolution that Cohen asked me to sponsor would let the people vote on amending the state constitution to cap any income tax enacted by the legislature at four percent, exempt the first $7,500 of income, remove the sales tax on groceries and medicines, allow greater tax relief for senior citizens, and authorize a lottery.[96] Of course, Cohen breezed through the horse-trading state senate with the resolution.[97]

As I worked to line-up votes, the *Commercial Appeal* reported Cohen's comments that appeared to insult the entire state House of Representatives.[98] When asked what kind of delegates might be elected if there were a state constitutional convention on tax reform, Cohen quipped wouldn't it be "scary" if they were "the House of Representatives?"[99]

Cohen and House Floor Leader Jere Hargrove had angry words on the house floor over the comments. Hargrove demanded an apology. At one point, I thought they were going to step outside to settle it with a fist-fight.[100] Speaker Naifeh and other house leaders warned that Cohen's remarks might have killed the resolution.[101] Cohen said he apologized and was merely stressed that the house had not yet adopted the resolution, but it was also reported that he didn't take his comments back.[102] Some house members said they wouldn't support any of his legislation, not just the tax reform resolution.[103] Perhaps as a karmic payback for his insult of the state house, the Citizens Against New Taxes group picketed Cohen's Memphis residence, with the senator coming out waving the American flag in high drama.[104]

With the resolution being the only chance for a constitutional amendment process to begin that year, I tried to smooth Cohen's behavior over with my house colleagues.[105] There was enormous pressure due to the significance of the measure since the governor's special session had been unsuccessful for tax reform.[106] If the resolution passed the state house, it would still have to pass both chambers by a two-thirds vote in 1993 and then be put on the ballot for the voters to decide in the next gubernatorial election of 1994.[107] If it failed, then three more years would be required to get it on the ballot.

The governor lobbied for the Cohen-Chumney tax reform resolution the morning it was scheduled for a house vote.[108] However, later, while on the house floor, I received a call from the governor's office. Cohen also was working to amend the governor's workers' compensation reform bill against his wishes.[109] I went downstairs to see McWherter as requested.

As the governor was a large man, all the chairs in his office were large as well. I felt dwarfed sitting across from the governor and his chief of staff. The governor told me that his agreement to support our tax reform resolution was off because of Cohen's efforts to amend the administration's workers compensation bill. This was just minutes before the tax reform resolution was scheduled for a vote on the house floor. Concerned that I was missing important votes while talking with the governor, I went back to the house floor to do my job. Needless to say, the resolution failed.[110]

Some Republican lawmakers voted against the resolution because the Democrats did not support a bill by Rep. David Copeland (R-Chattanooga) for a constitutional convention on taxes.[111] Many voted against the Cohen-Chumney resolution out of fear that it would be perceived as a vote for a state income tax and become a campaign issue.[112] And, of course, many were still mad at Cohen's remarks about the House of Representatives. Moreover, the governor had withdrawn his support, which cost votes. The issue of tax reform would be left unresolved due to the failure of both measures.[113]

Also left for the next year to deal with were education and Medicaid reform issues in the continuing national recession.[114] Yet, I did push through the state's first criminal stalking law.[115] In addition, I sponsored and passed legislation from the Tennessee Women's Political Caucus requiring the administration to publish monthly vacancies on state boards and commissions so that more women could apply for appointments. And I even ventured into international politics by passing a resolution urging respect for Kuwaiti women due to reports of their mistreatment.

4

Although fortunate not to have an opponent for the 1992 elections, my out of session legislative work continued. The McWherter administration announced plans to close the Memphis Mental Health Institute (MMHI) without consulting Shelby County legislators.[116] Due to the significant need for such mental health services in our area, I asked for a Tennessee Attorney General's opinion on whether the facility could be closed by the administration when the legislature had authorized funding.[117]

And, the National Democratic Convention in New York City beckoned, which I attended as an Alternative Delegate for Bill Clinton. Gail, my younger sister, attended as well, and we shared a tiny room with another delegate from Nashville in a somewhat rundown hotel where the Tennessee delegates were housed. Getting clean towels was an adventure, and Gail had to sleep on a rollout cot.

We enjoyed sight-seeing, as well as convention events. I secured a convention pass from Congressman Bart Gordon that we were to share with one of his friends. Gail went into the convention hall first, and we made arrangements to meet at a restaurant nearby at a particular time to hand off the pass. I was at the restaurant with the friend at the appointed time. Unbeknownst to us, there were two restaurants with the exact same name near the convention hall. After a couple of hours of frantic payphone calls (before the time of cell phones), we gave up, and all went back to the hotel. Thank heavens the next day, the congressman was able to take care of his friend with another floor pass, and we were able to get some passes as well.

We decided to visit the Statue of Liberty. My sister wanted to skip going to the top, but I convinced her to do the climb. Although the sign said six hours from this point, the line didn't look very long to me. Once we got inside the statue on the narrow stairwell, we couldn't turn around. Six hours later, an exasperated sister and I snapped a photo from the top and then climbed back down. The experience took on new meaning later, after the terrorist attack of 9/11 closed the statue tours.

Early one morning, I caught a cab to Central Park for the 5k Run for American Health for the DNC. A friend wanted to attend, but after a night of partying was very late meeting me for the shared cab ride. When we arrived, the race had already begun. Having already registered, I jumped out of the cab and ran around the park. Imagine my surprise when I was announced the winner in the women's elected official category, and Rep. Bart Gordon (D-Tenn.) for the male's elected official category.[118] I guess the early bird doesn't always get the worm!

We even got to see Ann Richards' famous "potato" speech where she poked fun of Vice President Dan Quale. I met her briefly backstage. A few years later, I contacted the Texas governor's office to ask if Richards had time to talk with me about politics. Governor Richards was gracious enough to take the time and gave me some good advice. Of course, she had a great sense of humor—asking about our "good-looking" single Governor Ned McWherter.

5

An opportunity arose to take advocacy for women overseas. With Cohen's nomination, I was grateful to serve as a delegate of the American Council of Young Political Leaders to Japan. Our ten-member delegation met with many leaders in Tokyo, including members of the National Diet (Japan's equivalent of the U.S. Congress), business leaders, state and local officials, high-ranking bureaucrats from the national government, and members of the press and media. The delegation toured factories, businesses, heard from experts in various fields, and even attended a baseball game and a watering hole that featured Elvis music.

Among those we met was Morihiro Hosokawa, Chairman of the Japan New Party, who the next year became the Prime Minister for Japan. When we learned of his selection, I sent a congratulatory note, commending him on his campaign pledge to include women in his cabinet.

Seeing that the Diet members on our meeting agenda were all male, I asked if we could meet a female Diet member. The hosts graciously added to the schedule Takako Doi, the former Chair of the Social Democratic Party of Japan and Member of the Japan House of Representatives. The next year, Doi was elected the first woman speaker of the Japanese Diet's lower house, and the highest position a female politician had held in the country's modern history.[119] As we encountered government and business leaders, we always asked about plans to include more women.

Another economist on the itinerary surprised me with his response to my question of whether the country's aging population would result in more opportunities for women in the workplace. He flippantly replied that the country would rely on Korean labor, and robots were being developed that will cook dinner, clean house, and "kiss you good night, too." Years later, in 2014, news reports came out of a robot named "Pepper," developed by a Japanese company that recognizes the people's emotions, dances, sings, and tells jokes.[120] Its billionaire developer wanted the robot to be "tender" as a possible companion for the country's growing elderly and lonely population. Now I know what that economist was talking about.[121]

With protocol of paramount importance, our hosts were very anxious about being on time for the morning tea scheduled with the Chief Cabinet Secretary. Although the schedule was intense, with virtually every minute booked from early in the morning to the evening, delegation members still managed to visit local nightclubs in Tokyo sometimes until the wee hours of the morning. Nonetheless, our ten-member delegation did arrive on time at the Cabinet Secretary's office and was seated at a long table with formal tea served.

Despite the seriousness and high honor of the meeting, it was still hard not to laugh when one hungover delegation member got up and, for what seemed an eternity, slowly walked down the very long length of the table and out of the room without explanation. We all suspected that he was lucky to make it out the room without having a George H.W. Bush-esque Japanese dinner upchuck experience.

Our delegation traveled through to Kyoto, toured an Imperial palace and enjoyed a traditional Japanese play. The last stop was the small town of Kaaga, where we toured an art exhibit center and a manufacturer. We even enjoyed a traditional bathhouse—where women bathed separately from men.

Returning to the United States from the neon, crowdedness, and limited green space of Tokyo, I felt very thankful for the beautiful trees, larger living spaces, and single-family neighborhoods in my hometown. Also, I was glad that even though more gains were needed, I lived in a country where women at that time had relatively more opportunities in the workplace than in Japan. However, I will never forget the wonderful hosts, beautiful countryside, and interfacing with Japan's top leaders.

6

Back in Memphis, I was re-elected to the state house in 1992 without opposition. In keeping with my belief that a woman can achieve anything if she works hard and plays by the rules, I ran for a state house leadership position, although I was only one of a few women in the Democratic legislative caucus. My freshman male colleagues were running for positions, so why shouldn't I? Wasn't I just as – or *more* – qualified?

So, I ran for House Majority Whip in the House Democratic leadership caucus elections. Believing I had the votes after polling caucus members, I asked another candidate on the eve of the vote to drop out of the race. He thought he had the votes. When we compared notes, to my surprise, many of the legislators on my list of supporters were also on his list as supporters! At least I had a head's up as to what was about to happen.

When the results were announced, it was the practice for the winners and the losers to make brief remarks. When my turn came, having lost the election, I calmly walked to the podium and said, "For those who told me you would vote for me and did, I thank you. For those who told me you wouldn't vote for me and didn't, I respect you. For those who told me you would vote for me and didn't…" *Long pause.* "…I know who you are." The crowd burst out with laughter, and several legislators ran up trying to explain to me why they told me they would vote for me and didn't, unwittingly showing their hand.

Over the next year, I openly told anyone who would listen about how sexist the Tennessee House Democratic caucus was since only one woman—House Speaker Pro Tempore Lois Deberry, had ever served in the top leadership. Also, no women were serving as chair of any of the thirteen state house standing committees.

Yet, I didn't give up and continued to hope that another door would open for me to move up and serve in a greater way. When Al Gore was tapped for U.S. Vice President, questions arose as to whom the governor would appoint to serve the remainder of Gore's U.S. Senate term. Mentioned were Rep. John Tanner, Rep. Jim Cooper, and Jane Eskind, who previously had run for the seat. Since Eskind also had run for governor against McWherter, she was promptly eliminated from the list.

Also mentioned as a potential appointee was the *Nashville Banner* publisher's wife, and—yours truly, Carol Chumney.[122] In an article in the *Memphis Flyer*, Jackson Baker referred to me as "highly regarded in the House for a first-termer," and "indisputably ambitious" based on the encouragement by my political consultant John Bakke who had advised congressmen and mayoral candidates.[123] Yet, the reporter ended his article by promoting me for a 7th congressional race in a highly Republican district, moreover, not one where I resided.[124] While I didn't get the U.S. Senate appointment, I hoped that there would be another Year of the Woman in the near future.

5

Standing Up Against Sexual Harassment

1

The year 1993 kicked off with the usual riverboat cruise for state legislators aboard the General Jackson showboat in Nashville on the Cumberland River and fireworks hosted by the Tennessee Business Committee. Then, the annual dog and pony show began with Cohen pushing a statewide lottery referendum without casino gambling and Mayor Herenton pushing casino gambling, which Cohen feared would kill chances of passing the lottery.[125] Herenton announced getting casinos in Memphis was his top legislative priority but ultimately backed off for the time being.[126]

But that wasn't the only hot issue. Women legislators contended gender bias when none were elected to the House Fiscal Review Committee despite two female candidates. Rep. Karen Williams, who had been a candidate, was even denied her attempt to address the disparity on the state house floor before the session adjourned.[127] My bombshell was filing legislation to define sexual harassment, require sexual harassment policies for all three branches of government, and mandatory workshops on the subject.[128]

With that, the legislature adjourned to allow most Democratic officials to attend the inauguration of Bill Clinton and Al Gore in Washington, D.C. Once again, my sister Gail joined me. We went to a concert featuring Barbara Streisand, and the actual inauguration, where we heard Clinton's promise of change.

The Tennessee Ball featured Paul Simon, with Bill, Hillary, Al, and Tipper jointly appearing. We all loved it when they danced, and then Bill put on shades and played the saxophone with Simon and his band. It didn't even bother me that two other women wore the exact same dress as I did or that there was nowhere to sit, nothing to eat, and we couldn't leave for the restroom and return due to security. We had a blast dancing and cheering with David Upton and other friends.

When the session resumed, saying that the reaction to my sexual harassment bill at Capitol Hill was chilly is an understatement. Yet, it was needed. The *Tennessean* editorialized in its favor reporting that only 377 of the state's 64,962 employees had received training on the subject, and neither the legislative nor judicial branches of government had policies.[129] As I explained, it was a pervasive problem, with some men not understanding that you're not supposed to pat a woman on the bottom at work. Women simply want to be treated with respect.[130]

An example of the need for the law was the federal criminal trial of Chancellor Judge David Lanier from Dyersburg, Tennessee. He was found guilty in federal court of two felony and five misdemeanor charges for criminally violating the constitutional rights of five women by assaulting them sexually while he served as a state judge.[131]

Paula Wade wrote a scathing column in the *Commercial Appeal* about her own experiences as a reporter and victim of sexual harassment at the State Capitol.[132] She reported comments made by some male legislators about her body, with one urging her to wear short skirts so he could stay awake in committee meetings.[133] Wade noted that I, and my cosponsor Rep. Henri Brooks, were "a formidable pair of serious-minded, outspoken professional women," and we had Sen. Steve Cohen as the senate sponsor.[134] However, in her opinion getting the bill through "the good-ole-boy gauntlet of the state legislature" might be daunting because these guys "just don't get it."[135] She was right; it would be difficult.

According to Wade, a male legislator had asked another female reporter in jest if he could "feel" her after she said she felt like actress Kathleen Turner that day.[136] And, Wade, herself, received sexually provocative anonymous and forged notes delivered to her by sergeants-at-arms on the house floor and during committee meetings, just as I had.[137] Because the female staff feared losing their jobs and did not comment, their experiences were probably worse.[138]

In fact, I filed the bill because a legislative secretary told me of pervasive harassment. She asked me not to reveal her name. After I filed the bill, a reporter wanted to interview her. I called and asked if she would agree to an anonymous interview. She was so afraid that she declined and begged me to remove anything from my files about her. I did, and shortly after that, my entire sexual harassment bill folder mysteriously disappeared from my office. To this day, I have never revealed her name to a single person.

Wade recognized in her editorial the pressure that female legislators, reporters, and staff members felt to laugh the incidents off as "boys being boys."[139] However, she also stated that the behavior was "demeaning, intimidating" and interfered with the legislative process, adding that this was "not a fraternity house."[140] I was glad she spoke out in support of the bill.

The story of the condom sent anonymously to me on the state house floor, and the "pink panties" episode, along with my sexual harassment bill, made statewide news.[141] Adding fuel to the fire were national allegations of sexual harassment by numerous women against U.S. Sen. Bob Packwood (R-Oregon).[142]

One male legislator opposed my bill because he didn't "like a sexual harassment policy being 'shoved' upon him."[143] Cohen predicted that some lawmakers would try to defeat the measure on the grounds that it would be too expensive to require all state employees to attend sexual harassment workshops.[144] I replied that we could amend the bill to make the workshops voluntary if it was necessary, to avoid that excuse for voting against the bill.[145]

The legislative session was lonely for me, with many colleagues angry about the sexual harassment bill. I soldiered on. The session became even more intense when Senator Cohen and I sent a letter to Chancellor David Lanier asking him to resign his judgeship so as to avoid waiting for the Tennessee Court of Judiciary to take action on his removal.[146] If he refused, we would then introduce a resolution for his removal, which required a two-thirds vote in each chamber of the state legislature.[147]

In the federal court trial, several women testified against Lanier, making national news. Their testimony included stories of his forcing a woman whose daughter's custody remained subject to his jurisdiction from a divorce proceeding to perform oral sex and grabbing the breasts and buttocks of several other women who worked at the courthouse.[148] Prosecutors argued that Lanier used his power to victimize the women; Lanier contended that the prosecution was politically motivated.[149]

Our action was prompted when several women called concerned that Lanier's victims would have to testify again before the Court of Judiciary and be personally cross-examined by Lanier. The trial court revoked Lanier's bond after finding he had contacted prosecution witnesses after the conviction.[150] Our resolution would be personally delivered to Lanier by a sergeant of arms, and he was afforded ten days' notice under the *Tennessee Constitution*. The process was much simpler than impeachment, requiring a trial in the senate.

Rep. Ronnie Cole (D-Dyersburg), the state representative for Chancellor Lanier's area, and several house legislative leaders argued that the state legislature should wait for the Court of Judiciary to act instead of passing a resolution ousting Lanier.[151] The Court of Judiciary was expected to take at least a month before rendering a recommendation. Cole asked us to stay out of matters involving his state legislative district and said a Tennessee Attorney General's opinion had been requested on the removal procedure.[152]

Cohen, not to be deterred, asked Tennessee Attorney General Charles Burson for his own opinion, and at a press conference, said that we would move ahead "full speed, damn the torpedoes."[153] Cole accused us of grandstanding.[154] Cohen replied that we were simply following the procedure authorized by the *Tennessee Constitution*.[155] Because there was a conviction, as opposed to mere allegations of impropriety, he argued that the Court of Judiciary hearing was unnecessary.[156] Even if the Court of Judiciary were to rule, the most severe penalty would be to ask the legislature to impeach Lanier, causing an additional delay, and possibly requiring a special session if not handled before the regular session adjourned.[157]

2

The 1993 session droned on with frustrated legislators finally voting to extend the half-cent sales tax increase to fund education reform.[158] The move left the tax reform debate for the next governor. Rep. Rufus Jones and others argued that this would simply add a greater tax burden on the poor. [159]

Cohen, also frustrated, withdrew his lottery resolution, and blamed the casino gambling supporters.[160] And, at the age of thirty-one, the local Memphis daily newspaper ran a photo of me with the caption, "As an ambitious freshman, Chumney sponsored and passed more bills than any first-term lawmaker in recent memory. She is outspoken on women's issues, individual rights, public schools, and colleges."[161] The fact that my work had been recognized was encouraging.

Besides the major coverage of the sexual harassment bill, the press and media had a field day with the debate on "potty parity" legislation, which Cohen asked me to sponsor in the state house. The bill would require restroom facilities for women at a higher ratio than men in new and renovated public stadiums and other buildings. It seemed like a no brainer since women often waited in long lines at the facilities. The architects did not factor in that it takes women longer to undress due to our anatomy or that babies and children are often in tow.

Sen. John Ford made the unfortunate error of commenting that women should just not drink as many soft drinks, beer or water.[162] Sen. Thelma Harper, an African American representing Nashville known for her prominent decorated hats, called him to task.[163] One editorial, although recognizing Ford's good voting record on women's issues, chastised him, saying he should undertake potty training to use the restroom while carrying a purse, coat, wearing pantyhose, and holding a baby needing a diaper change. [164] The image was hilarious, especially since he was known to be a lady's man.

In all fairness, Sen. Ford responded that his remark was made in jest and taken out of context.[165] He accused Harper of showing off, which she denied. Ford flatly refused to apologize saying that he respected women and was proud of his record of hiring females as both a state legislator and court clerk. [166]

3

The sexual harassment bill wasn't the only one that was difficult to pass. My bill to outlaw ticket scalping with a $500 fine was not yet moving in the House Judiciary Committee. When "Radio Ron," a radio reporter at the legislature, asked whether he should invite Garth Brooks to come and speak in support, I said, "yes" thinking that he was just kidding. A few days later, Brooks was on the Nashville newspapers' front pages about his expected appearance before the committee. I was surprised and a bit nervous.

During the session, college students will intern. My interns asked if they could ride in the car to pick up Brooks. Since there was not enough space for me to ride, too, I didn't have the heart to tell one of them, "no." In hindsight, I should have gone myself in order to brief Brooks on the legislative process.

Brooks showed up, black cowboy hat in hand. I introduced him to the committee members before a packed room. He testified that scalpers hired homeless people and teenagers to stand in line to buy the tickets and then sold them at enormous prices, calling the practice "evil." [167]Brooks said that the scalping robs his regular fans of the chance to see the show at a legitimate price.[168]

There was much debate on the bill and some joking. Rep. Jere Hargrove asked, "When you wrote about 'friends in low places,' did you have us in mind?" Not missing a beat, Brooks quipped, "It depends on how you vote on this bill."

Due to some of the legislators' questions about how the proposed law would operate, it was moved over to be considered again on another day. While this is standard practice in the state legislature, Brooks took offense. After the hearing, we gathered in the House Speaker's office for photographs with the country music star. Brooks gave an impromptu press conference and blasted the legislators for not passing the bill out of committee, saying the process "scares me to death."[169] The fallout continued, in news stories over the next few days, with the House Speaker defending the legislators. Brooks came under scrutiny with one report that he was not even registered to vote.

Despite the controversy, I finally was able to get the bill passed out of committee after the popular University of Tennessee and other college sporting event tickets were exempted. However, due to the fact that a legislator's family member had previously run into ticket scalping trouble in Kentucky and adamantly opposed the bill, it did not become law at that time.

Years later, in 2013, the issue resurfaced with a high-powered coalition including the FedExForum, UT, Tennessee Titans, Nashville's Grand Ole Opry, along with Garth Brooks, and others, pushing legislation to require internet ticket scalpers to disclose their identity, give the original cost of the ticket, and correct seat location, and to stop deceptive practices.[170] Pat Halloran, CEO of the Orpheum in Memphis, said that "rogue" scalpers were using fake websites to trick patrons into buying tickets that had not even gone on sale yet. They were also using software to buy up the best tickets before fans had an equal chance to purchase those tickets.[171] It was nice to see that a law was finally passed, albeit two decades later.

4

The debate on my sexual harassment bill continued. In the past year, when I had suggested to the house leaders that the legislature develop a policy, they seemed receptive but still had not publicly commented on my bill.[172] In an effort to garner their support, I explained that the legislation protected both employers and workers by educating them on what constitutes sexual harassment and the consequences. The bill's intent was not to keep men from complimenting women or telling a joke but to address offensive behavior that would have an impact on a person's job, particularly those in an unequal status.

Some legislators raised objections that employers might lose a customer if they had to prevent someone from sexually harassing an employee. My response was, "What if it was your mother, or your daughter, or your sister?" and "You might lose a client, but it is an issue of right and wrong." Workers are more productive where they feel respected and safe. Perhaps some of the pushback was a backlash due to recent gains made by women in the workplace.

Still trying to get the votes, I decided on a strategy to ward off any claims by legislators of insufficient knowledge about what sexual harassment was as an excuse to vote against the bill. Borrowing educational videos on sexual harassment, I reserved a room in the Old Supreme Court chambers in the State Capitol Building to continuously run the videos all day so the legislators and staff could watch when their schedules permitted.[173]

In the last days of the session, my sexual harassment bill passed after nearly two hours of debate on the house floor, with numerous parliamentary procedures to try and send the bill back to the committee (with forty house members even voting "aye"). One of the biggest opponents was another female colleague. During the lengthy debate, I took a quick break from standing in the well as the house sponsor and went behind the speaker's podium to get a cup of water from the water cooler. I recall my hands shaking. Finally, the votes were cast. One legislator later admitted that he stepped out on the balcony to avoid voting. Despite all the hoopla, nearly every house member voted "aye." The bill passed the house by a vote of eighty to eleven. [174]

The bill passed the senate with three no votes and two women senators abstaining.[175] Sen. Thelma Harper was the only female senator to vote "aye."[176] The first sexual harassment law for Tennessee would now be mailed to all employers, and workshops would be made available to all state employees, including judges and legislators.

The bill went further than federal law in requiring the legislature and judiciary to adopt policies.[177] To put it in perspective, in 2014, the house in the U.S. Congress still did not require training, although a federal statute was enacted in 1995 to create a process to report sexual misconduct after the resignation of Packwood.[178] As the *Tennessean* editorialized in 1993, the Tennessee law came about because of the anonymous condom sent to me by a colleague on the state house floor, which was an impetus for my introducing the bill that now led to protections for everyone in state government.[179]

The policy was updated in 2016 after two state legislators were accused of violating it, and one ousted with the other resigning. [180] The state senate and house sexual harassment policies were amended to include founded complaints to become public records and require supervisors to report any incidents. [181]And the House Speaker announced he would resign in 2019 after a *Tennessean* investigation revealed sexually charged text messages shared by his chief of staff, among other things. [182] Thus, it was clear that the policy was needed.

On the same day that my sexual harassment bill passed, the Tennessee General Assembly adopted the resolution to remove convicted felon Lanier from his judicial position.[183] Although he had sent me a creepy letter, ultimately, he chose not to appear and defend. It was good to have the issue behind us.

5

In addition to the sexual harassment bill, my advocacy for women included co-sponsoring a bipartisan bill requiring the party caucuses to have open voting on the state's constitutional officers' elections.[184] The Democrats were in control of both legislative chambers and used secret balloting on the caucus elections for nominations of the secretary of state, comptroller, and treasurer. Once the nominees were chosen, they were assured of election in the respective legislative bodies due to party loyalty.

My experience of vote counting in the House Majority Whip race in 1992 was similar to that of two candidates for Tennessee Secretary of State that year. Both Riley Darnell and Bryant Millsaps believed they had the votes needed, but as the *Tennessean* editorialized, "no one can spot a turncoat with secret ballots."[185]

My support of the reform measure was based, in part, on the fact that no woman in the history of the State of Tennessee has ever held one of those state constitutional positions. Keeping the vote secret seemed like an easy way to just keep the good ole boy network going. My support of the measure was not appreciated by some in the house leadership. Unfortunately, it did not pass. Tennessee, as of 2021, still has never had a female state constitutional officer.

6

Leading Crusader for Women

1

When the session resumed in 1994, women made more gains with the bill sponsored by Representative Hargrove requiring every other future guber-natorial appointment to each of the four state education boards to be the female gender until parity is reached.[186] Rep. Ron Ramsey (R- Blountville) attempted to amend the bill to make it non-mandatory and was quoted in the *Commercial Appeal* as saying, "…if we'd wanted to catch up [with parity], we would have done it by now."[187] Others joked about whether the new law would encourage men to cross-dress to get appointed, and there was even a tasteless joke about the man who had his private part removed by Lorena Bobbitt. [188]

The numbers were staggeringly gender skewed, with the powerful UT Board of Trustees only having one female member out of twenty-four; the eighteen member U.T. Board of Regents had only two female members.[189] Hargrove hit the nail on the head when he said that the bill's purpose was to include the "intellect, experience, heart, soul and perspective" of women on the boards.[190] As I said, it was more likely for a woman to be struck by lightning or killed by a shark than be appointed to one of the boards without the legislation.[191]

On the other side of the state, I was recognized in the *Johnson City Press* as being "the leading crusader for women's issues in the Tennessee General Assembly."[192] My legislative package, as one of now only fifteen women serv-ing in the state house, included wage equity legislation and divorce reform bills to allow battered spouses to list a mailing address instead of a street address in court filings and to ensure an equitable division of non-vested pensions.

Another significant measure for women brought all the female legislators united together in the well of the house chamber. The resolution I
prime-sponsored, along with Senator Cohen, created a commission to celebrate the 75th anniversary of the key vote cast in the Tennessee House of
Representatives approving the *Nineteenth Amendment* to the *U.S. Constitution,*
giving American women the right to vote. [193]The vote was called the "Perfect
36" because approval by thirty-six states was necessary. Tennessee was the
36th state to approve the amendment. The vote was extremely controversial
in 1920. We were about to find out in the year ahead that women's suffrage
still was controversial.

In a ceremony organized by my office, the legislature also recognized
in joint session the fifty-five women who had served as representatives or
senators in the 200-year history of the state. [194]Sadly, this group of female
legislators was comparatively a small number. Speakers included Dr. Dorothy
Lavinia Brown, a medical doctor and also the first African American woman
elected to serve in the Tennessee state legislature; Speaker Pro Tempore Lois
Deberry, who was the longest-serving woman; and Sen. Anna Belle Clement
O'Brien, who had held leadership roles in the state senate and run for governor.[195] It was interesting to meet some past trailblazers who served when it
was even more difficult for a woman to attain public office.

And the potty parity bill finally saw the light of day when it passed out of
the all-male powerful House Budget Subcommittee.[196] Although I was afraid
of "getting pottied on" by the committee, I had help from the executive branch,
house leaders, and lawmakers' wives and family members behind the scenes. The
potty parity bill required the state building commission to set the ratio of how
many more water closets and lavatories women would have than men. Later, on
the house floor, I asked for support so that women could "catch the big slam-
dunk at the basketball games, hear the great (guitar) lick at the concert, and
watch the winning touchdown at the football game."[197] It passed unanimously,
and I was thrilled in light of persistent teasing by my male colleagues.

Women's issues were also on the table with judicial reform efforts.[198] I
was a crucial vote in the House Judiciary Committee for the plan to allow
Tennessee Supreme Court justices and appellate judges to run in nonpartisan
retention elections.[199] Before the law, the executive committee of the party
in power nominated the justices. The reform measure passed by one vote
in the House Judiciary Committee and would require the judicial selection
commission that made recommendations to the governor for new appointees

to be balanced by race and gender. [200] In my view, it was the best chance for women to gain appointment to appellate judicial positions. Later, a wealth of women were appointed to judicial positions due to this legislation, which required the inclusion of women in the selection process.

On one occasion, at their request, I took several of the Tennessee Supreme Court Justices to the annual Memphis Barbeque Fest at Tom Lee Park at the river's edge. There they rubbed shoulders, ate pork, and shook hands with an assortment of people scattered amongst the colorful tents, trying to get re-elected. While some in the political parties disagreed, I believe in a non-partisan process for the election of judges. I supported the appointment of appellate judges with election thereafter on a simple "yes" or "no" retention vote. However, I believe that trial judges, who are often the decider of facts, should be subject to challenge by opposition candidates each election cycle. The measure eventually passed.

2

On the local front, Shelby County Commissioner Carolyn Gates lost to Jim Rout in her bid in the Republican primary to become the first woman Shelby County mayor.[201] And, in an odd twist of Tennessee history, Pam Gaia, after her unsuccessful run against Congressman Ford Sr. in 1990, switched parties and decided to challenge me in 1994 for the state house.

Gaia resurrected her trademark issue of nursing home reform, which had caused her to lose favor with Governor McWherter when she voted against his own reform proposal. In addition, Gaia now argued that the women's rights issue was "outdated" and "not as important as it used to be."[202] While I supported nursing home reform, my response was that women's issues are always relevant.

Gaia's independence was notable. Taking a much-needed vacation before the campaign heated up allowed me to consider the independence, bravery, and crusade of another woman and the consequences. I visited France. Paris was incredible, and the trip included visiting the Louvre, the Musee d'Orsay with its impressionistic paintings, Versailles, and the Eiffel Tower. I even ventured by bus to the home of Josephine, the wife of Napoleon. There, I was pleased to see a plaque on her carriage thanking Memphis for restoring it as part of the annual Wonders exhibition in the Memphis Pyramid Arena.

My French needed some work, so I relied primarily on a small digital translator device. One waiter at an upscale restaurant in Paris did not help me out with my confusion over the menu. Instead, he dutifully brought what I ordered: a soufflé for an appetizer, a soufflé for dinner, and alas to my chagrin, a soufflé for dessert. Thank heavens the German couple seated next to me had mercy on my error and traded their apple strudel for my chocolate soufflé, saving the evening!

My trip included the Loire Valley, with its lush pastures, castles, and six-course dinners. Traveling further into the countryside, I visited Monet's home and gardens, and the Normandy D-Day beaches, where just weeks before President Bill Clinton celebrated the 50th anniversary of the storming of the beach. I was never so thankful to our many brave soldiers who lost their lives saving our democracy!

One stop was the tower honoring Joan of Arc in Rouen, which contained memorabilia about her and the castle where she was imprisoned before her execution. Learning more about her incredible story, as a woman leading the French army in 1430 who would not renounce her cause, was inspiring. At the time, I had no idea that my reform efforts as a public official would be likened to her on more than one occasion in the press in later years. I recalled how Gaia had been chastised and sometimes ostracized for refusing to compromise on nursing home reforms. Although it was nice to later, like Gaia, be compared to the heroine Joan who was canonized a Catholic saint, I had no interest in being ostracized, or even worse, burned at the stake!

3

While I did champion many women's causes, my legislative work over the years included a wide range of areas. For example, I was glad to secure state grants for local needs, including repairs to a Midtown Memphis Williamson Park, for the purchase of playground equipment for children with and without disabilities at Kingsbury Elementary School, for the Randolph Public Library, the Lewis Senior Citizens Center, the Memphis Zoo, and the Memphis Youth Sympathy.[203] I love driving by and seeing the children play on the Kingsbury Elementary playground.

Sen. Jim Sasser, the U.S. Majority Leader at the time, joined me for one of my trademark town hall meetings while he campaigned.[204] On the agenda was a discussion of universal health care coverage and reform of TennCare, the $3 billion federal-state health plan that insured about 340,000 former Medicaid recipients and others who had no private health insurance. [205]I pushed for improvements in prescription drug reimbursement and coverage, adding more specialists, requiring audits of the managed care organizations, increasing funding for mental health, and providing greater access to physician care.

Domestic violence reform was also part of my platform in 1994. About that time, the country was gripped with the terrible stabbing death of Nicole Brown Simpson and the high-speed chase by law enforcement to appre-hend the famous NFL football star and TV announcer O. J. Simpson. The debate on domestic violence came to the forefront as the country speculated on whether or not he was guilty of the murder. My reform measures were well-received. [206] With estimates of hundreds of battered women killed and millions beaten every year, the O.J. Simpson case brought new attention to the serious problem. [207]

Besides legislative responsibilities, I had to play catch up to earn a living as an attorney after the session adjourned. One client, an international radio communications corporation, hired me to handle defending an appeal by the other vendor in a multi-million dollar bid for a contract to replace radio systems with the City of Memphis. Mayor Herenton heard the appeal, with twenty-six people present at the hearing, including the bidders, attorneys for the vendors, and the city officials. [208] Little did Herenton or A C Wharton (the local attorney for the losing bidder) know that each would face off against me on the ballot one day for the mayor's job. [209]In any event, this time, Herenton and I were on the same page. He denied Wharton's client's appeal.

Besides serving as mayor, Herenton was venturing into the real estate business. Through Herenton Investments, Inc., he developed Banneker Estates in southwest Memphis. [210] The developer emphasized that no tax incentives or concessions were sought for the development, geared to attract black pro-fessionals. [211] He even had his own home built in the development. Later, his development activities would draw scrutiny.

4

With the 1994 election underway, I ran as the "Can Do" representative. Apart from women's issues, my record included passing the law to authorize personalized state automobile license tags with proceeds to fund state parks, securing funding for the Tennessee Arts Commission, and supporting property tax relief for seniors. I also passed a law to establish reckless homicide as a criminal offense, cosponsored the Cohen-Kernell lottery referendum, and sponsored a bill with Lieutenant Governor Wilder to establish the Mississippi River Cycling and Hiking Corridor Trail for West Tennessee. As to ethics reform, I passed a law in the house termed the "Anti-Skullduggery Act" (conceived by Senator Cohen to prevent incumbents from handpicking their successors by withdrawing after the filing deadline without advance notice).[212]

Also, I had prime-sponsored and passed the law to provide immunity from civil liability for the condition of the meat for hunters who donate deer meat (unless negligent, reckless, or intentional conduct causes injury).[213] The Tennessee Wildlife Federation's "Hunters for the Hungry" program partnered with game processors who processed the meat for free (or at a reduced price) for donation to food banks and soup kitchens.[214] In August 2020, the Federation's website stated that since 1998, the program provided more than 7.6 million meals to those in need.[215]

During this time, on occasion I co-hosted *Legislative Report* on the local access library television channel with Senator Cohen and sometimes with Representative Kernell, discussing state issues. It was Cohen's show, and he graciously allowed me to co-host it. Cohen was extremely intelligent, fast-talking, and bullheaded. Kernell was very deliberate, considerate, and knowledgeable. The show was fun as we bantered back and forth over the topics of the day.

Due to my legislative record, visibility, and the Democratic demographics of the district, Gaia's challenge was not perceived to be strong, although I took it seriously. Accordingly, I spent the summer and fall knocking on doors, especially in the new working-class area added in redistricting. When I made it back to a higher income Midtown neighborhood to knock on doors closer to Election Day, one constituent chewed me out about his wife having to pay the new state privilege tax and my failure to stop by sooner in the campaign. Later, I found out that Gaia lived nearby and apparently walked that same street every day, which helped put in perspective his ire about not seeing me sooner.

Knocking on doors is the best way to connect with the voters. The house legislative districts contained about 50,000 people. I could knock on about 10,000 doors over six months. So, it made for long hours at the law office

during the day, and in the hot Memphis weather – with the temperature sometimes over 100 degrees – knocking on doors in the evenings and on weekends.

Although many voters asked me inside, and on occasion, I obliged, the
general rule was to spend only about 5 minutes on each house's doorstep.
Otherwise, I could not reach the number of voters needed to win the election.
Also, there were safety issues, as I was a woman often out by myself, sometimes
in high-crime areas.

One constituent in a working-class neighborhood came to the door, and
fearfully said, "What are you doing out here by yourself – there are gangs
out here." I tucked this information away to work on after the election. She
became a long-time supporter over the years.

Sometimes knocking on doors was frustrating, especially if I was tired
after a long day or chased by a pack of dogs. On one occasion, a man asked
my view on pit bulls. My literature contained a pledge to work on the issue
since an elderly woman had been mauled by one recently. As I looked down
at the half pulled back bottom of the screen door, I saw five pit bull dogs
poking their noses at me. I quickly got off the porch and felt lucky to be alive!

Another day when the weather was cloudy and about to rain, I made the
mistake of breaking the general rule not to enter the constituent's home. Once
inside, the voter began a long soliloquy on her opposite view on a major issue,
and I was stuck for about an hour. When I left, I called it a day and went
home after knocking on only one door.

Other times, knocking on doors seemed like a divine intervention by
God. Like the time I knocked on a lonely elderly man's door just after his wife
had died and the day happened to be her birthday. Or the time I sat with a
woman on her porch after she had just come home from brain surgery. I broke
the rule that day sitting with her for a long time. When I left, the thought
ran across my mind that I must be a lousy candidate for breaking the rule,
especially when the elderly woman wouldn't even vote. But I was glad to be
there to encourage her that day. As the saying goes, you never know who's
watching – years later, I ran into her son, who thanked me for spending so
much time with her that day.

After the primaries, the governor's race was now between Republican
U.S. Congressman Don Sundquist and Democrat Phil Bredesen (who had
been the mayor of Nashville). Bredesen also had built a small firm into a large
health care company. The *Memphis Business Journal* endorsed Bredesen and
me based on being better qualified than our opponents. [216]

And, the *Commercial Appeal* called me "one of the legislature's bright lights."[217] The editors recognized that I: "launched the drive for 'total quality management'" that the state government now used; was instrumental in securing funding for improvements to the Memphis Zoo; passed the Memphis Plan to help the Church Health Center expand volunteer health care for the working poor; sponsored Tennessee's first stalking law; "led creation of a registration and monitoring program for sex offenders;" helped push through McWherter's education reform for kids; "helped lead efforts to let voters decide the lottery issue;" and advocated for ethics reform and to remove the sales tax from food.[218] I appreciated the recognition of my efforts.

With an anti-incumbent mood sweeping the country, well-respected Rep. Jim Cooper (D-Nashville) had an uphill battle by running for the U.S. Senate against attorney, famous actor, Watergate presidential scandal investigator, and Republican nominee Fred Thompson. My challenge was to turn out the Democratic base in my legislative district.

Gathering support from various African American pastors, I organized a prayer breakfast at a local church for a Saturday morning. Both Congressmen Harold Ford Sr. and Jim Cooper appeared. Out of courtesy for his position, I let Ford speak first. He whipped up the crowd, telling them that I would be more effective than Gaia because she had burned bridges with the Democratic house leaders.[219] Then, the master politician gathered up the crowd before I even made my own remarks and carted them off on a bus to the election commission to early vote. This was Memphis election drama at its best, and another lesson learned—be sure to speak first at your own event.

5

Behind the scenes, another drama unfolded with a tug-of-war over what woman or women would lead the newly authorized Tennessee Women's Suffrage Commission. Cohen pushed one candidate who had a long record of advocacy for women, was well-respected and had supported us both. His arch-rival, Sen. Thelma Harper, wanted the job. Harper was supported by House Majority Leader Bill Purcell, who was also an ally. There were painful machinations and power plays behind the scenes and at public meetings.

Majority Leader Purcell resigned from the commission due to the controversy. Being pulled in two different directions, respecting both women candidates, and recognizing that both black and white women had led the effort for women's suffrage, I supported both women for a dual chairmanship. This seemed like a logical compromise to me.

The votes were very close between the two women. A meeting of the commission was scheduled for Memphis where the leaders would be elected, but there were concerns about whether enough members would attend to constitute a quorum. Then word came to me from Cohen's office that he would support the dual chairmanship for the two women. However, when I showed up at the meeting, that was not the case and those present voted in only his candidate.[220]

In his haste to get his candidate in, Cohen neglected to adhere to the state law requirements. Some members were allowed to vote by telephone, and others were not afforded the same notice and opportunity.[221] Having been misled that there was a compromise, I seriously considered resigning from the commission myself. However, I felt a responsibility to the legislators who voted to create the commission, my constituents, the past women suffragettes, and the people of Tennessee (in particular the women) to see it through. And it was a non sequitur that a commission established to celebrate the right to vote would disenfranchise members when electing its leadership.

Therefore, I requested a State Attorney General opinion on the legality of the Memphis proceedings, which put me at odds with Cohen. The Attorney General agreed that the correct procedures were not followed. At the next meeting of the commission in Nashville, both women were elected co-chairs.[222] The important work of planning the celebration moved forward.

6

Back on the campaign trail, I added the issues of addressing violence in schools and the eviction of drug dealers who live in rental properties to my platform. Gaia ran on her record of passing the law to allow pharmacists to substitute generic drugs for brand names. When asked why she switched to the Republican Party, Gaia said she did not want to be part of the local Democratic Party due to its "bossism," apparently a backhanded reference to Harold Ford Sr. and perhaps McWherter.[223]

On Election Day, November 1994, the voters put me back in, but it was a bittersweet victory. Although Gaia was my opponent that year, she also had been a mentor and a woman I admired as a high school student when there were very few women serving in public office. She will always be remembered for being a trailblazer on nursing home, generic drug, and other reform efforts.

While 1992 was the "Year of the Woman," reporter Emily Yellin wrote an article in the *Memphis Flyer* calling 1994 the "Year of No Women."[224] Yellin pointed out that there were no women in the race for Shelby County Mayor for the general election (since Carolyn Gates was defeated in the Republican primary), or U.S. Senate, or any serious gubernatorial candidates.[225]

I thought this was also more of a problem in the Southern states, which had the least representation by women in state and national governments. Also, Tennessee does not elect the constitutional offices of Treasurer, Attorney General, Secretary of State, or even Lieutenant Governor by popular vote as many states do. Thus, there are fewer opportunities for women to be elected statewide and build the name-recognition and track record for a gubernatorial or U.S. Senate bid. And there is always another male who is groomed and ingratiates himself with party leaders, waiting in the wings for appointment upon the next constitutional vacancy.

In 1994, the state senate had only three female members of thirty-three, and the state house 13 of ninety-nine members.[226] The only area where women were elected to executive positions in Shelby County [Memphis] was the county court clerk positions.[227] On the positive side, the obstacles that Southern women face when seeking higher office mean that those who do overcome them and reach the national level may be more difficult to defeat.

In November, Republican Don Sundquist was elected governor. He had pledged to appoint a cabinet and staff that would be representative of the people of the state. Yet out of twenty-seven department heads and senior staffers, he appointed eight women as opposed to thirteen or fourteen, which would be equal to the 52% female population of the state.[228] Thinking back on my wish list presented at the New Year's Day prayer breakfast in 1991 after Herenton made his nearly all-male mayoral cabinet appointments, all I could say was while some gains had been made—*deja vu.*

Progress was made, however, when the House Democratic Caucus elections were held. The House Majority Whip position came open when the current whip lost his reelection bid in his legislative district. Not a quitter, I ran again. This time I won.

7

Why Women's Suffrage Matters

1

The 1995 New Year brought the O. J. Simpson trial, the death of Vince Foster and resulting investigation, and the revelation by newly elected U.S. House Speaker Newt Gingrich's mom that he said Hillary Clinton was a "b..." according to the *Nashville Banner*.[229]

As the preparations began for the 75th anniversary of women's suffrage, we marked our progress. Women were doing better overall across the country in terms of gaining election to state legislative offices, increasing from 604 in 1975 to 1533 in 1995.[230] However, that was still only about a fifth of the positions even though women were more than half of the electorate.[231] Only 11% of the U.S. House members were women, 7% were U.S. Senators, and 8% of governors were women.[232] Tennessee ranked 40th among the state legislatures in terms of numbers of women members.[233]

Debate ensued over which political party women were gravitating toward and was more inclusive of women in leadership positions. Rep. Karen Williams was not successful in her bid to be the Republican Party candidate for the state's Public Service Commission. But, she defended her party saying that she did not want special treatment and that "if you weren't on the table, you elbow your way in."[234] The statewide Democratic Party was led by Jane Eskind, previously elected as a statewide Public Service Commissioner and an unsuccessful gubernatorial candidate.

Democrat Rep. Lois Deberry held the privilege of being the first woman elected House Speaker Pro Tempore. Sen. Thelma Harper became the first woman named Vice-Chair of the Senate State and Local Government Committee. Rep. Mae Beavers and Rep. Joyce Hassell were Republican

Assistant Floor Leaders, and Rep. Shirley Duer was the first female elected chair of the House Republican Caucus. And, although parity had not been reached, Beth Fortune, the governor's press secretary, still pointed out that Governor Sundquist's eight cabinet appointments of women were more than any prior administration. As Sen. Carol Rice observed, women needed to view their roles differently and see themselves as able to deliver the message, as opposed to just being background workers.[235]

With the issue of gender parity ripe for discussion, I pushed a legislative agenda in 1995 related to women's health. During the hot summer months of campaigning the year before, I knocked on the house door of a woman who wore a head covering and told me that she had gone through three bouts of breast cancer and was still fighting the disease. She wondered why new treatments had not been developed.

This prompted me to develop and sponsor legislation establishing a legislative committee to study women's health issues. The committee, among other things, would review whether state research facilities were giving women's health issues proper attention and assess how TennCare (Tennessee's Medicaid program) was faring in terms of servicing women's health needs.[236] The bill also would establish a Center for Excellence for Women's Health at the University of Tennessee Medical Center in Memphis to research breast cancer and other women's health issues. After discussion with the Chancellor of UT and other faculty, I asked UT to develop their own proposal.[237]

The proposed Center would focus on breast cancer, cervical cancer and heart disease, osteoporosis, and menopause. Part of the work of the Women's Health Study Committee would be to determine if the state's colleges and universities were including a proportional number of women in biomedical clinical research studies. It also would recommend specific legislative action to address women's health care, disease prevention, and research. Most troubling was that women relying on TennCare did not get epidurals during childbirth at the same rate as women on private insurance.[238]

2

The session also was exciting because the job of House Majority Whip was fascinating. I met in the private leadership planning sessions with the House Speaker, Majority Leader, Speaker Pro Tempore, and Floor Leader. My job was to help count the votes for Democratic Caucus-backed legislation, and I was good at it. I had seen how members would hedge and sometimes lie about their support in my first effort to become majority whip when I had compared votes with another candidate. As a silver lining to that defeat, it made me much more astute at determining when a "yes" was really a "yes" or just a "maybe."

One task the house leaders asked me to do was to call out the governor on the state house floor for his refusal to sign local tax bill authorizations.[239] Local governments are required to get state legislative approval for certain types of local taxes.[240] Usually, they are passed on the Consent Calendar in the house because they are local bills with no statewide application. The state legislative vote is merely giving the local body the authority to levy the taxes—or not.[241]

A local bill to extend the hotel-motel tax to pay for improvements to the Memphis Pyramid Arena was bottled up in committee in part due to the governor's position that he would not sign any tax bills. Also, some suburban Shelby County Republican legislators wanted to trade their support in return for a bill to form a special school district for the county schools. Lobbying for the hotel-tax bill were the local mayors and the hotel-motel industry in Memphis. For local bills, the signature of all of that county's state legislators usually was required. Sen. John Ford pushed it through the horse-trading senate, but it was stuck in the house.

The governor and some legislators were gun-shy on the fairly innocuous local tax bills. They had become fodder for opponents' unscrupulous campaign ads claiming that a vote to permit a local tax to be adopted or not in another legislator's county was a vote for a tax increase.[242] On the house floor, I likened the governor to a general who sends the troops into battle and stays behind the lines because he expected the legislators to take the heat for passing the bills without his signature.[243] And, in my next campaign, I found a way around the unfair tax increase accusations by having my staff add up every tax decrease I voted for and sending that to the voters in response to any attack by my opponent.

3

Apart from the tax bill debate, Ann Davis, a female constituent, asked me to sponsor legislation to require licensure for massage therapists, which were unregulated. They were tired of being lumped in with prostitutes in the public's mind and wanted licensure to demonstrate that they are legitimate professionals simply providing therapeutic massage.[244] Advertisements abounded by those who were in the other profession for "mirrored Jacuzzi room" with "beautiful masseuses." The confusion caused problems for legitimate massage therapists when a customer expected more than a massage. The bill required training for licensure and prohibited anyone with a felony conviction or a conviction for prostitution or sexual misconduct from qualifying.

Knowing that the conservative state legislature might misconstrue the bill, we pitched it as a law enforcement measure that would make it a criminal misdemeanor for anyone without a license to advertise or engage in massage for compensation. We also secured a Republican, Sen. Keith Jordan, to carry the bill in the state senate. When the bill became law, the police would be able to make arrests without having to prove an illicit act at "massage parlors" if they had no legitimate state license and were really "whoopee parlors" and fronts for prostitution. [245]

In addition to garnering support from Senator Jordan and Governor Don Sundquist (who already had a legitimate masseuse), we also planned a Massage Licensure Day at the State Capitol. At that time, massage therapy was a relatively new profession, and most of the state legislators had never received a professional massage. Massage therapists from around the state brought their chairs and gave free neck and shoulder massages in the halls of the underground Legislative Plaza in front of the legislative committee rooms. The bill breezed through the more relaxed state legislature. Later, a legislator from another conservative Southern state asked me how we got it passed, as his licensure bill had been balled up in their state legislature with fears that it would legalize prostitution. Today, licensed massage therapy is a commonly accepted profession.

4

My legislative package also dealt with domestic violence, AIDS screening for indigent pregnant women, and the growing gang problem. Recalling my constituent's concerns about gangs in her neighborhood, I called a town hall meeting at Kingsbury High School, inviting the neighbors, police, and school officials. One parent took the mike and said she had removed her child from the school because of threats and harassment from gangs.[246] A good-sized crowd of fifty parents, along with the principal, attended. A few years earlier, a youth had been shot in the neck at the school, and another's jaw had been broken after school. The parents were furious at the school officials.

At the time, I knew some school officials were mad at me for calling the meeting due to the bad publicity for their school. However, years later, a police officer who was there told me that due to that meeting, the police were able to get additional resources for gang intervention because the problem had finally been brought to the forefront.[247] Certainly, denying that a problem exists is not the way to solve it! Later, with Senator Jim Kyle, I sponsored the Kingsbury High School's championship basketball team at the State Capitol to ensure that the school received positive coverage for its students as well.

And, in the aftermath of the O. J. Simpson investigation and trial and at the request of advocates, I sponsored legislation to create a statewide council to develop policies and training programs on domestic violence for police, judges, and others in the criminal justice system. With several women battered by a husband or boyfriend every minute in the nation, a lot of work needed to be done to alleviate the problem.[248] It was estimated that 30,000 women and children were served in family violence shelters in the state in 1994.[249]

Another bill sponsored by Rep. Roy Herron and Rep. Brenda Turner would force the police to make an arrest when arriving at a domestic violence scene.[250] On why police did not routinely make arrests at the domestic violence scene, the *Chattanooga Times* editors put it best, saying "the problem is that wife-beating is still not universally acknowledged as a serious crime" and instead was seen as a "family problem."[251] Other reforms required doctors and medical professionals to report domestic violence and waived filing fees for orders of protection.

At an event at the National Civil Rights Museum, I was the keynote speaker on the topic of combatting domestic violence. It was on the same night that a television interview of Simpson was scheduled and then canceled. In my remarks, I said, whether or not you believe Simpson is innocent or guilty of the murder charges, it was never disputed that Brown had suffered domestic violence.

I urged the public not to ignore the truth like so many batterers do, and instead, as a society, stand up and say, "No way, O.J." Despite the acquittal, the Simpson trial squarely focused the public's attention on the issue, with reforms growing in the aftermath. This was similar to the sexual harassment reforms after Anita Hill's testimony, even though Clarence Thomas was approved for the U.S. Supreme Court. Never before had I seen a top gubernatorial candidate running television ads touting his plan to fight domestic violence in Tennessee. Many new state laws were enacted largely due to the awareness raised by the tragic Nicole Brown murder.

In addition to domestic violence reforms, the Women's Health Committee was approved, and we began hearings on the lack of sufficient standards in TennCare to protect pregnant women and babies. Funding had been cut to the Regional Medical Center in Memphis, and reports came back that pregnant women were no longer being screened for AIDs even though the risk that the baby would be born with the illness would drop two-thirds if given the anti-viral drug.[252] Also, the date rape bill did pass, even though some senators actually debated whether only a "chaste" woman could be raped.[253]

5

Sometimes being an effective legislator is about what you stop as opposed to what you pass. The Budget subcommittee of the House Finance Ways & Means Committee was the most powerful committee in the state house, where all bills with fiscal notes over $100,000 were assigned. The subcommittee was known as the "black hole" in that many of the bills never see the light of day again. The chair was Tommy Head (D-Clarksville), a very tall, influential figure, and the brother of Pat Head Summit, the famous University of Tennessee championship women's basketball coach. His clout put in proper context the pressure felt by the three-member House Judiciary Civil Practice subcommittee, on which I served when Head's environmental audit bill arrived for consideration.

Manufacturers and businesses backed Head's bill that would allow environmental audits they made of property to be confidential.[254] While more properties might be cleaned up, those harmed by the pollution would not have access to the information for any civil lawsuit. The bill initially also protected the polluters from criminal prosecution, but the sponsor dropped that.

Our subcommittee was on the line, worried that if we voted against Head's environmental audit bill, none of our other bills lodged in the Budget subcommittee would see the light of day. Therefore, we kept the ball in the air the entire session, continuing to consider the bill but never actually taking a vote. Head finally dropped the bill in exasperation. Later, we received the Tennessee Citizen Action and Tennessee Trial Lawyer's Consumer Protection Awards because of our subcommittee's efforts.

6

With the focus turned to the upcoming historic 75th year of women's right to vote, the Women's Suffrage Commission wasn't the only "brouhaha" for state-wide landmark celebrations. Tennessee's 1996 Bicentennial celebration plans were underway, with Vice President Al Gore as honorary chair. News reports came out that Gov. Don Sundquist and the First Lady Martha Sundquist wanted Gore to withdraw so they could head up the celebration.[255] With Gore and Lamar Alexander's sights on the presidency, some were concerned that the non-partisan celebration would become partisan during the U.S. Presidential election year. Sundquist was said to be having legislation drawn up to replace Gore.[256]

Some Democratic Party leaders wanted Gore to lead the event because he was the highest-ranking Tennessean in the White House in more than 100 years. As House Majority Whip, I suggested to the press that maybe they should be co-chairs. Martha Ingram, chair of the board of Tennessee 200, agreed.[257] There were concerns that if the matter were not resolved, Sundquist would send the million dollars allocated in the budget to a group other than the nonprofit, which could result in separate Republican and Democratic celebrations.[258] Eventually, it was worked out that the Sundquists would be honorary co-chairs of the event, with Al Gore chairing the advisory committee of current and past congressional leaders. [259]

7

It also didn't take long for the new sexual harassment law to get its first workout, with a twenty-eight year-old legislative assistant asking for an investigation of 58-year old Rep. Joe Bell. [260] Bell, who often sported a wide grin, was the House Agriculture Committee's powerful chair and had been a state legislator since 1977. He was known for conscientiously attending weddings and funerals in his rural district. The press quoted the legislature's personnel director as saying that the secretary had taped conversations with Bell.[261] The *Knoxville News Sentinel* quoted other sources that the tapes contained "graphic language" in which he offered to pay her car note and apartment rent in exchange for sex.[262]

Under the new legislative policy, the House Speaker could give an oral or written reprimand or refer the matter to a committee. To expel a member took a two-thirds vote of the state house. I reiterated that the law was passed to set up a procedure to ensure all rights were protected in evaluating the allegations, raise awareness and educate the the legislators and staff, and make sure that each legislator properly conducted his or her office.[263]

The next day, Speaker Naifeh issued a press statement that he found Bell had violated the new sexual harassment policy. The House Speaker decided that Bell had created an "offensive working environment with his inappropriate conduct" and by "unwelcome sexual advances and inappropriate and offensive verbal conduct of a sexual nature." The House Speaker removed Bell as chair of the House Agriculture Committee, reassigned him from his prestigious office in the Legislative Plaza to the less favored War Memorial Building where the Republicans and freshmen were assigned, and publicly reprimanded him for his behavior. The House Speaker added that he had taken the most severe actions possible within his authority. He would "support the rights of all women and men to work in a setting of mutual respect, void of behaviors that were offensive and demoralizing," and "sexual harassment would not be tolerated in the General Assembly."[264]

The legislative assistant's mother spoke out in support of her "gutsy" daughter calling Bell an "old goat" and comparing him to U.S. Sen. Bob Packwood.[265] She added that her daughter had asked Bell to stop, and he persisted and that her daughter needed the job.[266] According to the *Nashville Banner*, the mother further said that she was scared for her daughter because "we're little people" and "[t]hose guys can hurt you."[267] She added that her daughter went forward with a formal complaint if only to help other women.[268]

Bell responded by claiming that he was solicited and set up and that the audiotape had been edited.[269] Naifeh responded that the decision was based on more evidence beyond the audiotape.[270] When the press found out that Bell had requested per diem for the days he was in Nashville related to the investigation, the House Speaker refused to pay the expense.[271] I commended the House Speaker for taking swift and appropriate action because the person at the top has to set the standard for the conduct of all others in the workplace.

The legislative assistant was elated with the House Speaker's actions but was said by the *Tennessean* to wonder if she needed to work for a woman legislator because the males would be "scared of me now."[272] A few days afterwards the *Wilson County News* reported that she felt the punishment was not sufficient because it "doesn't matter to him."[273] However, she later called and thanked me for passing the law to require the sexual harassment policy, saying that it works.

While some questioned whether her later reassignment to the typing pool was a form of punishment, the actions taken overall by Naifeh were extraordinary in light of the past atmosphere that according to the *Tennessean* had included "even open sexual liaisons between lawmakers and secretaries," and legislative college student interns.[274] As editorialized by the *Nashville Banner*, Naifeh's swift punishment was appropriate, timely and brought a "new day" to the good ole boy state legislature, especially in comparison to the then still unresolved U.S. Senate's handling of the sexual harassment complaints against Sen. Bob Packwood which had been public more than two years.[275]

The litany of pranks that had grabbed the public's attention, such as the condom being sent to me anonymously on the house floor, and the "pink panties" incident, along with Chancellor Lanier's conviction, were reviewed again by the press about the pervasiveness of sexual harassment in government. According to the *Tennessean*, prior reforms in the early 1970s had included House Speaker McWherter requiring "secretaries to report to work, observe a dress code and actually type."[276] Later, Lt. Governor Wilder and House Speaker Naifeh took hiring and firing of legislative secretaries away from the individual legislators to be instead handled through a screening process by the personnel director with the decision-making by the speakers. However, they still were not subject to civil service protection.[277] My thoughts were that the legislature was growing more inclusive of women since 1990 with the aid of the new sexual harassment law, although there were still only seventeen women out of 132 legislators.

8

The Tennessee Women's Suffrage Celebration finally came together, with a special thanks to the help of many, including the Women's Suffrage Commission, my legislative assistant Donna Morgan and other members of the dedicated state legislative staff. Tipper Gore, the spouse of Vice President Al Gore, joined the festivities at a National Women's Political Caucus Convention in Nashville.[278]

However, some were not on board with the commemoration. On the national level, the U.S. House declined to move a 13-ton women's suffrage statue depicting Susan B. Anthony, Elizabeth Cady Stanton and Lucrecia Mott from the Capitol Crypt to the Rotunda due to its weight. [279] And when Dolly Parton's assistant was called to invite her to participate in the celebration, although still her fans, we were amused and disappointed when the word came back that "Dolly doesn't do causes."

Leading up to the historical reenactment, the Tennessee House of Representatives' exciting cliff hanging vote that decided women's right to vote in America was recounted by newspapers. The governor had called the special session at the request of President Woodrow Wilson, and suffragettes and anti-suffragists came from around the country to the State Capitol to lobby the Tennessee lawmakers. The legislators that opposed women's right to vote wore red roses while those in support wore yellow roses, hence the debate is called the "War of the Roses."[280] There was talk of bribes, or simply entertainment, to persuade the legislators.[281]

The deciding vote was cast in the Tennessee State House in 1920 by a young man, Harry Burn, age twenty-four, who wore a red rose on the day of the vote and had voted with the anti-suffragists on motions to table the vote.[282] Yet, Burns voted "aye" on the final ballot to the shock of the crowd observing the proceedings in the gallery.[283] Burns was reported to have said that he made his decision after receiving a note from his mother telling him to vote aye.[284] Burns explained, "I know that a mother's advice is always safest for her boy to follow, and my mother wanted me to vote for ratification." [285]

The women suffragists had prepared for years for the vote in the state legislatures. They were often made fun of in the press and at home. According to author Carol Lynn Yellin, as reported in the *Plain Dealer*, the anti-suffragists worried that giving women the right to vote would harm the states rights and lead to "petticoat government."[286] Some arguments were that only those who could bear arms in the military should have the right to vote, with the famous retort by Nashvillian Ann Dallas Dudley that "women bear armies."[287] The *New York Times* reported in its historical review that others argued giving women the vote would "enshrine nagging as a national policy." [288] But the suffragists argued back that women are taxpayers and deserve equality.[289]

With his vote cast, Burn, from tiny Niota, Tennessee, was also reported by *The New York Times* to have said, "I appreciate the fact that an opportunity as does seldom come to mortal man to free 17 million from political slavery was mine. I do it not for any personal glory but for the glory of my party."[290] Today, stories are still told of the historic vote, with some reports by suffrage historian Wanda Mathis that Burn had to jump from a window to escape the angry anti-suffragist lobbyists after the vote.[291] Tennessee Governor Albert H. Roberts signed the amendment on August 24, 1920, forwarded it to the U.S. Secretary of State, and the rest is history.

On August 19, 1995, more than 500 women and girls marched in the hot summer sun, some in 1920s attire, from Nashville's Union Station to the Legislative Plaza to commemorate the historic vote.[292] Then an overflow crowd in the Tennessee House of Representatives' gallery required some to watch the reenactment in a separate room with television monitors. Rep. Bob McKee (D-Niota) portrayed Harry Burn, with Rep. Don Ridgeway (D-Paris) portraying Rep. Joseph Hanover, and House Speaker Naifeh having a starring role as well. Actors were used for the anti-suffragist roles since none of the legislators wanted the parts.[293]

The crowd cheered, chanted, booed and jeered, as various actors made now humorous arguments against women having the right to vote: so that her husband could rule over her; because it would make men weak and effeminate; or that it might let prostitutes and foreigners vote. After the re-enactment vote, yellow roses were thrown from the gallery as was done seventy-five years earlier.

With a packed house, the historic re-enactment was a success. However, while Tennessee helped lead the way to make women's suffrage the law of the land, it still unfathomably lags in electing and appointing women to public office.

At the end of the re-enactment, I was honored that Speaker Naifeh recognized me as the one "very much responsible" for the reenactment celebration. In my remarks in the state house well, I stood wearing a white suit, and a yellow rose before the packed chamber and gallery and pointed out that women joined the workforce in greater numbers after gaining the right to vote in 1920. Women also made their voices heard in political circles to bring needed workplace reforms, such as better hours and conditions. Women are the majority of the voters and together can elect anyone to any position in government. But I lamented that in many ways, the political and economic power of women is unrealized.

At the seventy-five year point after winning the right to vote, I asked why only eight percent of the U.S. senators were female? Why were only ten percent of the U.S. house members women? Why had only nine women ever served as governor of a state? And why had there never been a female governor of Tennessee? I added that "because of Newt Gingrich, we still can't get the Women's Suffrage statue out of the basement of the United States Capitol." Mentioning that U.S. House Speaker Newt Gingrich was in Nashville that day, I joked that he "is probably sporting a red rose." The Democrats cheered and clapped; the Republicans weren't too happy with that remark.

At that time, women were about forty-six percent of the U.S. workforce and owned businesses that surpassed the Fortune 500 in numbers of jobs created with billions of dollars in revenues. Fifty-five percent of working women were earning one-half or more of the family income.[294] Yet, I noted that women still earned only seventy-five cents to the male wage dollar despite these facts. And, only a handful of women served as CEOs in America's 1000 largest public corporations.

I told the packed audience that "the glass ceiling is real and represents our next greatest challenge" and called upon women to strengthen their voices, make their presence felt, challenge the status quo, and continue the fight that our mothers and grandmothers began. I advocated for more women to be elected to office, promoted in the workplace, and for quality daycare. My remarks concluded by urging women to lead the fight for health care and education reforms and a better and more humane world.

Speaker Pro Tempore Deberry followed, paying tribute to former women suffragists but also calling for a new vision for the enormous challenges ahead. She noted that women were still behind as far as wages and participation in the board room were concerned. Deberry called for women to run for political office to address social injustices, saying that women are strong and the hope of survival of a civilized world. She ended with her oft-repeated saying that "roosters crow, but hens deliver."

In introducing the governor, Lieutenant Governor Wilder acknowledged that even though we had come a long way, he agreed with "Carol" that "we aren't there yet because if we were, there would be 17 women state senators and not three." Governor Sundquist ended the celebration talking about the women in his senior staff and bragging on appointing more women to his cabinet than any other governor.[295]

Looking back, I am proud of my speech in 1995, which marked in time our lack of progress in an effort to spur progress. [296] Unfortunately, in 2021, we still never have had a woman governor in Tennessee, and only in 2018 elected our first female U.S. Senator.

However, good news did follow after the suffrage celebration when the marble statue of three female suffragists in honor of the "Women's Revolution" would gain approval in 1996 to be moved from the U.S. Capitol Crypt upstairs to the Rotunda. [297] The depiction of these women in the Rotunda would be the first for women leaders, except for a mural depicting Pocahontas. [298] Perhaps Gingrich, while in Nashville that day, heard of my remarks on the state house floor at the celebration and decided to switch roses? In any event, this was indeed a victory of sorts—albeit not the same as breaking these political, economic, and social barriers for women.

9

While women still had not reached parity for serving in Tennessee public office, another group lost power. The Tennessee Democratic Party lost the governorship, both U.S. Senate seats, and control of the state senate, with two members switching parties to join the Republican ranks. [299] And, Governor Sundquist predicted that the GOP soon would take over the state house. [300] Yet, there were some bipartisan appearances by Republican Sundquist and Democratic Nashville Mayor Phil Bredesen in support of the issuance of state bonds for the construction of a football stadium for the relocation of the Oilers professional football team to Nashville.

But there were kudos in the press for progress made in creating the Joint Committee to Study Women's Health. Now, the health care policymakers were being forced to recognize that women had specific health care needs that often were not sufficiently addressed. As the *Tennessean* editors noted, less scientific research had been done on medical issues such as osteoporosis and menstruation compared to medical problems unique to men. [301] Other examples cited by the newspaper were clinical drug trials that did not include women, surgical instruments too large for women's arteries in heart surgery, and the lack of education for medical providers as to the signs of domestic abuse. [302] The opinion added that the "legislature was smart to establish this committee; it would be smarter still if it heeds its advice." [303]

Overall, it was a good year: having been effective as House Majority Whip; the successful use of the new sexual harassment law; a well-attended and exciting Women's Suffrage Celebration; speaking on a panel concerning women's health at the National Convention of the National Women's Political Caucus;[304] and earning the Legislator of the Year Award from the March of Dimes and Tennessee Perinatal Association and the Tennessee Task Force Against Domestic Violence. The fact that I and my female colleagues' reform efforts were successful in many instances highlighted the fact that a woman can make a difference in public office, and women's suffrage matters!

8

Breaking the Same
Old *and* New Ground

1

The year 1996 began with the reversal by the U.S. Sixth Circuit Court of Appeals of the 1992 conviction of Chancellor David Lanier, in a split vote of 9-6 due to differing opinions as to whether or not he acted under "color of law" so as to constitute a federal civil rights violation. [305] Lanier had been released from jail with no bond months earlier upon notification that the Sixth Circuit was reviewing the matter.[306] He had been sentenced to twenty-five years in prison for using his powerful office to violate the civil rights of female employees and women before his court by sexually assaulting them.[307] This was the first case nationally for a sitting judge to be convicted on such charges, according to the *Commercial Appeal.* [308]

Lanier's brother served as the local prosecutor in that county and had brought no state charges.[309] The U.S. Attorney promptly appealed to the U.S. Supreme Court. Editors with the *Tennessean* urged state officials to take action to charge him to ensure justice for the eight women who described how he "forced them into oral sex, squeezed their breasts and buttocks, held their jobs and even their children as hostages." [310] I was concerned about the victims now that he had been released, albeit temporarily awaiting the Court's review.

The 1996 legislative session also kicked off with potty parity on the agenda again due to reports that the new Nashville football stadium plans had only a ratio slightly better than one to one restrooms for women as to men.[311] Cohen and I had both pushed for a two to one "potty parity" ratio. The

State Architect and Building Commission had failed to promptly establish the ratio of women's restrooms to men for new public buildings as required by the "potty parity" law.[312] The state architect took responsibility, but the damage was already done as to the Nashville stadium to be under construction. [313]

What a shame it was that new ground had not been broken for women. Women would once again have to wait in line and miss a lot of what they paid to see in the stadium. The *Tennessean* editorialized that by dragging their feet, the commissioners had sent the message that they "believe this law which some male lawmakers scoffed at during the legislative debate, is not a priority" despite research that found women require more time than men.[314]

Because the $55 million in state bonds for the stadium were proposed to be repaid with sales tax revenues from purchases by women as well as men, we argued that women should not be short-changed with insufficient restroom facilities to meet their and their children's needs.[315] It is about convenience and health, and very few men would tolerate inadequate restroom facilities for themselves. I called for those in charge of the project to step up and do the right thing. Even though the commission had finally recommended a two to one ratio for large buildings, the stadium's construction managers would not pledge that they would meet that ratio.[316] However, eventually, things worked out for women at the stadium. But, lo and behold, not enough restrooms for men were included, which caused them to wait fifteen to twenty minutes— certainly a first for their gender. Eventually, adjustments were made to get the proper ratio.[317]

Women's health continued to be on the forefront by TennCare's reversal to now authorize funding for high-dose chemotherapy stem-cell treatments for breast cancer patients.[318] The decision affected thousands of breast cancer patients statewide and would also trigger coverage by insurance companies.[319] While the new treatment was harsh, it was the only hope of beating cancer for some women. Rusty Siebert, TennCare Bureau chief, announced the change at a hearing of the Select Joint Committee to Study Women's Health after it had pushed for the coverage.[320]

And protections for pregnant women were sought with proposed legislation to require the offer of a 48-hour hospital stay to women and newborns after delivery. One bill by Rep. Brenda Turner (D-Chattanooga) required insurance companies to cover a minimum of forty-eight hours in the hospital after a normal delivery and ninety-six hours after a C-section unless post-delivery care was provided.[321] Another bill, sponsored by myself, House

Majority Leader Bill Purcell, and Sen. Jim Kyle, required insurance companies to pay for the care ordered by the attending doctor in accordance with the guidelines of the American Pediatric Association and the American College of Obstetrics and Gynecology.[322]

Another gain for women was made with the passage of my bill sought by advocates to prevent insurance companies from discriminating, denying coverage, canceling policies, or raising premiums for domestic violence victims.[323] In presenting the bill to the state house, I pointed out that if women feared that reporting domestic abuse would lead to the denial or the cancellation of their coverage, they might make up another explanation for their injuries. They might never be referred to a shelter or service or get the abuse prosecuted.

After the Women's Health Committee had studied infant mortality the prior year, a law passed, with the support of the March of Dimes, requiring the TennCare Bureau and the Department of Health to provide the committee with detailed data about pregnant women.[324] The rise again in the infant mortality rate raised a red flag. While state officials downplayed the numbers, the data showed that black children were dying at triple the rate for white babies.[325]

2

In addition to pushing the women's health agenda, I also took action concerning the funding for a new professional football arena. While some might characterize Democrats as tax-and-spenders, I always am very frugal in my approach to budgeting. Perhaps it is due to my economics degree. I don't like to see money wasted when there are so many needs being unmet. For example, my economics degree was particularly useful when the Oilers bond deal came through with concerns about whether the financing proposal adequately protected state taxpayers.

The package included $55 million in bonds and about $12 million in road and infrastructure improvements toward the $292 million Nashville stadium.[326] The House Minority Leader, H.E. Bittle, said that team owner Bud Adams had pledged $117 million in collateral for the state and city bonds should the team break the lease.[327] From my calculations, the Oilers would make $2 billion over thirty years. My questions angered some, but Rep. Don

Ridgeway also had concerns as not all of the permanent seat licenses had been sold.[328]

When questioned by me, then Finance Commissioner Bob Corker testified that the state would turn a profit on the deal over the bonds' life through increased spending of consumers. [329]Corker also agreed that the Sundquist administration would back legislation that would capture sales tax revenues to improve the Liberty Bowl Stadium in Memphis if the Oilers played there while the Nashville stadium was under construction.[330] However, my efforts to amend the bill to give the sales tax to Memphis during the two years the Oilers would play at the Memphis stadium was not adopted in the committee due to the opposition of Rep. H. E. Bittle.[331]

Later in the session, Memphis and Shelby County sought legislation sponsored by Rep. Larry Miller and Sen. Steve Cohen to allow the Sports Authority to spend state sales tax rebates received on games the Oilers played at the Liberty Bowl Stadium on non-stadium improvements.[332] When it was reported that the Sports Authority had agreed to use half of the rebate money (approximately $1 million a year) for the Oilers' team travel expenses, I successfully amended the bill on the state house floor to prohibit such payment or any other payment to the team unless a majority of both the Memphis City Council and Shelby County Commission approved it.[333] My amendment also required the Sports Authority to file an annual public report on the use of the money. Adam's team certainly didn't need the money, and my constituents did.

The various issues legislators dealt with in this session ran the gamut, from health care to taxes, sports, and even to religion. Believe it or not, the session also included a debate on two resolutions about the posting of the Ten Commandments in homes, schools, businesses, and churches, with a Democratic and a Republican version. Defeated was a law to restrict the teaching of evolution, which garnered some international attention.[334]

3

The 1996 election session was gearing up as well, with the ground-breaking news that Congressman Harold Ford Sr. would not seek reelection but instead support his son, Harold Ford Jr., for the position. The press speculated whether Rep. Lois Deberry would seek the seat, with Herenton saying he was interested in supporting her.[335] Deberry was upset about Herenton's comments, saying it ruined her chances. Presumably this was because she was now considered his candidate in a long-running feud that had developed between Ford Sr. and Herenton, as opposed to being her own woman and possibly the first female member of Congress from Memphis.

Deberry did not run for Congress, and the other two major candidates besides Harold Ford Jr. were Sen. Steve Cohen and State Rep. Rufus Jones. Mayor Herenton later endorsed Jones. Herenton had been previously married to one of Jones's sisters.[336] Yet, Ford Jr. attributed the endorsement by Herenton to the fact that he and his father "have been under attack by the mayor in past months."[337] Cohen touted his more substantial experience and qualifications over those of the much younger Ford Jr., who had never served in public office.[338]

The Republicans found a candidate to challenge me in my reelection as well—an airline baggage handler, union member, and former professional wrestler who said he was ready to get in the ring with me. [339]

That was also the year that President Bill Clinton and Vice President Al Gore were up for reelection. When they, along with Hillary and Tipper, brought their campaign bus through West Tennessee, I was there along with Speaker Pro Tempore Lois Deberry. We flew in from a legislative convention, and I barely had time to run home from the late-night flight, shower, change, grab some water, and meet her for the ride to Union City. When we got there, the Clinton campaign bus was delayed, and we waited with the crowd in the hot sun. Suddenly my bottle of water became very valuable as people began to sweat. When she arrived, Clinton spent some time assisting one woman who fainted in the heat.

After they spoke, the Clintons and Gores got on the first bus, and we rode the second bus with other legislators and officials from the area. The accommodations were rough, with the bathroom on our bus being inoperable and out of running water. The buses stopped at various little towns along the way for speechmaking, and then we took a lunch break at a small restaurant. I was able to say hello to President Clinton and had my photo taken with him inside the restaurant.

Needing to use the restroom facilities, I went to the back and asked the secret service if I could use the restroom. They said yes. I noticed that the handle to the restroom door had no knob or lock. Inside the bathroom, I struggled to unzip my front zip culottes' outfit. Suddenly the door was flung open, and the secret service agent announced, "The Vice President needs to use the restroom." I was afraid Al Gore was going to walk in right then with my outfit undone. I quickly exited while the secret service agents snickered and laughed. Perhaps this was a regular prank?

After Bill and Al spoke to the crowd again, the buses left for Memphis. When we got to Memphis City Hall, Bill Clinton, Al Gore, and Rev. Billy Kyles, who was famed for being with Dr. King at the Lorraine Motel the last day of his life, and I were photographed together behind the stage. It was an amazing experience.

My own general reelection neared, and I campaigned throughout the district and community, as did my Republican opponent. One of the must-do stops was the annual Luau hosted by Democratic Party activist Annie Pruitt in her South Memphis African American neighborhood. She roasted an entire pig in a pit in her backyard, with a lavish spread of every dish imaginable on the Luau table. I loved Ms. Pruitt. She had a wicked sense of humor, was a devout Christian, and put on her heels and danced without a care as to her age. Candidates of both parties and all races stopped by and paid homage. Ms. Pruitt's event brought people together.

Besides the Luau, visiting the churches around the city was one of the most enjoyable experiences of my tenure as a public servant. I made a point not just to show up at campaign time but also to return and worship during other times of the year. One time, when I went back to worship after an election, the preacher recognized me and reminded the congregation of the Bible story of the ten lepers (where only one came back to thank Jesus after he had healed them all).[340]

The sermons and music were inspiring. In most African American churches, the congregation sings, shouts, and claps with genuine fervor. Sometimes, the spirit overtakes a congregant, who will dance or swoon. Some services lasted two hours. At one church in North Memphis, the elderly pastor preached so long that the service lasted about three hours. When the service ended, he looked at me, surprised that I was still in the church—the only white person in the room—and explained to me that Sunday had been the only day that his ancestors could express their feelings after picking cotton all week and that's why they spent most of the day at church.

But not all was serious. Having some fun with the election, I ran an ad in the progressive *Memphis Flyer* playing a spoof on the newly appearing Singles Ads in newspapers (precursors to online dating profiles).[341] The ad read:

SFW: Single Female Whip
Looking for you in all the voting places!
35-year-old attorney, ISO 18yo+ voters,
for special date election day, Nov. 5.
*House Democratic Majority Whip
*Public Education Important
*Takes Women's Health to Heart
*Enjoys Clean Air, Water and Outdoor Fun,
(Endorsed by the Sierra Club)
*Cosponsor of lottery referendum
(Life is full of chances)
*Sense of Humor a Must
*Always Available
*Call me,
*Don't You Deserve the Best?

I didn't know whether it was the ad or my record, but I was reelected.

4

Unfortunately, my experience with the House Democratic Caucus elections did not fare as well. The House Majority Floor Leader position opened up, and I decided to run, hoping to break ground as the first female to hold the post. Several of the other Democratic women legislators, having seen that I was able to win the whip position two years earlier, decided to run for positions as well. One could count the number of elected House Democratic leadership positions on two hands, so this was unnerving to the guys thinking that the women were taking over.

My opponent for the Majority Floor Leader position lived near Nashville and hung out by the elevators at the Legislative Plaza and campaigned daily while I was back in Memphis working at the law office. I tried to gain the endorsement of one house leader who had asked for my support in a prior leadership race. Although at the time he said he gave me an "open marker," he reneged, saying it didn't give license to have his "balls" cut off. Perhaps as another omen, the evening before the vote, I had a stomach virus and was up all night. When the votes were cast, my opponent won.

So did all of the other guys except for Speaker Pro Tempore Lois Deberry. Rep. Mike Williams (D-Franklin), the new House Majority Floor Leader, attributed his victory to a rivalry between Middle and West Tennessee. However, Rep. Brenda Turner wasted no time going to the committee room podium and calling the guys out with "deep-felt disappointment" that all of the women, except Deberry, had lost.

Turner reminded the caucus members that women helped reelect Clinton and Gore and remarked on the dearth of women in the legislative leadership ranks. Also losing were Rep. Kathryn Bowers (D-Memphis) and Rep. Mary Ann Eckles (D-Murfreesboro) for House Majority Whip and Rep. Kim McMillan (D-Clarksville) for Assistant Majority Leader.

Acknowledging the gender backlash, I simply said that the door for women might have closed, but it would open again. Sometimes it is a case of two steps forward, and one step back as women try to move ahead for parity in leadership. Because of the women's losses, there was a stronger clamoring for women to have more significant leadership roles in the committee positions. The state house Democrats held a wide majority of 61 out of 99 seats, and with the Speaker's appointments, controlled the committee leadership positions.

Embarrassed, the House Speaker pledged to create a new house standing committee to work on children and families' issues. He would appoint the first woman chair of a house standing committee in the history of the state. He had lunch with me in Memphis and promised it to me. It wasn't the position I had wanted, but it was an opportunity to serve in a greater way—so I was excited.

When the session resumed in January 1997, the Speaker had a bad fall and had to come to the office with a big bandage on his forehead. That wasn't the only reason for his headache. He called me into his large office with other house leadership team members and told me that Rep. Brenda Turner wanted to serve as chair of the new House Children & Family Affairs Committee. Because she had seniority, he asked if I would agree to disregard his prior commitment and instead serve as vice-chair. This was another huge disappointment. However, I saw this as an opportunity to ask for an additional assignment, as well.

Thinking quickly on my feet, I agreed to serve as vice-chair of the new committee as he requested. However, I also asked the House Speaker to put me on the most powerful committee in the state house—the House Finance Ways & Means Committee's Budget subcommittee. All bills with fiscal notes exceeding $100,000 had to be approved by the Budget subcommittee. The subcommittee was all male, except for the presence of the House Speaker Pro

Tempore, who was not an official member but had the privilege of voting on any committee in the House of Representatives.

House Speaker Jimmy Naifeh listened but explained that there was no vacancy on the subcommittee. No problem. I suggested that he just expand the seven-member committee. And, he did. So, after only six years in the legislature, by running and losing, and running and winning, and running and losing again, I managed to break new ground and help open the way for Rep. Turner to become the first woman chair of a house standing committee, and also for myself to become the first female to serve as an official member of the most powerful committee in the state house.

5

The Tennessee state legislature was a very masculine body, although years later, its members finally elected Rep. Beth Halteman Harwell as House Speaker. The Budget subcommittee, which informally gathered every week in the Speaker Naifeh's office was about as macho as it gets. Many of the members puffed away on cigarettes and cigars. At times, I put my hand in front of my face and could barely see it because the smoke was so thick. They relished the raw power of being able to debate and decide so many important matters. Contrary to the long-held belief that only women are petty, pettiness was fully permitted, embraced, and adhered to by a few of these immensely powerful and well-respected men.

While some of the male Budget subcommittee members might be annoyed by my assertiveness as a younger female attorney, there were other female legislators whom the good ol' boys viewed as downright offensive. A few of the subcommittee members killed those female members' proposed bills without any regard whatsoever to the merits but based upon a perceived slight, a show of disrespect, or simply out of spite.

The subcommittee's unwritten rules were that you said anything you wanted in the gathering in the speaker's office, but when the subcommittee voted in public, it was voice vote—and we all had to vote the same way, even if we disagreed. The subcommittee was called the "black hole" in the hallways because many bills were killed for lack of a motion or a second. The bills then were lost forever in a black hole—the legislative equivalent of quantum physics.

I spoke up for the bills which had merit, even if the legislative sponsors were not well-liked. This was not easy to do. I equated serving on the subcommittee as spending a few hours on the football field butting heads with the guys. Lois Deberry told the subcommittee members that I was their conscience.

Rep. Henri Brooks, one of the female African American legislators, appeared never to believe that I had spoken for her bills. She wanted us to make a motion for her Title VI civil rights bill in the public meeting. She knew that if the African American male member of the committee and I both supported her bill, it would be considered at the public subcommittee hearing.

But, as the saying goes, you can't hide the truth forever. One day when that male member was absent from the closed-door session, I asked if I could move to adopt the bill when the subcommittee met in public later that day. The Budget subcommittee's chair agreed, believing that there would not be a second since that member was absent. When the bill was called in the public subcommittee meeting, I made the motion. The absent legislator unexpectedly arrived late. There was a horrific look on his face as he did not know what to do since the house sponsor fully expected him to second the motion, which would then necessitate a public vote. Finally, after a long pause, he moved to second the adoption of the bill, and all hell broke loose. The chair abruptly adjourned the subcommittee. Even though he had agreed I could make the motion, I was in deep hot water.

The Budget subcommittee was rough, and some members even hazed on occasion. One of the perks of being on the subcommittee was an invitation to dine with the governor at his mansion late in the session when it was time to decide the state budget. As the only female on the subcommittee, I was the only woman at the mansion for dinner with the other subcommittee members and Governor Sundquist. At dinner, two of my colleagues begin to joke and imply over the fine china, crystal, and silver in front of the governor that I was having a sexual relationship with another one. Of course, it was a lie, but I felt totally humiliated.

Thank heavens, although of a different political party, the governor graciously changed the subject and asked me how my parents, whom he had met once before, were doing. My colleagues shut up. In the photo from the evening taken with the subcommittee on the steps inside the Governor's Mansion, the shell-shocked look on my face tells the whole story.

85

In any event, I managed to turn the subcommittee experience into good by getting a $200,000 appropriation as start-up funds to create a women's health center at the University of Tennessee at Memphis to serve the 2.5 million women in the state, among other things. While the gender bias was rough at times, I took on the tough battles fighting for my constituents.

6

There were a plethora of legislative skirmishes on other issues as well. During the 1997 legislative session, one victory occurred when the Shelby County District Attorney Bill Gibbons pushed legislation authorizing his office to file eviction actions against tenants who use rental properties for drug dealing. I also pushed an amendment to authorize prosecutors to evict prostitutes who operated in rental properties since there were several complaints from a low-income area in my legislative district where large church congregations were located. I also proposed an amendment that would charge a fine of $1,500 to landlords who refused to take eviction action after notification from local prosecutors. Some legislators opposed the part of the bill backed by Gibbons that authorized the courts to order that the landlord pay the attorneys' fees and court costs for the eviction.

Gibbons and the house sponsors initially opposed my amendment to add eviction of prostitutes to the bill. However, I pressed forward, in moving to amend the bill on the house floor, arguing that a similar law in New York had been successful. With the UT Lady Vols waiting to be honored in the state house gallery, the debate ended, a vote was taken, and my amendment failed.

Some news reports the next day were unfavorable on the vote against my amendment, that as I said, would help stop landlords from having prostitutes operating on their property. One reporter noted in the *Tennessean* that the crowd of mostly young girls in the balcony "got a look at even more role models than they came to see" with the defeat of my amendment.[342] Several legislators were upset that they had been told to vote against my amendment and now would face campaign attacks that they voted to protect prostitution. Afterwards Gibbons relented, the house members reconsidered, and my amendment became a part of the new law.

During the session, women's health was also on the agenda, with the TennCare Bureau under fire for some physicians' refusal to treat pregnant women. The Memphis Regional Medical Center reported that approximately 900 women who delivered babies at the hospital had received no prenatal care.[343] Physicians turned away many TennCare expectant mothers despite having presented their cards indicating that they were presumptively eligible for coverage. The doctors feared that the women would later be found not to qualify for coverage, and the bills for their treatment would not be paid.

The Sundquist administration stated that it had fixed the problem, but the new report showed that was still not the case. As chair of the Women's Health Study Committee, I called out the administration in light of another report from Nashville's Metro Health Department that nearly a third of 151 Davidson County pregnant women surveyed had been refused an appointment with a doctor or other health professional in a six-month period.[344]

Also of concern to women was the practice of drugs being used to facilitate date rape. A bill was written and introduced by Republican state Sen. Randy McNally (R-Oak Ridge), a hospital pharmacist, to make the use of drugs to incapacitate a person for the purpose of sex to be the criminal offense of aggravated rape. I was the prime sponsor of the bill in the state house. According to the DEA, the drug Rohypnol—aka the "Forget Pill," "Trip and Fall," and "Mind Eraser"—was being smuggled into the country and sold on the street for less than $5 per pill. [345]

The use of the drug for date rape was growing in other states, including on college campuses. While no such rapes had officially been reported at the Tennessee colleges interviewed, one police officer observed that women reported only 10% to 15% of rapes.[346]

The debate in the House Judiciary Committee raised whether the penalty for rape by incapacitation with a drug should be as strong as that for rape by force. My response was that a person never has a fighting chance if you put a drug in their drink. One legislator asked if it applied to a person getting drunk on a date and having sex. He was reassured that it only applied to the use of a controlled substance. Due to the fiscal concerns in the tight budget year, McNally agreed to amend the bill in the senate to instead make the use of a drug for the purposes of rape to be an enhancement factor for sentencing on the rape offense to ensure its passage. I further amended the bill to include the crimes of sexual battery and rape of a child. As we can see from the recent Bill Crosby scandal, this topic remains controversial even today.

Besides addressing date rape, Rep. Joe Kent and I held hearings in Nashville with Memphis police officers testifying about the growing gang problems. Their stories of gang initiation activities involving murder and home invasions of innocent victims shocked the legislators. One gang's members were said to leave the headlights off on their vehicles on purpose and then follow home and shoot citizens who flashed their headlights in response. The police reported that the gangs had infiltrated suburbs, all ethnic groups, and even smaller towns. The social fabric was fraying, and measures were needed to intervene sooner with youth to counter the gang culture.

Representative Kent was carrying legislation for Governor Sundquist to create new criminal offenses for gang activities with enhanced punishments if undertaken in connection with an underlying crime. The Memphis police estimated there were at least 3000 active gang members in the Memphis area.[347] Certainly, we had come a long way since my town hall meeting in 1995 in terms of raising awareness of this serious and growing problem when some had not wanted to admit that gangs even existed.

7

Besides sports, healthcare, and crime, children and family issues were now at the forefront. The new House Children & Family Affairs Committee, headed by Rep. Brenda Turner, the first woman standing committee chair, was off and running. As vice-chair, I found the work intense with all of the emotional family law issues and strong advocates on all sides.

Chairwoman Brenda Turner had a long legislative record supporting women and children. She received both praise and complaints about how the brand new House Children & Family Affairs Committee was handling legislation. While some legislators complained about delays in getting their bills through the new committee, Speaker Naifeh complimented its performance. Others noted that the committee members and officers represented the legislature's best experts on women and children's issues, as reported in the *Chattanooga Times*.[348]

The committee wrapped up its business as the frantic end of the session approached. While I focused a great deal on women's health and the new committee's work, I also advocated for men. At the end of the session, I was able to pass a law requiring health insurers to cover prostate cancer screening for men over age fifty. With studies by the American Cancer Society showing that early detection of prostate cancer results in a 99% five-year survival rate, the testing would save lives, as well as expensive medical costs for late-stage treatments.

Besides the usual end of session legislative drama, there were fireworks back home in Memphis as well. Jackson Baker, with the *Memphis Flyer*, reported that Mayor Herenton told him to "go to hell."[349] Baker had asked about the mayor's private business deals and some city contracts, implying a conflict of interest.[350] After an unrelated press conference, the *Memphis Flyer* reported the mayor said that it was "nobody's business how I make my money and who I appoint to do things for Memphis."[351] The newspaper disagreed, wondering how many other such contracts existed and further asking why the city council was not investigating the matter as well.[352] This was only the beginning.

When the session ended, I felt a lot had been accomplished. I had broken new ground as the first woman to serve on the House Budget subcommittee, served as vice-chair of the new children and families standing committee, and passed several of my bills, such as the date rape law. Little did I know that one bill had slipped through that could seriously harm Memphis.

9

Defender of the City

Not long after the 1997 legislative session adjourned, the legislators and the public became aware of an amendment slipped onto a bill in the hectic late-night legislative sessions that made the process easier for communities to incorporate and block annexation by an adjoining city. The powerful Lt. Governor Wilder wanted to protect the tiny Hickory Withe community in rural Fayette County from annexation by the nearby city of Oakland.

Yet, the bill that passed also would allow the huge new retail area of Wolfchase Galleria, scheduled to be annexed by Memphis, to become a "tiny town" called "Independence," along with other tiny towns of "New Berryhill" and "New Forest Hills" in suburban Shelby County. This move would cost Memphis, which had built the sewers for the new developments, an estimated $2 million a year in lost sales tax revenue alone. The *Commercial Appeal* called it a "slick and furtive" maneuver by Wilder that resulted in "mostly white suburban Shelby County communities to file for incorporation as cities."[353]

My response was promptly to band together with eight other legislators to begin a petition drive for a special legislative session to rescind or amend the law. Further, I boldly suggested that Memphians not shop at the mall until the issue was resolved as a way to get the mall owners involved in stopping the incorporations.

That weekend, while in a different shopping mall in Memphis, a person asked me about an editorial in the *Commercial Appeal* that morning calling me out for the suggested boycott. Having missed the editorial, I immediately went home to see what it said. To my dismay, the newspaper called my idea its choice, if there is an award, for the "summertime silly season."[354]

But not everyone thought my position was silly. Mayor Herenton admiringly told me that he liked my "curveball" in that the backers of the bill never anticipated that Memphians would just shop somewhere else if the mall were not annexed. He also fought the new law, analogizing it to the Civil War, saying that the issue was "about geography, it was about race, it was about class, and then people want to put it all under the guise of independence...."[355] The still unresolved feud between city residents and those in the county had reared its head, not for the first time—nor the last.

Thank heavens the *Memphis Flyer's* Jackson Baker came to my rescue and named me the "Defender of the City" in a column devoted solely to my role in playing "Horatio at the Bridge on the incorporation question."[356] I told him and the readers that the tiny town proponents were trying to bleed the city to feed themselves and were seeking a free ride while Memphians only wanted a fair shake. The City of Memphis lobbyist and Tennessee Municipal League Director Joe Sweat joined my petition drive.

The *Flyer* article waxed on about how I was outspoken within the context of the state politics' "Good Old Boy" system, insisting on being called "Representative" instead of "Lady" on the house floor. Also, it said that I had distanced myself from Senator Cohen who, due to his independent thinking with an "iconoclastic streak," was able to get things done even though somewhat isolated.[357] Story had it that another public figure initially declined to be called "Lady" when her husband was knighted – Margaret Thatcher. But she later became known as the "Iron Lady." So, I was in good company.

Baker added that I had good working relationships with house leaders such as Speaker Jimmy Naifeh and Majority Leader Bill Purcell. Also, he observed that I had served as House Majority Whip until the gender-biased defeats in the recent secret-ballot state house caucus elections.[358] He noted that I had passed many bills, including "potty parity" and the law mandating a 48-hour stay for mom and newborns after delivery.[359]

The columnist opined that I had gotten the "maverick habit" again and credited my amendment to prohibit the local sports authority from using the sales tax rebates to pay Oiler's team travel expenses while playing in Memphis as probably spurring the public backlash that forced the team owners to concede.[360] The column was one of the best setting out my record in my political career.

Still trying to find a way to stop the tiny town incorporations that would harm Memphis, in a salvo over the bow to Wilder, I simply asked whether a person had to be a member of the senate under the *Tennessee Constitution* in order to be elected lieutenant governor of Tennessee? In other words, maybe another person not a member of the state senate should challenge him—perhaps even me? While Wilder had helped me in my first election, the future of Memphis was at stake.

In a letter to the editor published in the *Commercial Appeal*, I pointed out that it's about leadership and urged the newspaper not to fiddle while Memphis was harmed in the governor's leadership vacuum. I asked the editors and public to get behind my petition calling for a special legislative session to fix the annexation law.[361]

Memphians subsidized the area's use of its roads, amenities, police, and fire protection. The law precluded the city's option to annex county residents who took full advantage of these services when working and playing within Memphis. It also hindered Memphis' growth and put new burdens on economic development. While smart growth was necessary, Memphis had invested substantially for this particular area to be developed, always with the understanding that it would ultimately become part of the city.

My guest column pointed out that unincorporated county residents would suffer, too, with higher taxes when the new tiny cities took half of the local sales tax revenue from the Wolfchase Galleria Mall and retail corridor.[362] The county also would lose portions of state-shared tax funds, and the tiny towns might levy heavy taxes on the businesses within their town to pay for the services.

An example of the gross inequity at stake was that the estimated 8,000 citizens of the new proposed tiny town "Independence" would benefit from the sales tax revenue generated by metropolitan area shoppers from the new $250 million Wolfchase Galleria mall, instead of the citizens of Memphis. The mall was a huge money-maker.

Calling this greedy and an insult, I pointed out that Memphians had paid millions in sewer extensions for those suburban areas. Yet, the tiny town proponents wanted Memphis to shop at the mall while they kept the local sales tax revenue. I encouraged the newspaper to turn up the heat on the governor to call a special session before it was too late.

Apparently, seeing the news coverage (and my question about who qualifies to serve as lieutenant governor of Tennessee), Wilder called me up to talk. I was polite, telling him how serious this issue was for Memphis. We ended the conversation cordially.

As the debate got dirty, Memphis officials announced that they would not provide new sewer services in the tiny towns if they were incorporated. The public utility studied whether it could shut off services in those areas.[363] But the proposed town of Fishersville still moved forward with plans to incorporate with about 5,000 residents.

Letters to the Editor of the *Commercial Appeal* poured in from all sides of the volatile debate, with many suburbanites complaining about the crime, poor schools, and blight in Memphis while others called the move for tiny towns greedy and racist.[364] Some wisely pointed out that all of the people in the area were dependent on a healthy Memphis in order to survive and thrive.[365] Even my Republican aunt Edith Russell Chumney wrote in, calling for metropolitan government and naming the tiny towns "Mistletoe" because they live "off the closeness to Memphis like mistletoe lives off the trees it latches onto."[366]

The African-American focused *Tri-State Defender* newspaper editors also went to bat with an editorial supporting my suggested boycott.[367] The paper applauded and stood "firmly behind" my "courageous suggestion to boycott, if necessary, the Wolfchase Galleria."[368] The newspaper called the tiny town proponents "selfish and unfeeling" while ignoring the huge amount of monies spent weekly at the Wolfchase mall by Memphians.[369] The paper went on to say, "You tell 'em Carol," noting that the galleria and its businesses did have a role in the controversy because they would be a significant source of revenue for the tiny towns – and wondering if there were a conspiracy. [370]

The *Tri-State Defender* editors added that the legislature had a vital role in the matter as well, and shame on those who called the challenge of the law "silly." [371] And, the editorial ended with the rallying cry, "Right on Carol, we'll be with you."[372] I appreciated their support in the battle for the future of Memphis.

Lt. Governor Wilder took more heat with conspiracy theories abounding and the revelation that his cousin was the mayor of Hickory Withe. The Tennessee Municipal League (TML) was under scrutiny with its own report that its lobbyist agreed to a version of the bill that would only apply to that town, but then the language of the bill was later broadened to include other areas, raising the question as to whether Wilder's hand was in the revision. Because the Tennessee Municipal League sponsored the bill, the stealth amendment slipped through unnoticed as legislators trusted it wouldn't harm their cities. Local officials around the state were angry.

Finally realizing the seriousness of the issue for Memphis, the *Commercial Appeal* editorialized that Wilder had to have known the harm that would come to the cities, including Memphis, and just didn't care.[373] Echoing my speculation about a possible challenge to Wilder even though they had called me "silly" at first, the editors now said that Memphis should say, "To heck with Wilder. We'll do our best to see that the legislature never re-elects him as speaker of the Senate."[374] I was glad they saw the light, although they never apologized about the prior editorial "dis" of me.

The City of Memphis, and four other cities, along with the Tennessee Municipal League, filed a lawsuit to fight the new law as unconstitutional because the bill caption did not provide proper notice of the proposed law's subject matter as amended. The large cities argued that they would suffer "irreparable harm" because the new law suspended for one year the annexation provisions prohibiting towns close to large cities from incorporating.[375] Four proposed towns sought to intervene to help defend the new law.[376]

The taxpayer-funded TML was the watchdog on issues for municipalities. A heated internal debate was underway within the group about whether staffers knew about the amendment that included areas Memphis sought to annex. They contended Wilder duped them. Wilder and the house sponsor, however, claimed in a story in the *Commercial Appeal* that the TML staffers were fully aware of the breadth of the amendment and approved it.[377] Yet, even Governor Sundquist said that he had not been aware of the bill's impact when he signed it into law.[378]

Wilder had served as lieutenant governor (elected by the state senate) for twenty-six years and was powerful. He was known to have helped African American workers in the 1960s when they were removed from land where they lived and farmed because they had registered to vote. Also, he had joined with Republicans to keep his position in 1987. And he stood by controversial Sen. John Ford when some attempted to strip him of his committee chairmanship after an arrest involving an alleged "road rage" incident with a trucker (of which he was later acquitted.)[379] Wilder represented a portion of the rural West Tennessee part of the state, and was wealthy due to business ventures, farming, banking and work as an attorney.

According to the *Commercial Appeal*, both Wilder and his son were in the waste disposal business.[380] In 1995, he had pushed through a bill in the state senate to require local government approval of a landfill proposed for Gallaway, Tennessee, all done within an hour and under duress when his constituents stormed the State Capitol. It was reported that his son was a business partner of the proponents of the landfill.[381]

Unwittingly, I had gotten tangled up in that matter due to a promise made to a constituent during my 1994 campaign for reelection. The constituent asked if I would attend a meeting at Gallaway after the election. Thinking he meant the Galloway Golf Course in my district in Memphis, Shelby County, Tennessee, I said "yes." After the election, the constituent called and wanted me to go to Gallaway, Tennessee, in Fayette County because he hunted in the area and opposed the landfill. Honoring my promise, I ventured forth to a meeting in an adjacent county, having no idea of the political landmine ahead.

Arriving at the meeting at a lodge, I first realized that the issue involved the two most powerful men in the legislature – Lt. Governor Wilder and Speaker Naifeh – as well as a room full of angry residents opposing the landfill. Wilder and Naifeh looked at me in bewilderment, wondering why I had made the trek to their district for the meeting. Later in the session, it was quite a show when the House Speaker Naifeh ceremoniously passed the bill requiring local approval in the state house, personally walked it over to the state senate, and dumped it in Wilder's lap with the crowd in tow.

If you go to the courthouse in Fayette County, Wilder's statue is in the atrium, which is a testament to his political acumen and clout. However, everyone was not a fan. He was also criticized for not doing enough to help Fayette County rise above its poverty and other social ills, according to one letter to the editor in the *Commercial Appeal*.[382]

Now, under siege from urban legislators and their constituents about the new tiny towns law, Wilder and Naifeh proposed to appoint a study committee to review annexation reforms. The *Commercial Appeal* interpreted this to be simply an excuse by Wilder and Naifeh to do nothing, and a signal that the called for special session would not occur.[383] The accusations continued to fly as to who was responsible for the amendment—Wilder's staff either alone or in conjunction with TML lobbyists charged to protect cities.[384] Even the press was upset that it did not catch the import of the amendment when the state house and senate voted on it, which the *Commercial Appeal*'s commentator now said had "devastating consequences to Memphis and other cities."[385]

In the wake of the revelation of the amendment's impact, new reports came that the credit rating for Memphis and other Tennessee cities might be adversely impacted. Standard and Poor's rating agency's analyst noted that the proposed incorporations of the tiny towns in Shelby County could result in the loss of millions of tax dollars by Memphis and limit its economic growth.[386] Mayor Herenton wrote an opinion editorial on how the tiny towns would adversely impact Memphis.[387] While annexation reforms might be needed to give county residents a greater voice, the study committee would not solve the immediate crisis for Memphis.

As the controversy continued, it became more apparent to all involved, including the press, that Wilder's amendment (as the *Memphis Flyer* said) was a city killer for urban areas like Memphis.[388] The *Flyer* editors joined my call for a special legislative session, urging Governor Don Sundquist, as a former Memphian, to reconsider since it was a "life-or-death matter" for Memphis.[389]

I appealed to Wilder to "do the right thing, be a statesman," and support the special session.[390] And, after some research, I also pushed two possible approaches to more equitably share tax revenue should the tiny towns be established.[391] Not giving up, I wrote an opinion editorial on how metropolitan Memphis's future depended on resolving the incorporation issue.[392] A public hearing was scheduled for a proposed tiny town in the Shelby County suburban area, and I attended to voice opposition.

The area benefited from the amenities in Memphis, the $700 million-plus in private capital investment, and the air, road, rail, and river transportation infrastructure.[393] Without continued public investment by the city, companies such as Federal Express might take their corporate headquarters elsewhere, costing jobs and millions of dollars.[394]

If the Memphis metropolitan area became riddled with a proliferation of governmental bodies that had to be navigated to get things done, business prospects would favor other cities with less red tape.[395] My opinion editorial drew a contrast between Nashville's higher economic growth and bond rating, with its consolidated government, and Louisville that had 93 incorporated suburbs and no metro government at the time.[396] If Memphis, the flagship city of the Mid-South, faltered, then the infrastructure supporting businesses in the entire metropolitan area was in jeopardy.[397]

Court proceedings continued, proposals for compromise were put on the table, and elected officials spoke with one another through sound bites subject to misinterpretation. But, I conveyed the urgency for considering reliable information from independent experts about the effects of incorporation. The tiny towns' proponents should consider the enormous costs to build a city government from scratch and potential liabilities for unexpected accidents, natural disasters, lawsuits, or inadequate services.[398]

The debates continued with proponents of the "toy towns" Chapter 98 law saying they simply wanted self-governance and some opponents claiming the law was racially motivated.[399] Mayor Herenton was reported to be angry that both the governor and Republican Shelby County Mayor Jim Rout did not support the city's efforts to undo the new law.[400] Rout would not take a stand, and the relationship between the two mayors was contentious, with Herenton said to have called him cowardly, spineless, and paranoid.[401]

Just two days before the first elections were to be held for tiny town incorporations, the Tennessee Supreme Court ruled that the law was unconstitutional.[402] Memphis was saved!

PART THREE

——

Daycare Reform

10

The Only Woman Chair

1

Apart from legislative and law firm responsibilities, I took some time to try my hand at another endeavor in 1997. That was the year of my film debut in the major motion picture *The Rainmaker*, based upon the novel written by a former state legislator from Mississippi – John Grisham. Matt Damon, the latest hot actor, was the star, and the crew was looking for local attorneys for casting in a scene shot at the Memphis Peabody Hotel where his character took the bar examination.

It was a long day, mostly spent standing and waiting or in a back room. My character was a proctor for the bar exam with no speaking role. Although I did not get to talk to Damon, I did get introduced to Coppola and chatted with actor Jon Vogt in the back room.

We were told not to wear makeup and to dress professionally for the shoot. However, being from the South, the idea of appearing in a film without makeup was unimaginable—so I did not show up barefaced. Perhaps, that's why in the movie I appear only from the neck down? In any event, it was great to be part of such a successful film partially shot in my hometown.

Another exciting event was the private reception for the opening of Elvis Presley's Enterprises restaurant and club on Beale Street. In attendance were both Priscilla and Lisa Marie Presley. Also, Jewel performed. I often enjoy sharing my mother's story about the time she met Elvis while in college in the 1950s. My mother was out on a date with my dad at the Strand Theater. When she went to the ladies' room, a guy with sideburns and a leather jacket was sitting on a couch in the lobby. Looking at her, he patted the couch and gestured for her to have a seat. This was when Elvis was just taking off. My mother walked right on by. Later, when they left the theater, his pink Cadillac was outside in a no-parking zone with girls writing "I love you Elvis" with lipstick on the windshield. My mom preferred my devoted father over Elvis, for which my father is eternally grateful!

I also took some time off to venture to Nassau with a group hosted by the Memphis Pink Palace Museum for a much-needed vacation. The Pink Palace is a cultural and historic mansion museum, originally planned to be the home of Piggly Wiggly founder Clarence Sanders. After his economic demise, it was eventually donated to the city by subsequent owners and became a landmark.

Even though the trip was pitched primarily as a shark dive, I planned only on snorkeling. I never thought I would scuba dive, having always watched on T.V. those who did, wondering how they were able to overcome their fear of being so deep in the water with only an air tank. However, when I went to the scuba shop to sign up for the trip, the salesman convinced me to take scuba classes. I decided to give it a try and took lessons at the shop. When we arrived at Nassau, I was still rather shaky on my scuba diving skills, having been out of town so much on legislative business.

In any event, I never intended actually to do the shark dive. Not wanting to hang out by myself on the shore, I did go out on the boat with the group for the shark dive. But, I planned to stay in the boat. However, when everyone got in the water, I changed my mind and jumped in as well. What a thrill!

We swam around where the sharks were. Then, on the second dive, we went to the bottom of the ocean. The divemaster had an iron glove and a cage filled with fish to feed the sharks. As we sat on the ocean floor in a circle with the divemaster in the middle, the huge sharks swam right at, around, and above us to get to the fish the dive master pulled out of the cage. What an amazing experience and excellent preparation for working with some shark public officials and lawyers in the years ahead!

2

At the end of 1997, with Memphis's future safe from the tiny towns law, there was more good news with reports that the University of Tennessee Health Sciences at Memphis was proposing a $4.9 million Center of Excellence on Women's Health.[403] The proposal was developed by the university at the request of the state legislature's Select Committee on Women's Health.[404]

And, to ensure that another stealth "tiny towns" amendment did not slip through, in January 1998, I filed proposed rules changes. My proposal required adequate notice of amendments and that bills seriously altered on the floor of the state house be returned to the appropriate committee for review.[405] The House Rules Committee met to review how to address better the issue of "caption bills," where a bill is introduced with little in the bill's body and then later amended with the text of what the proposed law would actually do.[406]

Also back in the news was Lanier, the former powerful judge from West Tennessee, with a new twist. Lanier had been released from federal custody in 1996 after the Sixth Circuit Court of Appeals reversed his conviction for criminally violating the civil rights of women by sexually assaulting them under the color of law as a state judge.[407] In March, the U.S. Supreme Court directed the Sixth Circuit to reconsider its ruling because it had erred and used the wrong legal standard for the reversal.[408] The Sixth Circuit ordered Lanier to surrender while it reconsidered the case, and he was a no-show, so an arrest warrant was issued.[409] A book had even been written about his case.[410] Now he was on the lam.[411]

While Lanier's saga continued, the Memphis metropolitan area's elected officials still held tremendous clout at the State Capitol. Most powerful West Tennessee officials had office buildings, universities, prisons, or facilities named after them. While I was the youngest in the bunch, I have the unique honor of probably being the only politician in history to have a Kubota tractor named after me. That's right—the "Carol C" is a diesel-powered tractor, for which I helped secure state funding for its purchase by the V & E Greenline in my legislative district.[412]

The V & E Greenline is the first greenline in Memphis, established in a railroad right of way. It is preserved and maintained by citizen volunteers. When I learned at one of my town hall meetings that the neighborhood group needed a tractor, I added a grant to the state budget. The neighborhood later honored me by naming the tractor after me—maybe because of my tenacity, who knows? And, years later in 2016, it was humbling to be recognized at their twentieth anniversary neighborhood event for being the "Guardian Angel" that helped secure the tractor to make the first greenline in Memphis a success. I'll gladly have my name on the tractor that maintains a public greenline where people can exercise and enjoy nature over having it on an office building any day.

3

As the 1998 campaign season commenced, once again, I spent evenings and weekends after my work at the law office knocking on doors to talk with constituents and ask for their votes. The same Republican wrestler that challenged me in 1996 ran again, but there was no primary opposition.

The election year was interesting, with County Mayor Jim Rout challenged by eccentric candidate Robert "Prince Mongo" Hodges. Hodges pledged to install a firing squad to execute those convicted of serious crimes, hire chefs and maids for the firehouses, and order a four-day workweek.[413] When I was in high school, "Prince Mongo" once came to a football game barefoot and in a loincloth in the middle of winter.

The Shelby County mayor's job was much more limited than that of the Memphis mayor, with county roads, a joint health department, the correction center, and funding for the Memphis Regional Medical Center being the significant responsibilities. Rout ran on a platform of no new taxes and pledged to develop a countywide economic development plan.[414] Hodges, a perineal candidate for county and city mayor, claimed to be from the planet Zambodia, which he said was nine light-years from Earth.[415] Based upon his behavior, we didn't doubt it.

The *Commercial Appeal* editors endorsed me for reelection to the state house for working "hard and well in areas such as women's health, legislation to combat domestic violence and gang violence, foster care, and related children's and family issues."[416] The endorsement also mentioned my push for state funding for mental health and long-term care services.[417]

On Election Day, there was the usual drama at the polls, with a poll worker for my opponent telling one of mine that I was a "b___." Not missing a beat, my loyal volunteer poll worker replied, "Well, she might be a "b___," but she's *our* "b___." Perhaps a future campaign slogan? In any event, I was reelected in November with about 70% of the vote.[418]

4

As it is said, God works in mysterious ways. In 1997, I had run for House Majority Floor Leader and lost, was offered the chairmanship of the new House Children & Family Affairs ("CFA") Committee and ended up being the vice-chair instead. Since Rep. Brenda Turner was relatively young from a legislative perspective, I thought she would serve as the chair of the House CFA Committee for another fourteen years or more, and I would not move up in the leadership ranks anytime soon. However, in 1999 the unexpected happened, and I was promoted to the chairmanship.

In a behind the scenes intrigue, several committee members grumbled privately to the House Speaker about how the chair was conducting the committee work, and two members spoke openly to the *Chattanooga Times*.[419] Turner was said to acknowledge discord and attributed it to many factors, such as being a new committee and a political rivalry.[420] When asked by the press, I responded that it was a new committee that had been assigned a lot of difficult legislation, and Turner had put the time in to do the job. Rep. Kathryn Bowers defended Turner, saying she did an admirable job. However, the newspaper reported that Rep. Tommie Brown, a colleague from her hometown, blamed Turner and also asked not to be reappointed to the committee.[421]

A few committee members even approached Speaker Naifeh, saying they would not serve on the committee anymore if he didn't make a change.[422] This was an awkward situation for the House Speaker, as Rep. Brenda Turner had seniority, was well-regarded by many, and had accomplished a lot in her years of service. The Speaker asked me what I thought, and I gave him a possible solution: promote Rep. Brenda Turner to the vacant position of Deputy House Speaker. And he did precisely that in addition to appointing me to serve as the new chair of the House CFA Committee.[423] Now, Turner became the first woman ever to hold that post.

Becoming the second woman in the history of Tennessee to serve as chair of a Tennessee state house standing committee was an honor, and I took the job seriously. At that time, I was the only woman chairman in both the senate and house out of twenty-two standing committees.[424] As noted in the *Commercial Appeal*, committee chairmen are "part of the legislature's influential leadership structure and play key roles in what bills pass and fail."[425]

However, Naifeh required me to relinquish my position on the Budget subcommittee as part of the change. But, I remained a member of the full House Finance Ways & Means Committee. Little did I know at the time how important my new role as chair of the children and families committee would be with regard to daycare reform in the years ahead.

5

While the House CFA Committee's work was my primary focus, the state's budget problems were growing and dominated the session. Governor Sundquist proposed tax reform that would enact a 2.5% tax on all businesses' payroll and profits while also removing the sales tax from grocery store food and repealing corporate excise and franchise taxes.[426] Democrats responded positively, calling the measure "intriguing" and "bold" but needing more details, while some Republicans were flabbergasted that one of their own proposed a payroll tax.[427]

In addition to the budget issues and my new position as committee chair, my legislative package included a bill backed by the Tennessee Education Association. The proposed law would punish adults who know but don't report that a juvenile is taking a firearm onto school property, including athletic stadiums and other facilities where school-sponsored events are conducted or any public park, playground or civic center.[428] The law at the time only applied to parents and guardians but would be expanded to include all adults.[429] After filing the bill, the tragic Columbine High School massacre occurred in Colorado, where two students killed a teacher, twelve classmates, and themselves.[430]

My proposed amendment to my own bill failed in committee. It would have made it unlawful for anyone to provide a rifle, shotgun, or handgun to a juvenile if they know there is a substantial risk that the youth will use the weapon to commit a felony. In the debate, I acknowledged that parents couldn't know everything that their child does. But, I stated, "if a parent is paying attention to their child and spending time with him, they are going to have some clue about whether he is building a bomb in the bedroom and writing a diary about how he is going to blow up something and fly to Mexico."[431]

During debate on the house floor, opponents called the bill just furthering the "snitch concept" and not in keeping with rural practices.[432] However, Rep. Don Ridgeway, from the rural city of Paris in West Tennessee, spoke in favor of the bill on the grounds that guns on school property is not just an urban issue.[433] Passing a gun restriction law in the Tennessee state legislature is nearly impossible due to the powerful gun lobby.[434] But, the state house voted overwhelmingly in support of my bill, and I had several cosponsors join me in the well on the house floor.[435]

Rep. Dan West, an ardent *Second Amendment* proponent, even withdrew his bill that allowed holders of handgun permits to carry the weapon in the parks, playgrounds, and other public property.[436] When Governor Sundquist signed my bill, I commented that when kids are killing each other in the schools, it's clear that adults need to take more responsibility.[437]

6

With no tax reform measure adopted, the governor announced that he would call both the senate and house into a second special legislative session. Former Governor Ned McWherter, who served as house speaker for nearly twenty years and governor for eight years, explained that the present tax structure was adopted after World War II when workers were primarily farmers.[438] He advocated lowering the tax rates and broadening the tax base to ensure that all citizens paid their fair share.[439] McWherter added that counties depended on state revenues for roads, schools, and healthcare.[440]

On the campaign front, in 1999, well-qualified Al Gore struggled in his presidential bid, due in part to being contrasted with the popular Bill Clinton.[441] Also, Memphian and well-known professional wrestler Jerry "The King" Lawler appeared on *Hardball* with Chris Matthews to discuss his Memphis mayoral candidacy.[442] Lawler claimed his primary qualification was that he was not a politician.[443] Memphis Mayor Herenton claimed he was in the lead for reelection as Memphis mayor with forty-two percent of the projected vote just before the filing deadline.[444] Joe Ford (brother of Harold Ford, Sr.), Mary Rose McCormick, Pete Sisson, and Shep Wilbun had joined the field. Religious Roundtable leader Ed McAteer, who had flirted with the idea of running, decided to pass.[445]

Although the national and local politics were interesting, my work was cut out for me as the new chair of the House CFA Committee dealing with complicated but needed family law reform measures. I was also pleased that the Memphis Partnership for Women's and Children's Health of UT Memphis, Methodist Healthcare, and Le Bonheur Children's Medical Center funded an endowed professorship in women's health.[446] I was gratified by the comments of Dr. Hank Herrod, dean of the UT Memphis College of Medicine, that my "work on behalf of women would make a difference for many generations to come." [447] His words made all of the hazing in the Budget subcommittee to get the start-up funds for the Center for Women's Health seem worthwhile. We ended the legislative session on a positive note, unaware of the serious issues that lay ahead.

7

Back in Memphis, I delved into work at my law office, trying to catch up after the session adjourned. The news came out about misused funds connected with the Memphis Police Department's property room that housed confiscated drugs, monies, and other personal property. In my capacity as a state legislator, I gave a T.V. interview that the officers and staff involved should be required to pay back the funds. Working very late the next day downtown at the law firm, I came out near midnight to find my car missing from where it had been parked on the street. I called the police to report that the vehicle was stolen, and my friend Oran Quintrell, who worked the late shift, drove me around the area to make sure it wasn't left nearby before taking me home.

A few days later, when the car still had not been found, I called in a report to the Tennessee Bureau of Investigation and rented a car. About ten days later, a friend called and asked me if everything was okay. I asked, "Why?" He said, "Well, your car is parked out front of the Kustoff Strickland law firm." David Kustoff was the local Republican Party chair, and Jim Strickland, the local Democratic Party chair, who happened to be law partners. I ran the three blocks to their office to find my car parked out front with a parking ticket on the windshield. The car door was unlocked but not broken.

All car contents were still there, except for a duffel bag of gym clothes and photographs of me shaking hands and talking with Bill Clinton in a crowd at an out-of-state political conference. Later, when meeting with the police chief, I told him what happened and asked if anyone had found the duffel bag because I certainly wanted to retrieve those photographs. He professed to not know about the incident. Who took the car? I guess we'll never know.

Despite the incident with the car, I was relieved to have successfully completed my first year as the only woman chair, with a special thanks to the other committee officers, and Sharon Peters, Shannon Romain, and others that ably staffed the committee's work. I was soon to find out that God had placed me at the right place at the right time to lead a major children's reform effort.

11

The Babies Died

1

Why is it important to have women in the political process? Some might feel that women are too independent and not team players. Yet if so, those same qualities are what often prompt real change for the better.

In 1999, two children tragically died in Memphis on the same sweltering hot day, when accidentally left in daycare vans. Brandon Mann, age two, was left for five hours by one daycare center and died an hour after being taken to the hospital.[448] Darnecia Slater, age twenty-two months, was left in a hot van for nine hours in heat reaching up to ninety-two degrees at the Children's Palace founded by County Commissioner James Ford, a member of the powerful Memphis Ford family.[449]

James Ford said in the *Commercial Appeal* that Darnecia's death was "devastating" and the "worst day" he "ever had in his life."[450] He could not explain why two employees did not do their jobs to double-check the van or why the child was not missed the entire day in the center serving over 150 children. [451]

One of the parents was said to have reported one worker for cursing the children on a bus; another parent at a different center was labeled a "troublemaker" for having reported a daycare van driver drinking at a convenience store.[452] The state suspended the licenses and closed the two daycare centers.[453] However, they were back in business after appealing and submitting written plans for correcting the problems that led to the toddlers' deaths.[454]

Years earlier, welfare reform had deregulated child care and increased daycare funding to assist parents working on getting their GED and to enter the workplace. This spawned new child care centers. Unfortunately, it also created a system that could foster neglect, or that some would abuse at the expense of children.

In 1998, near the end of the legislative session, I had tried to pass a reform measure to require criminal background checks through the Tennessee Bureau of Investigation ("TBI") for foster parents and daycare workers paid by the state. I had just learned from a news report that some foster parents for children in state custody had child abuse backgrounds.[455] Despite the seriousness of the issue, my amendment was stalled and left for another session by the subcommittee members after opposition by a statewide child care association.

Then, the next summer, the two babies died. There was a public outcry, and the story was reported in the national *USA Today*.[456] But no one wanted to do anything about it. Why? Because there were many influential politicians and religious leaders in the daycare business.

2

This was also the year two political factions butted heads when Memphis City Council Chairman Joe Ford challenged incumbent Memphis Mayor Herenton.[457] Jumping on the daycare reform issue, Herenton volunteered the city police department to perform criminal background checks and daycare workers' drug tests, even though this was not required under the current state law.[458] He directed city building inspectors to assess Memphis daycare centers to ensure compliance with building and occupancy codes. The mayor also announced a new city program to provide training and small business center loans for centers to help them achieve accreditations and correct health and safety violations.[459]

The mayor further urged the governor to conduct independent audits of all daycare centers' finances, and to inspect for compliance with state safety regulations.[460] He proposed to forward reports of any criminal activity to Shelby County District Attorney Bill Gibbons. Gibbons, however, responded to the hot potato that the Tennessee Bureau of Investigation was the appropriate entity to receive the reports.[461]

Ramping it up, Herenton wasted no time in blasting some unidentified daycare centers operated by "politicians" or their family members in low-income neighborhoods. He said some centers were "reaping enormous profits" and given "preferential" treatment as to the "placement of children."[462]

Councilman Joe Ford set up an ad hoc committee to review safety standards and make recommendations, which Herenton called politically motivated.[463] Joe Ford acknowledged that both of their actions would appear politically motivated due to the closeness of the mayoral election, but argued that action was needed to avoid another tragedy.[464] State Reps. Ulysses Jones, Larry Miller, and Joe Towns Jr. also held a press conference to call for more surprise inspections and for the state to require centers to have general liability insurance coverage. [465]

3

In the state house, the Health & Human Services Committee was charged with child care oversight. At the time, though, many public citizens believed that the House Children & Family Affairs ["CFA"] Committee had oversight of laws regarding child care because of its name. As chair of that committee, I felt a special responsibility to take action in the absence of action by others.

One of my mottos has always been, "If you do the right thing, you might catch hell in the short run, but it always works out in the long run." In this instance, as chair of the House CFA Committee, I had a moral responsibility to the children—even if it wasn't within my committee's actual jurisdiction. The moral responsibility required action even though it would be an uphill battle because the Senate Health & Human Resources Committee's chair was John Ford. His own family member was in the daycare business at the site where one of the two children had died that summer. According to the news, another Ford family member was the coordinator-supervisor for the area's child care broker, Cherokee Children and Family Services that held a large contract with the state.[466] There were also powerful politicians, judges, and churches across the state that were, or had family members, in the daycare industry.

It was a politically charged issue from the start. More horrors came to light, as a Memphis daycare van driver transporting several children was arrested on DUI charges, which he denied. [467] Later, he was found guilty of refusal to submit to a BAC test. [468] His prior record was not caught because the state did not require criminal background checks due to some centers' objections to the expense as excessive.[469]

Another child at a different center was left in a van asleep and unnoticed. The child woke up, climbed out a van window, and went inside, resulting in her parents calling for stronger protections.[470]

110

House Speaker Naifeh ordered a legislative review of the state rules and regulations for daycare centers by the House CFA Committee.[471] And, I scheduled House CFA Committee hearings for the next month. Welfare reform was moving families off welfare to work, but now the families were at the mercy of daycare operators and dependent upon the state to provide proper oversight. In response, the daycare lobby geared up to oppose reforms or request higher state subsidies.[472]

Now, the daycare issue was front and center, as the abuses revealed by the *Commercial Appeal's* investigative reporting further angered the public. The state had just tightened controls monitoring government monies spent at daycare centers to feed the children. It was reported that some centers spent only a third or less of each dollar given for food from the public program on food.[473] Most discrepancies were attributed to mismanagement and sloppy bookkeeping, but some centers were charged with crimes of falsifying attendance records to receive payment for children not served at the center.[474]

The *Tennessean* editors also called for reforms and reported that a twenty-three month-old Nashville child also had died in a hot daycare church van in 1994.[475] The editors urged immediate action to avoid another tragedy, noting the tougher emergency rules implemented by the Department of Human Services for checking the children on and off vans.[476] And, House Speaker Naifeh expressed support for my efforts to require background checks on daycare workers through TBI fingerprints.[477]

A joint meeting of the House CFA Committee and the Select Committee on Children & Youth (a joint special committee of the senate and house members) was held in Memphis in September 1999 with testimony by state officials, child care providers, and parents regarding inspections, violations, penalties, transportation procedures, and background checks.[478] As chair of the House CFA Committee, I asked citizens to call with any suggestions or to report problems.

Other legislators admitted regret for caving to industry pressure the prior year and not passing stricter rules proposed by the Sundquist administration to lower adult to child ratios for centers.[479] Parents testified about abuses, such as unattended children, mixed-up bottles, bruises, diaper rash, and even sexual abuse.[480] Natasha Metcalf, the state's Commissioner of the Department of Human Services ["DHS"], admitted that more aggressive enforcement of the rules was needed. The administration supported higher standards, as well as criminal background checks and drug testing of workers if the issue of funding could be resolved.[481]

The *Commercial Appeal* reported the Tennessee DHS's attorney as saying that the state did not require daycare centers to obtain general liability insurance partly because "child sex abuse was going on" in the 1980s before welfare reform, making it difficult for the centers to secure insurance.[482] Due to the need for "child care space," the attorney said that the state "had to balance those two things out."[483] The admission of sexual abuse as a prevalent occurrence only raised more serious concerns about the children's safety. And the lack of general liability insurance might leave parents without recourse if their child suffered an injury on site.

After chairing the hearing, I toured a daycare center in the Binghampton neighborhood in my district for a first hand inspection. The kids were darling and inspired me to press forward.

The Tennessee Child Care Center Standards Advisory Committee, chaired by Rep. Henri Brooks (D-Memphis), also held a hearing in Memphis. Parents complained about children being transported in vans with no seat belts, or even seats, and long van rides.[484] However, a representative from the Tennessee Child Care Association of center owners warned against stricter rules, calling instead for more licensed counselors to enforce the current rules and regulations.[485]

Then came the *Commercial Appeal* report of the large salaries paid to some daycare operators. Some of those centers also used public funds to give associates gifts, make political contributions, and even take trips to New York, Canada, Austria, Switzerland, Germany, Africa, and Italy for training, conferences, and educational purposes.[486] One center's two-person management team was paid $275,000 in salary from the $1.5 million received in government funding according to the newspaper.[487] Another daycare nonprofit founder was determined posthumously to have converted some of the monies to personal use, including purchasing personal property in the founder's own name (such as oriental rugs).[488] With an estimated $82 million being spent by the state for child care in the Memphis area alone, the state provided scant financial oversight due to its position that the daycares were independent businesses subject only to regular inspection.[489]

While some operators were taking lavish trips, most workers earned minimum wage and received no health insurance or other benefits.[490] At some centers, there was a considerable disparity between the workers' salaries and that of the officers and directors.[491] Yet, at others, the workers could earn up to $35,000 a year, highlighting that it was possible to pay workers more and improve quality.[492] Another center in a housing development in Memphis paid its workers $6 to $7 an hour (barely above the state's minimum wage rate of $5.15) but did provide retirement, vacation, health insurance and other benefits, calling the center a "family" and forgoing expenditures on new equipment or the rental space.[493] The heavy responsibility of caring for, teaching, and training the area's youth was not commensurate with the workers' pay.

4

Meanwhile, stories poured out about daycare abuses,[494] such as the state's failure to audit the centers that received public funds, with some not timely filing tax returns or still being paid subsidies although in bankruptcy.[495] One child care center received $1.5 million in state funds, although it did not file tax returns for three years until questioned by a reporter.[496] The owner had operated a prior daycare center dissolved after filing for bankruptcy with tax liens totaling more than $600,000.[497]

Despite these reports, state officials continued to take a hands-off approach to the daycare centers' finances claiming they were fee for service independent contractors.[498] Even though Arkansas audited its centers that received $100,000 or more in funding, the Tennessee DHS instead claimed amounts paid were not subsidies requiring audit because the parents received a certificate that guaranteed payment by the state to a center of their choice.[499]

The state's daycare broker system also came under fire. In Shelby County, the nonprofit Cherokee Children and Family Services ["Cherokee"] had a multi-million dollar state contract to match low-income families with daycare providers, determine eligibility, and issue the certificates that parents used to pay the daycare centers.[500] The state re-awarded the Cherokee contract in the midst of the daycare reform debate over alleged legislative conflicts of interest of this broker.[501]

The *Commercial Appeal* reported that WillieAnn Madison received $100,000 as the Executive Director at Cherokee. At the same time, the newspaper said that her husband earned $52,000 as Executive Director of one child care center and $36,000 as the treasurer of another.[502] According to the newspaper, Cherokee also paid another $72,000 to an entity controlled by WillieAnn Madison. [503] Unlike Memphis, the broker agencies in Nashville and Knoxville were divisions of their respective local governments. The Memphis broker compensation was more than double that of Nashville and Knoxville top executives.[504]

Memphis attorney Richard Fields was an ally of Mayor Herenton. Ultimately, he filed a federal court lawsuit on behalf of some child care centers against John Ford, James Ford, WillieAnn Madison, the Cherokee broker, and others.[505] The lawsuit claimed that the Cherokee broker and others illegally steered children and the state subsidy payments to specific daycare centers. [506] The defendants in the suit all denied any wrongdoing.

5

During the three months after the July tragedy of the babies' deaths, the governor announced the creation of a special legislative committee to review daycare regulation.[507] Sundquist named Sen. John Ford to the committee.

The focus of the *Commercial Appeal's* investigative reporting on daycare turned to Sen. John Ford's involvement with the industry. The newspaper reported that Ford had connections to two companies that handled the lion's share of insurance policy sales to daycare brokers in Shelby County.[508] The article reported that Ford had been an agent with one of the firms, and his 1992 campaign manager owned the other.[509] But there was no evidence that Ford had benefited directly from the companies' insurance sales with child care centers or of any wrongdoing.

One insurance agency also had provided employer's liability and workers compensation coverage to the Cherokee broker, to the center operated by WillieAnn Madison's sister-in-law, and to another operated by her sister, according to the newspaper.[510]

Sidney Chism, a labor leader who had been a major player in Herenton's mayoral defeat of Councilman Joe Ford in October, spoke up about Sen. John Ford's connection to the insurance agency.[511] When questioned, John Ford was reported to angrily respond, "It's none of your damn business."[512] As the state legislature is a part-time job, most legislators worked in various businesses or professions in addition to their legislative service.

In giving a history of daycare, the *Commercial Appeal's* Marc Perrusquia reported that insurance companies had previously bid for the state-subsidized daycare center business.[513] The centers had also been subject to an annual state audit.[514]

As I researched the issue, I found many more problems with the state child care regulation, beyond how children were transported and the conflicts of interest. The deregulation in the 1990s eliminated the requirement of general liability insurance and an appropriate rating system. There were insufficient safeguards in place for background checks for the van drivers and other workers. Better training was needed for child care workers and lower ratios of adults to children to ensure the children's proper development based upon new scientific research.

6

Amid the daycare scandal, the legislature went into another special legislative session called by the governor in November 1999 to work out a long-term budget solution.[515] The governor proposed reducing the state sales tax from 6% to 3.75%, eliminating the 6% sales tax on groceries, revising the business tax structure, and enacting a flat 3.75% state income tax. [516]Angry anti-tax protestors joined legislators at the State Capitol. Security concerns were raised. Some threats brought worries over the inadequate protections in the legislative offices and State Capitol, which had no metal detectors or means to identify persons accessing hallways or senate and house galleries.[517] We did our job, albeit disturbed about the lack of adequate safety precautions.

The special session turned up empty after a few weeks, with the budget impasse over tax reform still firmly in place.[518] We went home exhausted, scrambling to catch up at our respective workplaces after having spent most of the year in contentious budget debates.

With the budget crisis on hold for the time being, I researched and drafted bills for a major overhaul of child care across Tennessee. After the administration withdrew legislation in 1998 from a Senate committee to lower child to child care worker ratios, the Commissioner of DHS said they would bring legislation in 2000 to strengthen the laws. [519]

The community's outcry over children left in dangerous conditions continued in January 2000 just as the legislative session commenced. A thirteen-month-old was reported to be left alone at a daycare center for forty-five minutes after it had closed for the day in Memphis.[520] The owner was one of the three plaintiffs in the child care broker federal court lawsuit and dropped out of the lawsuit.[521] I was outraged that children were still being placed in danger and called DHS Commissioner Metcalf, asking her to take action. Per the department's zero-tolerance policy adopted only two months earlier, the Commissioner suspended the center's license and scheduled a hearing for permanent revocation.[522]

As the debate began on reforms, Senator Ford did advocate for improved basic training for daycare workers and the state to better monitor whether centers had more children than allowed under their licensure, which he felt constituted "imminent danger."[523] With only a high school diploma and limited training required to obtain a state operator's license, I argued that problems should be expected when there were no requirements for experience in business management and child development.[524]

As a member of Sundquist's legislative task force charged to review child care regulations, I was concerned that the committee would not complete its work in time to file reform legislation for the 2000 legislative session. In the task force and the House CFA's Committee hearings, I pushed for major reform, including fines on rule-breakers, criminal background checks on daycare workers and providers, greater financial oversight, and directors' training.[525] The *Commercial Appeal* reported that I had "emerged as the leading voice for change,"[526] with the editors writing that the proposals if enacted would bring the most comprehensive child care reform "in nearly a half century."[527]

Another reform I pushed was to lower the daycare worker to child ratios from five infants to four per worker, drafting legislation to effect this even though such changes were usually done administratively by regulation. My other ideas included developing a report card system for the centers to measure quality, stronger civil penalties for violations, and expanding the pilot program for at-risk children.[528] Drawing comparisons (based upon my own research) between Tennessee and other states, I was able to point to objective evidence that Tennessee's child care laws were too weak.[529]

Mayor Herenton now proposed that the City of Memphis become the daycare broker for the area instead of Cherokee, pointing out that both Nashville and Chattanooga local governments were the brokers in their areas.[530] He also proposed for the city to take over Memphis City Schools as well, which caused quite a stir.[531]

The lawsuit filed by attorney Richard Fields was still pending wherein the plaintiffs, among other things, alleged that the defendants schemed to siphon funds from the state and federal governments to deprive the daycare centers from receiving the broker child placement referrals. [532] Some saw Herenton's proposal for the city to be the daycare broker and the lawsuit against the Cherokee broker and James Ford as simply more of a "long-running feud" and a power struggle between Herenton and the Ford family.[533] Others saw the proposal for the city to take over the public schools as a "power grab" by Herenton, similar to the control exercised by former Memphis Mayor E. H. "Boss" Crump, the most powerful politician in the state during the 1920s and 1930s. But, as to the lawsuit, U.S. District Judge Julia Gibbons dismissed the RICO claims and the fraud claims against all but two defendants.[534] Later, the Judge dismissed all claims against John Ford and all defendants.[535]

7

With the governor's task force meeting only once and the bill filing deadline looming, I decided to move forward with my own daycare reform legislative package. In late January 2000, I filed ten daycare reform bills. Due to the politically powerful people connected with the industry, I sincerely believed that this action might end my political career. [536]

The bills required criminal background checks for workers, greater training for daycare directors, restrictions on who could drive the daycare vans, financial reporting, and audits for centers that received more than $50,000 a year in state funds. They also mandated report cards for the centers, general liability insurance requirements, and restrictions on the distance that a state would pay for a center to transport a child to and from home. My legislative package included stiffer penalties on aggravated assault by a daycare operator, employee or volunteer, and expansion of preschool program funding for better quality education. [537] One bill also provided civil penalties up to $1,000 as an enforcement measure and would allow state officials to partially restrict licenses, such as revoking transportation but otherwise allowing the center to operate.[538]

All agreed that any reforms faced an uphill battle in light of the powerful child care lobby that was already working to defeat any legislation to reduce child-to-worker ratios, although some groups were supportive.[539] Sensing the urgency, I pushed forward to secure senate and house cosponsors for the bills. I also built coalitions among legislators and some child care providers, meeting with the friendlier Tennessee Child Care Association, and the TAEYC leaders. And the *Jackson Sun* reported that legislators had begun to rethink their positions on child care reforms in light of the tragic deaths of Brandon Mann and Darnecia Slater.[540]

12

"I'm Sticking with My Bill"

1

As I pressed forward, I realized that another powerful politician, Lieutenant Governor Wilder, might be a major player in getting my child care reform package passed in the senate. Perhaps there was still bad blood from my calling him out on the "tiny towns" law in 1997? An appeal from a decision holding that law unconstitutional was denied by the Tennessee Supreme Court in January 2000, which affected his cherished Hickory Withe in Fayette County, as well as four other of the twenty proposed "tiny towns."[541] Wilder refused to comment on it in the press.[542]

Although the *Commercial Appeal* editors strongly advocated for reform, the chances of passing the child care bills in 2000 looked slim since it was a tough budget year. Right off the bat, the *Jackson Sun* pounced, writing a scathing editorial of how my daycare reform effort was insincere and hopeless. The newspaper was in Madison County, also in Wilder's legislative district. The editorial called me out by name, chastising my child care reform efforts as "just opportunism."[543] The editorial predicted that child care reform would fail, saying that from my "high perch as a lawyer" "less rhetoric" and "a more realistic approach" was needed because the problem would not be solved "through legislative edict from on high."[544]

The *Jackson Sun* editorial asked who would pay for the expensive reforms in light of the state's budget problems and whether the cost would drive up center operating costs.[545] The opinion accused my unnamed colleagues and me of "showmanship" and of being interested in daycare reform only "during legislative or election seasons."[546] I thought it a warning of sorts, or shot across the bow, perhaps coming from someone connected to the business or to one of the powerful legislators from that area.

While the editorial was disheartening and humiliating, it didn't stop me from trying. I couldn't sleep at night if I didn't push forward, thinking that another child might die if something wasn't done.

2

The Sundquist administration decided to introduce its own child care reform package that required criminal background checks of new daycare workers paid for by the state, fines for centers that violate the rules and increased licensure fees.[547] A second administration bill made it a Class E felony for anyone to obtain state child care subsidies fraudulently.[548] The package also included new proposed rules for more training and lower adult-child ratios to one adult for every four infants instead of five.[549] Absent from his legislative package was any requirement of financial reports or audits of daycare centers, which I promptly asked the governor's task force to consider.[550] With others pointing to the warehousing of children resulting from the hasty welfare reform earlier, some legislators openly wondered aloud how the tragedies could happen.[551]

According to the *Commercial Appeal*, Senator Ford immediately warned the governor that his bill would be amended substantially in the Senate General Welfare, Health & Human Resources Committee that he chaired.[552] The local press continued to remind the readers in news stories that Sen. John Ford's brother, County Commissioner James Ford, had interests in daycare centers that had received nearly $700,000 in state funds in the six months before the end of the year.[553] They also noted John Ford's connections to the insurance agencies selling policies to daycare centers.[554] The governor's bill was carried by Memphis Sen. Curtis Person in the senate and Speaker Pro Tempore Lois Deberry and Rep. Page Walley in the state house.

President Bill Clinton's administration was also pushing child care measures, proposing an expansion of Head Start funding and the child care tax credit.[555] The administration argued that child care improvements were necessary for welfare reform to work.[556]

The issue was volatile and contentious from the get-go at the Tennessee State Capitol. Sen John Ford, sometimes charming with a great sense of humor, also had another side and "blasted" my daycare reform bills in the Governor's Committee on Child Care. He publicly criticized my daycare financial audit and child care broker reform bills, warning that they would be before his committee.[557] He also argued that some of the reform measures were too expensive for child care providers.[558]

I replied that Arkansas had an audit requirement for daycares that helped to flag quality issues. Ford angrily responded, "I'm not going to let my twenty-five years of experience fly out the window based on what somebody in Arkansas" does.[559] I calmly responded, "I'm going to stick with my bill."[560]

My broker bill sought to address the conflict of interest issue where the Cherokee broker in Memphis had board members that owned interests in several daycare centers.[561] Competing daycare operators complained that the centers connected to the Cherokee board members benefited from a larger share of state-subsidized children.[562] Ford countered that the parents picked the center, not the broker.[563] However, there were still complaints, with some arguing that the broker could tell a parent the center they picked was full, thus manipulating the process.[564]

Meanwhile, Sundquist administration officials, including his former chief of staff, and current finance commissioner, testified before a federal grand jury in Memphis on a daycare probe.[565] And, the state comptroller's office was also auditing several of Shelby County's largest publicly funded daycare centers at the request of the U.S. Attorney in Memphis.[566]

The *Commercial Appeal* went after Sen. John Ford in one of many editorials to follow, saying that he should recuse himself.[567] The editors argued that he had a conflict of interest on the daycare issue, had business ties to the insurance companies that sell policies to daycare centers, and had a family member who had an ownership interest in daycares.[568] Since he would not recuse himself, they contended that his colleagues and the Sundquist administration should not let him "dictate the disposition" of daycare reform legislation as the chair of the senate committee that would consider the bills.[569] Noting that senate rules gave Ford, as a chairman, "wide latitude to advance or bury legislation," the editors urged the senate to exercise "bipartisan courage" and invoke the rarely used procedure of recalling the bills from the committee to the senate floor if necessary to safeguard the lives of young children.[570] Hopefully, it would not be required.

The child care lobby geared up with so many representatives that one article in the *Commercial Appeal* compared them to the gun lobby, well-known in Tennessee to be pro-NRA.[571] One newly formed group from Memphis brought 200 people to Nashville to oppose the daycare financial audit and other reform measures.[572] Roosevelt Joyner, who headed up the lobbying group, said he opposed the audits because the daycare centers were private businesses and not government contractors.[573] He did not oppose lowering the adult-child ratios, though, if the state provided additional funds.[574]

My daycare reform efforts were boosted when House Speaker Jimmy Naifeh pledged his support.[575] While Joyner called some of the reform measures a "knee-jerk reaction," Herenton also backed reforms in the county delegation meeting at the State Capitol, wanting the city to take control of daycare brokering, Head Start, and the public schools.[576]

To get everyone in the right frame of mind when the Shelby County delegation meeting began, I asked for a moment of silent prayer for the two children who had died in the daycare vans. The room grew quiet.

After the prayer, Sen. John Ford reiterated that he would block much of the legislation. Joyner and I agreed to try to work together on the proposals. He expressed his sympathy for the families of those who had lost a child.[577] Joyner continued to call daycares private businesses that should not be subject to a state audit. However, Herenton observed that "early childhood education has become subordinate to entrepreneurial interests."[578]

Meanwhile, the grand jury probe into the Cherokee broker system continued.[579] Cherokee had held the state contract for ten years, being selected the prior year again despite scoring lower than two other applicants.[580]

Again, the *Commercial Appeal* editorialized in favor of daycare reform, although noting that the likelihood of substantive reform appeared "bleak."[581] The crux of the issue was whether the legislators would put the children and families ahead of the "politically influential daycare lobby in Nashville."[582] The editorial mentioned House Speaker Naifeh's backing, but the absence of leadership by Lieutenant Governor Wilder on reform.[583] Political cartoons in the newspaper included a limousine marked "Lobbyist" at the front door of the State Capitol, with children and "Day Care Reform" at the back door.[584] I still hoped to get Wilder's support.

The progressive weekly newspaper, the *Memphis Flyer*, joined in, telling John Ford to "Butt Out."[585] The editors observed that corruption (a counterfeiting ring) and cozy deals were the norms in the daycare industry at that time, and because of the lack of oversight, "horrific child deaths" had occurred. [586] The editorial was clear not to accuse John Ford or his family of any wrongdoing. But it argued that due to his connection with the industry, it was a "no-brainer" that Ford should recuse himself (especially in light of his statements that he would personally stop some of the reform efforts.)[587] Yet, Ford would not stand down.

3

Part of my strategy in getting the reform measures through the legislature included traveling to the eastern part of the state to talk with newspaper editors and the media. Tennessee is a long and narrow state, with different time zones for Knoxville and Chattanooga than Nashville in the middle and Memphis on the western end. My office scheduled the media interviews, and after the week's legislative session ended, I traveled to Chattanooga for an overnight stay. My colleague, Rep. Brenda Turner, recommended that I stay at the historic Read House Hotel.

While I had heard stories that it was haunted, having been used as a hospital during the Civil War, I paid scant attention to the story. Supposedly Room 311 was frequented by the ghost of a woman jilted by her lover in the 1930s. [588] Al Capone had also stayed in the room during his trial. [589] However, I was in good company staying at the hotel since it also previously had hosted Winston Churchill.

I was assigned a room in the annex from the original hotel and turned in for the night. However, being cautious, I kept a light on in my room. At some point during the night, doors started slamming up and down the hall, although as far as I could tell, only one other room was occupied on the entire floor. I poked my head outside the door more than once to see who was making the noise but saw nothing.

Having a 6 a.m. radio interview scheduled, at about 1 a.m., I finally called the front desk and asked for another room due to the unexplained noise. It was a great story for the radio deejays the next morning who thought it was hysterical. However, it made for a really long day when with hardly any sleep, and after all of the Chattanooga interviews, I drove to Knoxville for more interviews, visited a daycare, and then made the long, nearly seven-hour drive back to Memphis. However, I was determined to get the reform measures adopted into law.

As reported in the *Johnson City Press*, with more than a quarter of a million Tennessee children enrolled in daycare at some 6,000 licensed facilities, this first major reform effort since 1953 of the daycare laws was the most important issue of the 2000 legislative session. [590] And, U. S. Sen. Bill Frist (R-Tenn.) proposed his own federal bill to authorize millions of dollars to establish grants to improve health and safety conditions of child care facilities nationally for training, criminal background checks, children with disabilities, and improving child care transportation safety. [591]

My proposals included common sense measures, such as to limit child care centers from transporting children for more than forty-five minutes one way without a state waiver, requiring the state department of human services and the department of education to share information regarding allegations of neglect, and to prohibit anyone convicted of a DUI or vehicular homicide within the past five years from driving a daycare van. My view was if the legislators kept the interests of the children at heart, there should be no problems in getting the reform measures adopted that year.

4

Another part of my strategy to get the bills passed was to counter the daycare lobby with action by everyday citizens. I scheduled a town hall meeting at the local board of education auditorium in Memphis to hear from the public and to get people involved in the lobbying effort to support my legislative package. Unfortunately, on the morning of the meeting, a 5k race blocked off easy access to the auditorium. I worried that no one would show up because of the difficulty of getting to the building.

Thank heavens, about twenty-five people showed up. We sat around a table talking about the reform efforts. I asked each person to explain why they had come that morning. Present were some daycare directors and workers, officials with the League of Women Voters, Memphis Chamber of Commerce, and several local Democratic and Republican party activists. As each person around the table introduced themselves, one African American young woman, Tomeka Williams, explained that her four-month-old child had died in 1997 when left in a daycare van in Memphis. The tragedy had received little if any, publicity at that time. This was my first awareness that another child had suffered the same fate as Darnecia and Brandon. I quickly asked Williams if she would come to Nashville to address the Shelby County legislative delegation, and she agreed.

At that point, Sen. John Ford had canceled every scheduled meeting in the senate subcommittee on the daycare reform package.[592] The house subcommittee was scheduled to hear the reform measures that week. I urged the group to call the seven legislators that were its members.

Having Tomeka, and her baby Destiny's father, Adrian Williams, join the effort was a godsend. The legislators needed to hear from them and keep in mind their child and the other children who had been hurt or killed when they voted on the reform package. Tomeka expressed gratitude that she was not alone in wanting safer daycare.[593] Her child had been left in a van for several hours, with the temperature inside estimated to be 112 degrees. After being rescued, the child died two days later from massive brain swelling caused by a heat stroke.[594] The driver pled guilty to criminally negligent homicide and was sentenced to one year in prison, suspended, and a year's probation.[595]

Every time we hit a roadblock, something else happened that helped convince the legislators to approve the measure. When some opposed my proposal to require general liability and accident insurance as too expensive for small daycare operators, news came out of a child scalded at a Shelby County daycare center.[596] I argued that the child might need ongoing medical care, and without insurance, there may not be funds for the medical care.

Rep. Gene Caldwell, a pediatrician, pushed to reduce the transportation time lower than the current ninety-minute one-way trip, on the basis that an infant would spend three hours looking at the ceiling, which was unhealthy.

The house subcommittee then approved requiring centers to purchase liability insurance and to have criminal background checks for workers.[597] They also voted to reduce allowed travel time for children in the vans and to ban workers with a DUI or vehicular homicide within the past five years from driving the buses.[598] Speaker Pro Tempore Lois Deberry worked on combining the governor's reforms and my legislative package into one final package.

The Commissioner of DHS, Natasha Metcalf, then announced that the state would phase out the daycare broker system that summer.[599] Senator Ford said it was an administrative decision and also voted the governor's reform package out of the senate child care subcommittee.[600] I commented that the bipartisan effort on the reform was very positive for Tennessee's children. However, a lobbyist for the child care brokers was not giving up on convincing the governor to keep the broker system.[601] My concern was that the industry would pressure the governor after the legislature adjourned to change his mind and keep the broker system. Therefore, I urged the house members to keep the conflict of interest prohibitions in the reform package, just in case.

Having agreed on most of the reforms sought by myself and Sundquist, the house subcommittee combined the bills into a single reform initiative. The *Commercial Appeal* reported a "flicker of hope" that "potentially life-saving daycare reform finally could become a reality in Tennessee."[602] The Sundquist administration now supported the adoption of rules for lower adult-child ratios, training, and transportation that could become effective within a matter of weeks as opposed to the usual eighteen-month rule-making process.[603]

The adult-child ratio reform was a sticking point for some legislators, concerned that low-earning parents who did not qualify for state daycare subsidies couldn't afford increased costs.[604] Facing an approximately $400 million shortfall for the next fiscal year, the state was in no position to increase the daycare subsidy amount or expand its scope.[605] Adding extra workers due to lowered adult-child ratios would cost parents of an infant about $25 more a week. But I warned the whole package might not pass if the legislation increased state subsidies.[606]

Additional expenses included liability and accident insurance, fingerprinting, and background checks for new employees.[607] The administration agreed to cover the cost of criminal background checks and enhanced training for center operators.[608] I continued to advocate for a bipartisan approach that would combine all of the reform measures from both chambers into one bill.[609]

In an effort to get the bill passed, the house subcommittee decided to phase in the lower adult to child ratios, starting with children two and under within one year.[610] Some argued that the reform would force parents to take their children out of daycare into unregulated caregiver homes. [611]Joining the fray, workers brought 200 pre-school children to the State Capitol to support worthy wages, calling for better pay in the daycare industry than its average of $6.12 an hour.[612]

Pressure for reform mounted with a new report in the *Chattanooga Times Free Press* of a child in Cleveland, Tennessee, who unlocked a door to a daycare center and walked onto a heavily traveled roadway while the caretaker slept.[613] The child was brought back safely after motorists called the sheriff's department.[614] The newspaper also reported other children dropped off at home without verification of an adult on the premises, left inside a center after it closed for the day, and hospitalized due to improperly administered medication.[615]

Not long thereafter, the Senate General Welfare Committee and the house subcommittee began tampering with the proposed financial disclosure and audit requirements for daycare centers.[616] The house subcommittee changed the bill to take out the financial disclosure requirements and audits, acting on the request of the Sundquist administration and state Comptroller John Morgan.[617] I pushed for annual reporting by child care centers receiving more than $75,000 a year in state subsidies, as to salaries and other compensation paid to directors and officers, spending on food and supplies, and payments to related parties including leases, consultants and subcontractors.[618] The comptroller offered to work with legislators to forge a compromise, while Speaker Naifeh and I stood our ground on requiring accountability for how the funds were spent.[619]

Disappointed, I told the house subcommittee that it had watered the measure down so much that the bill would not be worth doing. I reminded them that many financial irregularities in the daycare business in Memphis had been disclosed only due to investigative reporting. The removal of financial disclosure requirements could appear as the legislature's attempt to keep any misspending secret.[620] While opponents argued that increased inspections alone would be sufficient, Speaker Pro Tempore Deberry agreed with me, telling the committee that the bill would not fly without an audit provision.[621]

The next day, the senate committee removed the plan to expedite rules on lowering adult-child ratios at daycare centers and removed the financial disclosure provisions, with a battle now predicted between the house and senate versions of the reform bill.[622] However, the fact that the reform bill had advanced out of the committee chaired by Sen. John Ford was deemed a "milestone."[623] Then a miracle happened: Sen. Ford not only voted for the reform bill but signed on as a co-sponsor.[624]

The senate bill still had to pass through the Senate Government Operations Committee and Finance Committees but was moving forward. The fact that the senate and house versions were different now created the possibility that the measure might not be passed at all in the late, busy days of the session if the joint conference committee could not resolve the differences upon the bill's passage by both chambers.

Trying to save the financial reporting provisions in the daycare bill, I reluctantly agreed to a more narrowly drawn amendment proposed by the comptroller and house leaders. The amendment required the twenty-six largest daycare centers that received more than half a million in state funds to have annual audits. Centers receiving more than $75,000 a year in state funds would be required to report how the funds were spent in categories, including the total spent on salaries and benefits. The compromise wasn't perfect, but it was better than the amendment the subcommittee had previously approved without any specific audit or financial disclosure requirements. That amendment gave the administration and comptroller only the power to ask for financial information if deemed necessary.[625] The compromise amendment included random audits of centers receiving more than $250,000 in state funds to determine whether the centers efficiently spent the public monies for quality child care. The audit and financial disclosure information would be used to develop a new report card system for daycares that would reward higher quality centers with higher subsidy payments.

When the bill passed out of the House Health & Human Resources Committee after two hours of debate, due in part to filibuster efforts, there was applause and whistles. However, there was still a terrific battle ahead in the senate regarding lower adult to child ratios and to find the funding for the improvements.[626] Others spoke in support of the financial accountability measures, including Rep. John Deberry and Rep. Tre Hargett.[627] While the bill did not include all of my proposed reforms, it was comprehensive. Major reforms included the requirement that the DHS develop a report card licensing system, background checks for workers, audits (now paid for by the state), and financial disclosures. The bill headed to the House Finance Ways & Means Committee with the hope that the senate would adopt the house bill, which could be a model for other states.[628]

5

At this time more revelations were forthcoming on the Cherokee broker business dealings. The *Commercial Appeal* reported that the executive director, WillieAnn Madison, bought $1 million worth of real estate two weeks after the agency's board of directors voted to pay $437,000 in back rent to Madison's Affordable Properties Management for the building that housed the agency.[629] According to the story, she and her husband bought five buildings and then they sold one of them to her sister and another to daycare operator Joyner.[630] The lump-sum payment for back rent for an alleged miscalculation of the building's square feet was calculated retroactively to 1995.[631] Their attorney, Allan Wade, defended the real estate transaction as unrelated to the back rent payment and the back rent payment as appropriate.[632] A CPA was reported to have warned the agency that some of the transactions between the board and its employees and related entities could jeopardize its nonprofit status if the IRS found that it was for the benefit of the individuals and not the stated charitable purpose.[633]

Questions were raised about whether the agency needed such a large space, with the building containing a swimming pool and a theater for some twenty employees.[634] The agency claimed it needed the space to house about 100,000 records on nearly 40,000 clients.[635] The agency's auditor was reported to raise questions about the investment of some $300,000 in the stock of a start-up bank of which Cherokee's executive director, WillieAnn Madison, served on the board of directors, with concerns that the investment could harm the nonprofit if the bank failed.[636]

In light of the news reports, state officials sent an employee to inspect the building. The *Commercial Appeal* broke the story that the office space was actually one-half of the 20,000 square feet identified in Cherokee's lease with Affordable Properties Management.[637] More cartoons appeared in the newspaper, with one of a small child holding a sign with the words "Day Care!" changed to "They Don't Care."[638]

Back at the state legislature, Sen. Doug Henry came to the rescue of the proposed lower adult to child ratios by amending the bill in the finance committee to add the removed language allowing DHS to adopt the rule changes immediately.[639] Senator Ford voted "no," but the amendment passed on a voice vote, and then the bill was approved with all, including Ford, voting in favor, with one abstention. [640]

6

To rally the troops, our citizens' group chartered a bus for the trip to Nashville. We had white and red stickers printed with "Child Care Reform Now" for supporters to wear. I divided up the citizens, with each assigned a certain number of legislators to visit in their offices to ask for support. Tomeka Williams also came and was scheduled to address the Shelby County legislative delegation. Lieutenant Governor Wilder agreed to see the group, but when the delegation meeting ran late, he refused to see the citizens without me present. Not wanting to leave Tomeka alone to testify before the delegation, I was worried that we would miss the opportunity to talk with Wilder. We finally were able to attend that appointment, hoping that it would sway him to our side. We were encouraged when the house approved the bill 96-0 and sent it to the senate, which approved a different version thirty to one.[641]

There were discussions before the vote about who would lead the bill in the house since the governor's bill and my legislative package were combined. While I had been willing to forgo taking the lead in the state house to get the resolution removing Judge Lanier passed, this time, I remained the lead sponsor. I appreciated the many other sponsors who helped in the effort, such as Speaker Jimmy Naifeh, Rep. Lois Deberry, Senators Curtis Person and Roy Herron, and Rep. Page Walley.

When I presented the bill on the house floor, I acknowledged all who had helped. However, I dedicated the bill to Destiny Williams, Brandon Mann, and Darnecia Slater and their families, along with the many other babies and children who had suffered at others' hands. The three babies had died in vans, forgotten, helpless, and afraid. In my remarks in support, I said that we "bring this bill so that their deaths will not be forgotten, in the hopes that other children will not suffer similarly." The new proposed law would make the child care system in Tennessee safer and more accountable.

I reminded the legislators of many tragedies, including incidents in several counties across the state. A two-year-old was disciplined with a flyswatter and a three-year-old bitten on the arm by the owner in one county. Children were found unsupervised on busy streets in two other counties. The U.S. Secret Service made a daycare raid on one center for counterfeiting, a child was given the wrong medicine resulting in serious illness in another, and an 8-month-old infant was seriously burned from a bottle warmer while unsupervised.

I reviewed the state comptroller audit report on the improper billing for food by some child care centers, the criminal investigation by the federal grand jury, and the investigative reports of some primarily publicly subsidized centers spending money on overseas trips and large salaries for owners. With state subsidies of 70% of the market rate, every dime should go for the children.

In requesting adoption of the reform legislation, I asked, "What if it was your child? Wouldn't you require more?" I reminded them that it *was* Tomeka William's child, and she supported the reform measures. The bill was the first step to better protect the 267,000 children in licensed facilities in the state.

With the house and senate votes, the reform bill was forced into a conference committee, with the major difference being the lower adult-child ratios. The final bill contained a compromise of many of my bills, parts of the Sundquist administration bill, and proposals from other members.[642]

On the same day, it was reported that Cherokee would repay the state for rent overcharges and that federal prosecutors had issued subpoenas.[643] Because the entity was more than 99% publicly funded in the approximate amount of $7 million, the public was outraged.[644] Cherokee's attorney, Allan Wade, fought demands from the Memphis Publishing Company and a citizen who sued for access to the agency's financial records under the state open records act.[645] Judge John McCarroll ruled that the documents were public due to the broker's contract with the State.[646]

Later, on appeal, the Tennessee Supreme Court upheld the ruling that the entity's records were public and held that the state comptroller had the right to audit. [647] WillieAnn Madison and Joyner contended that they had done nothing improper, and the building's size had been miscalculated by subtracting the size of a parking lot from the total 47,000 square-foot lot.[648]

Near the end of the session, since both the house and senate had passed the reform bill, albeit different versions, the push was on to keep the stronger house provisions and get it passed by both chambers before the session adjourned. Both the house and senate had to pass identical versions of the bill, and the governor either had to sign it or at least not veto it for it to become law. The *Commercial Appeal* chimed in, urging the legislature not to water the bill down and to pass it the same session.[649]

The next day both the house and senate passed the bill and sent it to the governor, with the audits, the speedy adoption of the lower adult to child ratios, and higher training for workers.[650] The *Commercial Appeal* called it a "hard-won triumph for Rep. Carol Chumney" after the bill sponsors fought back heavy opposition and noted that I "beamed" upon its passage.[651] I hugged and thanked House Speaker Naifeh for his support. The governor signed the bill into law, calling the reforms "monumental."[652] I was ecstatic.

7

Though the daycare reforms were decided, unfortunately, the state's fiscal problems remained unsolved. Tax reform protestors continued to circle the State Capitol, honking their horns to oppose a state income tax. A 5% income tax on adjusted gross income above $100,000 for single filers and $200,000 for joint filers had been proposed, but it went nowhere.[653] The legislature adjourned on a Saturday and agreed to return the following day to continue working, although gridlocked, with a June 30th budget deadline looming to avoid a government shutdown.[654]

Finally, the exhausted state legislature adopted a budget spending nonrecurring funds for recurring expenses and raising revenue projections beyond the State Funding Board's official estimates.[655] While Sundquist vetoed the measure calling it a "Fudge-It Budget," the legislature overrode his veto and adjourned to take up the fiscal crisis another day.[656]

After that, Tennessee's child care tragedies, political connections within the industry, and reform efforts were the subject of national attention in the July 10, 2000, *TIME* magazine issue on the pulse of America.[657] The article noted that you couldn't have successful welfare reform without good day-care.[658] The tragedy of Destiny Williams' death was reported, along with that of Brandon Mann and Darnecia Slater, all of whom had been left to die in sweltering hot daycare vans.[659] The obstacles of getting reform passed, and then my victory in passing reform was noted in the article, although I cautioned that "change takes time."[660]

Some of those responsible for the death of twenty-two-month-old Darnecia Slater, whose body temperature was 108 degrees when found in a van, were held accountable, with each receiving two-year sentences and $500 fines after pleading guilty to reckless homicide.[661] According to the Associated Press, one defendant claimed to suffer from a mental health condition. The other claimed that the daycare had her falsify employee records to state that she had graduated from high school when she had dropped out.[662] The *Commercial Appeal* also reported that a worker had been placed on probation in 1989 for selling cocaine, which might have been flagged if there had been a background check.[663] The daycare denied that any records were falsified, and the state declined to investigate.[664]

Relatives of Darnecia spoke out on the anniversary of her death, still wondering why center workers never realized she was left in the van all day and how stricter training requirements had then been in place for hairstylists than child care workers.[665] The new law required pre-service training for workers and greater training for directors. Advocates such as Linda O'Neal with the Tennessee Commission on Children and Youth, and Nancy Jones, an educator, continued to speak up for higher wages for workers. I hoped that the law's provision for more public-private partnerships to encourage corporations and charitable organizations to help finance improvements and higher wages would work.[666] Later, the *Commercial Appeal* reported that both the families of Darnecia Slater and Brandan Mann filed multi-million dollar wrongful death lawsuits against the respective daycare centers.[667]

The Tennessee child care bill accountability provisions also were selected for the national Democratic Leadership Conference's "Idea of the Week." The DLC called Tennessee's decision to invest in public subsidies for child care as part of welfare reform "admirable" but also noted the neglect and mismanagement in some child care centers.[668] The DLC thanked me for making

Tennessee "one of the first systems" in the nation to add an evaluation of child care centers "based on universal standards and clear, parent-friendly criteria."[669]

The article pointed out that the new law required the state to develop, by fall, spending guidelines and benchmarks for centers that receive $75,000 or more a year in state subsidies to ensure that they properly spent the funds to care for children, along with the audit requirements.[670] Noting the "long fight with industry lobbyists," the DLC also acknowledged that after the "successful effort to engage the initially reluctant Sundquist administration in Nashville, Chumney won the day in late June with the enactment of major portions of her legislation."[671] The national publication ended with the statement that "Carol Chumney, and her state of Tennessee, are getting accountability right."[672] The accolades were appreciated, but I give the credit to God for making a way where there did not seem to be a way.

8

My reform efforts continued when I was elected to serve as a member of the National Democratic Convention Platform Standing Committee. Because inclement weather delayed my flight to Cleveland for the meeting, I faxed in my proposed amendment to the platform, which said that Democrats believe "in requiring accountability so that federal moneys and subsidy payments are effectively used to provide quality in child care."[673] With the federal government spending about $3.6 billion on child care, mostly for subsidies for low-income families, I felt the plank was needed to avoid abuses in other states similar to what had happened in Tennessee. [674]Despite delayed flights, I made it to Cleveland at 2:30 a.m. in time to attend the meeting later that morning and get the amendment adopted after some negotiation with party leaders.

In August, I attended the National Democratic Convention in Los Angeles and made sure that the amendment was approved for the official platform. As reported in the *Tennessean*, the new plank to the National Democratic Party Platform put the party "squarely on the side of children and safety when it comes to dealing with the child-care industry."[675] Calling my effort a "crusade," the newspaper endorsed the premise that the "key" to quality child care is "accountability."[676] The editorial called for the same reforms in Tennessee to be raised on a national level for the "well-being" of all children.[677] I was happy that the new law might help families and children across the USA.

13

More Daycare Reform Battles

1

The 2001 session brought proposed state legislation by others to reauthorize the Memphis daycare broker system over my strong opposition. There were powerful political forces in the state seeking to undo what we had done the prior year. I, and others, continued to fight to keep the reforms and ensure their implementation.

At the end of the session, the cliffhanger was a late-night vote by the legislature to delay the rules for the reduction in adult-child ratios until February 1, 2002, for infants or children through the age of two.[678] Rep. Gene Caldwell, a pediatrician, opposed the delay due to the negative impact on child brain development.[679] The house refused to concur in the senate proposal on the omnibus rules bills that involved many other state department and agency rules. Rep. Mike Kernell, the Chair of the House Government Operations Committee, recalled only three other times in the past fifteen years where the rules bill had been the subject of efforts to alter the rules on the floor substantially, calling this the one "the most critical."[680]

In the senate-house conference committee formed to work out differences on the rules bill, house leaders, including me, sought a compromise by having the reduction in ratios go into effect for infants only and delaying the ratios for older children. Senate opposition was led by Sen. Marsha Blackburn (R-Brentwood) and Rosalind Kurita (D-Clarksville), who insisted on a delay for all age groups.[681] The delay for all age groups until February 1, 2002, was the best that could be accomplished and at least kept in effect all other state government rules.

The reduced ratios would go into effect by default on February 1 if opponents didn't pass a delay bill before then. As Representative Kernell said, when the session resumed in 2002, "there will be only three weeks to pass a bill to stop (the ratios)." "So those who want better ratios lost some time but got the near certainty of the ratios going into effect then."[682]

In Memphis, an association of about 50 for-profit and nonprofit daycare operators also filed suit in July to stop the new law's requirements for financial reporting and audits.[683] Circuit Court Judge Kay Robilio denied the request for an immediate temporary restraining order to block the audits.[684] Allan Wade, an attorney for the daycare association, argued that public money was not involved because the parents received a certificate instead of direct payments by the state to the operators.[685] I advocated for moving state funds into Head Start and public schools if the daycare accountability measures were removed. This was heralded by the *Commercial Appeal* editors, who asked what the operators had to hide that necessitated the lawsuit.[686]

The daycare reform fight continued in the courts with lawsuits by Tennessee Attorney General Paul Summers against certain daycare nonprofits and operators, alleging improper personal gain concerning compensation, leasing arrangements, and loans.[687] One lawsuit alleged that the owners used nonprofit assets as collateral for a half a million-dollar loan to open a for-profit daycare in Arkansas.[688] Other allegations of misused funds included personal use of a 2000 Lexus 470 sport utility vehicle.[689]

Another lawsuit by the state Attorney General alleged misuse of nonprofit funds for excessive salaries, rent, and personal use of the daycare's two Mercedes Benz vehicles.[690] The defendant's attorney, Allan Wade, filed a suit to dissolve the nonprofit, and the operator reopened two centers as for-profit operations.[691] The lawsuit by the Attorney General alleged that the operator had used nonprofit funds to pay for loans on real estate in her name, personal utility bills, tuition for her children, personal credit card expenses, and birthday parties, as well as paying personal debts.[692]

Upon the advice of their attorney, A C Wharton, WillieAnn Madison and her husband pled the *Fifth Amendment* and refused to answer questions from state lawyers about the broker's finances and operations.[693] A Nashville chancellor dissolved the broker entity and appointed a receiver, finding, among other things, that the entity had spent about $24,000 on a trip for relatives and an employee to London.[694] The entity appealed the Chancellor's ruling.[695]

The daycare reforms were under siege in the state legislature in 2002 as well, with a bill filed by Sen. Marsha Blackburn (R-Brentwood) and Rep.

Diane Black (R-Hendersonville) to roll back the increased adult-child ratios for all children except infants.[696] The legislators claimed that the increased costs for the added staff would close some centers, but Blackburn did not identify any by name.[697] I countered that the measure was needed to ensure children's brains develop properly.

The attack on the law continued with a senate committee voting to revoke the new lower adult child ratios and another bill scheduled to delay implementation of the report card evaluation system.[698]

I, Rep. Gene Caldwell and others, the Sundquist administration, and child care reform advocates around the state rallied to keep the reforms, pointing out that only ten centers statewide had closed after the implementation of reforms over the past year.[699] One estimate showed that the lower adult-child ratios would add only about $6 a week to daycare costs. [700]

New state reports stunned the public, as 131 daycare workers were terminated after the now-required background checks.[701] Among those terminated were a man formerly imprisoned for a decade in another state for aggravated sexual assault, a former hospital employee with a conviction for abusing patients, a woman convicted of vehicular homicide, and a man convicted of rape.[702] Another worker had been convicted in another state of smothering her newborn and hiding the body in the garbage.[703] There were also drug and DUI charges, and some with prostitution records.[704] It was shocking to think that these people would still be employed as child care workers without the reform law.

I pushed for an increase in the child care subsidy amounts for low income and poor parents, which would be earmarked to increase the salaries of center workers and van drivers for higher quality hires.[705] The *Commercial Appeal* editorialized about the inconsistency of some legislators' harsh words, given their failure to support my proposal for increasing and earmarking subsidy funds for van drivers, as well as their support of delaying other reforms.[706]

Lawmakers were livid about the deaths of four more Memphis children in a daycare van crash, where the driver (who also died) had a prior misdemeanor drug conviction and was found with marijuana on his person at the accident scene.[707] The center's operator leased from an owner who had prior problems for a center at the same site. [708]

The owner's license had been revoked at one center after she and a son were indicted on a counterfeit money scheme.[709] Charges against her were ultimately dismissed after pretrial diversion, but her son pled guilty to one count of conspiracy.[710]

As far back as 1992, one of her centers had been cited after an inspection found only two workers supervising 26 toddlers in one room.[711] The owner and her then husband lost their license for a Mississippi daycare center after allegations of drugs being sold out of the center by a night watchman related to the operator. Dope was found in wooden cubicles where the children stored their sleeping mats, and a gun left in an unlocked filing cabinet accessible to the kids.[712] The night watchman served time on one of the drug charges.[713]

In 1998 another son at a different center owned by the same person had been charged with reckless endangerment while driving a busload of children.[714] Later, he pled guilty to reckless driving and driving without a license, with the other charges dropped.[715] He had a prior record, and the state oversight officials scrambled to determine why the required criminal background check had not been done.[716]

Continuing my efforts at daycare reform, I proposed a national registry for child care operators so that officials in one state would be notified of actions against operators in another state. This would help officials considering license applications.[717]

The *Commercial Appeal* raised new questions by revealing that the back rent paid to the Shelby County child care broker included not only $437,000 but also another $141,000 check paid a month before the board's approval in March 1999.[718] The Tennessee Court of Appeals upheld the receivership for the entity in the lawsuit by the Tennessee Attorney General Paul Summers.[719] The Court referenced interest free loans given to employees by the non-profit, including one to pay off a student loan of the stepson of the executive director.[720] Also, the entity had paid for personal expenses on trips that had no business purpose, including to Hawaii and London for the executive director, other relatives, and employees, and cleaning services for her and her mother's home.[721] After the auditor flagged the trips, the value of the personal expenses was added to the employee's salary.[722] Yet, the appellate court noted the individuals were not required to pay the monies back.[723] Ultimately, the court of appeals held that the Cherokee entity was "operated for the private gain of Mrs. Madison, her family and/or other individuals in control."[724]

After it was reported in the *Commercial Appeal*, the Cherokee board passed a resolution requiring the $502,838 overpayment of rent to be repaid by the Madisons or the building transferred to the entity with payment for any amount due greater than its appraised value.[725] The Madisons executed the deed, and WillieAnn Madison repaid over $30,000.[726]

Later the Madisons were tried jointly in federal criminal court.[727]WillieAnn Madison was found guilty of tax evasion, false statements on tax documents under penalty of perjury, false or fraudulent claims, theft from programs receiving federal funds, among other charges. [728] She was ordered to serve 23 months in jail and make restitution of $751,832. [729] Mr. Madison, who had been paid as the accountant for the broker entity, was convicted of tax evasion and aiding the preparation of tax documents containing false or fraudulent statements. [730] He was sentenced to 10 months and to pay restitution of $564,832 (jointly and severally with his wife). [731] The convictions were upheld on appeal, with the Sixth Circuit finding that the "defendants treated their personal property and the property of the business for which they worked as substantially interchangeable."[732]

2

Once again, in 2003, daycare reform opponents tried to delay the lower adult-child ratios for children ages four and five and mixed-age groups.[733] Governor Bredesen's staff at first supported the delay. Other bills were pending to remove or scale back other reforms that had already passed and been implemented.[734] The mandatory drug testing for daycare employees had not been implemented yet, despite the tragic deaths of four children the prior year when their driver had a previous misdemeanor drug conviction.[735]

The *Commercial Appeal* again editorialized in opposition to the efforts to delay the new rules.[736] The editors noted that the reform movement "led by state Rep. Carol Chumney (D-Memphis), made important gains," but much effort since then had been required "beating back efforts" to delay or undo the 2000 law.[737] It seemed that the battle would never end.

A compromise was reached shortly thereafter with the lower ratios for four-year-olds to take effect in six months, and the five-year-olds a year later.[738] I agreed to the compromise to allow state officials and daycare operators time to catch up with the many reform measures. However, Senators Kurita and Ford pushed an amendment to a bill to lower the ratios for those ages indefinitely.[739]

Daycare reform advocates, including me, once again played defense, trying to stop the bills and amendments that would scale back or repeal many of the hard-fought reforms.[740] We succeeded in keeping the key reforms, but it took herculean efforts.

Because of my battle to pass landmark child care reform, I was selected as one of the Democratic Leadership Council's (DLC) top 100 Democrats to Watch nationally. The selection was part of the group's passing of the torch to a new generation of "innovative" "pragmatic" leaders. As one of the top 100, I attended a private roundtable discussion with former President Bill Clinton.[741] Later at the conference, I spoke with him about the state child care reforms, possible national child care reforms, and the need for the Democratic Party to increase support for female candidates. In his typically charming way and oblivious to the surrounding crowd, he held onto my hand, looked into my eyes, listened intently, and agreed. I hoped it would make a difference.

14

The Death of Tax Reform

1

While daycare reform had succeeded, the tax reform battle suffered a different fate. In 2001, the governor continued to push for an income tax to fund education and warned that massive cuts or a sales tax hike would result otherwise.[742] The projected state budget shortfall was about $800 million.[743] The state's sales tax was one of the highest in the country.

The state senate and house were logjammed over whether to pass a half-cent sales tax increase or Sen. Bob Rochelle and Rep. Tommy Head's proposed graduated income tax with high exemption rates, repeal of the Hall Tax on investments, and removal of all sales tax on food. Also on the table was how to fund the governor's education "reading initiative."[744] Some house leaders opposed the proposed sales tax increase as only a short-term solution.

Attorney General Paul Summers warned legislators that many of the budget cuts proposed by some would contravene court orders and spur lawsuits related to social service programs, public education, and corrections.[745] An example was the TennCare program's failure to pay millions to regional hospitals for mental health services provided.[746] Insufficient funding of programs caused patients to be dismissed without an adequate community support network and others to remain in local jails.[747]

The differing placeholder budget bills passed in the house and senate were sent to a conference committee to work on a compromise after a majority of the senate voted against an income tax.[748] There was not a majority in either chamber for any of the proposed revenue plans.[749] Ardent tax reform supporter Republican Lewis Donelson did not give up. He informed citizens in an op-ed that Tennessee had the highest business taxes in the South, a high sales tax rate that hurt low-income citizens, high local property taxes that burdened businesses, and the Hall Tax on investment income that disproportionately affected retirees.[750]

The impasse over a budget solution forced the session into June, with an end-of-the-month deadline to avoid a state shutdown.[751] Sen. John Ford proposed a 2% flat tax on all adjusted gross income with no deductions for most citizens; removing the state sales tax on groceries, clothes, and nonprescription medicines; reducing the Hall Tax on investments; and providing funds to local government for losses in sales tax revenues under the plan.[752]

The governor challenged the legislators to have the courage to solve the budget problems and warned of the consequences of the "Armageddon" budget proposals that would adversely impact local governments.[753] A new plan by Sen. Joe Haynes and Rep. Gene Davidson emerged to raise the sales tax and set aside monies for agriculture programs and health programs, but not fully fund the governor's reading initiative.[754] As the budget debate continued, Sundquist signed into law his education bill while surrounded by kindergartners and pledged to veto any financing plan that raised the sales tax, especially on food.[755]

The session dragged on into July with angry anti-income tax protestors flooding the hallways outside the house and senate chambers. One angry agitator got in the face of a large state trooper positioned in front of the house chamber right in front of me.[756] There was scant security at the time, with citizens allowed in the balconies overlooking the legislative chambers without having to pass through metal detectors. The trooper dragged the protestor across the floor. The protestor got up and went right back to the trooper invading his personal space again. Later, I submitted an affidavit on the trooper's behalf. Security concerns grew along with the crowds.

On July 12, 2001, state Sen. Marsha Blackburn incredibly sent a fateful email to a conservative radio talk show host calling for "troops" to stop the senate from voting on an income tax reform proposal.[757] Thousands of angry citizens stormed the State Capitol in protest, even knocking on the doors to the senate chamber. Some threw rocks and broke a window in the governor's office.[758] Needless to say, the senate delayed the vote until the state troopers could maintain order. Yellow tape was placed in the aisles outside the legislative chambers to separate the legislators from the crowd. It felt like walking through a crime scene as we ventured onto the house floor for work, not knowing whether an angry citizen in the gallery might pull out a gun and start shooting.

Shortly thereafter, the senate ended its longest session in state history and passed a budget that used $560 million of a one-time windfall tobacco settlement fund to balance the books.[759] The house concurred and adjourned as well.[760] Governor Sundquist was critical of the disruptive behavior of the protestors and those who encouraged them, which even resulted in troopers being dispatched to Sen. Bob Rochelle's home for protection.[761] Yet, the problems were left for another day as all of the weary legislators went home.

2

In 2002, weak franchise and excise tax collections were reported in March with an already projected $310 million deficit.[762] As a result, the senate passed a temporary sales tax increase as the legislators again sought a permanent solution.[763] However, it was not put to a vote in the house due to a lack of votes.[764]

The tax debate intensified. After around-the-clock budget discussions in committees, hallways, and side rooms at the State Capitol, Naifeh finally put his tax reform plan up for a vote in May. It was a 4.5% flat tax on adjusted gross income, with some exemptions, increases in sin taxes, removal of the sales tax on grocery store food, clothing, and nonprescription drugs, and elimination of a tax on investment income.[765] The measure failed with only 45 votes for the plan, but Speaker Naifeh froze the electronic vote board.[766] The legislative leaders adjourned to the hallway, scrambling for over two hours to sway the holdouts.[767] The word was that five legislators who had pledged to support the measure reneged when it came time to vote.

The vote was the legislative death knell for some of those voting "aye," knowing that it would cost them their reelections. Even some members of the House Democratic leadership voted "nay" on the historic vote that might have changed the tax structure of Tennessee for years to come. Finally, the electronic vote board was cleared after Speaker Naifeh convinced four "no" votes to switch to "abstain."[768] This allowed the bill to be referred back to the Calendar and Rules Committee for possible consideration at a later date.[769] The debate continued, but the names of those voting "aye" were etched in time forever.

During the budget battle thereafter, one legislator was lost due to a scandal.[770] When the news of the scandal broke, the press had a feeding frenzy. He was a tough, hard-drinking, and joking former sheriff from the rural eastern part of the state, and well-respected for working in a bipartisan way. As the press and media hounded him, more stories were forthcoming about a prior Nashville investigation.[771]

He returned to the house floor briefly, maybe to see how he would be received, with many legislators from both sides of the aisle welcoming him back. He then went home, and his death was reported. With the hundreds of angry anti-tax protestors and the serious budget issues, perhaps he felt that his personal scandal would only make it harder to solve the state's fiscal problems. However, he had been considered a key vote in support of tax reform.[772]

A few weeks later, there were reports that House Speaker Naifeh was only three votes short of passing major tax reform, including a 4.5% flat income tax. [773]The June 30 budget deadline loomed. Throngs of anti-tax protestors gathered on the streets outside the State Capitol honking horns nonstop, with tax reform supporters also present and planning a march.[774] Governor Sundquist and others worked for the vote and discussed compromise measures. The house legislative leaders warned of a back-up Downsizing Ongoing Government Services ["DOGS"] budget plan with catastrophic cuts if no new revenues were adopted.[775] New plans came forth daily from both sides of the debate, including the Continuing Adequate Taxes and Services ["CATS"] budget plan of Rep. Frank Buck and others that would raise sales and other taxes with $100 million in budget cuts. [776]

Candlelight vigils were held at the State Capitol by tax reform supporters, including state employees. The anti-tax protestors were encouraged by local radio hosts Steve Gill and Phil Valentine, who broadcasted from a booth outside the State Capitol.[777] A 6% income tax plan with a state sales tax reduced to 2.75% emerged in the state senate, proposed by Lieutenant Governor Wilder. [778]

Reports spread that it could be voted on the same day, and if it passed both chambers would be put to a statewide vote in 2004 for a constitutional convention on the issue. The measure also repealed the Hall Tax on investments. Naifeh tweaked his tax plan to add a constitutional convention in an effort to pick up five to seven votes.[779]

The word spread that the house might vote the same day on Naifeh's plan as well. Wilder's turn-around from his prior position that the income tax was unconstitutional was of major significance, according to Sen. Jim Kyle, because he had never seen Wilder lose a bill.[780]

With only two days left until a government shutdown if a budget were not passed, the urgency of the situation grew as the Senate Finance Committee rejected the "CATS" conceptual budget.[781] The sponsor, Sen. Doug Jackson, said he would bring it back up again because "a cat has nine lives, and we've only used one."[782] The stopgap plan raised the state sales tax, added new business taxes, and increased sin taxes. Some members objected that the proposal had no details, and Jackson claimed that another member had reneged on a pledge to support the measure.[783]

With the deadline expired, the house narrowly voted down the CATS budget on July 2nd.[784] Naifeh prepared to present his tax reform plan with a partial shutdown of state government continuing.[785] About 22,000 government workers were furloughed while the tax debate raged.[786] Representative Buck chastised some members who would not vote for any budget, telling them that they were stringing the others out and that "we're destroying ourselves."[787] Deputy Governor Alex Fischer appeared before the house and begged for a solution, with several Sundquist cabinet members also explaining how the partial government shutdown was harming Tennesseans.[788]

After the surprise 1999 announcement by the governor proposing a payroll tax and removing the sales tax from food, which was not adopted; his support of an income tax after that; three years of patch-work budgets, or rosier than projected revenue projections to balance the budget, and the spending of reserve funds and windfall tobacco settlement funds; the legislature was still divided in 2002 on how to devise a permanent budget solution.[789] Because the fastest-growing part of the economy was services that were mostly not taxed, and the growing Internet sales were untaxed, the state's tax structure was not producing enough revenue to cover its expenses.[790] The crisis had only worsened.

The legislative session finally ended, although not with any meaningful tax reform. Instead, the legislature raised the sales tax and increased taxes on businesses, alcohol, and tobacco.[791] The result was a sales tax, that with the local option added, was as high as 9.4% in some counties and among the highest in the country.[792] I voted no.[793] The loud car horn honks ceased with anti-tax protestors taking credit, including the radio talk show hosts.

Years later, in November 2014, the Tennessee voters approved the Tennessee Income Tax Prohibition Amendment 3.[794] In the now Republican-controlled state senate and house, State Sen. Brian Kelsey and Rep. Glen Casada had passed the resolution for the amendment that outlawed a state or local payroll tax or personal income tax. After years of battles, tax reform was truly dead absent any future constitutional amendment adopted by a majority of the voters.

PART FOUR

First Effort at Higher Office

15

Kicking off Race
for County Mayor

1

While the efforts to keep day care reforms and address tax reform were ongoing in 2001-02, I also was a trying to bring reforms to local government. My state legislative work on annexation and other issues had raised my awareness and concern over the inadequate growth and other county policies. The decisions being made at the local level would financially bind generations to come. Also, with over a decade of experience in government, including shaping health care, financial, education, and criminal justice policy, I believed myself the best person to lead the county in the full-time executive position. I wanted to make a difference as county mayor and bring the needed local reforms to the Memphis metropolitan area, just as I had led the effort in 2000 to reform statewide child care. Little did I know how extraordinarily difficult it would be for a qualified woman to win the Shelby County mayorship.

In 2001, I boldly announced my candidacy for Shelby County Mayor for the 2002 election.[795] Supporters gathered at Garibaldi's pizza parlor near the University of Memphis campus for the announcement.

Senator Cohen was also considering a bid, especially in light of reports of the current administration's problems managing the county jail.[796] Another candidate was prominent suburban banker Harold Byrd, who had served as a state legislator for six years and lost a congressional bid in 1994.[797] A University of Memphis booster, Byrd's trademark in the mayoral campaign was to jog through neighborhoods, literally.

This race was significant in that the victor would set growth and fiscal policy for years. It was also an opportunity for metro Memphis to have female executive county mayor leadership for the first time.

My platform included reforms regarding the county debt, Head Start, the jail, and improving mental health services. I eagerly called upon students at the University of Memphis to get involved in my campaign and pass the torch to a new generation. The students would have to repay the county's high debt in the future. One student called me a fighter in the *Daily Helmsman* campus newspaper and someone who listens to the people.[798] Shelby County Mayor Rout, evaluating whether he would seek reelection, said that he respected my right to run but that more candidates would enter the race.[799] My dad replied in the campus article, "As biased as a father can be, I think she'd be a great Mayor!"

The county could be better managed. It was under fire from federal Judge Jon McCalla for running a dangerous jail.[800] Bill Gibbons, Shelby County District Attorney, was questioned about delays in processing criminal cases. He primarily blamed the Memphis Police Department for not timely turning over investigative files.[801] At that time, nearly 1,900 people were incarcerated in the jail designed to house 1,200 inmates.[802] Of those detained, 400 had been charged but were awaiting indictment, while another 300 had been indicted but were awaiting indictment on other charges.[803] While public and nonprofit funds had been allocated to purchase a new computer system to assist in processing the cases, Gibbons admitted that it was not used by the prosecutors due to performance issues.[804]

Besides the jail problems, the county capital debt had tripled to $1.2 billion or more since 1990.[805] Republican Sen. Mark Norris and I teamed up and introduced state legislation that required the Shelby County government to adopt a policy limiting the type and amount of its debt.

County budgeters were strapped trying to fund new schools being built in the developing suburbs. Mayor Rout, a Republican, was critical of us for not consulting him first about the debt policy bill. He blamed the high debt on the state school funding formula that required three dollars to be spent for city schools for every dollar spent on county school capital funding.[806] My concerns were that future annual payments on the debt would require higher property taxes, thus negatively impacting taxpayers, especially senior citizens and those on fixed incomes. Better solutions were needed.

2

At odds with the state and county's fiscal woes was the new proposal by Memphis AutoZone founder J. R. 'Pitt' Hyde III, and two others to build a new $250 million downtown arena in Memphis. The plan was to buy a share of the NBA Vancouver Grizzlies from Chicago billionaire Michael Heisley and move the team to Memphis.[807] The arena proposal quickly became an issue in the county mayor's race that was heating up.

Memphis already had a Pyramid arena. However, FedEx Corp was on board, offering to buy the naming rights for the team and new arena, and those monies would go to Heisley.[808] The Memphis group proposed using sales tax rebates, tax-increment financing, and some 70 million public dollars.[809] The Memphis Pyramid arena was not deemed suitable by them due to lack of sufficient luxury suites based upon its unusual size, with retrofitting estimated at $190 million. [810] Poor acoustics were also cited with respect to the needed retrofitting and were attributable to the building's odd shape.

More detailed proposed financing plans for the arena released thereafter included a $30 million tax break on MLGW (public utility) water bills, surcharges on car rentals, $24 million from the city and county governments, and allocation of millions from the local hotel/motel tax.[811] Added to the mix were some $100 million in private funds from a local ownership group, $100 million in naming rights from FedEx, and $65 million more in proposed corporate contributions.[812] The state comptroller questioned the proposed state assumption of the $40 million remaining Pyramid Arena debt and another $70 million in state bonds to be repaid by the sales taxes generated from the new arena.[813]

The Memphis Pyramid, a huge pyramid-shaped arena on the Mississippi River banks, was still operating as the "Tomb of Doom" for the University of Memphis "Tigers" men's basketball team, as well as a concert and exhibit hall. Costing $62 million to build, the Tigers paid $7 million annually to play in the facility.[814] Apparently, the facility was turning a profit, albeit not the tourism boon promised by the developer to draw three million people annually.[815]

Some likened the Memphis Pyramid to a tomb built for a modern-day pharaoh or monument to the ancient Egyptian god Ptah. For many years, a statue of Ramesses the Great, created from a mold of the actual Ramesses statue in Egypt, guarded the front. Plans for a 321-foot glass inclinator to a top observation deck; various music and sports halls of fame; a movie theater, a restaurant, and an Eco park had not materialized. All such plans were scrapped when the developer, Schlenker, had declared bankruptcy.[816]

City and county leaders moved forward with plans to build the new arena even though the Memphis Pyramid was not yet paid for, and there were no plans for its further development or reuse should the U of M Tigers vacate its lease. Herenton and Rout both supported the arena project. However, Memphis Mayor Herenton raised concerns about Heisley and FedEx striking private deals without his participation, which might preclude using nontax revenues from the arena to pay off public bonds.[817] I asked for copies of all agreements and the architectural study regarding the Pyramid retrofitting.

I also sent both the city and county mayor a list of questions asking why the fees for luxury suites and club seats could not be increased commensurate with higher prices paid in other cities to aid with construction financing and lessen the burden on taxpayers? Also, I asked what would happen if the team left Memphis before the bonds were paid and who would pay for construction cost overruns? Rep. Curry Todd also raised concerns that there was not yet any agreement that the team had to stay in Memphis until the bonds were repaid.[818] The citizens deserved answers as to the costs, and protection for any investments of public monies. And, a solid plan was needed on how to address the huge county debt that was now proposed to be substantially increased.

3

In the summer, Sen. Jim Kyle and Harold Byrd had joined me in announcing for the county mayor's race, and Republican Mayor Jim Rout bowed out. Then, AC Wharton entered the field.[819] His profile in the *Memphis Flyer* curiously asked, "What AC Stands for," with the answer that the letters of the name "AC" "don't stand for anything."[820] As an attorney, Wharton had represented many prominent criminal defendants over the years in his private practice. Some of his clients included Mayor Herenton in defending against charges of breach of promise as the city schools' superintendent; WillieAnn Madison in the Cherokee broker grand jury investigation; County Commissioner Michael Hooks Sr.; and a former Tunica, Mississippi, county sheriff who pled guilty to extortion.[821]

As the *Memphis Flyer* article noted, Wharton had managed Herenton's 1999 mayoral campaign.[822] He patted Herenton on the back as doing a fine job as Memphis mayor.[823] Herenton reciprocated by saying Wharton would make an excellent county mayor.[824] Even TV celebrity "Judge" Joe Brown said he might vote for AC, having been recruited by him years earlier when Wharton headed the local legal services office.[825]

Rebecca Gleaves, a reporter for the *Memphis Flyer*, described Wharton as an "impeccable dresser," with laughable stories of him mowing the grass in his expensive dress suit, tie, and shoes.[826] He even kept a shoeshine machine in his office.[827] He might be a formidable candidate. But, as Paula Wade with the *Commercial Appeal* observed after the Gridiron show parody in 1991, I am nobody's shoeshine girl!

As the field shaped up, Kyle announced a poll showing himself in the lead, with me second, and Byrd way behind.[828] His poll found me benefitting from being the only woman in the race, and Byrd's support limited to the suburbs.[829] The poll did not include AC since his entry into the race was a surprise. [830]

Not deterred by Kyle's poll, Harold Byrd proceeded with fundraisers and jogging through neighborhoods.[831] He was backed by former local Democratic Party Chair Sidney Chism, a labor leader and African American, who often wore a white cowboy hat.[832] Chism denounced Wharton's candidacy as a product of Rout's Republican supporters' desire "to keep the status quo."[833]

Wharton, the part-time head public defender as a Rout appointee, claimed support of prominent lobbyists for the Rout administration and even the county mayor's executive assistant Bobby Lanier. Yet, political columnist Susan Adler Thorp opined that Rout was "furious" about being tied to Wharton's candidacy, saying he had told AC that he would support the Republican nominee.[834] Wharton also was backed by bond attorney Charles Carpenter and Herenton aide Reginald French.[835] Columnist Jackson Baker immediately reported that most observers dubbed Wharton as the "man" to beat.[836]

Byrd and many of his supporters, including local civil rights leaders Maxine and Vasco Smith, were angry about Wharton entering the field.[837] Byrd claimed that Wharton had misled him about his intention of entering the race.[838]

Kyle quickly exited the race after Wharton entered. The three Democratic candidates left were all "credible" and "serious people," according to David Kushma, an editor of the *Commercial Appeal.*[839] He noted Wharton's work to improve the local criminal justice system; Byrd's service as a booster for the University of Memphis; and my leadership for daycare reform "often over the opposition of other Memphis Democrats in the General Assembly who place the interests of daycare operators ahead of those of poor kids." [840] He urged the candidates to address critical issues of the enormous county debt, smart growth, funding the schools, fixing the overcrowded jail, tax reform, and consolidation of city and county governments and schools. [841] That's why I was running for the job.

While a county mayor candidate, I also was beating back the efforts to undo child care reform in the legislature, a part of the serious state tax reform debate, and continuing to practice law. It was a busy time.

While the race was developing, the World Trade Center bombing on September 11, 2001, overshadowed everything with the country aghast at the terrorist attack, horror, and death toll. I recall watching in disbelief from home due to a scheduled campaign photoshoot later that morning. The men and women who worked to save others in the crisis were heroic. The attention of all was on the rescue efforts, mourning for those lost, gratitude for the first responders, and demands for justice. Ultimately, the election contest moved forward even though it seemed our country would never be the same.

A boost to my candidacy in 2001 were awards from the Association for Women Attorneys; Memphis/Shelby County Children and Youth Council, Tennessee Sierra Club; and receiving the UT Health Science Leadership Award. Not so auspicious was my fundraiser hosted in December to capture as many funds as possible for the county mayoral race before a fundraising ban began the next month when the state legislative session resumed. The event scheduled for an upscale restaurant in Midtown ended up coinciding with a rare ice storm. We had a Santa on hand, plenty of food, and a few good friends who braved the storm out of kindness. In any event, I hoped that the voters would give me the opportunity to reform county government in light of my strong state legislative record.

16

Why Does She Stay In?

1

In January 2002, a poll released by consultant John Bakke commissioned for Wharton claimed he led the county mayor Democratic primary with 51%, Byrd 13%, and 11% for me.[842] According to the poll, Wharton would also defeat well-respected Republican candidate Larry Scroggs two to one.[843]

Wharton's history of defending WillieAnn Madison in the Cherokee daycare broker scandal had scant impact on his support in the election, despite the public outrage over the entity's misuse of public monies. Some said he benefited from his calm demeanor, in stark contrast to Memphis Mayor Herenton's aggressive bravado.

In his usual abrupt fashion, Herenton boldly took the limelight by announcing his support for a consolidated government at Councilman Myron Lowery's annual prayer breakfast. His plan included keeping the city and county schools separate, freezing the school boundaries, and establishing a single funding source to equalize spending and allocate more funds to at-risk students.[844]

Memphis encompassed nearly 70% of the county yet still had a separate county government and different city and county school systems. At that time, the Memphis City Schools had very few white students proportionally due to an exodus after the federal court-ordered busing. The higher-performing county schools, generally located in more affluent areas, had a majority white student population. Most folks in the suburbs believed that consolidated government would ultimately lead to a consolidation of the schools, which they vehemently opposed.

I supported a metropolitan government that would unify the citizens. I also endorsed balanced growth with impact fees on developers to pay for the county's growth that was driving up its enormous debt. Byrd was for consolidating law enforcement, freezing school boundaries, and single-source funding of the schools.[845] Herenton warned that if the merger did not occur within the next five years, then the county's high taxes would drive citizens and investment to adjoining counties and across state borders.[846]

2

As Wharton continued to build support, rumors spread that Byrd would drop out of the race, which his campaign co-chairs, attorney Jim Strickland and Sidney Chism, denied.[847] Byrd had already raised $300,000 and scheduled a campaign headquarters opening.[848] The banker, who is white, had cross-racial support, including superstar Isaac Hayes.[849] An estimated 70% of the voters in the county Democratic primary were African American.

Sen. Jim Kyle broke with "political tradition among party leaders" to not endorse in a primary and endorsed Wharton, joining Sens. Steve Cohen, Roscoe Dixon, and John Ford.[850] Despite my campaign's internal strong polling and solid record, Jackson Baker with the *Memphis Flyer* opined that many watching the race had not been convinced "that she's a serious player."[851] But Baker did report my endorsements by the local Women's Political Caucus and the AFL-CIO. [852]

His article contended that Byrd was the frontrunner until Wharton entered the race, with me as more of a "sleeper" than a "spoiler."[853] Kyle's poll had shown me ahead of Byrd, and the poll by Wharton's campaign showed Byrd and me only 2 points apart. Whether the unsubstantiated perception of a prior frontrunner status for Byrd was due to a banking background that benefited his fundraising, an unreleased Byrd internal poll, or subconscious stereotypes about a women's efficacy to win a historically male-held office was unclear. In any event, rumors still swirled that Byrd would drop out, which he denied. [854]

My own pollster dubbed me "Rocky," aka Balboa, for my tenacity. Thereafter, *Memphis Flyer* reporter Jackson Baker dubbed Byrd "Rocky" for pushing forward. [855]

Wharton downplayed the merger issue, instead claiming the top issues to be overcrowded jails and the need for investments in long-term prevention programs to reduce juvenile and adult crime.[856] Byrd advocated raising teacher salaries. He supported merging duplicate services, arguing that the county's budget problems necessitated a more immediate solution than consolidation.[857] Reminding voters that Memphis continued to annex and there was less and less unincorporated area in the county, I advocated for consolidation. I also supported smart growth, as opposed to rubber-stamping every development. The debate and results of the county mayor's race in 2002 were precursors to the serious financial and political issues that would continue to impact the metropolitan area's growth for years to come.

Baker with the *Memphis Flyer* reported that Wharton had the backing of former Congressman Harold Ford Sr.; candidate Rep. Larry Scroggs by the Republican party leadership; and observed that Byrd benefited from name recognition. [858] Wharton acknowledged that political operative and Rout mayoral aide Bobby Lanier had encouraged him to enter the race when the county mayor was not certain to seek reelection.[859] While Byrd had approached him about his own candidacy, Wharton professed never to have pledged his support.[860] Byrd apparently felt betrayed that Wharton did not reveal at that time that he might run himself.

Along with the accolades for the other candidates, Baker reported some were "mystified" at my not dropping out of the race. [861] This was *deja vu*, recalling the efforts by some to get me to drop out of the state legislative race in 1990. Since my polling had shown me ahead of Byrd, Baker gave my pollster credit for my decision to stay in the race.[862]

In fact, my campaign's poll found Wharton at 37%, myself at 27%, and Byrd at 6% among Democrats polled. According to the results, the voters overwhelmingly wanted tougher daycare standards, a new funding system for public education, and total consolidation of the city and county governments—all issues included in my platform. Moreover, I had the highest job approval by the voters.[863] And, based upon the poll even Baker now admitted, I had a basis for challenging Byrd as well due to his third-place status.[864]

However, a real obstacle was fundraising due to the "bandwagon strategy" underway on Wharton's behalf.[865] But, I pressed forward. Touting my stronger credentials and experience, I called out the backroom politics that was a by-product of the "good ole boy system," causing a $1.4 billion county debt, higher property taxes, and poorly planned growth.[866] I pledged to clean house, bring in a new team, better manage the growth, and make developers pay their fair share.

Indeed, developers' relationships with the government officials were "cozy." Pointing out these two close relationships was a centerpiece of my campaign. So, I refused to accept donations from developers and called for ethical reforms. One prominent developer backing Wharton was a large political donor and fundraiser. He had sold the land to the county for several new suburban public schools, built homes, and benefited from the commercial development.[867] In 1996, he and Mayors Rout and Herenton had agreed that the City of Memphis would extend sewers to enable the suburban development, with approval of a new joint city-county high school in the eastern part of the area.[868]

Two former Memphis mayors, Wyeth Chandler and Dick Hackett, endorsed Wharton. Hackett, who was defeated by Herenton in 1991, said Wharton would look better to bond rating agencies as someone who would make the tough decisions to raise taxes if needed, rather than make a political decision.[869] This was an unusual endorsement message since most voters opposed property tax increases. And, Chandler said Wharton, who had never held elective office, had more experience in the areas of education, health care and the county jail, disregarding my twelve years of successfully working on those issues as a state legislator.[870]

Yet Mayor Herenton declined to endorse Wharton for the Democratic primary due to his failure to support city and county consolidation whole-heartedly. He praised me for being "courageous and forthright" on the issue.[871] A Herenton endorsement could cut both ways because his brash attitude had alienated most suburban county leaders. The disharmony was so bad that the usual state legislative county delegation dinner at the State Capitol with the mayor of Memphis, the county's suburban mayors, and the Shelby County mayor morphed into separate urban and suburban dinners scheduled on the same night. This forced some, such as me, to trek to two dinners for the sake of harmony.[872]

3

With the candidate withdrawal deadline looming, the press took note of Wharton's lack of a substantive platform, saying that he seemingly relied on his charm.[873] A supporter of his was reported to be worried that Wharton had not galvanized enough of the black vote.[874] Byrd was also reported to be vague in terms of his platform. These contrasted with my direct positions on issues ranging from consolidation to smart growth.[875] Meanwhile, Republican George Flinn prepared to spend half a million dollars of his own money, if necessary, to beat Larry Scroggs in the Republican primary.[876]

Byrd's supporters contacted my pollster asking me to withdraw, claiming that the Byrd pollster showed us tied at 22% and Wharton in the lead at 41%.[877] However, my campaign poll showed me ahead of Byrd. They argued that we had similar platforms and that this was a reason for me to drop out and back Byrd, which was not valid. And, despite Wharton's lead, one of my key advisors, Barbara Lawing, encouraged me to continue because dropping out would only perpetuate the stereotypical belief that a woman did not belong in the mayoral arena.

On the withdrawal deadline, a tense two-hour meeting took place at my pollster's office, with Byrd's supporters on the speakerphone with my team leaders. [878]Byrd's team explained that his financial backers would only contribute more money if it were a one on one contest between him and Wharton. There was even a shocking veiled threat from one Byrd supporter that if I stayed in the race, my tenure with the law firm, where I was a partner and had practiced for sixteen years, would be in jeopardy. Ultimately, I left the meeting to head downtown to court, bypassing the election commission office where a withdrawal from the race could be effectuated by noon. Obviously, the stakes were high.

Thereafter, Byrd called his campaign advisor, Jim Strickland, to end his mayoral bid only five minutes before the noon withdrawal deadline.[879] After eight months of campaigning, he explained the reason to exit the race was to avoid the primary from becoming racially divisive with "two white candidates and a black candidate" in the race.[880] His own campaign manager, Sidney Chism, however, admitted that even in a one-on-one with Wharton, Byrd still would have had to run a divisive campaign to win.[881] Silver-haired Byrd's face in his campaign advertising on the side of city buses now abruptly disappeared, after spending hundreds of thousands of dollars. Despite his campaign supporters having said that we stood for the same things, Byrd refused to endorse me.[882]

Jackson Baker with the *Memphis Flyer* excitedly wasted no time writing that most observers believed that Byrd's withdrawal would assure Wharton the Democratic nomination even though a single vote had not yet been cast. [883]He called me "underfunded but determined."[884] Another reporter wrote that Byrd was considered the main primary threat to Wharton, even though my polls had shown me ahead of Byrd. [885]

Pundits began piling on with the pitch that Wharton couldn't lose the county mayor's race, unless, as Jackson Baker said, "arguably," he was "run over by a truck."[886] Obviously, this adversely affected my fund-raising. Perhaps it was due to his financial and political backers, polling, or race, but I wondered why they didn't factor my gender into their analysis, with women more than half of the voters?

Since Byrd had withdrawn, there also was speculation that the independent candidate Sir Isaac Ford, son of power broker Congressman Harold Ford Sr., would not seriously campaign since his father was supporting Wharton.[887] Yet, Sir Isaac told the *Tri-State Defender* that if I, or lesser-known African American mayoral candidates C. C. Buchanan and C. J. Cochran, did not win the Democratic nomination, then "the democratic party ...will have a democratic puppet controlled by republican money and their conservative ways."[888] Wharton retorted that he was a "lifelong democrat."[889]

Sir Isaac further "hinted" at the possibility of fraud at the Shelby County Election Commission as far back as 1974 when uncounted ballots were discovered at the last minute after pressure, giving his father the victory in his first congressional election.[890] This issue would resonate more in the years ahead.

In any event, I pressed forward. How could a woman ever win if she didn't stay in?

17

Focused and Deliberate

1

With Byrd out of the race, my focus was squarely on getting the message out about my platform that included support for a metropolitan government that would bring efficiencies and better manage growth. True to the rumors, Wharton wryly trotted out a proposal to consolidate the county correction division with the county sheriff's department. He touted it as jail consolidation, although it had nothing to do with a city/county merger.[891] The venue for his pronouncement was the age-old Henry Loeb Dutch Treat Luncheon, a holdover from the arch-conservative mayor who had served during the turbulent 1960s.

My point was that consolidation, with cost-cutting and less insider politics, could reduce the spiraling out of control county debt and help avoid property tax hikes. Wharton instead proposed to slow down certain projects; Scroggs to change the school funding formula; and Flinn to reassess spending and emphasize public safety, education, and economic development.[892] Wharton and I also sparred at the luncheon discussion over my concerns that the city and county would be on the hook if local private investors did not provide the funds pledged for the new FedExForum arena.[893]

While the other candidates tried to side-step the issue, I continued to face the merger issue straight on.[894] However, an impediment to supporting a consolidated government for some was the speculation that Herenton would run for metro mayor if the merger went through, which he would not rule out.[895]

At a Whitehaven school forum in South Memphis, I contended that Wharton was beholden to developers due to their large contributions to his campaign. He retaliated by calling me "strident" and "lacking the ability to garner a consensus on issues like growth and development."[896] This was not to be the only time that a gender-biased stereotype would be used against me, *i.e.,* a woman who speaks her mind is too pushy or demanding—while a male who does is deemed decisive.

My response was that Wharton wanted to hold a summit to develop a growth plan, instead of merely articulating a plan that included impact fees on developers and a more independent planning office. Wharton responded that I was "casting aspersions" and acting like a legislator that only had to cast one vote instead of a chief executive.[897] I responded that Wharton, despite his claims, had never passed a law and had been silent as to daycare reform when babies were dying. Moreover, the county mayor must have a firm grasp of the legislative process in order to get *her* agenda through the county commission.

At a forum, I pressed forward mentioning that Sen. Norris and I had passed the law requiring a county debt policy. Apparently, Wharton wasn't aware of the new law when he pledged he would adopt a debt policy or was simply continuing with an obfuscating "me too" strategy.[898] In my answers, I drew a strong contrast between myself and Wharton since I alone had the fortitude to stand up to the developers for smart growth.

Wharton opposed impact fees on development, saying that would make a bad situation worse.[899] The developers had "vehemently opposed" impact fees in the prior year's debate before the county commission, arguing that they would slow residential development.[900] But, the fees would shift the tax burden off regular citizens countywide.

At a subsequent meeting, I pledged a two-year county property tax rate freeze and complete county government reorganization if elected. Wharton said the tax freeze promise bordered on irresponsibility.[901] In reply, I argued that Wharton's close ties to the Republican Rout administration would prevent him from making the hard decisions for staffing cuts needed to avoid a property tax increase. Ironically, Wharton blamed me for the failure of tax reform despite my prime sponsorship of the major tax reform resolution in the state house.[902]

My campaign team was motivated, including co-chairs Steve Steffens, a white Democratic blogger, and Coleman Thompson, an African American nonprofit head, and others from diverse backgrounds, including Bob Hatton, Mila Borden, Joyce Akehurst, and Bonnie Blair. However, we had little experience in running a countywide campaign.

As the early voting period neared, the usual profiles ran in the *Commercial Appeal*. One had the interesting subhead about Wharton, "Little-known fact: First name was A space C space. It doesn't stand for anything."[903] The article discussed Wharton's background as a public defender of the low-income accused, which contrasted with his high-profile criminal defense representation of powerful figures in the courts through his private law firm on the side.[904]

My profile called me "focused" and "deliberate," as the leader of the fight to reform daycare in the state, and winning election to the state house six times.[905] My various hobbies of Spanish, banjo, ballroom dancing, and sculpting classes were mentioned, as well as my civic service on nonprofit boards.[906] My political campaign experience helping Governor McWherter and Al Gore was noted, with their support later returned in my first election to the state house. And my academic credentials were described.[907]

My leadership positions in the state legislature were correctly set out. My election as majority whip and appointment to the "Black Hole" Budget subcommittee was explained as a "move indicating she was on a path to a leadership position in that chamber."[908]

Lois Deberry (D-Memphis) talked about my "bulldogging" of the "mammoth" daycare reform package and ability to know how to pick my battles and compromise when needed still to make a difference.[909] Even the fact that I forewent greater earnings as a partner at my law firm due to time devoted to public service was mentioned.[910] While some expressed differing opinions in the article, overall, it was a fair presentation of who I was, what I stood for, and what I had accomplished.

Yet, the catch-22 remained, how can a woman effectively compete to be the first female elected mayor if no one believed a woman could ever win? The bias based upon stereotypes, historical results, and pundits' projections, significantly impeded our fundraising.

2

My platform in the county mayor's race also included implementing local government daycare grants for training and using law enforcement to eliminate corruption. I also promised to stop cronyism, including developers' gifts to elected officials. Once again, I called out Wharton for taking large campaign contributions from developers and for representing the Cherokee broker when the public had cried out for daycare reforms.

Wharton responded in the *Commercial Appeal* that he had only taken the "tough" cases, had experience and character, and had "not lived a boutique life."[911] His distinction was incorrect. I had demonstrated character in my legislative endeavors. And by virtue of my legal and public service positions, I had the requisite experience. Also, I was in no way a debutante, having worked my entire life since a teenager flipping hamburgers at a fast-food restaurant, serving customers at a local department store, and representing clients as an attorney and constituents at the state legislature. AC's implication that my lifestyle revolved around shopping at high-end clothing stores appeared merely an effort to falsely typecast me as frivolous and entitled in a gender-biased way as a guise to detract from my hard-earned serious record and credentials for the job. If anything, based upon his own expensive attire, Wharton lived the boutique lifestyle.

But Wharton wasn't the only one playing the gender card. Somehow, the press thought it worth reporting that I referred to the next county mayor as "she."[912] As the only major female candidate in the race, the "backdrop" story remarked that I was not "lacking in confidence."[913] Was I supposed to refer to myself as "he"?

Jackson Baker, with the *Memphis Flyer*, wrote that since Byrd had withdrawn, I was on the offense against Wharton for taking developers' campaign contributions and for dodging the consolidation issue.[914] And, he reported that Wharton was "hitting back" with the race becoming a "real contest" as opposed to an "inevitable Wharton victory."[915] In response, Wharton trotted out two female supporters after the next public forum to defend his representation of the child care broker director.[916]

To its credit, the *Commercial Appeal* did an in-depth story on the challenges of the rapid development in the county, sprawl, and the candidates' positions.[917] Flinn, Scroggs, nor I were reported to have received contributions from developers, but substantial developer donations were fueling Wharton's campaign.[918] Wharton claimed that it was "Hogwash" to believe they would make a difference in his decision-making and didn't "give a damn" if the developers contributed or not.[919]

The Tennessee Sierra Club raised alarms about the money spent subsidizing growth when the infrastructure in place was decaying.[920] The population growth in the area was only about a fourth of the increased land development rate.[921] And, concerns were raised about growing traffic congestion, pollution, loss of trees, and spiraling costs to taxpayers for building new schools and services. [922]

The *Commercial Appeal* editors pointed out that the county's "haphazard, unplanned" growth had been mainly due to the "wide influence" of property developers, which had resulted in property tax increases.[923] The newspaper called upon the candidates to articulate their opinions on the issues of impact fees or a county real estate transfer tax, as opposed to saying they'll "look into" the problem.[924] While they called me "excessively purist" for refusing campaign contributions from developers and criticizing those who did, the editors urged the candidates to tell the truth about how their connections with developers would affect their decision-making as county mayor.[925] While it might have bucked traditional norms for those holding and seeking the county mayor's office at that time, my arms-length relationships with developers in an election that would define future growth patterns for years to come was a step in the right direction.

Another forum was held for both the Democratic and Republican candidates only a few weeks before the election. My nearly all-volunteer team was so tired that they did not appear. The Wharton supporters were out in full force, and some moved their chairs right in front of me at the head table of candidates. When I answered a question, they frowned and shook their heads "no," trying to distract and rattle me.

Inaccurate and misleading questions were permitted from the audience. Misstatements were made by the other candidates about my positions that I was not allowed to rebut. Wharton got the last word again using coded language claiming that I was a "boutique" candidate.[926] It was a very discouraging day to be alone at the debate with so many false statements being made and little opportunity to set the record straight.

My last campaign fundraiser was scheduled at the Memphis Botanic Garden to present my new vision for the Shelby County of the 21st century. Not to leave any shot unanswered, I called Wharton out for development and daycare conflicts of interest and thanked the *Commercial Appeal* for calling me a "purist" as a compliment. [927] The diverse event host committee included friends from professional fields, businesses, party leaders, women and children's advocates, and union leaders. I appreciated their support!

3

During this time, *The New York Times* reported that babies again were dying in Memphis daycares, noting the community's outrage as teddy bears and flowers memorialized the graves of the children in one neighborhood.[928] The paper remarked that the city's "political elite" was "strangely muted" on the tragedies because its "power structure is wrapped up in it," just as in 1999 when the two babies had died on the same day in different daycare vans.[929] As acknowledged by the editor of the *Tri-State Defender*, Audrey McGhee, "too many lawmakers, preachers, judges, and other prominent leaders" were in the daycare business.[930] Greater enforcement of the new reforms was needed.

One of the difficulties in the county mayoral election was that some voters wanted me to stay in the state house, in part because of my successful child care legislation. The new daycare tragedies only brought that issue back to their attention, making the campaign harder for me to win. Obviously, I could not stay in the state legislature forever. And as the county mayor, I wanted to bring the growth policy and other reforms needed. Yet, despite my demonstrated state leadership, many oddly favored instead the attorney who had represented the past daycare broker's executive director who had been accused of financial abuses.

As Election Day neared, the top candidates from each county mayor primary were asked by the *Commercial Appeal* and *WREG News* Channel 3 to debate together live.[931] The televised debate was a first for me as the only female debating three other male county mayor candidates who were all at least thirteen to twenty years older.

Given the newspaper's glowing coverage of Wharton and Scroggs, it was no surprise that the *Commercial Appeal* editors endorsed them in the respective primaries.[932] The editors relied in part upon Wharton's Republican connections as an indication of bipartisan coalition building.[933] While noting that I had worked "hard and well" to reform daycare and "sounded important alarms about the undue influence developers exert on county government," the editors found my criticisms of Wharton too strong to exemplify consensus-building ability.[934] They conveniently ignored my passage of the daunting child care reform nearly unanimously with a bipartisan coalition. And why was I supposed to debate Wharton with my hands tied behind my back?

Since I also had filed to run for reelection to the state house, the editors opined "for now" that it was the "best place" for me to fulfill my "considerable capacity for public service."[935] However, finding Rep. Larry Scroggs, *like me,* to be an "experienced and productive lawmaker, respected by members of both parties," he was given the paper's endorsement over Flinn.[936] They noted that if Flinn advanced to the general election, he "would have a great deal of homework to do to match either of the major Democratic candidates in mastery of the nuts and bolts of government."[937] Hmm...

Flinn, a wealthy doctor and inventor in the field of radiology and owner of several radio stations spent a lot of his own money in the campaign alarming Scroggs' supporters.[938] After Flinn made a large TV ad buy, a panicked-looking Scroggs held a press conference claiming that Flinn was trying to buy the election.[939] Scroggs began running a hastily put together TV ad desperately asking for money, realizing that he was about to be seriously outspent.

My ad in the *Tri-State Defender* (a newspaper focused on the African American community) was populist, "Working for People, Working for Change." It set forth my platform of getting control of taxes, reorganizing county government, better funding public schools, making developers pay their fair share, stopping waste from backroom deals, providing better law enforcement, and moving toward a metro government. [940]

Wharton's ad in the *Memphis Flyer* stated that he was a "friendly fighter" who supported better funding of schools, more affordable and quality health care, and reducing the county debt.[941] This contrasted with his advertising in other venues that he was a "consensus builder." Later, an advisor on Wharton's team told me that there was a difference of opinion in the campaign over which theme to use—with the ad agency going with one and the campaign others.

Not letting up on Wharton's positive publicity, Baker with the *Memphis Flyer* praised him and noted his service "in positions of authority" such as boards and commissions.[942] Even his refusal to articulate positions was lauded as not "waffling" but instead "independence from causes," using Herenton's task force on consolidation as "cover" to avoid taking a position.[943] And, as a man dubbed "uncommonly unthreatening to whites," his race was explained as a plus in the county population that was growing more African American.[944] I and others viewed all of this as just giving him a pass for dodging the real issues.

The *Flyer* dismissed Pastor C. C. Buchanan, who repeatedly called out Wharton as a "tool of Republicans and special interests."[945] My campaign themes, however, were cited as unexpectedly effective, especially when calling Wharton out at the forums.[946]

Yet, this time Baker marginalized some of my credentials. He wrote that I was the chair of a special joint legislative committee for children—as opposed to being in a position of authority as the only woman to chair a regular standing committee in the entire state legislature (and only the second woman to do so in the state's history).[947] Ironically, in 1997, Baker had reported that my lost bid for majority floor leader was in a secret ballot election process "unkind" to other female legislators seeking house leadership positions too, and had noted my good working relationships with house leaders.[948] This time around, he instead blamed that loss on not being a "team player."[949] These were just more examples of how the press can spin the story based upon which candidate they favor.

The fact that I was independent, "driven and highly focused" was coupled with a comment about "an infectious giggle" giving me "like Wharton, a well-rounded personality."[950] But, despite some of the stereotypical comments (perhaps subconscious due to our culture), Baker added that support had grown for my argument that Wharton was too connected to the developers and that sprawl needed to be addressed.[951]

With only a week to go in the primary race, a low voter turnout of only 10% was expected despite the high-profile debates. There was even a battle between a brother and sister—Joe and Ophelia Ford (also from the powerful Ford family)—to replace a county commission seat vacated due to their other brother's passing.[952] The *Commercial Appeal* hyped that the county mayor's race could elect the first black or the first female county mayor.[953] This was the first time the Democrats would elect a nominee in a county primary.[954] I was described as having "mounted an aggressive campaign," with Wharton still identified as the frontrunner.[955]

During this time, a forum was held where three African American mayors from other cities were brought to town to discuss issues. This event was likely a public relations strategy to make the possibility of *two* black mayors— Herenton as city mayor, and Wharton if elected county mayor—seem less threatening to some white voters or out of the ordinary. I tried to get a former big-city female mayor to come to Memphis to no avail.

The *Commercial Appeal* asked a University of Memphis political science professor, Ken Holland, for his opinion on the election. Holland noted my remarks implying that Wharton was in the pocket of developers who substantially contributed to his campaign.[956] The professor also mentioned stereotypical claims by Wharton that I did not have the "personality of a leader" and was too "fixed in her positions to make a good leader."[957] While Holland was only commenting on others' claims, I had to ask, when did conviction become a negative? And, when will assertive women leaders be deemed strong and decisive as are men, and not shamed for purportedly not being reasonable enough?

As Baker with the *Memphis Flyer* commented, the "persona of a candidate can be perceived in radically different ways" depending on the circumstances, and office sought.[958] But, perhaps it is the lens of the media and press that distorts the true picture of a candidate based upon conscious or subconscious gender biases and cultural norms associated with the position sought.

The *Tri-State Defender* ran profiles of Wharton and me on Election eve. Wharton was called a "gentleman politician," "particularly likeable," "dapper," "articulate" with "honed vital political savvy."[959] The reporter, Wiley Henry, mentioned the rumors that Wharton had been "bought and paid for" by "Republican masterminds."[960] During the campaign, I had commented on Wharton's "styling, smiling and profiling," to highlight that, instead, a serious independent mayor was needed.

Henry described me as "smart, assertive," and not afraid to speak out or take on the tough issues.[961] The reporter said that sometimes people see me as "stiff-necked" and "unflinching on issues" but also exercising forbearance depending on the circumstances.[962] He described me as having that "next-door-neighbor-appeal," but also a "bundle of energy" and an experienced defender of the people.[963] My platform was set out in-depth, with Wharton now claiming a general twenty-point plan to create various unnecessary new offices and boards, apparently patronage positions.[964]

Henry noted that I was the only elected officeholder in the Democratic primary, with a "feather in her cap" as to family issues due to chairing the House Children & Family Affairs Committee, as well as "fearless" and a "warrior."[965] Among other things, my platform included improving housing for the mentally ill to keep them out of jail and ending the cronyism and backroom deals of the "Good ol' Boy Network."[966]

Despite my good profile, the *Tri-State Defender* editors endorsed Wharton, saying it was one of their "most difficult decisions" in that we both had "commendable platforms" and were both "passionate" about public service.[967] The acknowledgment of the difficulty in making the endorsement was appreciated. Of course, the endorsement would have been better!

When the early vote results came in on election night, I doubted their accuracy due to my internal and exit polling showing me with a higher percentage, although in second place. Still, I was proud of our effort in the Democratic primary, where less than 13% of voters identified themselves as white, realizing that I was going up against perhaps more than one bias in the election as a white female. Eventually, I called Wharton that night, giving him my support for the general election. However, I also let him know that the "boutique lifestyle" comment was out of line. He denied saying it, although it was reported in more than one venue, and I heard him say it myself.

I then went outside my headquarters, hugged my many African American poll workers and supporters—some of whom were crying on TV—conceded the election before the media, and publicly announced my endorsement of Wharton for the general.[968] In my remarks, I attributed the loss in part to being outspent three to one by Wharton. I was proud of the campaign we ran and its impact in shaping the election debate. However, out of respect to my supporters who fought hard with me, I declined Wharton's request to appear at his headquarters that evening.

Herenton did appear at Wharton's campaign headquarters on election night and pledged his support with both raising their hands in a victory salute, as well as Sidney Chism and Senators Kyle and Cohen.[969] In his remarks to the crowd, Wharton was quoted as saying, "I just want to be known as a good guy."[970] That was the problem in a nutshell.

Despite the result, I remained proud of my truthful and consistent platform that set out my vision for the people of Memphis and Shelby County. And, perhaps by running a strong campaign, I had demonstrated women's ability to compete in the mayoral arena and one day win.

4

The day after the election, I was back at the state legislature in Nashville on the house floor doing my job.[971]

Wharton and Flinn each had won their respective primaries in a bitterly fought battle on both sides. Scroggs also attributed his loss to being outspent by Flinn who pumped large sums of personal funds into his own campaign.[972] Flinn's problem now was that the rank and file Scroggs' supporters were furious over the negative campaign ads, which made it hard for party leaders to get Republicans to close ranks for the general election.[973] Yet, contrary to the accusations that I was not a team player, I had endorsed Wharton as the Democratic nominee.

In the aftermath, one suburban columnist praised my forthright "refreshingly amateurish" statement of my support for a metro government, while Wharton had hedged.[974] Later, a local Democratic activist told me how impressed he was about my support for tax reform as a state legislator, even though running for county mayor at the same time. Integrity and transparency should be the norm in politics rather than a surprise.

In a post-election analysis, Baker with the *Memphis Flyer* graciously opined that I had handled my campaign issues well, kept Wharton "off-balance" in candidate forums, and took firm stands articulating a solid platform.[975] He found that Wharton was "ambivalent" as to city-county consolidation and reluctant to take fixed positions.[976] This was explained as part of Wharton's "cautious makeup" inherited from his father, whose first name was also "A C."[977]

However, Baker then rubbed my loss in, saying that none of it mattered to women voters in particular, including my strong legislative record on daycare reform.[978] The fact that Wharton's party affiliation was "ambiguous at best" was seen as a "plus" by the voters, according to Baker.[979] He then ventured into a horse-racing analogy, writing that voters generally ignore the issues and ideology and focus primarily on "how the horse bears up under the stress and drama of a race."[980] But, he had already said that I had run the race well.

Wharton laughed about the fact that he was "*definitively* indefinitive."[981] At least he was consistent about being opaque.

When asked about seeming to get his "ire up" in some debate exchanges with me, Wharton admitted that at times he was too "thin-skinned."[982] He explained it as frustration about the time wasted for candidates like Buchanan to attack him, taking time away from my plans on addressing urban sprawl or his ideas on reforming the jail.[983] He added that "It wasn't a case of I'm mad at her and will stay mad forever," but he vowed not to be a "doormat" and "just lay down" either.[984] Yet, somehow, he inexplicably managed to escape the "strident" label.

Wharton further claimed that a "lot of Republicans" said they voted for him in the Democratic primary."[985] When asked if having a black city and a black county mayor would increase white flight to the adjoining counties, Wharton replied "not necessarily."[986] He attributed the flight to "failure" to address problems such as schools and crime, pledging that he was going "to stop" the outrageous crime.[987] It was another promise that came back to haunt him in the years ahead.

In hindsight, the county mayor race was an uphill battle for me. Voters were not ready for female leadership or a metropolitan government. Nor were some in power ready for a strong independent woman who can't be bought.

I also attribute Wharton's primary nomination in part to the band-wagon effect. The press and media anointed him. There were the subtle sexist references to my "personality,"' alleged "boutique" lifestyle, along with the perception that a woman could not win. The endorsements of Wharton by Kyle, Cohen, Ford Sr., and the former city mayors added to the narrative. And he benefitted from the large donations of developers to his campaign. My campaign also would have benefited if Herenton (who agreed with my position on a metropolitan government), and Byrd (whose supporters said we had similar platforms), had each endorsed me. Although the glass ceiling remained firmly in place, I had been a woman in the arena who fought for metropolitan Memphis's future and survived to fight another day.

18

Back to the State House

1

After the county mayor primary, I geared up a reelection effort for my state house seat. And I was starting my own law firm. After losing the county mayor's primary, my partners at the firm where I had worked for sixteen years wanted me to devote myself full-time to the practice of law. Of course, since public service was my passion, I left the firm and opened my own law office. The silver lining of running my own law office was that it enabled me to take some public interest cases and also become a much better attorney as a result to boot. But, the year was extraordinarily hectic – running for county mayor, serving as a state legislator during the most severe fiscal crisis in our state's history, opening my own law office, and running for reelection to the state house.

The past four years had been tough, in fact, with long legislative and special sessions that had turned the part-time job into a nearly year-round endeavor. Not to mention that some of our work was done *per gratis* when the authorized ninety days for legislative session expired.

I faced a November general reelection campaign to the state house with a female Republican opponent. My Republican house opponent from the 1996 and 1998 elections opted not to challenge me in 2002, saying that I was a "very intelligent lady with lofty goals" who always returned his phone calls.[988] He added that running against me was like "trying to cut a redwood forest down with a fingernail file."[989]

In the general election, my opponent, a substitute teacher in the city schools, supported sin taxes for better education funding, but not tax reform.[990] My platform included funding public education, fighting off efforts to undo daycare reform, and environmental issues.

Although now campaigning for the state house, I did watch with interest the county mayor general election. Flinn had come out against the state income tax while Wharton said it appeared to be the only alternative to a higher property tax rate, each playing to their respective bases of support.[991] Yet, Flinn's no new taxes stance did not square with his platform that included additional expenditures for education, roadbuilding, and law enforcement.[992] Wharton was disappointed that Flinn refused to debate.[993] Neither of them had ever been elected to public office. In fact, Wharton had lost a prior bid for district attorney.[994] And, he had not been selected at the People's Convention in 1991, which instead chose Herenton, who went on to win election as the first elected African American mayor of Memphis.[995]

Due to what I perceived as occasional gender-biased coverage about my "personality" in the past campaign, an editorial in the *Commercial Appeal* raised my ire even though a well-meaning progressive editor wrote it. He asked, "What do women want? Can we talk?"[996] The op-ed discussed how everyone needs to learn how to "communicate across the gender barrier," referring to a Russian man's arrest for trying to fix an Olympic ice skating contest in a conversation with a female French skater.[997] The op-ed further discussed how Bill Clinton speaks in the feminine mode and that women "look for emotional support in conversations, not solutions."[998] He added that men often talk in the masculine mode, with examples of Ross Perot coming up with solutions for the economy and Donald Rumsfeld taking out Saddam Hussein.[999] In addition, he implied that Clinton persuaded Madeline Albright and Janet Reno to join his administration by his feminine communication mode.[1000]

My published letter to the editor challenged those assumptions, regardless of whether they were tongue-in-cheek or an honest effort to understand the sexes. They unwittingly perpetuated a gender stereotype by implying that women communicate only in a "feminine" mode and are not decisive.[1001] Reno and Albright had accepted their jobs as smart and logical career moves any "person" would take with a solid track record, and not to pander to Bill Clinton. My letter observed that some women across the country had served well as governors, U.S. senators, big-city mayors, on the U.S. Supreme Court, and as CEOs, but in Memphis, the doors still were closed.[1002] In the letter, I challenged the press to put away limiting gender stereotypes about women's "personalities," to "respect their hard-earned credentials," and to accept us as "equal leaders who can communicate effectively with everyone, and are worthy to serve in both higher office, the boardroom and the editorial ranks."[1003]

My concerns were substantiated only a few months later with the news that Tennessee, Mississippi, and Arkansas ranked at the bottom of the nation in terms of social, political, and economic progress of women according to the *Status of Women in the States* report from the Institute for Women's Policy Research. [1004]In fact, Tennessee ranked 50th of the states and the District of Columbia.[1005]

2

While the campaigns and the legislative session were intense, I did enjoy the Democratic Leadership Council National Conversation in New York during 2002. Moderate Democrats from around the country came together to talk about child welfare, economic development, school reform, the environment, winning elections, health care, transportation, and homeland security.

My service as a state legislator led me to many places, including a seated dinner in the dining hall at the U.S. Capitol hosted by Republican House Majority Leader Trent Lott for a bipartisan women state legislators' conference. At another DLC conference, then Virginia Governor Mark Warner hosted the delegates at his home. On the way to the event, the cab driver told me that he had supported Warner in the past election and wanted to meet the governor. So, when he returned to pick me up, I invited him inside to meet Warner. To my chagrin (and Warner's), the cab driver proceeded to tell him that he had not fulfilled a promise to a relative. Of course, this happens to every politician from time to time. However, Warner, a likable guy with smooth charm, handled it with style, saying he would check into it when he got back to the office.

On one trip to Washington D.C. for a conference, I decided to contact a veteran editorial reporter nicknamed "Woody" for a cup of coffee. Woody, who had clout, wrote a political column for Scripps Howard, the entity that owned the *Commercial Appeal* at the time. I wanted to talk to him about my concerns regarding the sometimes gender-biased Memphis coverage. But Woody was too busy to meet. Not to be deterred, I went by the Scripps Howard D.C. offices in person and gamely asked to speak to Mr. Scripps. Since Mr. Scripps had been deceased for many years, instead, the D.C. bureau head graciously sat down and chatted with me. He also invited me to the office Christmas party later that day. The look on Woody's face when I walked into the party at his boss's invitation was priceless. We got to chat after all.

3

In the county mayor general election, Sir Isaac Ford dropped out as predict-ed.[1006] Flinn sent a letter to voters warning that Wharton would raise taxes.[1007] But, Wharton claimed that the proposals in his twenty-point plan would not cost more money.[1008] Wharton, who had print ads saying he was a "fighter" in the primary election, now ran other print ads touting him as a "Bridge Builder."[1009] While I respect his seeking public service, I wonder whether he couldn't figure out which he really was, or perhaps that would be taking too much of a position?

In August, Wharton beat Flinn with 62% of the vote.[1010] The *Commercial Appeal* dug in with an article calling Flinn's campaign "mean-spirited" and said it hoped he had learned a lesson on how not to campaign.[1011]

During the weeks before the election, Flinn had attacked Wharton on TV about his connections to the Memphis NBA franchise supporters and their alleged "backroom" deals to fund the new arena.[1012] Flinn's campaign aired ads implying that Wharton was a "hand-picked" "crony" of the establishment.[1013] Anonymous robocalls went out alleging conflicts of interest by Wharton over his representation of the child care broker director in the daycare scandal.[1014] Wharton's supporters defended saying he was simply giving legal represen-tation as allowed by the *U.S. Constitution*.[1015]

In the end, Flinn spent about a million of his own dollars on the general election.[1016] On Election eve, a defeated Flinn appeared at Wharton's victory party, pledging his support.[1017] However, he did not apologize for his campaign ads, calling them "honest" and "hard facts."[1018]

4

Despite my pointed letter to the editor about gender stereotypes, the *Commercial Appeal* still endorsed me for reelection to the state house. The editors found me to be "one of the most accomplished lawmakers in the local delegation," a "staunch...advocate on Capitol Hill of reform of Tennessee's corrupt, occasionally deadly system of tax-subsidized child care," who "worked effectively to pass legislation aimed at promoting neighborhood revitalization and environmental protection, public health and consumer rights."[1019]

The endorsement was appreciated, even though the attorney who had represented the Cherokee executive director had just been elected county mayor with the newspaper's help. Wharton had represented WillieAnn Madison regarding the federal grand jury investigation about the child care broker's misuse of funds.[1020] While I understand and affirm the right to legal representation, the newspaper's editors' support for Wharton who had represented WilleAnn Madison seemed incongruent with their overwhelming support for local daycare reform.

In my reelection bid for the state house, there were last-minute campaign dirty tricks. Incredibly, one flyer in support of my opponent claimed that I was "suspiciously quiet" about the Cherokee daycare broker scandal. On the contrary, I was the leader in the entire state legislature in successive sessions addressing the issue.[1021] Somehow, my role was also edited out of an article in the *Commercial Appeal.* I wrote the editor asking that my record be set straight by the newspaper and called the mail piece absurd. [1022]

An ultra-conservative congressional nominee, Marsha Blackburn, campaigned on behalf of my Republican opponent.[1023] I countered with endorsements from the Memphis Police Association, Memphis Education Association, Memphis AFL-CIO labor council, and Tennessee Sierra Club.[1024] My opponent's campaign sent out mailers in key areas with the photo of an African American female activist on the front, leading some voters to mistakenly assume that the activist was the candidate as opposed to the white female running against me.[1025] While she is an intelligent, articulate person, even the press noted her differing pitches to different parts of the district, as a Republican low-taxer or as a progressive.[1026]

In any event, I was pleased to win reelection handily!

5

Having won reelection to the state house, I was also unanimously elected to serve as the Shelby County legislative delegation chair.[1027] I planned to bring together legislators from the other counties in the metropolitan Memphis area to give the delegation a regional focus and more clout. Although I could not do it as county mayor, I was still interested in building bridges for the area. The House Speaker said that he liked my approach.[1028]

During this time, I continued to produce and host *Tennessee Lookout,* a local cable access television show on state and local governmental issues.

Over the years, guests varied from long-famous "Funky Chicken" blues singer Rufus Thomas to the first female African American preacher of a large Baptist Church, Rev. Gina Stewart. I had come a long way from that first hosting of the Democratic Women show with Rep. Mike Kernell.

As the legislative session neared, the state's fiscal situation was still a mess despite the sales tax increase, with a half-billion dollar shortfall disclosed by Phil Bredesen at his gubernatorial inauguration.[1029] Bredesen proposed painful budget cuts of 9% in discretionary spending for a $21.5 billion budget.[1030]

The state budget problems prompted Memphis Mayor Herenton to push for consolidation, proposing to eliminate the city school board. He claimed that consolidation of the Memphis and Shelby County school systems would reduce city property taxes overall by thirty-five cents per hundred dollars of assessed value.[1031] Wharton characteristically hedged.[1032] I asked if Herenton were serious due to his habit of announcing a new initiative and then abruptly dropping it like a hot potato.

Wharton moved forward with a summit on development to manage county growth. Now that the election was over, he came clean, admitting that "poor planning by government and developers" had caused overcrowded suburban schools.[1033] My position was that impact fees or development taxes should be considered to fund the new suburban schools, so that the taxes would not unfairly burden city and suburban residents that did not live in the newly developed areas. In an opinion editorial to the *Commercial Appeal*, I reminded the citizens that the leapfrog development would harm seniors and those on fixed incomes when property taxes were raised to pay for the resulting new schools.[1034]

The city council and Memphis City School Board were undecided on whether the school board should call for a public referendum to merge the city and county schools.[1035] The Tennessee Attorney General opined that only the city school board, and not the city council, could authorize a referendum or surrender the Memphis City School's charter.[1036] Disappointed, this left Herenton pondering legal action in the courts to determine whether the school board had lost the right to exist based upon another opinion of the Tennessee Attorney General. [1037]

County Mayor Wharton presented his proposed budget with a thirty-five cent property tax increase. [1038] In a gutsy move, Herenton appeared at the county commission's meeting to pitch consolidation, saying he was not speaking as the Memphis Mayor but as a regular citizen.[1039] As a result, the commissioners called for a summit by all local elected officials on the issue.[1040] Herenton was critical of the prior Rout administration's management, which had resulted in an approximate $1.5 billion in debt and high taxes.[1041]

Albeit after the election, even the *Commercial Appeal* agreed with my platform issue that the county should consider adequate facilities taxes and impact fees.[1042] Wharton now finally proposed an adequate facilities tax opposed by many real estate brokers and delayed at the request of the Memphis Regional Chamber of Commerce.[1043]

With cement mixers honking outside sent by homebuilders in protest, the county commission proposed to delay consideration of the development tax capped at 1%.[1044] The heavy opposition to the tax by developers and homebuilders at the county commission meeting resulted in high drama, with the public room ultimately cleared by the fire department purportedly due to bad weather sirens.[1045] Wharton agreed to wait a year before approaching the state legislature with the plan, which gave opponents more time to organize against the proposal. [1046]He ran up to the State Capitol to make a show of pushing the tax, but it was obvious that his support of the measure was half-hearted. Wharton appeared to be glad of the delay, now promising a study of the county government's operations similar to my proposal in the county mayor race.[1047]

Without a development tax, smart growth, consolidation, or deep cuts in expenditures, the only viable alternative was to raise the already high property taxes to pay for suburban growth.[1048] While Wharton had professed to be in favor, he had been elected with strong financial backing from developers who opposed the development tax.[1049] This was the exact conflict I had raised in the county mayor primary campaign.

Some pushed controversial alternatives, such as: selling the public utility for an estimated $800 million; developing a portion of the pristine, 450-acre Shelby Farms Park; privatizing the jail; or putting a casino in the Memphis Pyramid with tax revenues estimated at $25 million a year.[1050] Ultimately, Wharton proposed a property tax increase even though the combined Memphis and Shelby County's property taxes were 60% higher than sister city Nashville. [1051]

As to consolidation, some were critical of Herenton's intentions deemed as only wanting to be "King" of Memphis and Shelby County.[1052] Yet some lauded Herenton with the unveiling of a statue in his honor across from the historic Lemoyne Owen College. In the end, the property taxes were increased in 2003, just as I had predicted in the county mayor democratic primary.[1053] A chance for meaningful local tax reform had passed the county by.

PART FIVE

——

Memphis
City Council

19

―――

Taking Reform to City Hall

1

The nonpartisan Memphis City Council District 5 seat opened up in 2003, with possible candidates including George Flinn and local attorney Jim Strickland.[1054] The Republican Party formally endorsed Flinn.[1055]

I prayed for a sign about whether or not to run for city council, still wanting a new challenge and to bring needed reforms to the local level. After exhausting weeks of traveling back and forth to Nashville during the legislative session defending daycare reform, I came home one evening and called a friend, Joyce Akehurst, before unpacking. Suddenly I heard a noise on the other side of the den. I timidly took a look and found a bird stuck to insect paper behind the stereo. I took the bird outside and then turned in for the night, wondering how the bird had entered my house.

Loud noises woke me up the next morning, and I rushed downstairs. Another bird was in the house, flying around the den and kitchen. I grabbed the kitchen broom and opened the back sliding glass doors to steer the bird outside. When it flew to the front of the house, I opened the front door and ran around flailing the broom, trying to get the bird to fly outdoors. Finally, it did. After reflection, I decided that my prayer was answered. I needed to work and live full-time in Memphis since birds had begun to inhabit my house in my absence.

My decision to enter the city council race took some by surprise. Reporter Baker with the *Memphis Flyer* apparently favored Strickland. In reporting the news, he posted an unflattering photo of me with what appeared to be a sneer on my face.[1056] Flinn, who had already announced, showed class saying, "Carol's done a real good job at the state level."[1057]

In my announcement, I acknowledged that there were many good candidates in the race, but none with my experience as to the issues the council would be dealing with, such as child care and smart growth. Nearly half of my council district included portions of my legislative district, as well as another East Memphis area where I had grown up, attended the public schools, and had my law office.

After announcing for the council seat, one of my first stops was the mayor's office at City Hall. I showed up without an appointment. Herenton invited me into his spacious office that had two long black leather couches facing each other. The mayor sat on one couch and I on the other. He said, "You're just kidding about running for the council," with a laugh. Then, he sprawled his 6' 6" frame lengthwise across his couch.

Not to be intimidated, I tried to move from an upright seated position to a similarly more leisurely and reclining position—but it just didn't work for me. I sat back up, saying that I was dead serious about running, intended to win, and wanted his support. We ended the meeting cordially.

2

Meanwhile, Jim Strickland geared up his campaign. He announced Democratic County Commissioner Deidre Malone, Republican District Attorney Bill Gibbons, two former Shelby County Republican chairs, and two Democratic Party activists as his campaign co-chairs. [1058] Strickland was identified with the Herenton faction of the Democratic Party and endorsed by vacating District 5 Councilman John Vergos. [1059] Other candidates entering the race were lobbyist Joe Cooper, arborist Mark Follis, and Kerry White.

Good news came with a poll showing me well ahead of the pack, at 43%, Flinn at 20%, and others further back. [1060] Also, my favorable rating was 62%, with Flinn at 32% and Strickland at 14%. [1061]

Shortly after that, word came back that the Memphis City Council's last-minute redistricting efforts could draw my home precinct out of District 5. [1062] When I contacted the U.S. Attorney's office to ask some questions about the issue, some councilmembers were upset and claimed pressure. [1063] Perhaps so—to do the right thing. In any event, it worked because they left me in District 5.

Despite my frontrunner status in the poll, the press reported that some pundits considered the council District 5 race to be between myself and

Strickland.[1064] While conventional thinking was that Strickland would have better funding by virtue of Republican connections, I had stronger name recognition.[1065] Campaigning was in full swing in summer 2003 at various picnics and community events.

A real concern was whether the voters would allow me to come home and serve on the city council when the poll showed high approval for me as a state legislator, particularly concerning my child care reform work. Every year since the major reform measures became law in 2000, I had continued leading the effort to ensure the reforms were implemented and not undone. Also, reports continued to bring the issue to the public's attention, such as the suspension of transportation services at one daycare in the hot July summer of 2003 after inspectors found overloaded vans and some children buckled together in the same seat.[1066]

Another tragedy occurred when Amber Cox-Cody, age two, was found dead in June after spending eight hours alone in the 90-degree summer heat in a daycare van.[1067] The death was not only sad but mind-boggling, in that the new laws required the drivers and on-board monitors to make headcounts and cross-check roll sheets both on the van and again inside the center. Most telling was that the center had received only a one-star quality rating out of a possible zero to three rating system. [1068]

Although the reforms were working at most centers, more time was needed for all centers to come into compliance. Governor Bredesen announced that the state would no longer subsidize daycare transportation.[1069] Some saw this as a move to simply cut costs for the state, as opposed to protecting the children's safety for necessary long-distance trips to centers in some areas. [1070]He later backed down. With the new reforms, it was time for state regulators to do their job, including the audits to ensure that funds were used to care for the children. [1071]

As chairwoman of the House Children & Family Affairs committee, I called a hearing. A mother testified about her child's abuse at a daycare with little assistance from the state. [1072]Although the alleged perpetrator had been reported three years earlier for abuse at a different child care center, he was not prosecuted, thereby enabling him to get a job at another center since he had no criminal record.[1073] Questions were raised about whether the division of children's services had submitted a form to the department of human services that the charges were founded. [1074] Ultimately, he pled guilty to aggravated sexual battery.[1075]

The need for abuse reports to be shared between the state's departments of children's services and human services was a focus of the hearing. The mother, outraged, spoke out that "enough is enough."[1076] After a prior public panel discussion by the *Commercial Appeal* and *WREG News* Channel 3, there had been calls to end the "attitude of carelessness."[1077]

Perhaps to send a message, District Attorney Bill Gibbons asked the Shelby County grand jury for first-degree murder charges against three employees at the daycare center where Amber Cox-Cody died.[1078] The *Commercial Appeal* editorialized that "constant pressure" was needed by government regulators, daycare owners, and supervisors, and even elected officials to prevent another child from dying.[1079] Recognizing the hard-fought gains already made with the new laws and rules, the editors also agreed with my recommendation that the model for four and five-year-old children in child care should change from babysitting to early childhood education.[1080]

3

While juggling my law practice and legislative duties, my city council campaign received a boost when elderly Republican former District 5 City Councilman Bob James endorsed me. We had met at a Toastmaster's meeting on a campaign stop. Although conservative, he favored state tax reform.

Another unexpected occurrence in the hot summer months was a massive windstorm that swept through the city, leaving thousands without power for over a week.[1081] Yet, Mayor Herenton left town during the crisis to attend a fundraiser in Arkansas.[1082] MLGW, the public utility, declined assistance from the Mississippi private Entergy utility, which angered many citizens left in the dark.[1083] John Willingham, a Republican county commissioner who was running against Herenton for Memphis mayor, made hay about the failure of the city and MLGW to provide sufficient emergency services.

Oddly, Republican Party Chair Kemp Conrad asked Willingham to drop out of the mayoral race against self-professed Democrat Herenton, which he declined.[1084] Conrad also pooh-poohed Willingham's "conspiracy theories" as to why MLGW did not accept help from the neighboring private utility in the crisis.[1085]

Herenton attempted to rectify the complaints by announcing a new emergency phone number. But his opponent, John Willingham, chastised him for not being visible or showing leadership during the crisis.[1086] Citizens wrote angry letters to the editor, saying that the MLGW president Herman Morris and his top executives should go a week without power before deciding to turn down assistance.[1087] Some of Morris's neighbors wondered if favoritism were at play because his large Midtown home had lights while they were in the dark. One unfavorably contrasted Herenton's inadequate response to the power outage with that of Mayor Rudy Giuliani's attentive response after the 9/11 attack on the World Trade Center. [1088]

After the crisis abated, my campaign headquarters kick-off boasted famous opera singer Marguerite Piazza singing the national anthem. Republican former city council member Bob James gave remarks, along with a host of other Republican and Democrat elected officials for the nonpartisan election.[1089] In my speech, I reminded voters that they had reelected me six times as a state legislator who gets the job done. I pledged that as their city councilwoman, "when someone needs to care...Carol will care; when someone needs to speak out...Carol will speak; when someone needs to take a stand... Carol will stand" and that they can *Count on Carol*!

The *Commercial Appeal*, which usually profiles each candidate, announced a new policy for the election. The newspaper would only feature candidates who presented a unique angle. A feature ran for each of Strickland, Flinn, and the other male candidates in the race, but none of me. Although my team pitched several worthy stories, nothing was printed.

Some of my female supporters, such as Lois Freeman, were livid. They called the reporter assigned to the race and wrote scathing letters to the editor about the gender bias. Under duress, reporter Blake Fontenay relented in exasperation. He called to interview me with the trite angle that I was the "female" candidate in the race. Since I had the most experience and a solid record, I was reluctant to be defined solely by my gender. However, a profile was better than no profile, so we cooperated.

Based on these events, we were not surprised when the *Commercial Appeal* endorsed Strickland even though he had never held a day in public office.[1090] The editors used gender-coded language that he could speak "authoritatively" about smart growth issues, although I had championed those issues only a year earlier as a candidate for county mayor.[1091] They wrote that he was "especially well-versed in city tax and spending matters" with no explanation as to why when I had an economics degree and served on the state's House Finance Committee that had a much larger budget to balance.[1092]

The editors acknowledged my "usefully" proposing the creation of a Children & Youth office at City Hall and that I "would make an excellent addition to the city council," but argued my "principled leadership" at the State Capitol was "too valuable to lose."[1093] In response, my campaign emphasized that after thirteen years of traveling to Nashville, as the more experienced candidate, it was time for me to come home and do more serving the people at City Hall.

The *Memphis Flyer*, although not endorsing candidates, did opine that my name-recognition and constituent base would more than likely result in a majority of the vote or a runoff with either Strickland or Flinn.[1094] My campaign team pushed hard. We posted signs all over the district, and a few supporters stood with me on strategic street corners waiving to voters during rush hour traffic.

Debating at the public library in September were Strickland, Flinn, another candidate, and me. Strickland opposed my children's and youth office on budgetary concerns, despite the continual daycare problems.[1095] We previously had been associate attorneys at the same law firm, although he left while I had stayed and made partner. Yet, he bragged about having the support of lawyers from the firm, as if he were part of a club. In response, I chided him that some of those lawyers were supporting me.[1096]

Strickland took a shot at Flinn and me, implying that we were each extreme in ideology on the liberal-to-conservative spectrum, despite my moderate voting record.[1097] Flinn was considerably toned down from the 2002 county mayor's race, pitching simple proposals such as having educational videotapes for moms at medical clinics.[1098]

As the council race continued, I pushed early childhood and public education reform, while Strickland said he would only address budgetary issues.[1099] I called it a cop-out because the council's role in approving the city schools' budget gave it a bully pulpit to push for reforms. Strickland proposed closing low-populated schools, while Flinn said he would go after private donations of equipment for the schools.[1100] We duked it out across the district.

4

Herenton, seeking a fourth Memphis mayoral term in the municipal elections, was perceived as invincible by the local press in part due to his 1999 defeat of challenger Joe Ford.[1101] Even the GOP leaders said he would be tough for either a white or black candidate to beat.[1102] A *Commercial Appeal* cartoon bore an "S" for Superman on Herenton's chest.[1103] His absence during the windstorm for a fundraiser and other gaffes did not appear to stick, nor did the newspaper editors seem to care.[1104]

Part of Herenton's support was due to recent downtown revitalization and only one property tax increase in the past ten years.[1105] Vacating Councilman John Vergos complimented Herenton for not playing the race card and improving Memphis' national image.[1106] While some still said that the city was racially polarized, Herenton claimed that his election as the first elected black mayor showed that Memphis was now progressive.[1107] Progressive enough to one day elect a female mayor? That wasn't even a topic of discussion.

Despite the *Commercial Appeal* endorsement of Strickland, my candidacy was boosted with the endorsement by the historic African American-focused newspaper, the *Tri-State Defender*.[1108] The editors based the endorsement on my experience as a state legislator and "the genuine concern she has exhibited for the least of those among us."[1109] At least one newspaper was willing to go all out for the candidate who had the most experience and was female.

As Election Day neared, I remembered my unease about the accuracy of the county mayoral primary election results. Thus, before voting began, I teamed up with Rep. Mike Kernell to take advantage of a rarely used provision in state law that allows candidates to inspect the voting machines. At the election warehouse, we looked at one of the machines under the watch of a puzzled election official, asking if we could inspect the software for the touchscreen direct record electronic (DRE) voting machines.

The state voter laws were enacted years before computerized voting and had not kept up with the times. A resolution by state Senator Rochelle passed the senate in 2001 to review election processes in light of automation and the 2000 presidential election that came down to a few hanging chads.[1110] However, despite support by Reps. Ulysses Jones, Mike Kernell, and myself, the measure was taken off notice in the state house subcommittee due to budget cuts limiting out of session study committees.

Despite our requests, we were not allowed to inspect the voting machines' software. The interior software was just as significant in determining the election's accuracy as the exterior of the voting machines. We hoped that stopping by would at least make an impression on election officials that we intended to challenge the election if there were any irregularities.

On October 9th, although the top vote-getter, I faced a runoff with millionaire George Flinn. Strickland's endorsements by Vergos and other "political heavyweights" were to no avail with his third-place finish.[1111] Since both Flinn and Strickland had outspent me substantially in the election, I was glad that my message had reached the voters.[1112] One voter wrote a letter published in the *Commercial Appeal* wondering why the headline on the day after the election had Flinn's name listed first when I had received more votes, and my name came first in the alphabet?[1113]

The election was nonpartisan, but Flinn was a Republican and myself a Democrat. The Republican Party endorsed Flinn, but the Democratic Party had remained neutral in the first election. Now, it endorsed my candidacy for the runoff election set only a month later.[1114]

The press was already looking ahead to the 2007 Memphis mayoral race, predicting that the runoff winner in District 5 – either myself or Flinn – could be a candidate for mayor.[1115] Even now, some twelve years after giving my "wish list" at the Lowery New Year's Day Prayer Breakfast, there was still not parity at City Hall. Herenton's administration now boasted only two females at the top – Gail Jones Carson as the mayor's spokesperson and Sara Hall heading up the personnel department.[1116] In any event, I was entirely focused on winning the city council election and not on a potential mayoral election four years off.

With the runoff election campaigning underway, I honored my pledge to resign from the state house if elected to the Memphis City Council. Flinn and the Republican Party leaders were shocked by my state house resignation on October 23rd, three weeks before the November 13, 2003 city council runoff election.[1117] Taking action more than a year from the November 2004 general election ensured that the voters could elect a representative to the vacant state house seat instead of it being filled by a vote of the Shelby County Commission.

At a press conference, I announced that the people, not politicians, should select my replacement. I was willing to assume the political risk by resigning before the runoff election to ensure they had that right.[1118] House Speaker Naifeh praised my years of service, saying, "She has served her constituents and the people of Tennessee very well in her capacity as state representative" and that he looked forward to working with me in the future regardless of the office held.[1119] I faxed the resignation to the governor's office, not knowing whether or not I would win the city council runoff. I thought back to when I went with trembling hands to file for the state house for the first time in 1990. I remembered and was thankful for so many family members, friends, campaign coordinators, volunteers, contributors, constituents and colleagues of both political parties who had helped me over the years, including Kristina Ryan, Liz Landrigan, Beth Dierrson, Lisa Incardona Rachelle Burgins, Lupe Gonzalez, Francis Issacs, Charlie Caswell, Ginny Shea Dunn, Betty Isom, Jocie Wurzburg, Karen Shea, Arthur McArthur, Myra Stiles, Virginia Reynolds, Bobbie Morris, John Freeman, Chip Armstrong, and Charles Boone.

Strickland, who claimed to be a Democrat, did not return my calls, but former Councilman John Vergos did endorse me. Apparently, Strickland was not a "team player," or else he was not really on the Democratic team. While Flinn and Kemp Conrad, the local Republican Party chair, criticized my actions in resigning as "political," conservative local talk show host Mike Fleming said that it was a sign of my confidence of victory.[1120] And I was pleased when others spoke out with their view that the action showed "integrity and character" rarely found in local government.[1121]

The *Tennessean*, a Nashville-based newspaper, wrote an editorial that "few state legislators were as effective in their service to all Tennesseans as Rep. Carol Chumney."[1122] The editors added that my "name would long be associated with a host of child and family issues throughout the state," including my work as "a tireless advocate for better child care" and "chief architect of the legislation that dramatically changed Tennessee's child-care laws."[1123] The editorial also noted my "leadership and courage" on many issues such as insurance coverage for divorced or widowed spouses, domestic violence, and women's health.[1124] Calling me a "valuable asset" to my party, the editors also wrote that "she's also had a bipartisan ability to bridge the gaps on important issues" and that my departure created a "void that other lawmakers must fill."[1125] I was thrilled with the editorial! Later, I would think back to their assessment of my work, when some local politicians and columnists made unfounded charges about whether or not I could work in a bipartisan way.

On the heels of the *Tennessean* editorial, the Memphis *Commercial Appeal* now endorsed me for city council in the runoff, citing my legislative experience and "hands-on knowledge of city issues."[1126] The editors now found me "one of the most accomplished lawmakers in the Shelby County delegation during her 13-year tenure."[1127] They cited my "valuable expertise in such areas as early childhood education, metropolitan development and 'smart growth,' and public school funding and governance."[1128] If that endorsement had run in the general election, there probably would not have been a runoff.

Flinn was avoiding joint appearances. I pointed out that he was ducking debates when the voters needed to hear the candidates' positions. Flinn countered there was no need since he had debated in the first election.[1129] I criticized his use of his own money to send mailers to the voters without appearing in-person to answer questions he might not want to address.[1130]

The local Democratic Party delivered its own newspaper to voters with an article addressing my candidacy and record. The piece set forth my progressive positions on education, children and youth, community policing, revitalizing neighborhoods, tax reform, and my fiscal conservatism, push for efficiencies, and endorsements by groups such as the Sierra Club, Memphis Police Association, and Memphis Fire Fighters.[1131]

At this point, Jackson Baker with the *Memphis Flyer* called the race too close to call due to projected low voter turnout.[1132] The Republican elected officials who had endorsed Strickland now backed Flinn, and many Democratic elected officials, such as Deidre Malone, now supported me.[1133] Useful in the absence of a Strickland endorsement was his own mailer in the first election suggesting a "winning combination" to be me in the state house, Strickland on the city council, and no position for Flinn.[1134] Strickland tried to backpedal from the mail piece, but it was too late.

Feeling in some respects like David against Goliath due to Flinn's enormous wealth, I campaigned tirelessly. Meanwhile, the *Commercial Appeal* ran a last-minute article on our similar positions on smart growth and keeping cell towers out of parks.[1135] We both focused on how better to manage a response to natural disasters, such as the recent June windstorm.

The *Memphis Flyer* opined that the early voting turnout might point to an upset for me because only 154 black voters had participated versus more voters from traditionally Republican East Memphis precincts.[1136] My prior legislative service, endorsement by Republican Bob James, East Memphis childhood roots, and Flinn's refusal to appear with me even at the conservative Dutch Treat luncheon gave me the edge.[1137] It didn't help Flinn either when one of my industrious campaign workers, Jody Hurt, delivered to election officials a hilarious photo of him crossing a polling place boundary in violation of the law. Conrad was forced to respond to the accusation.[1138]

Election night was exciting when I won the runoff by over 55%. I vowed to move forward immediately with my platform issues. The *Commercial Appeal* reported that I "campaigned as aggressively as an underdog in the runoff," resigned my state house seat held for thirteen years, and called Flinn out for refusing to debate.[1139] It was nice to read the positive words of constituents who said they voted for me due to my availability, including answering my own phone calls, constituent service, and strong legislative reform record.[1140] Some sheepishly admitted they initially voted for Strickland only because they wanted me to continue as a state legislator.[1141]

The *Democrat* newspaper claimed the victory as being over the "power of money," the "powers that be," and even "divisive powers within your own party."[1142] I was pleased that the editorial complimented my "record of excellence" and "ability to reach out to voters and give them a straight and honest message," and "commitment to personal independence and devotion to service, not homage to special interest" as a "model all Democrats can be proud of and seek to emulate in future elections."[1143]

The *Democrat* editorial noted my "smart and positive race," overcoming endorsements of Flinn by Mayor Herenton, Councilmen Myron Lowery, and Rickey Peete, "supposed Democrats, who, for some reason, felt a Republican millionaire was a better choice."[1144] Interestingly, Jackson Baker, with the *Memphis Flyer* attributed those endorsements possibly to the fear that my "diligence and determination" could become a "caveat" to other city politicians.[1145]

The victory was great, but little did I know what lay ahead as a new member of the Memphis City Council. An inkling came with Herenton's New Year's Eve announcement of his administration "picks" for the next term, with Joseph Lee nominated to replace Herman Morris as head of the public utility.[1146] Lee was the current finance director for the City of Memphis. Surprised councilmembers began weighing in on the lack of any utility experience by Lee, as well as some other controversial mayoral nominations.[1147] The mayor also proposed an $11,000 raise for the position.[1148]

In my view, the proposed salary of $195,000 for the MLGW president was high, especially in light of the inadequate response by the public utility in the past summer windstorm. I called for a national search for potential candidates to lead the utility as the best way to find qualified applicants. Councilman Jack Sammons, on the other hand, defended the raise saying that a $200,000 salary was commensurate with the wages paid to CEOs to run major corporations.[1149] And we were off and running…

20

"You're Just Stupid"

1

On New Year's Day 2004, Mayor Herenton ominously sounded off about his "enemies" who were plotting against him,[1150] and warned councilmembers and others in the "political establishment" "don't bring me no mess and there won't be no mess."[1151] Although he traditionally addressed Myron Lowery's prayer breakfast, Herenton held his own breakfast that year. His pronouncement that he was "somebody" and some councilmembers were "nobodies" without their council position set off a running feud.[1152] Baker with the *Memphis Flyer* interpreted it as a declaration of "war" on the city council "while seeming to claim divine sanction."[1153] It sounded like one.

Herenton aggravated the councilmembers by remarking that he might have to keep running for mayor because there wasn't another "elected official in the City of Memphis I would have confidence in doing this job."[1154] Councilman Brent Taylor observed that the mayor began every year with controversy. Still, this year Councilwomen Tajuan Stout Mitchell and Barbara Swearengen Holt and others expressed shock at his remarks.[1155] Whether Herenton's spouting off was simply an aspect of his "alpha male" persona or rumored "darker issues" was a matter of debate in the *Memphis Flyer*.[1156]

I was sworn in with the other councilmembers at the convention center, with my mother holding my Bible and my dad in the audience. With Herenton's erratic behavior, we didn't know what to expect.

My pollster had jokingly compared my election to the blonde-haired sorority sister character Elle played by Reese Witherspoon in the movie *Legally Blonde*. Instead of going to Congress, I was going to City Hall. While I disagreed with his comparison, I did feel that after the raucous but professional state legislature, City Hall seemed like a kindergarten playground. Little did I know at the time how eventful the year would be or the landmines that lay ahead.

After the breakfast, the mayor downplayed the council's role in approving his nominations. He pushed Joseph Lee for President of MLGW and defiantly said that he would appoint his nominees as interim division directors without council approval if necessary.[1157] Due to council objections, Lee initially withdrew his name from consideration.[1158]

Although no one was certain what had prompted Herenton's outbursts, Councilman Taylor believed it was because the council had delayed a pay raise vote for the mayor until after the election.[1159] Ultimately, Herenton was given a $20,000 pay raise, but he complained that Councilman Rickey Peete "mismanaged" the proposal.[1160]

Because of the mayor's comments, Taylor proposed a resolution requiring council approval of interim directors and restricting their pay to forty-five days.[1161] Upset, Herenton announced that he would fight for his nominees and didn't "need no damn friends on the council."[1162] Perhaps to appear more reasonable, the mayor reached out to suburban mayors about taxation and school consolidation. Yet, Herenton admitted that some had perceived him as arrogant when pushing school consolidation.[1163]

Herenton's remarks angered councilmembers. Only a few days later, the new city council rejected four of his nominees and delayed action on Lee's nomination.[1164] The council approved the minutes at the same meeting, which meant that it could not reconsider the rejected nominees.[1165]

Even Councilman Edmund Ford Sr. said that the council should do a thorough search before voting on Lee.[1166] As I pointed out, the best candidates would not apply if the mayor were not on board with the search objective. Councilman Jack Sammons and others voted against the delay on Lee's nomination, with Sammons calling Lee a "hometown success story."[1167] Herenton brushed off the council's action as "envy and jealousy."[1168]

Herenton doubled-down, refusing to exclude even his friend County Mayor A C Wharton from his assertion that he was the only person fit to serve as Memphis mayor.[1169] He contended that the other elected officials should simply be more like him and stop being politically expedient.[1170] The mayor infuriated virtually every political leader in the city by claiming he had not seen a single elected official "who wasn't for sale" (later qualified to a "very few" that did not have a "price").[1171] He touted his own self-professed integrity, oddly claiming that no one had solicited him as mayor even though he had the sole contracting authority.[1172] Herenton claimed he was serving as mayor out of civic duty, complaining that the mayor's job was not a money-maker, precluded the pursuit of business opportunities, and only afforded a small pension.[1173] Yes, that is what public service often means—sacrificing personal business pursuits for the greater good.

The mayor admitted in the *Memphis Flyer* that some would see him as an "egomaniac," but added that unlike some other elected officials, he was "steady" and "on course."[1174] Aware that some councilmembers were plotting to defeat his nominees, Herenton believed that they were trying to teach him a lesson because he was "arrogant."[1175] He explained his remarks on New Year's Day as faith-based, which others construed instead as a messiah complex.[1176] He certainly had an unusual way to secure his cabinet nominees' approval by the council.

Splattering his remarks liberally with "damn" and "shit," the mayor admitted involvement in trying to "take control" of the huge $1.5 billion public utility prepayment bond deal with the Tennessee Valley Authority. He explained that MLGW President Herman Morris selected a mostly out-of-state Wall Street team that lacked in minority participation.[1177] However, Herenton denied allegations that one of his sons, who worked for a First Tennessee Bank affiliate, was ever involved with the deal.[1178] This revelation about the deal and its players by Baker in the *Memphis Flyer* would be the subject of scrutiny by the council and others.

Herenton vowed to fight to ensure that his "awesome powers" as mayor, were respected. He hurled a veiled threat to any councilmember who interfered with his administration that such action could result in that councilmember's seat being declared vacant.[1179] The mayor shrugged off his losses on the council nominee votes but warned that the fight was not yet over.[1180] Indeed, this was only the beginning of a contentious fourth term for the mayor.

2

Shortly after that, Councilman Jack Sammons called for a "Watergate-style investigation" by the city council regarding whether Herenton improperly steered business on the $1.5 billion MLGW bond issue.[1181] Herenton had sent a memo in August 2003 to MLGW President Morris asking to include a Little Rock law firm and FTN Financial (a subsidiary of First Tennessee National Corp) in the deal.[1182] The Little Rock law firm had held the controversial campaign fundraiser for Herenton during the major windstorm crisis, where he was reported to have raised about $25,000.[1183] At a press conference, Herenton retorted he only sought to ensure minority firms participated in the MLGW bond deal.[1184]

The mayor also suggested rescinding the MLGW severance package for Herman Morris, exceeding $200,000 taxpayer dollars.[1185] On the other hand, Councilman Jack Sammons wanted to explore whether the mayor even had the power to fire the MLGW president. He speculated that Morris might legally still be employed by MLGW even though Herenton *disap-* pointed (colloquial for not reappointed) him from his position after his 2003 reelection.[1186]

With a unanimous vote, the Memphis City Council moved forward to investigate whether any work was steered by the mayor to firms that had raised money for his reelection campaign. [1187] Since council attorney Allan Wade had also worked on the bond deal, the council considered other legal counsel.[1188] In my view, even if an outside attorney opined that Wade did not have a direct conflict, the public perception still militated in favor of other legal counsel. Councilman E. C. Jones agreed.[1189]

At a special meeting, the city council continued to buck the mayor by approving an ordinance that stopped pay for any interim administration appointees after forty-five days without council authorization.[1190] Some temporary appointees had served a year or more, sidestepping council and public scrutiny.[1191] The mayor contended that interim appointees did not require council approval under the city charter.[1192]

In an effort to forge a compromise and avoid an adverse decision to the council by a lawsuit, I suggested a referendum to clarify the city charter along with a term limit amendment for the city mayor. Herenton, uninterested in a compromise, vetoed the interim appointee ordinance stating that it was an unlawful attempt by the council to exercise executive or administrative powers.[1193] With less than seven reported mayoral vetoes since 1967, my view at the time was that a public referendum on a charter amendment was a better way to resolve the matter. [1194]

A group of ministers, who were African American, came to Herenton's rescue calling the feud a "crisis." They asked him to drop one of his nominees and for the council to forgo the bond deal investigation.[1195] The ministers also urged the council not to look into changes to the city charter due to purely "personality differences" with the mayor.[1196] Sammons responded that the ministers should run for office if they differed on how the council's job should be done.[1197]

My response was that the charter review did not personally target Herenton, who was likely to retire before any term limits would take effect. Moreover, because any proposed charter amendments would require a year or more for a public vote, there was plenty of time for a healing process between the mayor and the council.

The *Commercial Appeal* editorialized in favor of the bond deal investigation, wondering if the lack of public bids for the underwriting group cost the taxpayers more because of the mayor's involvement and whether those who worked on the deal were qualified.[1198] The editors also questioned the propriety of Herenton suggesting in a letter to Morris that FTN Financial partially replace Lehman Brothers, when it as a subsidiary of First Tennessee National Corp. purportedly had "business ties" to one of Herenton's sons.[1199] These were valid questions since the public's money was involved.

3

With the controversy boiling, Herenton made nice with the mayors from the county's seven small suburban towns with a meeting after years of complaints that he ignored their interests.[1200] Forming a metro government was off the table for the meeting. Instead, the main topic was the migration of citizens to outlying counties. The county was experiencing not only outward migration but also a shift of the remaining population from the city to the county, increasing costs for new county schools and resulting in inner-city schools operating below capacity. [1201]

The citizens were lured to migrate to the suburbs with inexpensive new housing developments subsidized with government bonds for the infrastructure.[1202] Memphis struggled to revitalize downtown and encourage infill development. However, neither the city nor the county government had done much to stop the exodus of citizens. Nor had the county enacted impact fees or adequate facilities taxes to help pay for the new schools, as advocated by me in the 2002 county mayor's race.[1203] The result was a growing $1.6 billion county debt paid by both those inside and outside the city.[1204]

As one suburban mayor said, neither Memphis nor the suburban towns could survive without the other.[1205] And, as the Memphis Director of Housing & Community Development Robert Lipscomb later admitted, the city made it "too easy to move" with "some of our policies," resulting in serious blight in Memphis.[1206] This was the cost of not setting smart growth policies early on.

After the interlude with suburban mayors, Herenton returned to the fight, apparently upset about legal advice given to the council. He froze payments to and requested an audit of the former law firm of the city council's attorney, Allan Wade.[1207] City Attorney Robert Spence, perhaps getting the hell out of Dodge, announced that he was leaving his $122,000 city attorney job to return to full-time private practice.[1208] Both attorneys had vibrant private practices in addition to their city work. An audit found unsound business practices by the city due to insufficient guidelines for inside and outside attorneys, with a push to tighten up the rules. Over the years, the city allowed part-time city attorneys, due in part to the fact that highly qualified attorneys could earn substantially more in the private sector. However, on occasion, this practice was the impetus of charges of conflicts of interests when the City work and private sector work overlapped in some regard, whether the allegations were valid or not.[1209]

The dispute worsened when Mayor Herenton asked Councilman Brent Taylor to step outside, apparently to resolve the mayor-council differences the old-fashioned way.[1210] Taylor, shorter and smaller than Herenton in size, sarcastically replied that he didn't want to meet the mayor outside but rather at the health department for him to "piss in a cup so we can see what he's on."[1211]

As one commentator with *WREG News* dryly noted, the "raucous to bizarre" turn of events and Herenton's failure to get appointments and other matters approved by the council might have taught him that "he's nobody without the city council."[1212] It was ironic that years later, in 2012, Taylor was called out by a colleague for agreeing to serve on the private charter school board proposed by Herenton.[1213] Apparently, over time, they patched things up.

Moving forward, Herenton announced at a not so cordial meeting of the council's utility oversight committee that he would not do a national search for the MLGW vacancy until a court of law resolved the issue of the interim appointments.[1214] However, in a light-hearted moment, he did give Councilman Edmund Ford Sr. a hug, with the proviso that he wasn't committing to hug any other councilmembers.[1215]

The council also voted down the request by the University of Memphis and Herenton to give the college an annual $125,000 payment for twenty years to help cover the costs for the Tigers basketball team to play in the FedExForum.[1216] While Herenton and Joseph Lee encouraged the proposal as a means to free up the Pyramid for alternative uses, some councilmembers logically asked why the city would pay the only tenant to break the lease with no replacement tenant identified.[1217] Although the council passed a resolution asking the university to keep the Pyramid as the venue for Tigers basketball games, the body later quietly approved the move to the FedExForum without the annual payments, with only myself abstaining because there was no replacement tenant.[1218]

Now, the Pyramid was left without a tenant, and as the major landmark on the city's waterfront was truly an empty tomb. I advocated an open bidding process on the use of the Pyramid. However, the prior deal with the Grizzlies (HOOPS) and the local governments appeared to give its owner, Michael Heisley, the right of first refusal for most events at the Pyramid which severely limited development interest.

4

In March, the council finally overrode Herenton's veto of the interim-appointee ordinance, with my sole no vote.[1219] In an opinion editorial in the *Memphis Flyer*, I wrote that the people should decide the matter in a referendum due to the unclear charter language, which might prompt an expensive lawsuit.[1220] Furthermore, the controversial and continuing feud between the mayor and the council harmed the city's national image, and the billion-dollar MLGW public utility was rudderless.

Due to the mayor and some councilmembers' angry public name-calling, I called for the petty infighting to stop. City leaders needed to focus instead on improving schools, reducing crime, revitalizing neighborhoods, and economic development. The MLGW presidential vacancy was a ticking time-bomb should there be another power outage or crisis, with no one to lead the utility. My research found that the leaders of other public utilities in the nation had extensive utility experience. Again, I pushed for a national search.

Ultimately, the mayor decided not to litigate the new interim appointee ordinance as his "mea culpa" to the council. [1221] With that issue behind us, I took my push for a national search for the MLGW presidential replacement a step further. I wrote to the mayor asking for a meeting. Having gained some leverage with the recent council vote, we met, and he agreed to consider my request.[1222]

5

During this time, it was also revealed that in January 2001, the prior city council had surreptitiously approved a cushy twelve-year pension rule for elected and appointed city officials to commence upon retirement regardless of the recipient's age. [1223] The prior rule for elected and appointed officials had required fifteen years of service, and they could not draw benefits until the combined age and years of service equaled seventy-five. [1224]

The forty-year-old finance director at the time left employment just one month after the twelve-year pension rule's approval, reportedly drawing $32,563 annually.[1225] Within six months of the rule's enactment, nine other city officials retired with an estimated $2 million price tag.[1226] Councilman Tom Marshall's professed belief that it applied only to about one hundred people was rightfully called "gullible at best" by the *Commercial Appeal*, as the city boosted about 300 appointed positions.[1227] Pricewaterhouse Coopers, an accounting firm, estimated the city's increased pension liability from the twelve-year pension as approximately $17 million.[1228]

While some councilmembers proposed that the mayor simply reduce the number of appointed positions, I wanted to address the actual pension eligibility provisions even though it would affect some councilmembers.[1229] Shortly after calling for the petty infighting to stop, I introduced an ordinance to repeal the twelve-year pension rule. Some councilmembers struck back the same day. Two members publicly accused me of grandstanding, along with two others complaining that I overworked my shared staff members. [1230] However, Councilman E.C. Jones admitted to the *Flyer* reporter that he resented my allegations that some councilmembers were petty.[1231]

My capable council staffers had never raised any concerns whatsoever to me. I conducted my council duties in the same manner as I had done during my service as a state legislator for more than thirteen years. Thus, in the same fashion, I had scheduled town hall meetings and also ten neighborhood "Coffee with Carol Chumney" meetings around the council district to hear from constituents. I even told the staff they did not have to attend.

Incredibly, I learned that the Council Chair Joe Brown and the council attorney Wade were reading some of my constituent emails, to which I promptly objected.[1232] And, not backing down, I personally issued a press release about the new "work ethic" being brought to City Hall, asking for a higher standard of professionalism and accountability, and refusing to be bullied into mediocre work.[1233] My constituents wanted me to get things done, expose the misuse of public funds, and demand accountability. In conclusion, I pointed out that the staff worked for the people of Memphis. If the councilmembers all worked hard and focused on constituent service, we would all get along just fine.[1234]

False accusations continued. At a televised council committee meeting, Chairman Brown claimed there were reports that I acted unprofessionally, which was not true.[1235] In shock, I defended myself, remaining steadfast to continue speaking up for the people of Memphis. With the TV cameras rolling, Councilman Jones angrily called me "stupid."[1236]

The two councilmen continued to harangue and finger point at me for what seemed to last about twenty minutes, in full view of the press and media.[1237] I responded that they had an ax to grind, relied on false accusations, and interfered with *my* staff relations. One news station ran the clip of me being called "stupid" as the "big story" over and over again for days.

After the incident, I took the time to compose myself in my office before appearing for the full council meeting that night. One news reporter inquired if I had gone home, apparently thinking that the verbal accusations would send me packing. On the contrary, I appeared and did my job.

The next Sunday, the public came to my rescue. The entire editorial page of the *Commercial Appeal* was full of letters to the editor praising my work ethic, "smarts and energy," and criticizing the councilmen for "childish" and "unbecoming fits of temper," "personal vendettas," as "bullies" "attacking" me, and for their "arrogance," and rudeness.[1238] Another person added that the other councilmembers were jealous of my "experience, respect" and the thirteen years of "dedication" and "attention" given to my constituents as "the only bright spot we had on this council."[1239] The letters were heartening.

To his credit, years later, Jones apologized to me, which I whole-heartedly accepted, and we stay in touch over Facebook. A former police officer, he served twelve years on the Memphis City Council, and points to his securing neighborhood grants for the council district as a major accomplishment.

And Joe Brown also made peace with me, as later explained in this book. Brown served five terms, and ultimately was elected Shelby County General Sessions Court clerk in 2019. As a councilmember, he cites his record for advocacy for a living wage, support for working men and women, and protecting seniors in independent living facilities.

A woman submitted a letter to the editor commending my "grace, dignity and decorum," intelligence and experience that deserves "respect" of all other councilmembers.[1240] A man wrote that "finally we have a new council member who is not afraid to speak the truth" with "impeccable" credentials.[1241] Others applauded me as an "honest workhorse" with "vision to think outside the box" who had "lit a fire" under the members, hoping that I could "break the cycle of conflict between the council and the mayor and get the council to pay more attention to the people they represent."[1242] Others simply expressed support for my efforts to repeal the twelve-year pension. The letters inspired me to press forward.

In addition, I received tremendous support from my constituents with emails, letters and phone calls, words of support such as "you go girl" at the post office or grocery store, an elderly missionary calling to pray with me over the phone, and even flowers.[1243] My response was to consistently speak well of the staff members assigned to me and advocate that council staff be brought under city civil service rules to avoid political manipulation or intimidation by anyone.

Not knowing what else might be said or done, I asked an Episcopal priest to stop by my council office to pray and placed several angel figurines on prominent display. Later, renowned Memphis artist Louise Dunavant autographed for me her painting of a family in a horse-drawn carriage and added a tiny blonde-haired angel in a pink robe at the bottom with the words "To Carol Chumney who is heaven-sent." The prayers and words of support encouraged me.

6

The tensions continued as I pressed forward to tighten up the twelve-year pension rule. Obviously, this did not make me popular with some council colleagues who might be affected by my proposed rule change. Yet, one retirement plan consultant described the twelve-year rule as "extremely rich." [1244]

The *Tri-State Defender* editors called me "feisty" and the council's "snub" of my efforts to fix the pension "one of the most self-serving attitudes exhibited by this body to date" and an "insult to our city's electorate."[1245] For example, Councilman Taylor, age thirty-five, could retire in four years and draw more than $9,000 a year, to total by age sixty about $190,000 (not including payments for the remainder of his life).[1246] And, another appointed official who had just retired at age forty-one was reported to draw over $22,000 a year (about $400,000 total through age sixty).[1247] The *Tri-State Defender* gave me a resounding endorsement as a "breath of fresh air," saying "RIGHT ON!"[1248]

However, some in the press took shots, with the *Memphis Flyer* editors accusing me of grandstanding for showing up to a county commission meeting (as an invited council member) and giving a TV interview.[1249] Referring to the "big story" of being called "stupid," they claimed it was a "highly public verbal walloping."[1250] Yet, they admitted that my position on the twelve-year pension was right because it was "a potential boondoggle for political appointees."[1251] Commenting on my "general assertiveness" like a "deer who races in front of the headlights and chooses to stare into them," they urged me to exercise "caution." [1252] Were they saying that I was too assertive as a councilmember or as a woman?

My response to the editors stated the obvious: Why on earth was I being ridiculed and accused of grandstanding for simply showing up for important meetings on public business?[1253] That some still believed it was in vogue to give a woman a public tongue-lashing was mind-boggling and disappointing. How was it that an individual with a bachelor's degree, a law degree, who was a thirteen-year veteran legislator, and a public servant rated public ridicule and verbal abuse from anyone for doing what I was elected to do?[1254] What Neanderthal and childish mindset would think that a man has a right to give a woman a public verbal walloping?[1255]

My letter added that while some might still prefer a giggling, silly, barefoot girl that they could control by making demands, this mindset creates problems for women in business. [1256] My response put everyone squarely on notice that I would not take verbal abuse or a "public walloping" from anyone without walloping right back. [1257] I concluded by adding, "thank goodness" that the newspaper had the sense not to put anyone's name on its editorial. [1258] Finally, since the editors agreed on my position on the pension rule repeal, I asked was the real reason for the editorial that they preferred a man to make the statements? [1259] Maybe in the future instead they would call out the offensive rhetoric and commend my assertiveness on behalf of the public for the repeal.

7

Yet, despite the continuing barrage of attacks, I stayed focused on my constituents. My first town hall meeting was on MLGW, the public utility.[1260]

My parents expressed concerns to me that their lights were always the last to be restored for service in power outages. Treating them the same as any other constituent, I told them to attend the meeting and ask the utility officials "why" directly. Later, this turned out to be a wise move on my part.

At the meeting, constituents voiced their disapproval of Joseph Lee's possible appointment as MLGW president, urging that a "seasoned executive, not a political appointee" be selected.[1261] In a reversal, Herenton had opened up the process after all with a two-week application period and a screening panel. Of the sixty-four applicants, the field would be narrowed to five, with Joseph Lee back in the running.[1262]

But Lee withdrew his name from consideration again, claiming to be too busy performing job duties as city finance director preparing the city's budget proposal.[1263] The other finalists had a wealth of utility experience. One applicant had served as president and CEO of the Nashville utility, and another as vice president and chief operations officer of MLGW with forty years at the utility.[1264] It would be interesting to see if the mayor would select from the qualified field or instead try to nominate Lee again.

8

The public debate on the repeal of the twelve-year pension rule continued, with city council attorney Allan Wade writing his own opinion editorial. Wade claimed that my proposed ordinance given to the press before distribution to councilmembers was an "attempt to influence public opinion" that was "contrary to the council's established rules of procedure."[1265] Yes, it certainly was an attempt to influence public opinion, and for transparency in a marked departure from the usual practice of some councilmembers to confer in backroom meetings in violation of the open meetings act.

Wade also called out the *Commercial Appeal* for editorializing against the twelve-year pension before hearing all of the facts.[1266] He submitted the op-ed at the request of several councilmembers. [1267]The city council attorney claimed that the number of elected and appointed officials who qualified for the twelve-year pension was comparatively small, calling me "petty" and "short-sighted" to "begrudge" them the benefit.[1268]

Wade contended that the city's pension plan was "actuarially sound." [1269] He claimed that the repeal of the twelve-year pension rule would "emasculate" the council's attempt to "promote equality in treatment among all plan participants."[1270] He opined that my proposed repeal ordinance was against the public's interest. [1271] Overall, it was an amazing effort to spin the outrageous twelve-year pension rule as good government.

When my proposed ordinance was presented to the council committee, only one councilmember moved for its passage, saying she did so to kill the proposal due to the lack of a second.[1272] While city officials argued that the twelve-year pension rule for elected and appointed officials did not affect taxpayers, I rhetorically asked if that were the case, then why not extend it to all city workers?[1273]

The next day, the *Commercial Appeal* ran an article with the headline that my pension repeal proposal was "not going anywhere." [1274]To the contrary, I was just warming up my efforts to build public support. Apparently, the reporter, Blake Fontenay, did not recall my daycare reform effort that had appeared hopeless at the start but later passed overwhelmingly.

Then the cartoons began. The *Memphis Flyer* included images of me posted by a local blogger.[1275] One was a cartoon of Herenton and me wearing a black wig with the words "Carol Chumney in That Girl" as a spoof of the famous Marlo Thomas character.[1276] The words "Daddy's Little Girl" were by my image. The accompanying article called me the "perfect modern woman (in an antiquated post-Jackie O sort of way)."[1277] It went on that she's "pretty, ambitious, stylish, and just a little ditzy. She's completely lost without a good, equally modern fella to help her figure out life's little mysteries—like how money works. She's just the kind of person to get way overdressed and tell the rest of the City Council to 'go fly a kite.' See if you could find the steamy if incestuous undertones that function as a leitmotif in this whimsical piece."[1278]

While as a youth, I had enjoyed the sit-com, the comparison and commentary was the stereotypical undermining of women's intelligence, independence, and financial acumen.

The second image was of me on a horse with the words "Lady Chumney Leads the Way."[1279] The depiction was described as "Lady Liberty leading the scruffy French rabble against their aristocratic overlords—an event that certainly foreshadows a dark reign of terror where blood tints the corpse-polluted Seine and heads roll in the street."[1280] While the newspaper's image was too small to see fully, the one posted on the blogger's site had my head superimposed on the body of a topless woman. I thought back to the "boutique lifestyle" claims in 2002 by Wharton and the stereotypical comments about my "personality." However humorous the images and commentary might be to some readers, it appeared that the sexist view of my assertive reform advocacy and coverage of me was not just continuing but swelling.

Instead of being depicted as a ditzy girl, or a topless blood-thirsty heroine, the *Commercial Appeal* political cartoonist Bill Day portrayed me as a damsel in distress at the top of a tower that poked through a circus tent identified as the Memphis City Council. [1281] The banner for the tower read "Carol Chumney."[1282] While Day's cartoon was better, and the council did seem like a circus at times, I was woman enough to fight my own political battles with or without assistance.

Yet, the *Commercial Appeal* editors did call on the council to revisit the proposed repeal of the pension rule out of respect to taxpayers.[1283] The editorial noted that an appointee had retired the week before after twelve years of city service and would immediately draw over $22,000 annually.[1284] Under the old rules, she would have had to retire three years later and wait sixteen more years before drawing her pension.[1285] The difference in taxpayer cost for just this one employee was more than $350,000.[1286]

Councilmembers who served twelve years would immediately draw $9,180 annually for life, regardless of age.[1287] The editors wondered if the council had created an "unfunded city liability" should an exodus of appointees raid the system.[1288] These words would resonate even more strongly less than a decade later when the state comptroller warned that the city pension liability was seriously underfunded.

The *Commercial Appeal* editors added that while my work on the issue had angered some of my colleagues, it also "demonstrates a degree of political courage that is in short supply in local government."[1289] They reasoned that the public deserved a fair hearing on the twelve-year pension repeal proposal at the next meeting, instead of what some might perceive as a "self-serving dodge" by the councilmembers.[1290] I appreciated the support for my efforts.

And, once again, members of the public defended me in letters to the editor of the *Commercial Appeal* saying that I understood the true meaning of being a "public servant" as opposed to a "politician" and was simply doing what my constituents wanted instead of trying to win "Miss Congeniality" or be a "Big Shot Public Figure."[1291] Another writer wondered why the supposedly fiscally conservative Republicans on the council did not back my pension repeal proposal.[1292] That was a fair question.

One writer called Allan Wade unprofessional as an attorney for calling me "petty and shortsighted" because I was one of his clients in my official capacity as a city councilmember.[1293] And, the president of the local Democratic women's group wrote that she admired me for refusing to respond negatively to the verbal attacks, noting my character, experience, youth, diversity as a woman, skills as an attorney, and "strong work ethic."[1294] I felt gratified by the words of support.

Not giving up on my pension reform proposal, I intended to bring it up again before the city council committee. I had a long-term commitment to pushing it through and would be persistent, taking the time to build more public support.[1295]

9

At City Hall, Mayor Herenton presented his fiscal year budget to the city council, proposing to hire new police officers, pay raises for city workers, and other new expenditures, but no new taxes, and received a standing ovation.[1296] And the council reached a compromise with the mayor, approving twenty-six additional appointed positions to the 119 authorized by the city charter.[1297] The remaining 169 appointed during his term would remain until the end of 2007 and then revert to civil service.[1298]

With Joseph Lee out of the running for MLGW president, the Herenton administration pushed the city council, over my objection, to raise the salary for the position not to exceed $230,000.[1299] The field of candidates might have been different if the compensation had been set before advertising the application process.

As the council's MLGW bond probe continued with written questions sent to various players on the deal, Herman Morris (former MLGW president) responded that he had objected to the use of some firms Herenton recommended in favor of more experienced firms.[1300] But ultimately, Morris had acquiesced by adding FTN Financial with 20% of the bond work and another 10% divided between four small local or minority-owned firms.[1301]

As events continued to unfold, the *Democrat* newspaper, in an interview, re-explored the "big story" where I was called "stupid" by a council colleague after calling for an end to the "petty infighting," along with my push to repeal the twelve-year pension.[1302] I thanked my constituents for standing up for me, vowed to continue standing up for what was best for them, pledged to hold the line on property taxes, and reaffirmed my faith in the people and the democratic process. Ann Perry, the reporter, concluded in the story "that I was an independent Democrat with a strong desire to do what she thinks is best for Memphis."[1303]

With a different take, the *Memphis Flyer* sounded the alarm telling Herenton to "Watch Out, Willie!"[1304] Jackson Baker reported unsubstantiated rumors that I was considering a run for mayor and would count "on the gender factor which has propelled so many women, especially judicial candidates, to success in recent years."[1305] The article was curious, especially since the gender factor had never elected any women to the Memphis mayor's office. And why did the *Flyer* need to warn Herenton?

There being never a dull moment, Joseph Lee re-entered the field for MLGW president a *third* time for consideration, which presumably was orchestrated by Herenton.[1306] One outside candidate was quick to say that it seemed like Lee and Herenton were "joined at the hip."[1307] And an editorial by Wendi Thomas in the *Commercial Appeal* blasted the mayor.[1308] I said that the city's image could suffer if Lee were selected after appearing to have "favored son" status with "inside politics" as opposed to judging applicants by their actual qualifications.[1309] Others spoke out as well, including a suburban mayor on the screening committee arguing that the MLGW presidency should not be a training ground for a person who was inexperienced in the utility field.[1310]

Lee's supporters included councilmembers Edmund Ford Sr., Tom Marshall, and Stout Mitchell, citing Lee's recent work on the city budget with no new taxes that also increased spending.[1311] The letters to the editor of the *Commercial Appeal* claimed shenanigans by the mayor in pushing through the large pay increase during the time Lee had briefly withdrawn from consideration and a ruse with the real agenda being to put the utility up for sale.[1312] The newspaper editors agreed that Memphis' image was harmed "by the clumsy, convoluted path the selection process has followed."[1313] Clearly, Herenton never intended to nominate anyone other than Lee for the job.

Lee was approved at the next council meeting at a salary of $215,000, over my objection that the lack of notice of the vote blindsided those in the public who might have appeared to voice their objections.[1314] Herenton, speaking in support of Lee's nomination, admitted he had a bias against MLGW internal candidates. [1315] The mayor also complained of racism, comparing Lee to Marvin Runyon. The latter had served as chairman of TVA with no prior utility experience.[1316] But Runyon had been a CEO of a major automobile manufacturer. Herenton said that he had withdrawn Lee's nomination earlier due to the unfair targeting by the press.[1317]

In my remarks, I pointed out that Lee's salary would increase $95,000 from his city finance director position, and there was another more qualified applicant who had thirty-five years of utility experience. The selection process was a "sham," and there was not a real national search. Several other colleagues joined me in voting against the nomination, but Councilman Marshall decided to support Lee because of the way he had handled the city budget.[1318] Councilman Lowery agreed with me that Lee lacked utility experience, and the selection process was flawed.[1319]

Amidst rumors that he might resign as Memphis mayor due to ongoing unidentified FBI investigations, Herenton immediately proceeded to direct Lee to look into integrating functions of the separately run utility with city government.[1320] This raised a red flag with many utility employees and others about whether the mayor's real intentions were to dismember parts of the utility for sale.

As I observed in a letter to the *Tri-State Defender* that had editorialized in favor of the appointment, Lee went from supervising 83 employees in the city finance department to 2,700 at the largest three-service utility in the nation.[1321] Also, Herenton's playing the race card was disinguous since African Americans held all key government positions – the county and city mayor, superintendent of city schools, the city police director, and the former utility president whom Herenton had *dis*appointed.[1322]

My letter to the editor noted that the issue was not just Lee's appointment, but a matter of principled leadership instead of the continuing Memphis history of absolute mayoral control.[1323] I asked if the old system of oppression and doing something simply because you were the mayor was still alive today?[1324] Would the newspaper that had bravely and vigilantly "defended" those African Americans who were oppressed and not given a voice in the past ignore its long-standing articulated principles of equal justice?[1325] The sham nomination process orchestrated by the mayor was reminiscent of complaints made about past Memphis machine politics and autocratic city leadership in the first half of the 20th century.

With Lee's appointment finalized, Herenton abruptly announced that he was the target of an FBI investigation on the MLGW bond deal.[1326] Councilman Tom Marshall called for an end to the council's investigation, saying that the FBI was better suited to handle the matter even though the FBI had not contacted him.[1327] Councilman Sammons backpedaled from the "Watergate-style investigation," now claiming in the *Commercial Appeal* that it was never meant to be a "criminal inquiry."[1328] Rumors of a backroom deal to get the council to back off followed.[1329]

I opposed ending the council's inquiry on the basis that the FBI would only investigate criminal law violations and not violations of the city charter and oath of office. Further, if the council did not proceed, records might be sealed from the public on the matter for years.[1330] Allan Wade, the city council attorney who was a co-counsel on the bond deal, advised the council to suspend the investigation.[1331]

10

Changing the subject, Herenton floated a proposal for the city to take the $86 million provided annually to the city schools and instead use it to lower property taxes, fund preschool education and other city needs, and bolster the reserve fund.[1332] My concern, among other things, was that the city legally could not reduce its school funding, although not required to provide the monies initially. Also, the timing was puzzling since Herenton's budget for the year did not raise taxes but increased spending and was presented with rosy financial projections for the city. Councilman Sammons likened Herenton's proposals to a "Molotov cocktail approach of throwing a bomb in a room" to try to generate debate and then shelving the proposal with everybody going back to sleep.[1333] The analogy was not far from the truth.

The news also was that a group called Concerned Citizens of Memphis proposed a referendum for the November ballot that would return the pension requirements for city elected and appointed officials to at least fifteen years of experience, commencing when the age and years of experience equaled at least seventy-five.[1334] John Lunt, a financial consultant led the effort with others to collect over 67,000 signatures for a November referendum. However, the city legal staff issued an opinion the next day that the referendum did not comply with the state constitution and therefore it was rejected.[1335]

Unfazed, the group filed another petition with the election commission to establish a charter commission to review the pension rule issue. It also considered a lawsuit to force the referendum to be placed on the ballot.[1336] But, as opposed to a simple vote by the council to repeal the cushy twelve-year pension rule, it might take two years to be undone through the charter commission process. [1337]

My first year on the council certainly began as a wild ride, with all of the accusations, efforts to reform the pension abuses, investigations, and name-calling. But I pushed forward with my focus on doing the job the voters elected me to do.

21

Iraqi Delegation Banned
from City Hall

1

While the council job generally involved only local politics, in 2004, an international issue took the spotlight. In late July, the Memphis Council for International Visitors ["MCIV"] contacted me to participate in a meeting with a delegation of Iraqi leaders touring the United States. The group, including mayors, state officials, and community officials, represented diverse religions and factions.[1338] They were in America to learn about how to set up democratic processes in Iraq.[1339] They also wanted to know how to navigate civil rights conflicts.[1340] Accordingly, my office notified the appropriate City Hall office and sent out a press release to invite council colleagues and inform the press and the public about the opportunity.

The mayor's office never responded. And council chairman Joe Brown asked that the group meet elsewhere than City Hall. So, the organization reserved a room at the Memphis Convention & Visitors Bureau offices.[1341]

The seven-member delegation was sponsored by the U.S. State Department, having met with U.S. Secretary Donald Rumsfeld and Deputy Secretary of State Richard Armitage before arriving in Memphis in early August.[1342] Apparently, their driver did not get the memo on the venue change and delivered the Iraqi delegation to City Hall. They were then barred from entering City Hall by the edict of City Council Chairman Joe Brown, who claimed it was too dangerous to let them enter the building.[1343]

Jody Callahan with the *Commercial Appeal* reported Brown to have said that he would "evacuate the building and bring in the bomb squads" if the

208

delegation entered, which he denied. [1344] He admitted saying, "We don't know exactly what's going on" and "Who knows about the delegation, and has the FBI been informed?"[1345] and "We must secure and protect all the employees in that building."[1346]

The police chief even met the delegation at the entrance and denied them entry. The group was then taken to the Memphis Convention & Visitor Bureau offices, where I was the only public official to meet with them and answer their questions.[1347] At the convention bureau's offices, I did not know of Brown's comments and that the official delegation had been treated as if they were terrorists at City Hall. Callahan's report was quite extraordinary. In the city and county mayors' absence, I gave them keys to the city, cufflinks, a book about city government, and council certificates.[1348] The story of their ban from Memphis City Hall made international news.[1349]

Members of the delegation were later robbed at gunpoint on the Memphis Mid-America Mall.[1350] As the negative news coverage spread, other local elected officials scrambled to find and greet the delegation before they left town to avoid the public fallout.

The public was outraged. There were numerous letters to the editor of the *Commercial Appeal* expressing shame and embarrassment that Brown "was so stupid" as to ban from City Hall the delegation "from a war-torn land that has had little or no freedom, hoping to learn from us about freedom and democracy."[1351] The mayors were criticized as well for not making time to meet with them, although Wharton ultimately did.[1352] I was praised for "graciously" welcoming and caring about the group, doing my best to give a positive impression of Memphis, and salvaging "a little respect for the city."[1353] It was my pleasure, as the delegation members were warm and cordial despite the City Hall slight.

One writer nominated Brown for a "Most Embarrassing Moment by a City Official" award.[1354] A tongue-in-cheek writer encouraged the city to adopt a policy of general racial profiling.[1355] Another letter to the editor called the city leaders "childish, moronic and rude."[1356] A local pastor called Brown's actions "boorish, unpolished and unsophisticated."[1357] The writers said that Brown should apologize to the delegation.[1358] The pressure mounted as to how to rectify the uncalled for City Hall ban.

One writer wondered whether the Iraqis were provided with separate water fountains and bathrooms.[1359] *Commercial Appeal* cartoonist Bill Day wasted no time with a cartoon the next day showing doors to the Memphis

City Council with the words "No Coloreds" on one representing past segregation, and another with the words "No Iraqis." [1360] In the letter, the writer added
that only I understood "the concept of the conflict in Iraq and how to greet
visiting dignitaries who have nothing to offer us." [1361] He wondered, "would
Nelson Mandela have been treated in a similar fashion?" [1362] I only hoped that
the remainder of the delegation's visit would be conflict-free.

A writer's comments, published in the *Los Angeles Times,* stated that it
probably was a blessing that the delegation was not admitted to Memphis
City Hall. [1363] James Woodward wrote, "Can you imagine how much longer
this rebuilding [in Iraq] might take had they been allowed to observe the
messed-up political machine in Memphis?" [1364] Certainly, this was not the
image Memphis wanted to project to the delegation or the world.

The editors of the *Commercial Appeal* commended the group's "resilience,"
"grace," and "good humor" after living under the regime of Saddam Hussein
and then being humiliatingly snubbed at the Memphis City Hall. [1365] Deputy
Secretary Richard Armitage, in a conference call, expressed regret to the delegation when they arrived in Los Angeles. [1366] The head of the U.S. State
Department's Office of International Visitors joined them, and the Santa
Monica councilmembers greeted them with roses for the women and pins for
the men. [1367] The delegation asked questions about how to manage the diversity
of race and religion in local government. [1368]

After a call from Secretary of State Collin Powell's office, Mayor Herenton
and all of the city councilmembers, except me, signed a written apology to
the delegation. [1369] Since I did meet with the delegation, there was no reason
for me to apologize.

Some councilmembers, such as Jack Sammons, incredibly attempted to
cast blame on me for the fiasco. [1370] One news station even ran a hatchet job
story about my perceived aggressiveness, which was clearly an effort to divert
attention from those responsible for the international embarrassment and
make me a scapegoat. I couldn't believe the attack on the only politician who
handled the situation appropriately.

So, I sent out a press release containing the irrefutable proof with my
emails and a report by my legislative staff member Danielle Spears, showing
that we did notify the appropriate persons at City Hall well before the delegation arrived. My memo to the news station chastised it for succumbing
to the pressure in this particular "closed society" to adhere to "groupthink,"
instead of simply telling the truth.

My memo expressed that the media should show the advances that women have made in education, business, politics, the legal profession, and medicine, and tear down the walls of stereotypical perception, name-calling, and plain old-fashioned disrespect. Instead, the news station had perpetuated sexism with its news story's negative connotations attributed to me for the same assertive behavior for which it praised men. I called for the news station moving forward to adhere to its highest professional journalistic standards and to its responsibility to all people to present the truth.

With efforts to make me the scapegoat blocked by my irrefutable proof, Councilman Brown held a press conference nearly a week after the delegation had left town and apologized for his "misunderstanding."[1371] But he still maintained that he had acted to ban the delegation from City Hall not out of prejudice but to protect them and City Hall employees. [1372] His apology was denounced by the *Commercial Appeal* editors as "inadequate, unhelpful and left the impression that he would do the same thing again under similar circumstances."[1373] Also, they noted that Brown did not admit his own "error in judgment" and that the incident "reinforced unfortunate stereotypes about Memphis and the South."[1374] Brown's apology didn't fly with the editors, or with the general public for that matter.

The *Los Angeles Times* editorialized that "one of the unplanned, perhaps fruitful lessons the Iraqi visitors might now learn about American democracy is that it permits all sorts of freedoms, including the freedom to be stupid."[1375] While Brown was smart on many issues related to serving his constituents, in my view this was not his finest moment. In fact, it was poetic justice that Brown, who only months earlier had been part of the local public lashing out where I was called "stupid," was now called out by that newspaper as "stupid" internationally.

And the *New Orleans Times-Picayune* criticized Brown's actions as an example of "how easy it was for ill-informed demagogues to commandeer a microphone" and that it lacked in Southern hospitality. [1376] The *Memphis Flyer* in Chris Davis's column found "no excuse" for the delegation to have been "stood up, robbed, and turned away at the door of local government."[1377] Brown's apology didn't quell the editorial condemnation of his actions.

More letters to the editor poured into the *Commercial Appeal*, now outraged at Brown's "half-hearted apology," questioning his motives, and calling for him to resign.[1378] One writer said that Memphis now had a "black eye" nationally, with me as "the only one with enough dignity and acceptance to act as an ambassador for our city."[1379] I appreciated her compliment and was glad to have been there to help the delegation see that some in Memphis wished them well.

Thereafter, at the U.S. State Department's request, the city council mounted a letter-writing campaign apologizing to the Iraqi delegation and inviting them back to Memphis. Hundreds of these letters were hand-carried by the department of state to the delegation before they left the country.[1380] They certainly got an eye-opening experience on how the freedom of democracy can also be messy.

22

—

A Reformer

1

With the Iraqi delegation fiasco behind us, a new pension scandal erupted involving a former long-time county employee. Tom Jones, the former top county mayoral aide to Rout and others, had pled guilty to federal and state criminal charges for misuse of his county credit card. [1381]He now was reported by the *Memphis Flyer* to have been rehired briefly and approved "administratively" for a nearly double monthly pension. [1382]

Although the board subsequently voted to rescind the pension increase, the press openly wondered how Shelby County Mayor A C Wharton, chairman of the retirement board, could claim that he didn't know about the prior approval.[1383] The public was already in an uproar about the city's twelve-year pension rule for elected and appointed officials, with efforts underway by a citizen's group to put that matter up for a public referendum.[1384]

As John Branston with the *Memphis Flyer* noted, Wharton was elected "pledging that honesty and openness would replace the culture of entitlement."[1385] Instead, he wrote, it was replaced with a "culture of suspicion" of a "back-door way for insiders" of getting things done in county government.[1386] This was precisely the reason why I had run for county mayor in 2002 on a reform platform.

The report on the resulting investigation implicated two of Wharton's aides, and several other county officeholders.[1387] Aide Bobby Lanier's close association with Wharton was well-known. [1388]The *Memphis Flyer's* Chris Davis opined that the county mayor was either "disingenuous to a fault" or "astonishingly naïve and uninformed."[1389] Even the other aide, Susan Adler Thorp, was reported to have contradicted the county mayor's claim that he didn't know about the approval before the story broke.[1390] Lanier resigned as Wharton's executive assistant.[1391] Yet, it was apparent that the backroom politics was still the modus operandi in county government.

On the City Hall side, the press pondered whether or not Mayor Herenton, who professed to be a Democrat, would endorse George W. Bush in the 2004 U.S. Presidential race. [1392] Herenton had endorsed Republican Lamar Alexander for the U.S. Senate (even appearing on the stage election night).[1393] However, instead of fooling with national politics, the mayor became embroiled in a new controversy of his own by firing his fifth police director. [1394]The termination was prompted by the mayor's intervention (or interference depending on whom you asked) in the arrest of a drug-dealing suspect not far from City Hall. [1395]

In the aftermath, John Branston analyzed similarities between Herenton and former Memphis Mayor "Boss" Crump but did not find Herenton to be a dictator. [1396] Crump had ruled the city for decades, with mixed reports of his strong-arm tactics that also helped the city be dubbed as America's Cleanest City and Quietest City at the time. [1397] The fact that the question had to be asked whether Herenton was autocratic spoke for itself.

As the controversies swirled in both county and city government, news reports emerged about the growing support for a 2007 mayoral candidacy by me. Once again, my credentials were marginalized in an article by Baker with the *Memphis Flyer*, writing that I had occupied only a "lower rung of the Democratic leadership" for a "brief period." [1398] In fact, I had served as the House Majority Whip for two years and also as one of only thirteen standing committee chairs in the state house. Moreover, I had held other committee leadership positions the other years, except for my first term.

My efforts to repeal the twelve-year pension for elected and appointed officials were now said to be "abrasive" or "showboat tactics," as attributed to Herenton and some colleagues.[1399] My growing support outside of Democratic circles with local conservatives who simply wanted good government was reported to baffle some others.[1400] However, in the end, Baker acknowledged that my "doggedness" and "reputation as a reformer" had enabled daycare reform. [1401] The columnist further admitted my viability as a serious mayoral contender. [1402] The idea of bringing needed reforms to the mayor's office excited me, despite the distortion of my hard-earned record and local reform efforts.

2

Meanwhile, Herenton pushed forward with his effort to make the separate MLGW public utility a city division, now seeking to eliminate golden parachutes for its executives.[1403] He criticized the $200,000 severance package for Herman Morris, in particular, who also was awarded a full pension.[1404] Perhaps this was Herenton's way to get back at Morris for questioning his recommended changes in the huge MLGW bond deal transaction. The city mayor wrote MLGW President Joseph Lee that Morris's staff had developed severance packages more suitable to the private sector.[1405]

The *Commercial Appeal* editors used this opportunity to take up the banner again for restoring "sanity" with a repeal of the city's twelve-year pension rule for elected and appointed officials as an "inestimable" obligation.[1406] They noted my efforts, as well as that of Concerned Citizens of Memphis, which was gathering signatures for a charter commission referendum.[1407] I was still pushing my repeal ordinance.

Councilman Scott McCormick proposed increasing to twenty-five years the time elected and appointed officials had to serve to qualify for a pension. But his proposal to only apply it to any employees hired after the the resolution's adoption was called "probably too lenient" by the *Commercial Appeal*.[1408] This would allow all current elected and appointed officials who served the requisite time to keep the twelve-year pension.

The newspaper editors found McCormick's explanation that the legal staff advised him to draft the proposal so as to not apply to any current city employee "an overly conservative interpretation of the law."[1409] They reasoned that a state attorney general opinion should be sought as to whether a revised rule could include some of the city's current elected and appointed officials.[1410] In their view, the council would be "particularly courageous" if it expanded the proposal to include some current city employees "since some council members could be personally affected."[1411] Unfortunately, city councilmembers are not authorized to ask for a state attorney general opinion.

3

With the pension and MLGW reform efforts underway, in August 2004, the Herenton administration unexpectedly sought approval of a payroll tax from the city council. The push for a payroll tax did not square with the catapult of Joseph Lee into the office of president at MLGW on the heels of praise for his no new taxes city budget prowess and assurances that the Herenton administration could manage a $27 million shortfall.[1412] The mayor also had the city file a lawsuit against the Shelby County Election Commission for refusing to put the proposed payroll tax on the November ballot.[1413] The constitutionality of the tax was in question, as well as whether it could be enacted by the council with a referendum, without state legislative approval.

I called the payroll tax proposal a "half-baked idea" without justification based upon the city administration's representations that no new taxes were needed in the recent budget process. There were no parameters in the mayor's payroll tax proposal regarding how much the average family would pay, how much property taxes would be lowered, or analysis of the impact on business development.

Herenton, after losing the first round in court on the proposed payroll tax referendum, suddenly came clean to the city council and public by announcing that he had taken $30 million out of the city's rainy day fund to close the year's books.[1414] Only two months after the council had approved his budget with no new taxes, Herenton now said that the city needed "austerity measures" and a property tax increase.[1415] The mayor blamed the 2003 windstorm, overtime costs, and low sales tax collections.[1416]

Skeptical, I believed the mayor's revelation to be either a manufactured crisis or evidence that the administration had not given the council accurate information during the year's budget process. I immediately asked the administration's finance director for a comparison of sales tax collections from the past two months with the past two years.[1417]

I, along with Councilmen E.C. Jones and Brent Taylor, accused Herenton and his staff of deliberately withholding budget information.[1418] Taylor speculated whether Lee would have been approved as MLGW head if the city's true budget picture had been disclosed at the time of the vote on his nomination.[1419] While a financial report was said to have been presented in April, Joseph Lee had claimed that the city could make up the projected deficit with cuts in expenditures and a hiring freeze.[1420]

While Joseph Lee maintained no flaw in his budget analysis, city officials reported that another $28 million shortfall was projected for the fiscal year 2005.[1421] The revenue projections fell short in every revenue category, including parking fees, court fines, and property taxes.[1422]

Shocked at the mayor's announcement, I investigated independently. I found that the University of Memphis's Sparks Bureau of Economic Research had forecast much lower anticipated revenues for the city than were followed in the budget. When I contacted the Sparks Bureau, I found that the city administration had used the most optimistic revenue projections. Yet, the city policy required "realistic" and "conservative" revenue projections "in order to minimize the adverse impact of a revenue shortfall."[1423] During the budget hearings, the council was never told that the city administration's $493 million revenue projection for 2005 was $28 million above the Sparks' Bureau's mid-range forecast of $465 million.[1424] No wonder there was now a shortfall!

After weeks of asking the city finance department for its own worksheets and back-up documentation for the higher revenue projections that led to the city budget crisis, I was finally told there was no such thing. Apparently, the administration decided to ignore the city policy and use the Sparks Bureau economists' higher revenue projections. I presented my own report to the city council, analyzing budget data back to 2003.[1425] I believed that the mayor and Lee had known of the city's revenue problems long before they told the council and the public.[1426] I demanded answers and accountability. The council demanded quarterly budget reports from that day forward.

The mayor wrote the councilmembers a letter on September 21, 2004, which called for the council to adopt alternative revenue sources. In his letter, the mayor set out that he had tried to bring in new revenues by proposing a merger of the city/county governments, advocating for casino gambling, and suggesting utilizing assets at MLGW, which he said were all rejected. The mayor called the *Commercial Appeal* editors and local "timid" politicians "Monday morning quarterbacks" in addressing the financial issues facing the city. He said that some elected officials "are consumed with other political agendas and aspirations" and that "getting on television grandstanding and criticizing the administration would not address the challenges."

In his letter, Herenton asked that the council work "cohesively" with his administration and consider withholding any city funding of the schools to add another forty to eighty million dollars to the city budget. He believed such action might force consolidation of the schools.

The letter was not well-received. Both Councilman Brent Taylor and I fired off our responses to the mayor.

Taylor found the mayor's condemnation of anyone who disagreed with him "tiresome." He further spelled out what he termed a *"pattern of deception* emanating from" the mayor and his administration. Taylor claimed that the mayor "intentionally withheld plans to terminate Herman Morris and install Joseph Lee as president of MLGW" from Taylor and two other councilmembers, causing them to give "inaccurate testimony before the bond rating agencies" regarding the MLGW bond transaction. He added that the mayor "duped" the city council about the city's fiscal condition to get Lee's nomination approved.

Taylor also referenced the mayor's denial of attempting to "steer bond work" to the Little Rock law firm. Taylor no longer trusted the mayor, questioned his judgment, and had lost respect because of his "ill-advised comments." Taylor's philosophy on how to address the budget problem was simply to reduce spending.

My letter mentioned the standing ovation given to the mayor in April when he stood before the city council and presented what he said was a balanced budget. The budget was approved in the summer with no new taxes, new police officers, and pay raises for city employees. Yet, he now announced in September that "austerity measures" were needed, the administration had taken $30 million from the reserve fund and called for tax increases. I did not support his solution of a city money grab by cutting funds for kids in the schools. Nor did I support taking cost-savings from MLGW instead of passing them onto all ratepayers, many of whom were struggling to pay their high utility bills.

From my own subsequent independent research, I found his budget was based upon liberal and creative revenue projections. The city administration had yet to provide any rational basis for its high revenue projections, which were the real reason for the now exposed budget shortfall. No one had been held accountable for the actions that violated the city's fiscal policy.

Next, I recited the series of fiasco's since January 2004, including (1) the nomination of Mr. Lee as head of MLGW despite a national search that produced candidates with far superior qualifications; (2) the FBI investigation of the MLGW bond deal; (3) the interference with a drug bust by the mayor personally and the sudden firing of the police director; (4) the failure of his administration to respond to requests for assistance to meet with the local Iraqi delegation which resulted in international embarrassment to our city; (5) bringing the city council and the people a budget that didn't hold up after only two months; and (6) continuing a controversial appointment for chair of the Alcohol & Beverage Commission who was a key witness in a federal investigation involving a city contractor.

My letter pointed out to the mayor that when I raised questions about these matters, his general response was not to "cohesively work together" but to disparage my character, demeanor, and call names. He publicly chastised anyone who had an opposing view as having ulterior motives, but we were supposed to accept anything he said as gospel.

I found it ironic that he accused councilmembers of "grandstanding" when we simply asked why *he* had "grandstanded" in his April budget speech, misrepresenting that the city was in sound financial shape. I found it ironic that he now raised the issue of "timidity" for not blindly accepting his new budget recommendations when only a few months earlier, he had called me a "mean, angry and reckless" woman for refusing to support his nomination of Lee. I found it ironic that he called for leadership in his letter when he was the one who had led the city into this "mess." I found it ironic that he said now was the time to be proactive and make leadership decisions when the appropriate time was back in April when he presented his budget. I found it ironic that he now claimed that reducing expenditures further would impose serious disruption to government when earlier he had forced through huge pay raises for himself and his chief of staff.

I wrote to the mayor that he had forgotten himself. The City of Memphis did not belong to him but all of the people. Somewhere he had crossed the line from serving to dictating. Understandably, this did not create an atmosphere for "working cohesively together." In any event, I had consistently avoided retaliating with the same unprofessional tactics. Instead, I had acted responsibly by putting several proposed budget cuts on the table and called for other councilmembers to do the same. While I would continue to work with anyone and everyone who wanted to move Memphis ahead, in my opinion, where there is smoke – there is fire. Because of the smoke at City Hall, I called for a state audit of the books and continued to push for answers and accountability and expect answers like the rest of the public.

Wendi Thomas, a columnist with the *Commercial Appeal,* set out the dramatic events since the first of the year, and Herenton's erratic behavior at the time, calling him "consistently crazy" for his letter.[1427] She referenced Herenton's offer to "meet" Taylor outside in a "contentious" council committee meeting in February, his calling me "mean, angry and reckless," and his press conference in August to talk about the prior police director's alleged poor performance after his *dis*appointment related to the drug bust.[1428]

In my op-ed to the *Memphis Business Journal*, I reminded the public of (1) the mayor's $20,000 pay raise in 2003; (2) the nearly $16,000 pay raise for his chief of staff in 2004; and (3) that the city finance director, who put the inadequate budget together, was now making $215,000 as MLGW president.[1429] My conclusion was that the multi-million dollar shortfall was no surprise to the mayor or his finance team, bad news for the people of Memphis, and "[n]ot too bad for those at City Hall who got what they wanted when the real numbers and the rest of us were kept in the dark."[1430] Asking questions and scrutinizing the budget might not make me popular with some at City Hall or media reporters who want to go along with the status quo, but the $28 million budget gap was another example of why "groupthink" was harmful to the public.[1431]

Ultimately, the *Commercial Appeal* editors agreed with me that the budget deficit had grown because of the "badly miscalculated" revenue and expense projections during the budget process.[1432] They also ran a sarcastic cartoon of the mayor seated in front of a flow chart with "The Honorable Dr. Willie Herenton, CEO and Mayor of Memphis, Genius and Infallible Leader Extraordinaire" at the top of the chart, followed underneath by "God the Creator," then under it, the "United Nations," "U.S. President" and "Congress."[1433] At the very bottom of the flow chart was "Dog Catcher," "HFord Jr." and "City Council."[1434] The financial mismanagement of the Herenton administration and his prideful response to criticism were front and center.

4

Perhaps because of the controversy from the budget crisis, my and others' continued calls for reform of the twelve-year pension rule and the pension charter referendum drive, the city council finally adopted Councilman Scott McCormick's pension rule change proposal.[1435] My motion to apply the new rules to as many current city officials and councilmembers as legally possible did not receive a second.[1436] After the vote, some 300 eligible employees already employed still qualified for a pension after twelve years of service regardless of their age.[1437]

McCormick was given a slap on the back by the *Commercial Appeal* editors for his proposal as a "fast learner," although he had decided to fold instead of holding out for more comprehensive reform. [1438] However, the editors admitted that "it's not so clear that the rules couldn't have been changed to include at least some employees who haven't reached the twelve year mark."[1439] The legal advice relied upon by councilmembers was from some city attorneys who might gain from the twelve-year pension.[1440] The council disregarded my outside attorney's opinion provided to them that my proposal to apply the repeal more broadly was legal.[1441]

In the newspaper, McCormick said that his primary reason for proposing the measure was to reduce city insurance coverage liability for the twelve-year retirees.[1442] He admitted that the purported purpose for the twelve-year pension rule plan of keeping good employees, was in fact, an incentive for those employees to leave early.[1443]

Of twenty-seven others who had already retired under the rule, the *Commercial Appeal's* Jacinthia Jones reported that the former finance director was drawing over $30,000 annually for life.[1444] The article noted that the former comptroller, city treasurer, city attorney, chief prosecutor, and city engineer were all receiving salaries in the same range.[1445] Many had only twelve years on the job at City Hall and were well below age 55.[1446]

It had been a bloody reform battle, but in the end, the cause was partly won.

23

Veritable Tribune of the People

1

Continuing to grapple with the budget crisis, Herenton proposed hiring freezes, cuts, and layoffs of temporary workers to save about $32 million. However, I projected the shortfall to be closer to $36 million and advocated for additional cuts, including food, riverfront development funds, and non-essential computer purchases for an additional $13 million in savings.[1447] I reasoned that the leaders should first propose a reasonable budget and make cuts. Only after doing that did you go to the people and ask for a tax increase.

My concern was that if additional cuts were not made and the Sparks Bureau figures were again accurate, then there would be another huge shortfall in the spring, and the rainy day fund would be depleted further.[1448] The city administration claimed that it had hired an expert consultant to help stave off a reduction in the city's bond rating. Yet, I pointed out that there was no room for error to preserve the city's bond rating and that making additional proposed cuts was the most prudent fiscal policy. Because this was not Monopoly money, but the "people's money," I advocated for greater stewardship, a more straightforward and less adversarial and politicized process, with the setting aside of personal agendas and animosities even though it might not be politically convenient.

As the council struggled with the budget dilemma, I called for the Tennessee Comptroller to audit the city's books.[1449] The council would have to redo the current year's budget, and make cuts for the new fiscal year, which would adversely impact each department's operations. Because the mayor already had used reserve funds designated for a crisis, the task was much more complicated since cuts were needed to be made in the middle of a fiscal year.

More abuses came to light when the new MLGW president disclosed that the utility had expensive perks for high-ranking officers. A million-dollar life insurance policy had been given free to the president that cost ratepayers $45,000 a year.[1450] Fifty-nine managers were privileged with eight hundred dollars a month car allowances, included in their pension calculation.[1451] The revelations angered many citizens and fostered rumors that Herenton asked Lee to make cuts at the utility to prepare it for sale.[1452]

New alarms were also sounded about whether MLGW executives were leaving *en masse* after the resignation of three vice presidents and the elimination of the senior vice president positions.[1453] Instead of calling Lee on the phone, Herenton oddly sent a letter to the MLGW board asking it to tell Lee to slow down on the reorganization.[1454] The board delayed action on the elimination of the costly life insurance policies for executives for further study.[1455] I asked Lee so many questions at the next city council meeting, including whether or not he had plans to cut two more MLGW vice president positions as part of a "groupthink" purge, that some of his councilmember supporters were angry.[1456]

2

Thereafter, new revelations from the FBI's MLGW bond inquiry hit the press. Councilman Tom Marshall disclosed that a New York attorney for J. P. Morgan had received an FBI grand jury subpoena for business records.[1457] While rumors of Herenton's recent unexplained absence from City Hall grew, he hastily reappeared, claiming he had been busy at work on a planned reorganization to consolidate certain MGLW and city functions.[1458] He further claimed that the city's projected $27 million shortfall would be absorbed.[1459]

In response, I turned in new questions to City Councilman Tom Marshall, which he then sent to the various players in the MLGW bond deal. Herenton responded that his son was not involved in the deal. However, the mayor admitted that he had discussed his view with his son that local and minority firm professionals should be involved.[1460] Former City Attorney Robert Spence claimed attorney-client privilege, even though the questions were from the city council.[1461] Herman Morris and Joseph Lee had not responded.[1462] First Tennessee Bank had only provided a partial response. Due to the lack of responses, Councilman Marshall indicated that he would ask the council to issue subpoenas if they were not forthcoming.[1463]

The *Memphis Flyer* reported that all of the documents produced probably would end up on my desk as the only attorney on the city council.[1464] While the reporter, John Branston, claimed the documents produced showed no "smoking gun," my concern was the lack of responses by the attorney with the Little Rock law firm, and also J. P. Morgan, who both asked for more time.[1465]

Herman Morris finally responded that Herenton had said his son could not be involved in the deal.[1466] Morris also said he had no tape recordings about the deal in "my possession," which led some to wonder if he had turned some over to the FBI.[1467]

Councilman E.C. Jones and I both pushed to no avail for the council to hire an outside attorney and forward any council findings to the U.S. Attorney's office.[1468] The council did agree that members could turn in final questions by noon the following day for MLGW, attorneys, underwriters, and others involved in the deal to answer within two weeks.[1469] However, only a few weeks later, Councilman Jack Sammons stated that he regretted calling for a "Watergate-style" council investigation.[1470] The council voted to suspend the investigation without even receiving the answers to the questions outstanding.[1471]

Herenton labeled the investigation by the council and the FBI nothing more than "personal vendettas" by those trying to get him kicked out of office.[1472] He claimed that the news media, U.S. Attorney's office, and FBI were all "allies" "conspiring" to remove him as mayor.[1473] Herenton denied any connection between the Little Rock law firm's fundraiser and his pushing for its inclusion in the bond deal.[1474]

In the wake of the terminated council investigation, Baker with the *Memphis Flyer* reported divergent views about whether I was "a shameless showboat and opportunist, hell-bent on running for mayor in 2007," or "a gallant seeker after truth, justice, and good government—a veritable tribune of the people."[1475] Not to be deterred, I opposed the council dropping the MLGW bond investigation.

Although I had submitted questions for the mayor's son, Councilman Marshall claimed that it was his decision alone not to forward them for a response (but acknowledged conferring with other council members first).[1476] So, the mayor's son inexplicably was given a pass. Years later, when reminiscing about the abrupt ending of the "Watergate-style" MLGW bond deal investigation that had been called for by Sammons, Marshall would joke that it was "water under the bridge."

3

With the council investigation behind him, Herenton unveiled a plan to the city council to consolidate the auditing, legal, IT, and human resources functions of MLGW and the city. It appeared that Herenton's administration designed this as a way to find the extra $28 million he had said the city would absorb from the budget shortfall.[1477]

His plan included a forty-eight cent property tax hike and added two new senior-level city positions – deputy CAO and deputy COO with both earning $160,000 (the same salary as the mayor).[1478] This would obviously result in a raise from the $133,600 paid to the current CAO Keith McGee, with speculation that this might be an effort to increase the mayor's salary ultimately.[1479]

Herenton further called for freezing some MLGW management salaries and benefits as extravagant and not commensurate with comparable positions at City Hall. He criticized previous MLGW management for enriching itself at the expense of the ratepayers.[1480]

Finally, he proposed an MLGW rate policy based upon the income of customers. This was immediately questioned as being contrary to the TVA contract prohibiting any discrimination among customers.[1481]

The budget fallout continued. Many had trouble understanding how adding city positions at high salaries squared with the mayor's own statement that "austerity" measures were needed.

4

Despite the severe budget predicament, Herenton still moved forward with plans for his swank Christmas bash. His special city assistant, Pete Aviotti, sent letters on city stationery to seventy major contributors to the mayor asking for $1,000 each to pay for a "lavish" buffet, ice sculptures, decorations, and an open bar.[1482] As corporate donations were solicited, the press questioned if it was a campaign event since direct non-PAC corporate contributions to campaigns were prohibited under state law at that time. [1483]

All councilmembers, except Scott McCormick, skipped Herenton's annual bash at the Memphis Peabody Hotel.[1484] My absence was duly noted by one reporter, calling me the "councilwoman who would be mayor."[1485] I also did not attend the council Christmas dinner at the high-end Folk's Folly steakhouse feeling it was out of touch with the city's budget problems.

Instead, out of frustration with the "groupthink" at City Hall, I wrote an op-ed pointing out the inconsistencies in the press calling for "unity" between the council and the mayor.[1486] Only a few months earlier, the *Commercial Appeal* editors had criticized councilmembers for not asking enough questions to expose the false revenue projections in the administration's proposed budget, which were the genesis of the current mid-year budget crisis.[1487]

Even though Jackson Baker with the *Memphis Flyer* called my remarks spouting off again,[1488] my expressed view was that the desire for consensus was worthy. But the councilmembers should not check their brains or independent thinking at the door merely for the sake of "unity" in the budget talks. Instead, the council should leave its rubber stamp at home and bring common sense, professionalism, and civility to the table for an honest debate on what was needed.

When councilmembers forgo their independent civic responsibility, then the people lose the valuable democratic principles of well-reasoned debate, oversight, accountability, and checks and balances for their protection. From my perspective, when serious discussions involving a difference of opinion arose at City Hall, all too often the childish response was name-calling, character assassination, personal attacks, and threats. The result was a stifling of healthy debate, leaving the public upset over the antics and outbursts broadcast all over the Memphis region (and sometimes internationally).[1489]

My editorial pointed out that when I pressed for the council to send questions to the mayor's son about the MLGW bond deal, Councilman Edmund Ford Sr. gave fair warning that I had better watch my back.[1490] Only a few weeks earlier, he had raised his voice at a lobbyist after a council committee meeting. It came so close to a fistfight that the security officer on duty looked like he was about to draw his gun.[1491]

Some might see the lack of professionalism at City Hall as a hostile work environment. Herenton had set the tone at the beginning of the year, with his bullying, name-calling, browbeating, and personal attacks seeking to intimidate anyone who disagreed with him.

In my view, the behavior of Herenton was unprofessional. As I pointed out, no wonder some of the children and teenagers at a city school were beating each other up in school bathrooms and throwing food and chairs in the cafeteria – they were following the poor example set by some city leaders.[1492]

Since the council was responsible for nearly half a billion dollars of the people's money, it could not let the mayor dictate the corrections to the budget in light of his administration's flawed revenue projections. Otherwise, the council would be culpable as well for the city's fiscal problems. My editorial ended with a call for standards to be set by the council on how to conduct business more professionally.[1493]

5

In the wake of public outcry, MLGW President Joseph Lee announced that he and his management team would not take salary increases, and he would drop the proposed income-based rate structure for customers.[1494] Yet, despite the city's serious budget issues, Joe Brown and Edmund Ford Sr. were not so careful as outgoing and incoming council chairmen respectively. They unilaterally approved a whopping $12,000 pay raise for the council administrator to $99,999 and a $17,000 increase for the council deputy director to $75,000.[1495] Other staff members received large pay raises as well, in addition to a 3% city employee pay raise.[1496]

The mayor signed off on all the raises without the knowledge or consent of other councilmembers. He then spilled the beans during a budget committee meeting held to discuss the city's fiscal crisis.[1497] Herenton also now announced that he had decided to forgo his proposed promotion of two deputy directors at $160,000 a year.[1498] I called for a special meeting to rescind the council staff pay raises, which Brown refused.[1499]

Still trying to close the financial gap, Herenton presented four different budget choices to the council at a meeting just before the holiday break. He pitched a new stormwater fee, a fifty-four cent property tax increase, cutting the city school funding, or layoffs.[1500] Councilman Joe Brown opposed layoffs; Tom Marshall wanted to examine increasing fines and fees; Stout Mitchell called the proposed property tax increase "Wonderland;" and I pushed for the city to reexamine the tax breaks to selected companies.[1501]

With the year coming to a close, the budgetary problems still loomed, as I and a few others held out for cuts, while some on the council advocated for a tax increase.[1502] All watched for the New Year's Day prayer breakfast to see what mood Herenton would be in and whether he would blast away or strike a conciliatory tone with those with whom he needed to work on key issues.

Even Herenton admitted to the *Commercial Appeal* that he had considered quitting as mayor to devote full time to his real estate ventures because of the stress of the federal investigation and increased media scrutiny by the newspaper in particular.[1503] However, he also was said to want to preserve his "legacy" and decided to keep doing the job due to "immense pride" and because the "bastards against me...can't win."[1504] But, his comments were couched more in terms of his interest, as opposed to the public's interest in having a mayor with the fire in his or her belly to get things done for the people.

Overall, I felt good about my efforts for the year, and the fact that the public had voted me second best Memphian in the *Memphis Flyer* annual poll, just behind the Shelby County Mayor A C Wharton, and before Elvis![1505] Herenton didn't fare so well, being voted by the readers as Memphis Best Failure, ahead of the Pyramid and the Iraqi Delegation Visit.[1506] He also dominated the Best Nickname for a Politician category, with monikers such as "King Willie," "Slick Willie," "Wee Willie," and "Whacko Willie," among a few.[1507] It was a shame that matters had sunk so far from his prior popular support.

On a sad note, former State Rep. Pam Gaia, who was one of the women who had inspired me to run for office, passed at the age of fifty-eight. I attended her funeral and remembered the day I had met her in high school, as well as her kindness in giving me her pass to attend the Democratic Party's Midterm Convention in Memphis. She was one of the few positive role models at that time for a young girl like me who was interested in politics.

Gaia was remembered for her effectiveness, for her "crusades" to made generic drugs more available, and for nursing home reform.[1508] The *Commercial Appeal* editors took the opportunity to call me a "crusader" in my own right,[1509] in an apparent attempt to reinforce the Joan of Arc mantel they often cast upon me for merely speaking my mind and advocating for the truth—apparently oddities in local government.

24

You're Looking Good Carol!

1

Herenton began the 2005 New Year with a different tone, admitting that the city had been through a storm and that he had gotten "distracted" and "lost focus." [1510] The mayor boasted about the city's improved bond rating and other achievements at his own prayer breakfast. [1511] Comparing himself to the biblical figure Nehemiah, Herenton alluded to seeking a fifth term of office.[1512] But, he was also still reported to be considering leaving office to pursue real estate ventures. [1513]

At the breakfast, Herenton warned of upcoming reductions in city expenditures, such as garbage and police, and more unfilled potholes and uncut grass. He continued to advocate for eliminating the $86 million that the city provided annually for public school funding. [1514]Again, he pitched city and county consolidation, referring to the suburban municipalities as selfish. [1515]

Some questioned Herenton's stability, with John Branston in the *Memphis Flyer* reporting unsubstantiated rumors that Herenton was close to resigning.[1516] Herenton pledged to be more diplomatic in the upcoming year. [1517] Yet, Branston reported him to say that while most of the councilmembers are "basically good people and they don't have any animosity toward Willie Herenton," a few others "are not such good people" with "hidden agendas." [1518] It was not clear which people were good and which not so good in his view.

Not believing the administration's representations that the City of Memphis's bond rating held firm, I undertook my own internet research. In a press release, I was the first to advise the public that the Fitch bond rating agency had downgraded the city's general obligation debt rating from AA to AA -.[1519] Two other bond rating agencies had revised their outlooks from stable to negative.[1520] The downgrade was attributed to the city's poor planning, excessive spending, overly optimistic revenue projections, and diminishing reserves.[1521] The city reported only $27.5 million in reserves, about $20 million short of the 10% of the operating budget recommended standard.[1522] Thirty million had been used to cover the 2004 fiscal year shortfall. [1523]Another $28 million shortfall for the 2005 fiscal year was projected by city officials, which might deplete the city's entire reserves![1524]

Norm Brewer, with *WREG News*, complimented my "ever vigilant" work.[1525] He opined that although the failure to disclose the negative action by the rating agencies might not be a "full blown cover up," it raised questions as to the administration's "forthrightness" and whether the finances were in worse shape than admitted. [1526] Reminding readers of the adage that the cover-up is worse than the crime, the *Commercial Appeal* editorialized that the administration should immediately advise the council of any new adverse financial developments. [1527] Meanwhile, controversial radio talk show host Thaddeus Matthews began a petition recall drive to gather the needed 70,000 signatures to vacate the office of Memphis mayor.[1528]

With the budget issues at the forefront, action was taken on my call to repeal the large council staff pay raises unilaterally made by former Council Chair Joe Brown and approved by new Council Chair Edmund Ford Sr. The council revoked the raises (apart from the 3% given to all city employees) over Brown, Edmund Ford Sr., and Sammons's objections. [1529] Herenton had approved a $21,000 pay raise for the city council attorney, $20,000 for an administrative assistant, and $15,000 for a manager the previous year. [1530] Councilwoman TaJuan Stout Mitchell called the raises an "insult" to taxpayers and other city employees. [1531]

Citizens wrote letters to the newspaper complaining that Herenton had proposed cuts in public services and school funding, yet his and Lee's salary increased.[1532] Also, expenditures were made for the FedExForum, while police went without replacement equipment.[1533] And, the City of Memphis still owed millions in debt service on the empty Pyramid—now truly a tomb.[1534] The high crime and gangs were cited by many as the reason for the exodus of some to adjoining counties, with property values decreasing in the city, and increasing in the suburbs. [1535] They were right. The large pay raises made no sense in light of the financial crisis and the need to improve public safety and other essential city services.

2

Looking for a solution, Herenton proposed a meeting in the Pyramid to discuss education funding along with the consolidation of Memphis with Shelby County. Suburban mayors claimed they did not receive notice of Herenton's plans for a meeting, defended their towns' contributions to services funding, and reiterated their opposition to a consolidated government.[1536] Suburban citizens submitted vehement letters to the editor opposing the proposal. [1537]

Elected officials from state and local government, school board members, and even some suburban mayors attended the meeting. Herenton warned of a fiscal crisis in the county, claiming that the school funding formula would increase the county's required match for city school spending once annexations were completed.[1538] The mayor outlined his plan to consolidate city and county schools to create five school districts, each with a separate school board and superintendent, all headed by a chancellor of education.[1539] He asked for a twenty-member task force of city, county, suburban, and business leaders to study the proposal and make recommendations.[1540] Herenton pronounced that if the metropolitan government were formed, he would resign as mayor. [1541]

However, the meeting ended abruptly shortly after my suggestion that the consolidation of the police and fire departments be included in the work of the task force.[1542] I reasoned that County Mayor Wharton, under pressure, had ultimately said that he was open to the consolidation of law enforcement in the 2002 county mayor's race. Therefore, he should already be on board. Herenton angrily interrupted, saying, "I don't want to hear about her political campaign that she lost."[1543] He rudely added, "if you run again, you're gonna lose the next time too." [1544] With that, Councilman Brent Taylor stormed out of the meeting, and it adjourned. [1545] I was shocked at the mayor's harsh words toward me, merely making a recommendation on the best way to proceed. Wasn't that why the meeting was called in the first place?

Suburban mayors criticized Herenton's plan, while Wharton said he would first consult the county commissioners. [1546] In the aftermath, the county schools superintendent agreed that there was a funding crisis, and monies were needed to build new schools in the county due to the migration from the city. [1547]

However, although Herenton continued to push for consolidation of the schools after his outburst, the media and other councilmembers conceded that the issue needed a new messenger. [1548] Even Herenton agreed that the message was getting lost, calling himself "tall, dark and arrogant" and a "lightning rod." [1549] The consolidation issue had percolated for years in the community, with urban African Americans primarily opposing it in the earlier years and more white suburbanites fighting it later. [1550]

In the wake of the meeting, Herenton unilaterally undertook substantial cuts in services. He laid off 198 permanent full-time workers and about 1900 part-time temporary workers. [1551] Councilmembers had many suggestions on cuts that might have avoided some of the layoffs, such as forgoing the 3% pay raise, eliminating a proposed more than half a million dollar efficiency study, reducing work hours, and delaying other projects. [1552] The AFSCME union complained that they were not consulted about the layoffs as required in their Memorandum of Understanding with the City of Memphis and would have agreed to reduced hours as a concession. [1553]

Herenton claimed that the council's proposed cuts were too late, but the layoffs would only be temporary if the council adopted his hefty fifty-four cent property tax increase or cut millions in school funding. [1554] Indoor city pools were closed, summer camps and spring athletic leagues eliminated, grass not cut, and street repairs not made. [1555]

As I pointed out, my call earlier in the year for the mayor and council to cut an additional ten million dollars had gone unheeded. Because of the failure to act then, the choices were now more limited. In fact, the council had presented twenty-six cost-cutting recommendations to the mayor. Twenty-one of the recommendations were my proposals, including a pay raise rescission; review of millions in unspent monies for travel, food, furniture, professional services, cell phones, advertising, and computers; delay of some city construction projects; repeal of college tuition reimbursements for workers; and restructuring the government. [1556]

While the *Commercial Appeal* opined that state law might restrict the transfer of debt service funds for use in the operating budget, I proposed to delay construction projects to reduce the portion of the property tax allocated for that purpose and free up a larger allocation for operating expenses. [1557] The council decided to look, after all, to see if there were projects in the capital improvements budget to cut. [1558]

3

My efforts for accountability had not gone unnoticed. In the past, I had borne the brunt of some jokes, which was part of the price to aid journalism college students and be a good sport. The annual Gridiron show poked fun at politicians to raise money for journalism scholarships. In 2005, my potential mayoral candidacy was featured as the headliner.[1559] The chorus sang an entire number based upon the Broadway musical *"Hello Dolly,"* substituting the lyrics "You're looking Good, Carol." Another skit suggested that I might be a "nerd," but overall, the actress who played me was presented as the next mayor. Jackson Baker called it an "unofficial campaign launch." [1560]

Not letting the attention go to my head, I focused on the mayor's upcoming budget presentation. I proposed cutting the $27.5 million Beale Street Landing project ($17.5 million city funds); and the $238.8 million MATA light rail project that included tracks from the airport to downtown ($70 million city funds).[1561] While I support quality public transportation, one of my concerns was that light rail could decrease the car rental tax revenues dedicated to repayment of the FedExForum arena bonds. This would result in the city being on the hook for the difference. The light rail proponents apparently had not considered the bond funding issue.[1562] Also, the city's precarious financial situation made the timing of the enormous expenditure inappropriate.

The Riverfront Development Corporation ("RDC") ultimately withdrew its proposal from the riverfront's master plan for a land bridge that would require a dam and cost an estimated $78 million.[1563] Herenton had proposed it as far back as 1996. The expense of damming the harbor to create a lake and fifty-acre land bridge made it unpalatable in light of the city's serious financial situation in 2005. [1564]

Herenton formally presented his budget to the council with the proposed fifty-four cent property tax increase that would restore cuts, replenish reserves, give pay raises, and keep school funding. [1565]The mayor insisted that the city's financial crisis was a revenue problem and not a management problem. Others noted contrarily, pointing to the raiding of the city's reserve funds and abrupt layoffs of over two thousand city workers, while at the same time investing in a $250 million new arena with $30 million still owed on the empty Pyramid. [1566]And, to boot, Herenton's "flippant" statement to critics that "For those who want to leave, – *goodbye*" was perceived as a slap in the face to thousands of taxpayers who did not want a huge tax increase. [1567]

Councilwoman Stout Mitchell acknowledged there were some "management problems" with the administration. [1568] And Councilman E.C. Jones questioned why the city administration forecasted interest on investments for 2005 at $184,369 but budgeted over $2 million. [1569] The city finance director explained, without blinking an eye, that this was not an error but instead "cautiously optimistic" projections. [1570] I also questioned why the city administration did not comply with the city's debt service policy. [1571]

Pushing forward, Herenton again pitched a proposed merger of certain departments of the public utility with the city to bring projected cost-savings in the range of $4 million. MLGW board members complained of not being briefed about the proposal before the city council presentation. [1572] Councilman Joe Brown opposed the merger because it would violate the city charter. [1573] One retired MLGW executive wondered if the city was trying to siphon off funds from the public utility to solve the budget crisis. Others worried that the proposed merger would adversely impact their pension plan. [1574] As I observed, the purported savings from Herenton's proposal might not be realized because another half a million would be needed to equalize utility and city official salaries after the merger, including raising the mayor's salary.

Fears abounded that Herenton was proposing the merger in order to sell the public utility. A newspaper quoted him as saying that there are components of MLGW that lend themselves to spinning off for a big dividend. [1575] The mayor even sent the city attorney to oppose a bill in the state legislature that would require a public referendum before MLGW could be sold. [1576] The council quickly voted against the proposed merger of utility and city departments. [1577]

It didn't help Herenton that a report made the council aware of possible conflicts of interest by Yo! Memphis, a youth charter school funded with a federal grant administered by the city. The entity contracted with well-connected entities, including the City of Memphis CAO's brother (as a karate vendor), without competitive bids. [1578] As chair of the council oversight committee, I put it on the agenda, and the committee authorized another review.

The new audit revealed that the Yo! Memphis nonprofit spent grant funds for a night at the Ritz Hilton; $1,400 at a tanning salon; expenditures at local malls; and $2,400 for formal wear. [1579] The auditors reported that the job training program had no records for $5,000 in mall gift cards. Incredibly, they found that the more than $63,000 spent on formal wear, flowers, catering, photography, Grizzlies' tickets, and karate lessons were allowable expenditures under the federal government's job training program guidelines. [1580] Later, in 2007, the school had its charter revoked by the Memphis Board of Education for failure to meet math benchmarks. [1581] The entity filed a lawsuit claiming that the student performance evaluations were flawed. [1582] The case was dismissed in 2010 when the court granted summary judgment for the defendants. [1583]

As with the case of the Yo! Memphis expenditures, the city's budget needed oversight as well. The proposed initial funding for a new city and county $63 million 911 call center was put on hold by the council budget committee. But my efforts to remove the expensive light rail project from Herenton's $173 million proposed capital improvements budget in favor of devoting more resources to neighborhoods was defeated. [1584] Herenton had substantially increased capital spending during his tenure, with the city's debt nearly tripling to almost a billion dollars in the past ten years. [1585]

The administration and council had a practice of approving more capital projects than the city could handle in a year and then carrying them over to the next year. [1586] As I observed, that practice made it more likely that the glitzy projects would get done, with the more basic maintenance and neighborhood projects continuing to get put on the back burner. The *Commercial Appeal* editors agreed. [1587] Cutting development projects also made sense to improve the city's credit rating and lower interest rates for future projects. [1588] The city's debt had been flagged by one of the credit rating agencies during the past fall. [1589]

During the council budget debates, I proposed 5% across the board cuts to close $25 million of the funding gap. Other councilmembers did not back my plan, arguing that it would reduce services too much. [1590] Sammons's proposal for a twenty-three cent property tax increase, which would keep the layoffs, also did not garner support. [1591] As the night waxed late, Herenton appeared after 10 pm and spoke with Councilwoman Hooks in the back room. [1592] Finally, E.C. Jones proposed a 27 cent property tax increase, which was adopted. I and five others voted no, and the councilwoman and six others voted aye. [1593] The council had temporarily stayed the budget crisis, but my reform efforts were only beginning.

25

The Incredible,
Unshrinking Violet

1

In the hot summer of 2005, the bombshell hit with the news that former state Sen. Roscoe Dixon and six others, including state Sen. John Ford, had been indicted.[1594] Dixon was accused of a conspiracy with Barry Myers to obtain about $9,500 in bribes in 2004 to assist with legislation for the fictitious company named E-Cycle Management, Inc. ("E-Cycle"), which was part of the FBI sting operation called Tennessee Waltz.[1595] John Ford was indicted by a federal grand jury for alleged acts of corruption, intimation, and extortion as an elected official.[1596] Tim Willis, who had come under scrutiny regarding his dealings with the county juvenile court clerk's office, cooperated with the feds.[1597] He was paid $77,000 a year, plus expenses, to lobby on behalf of the fake E-Cycle.[1598]

A retired FBI agent whose alias was Joe Carson worked with Willis to tape and videotape conversations with state Sen. Roscoe Dixon and others regarding alleged payoffs for a bill filed in the Tennessee state legislature at E-Cycle's request.[1599] A video was played on T.V. of an undercover agent purportedly handing Sen. John Ford money in an office. Of course, under the justice system, one is presumed innocent until proven guilty.[1600] John Ford claimed the video was edited and that it was entrapment.[1601] Dixon and Ford denied the charges. John Ford resigned from his senate seat, and Dixon resigned from his county position as Wharton's CAO, to focus on their respective criminal defenses.[1602]

Yet despite the controversy, in a strange article Jackson Baker in the *Memphis Flyer* opined that indicted Sen. John Ford was "Cool," and former

Louisiana Governor Edwin Edwards (who had been charged with racke-teering and tax evasion, among other things)[1603] was "Supercool" for each of their excuses as to their legal problems.[1604] Also, a former mayoral candidate was dubbed "Cool" for accusing famous wrestler and mayoral candidate Jerry Lawler of "fixing fights."[1605] And, I was labeled "way uncool" for my perception of gender bias in some of the newspaper's coverage.[1606]

In a letter to the editor my response noted that despite having been regularly berated, called stupid, and cussed at by the mayor and a few of my colleagues since my election to the council, I had always kept my cool.[1607] Yet, as the only never-indicted elected official mentioned in the article, it was ironic that I was deemed "Uncool" with "sometimes over-the-top political ambition" for remarking on gender-biased coverage.[1608] In my mind, the article only demonstrated the backward thinking of glorifying the arrogant bravado of some men and castigation of women who merely ask for equality.

Pointing to powerful women, such as Indy 500 racecar driver Danica Patrick, Madeline Albright, Condoleezza Rice, and three-star U.S. Army General Claudia Kennedy, I called out the columnist as "Super-Uncool" for suggesting that a woman should not have the same opportunity to compete for a promotion as a man.[1609] The *Memphis Flyer* backtracked, claiming that the article was "tongue-in-cheek" due to my responding "to others' criticisms with unsubstantiated allegations of gender bias."[1610] But in any event, the readers of the *Memphis Business Journal* found me "cool," as they voted me their third favorite local politician, only after Wharton and Harold Ford Jr.[1611]

2

More financial problems loomed with Memphis Networx seeking another $3 million from the council.[1612] The entity was building a fiber-optic network to serve businesses and institutions.[1613] The chairman of the Networx board (also MLGW's chief financial officer) claimed that there were no financial problems at the company and the funds were needed to extend service to some large customers.[1614] Thirty-six million dollars had already been spent – about twenty-nine million of public money and seven million private funds.[1615]

Chris Davis, with the *Memphis Flyer*, wrote a thoughtful analysis. He pointed out that Memphis Networx had lost money every year since

1999, although initially projecting a sixteen million dollar annual profit. [1616] Suspicions were further raised when it refused to allow the local press to review its books, claiming that it was a private firm not subject to the open records law. [1617] The three goals set for the venture had not yet been accomplished - improving broadband accessibility for Memphis, providing service to poor citizens, and generating a profit for MLGW's investment. [1618]

Only a few months later, Memphis Networx sought a six million dollar increase in its line of credit from the city council, reporting that it had lost at least twenty-one million and spent twenty-nine million of the MLGW loan.[1619] Networx officials claimed that MLGW would give up its majority interest in the entity valued at eight to twelve million without the line of credit. [1620]

I proposed an amendment to back a loan in the range of two to three million that would ensure the city investors retained a majority interest, conditioned upon public disclosure of the company's financial statements.[1621] When Networx's CEO offered to allow me to review its books, I took a volunteer local accountant and learned of the Who's Who list of Memphis business elite involved in the venture.

The council voted against the loan.[1622] Not giving up, President Joseph Lee called for the council to reconsider because MLGW had not gotten "one dollar back yet" from the investment. [1623] Prominent developer and MLGW board member Nick Clark continued to urge approval of the loan request. [1624]

Due to the denial of the loan request, the public's share of Networx would drop from about 80% to about 40%, giving control to the private investors. [1625] Lee hired attorney Charles Carpenter to explore selling the company, buying out the private investors, or letting the private investors sell the company. [1626] The Networx financial mess was far from over.

3

Mindful of the city's financial problems, I pushed forward with budgetary reforms. My proposal to eliminate the large $800 a month vehicle allowances for ten city division directors and the $400 a month allowance for fourteen deputy directors, and allow only a mileage reimbursement, passed a council committee. But it was reinstated by the full council only a few hours later. [1627] It was finally sent back to committee, with my speculation that some councilmembers were merely trying to vote for it so as to be on record, then delay and defeat it.

While Stout Mitchell and Taylor were supportive of my measure, Sammons opposed it claiming the high car allowances were income for people who run the city government. [1628] Councilman Lowery, however, pointed out that the administration had given the allowances without the council's knowledge or approval. [1629]

Herenton's CAO proposed cutting the city car allowances by 25%, returning with recommendations later, or creating a fleet management manager position.[1630] Other councilmembers suggested a pool of cars and a reduction in the allowance by 50%. Herenton drove a late model Cadillac Escalade which was leased by the city for over $1,100 a month.[1631] He had received over $5,000 for a car allowance the prior year. [1632]

The MLGW president and seven vice-presidents received a $1,073 per month car allowance, and about fifty other managers received $857 a month in car allowances. [1633] To press the matter further, I showed up at the next MLGW board meeting, filled out a card as a citizen to address the board members, and asked them to review the car allowance policy.[1634] I added that the council had the power to restrict the car allowances, but the MLGW board should have a chance to address it first. With the heat on, the MLGW officials decided to review the car allowance policies. [1635]

Letters to the editor of the *Commercial Appeal* supported my position, especially in light of the layoffs of almost 2,000 city temporary workers and the fact that MLGW is not a profit-making entity. [1636] Sammons was criticized for calling my effort "a chance for camera time." [1637]

The *Commercial Appeal* also editorialized that mileage should replace the car allowances.[1638] The editorial noted that some MLGW officials were getting a monthly allowance that would be large enough to lease a Cadillac, Mercedes, or Porsche. [1639] The newspaper calculated that the $1,073 paid monthly to eight of the officials would equal reimbursement for each at forty cents per mile for over 2,500 miles (about the distance from Memphis to Seattle). [1640] The newspaper's examples brought home the extravagance, where low-income citizens struggled to keep their power and lights.

Finally, the council voted to discontinue the city car allowances, but approved the fleet office with the CAO's representation that it could be funded within the current budget.[1641] I tried to divide the issue on the votes, questioning the need for the fleet office.[1642] No specifics were provided on how much the fleet manager would be paid or the number of staff members assigned to the office.[1643] Sammons warned that some directors might leave if the allowances were eliminated. [1644] E.C. Jones disagreed, responding that 2,000 people had been laid off, and the affected directors were earning over $100,000 a year.[1645] Ultimately, Jones, Sammons, and I all voted against the measure, albeit for different reasons in that the proposal contained the fleet services proposal. [1646]

On the heels of the city council's decision, the MLGW board voted to discontinue car allowances for any new hires and to require mileage instead.[1647] For the forty-three executives and other management personnel whose annual car allowances totaled $425,000, the board eliminated the allowances. It then gave them the funds back as part of their base salary. [1648] This increased Lee's salary to over $227,600 annually, and others in management were given an additional $12,610 a year to their salaries that ranged from $136,000 to $175,000. [1649]

Besides car allowance reforms, the pressure was on for Lee to make good Herenton's claims that his budgetary skills qualified him for the job. MLGW officials projected gas and water rate increases within a year.[1650] Ratepayers were further outraged at MLGW's proposal to hire a speechwriter for Lee at a $90,000 salary and advertising expenditures for new management positions.[1651] At the same time, they were told that their utility bills would increase substantially. [1652]

Controversy also arose at MLGW when Lee reneged on rank and file worker pay raises negotiated by the union months earlier, with the union attorney alleging bad faith bargaining. [1653] As chair of the council's MLGW committee, I opposed the proposal from MLGW management as "lowball." The MLGW management came back with a different proposal, which eventually was accepted.[1654] However, tensions were high as councilmembers took Lee to task for huge car allowances and executive salaries. At the same time, he accused the council of holding up his budget and creating a hostile environment.[1655]

Finally, Lee announced that he would forgo his own $12,600 salary increase based upon his annual car allowance and instead use a mileage reimbursement.[1656] Many other top managers also passed on pay raises after council complaints that the monies that were to be rolled into base salaries were subject to council ratification. [1657]

4

Budget problems continued, with Herenton's administration announcing in the fall that the city was already facing a $10 million deficit despite the new property tax increase and much higher trash fees.[1658] The CAO claimed that the deficit would be absorbed, and the reserves replenished, but others expressed skepticism. [1659]

Councilmembers and the public were upset because in the summer parks and medians had not been mowed for months, with grass as tall as a person.[1660] The city had already been penalized by bond rating agencies for not keeping the reserve fund at an appropriate level. I asked for more information on how the city administration proposed to make up the shortfall. My concern was that the financial problems would continue until there was a major shift to address the city leaders' entitlement attitude for perks and excessive spending.

The next day the story changed. The administration now said that it needed to dip into the reserves but would later absorb the deficit. [1661] The administration blamed the new deficit on higher health insurance costs for retirees when expected cost-savings from a new plan were not realized, and the failure to collect another $4.6 million in franchise fees from BellSouth telephone when the city lost a ruling in court.[1662] Understandably, Councilwoman Hooks criticized the administration's overly aggressive budget forecasting.[1663] I questioned the timing of the shortfall because the deficits were known by city finance officials before the council had approved the current budget. Stout Mitchell, the council's budget chair, could not understand how the city administration reported a $12 million surplus in the third quarter, and then a $10 million deficit at the end of the fiscal year. [1664]

A few weeks later, new CFO Robert Lipscomb brought more bad news that the budget was in worse shape than previously reported.[1665] On September 6, Herenton told the council that his administration had miscalculated past budget projections and that he was concerned about whether the budget forecasts were credible, reliable, or accurate. [1666] Herenton admitted that the city's reserve fund might be in jeopardy and vaguely referenced other unidentified "minefields" that could increase the now $10.3 million shortfall. [1667] He pitched a "fiscal recovery strategy" to include a hiring freeze, a review of corporate tax breaks ["PILOTS"], and possibly selling certain city assets, such as parks and space on cell phone towers. [1668]

I called for the truth and an audit of the city's budget.[1669] After the city's bond rating had dropped, depletion of the city's reserve fund, layoffs, and tax hikes, the mayor of fourteen years could not even tell the public the actual city budget numbers. My sources advised that the current deficit was actually in the range of $20 million, with another $9 million of revenues that might not be realized as well. When I asked the mayor's new finance team how much money was left in the city's reserves, after a long *pause* - they replied $9 million. [1670] My sources advised that, in fact, the reserve fund had been nearly entirely depleted.

With a tiny or nonexistent reserve fund for unexpected emergencies or contingencies, if substantial cuts were not made or higher revenues received, then the city could end up the next year in the red with insufficient monies to pay the expenditures that exceeded budgeted amounts. Now the citizens, who were weathering higher city taxes and fees with the promise of the restoration of city services, would have to face serious cuts in services again. Of course, the bond rating agencies would negatively react to the city's precarious financial situation, which would increase the city's cost to borrow funds. If the city experienced an earthquake from the New Madrid fault or a terrorist attack, its people were left exposed without any monies in reserve to handle the crisis.

The mayor wanted to simply talk about solutions and ignore how the city got into the financial mess. But the public had a right to know about the reason for the past two years' budgetary shortfalls, why the city finance officials failed to provide accurate data to the council, and the current status of the budget with a full accounting of all revenues and expenditures. My proposed budget resolution would have the city council appoint an independent auditor or ask the state comptroller to examine the city's books so that the public would know the truth.

Lipscomb asked for more time to get accurate budget numbers, and the council did not adopt my budget resolution. [1671] I argued that every time there was a budget problem, somebody from the administration left, and a new person showed up asking for more time to review the books. I was pleased that veteran news reporter Norm Brewer backed me up on the audit in his *WREG News* Channel 3 commentary, calling it needed and "right."[1672] He added that my motion "got exactly nowhere" with councilmembers only because it was my idea. [1673]

Lipscomb also asked the council to consider a moratorium on corporate tax breaks ("PILOTS"), which cost the city about $45 million a year in foregone property taxes.[1674] Even Republican Shelby County Trustee Bob Patterson raised concerns in a letter to Lipscomb that there were about seventy PILOTS that had ended, but the companies were still receiving the tax breaks estimated at millions of dollars.[1675] Most councilmembers supported the proposed moratorium.[1676] However, I was concerned that there would be another two-week delay without an action plan. Due to the serious situation, I pushed for cuts as soon as possible.[1677]

Although nearly a billion dollars in debt, the city administration's budget proposed to spend approximately another two billion over the next five years.[1678] With the city's problems in paying its day to day operating expenses, the *Commercial Appeal* editors likened it to a homeowner who had trouble paying the monthly bills buying a brand new Lexus.[1679] The editors observed that the city's growing debt, and the council's failure to say no to capital projects, would make it more likely taxes would be raised in the future. [1680] They were correct in that the failure to manage the budget properly and for long-range planning was a financial train-wreck in the works.

As part of his plans to solve the budget problems, Herenton decided to sell some city parks.[1681] So, to build support, he scheduled a tour of several neighborhood parks for councilmembers and the media. Neighbors showed up at the stops pleading for the city to keep their parks and pointing out the improvements they had made at their own expense. At one urban park, we were amazed to see four horses grazing. In the meantime, trash piled up on city streets and grass continued to grow several feet high in city parks and properties.[1682]

Letters to the editor of the local newspaper supported my call for an outside independent auditor to review the city's books.[1683] There had been a substantial decrease in city services, an increase in taxes, a decline in the city's credit rating, and the use of most, if not all, of the city's emergency reserve funds. There were fears that the city was headed for bankruptcy. [1684]

With the reserves depleted, two of the bond rating agencies took negative action.[1685] Fitch noted the city's reporting of a larger than expected operating deficit in the fiscal year 2005 and overestimation of revenues for the fiscal year 2006. [1686] In the face of reports that Memphis was in its third year of operating at a deficit and had no reserves to handle any unforeseen emergencies, Herenton blamed his previous finance team for accounting and forecasting errors.[1687] Other citizens blamed the mayor. They compared his raise and that of his "cronies" while regular workers were laid off to abuses by large corporations giving huge bonuses and golden parachutes while workers' salaries and benefits were cut.[1688]

More questions were also raised about the PILOT corporate tax abeyance program, with a state study showing that more than half of the PILOTS granted in the state were in Shelby County.[1689] As one citizen observed, the practice shifted the tax burden from businesses to homeowners with exemptions granted to "virtually" every applicant.[1690] The debate raged as to whether companies such as International Paper would stay in Memphis if it didn't get its $15 million and fifteen-year tax freeze for its corporate headquarters and whether or not the city benefited.[1691] Even small companies were getting approved, with one creating only twenty-five jobs at $40,000 a year.[1692]

After reviewing the books, Herenton's finance team reported a projected fiscal year 2005 budget deficit of at least $25.8 million and a reserve fund of only $598,000. However, rating agencies recommended at least $48 million should be held in reserve by the city.[1693] Herenton's own finance director, Lipscomb, admitted that the city had been "overspending for three years" despite lower revenues and was "like an oil tanker without brakes." [1694] He made $12 million in cuts and found $21 million in inflated revenue projections.[1695] The city also had no long-range planning for its operational spending.[1696] With things out of control, a local blogger announced that he would jumpstart the recall effort for Herenton that he had abandoned earlier.[1697]

The council balked at my renewed request for a state auditor, instead choosing to submit a list of questions to the current city outside auditors.[1698] The budget crisis caused one rating agency to place the Memphis and Shelby County Sports Authority's revenue bonds on a "rating watch negative."[1699] Another firm lowered the city's general obligation bonds rating two notches. [1700]

Despite the serious budget problems, the council approved half a million dollars in state grant funds for dredging work to begin for the Beale Street Landing planned boat dock and park.[1701] The city administration also gave the Riverfront Development Corporation a green light on the $27 million project.[1702] It began work only a few weeks later to widen the Wolf River Harbor for the boat dock.[1703] The project was slated for completion by 2008.[1704] I was one of only two councilmembers who voted against the appropriation. [1705]

As Memphis grappled with the budget crisis and imposed a moratorium on new capital improvements projects, I proposed my own list of spending cuts totaling nearly $30 million.[1706] The list included scrapping the MATA light rail, police headquarters renovation, and dropping the Beale Street landing project as "budget-busters."[1707] E.C. Jones scolded some councilmembers who had rubber-stamped too many of the mayor's projects in the past. [1708] The *Commercial Appeal* editors agreed that these were legitimate projects to review with the high city debt and the low reserves. [1709] I pushed for my proposed cuts, but no one on the council would second my motion.[1710] The city administration now blamed the deficit on fire department overtime, while I warned that the City of Memphis could go into receivership if drastic action was not taken[1711]

Norm Brewer with *WREG News* opined that no matter how "important the issue" or "how logical or right" my position, even if I proposed the Ten Commandments as a resolution, the council would not second my motion.[1712] He attributed it to the fact that from day one I "dared to speak out, dared to be an independent thinker and activist on a body much more given to group thought and action."[1713] He called the treatment of me "grade school, playground stuff," and "low grade, political spite," saying those councilmembers should be ashamed.[1714] I agreed with Brewer that a more independent acting council was needed, especially in light of the severe financial crisis.

I was forced to call out councilmembers in the media, saying that the body's passive inaction on the budget crisis put taxpayers at risk.[1715] Every time I tried to do something to address the problem, I found myself standing alone. I pushed for budget hearings. If the city ended up in the red with a serious shortfall or defaulted on bonds, it could be forced into receivership and have someone else operate the city. Since state law required that a balanced budget be submitted to the state comptroller by the year-end, the council should oversee any changes made by the administration before its submission.

With a closer look at the budget, Blake Fontenay with the *Commercial Appeal* came to the conclusion that much could have been avoided, such as the city's use of overly optimistic revenue projections for several years instead of using the low or mid-range projections of the Sparks Bureau of Business and Economic Research (which I had written op-eds on earlier in the year). [1716] He noted several areas where the city had miscalculated revenues, made accounting errors such as on encumbered expenses, and delayed actions to address the shortfalls that aggravated the crisis. [1717] The columnist pointed out that monies available for operating expenses would increase if major capital projects were cut, which was the exact position I had advocated.[1718] Herenton also admitted that action was delayed in addressing the budget deficit due to not wanting to raise taxes before the 2003 municipal elections.[1719]

As the city and county both struggled with budget problems, the median income had dropped nearly 5% in the county during the past three years. [1720] Many middle-class citizens had left the city, and also the county, for greener pastures in surrounding counties. They sought to escape high taxes, crime, and, as one said, the "dysfunctional politics of Memphis." [1721] Action was needed to stop the exodus and attract the middle class back.

5

In addition to the growing budget crisis, the Tennessee Waltz scandals continued with guilty pleas by former state representative Chris Newton for taking a bribe, and citizen Barry Myers, and Chattanooga school board member Charles Love for passing payoffs. [1722] Newton, a likeable person, had been a cosponsor of the successful lottery resolution. He was a Republican and known to work in a bipartisan way. After apologizing and serving time, he resumed his private-sector business career in East Tennessee.

As a result, the state legislature proposed reforms that required cities and counties to enact new local ethics rules with teeth.[1723] Memphis City Council and Shelby County Commission rules only provided for censure by colleagues and were advisory.[1724]

Some councilmembers pushed back, claiming reforms were not needed or would not help. Councilman Brent Taylor claimed that the lack of teeth in the city's policy came from the advice of Council Attorney Allan Wade. [1725] Councilman Jack Sammons preferred to pass the buck in favor of a state ethics law and argued that "you can't legislate morality. If a guy's a thief, you can pass six volumes of ethics laws, and he's still going to be a thief." [1726]

But the discussion of ethics did not stop Herenton's fourteenth annual holiday party at the Memphis Cook Convention Center, with the Memphis business elite as the "host" committee. [1727]Pete Aviotti, the special mayoral assistant, dutifully collected the $1,000 from the hosts, and speculation abounded that Herenton would be tough to beat in 2007 for reelection due to the blue blood donor list for the event. [1728] The movers and shakers attended despite the drop in the bond rating, depleted reserve fund, shake-up in the finance department, and indictments of several police officers. [1729]

On Herenton's side for reelection was the growth of downtown development, the creation of affordable housing where several public housing developments once stood, and a base of support that would vote for him no matter what.[1730] Noticeable was the lack of progress in several key areas promised, such as minority business development, stronger neighborhoods, consolidation of governments, and the lack of enough population growth downtown to attract a variety of large retailers, including a supermarket grocery store.[1731]

In a year-end review, Baker with the *Memphis Flyer* listed his top highlights for 2005.[1732] He included Herenton's repeated unexplained absences from his mayoral duties and my "high profile undeclared campaign for mayor" which had growing support. [1733] Accordingly, Baker dubbed Herenton as the "incredible shrinking mayor," and me the "incredible un-shrinking violet." [1734] In the same piece, he complimented Wharton on his job as county mayor and revealed that some were "touting" him for Memphis mayor. [1735] His article heralded the musical chairs of recycling status quo politicians that was about to commence again.

26

A Lightening Rod

1

After a rough past year, Herenton began 2006 gamely pledging that the city would end the fiscal year with a surplus and begin to restore its bond ratings.[1736] Having depleted the city's reserves, he again pushed for consolidation but expressed his support of the PILOT tax abatement program.[1737] He also undertook a multi-million dollar restructuring of the city's bond indebtedness, which I opposed.[1738] The deal extended payment terms from six to nine years to increase cash flow for 2007 and 2008.[1739] Herenton's finance director claimed that Memphis would pay half of its debt within ten years.[1740] Interestingly, nine years later, the city reported about the same amount of 1.2 billion debt, plus another half billion for the unfunded pension.[1741]

Yet, Herenton had other matters on his mind. In February 2006, he traveled to Atlanta under subpoena as a possible witness in a racketeering, bribery, and tax invasion trial of former Atlanta Mayor Bill Campbell, but was not called to testify.[1742] Campbell had made trips to Memphis to gamble at the nearby Tunica, Mississippi casinos, as verified by Herenton's former bodyguard.[1743]

Campbell was acquitted on the corruption charges but convicted of tax fraud.[1744] Although Herenton promised to explain why he had been subpoenaed after he testified, he now refused, saying that there was no need because he was never called to the stand by the prosecution.[1745]

2

Even though the mayor had other distractions, I stayed focused on the budget crisis. Once again, after my own independent research, I was the one who notified the public and the city council of another downgrade of the city's credit rating by Standard & Poor's.[1746] After my release of the information, the council was told later that day by the administration that all three bond rating agencies had downgraded the city's credit rating, two with negative outlooks.[1747] This meant higher interest rates on future borrowing. The ratings were based, in part, on the city's report of only about a million dollars in its reserve fund at the end of the 2005 fiscal year, inflated revenue projections and rising debt levels, along with a large capital improvement budget. [1748]

CFO Lipscomb claimed that the administration had planned to advise the council of the downgrades before my release but admitted that it would take three or more years to regain credibility with the rating agencies.[1749] In light of the downgrades, I questioned the issuance of bonds at that time when the city was in financial trouble.

The *Commercial Appeal* editors admonished Herenton for misleading the public by claiming at the first of the year that the city's financial mess was a "short-term fiscal aberration." [1750] The fiscal year report showed that the city's reserves were almost completely gone, with increased costs for health benefits and the mayor making a no new taxes pledge. [1751]

I pointed out that the city administration was using questionable methods to address the crisis, such as borrowing money to close the deficit for the current fiscal year, which would increase costs in 2009-2011.[1752] There was virtually no margin of error in the budgetary calculation, with some $1 million in reserves for a half-billion-dollar budget being analogous to trying to land a 747 airplane on a postage stamp.

3

Not only was the public outraged about the continuing financial misinformation coming from the administration, but also the corruption scandals of the Tennessee Waltz sting. Details became public with videos of the FBI undercover agents counting out cash to "bagmen" who then were instructed to give the money to elected officials. [1753] One FBI agent used a hidden camera along with phone taps to record conversations, posing as the CEO of E-Cycle. [1754] State Sen. Kathryn Bowers, a fireball as a state legislator, pled not guilty. Reports were that two other state legislators had accepted a free trip to Miami on a yacht, which another legislator had refused after seeking a legal opinion. [1755]

Roscoe Dixon, who had been an often capable legislator, moved for dismissal of his indictment alleging selective prosecution.[1756] The federal judge denied the motion in that Dixon had "failed to show the existence of any individuals who are not African American, and who could have been prosecuted for the offenses for which" he was charged, or discriminatory intent. [1757] A jury convicted him on all five counts, including conspiring to interfere with commerce by extortion and bribery in the Tennessee Waltz trial related to his service as a state senator.[1758] He was sentenced to over five years. [1759] Michael Hooks Sr. (nephew of civil rights leader Dr. Benjamin Hooks) pled guilty a few months earlier to bribery concerning programs receiving federal funds and received a twenty-six-month prison sentence. [1760] These convictions would mark the end of their public office careers.

Meanwhile, controversial talk show host, Thaddeus Matthews, spearheaded a recall Herenton effort named "Operation Fedup."[1761] Organizers needed to collect more than 65,000 signatures from Memphis voters in 75 days to get it on the ballot.[1762] But, even if Herenton were recalled, his CAO would take over under the city charter if the council could not agree on an interim mayor. And Herenton could run again for mayor in 2007.[1763]

The same blogger asked, "Does Carol Chumney Have the Biggest Set on the Council," to which there were many positive responses.[1764] One person applauded me as the only one in city government who spoke out and held my ground. He added that if this woman runs for president of the U.S., he will vote for me, which was flattering.[1765]

And Herenton, who had called me "crazy," was himself the one acting odd. The mayor was reported to say that he was called by God to serve as mayor, reiterating his 2004 New Year's Day prayer breakfast speech likening himself to King David of the Bible.[1766] He also defended the "holy dance" he did at a church (displayed on YouTube) as a celebration because he had avoided a serious accident by dodging a car recently. [1767] And the self-proclaimed Democrat was also seen sporting the campaign sticker of Republican U.S. Senate candidate Bill Frist and poo-pooing Congressman Harold Ford Jr.'s possible candidacy for the seat.[1768] According to Jackson Baker with the

Memphis Flyer, Herenton retorted as to the positive national coverage of Ford Jr., that out-of-state media persons, "don't have a damn vote." [1769] Apparently forgetting the significant role Harold Ford Sr. had played in his first hair-splitting mayoral election in 1991, Baker reported the mayor even to remark about a photograph in his office that showed the former congressman standing *behind* him on the stage on the historic election night—apparently a jab. [1770]

4

After Herenton gave his glowing budget address in April, I countered reminding the public of the three years of budgets in the red that led to the use of all but a pittance of the city's $70 million emergency reserve funds. Herenton claimed to know what he was doing and shrugged it off as merely an effort on his administration's part to avoid raising property taxes. [1771] He promised now that he had a plan that would hold the line on taxes for two years and restore the city's reserve fund with the same level of city services. [1772]

The mayor also warned unions and councilmembers that any efforts to "molest" his budget plan might result in lay-offs. [1773] The unions and the city began twenty-two impasse meetings. Herenton called the union leaders "irresponsible" in not accepting that Memphis had less revenues due to the exodus of many wealthy and middle-class taxpayers and businesses to the suburbs. [1774] Yet, some of this had been spurred by his own administration's policies and the continued drama at City Hall.

As the summer months ensued, I worked on several issues in addition to the budget crisis. Among other things, I pushed to keep the Mid-South Coliseum open as a venue for musical and community events by proposing shifting some funds from the vacant Pyramid. [1775] The funds could be used for upgrades to make the Coliseum ADA compliant, estimated to cost about $2 - $4 million. [1776] Revenues would be generated after it reopened. Elvis, Johnny Cash, and the Beatles are among those who had played in the historic venue. Music is what makes Memphis unique, and the Coliseum could fit into the city's tourism plan.

The rising crime was also an issue, with one survey showing nearly one in ten children in high school in Memphis schools reporting threats or injury by a weapon on school property. [1777] Due to a lack of promotional testing, the city was also short on higher-ranking police officers to oversee the rank and file officers, thereby making the force less effective. Also, the officers were not sufficiently paid, which impacted morale. And the roots of crime needed to be addressed.

Police Chief Larry Godwin opposed my belief that the city should shift more police officers from desk jobs to the streets. [1778] However, the head of the Memphis & Shelby County Crime Commission, national expert Michael Heidingsfield disagreed. He said that many police departments around the country were using civilians to handle certain investigations, man crime labs, and cover other positions where police officers worked out of a sense of tradition. [1779] This action would also have a positive impact on the budget.

As the summer proceeded, I called for a real crime fix.[1780] I pointed out that Herenton had denied the police and fire workers pay raises but filled hundreds of nonessential positions and created some new unessential jobs as well. Meanwhile, more and more children were caught in the cross-fire of crime.

In my view, the mayor should allow police and fire to come back to the negotiating table the next year if the financial picture improved so as to boost morale. Also, the mayor's calling the union leaders "irresponsible" for asking for a cost of living raise was irresponsible when he did not do his own belt-tightening. And the city's canceling of the police promotional test was a mistake because you do not send troops into battle without sufficient lieutenants to lead the way.

The city's decision to forgo a youth summer job program and to close Liberty Land amusement park, which had employed hundreds of youths, was unwise in that they were more likely to get into trouble fending for themselves on the streets. Instead of adequately addressing the problems, incredibly, the mayor instead planned a charity boxing match with former heavyweight champion "Smokin' Joe Frazier."

5

Another scandal broke in the summer, with a state report that the city had mishandled the FedExForum parking garage project and had to forfeit $6 million in federal funds. [1781] The Executive Director of the New Memphis Arena Public Building Authority (for the FedExForum), David Bennett, had raised concerns that the garage was not legally allowed to be a profit maker. [1782] But the state Department of Transportation released an audit showing that the city administration had turned the garage over to the Memphis Grizzlies, which was operating it as a for-profit venture. [1783]

The city also had signed a contract in 2002 with the state to receive $20 million in federal funds for an intermodal transfer facility to be located at the FedExForum. The new state audit revealed that the Memphis Area Transit Authority ticket office at the garage was vacant, and the bus terminal was not operational. [1784]

Herenton met with the councilmembers to answer questions about the garage, which was supposed to be utilized in connection with public transportation. The mayor claimed that no laws were broken and that the media and council were overreacting. However, he admitted that there were "some serious omissions."[1785] Councilmen Lowery, E.C. Jones, and Taylor called for a federal investigation. [1786]

Also, calling for an investigation, I handed out a transcript of a council committee hearing from the previous fall where attorney Charles Carpenter had stated that "we feel that there is little or no exposure." [1787] And, in November 2005, the City Attorney Sara Hall, had stated that she had reviewed the PBA records in detail as to communications with the state, and the intermodal facility was "a work in progress" as opposed to a requirement for the federal funding. [1788] But at the June council meeting in 2006, Hall now said that she was unfamiliar with most of the records and would need more time and assistance to review them. [1789]

The FBI opened a criminal investigation about the garage, which Herenton called "ridiculous." [1790] Councilman Myron Lowery responded that if nothing had been done illegally, why was over $6 million in federal funding forfeited?[1791] The state comptroller and state Senate Transportation Committee were also investigating the matter.

6

Stymied by the mayor's lack of initiative, I took a much-needed break from local politics. This time, I joined a small group of past delegates to represent the United States at the ACYPL East Asia-Pacific International Alumni Summit in Tokyo. It was an exciting event with political leaders from South Korea, the Philippines, Malaysia, Thailand, Indonesia, Taiwan, Australia, and other countries.

Just before the trip, Prime Minister of Japan Junichiro Koizumi traveled with President George W. Bush on Air Force One to visit Graceland, the home of Elvis Presley in Memphis. I faxed a letter, asking to meet with him when he arrived since I would be in Tokyo for the summit shortly thereafter, but he declined.

Although not meeting Koizumi in Memphis, the respective hosts did select me to make a presentation in Tokyo on behalf of the entire delegation to Yohei Kono, Speaker of the Japanese Diet (House of Representatives). During the trip, I met with political leaders from Japan, toured the National Diet Building, and even ventured out on my own to visit a shrine. I also presented Speaker Kono with a boxed set of Elvis CD's donated by Graceland, which he received with a huge smile. Through an interpreter, Kono then sagely remarked to the entire group that his father always told him to be gracious to all people because you never knew who that person might be. A very profound statement and a practice worth emulating. I was glad to represent Memphis and the USA at the international summit and remind the world of our "King."

7

Back in Memphis, I casually mentioned at a "Coffee with Carol" at a local bookstore that I planned to run for Memphis mayor, although a formal announcement would come later. The *Commercial Appeal* reporter deemed me a "lightning rod." [1792] A *Memphis Business Journal* online poll only a few days later showed me with 68% support, Herenton at 10%, and 22% for several other possible candidates. [1793]

Shortly after I announced a town hall meeting on crime, Herenton now called a press conference and proposed to add 650 police officers and other law enforcement improvements, with a corresponding fifty-cent property tax increase. Memphis had just been ranked 2nd in the nation for violent crimes. [1794] Part of his plan was to eliminate two years of college education and city residency as requirements for recruits.[1795] He also wanted to add 5,000 youth jobs, with the entire package costing nearly $50 million.[1796] While I supported more officers, indiscriminately raising taxes without addressing the police department's lack of sufficient management concerned me.

At my town hall meeting on crime, the public spoke out about the difficulty getting through on 911 emergency calls and a litany of other issues. I reminded the group that only two months ago, the Police Director Godwin told the Crime Commission that he did not need more officers. Now he was saying that the lack of sufficient manpower was causing lieutenants to respond to calls.[1797]

John Branston with the *Memphis Flyer* noted that Godwin had "done a complete turnabout on overtime and more cops this year" and called the mayor's new crime plan "slapdash." [1798] With an overcrowded jail, concerns were raised about how to handle more arrests with the proposed larger police force. [1799] And Heidingsfield, president of the Crime Commission, reasoned that more officers couldn't hurt, but this was not a long-term solution.[1800] It did seem like a hastily put together, not well-thought-out, plan.

Herenton responded that he had instructed Godwin that balancing the budget was the priority, which is why he did not ask for more officers in the summer hearings. [1801] In essence, the mayor was admitting that the administration had misled the council and the public about the city's real public safety needs.

But there was another way for the city to secure needed funds to hire more police. For many years annexation of surrounding areas had initially brought in more tax revenues than would be expended on extending city services to the areas. At year-end, plans were presented to annex two such choice areas, one near the exclusive Southwind Golf Course. Together they would bring an estimated $100 million a year into the city's coffers, according to the *Commercial Appeal*. [1802] Perhaps this was why Herenton wasn't more worried about the budget.

8

In the midst of the crime debate, a strange moment in Memphis history occurred when Herenton, age sixty-six, squared off in three 1 minute rounds against former heavyweight champion "Smokin' Joe Frazier" at the Peabody Hotel. The proceeds from the fight were to go to the county drug court foundation. The *Memphis Flyer* newspaper deemed it a "national embarrassment" to the boxers and the city. [1803] While the cause was worthy, I contended that the mayor's training for the match was grandstanding.

And despite the levity of the boxing match, the serious investigations and indictments were not over. In December, news broke of the federal complaints against Memphis City Councilmen Rickey Peete and Edmund Ford Sr. on charges of accepting bribes and extortion.[1804] Joe Cooper, a political operative, former county official, and convicted felon (bank fraud), cooperated with the FBI in connection with his own federal money laundering charges stemming from his contractual dealings allegedly selling cars to drug dealers.[1805] Cooper then wore a wire to secretly tape the two councilmembers' conversations about zoning and billboard issues.[1806]

A local developer had a proposed real estate development approved by the council on October 3, with myself and Councilman Scott McCormick among those voting no.[1807] The FBI provided cash for payments to Peete and Edmund Ford Sr.[1808] Of course, under the law, they were presumed innocent unless proven guilty in a court of law. Edmund Ford Sr. pled not guilty, characterizing any cash payments received from Cooper as legitimate car payments and down payment on a loan for a new funeral home.[1809] He also said loans from one prominent developer for his funeral home business and another developer's co-signing for his Cadillac were legitimate.[1810]

Peete, who has a charming demeanor despite his brushes with the law, had served time previously on charges of soliciting and receipt of a bribe when a local homebuilder cooperated with the FBI with audiotapes.[1811] The allegations in that matter were that he accepted a $1,000 bribe related to his council position under the table at a Shoney's restaurant.[1812] However, as a testament to his popularity with his constituency, he was elected again to the city council in 1995 after the restoration of his voting rights.[1813] He was even said to be a possible mayoral contender days before this new complaint. [1814]

The complaint against Peete alleged that Cooper had met with him and left cash payments of about $12,000 total in the bathroom at the Beale Street Merchants Association where Peete had an office. [1815] Ultimately, Councilman Rickey Peete pled guilty to one count of extortion under color of official right and was sentenced to fifty-one months in federal prison in the FBI sting called Operation Main Street Sweeper. [1816] Joe Cooper said he had left the cash payments after assurances that Peete did not need to worry about what he called the "alphabet boys."[1817] Peete resigned from office and began drawing his twelve-year pension. [1818] Later, he would become a GOTV consultant for various candidates after serving his sentence.

Another public official, Bruce Thompson, who had served on the Shelby County Commission, was later indicted on extortion and mail fraud charges.[1819] The charges related to a consulting contract with a contractor seeking a $46 million Memphis City Schools contract to build three schools. [1820] The allegations were that Thompson used his public position to falsely represent that he could control votes on the school board with monies paid to a minority contractor to use as campaign contributions for various school board members. [1821]

My Harrison, the special agent in charge of the Memphis FBI office, held a press conference with the U.S. Attorney to announce that they were "watching" the actions of public officials. Some thought that the indictment of white conservative Thompson was also an effort by federal justice officials to counter criticism that black Democrats had been unfairly targeted. [1822] Thompson denied any wrongdoing.

The year ended on a not so positive note after the "garage gate" revelations about the FedExForum garage, indictments, continuing budget crisis, and with Memphis now recognized as one of the nation's most violent metropolitan areas. [1823]

PART SIX

—

Memphis Mayor's Race I

27

The City

The City
Not by her houses neat
Nor by her well-built walls
Not yet again
Neither by dock nor street
A city stands or falls
But by her men
Not by the joiner's skill,
Nor work in wood or stone
Comes good to her or ill,
But by her men alone.
ALCAEUS

Engraved on the Wall at Memphis City Hall- 1966 A.D.

1

On New Year's Day of 2007, Memphis Mayor W. W. Herenton announced that he would seek reelection for a fifth term. Herenton, a towering six foot six, bore facial marks from taking some punches in his youthful boxing days. And he was never one to hold his political punches either. With his announcement, the mayor also proposed that the city tear down the Memphis Liberty Bowl Memorial Stadium and build a $175 million new football stadium.[1824] Touting the revitalization of downtown, improved public housing, and the city's fiscal health, he claimed that he was "on the wall" (likening himself to the biblical character Nehemiah who led the effort to build a wall around Jerusalem), and empowered by God to lead the city.[1825]

Memphis has long chased the dream of an NFL team, with the Houston Oilers [now the Tennessee Titans] having played in the Liberty Bowl for two years during the construction of Nashville's new stadium. Yet, only three days after Herenton's bombshell announcement, millions of dollars of previously approved city upgrades on the Liberty Bowl for ADA compliance, sound system, and restrooms were already underway.[1826]

Like many others in the city, I was shocked at the mayor's announced plans for a new stadium. First, why were the millions in upgrades approved if the mayor planned to push for a brand new stadium? Second, many needs would continue to go unmet if city funds were used for the proposed new stadium, such as leaky roofs in community centers, growing blight, and high crime. And third, the mayor's tendency to liken himself to biblical figures made some wonder if he had a messiah complex.

As a possible candidate for mayor, I responded that the timing was wrong for any public contribution for the proposed project. City leaders needed to be chasing jobs and criminals. Even Herenton admitted that building the case for a new stadium could get "ugly."[1827]

At this point, Herenton had won every election since he beat Mayor Dick Hackett in 1991 to become Memphis' first elected black mayor in a cliffhanger, decided by only about 142 votes. Speculation grew as to whether a formidable challenger would appear for the 2007 mayoral election. Some local developers and business leaders searched for an alternative candidate due to the high crime, high taxes, erratic behavior of Herenton, and exodus of many from the city.[1828]

In addition to me, others mentioned as possible mayoral candidates included Republican County Commissioner John Willingham (a former President Richard Nixon appointee). Also, possibly joining the field was former MLGW public utility president Herman Morris (appointed by Herenton until he was later unceremoniously *dis*appointed). In his sixties, Willingham was amiable when we crossed paths at the Memphis in May BBQ festival, where he hosted a tent with his own specialty barbeque sauce. Morris, who graduated from the private Rhodes College (Memphis), was a quiet attorney, an African American, and lived in the progressive Midtown part of the city in a mansion.

Herenton saw the lay of the land and took a preemptive strike. He sent a letter to County Mayor A C Wharton asking for his support in the election, despite the push by some to get Wharton to enter the race.[1829]

The *Daily News* featured my possible mayoral candidacy and my strong beliefs in democracy, justice, equality, and fair play.[1830] Often dubbed the "voice of reason" on the city council, I wanted the job.[1831] My platform was ethical leadership, to bring jobs, get control of crime, revitalize the neighborhoods, implement better code enforcement, and hold the line on taxes. Even though politics was often brutal, as mayor of Memphis, I would be able to do more to protect children in child care centers, improve public education, ensure wiser financial spending, and let the people's voices be heard. I was excited about the opportunity.

Marcus Pohlmann, a political science professor at Rhodes College, now speculated that Herenton's support in the business community was so strong that he could raise half a million to two million dollars by just announcing a reelection bid.[1832] He added that I was one of the few possible candidates that could give Herenton a run for his money (even though a white female in the majority-black city with historical racial and gender voting trends that favored the incumbent).[1833] I was encouraged. However, another conservative commentator, Susan Adler Thorp, opined on *WMC Action News 5* that Herenton was unbeatable.[1834] I replied that the same thing was said about the Titanic being unsinkable.

In February, I announced my candidacy for mayor of Memphis at the Kemmons Wilson Holiday Inn. Wilson, an amazing innovator, was the first to develop the modern-day hotel, with the first Holiday Inn in Memphis. Memphis is known for several successful and innovative entrepreneurs, such as Fred Smith, who founded Federal Express. Also, Clarence Saunders's Piggly Wiggly grocery stores revolutionized how people purchase groceries and other goods.[1835] I truly admire their accomplishments. That's why my announcement was in the Kemmons Wilson room, covered with photos about his life and his famous sayings.

My remarks highlighted the $6 million of federal money misused in a for-profit parking garage for the FedExForum; and the Memphis Networx "boondoggle" where MLGW invested over $25 million of public money to create a financially struggling fiber-optic plan. A good crowd showed up, and I felt that the speech went well.

However, some in the press used the setting as a way to poke fun. Jackson Baker, with the *Memphis Flyer*, commented on the homemade Chumney for Mayor yard sign recycled from my previous city council campaign (since fundraising had not begun yet for the mayor's race). He also portrayed me as a "maverick" apparently because I dared to stand up to those in power against misuse of public funds.[1836]

According to the dictionary, the word "maverick" originally described an unbranded calf. Certainly, no one has ever branded me.

Later, the word's meaning expanded to describe independent thinkers who stand apart from their associates. That's often true of me as well.

And, the label certainly was not negative in the famous 1986 movie *Top Gun,* where Tom Cruise played the ace navy fighter pilot named "Maverick." Maybe having been born on an Air Force base, and with a father who was a pilot, had rubbed off on me? However, some in the local press use the label to marginalize those who speak truth to power, implying they lack support or are eccentric.

The *Memphis Flyer* article also implied arrogance in using the Kemmons Wilson room for the announcement. Baker also used one of the entrepreneur's characteristically corny sayings to suggest eccentricity. The press had the power to shape public opinion about the efficacy of my chances at the polls, which impacted fundraising, endorsements, and turnout. I only wanted a fair chance.

On the other hand, the *Commercial Appeal* editors called my announcement "good news" because it would force an evaluation of Herenton, who presumably would now have to debate the issues.[1837] The editorial noted many good things were happening with the relocation of the corporate headquarters of two Fortune 500 companies to Memphis, but also the need to improve workforce development, address blight, and reduce crime that was "by anyone's standards" too high.[1838] If left unaddressed, these problems impacted the "city's future economic and social progress."[1839] Other issues included the reuse of the empty Pyramid arena and Mid-South Coliseum, the decision whether to build a new football stadium and the redevelopment of the Mid-South Fairgrounds in the heart of the city (where the amusement park which had employed many of the city's youth in the summer months had been dismantled). [1840] The editors appropriately reminded the public of the many issues that called for a strong and stable leader.

Blake Fontenay, with the *Commercial Appeal,* mentioned as liabilities for the mayor the huge property tax increase levied during the past term, the city's bond rating drops, and the investigation over the use of grant funds for the FedExForum parking garage.[1841] Herenton's focus instead had been on an ego-driven charity bout with former heavyweight champion Joe Frazier. [1842] However, he had a half a million dollar war chest. Even his former powerful opponent, Joe Ford, predicted that Herenton's big contributors would not donate to the other candidates to hedge their bets. [1843]

As Fontenay speculated, a crowded field might be an advantage to Herenton with the anti-vote split. [1844] The commentator referred to Herenton as a "12-foot-long alligator" and downplayed my candidacy.[1845] He doubted my ability to raise enough money or generate sufficient grassroots support based upon views of undisclosed "political observers." [1846] However, I believed that Herenton could be beat based upon his recent poor performance as mayor, and I was the one to do it.

As to the other possible mayoral candidates, some wondered whether Morris could connect with voters or garner enough support to avoid being only a spoiler. [1847] Willingham was discounted as unlikely to win and had not performed well in his prior city and county mayoral races. [1848] Both Herenton and Morris had baggage related to MLGW, including the poor response to the 2003 major windstorm, which left citizens without power for days; millions funneled into Memphis Networx with no return; and use of PILOT payments in lieu of taxes towards the financing of the FedExForum arena.[1849]

Some citizens called me the candidate with the most "backbone," "honest and forthright leadership," and able to make the necessary fiscal decisions. Some mentioned that I was experienced, independent, had "progressive ideas," "integrity," "intelligence, and compassion for all Memphis constituents." Others thought I had "courage" and level-headed "common sense" and would bring a "fearless attack on the problems facing Memphis to the campaign, and then to the future position as Mayor." [1850] Others mentioned Harold Ford Jr., Herman Morris or Myron Lowery, all African American men, with some implying that I could not win because "this is Memphis" (an apparent reference to my race or gender). [1851] The compliments were heartening; the discounting of my chances due to my race and gender the opposite. But I would not be deterred.

2

On the heels of my announcement, it was reported that the federal grand jury had subpoenaed three years of billing records from the MLGW public utility for City Councilman Edmund Ford Sr.'s accounts. [1852] Edmund Ford

Sr., a funeral home director, was an African American in his fifties, from the more flamboyant side of the politically powerful Ford family. He was passionate, dramatic, and long-winded when riled up, but also could be humorous and forthright. City Council Chairman Tom Marshall, an architect who was white and in his forties, was generally measured in his temperament. However, in light of the subpoena, he now called for the council to investigate.[1853] As chair of the council's MLGW oversight committee, I placed the matter on the calendar for the next meeting and asked the lawyers for the council and MLGW to advise what records the body had the right to inspect.

Edmund Ford Sr. previously chaired the council's MLGW oversight committee but no longer did after his prior indictment.[1854] That case, unrelated to the utility matter, was still pending.

Top executives at MLGW, including President Joseph Lee, were subpoenaed to testify before the grand jury. Various memos produced reflected that they had known of the alleged delinquent accounts of Edmund Ford Sr. for some time.[1855] At first, Edmund Ford Sr. refused to comment.[1856]

News reports claimed that Councilman Edmund Ford Sr. owed the utility $16,000 related to a business account, and his account was coded for inclusion in an MLGW program designed to aid impoverished customers having difficulty paying their bills."[1857] Inclusion in the "On Track" program would prevent the utilities from being disconnected.[1858] The newspaper claimed that his funeral home account was "flagged as not subject to service disconnection" by an assistant to Lee, "even though businesses are not allowed in the program."[1859] If this were true, he would have an advantage not afforded to other businesses similarly situated, raising a red flag.

However, in a press release, MLGW denied that Edmund Ford Sr. was a participant in the On Track program. It said that instead, the account was on hold due to a dispute over the bill.[1860]

Another *Commercial Appeal* news story reported that a MLGW vice president was notified whenever Councilman Edmund Ford Sr. received a disconnection notice.[1861] The notification list also included the potential service cutoffs for two other elected officials and one former city councilmember. All professed the notifications had been done without their knowledge.[1862] The utility officials denied any special treatment for Edmund Ford Sr.[1863] But, unexplained was why some citizens were on a special list from the general public.

Chairman Marshall appointed two outside lawyers as independent counsel to investigate.[1864] I requested that Joseph Lee appear and answer questions before the council's General Services and Utilities Committee.

Meanwhile, Herman Morris announced his candidacy for Memphis mayor in late February, pledging to stand up to "ad hominem" attacks by Herenton.[1865] An embarrassing memo Morris wrote when he was MLGW chief was leaked to the press by unknown sources. In the memo, he directed his staff to personally notify him of any utility cutoffs for certain elected officials, media figures, and prominent citizens.[1866] Not all elected officials made the special list, as I can attest. One night years earlier, I returned from the legislative session in Nashville to a dark house, having overlooked the payment during the heat of the session. The "VIP list" became a symbol of improper favoritism and the need for change.

Professor Polhmann now opined that the mayor was the man to beat due to his large war chest.[1867] He suggested that a one on one between Morris and Herenton might be a real contest, although his "betting money" would be on Herenton.[1868] He believed the MLGW scandals could harm them both, but that Morris might run as an outsider since he had never held elective office.[1869]

These "expert" opinions were apparently not based upon any reported polling data but influenced readers. I wondered how many votes I might pick up if a pundit said, "Carol's going to win hands down?" Because there had never been a woman mayor of Memphis, the odds of such a prediction were unlikely. This perpetuated an immediate gender bias right out of the gate in a mayoral campaign.

In the face of controversy over the special treatment for some elected officials with calls for him to quit by Councilman Myron Lowery and others, MLGW President Joseph Lee apologized.[1870] Even though having opposed Lee's appointment by Herenton, I wanted to be fair. My responsibility was to lead the council committee's investigation in such a way, as to ensure due process and protect the public's interest. Yet, regardless of the result of the investigation, it was obvious to me that MLGW needed new leadership due to the erosion of public confidence.

The federal grand jury's investigation as to the Lee/Edmund Ford Sr. utility matter continued. Council Chair Marshall advised that if Lee did not resign, he could be removed with Herenton's recommendation and a majority vote of the city council.[1871] Some councilmembers researched whether Lee could be ousted without Herenton's approval, with a report that under the

City Charter, nine of thirteen council votes were required for such action. [1872] Marshall later said eleven of the thirteen councilmembers were required to oust Lee without mayoral approval. [1873] In response, Lee submitted his resignation to Mayor Herenton, effective upon the mayor's acceptance. [1874]

Lee's attorney, Robert Spence, released internal documents from Morris's tenure as MLGW president to aid his client's defense. One 2002 letter from Angus McEachran, the former *Commercial Appeal* editor, concerned his own personal billing dispute. [1875] Morris had written his staff that "this could set editorial policy toward MLGW for years and must be handled with touch." [1876] McEachran claimed that he received no special treatment, only working out a payment plan due to errors by the utility. [1877] However, some felt that it was just another example of the utility's mission requiring equal treatment, run amuck.

As the Lee controversy exploded, Herenton abruptly announced, "To have the *Commercial Appeal*, Myron Lowery and Carol Chumney all in concert call for Joseph Lee's resignation speaks to an array of evil."[1878] Apparently, we were the "axis of evil" to Herenton, a phrase coined by former President George W. Bush for U.S. enemy countries Iran, Iraq, and North Korea. Herenton explained that he had not accepted Lee's resignation in order to wait until the investigation was complete. [1879] He called for the inquiry to be unbiased and professionally done, claiming that it was a "media, political witch hunt." [1880]

The report of Herenton's personal attack stunned me. My only action had been to call for a fair investigation and hearing by the council. Being publicly called evil was verbal abuse. First, I took a few minutes to compose myself. Then, I calmly responded to the press that the real evil was allowing some prominent citizens, whoever they were, to get utility service without having to pay their bills, while others who couldn't pay were left in the dark.

Apparently trying to regain public support, the mayor proposed a $5 million budget appropriation to assist the poor with their utilities.[1881] The general public opposed the measure, suspecting that their utility bills would increase if others got a free ride.

The MLGW board took no action to reprimand Lee or call for his resignation, deciding to wait until all the facts were presented. Instead, the board passed resolutions instructing staff to end any VIP lists and stop any special treatment of elected officials or other prominent citizens. [1882]

When asked, I observed that Herenton should have accepted Lee's resignation for the public's good. Now the controversy would continue indefinitely, detracting from the public's business. I again promised a "fair" council hearing for Lee despite Herenton's baiting me to retaliate to his name-calling.

In light of the public outrage over the preferential treatment of some, the mayor's refusal to accept Lee's resignation was a lost opportunity to regain the trust of the voters. Citing the Tennessee Waltz FBI sting of public officials, the indictments of the two councilmembers, and the FedExForum garage "debacle," the editors of the *Commercial Appeal* called for the mayor to "put his pride aside" and accept the resignation. [1883] They believed that it would help the city move beyond the "perception" that Memphis is controlled by politicians "steeped in corruption," and "movers and shakers who bestow financial perks" to them to gain a business advantage."[1884] I agreed.

Not backing down, in a radio interview Herenton went on the offense calling for an investigation of the meter-reading process to determine whether MLGW employees were sabotaging Lee by raising utility bills for the public. [1885] The mayor referred to himself as a "man" and Morris as a "boy" who "ain't going to enter this [City Hall] gate." [1886] He steadfastly refused to accept Lee's resignation despite the growing scandal, arguing that it "would be a miscarriage of justice" for Lee's career to be sacrificed because of the newspaper and some "hypocritical politicians, who many of them are crooked." [1887] Herenton pointed out that the justice system treated people differently based upon their race and economic class and warned that he would demand equal treatment under the law. [1888]

The MLGW union leader, Rick Thompson, admitted that the utility was using more temporary workers, who might increase billing errors. But he worried that Herenton's call for an investigation was instead "a back door" effort to bring in automated meter reading with a resulting loss of employees. [1889] Chairman Marshall doubted any intentional sabotage in billing practices, attributing any errors to negligence. [1890]

With me being called "evil," and now Morris called a "boy" by the mayor, I wondered what was next. The political name-calling was like that on a playground, rather than serious city business. Herenton occasionally smiled, expressed concern for youth, and was engaging. But, he also often acted like a dictator and bully, invoking race whenever challenged. My experience is that the only way to stop a bully is to stand up for the truth and let the chips fall where they may.

With the scandal growing, the *Memphis Flyer* reported that several public and private entities, including the Memphis Publishing Company [dba the

Commercial Appeal], had large outstanding MLGW balances due. [1891] The MLGW's books reflected that the Memphis Cook Convention Center owed over $800,000. [1892] Various explanations were given by all, such as a disputed bill, errors, or payment plans to bring the amounts in arrears current.

The fact that the former editor of the major daily newspaper was on the VIP list raised the specter of conflicts of interest regarding the coverage of the Lee issue and stories on Herman Morris and the utility. The claim by a former executive that the MLGW board deviated from the usual practice by allowing Joseph Lee to apply eleven years of his city pension time to his MLGW pension only aggravated the controversy. [1893]

The high drama continued at the city council committee meeting. I tried to maintain decorum, but during a discussion about his utility bills, Councilman Edmund Ford Sr. yelled, "don't make me no punk," claiming that it wasn't even his utility account. [1894] Councilman E.C. Jones, a white, middle-aged man who represented a primarily working-class district, wanted the council to rescind McEachran's Morris-approved MLGW payment arrangements. [1895]

Since the council had hired lawyers, I urged that the members first hear the results of their investigation and be counseled as to the proper legal procedures before acting. We adjourned. Later, when the lawyers stopped by my office, I showed them my stack of MLGW receipts for payment of my own utility bills kept by me over the years. They moved on to question other councilmembers. Thinking back to my first MLGW town hall meeting, having made my parents show up to get their complaints answered directly by MLGW officials, I was glad that no one could accuse me of asking for or receiving any VIP treatment for myself or my family.

The MLGW controversy became a national news story. The *New York Times* accurately reported the mood that "shielding the powerful from utility bills when many are struggling after a cold winter seems to have pushed public opinion over the edge" in Memphis. [1896] Again, I spoke out against favoritism at the public utility. A few days later, angry city council members upset with the negative national coverage confronted Lee, who was advised by Spence not to answer questions. [1897] Some called for Lee's resignation, although he had already given one to the mayor. [1898] I recommended a resolution asking the mayor to accept Lee's resignation when the council met in two weeks. [1899]

3

Perhaps to bolster Herenton, Baker with the *Memphis Flyer* warned potential mayoral opposition candidates of a "mauling" and "verbal" abuse by Herenton, described as a "proud alpha male" and former boxer "undefeated in the boxing ring and in the political arena." [1900] Examples given were the mayor's request that Councilman Brent Taylor step outside after a dispute over the council's failure to approve some of his proposed director appointees; telling a TV news anchor who touched his arm to remove his hand or he would "drop" him; and calling me part of an "array of evil" even though my comments about the Lee matter were reasonable. [1901] Baker pointed out that Herenton had called other black politicians "boys" and "clowns" who had considered or run for mayor against him, as he now called Morris. [1902] Baker was right that Herenton would be aggressive. But why there was a need to warn or ward off other potential candidates was unclear. Indeed, we all already knew the mayor's propensity to name-call.

Not intimidated, I intended to be the best mayor Memphis ever had and would not let verbal abuse or implied threats of violence stop me from putting my name on the ballot. If Herenton wanted to fight me, he would have to do so in the political arena.

The *Commercial Appeal* took Herenton head-on, running reports of the mayor's limited liability company private real estate ventures. [1903] At issue was a vacant lot sold by Herenton Investment Company to an engineer, whose engineering company had also received hundreds of thousands of dollars in no-bid road design projects approved by the city during the past five years. [1904] According to news reports, the purchaser later deeded the property back to Herenton's company for nothing. [1905] Those involved responded that he planned to buy the house when it was finished, and the $50,000 initially paid for the lot would then be a down payment, denying any favoritism with the city contracts. [1906]

Also reported by the *Commercial Appeal* was Herenton's prior sale of a house, through his business ventures, to a city administrative assistant. She was said to have received a salary increase of over $20,000 only months before the purchase, although no *quid pro quo* was reported. [1907] And, in 2002, Herenton's investment company sold land to his special city assistant, Pete Aviotti Jr. [1908] The multitude of real estate deals with city players laid out by Marc Perrusquia with the newspaper created more doubt in the minds of many citizens as to whether Herenton was devoting full time to his mayoral duties and if that role conflicted with his private endeavors.

On the heels of the real estate stories and Lee controversy, a new poll found Herenton vulnerable, with only 20% for him; 32% for me (in the lead); and 62% responding that Memphis was heading in the wrong direction.[1909] Those polled cited high unemployment, crime, and taxes, corruption, inadequate public education, and population loss as factors in their discontent.[1910] The poll found me to be a "serious challenger" with the highest support of the four candidates polled.[1911] Yet, speculation still grew as to whether Morris's addition to the field and Willingham would divide the "anti-Herenton" vote to give Herenton another victory.[1912]

Not fazed by the poll, Herenton characteristically replied that the *Commercial Appeal* was simply trying to control him and treat him like a "boy" as opposed to "the Chief Executive Officer of this city who happens to be a man."[1913] Morris added John Ryder, a Republican activist and attorney, as a co-chair of his campaign along with former Judge Russell Sugarmon and long-time public servant Minerva Johnican.[1914] My team worked on selecting a campaign finance chair to raise money and a campaign manager.

The fact that Herenton continued to hit on the "man" "boy" theme, along with other verbiage, left the female gender totally out of the equation. But, if I pointed that out, would I be said to be imagining gender bias again? This is the catch-22 women candidates often face: ignore subtle sexist innuendo or call it out and be accused of being overly sensitive. We left it alone.

Rumors abounded that County Mayor A C Wharton might be drafted to run for city mayor. Wharton professed no interest in running against Herenton.[1915] But, the conservative *Main Street Journal* magazine opined that the "wheels are already in motion" for Wharton to run as city mayor in 2011 as an "almost-lock to win."[1916]

In late March, the new polls showed Herenton lagging in both black and white neighborhoods with me leading all the candidates who had announced and doing well among both white and African American voters.[1917] I was ahead of both Herenton and Morris, with Willingham trailing at 3% and 25% undecided.[1918] The pollster also found that both Morris and I had a "high ability" "to get crossover support from voters of other races."[1919] As one voter said, "she's honest, she speaks her mind, and she's not afraid to stand up against anybody."[1920] My campaign team and I were elated!

However, surprisingly and perhaps as an effort to nudge him into the race, also polled was a field with Wharton in the mix, showing him at 31%, my support at 20%, Herenton at 12%, Morris at 9%, and Willingham at 3%. [1921] Some speculated that Wharton was rethinking his position on whether or not to enter the city mayoral field. The arrest of his oldest son in Knoxville was a distraction. [1922] Why was it that every time I led in a mayoral poll, Wharton appeared?

According to the poll, two-thirds of the voters were critical of Herenton's job performance and character and did not support his reelection. [1923] Rhodes College professor Pohlmann spun it as not a good report for Herenton but also said that my 32% (in the poll without Wharton) was not strong either, even though in the lead. [1924] He opined that Herenton could turn it around with his war chest. [1925]

However, I was glad that the *Commercial Appeal* editors said that the candidate's message mattered more than the amount of money raised as long as there was enough to get the message to the people. [1926] The fact that over a third of the citizens polled would leave town if given the opportunity was deemed a "sad truth" by the editors. [1927] Another poll by a Herenton supporter also showed him to be in trouble. [1928]

My response to the poll was excitement, believing that my message of budget cuts before tax hikes, greater accountability, and government efficiency resonated with the voters. I also pushed for more transparency and to stand up against abuses based upon "power and privilege." I had spent years working for the people at the state legislature and City Hall. The poll reflected support due to my consistent effort of listening to the voters and getting results.

On the heels of the good poll, Wendi Thomas, writer for the *Commercial Appeal,* warned not to get too hasty in replacing Herenton despite his "ghetto playground behavior" in calling Herman Morris a "boy." [1929] She argued to "resist the urge to choose his polar opposite and elected nemesis," claiming that I was a "contrarian" who "hasn't met a TV camera she didn't like." [1930] Thomas advocated for Wharton due to consensus-building skills needed for the job, or Morris instead of me. [1931] Her statement that "the devil we know could be preferable to the devil we don't" was apparently a reference to me. [1932]

Whatever happened to sisterhood? I was baffled and flabbergasted at Thomas's negative portrayal, especially since we had gone to lunch once and had a very cordial conversation. In her article she never even mentioned what it was in her view that merited calling me a devil. I had always treated her with respect.

The public's letters to the editor in response called Thomas's comments "childish" and premature, a reversal of her prior disdain for the mayor, and asked if Herenton wasn't, in fact, the real contrarian. [1933] One writer even wondered if Thomas's comments were racially motivated since all the candidates she preferred to me were black. [1934] In any event, I pushed forward with the campaign.

4

When the report of the independent lawyers investigating the Edmund Ford Sr.-Lee matter was scheduled for a council hearing, Lee's attorney advised that the MLGW president would not appear before the council until the federal investigation ended. [1935] Councilman Marshall expressed disappointment, noting that Herenton said he would wait until the council finished the investigation before deciding whether Lee should be replaced. [1936] Obviously, this delayed a decision indefinitely since the feds rarely disclose to the public whether an investigation is closed (as perhaps Herenton intended all along). Again, in the interest of fairness and due process, I reserved judgment on the outcome of the matter until after hearing the lawyers' report.

At the next council meeting, the investigators reported that Lee had prevented the disconnection of some utilities billed to Edmund Ford Sr. totaling nearly $16,000 during the same time that the councilman was serving as chair of the city council's MLGW oversight committee. [1937] However, Edmund Ford Sr. claimed they were not his charges due to a shared power outlet.

As chair of the council's MLGW committee, I logically recommended that the council ask the mayor to accept Lee's resignation, which would avoid a nasty trial before the city council on his removal. [1938] Councilman Sammons, a businessman connected by marriage to the influential FedEx founder, Fred Smith, instead introduced a resolution to demand that Lee tender his resignation a *second time*. [1939] My substitute motion for the mayor to accept the resignation Lee *had already submitted* died for lack of a second. Keep in mind that neither resolution, if adopted, would actually remove Lee from office. [1940]

Tensions boiled over at the meeting over the removal of Joseph Lee, with allegations of racism. [1941] The council had seven black and six white members. Certainly, Sammons's resolution could be perceived as offensive by alleging that Lee had not cooperated, even though Lee had finally appeared and answered questions directly from councilmembers over his attorney's objection. In the end, the Sammons resolution failed by six to six with my abstention.[1942]

Councilman Edmund Ford Sr. blasted that the Joseph Lee MLGW investigation was racially motivated. He explained that he was not prejudiced, but looking towards Marshall, added that he would "just have to get a white sheet." [1943]Three days after the "white sheet" comments, Edmund Ford Sr. reported that his office incredibly had received a package in the mail containing a white Ku Klux Klan robe with an anonymous note accusing him of being a bigot, hypocrite, and coward.[1944] He asked the police to investigate.[1945]

Although some in the press blamed me for Lee still being on the job due to the failure of Sammons' resolution, in fact, he could only be ousted with nine or more votes as Chairman Marshall had previously advised.[1946] As reporter Mary Cashiola with the *Memphis Flyer* explained, "to remove Lee, charges would have to be written," and the council would need to "essentially hold court proceedings to establish cause," with even then doubts over whether it had the authority to terminate him. [1947] The reporter called it a "surreal tug-of-war" about "asking a man who has already resigned to resign or accepting a resignation that isn't the council's to accept." [1948] I was glad that at least she mostly got it!

In the aftermath of the Lee vote, Republican Councilman Jack Sammons went on the attack accusing me of "playing high school politics at its worst level."[1949] And, councilmembers Brent Taylor and Tom Marshall impugned my motives, claiming that my abstention on the Sammons resolution was in retaliation for their lack of support on my substitute resolution.[1950] Even though Sammons and Marshall were both reported to have considered mayoral runs themselves for the 2007 election, the possibility that they were the ones playing politics in not supporting my substitute resolution was never mentioned by the media or press. [1951] As one local blogger commented, the "Sammons' resolution was there to A) take the pressure OFF the Mayor, B) try and trap Carol in piling on to Lee, and C) make Carol look bad, because he's [Sammons] in the pocket of the developers who want to keep Carol out of the Mayor's office." [1952]

It was a tough vote—but I voted my conscience based upon due process concerns that the city council lacked the authority to remove Lee independently of the mayor without written charges of criminal wrongdoing or malfeasance and a trial. My resolution would have sent the matter where it belonged, back to the mayor to accept Lee's resignation. Afterward, I had an inkling of how Atticus Finch might have felt even though Lee was not my client.[1953] Although Lee's actions were worthy of question, he *had* submitted his resignation, which *Herenton* had refused. It was impossible to fully explain my abstention vote in the highly politicized and racially charged public environment. But, in addition to the due process concerns and inaccurate wording of the Sammons resolution, I just didn't think Sammons would have asked Lee to resign twice if he were white.

The vote bothered some of my supporters and friends. One campaign contributor couldn't understand why I did not vote for the Sammons resolution. Another supporter said I should have just skipped the meeting. However, that's not what I was elected to do. I am sure they privately wondered why I stood up for due process for Lee, whom I didn't support for the job initially, and even wanted him to be replaced. I stood firm because we all have due process rights. If they are overlooked for one person, then they can be ignored for any of us. I had to do the right thing regardless of the judgment of some of my supporters or consequences for the election. Otherwise, I would lose respect for myself.

With the Lee vote over, some pundits, in apparent shock over my double-digit lead over the powerful long-serving Herenton, scratched their heads and tried to figure out how it could possibly be? Instead of attributing this to my solid record of public service and speaking truth to power, one reporter credited it instead to my "singlemindedness," noting that my "very independence scares defenders of the status quo."[1954] That might be true, but the status quo had left many people behind and fostered some corruption as well. Why not have leadership that would do what was best for all Memphians?

Reports grew of a "Draft A C" movement due to Herenton's weak showing in the polls, high crime, the reports of grand jury investigations, perhaps my good showing in the polls, and Herenton's ditzy promotion of new projects or proposals—only to lose interest, drop them like a hot potato and fail to make them concrete realities.[1955] And, attacks on me flew with a high profile Republican disc jockey and newscaster claiming that I was losing support in the mayor's race for abstaining on the Sammons resolution and that Sammons might enter the mayoral field. [1956] So, was this the plan all along?

5

After that, new revelations came forth of an agreement previously struck by MLGW (through its VP and General Counsel, Odell Horton Jr. upon the advice of the City Attorney Sara Hall) and Lee, that the utility would pay for Lee's attorneys' fees for the federal investigation and his testimony before the grand jury.[1957] The bill to date exceeded $60,000, with Spence keeping each statement under $25,000. The MLGW attorney disputed that this was done to avoid the need for city council approval and defended that it was the usual practice to provide a defense for MLGW employees when acting in their official capacity.[1958] MLGW board member Nick Clark, a prominent developer, was dismayed. He called for the cancellation of the agreement.[1959]

Questions were raised about why MLGW would pay for Spence to represent Lee during the city council's investigation, where he advised his client not to answer questions.[1960] However, Lee had disregarded Spence's advice and did answer questions through another attorney who had conducted the investigation for the council. The controversy worsened when MLGW refused to release the attorney's billing statements to the public.[1961]

Sammons contended that a double-standard was in play, with Lee getting an attorney paid for by the public for his indictment, but Councilmen Ford Sr. and Peete having to bear their own legal expenses related to their charges.[1962] He also called the $25,000 billing threshold a "premediated attempt" to get around council review.[1963] Many citizens were angry that Lee was still on the job, and they were paying his legal bills too.

It came to a head when MLGW board member Nick Clark reported to the FBI that Lee allegedly tried to blackmail him with misinformation.[1964]Clark claimed that the reason was so he would stay silent about the request for payment of Lee's legal fees.[1965] The allegations attributed to Lee by Clark were the proverbial straw that broke the camel's back. Herenton finally did what my resolution had requested—he held a press conference and accepted Lee's resignation.[1966] The MLGW board now reversed course on the payment of Lee's legal fees, and the MLGW general counsel also resigned.[1967]

Morris, who himself had been a Herenton MLGW appointee, now called the utility under Herenton's administration to have become a poorly managed "nest of cronyism and gangster management at the top" who are "friends of Willie."[1968] One local blogger wryly observed that Herman Morris at one time was also a "crony" of Herenton.[1969]

My letter to the *Commercial Appeal* editor explaining my Lee vote on the grounds that good government requires professionalism in hiring and firing went unpublished.[1970] Why wouldn't the newspaper allow me to explain my vote? In my view, the hiring process of Lee as MLGW president was a sham by the mayor; and the termination process was delayed by the mayor's initial refusal to accept Lee's resignation. Ultimately, after all this damage was done, Herenton did what I proposed; he accepted Lee's resignation.

Under enormous pressure, I did not take the easy way out but held firm that the mayor had the power to remove Lee by simply accepting his resignation. The council could only remove him after a due process hearing and ouster vote. I did the right thing but was not allowed the opportunity to explain it. With race being so much of a factor in Memphis, my principled stand was hard to explain to some voters who viewed everything in black and white. It was a very frustrating and lonely experience, but I voted my conscience.

With so much angst over the leadership of the "men" of the city, maybe it was time to amend the engraving on the wall at City Hall to include *wo*-men too!

28

The Sex-Plot Thickens

1

As I campaigned around the city, Andy Meeks with the *Daily News* dubbed me a straight-talking "results-driven politician" with "personal and professional ethic[s]" who was "perfectly capable of swimming with all manner of sharks."[1971] I was used to it after actually having been on a shark dive. In fact, these political sharks were worse than the real ones in Nassau, who swam within inches of me and never attacked.

With city budget discussions underway, I questioned Herenton's proposal to transfer $18 million from the city's debt service fund to spend on operating expenses, citing an 1897 Tennessee Supreme Court decision to support my position.[1972] The better approach would be to reduce capital projects to free up funds for operating expenses. Herenton's approach allowed him to roll-out an election-year budget with no property tax increase, adding $4 million to the reserves and one hundred more police officers.[1973] But there would be a payback down the road if sufficient funds were not available to pay the enormous city debt. Unfortunately, the press either just didn't care or wasn't reporting on it for some other reason. Later the chickens would come home to roost.

My opposition to the proposed capital project of the $29 million Beale Street Landing project initially prevailed with a committee vote of three to two to remove it from the budget.[1974] With an underutilized Mud Island river park, and empty Coliseum and Pyramid, for once, Memphis needed to take the time to fix what it had before investing millions in a new project.[1975] The city had a history of spending millions of dollars on a project and then, when it didn't work, moving on to a huge new project instead of fixing the ones already built.

The Beale Street Landing project was opposed by many environmentalists, river experts, and regular citizens. Councilman Tom Marshall, an architect, spoke in support of it as "an important piece of the Downtown restoration puzzle," claiming that to forgo it would set the city back a number of years."[1976] The Riverfront Development Corporation ("RDC") President added that "this is to allow Memphis to connect to the water" even though the Mud Island park already had a river walk and boat dock ramps.[1977] I continued to oppose it based upon the city's high debt.[1978] Only a few weeks later, the project was added back into the budget with the committee's reversal.[1979] Ultimately, it was approved, over opposition by me, Councilmen E.C. Jones and Jack Sammons, Memphis Heritage, the Sierra Club, Friends for Our Riverfront, and others.[1980] Some called it a $29 million boat dock.[1981] The RDC head optimistically projected that the project would be finished within two to three years.[1982]

Prophetically, the *Commercial Appeal* editors called upon the councilmembers to provide greater oversight to the project's financing, design, and progress.[1983] It reminded the public of past fiascos, including the convention center expansion that ultimately came in double the projected costs, the misspent grant funds on the FedExForum parking garage costing the city $6 million from future projects, and the $28.6 million lost in the Memphis Networx investment. [1984]

The Beale Street Landing grand-opening was finally held seven years later in May 2014.[1985] The project cost had grown from $29 million to $42 million and was four years behind schedule. [1986] Also, of concern was that no restaurant owner initially stepped up to operate in the new facility due to the lack of a natural gas service line, among other things. [1987]

The RDC ultimately was forced to open its own bar and grill at the new facility. However, the *Commercial Appeal* editors called for a first-rate quality restaurant by an experienced operator instead. [1988] In 2016, it was subsequently reported that the facility operated at a $90,000 deficit.[1989] Finally, two experienced restaurateurs stepped up in 2017 to give it a try on a short term contract. But, in 2018, the RDC, renamed Memphis River Parks Partnership, announced that the restaurant would not reopen, and the premises would be used instead for catered events.[1990]

While the facility did provide a boat dock and a concrete landing for folks to throw frisbees and sit, it had not fulfilled all the attraction features promised by its proponents. Even the RDC head admitted that the project should have been scaled back. [1991]

On debating items like the Beale Street Landing, the city council at times was like a snake pit. You never knew what was being plotted behind closed doors that might bite the next meeting. Some councilmembers opposed my mayoral candidacy calling me challenging to work with because I wouldn't violate the open meetings law by cutting backroom deals before the meetings. The practice was brought to the public's attention years later in 2014 when there were allegations that some councilmembers had violated the open meetings act prior to a vote. [1992] One councilmember, Janis Fullilove, claimed that the backroom meetings resulted in women being shut out of leadership positions.[1993] She contended that the secret meetings were a regular practice by white male councilmembers, which the called-out members denied. [1994] Several councilmembers, such as Harold Collins and Shea Flinn, defended the practice of private discussions on the selection of a chairman, which was promptly rebuked by an editorial in the *Commercial Appeal*. [1995]

Later, one councilmember announced that private meetings had preceded important votes on pension reform and health care cuts for workers.[1996] A former councilmember was reported to say that it was a common practice for some other councilmembers to cut backroom deals when he had served on the body. [1997] I believe that the public has the right to be present for the local legislative body's deliberations as required by state law and for such proceedings not to be merely a pre-planned charade.

Despite the opposition by some of my colleagues, John Branston, a reporter for the *Memphis Flyer*, wondered if the negative traits attributed to me by them were actually positives that would win over voters. [1998] He cited my being "independent to a fault" and straight-forward, with supporters seeing a "diligent council member who is demonstrably not better off financially for having been a public servant." [1999] That was true.

Branston called me "radical in a way that has nothing to do with feminism or war or national issues and everything to do with local issues and priorities."[2000] And, he acknowledged that my "refusal to join in the censure of Joseph Lee because it was irrelevant was unpopular but turned out to be correct." [2001] I appreciated his perspective.

It was hard speaking truth to power. I wanted what was best for Memphis, but the city council was a tough job, in part, because of the dynamics of the city. The council interactions were often dysfunctional. For example, there were only three female colleagues on the council, which put us at a disadvantage out of the gate. A more balanced council would better reflect the male and female citizenry.

Meanwhile, Herman Morris fundraised and took his jabs at the other candidates, saying he was the only mayoral candidate to have a "real first lady" in his wife. Herenton and I were single.[2002] Baker in the *Memphis Flyer* gave a few jabs himself. Again, he called me a "maverick" with a "go it alone reputation," but also acknowledged my grass-roots support even among the GOP.[2003] He further questioned Morris's comfortability with voters, and judged Willingham a well-informed eccentric.[2004]

With the John Ford trial for alleged bribery underway, Herenton now grabbed the spotlight and turned the tables. The mayor claimed that *he* had been offered positions and money not to run for reelection that *he* felt bordered on bribes.[2005] In his typically blunt fashion, he professed that he didn't "give a damn if you like me, but respect my leadership" and vowed to stay in the mayor's race.[2006] The mayor called out those who wanted him to step down as "just a few guys" "consumed with power and control."[2007] And, he morphed the presidential candidate Barack Obama's phrase "Audacity of Hope" into the "audacity" to think that Herenton could be controlled, likening it to "an old Southern slave master mentality" that he had rejected all of his life.[2008] I suppose my audacity was to think that a woman could be the mayor.

2

Herenton next abruptly dropped another political bombshell, claiming that he was the victim of a "sex-plot."[2009] He claimed that Nick Clark, the MLGW board commissioner who accused Lee of blackmail, had given money to Richard Fields, a Herenton long-time supporter and civil rights attorney, in a new alleged blackmail plot.[2010] The mayor claimed that a former waitress for a topless dance club was paid to video a sexual encounter with him secretly.[2011] Instead, according to Herenton, she went to the police and revealed the plot to the mayor.[2012] Herenton produced a letter by the waitress to the local district attorney, Bill Gibbons, wherein she claimed that she was offered $150,000 to seduce the mayor into a videotaped sex sting.[2013]

Some speculated that Herenton contrived the plot himself, as a ruse to gain sympathy and ensure a large turnout of his base.[2014] Certainly, the drama detracted attention from the major issues of high crime, poorly performing schools, and the MLGW scandals.

The whole story was bizarre. Fields had been a long-time Herenton supporter. Clark had been appointed to the MLGW board by Herenton. Why did they now purportedly turn on him? What did a sex-plot have to do with the mayoral election? When would the voters' real concerns be addressed?

Amidst this backdrop, on a hot sunny day, a large group of sign-waving supporters accompanied me to the election commission to file my official petition for Memphis mayor. In my remarks, I pledged to restore trust in government and clean up the crime, cronyism, and corruption that had taken root.[2015] I felt good about filing for mayor and hoped that we would win. However, the sex-plot story seemed to dominate the news.

Thereafter, Herenton also held a press conference, calling the alleged sex-plot the "2007 Political Conspiracy." He claimed that the conspirators included key business leaders, one high-level elected official, and even some members of the U.S. Justice Department.[2016] Quoting the Bible, Herenton called them "self-righteous, hypocritical do-gooders" who were trying to embarrass him as mayor by suggesting that he had connections with topless clubs and drug dealers and only "want to control Memphis."[2017] He announced that he couldn't be controlled. Also, he shared a personal warning from a friend to beef up his security, alluding to the assassination of Dr. Martin Luther King Jr.[2018]

Political science professor Pohlmann now suggested that Herenton might garner sympathy for the story, with harm to any opponents taking contributions from those involved. [2019] Other Herenton allies agreed, predicting that the alleged sex-plot would backfire on those involved. [2020]

On a roll, Herenton accused the *Commercial Appeal* of biased polling and reporting and went on the offense, saying that "Carol Chumney does not need a war chest" because the newspaper "give[s] her all the free news she needs."[2021] Talking in racial terms, he warned that African Americans shouldn't be divided and conquered and complained that "white people have wealth in this community" while black people "are basically economically disenfranchised." [2022]

With my solid record of helping people of all races and modest upbringing, Herenton had no basis for attacking me on racism or economic classism. Instead, he attacked the predominately white media and press. But his drawing race into the campaign more than likely still had a negative effect on my campaign.

Herenton further stated that he had filed a complaint with the U.S. Attorney General Alberto Gonzales, and had written the governor of Tennessee asking for a special prosecutor to provide investigatory monitoring of his complaints, along with letters to U.S. Sens. Corker and Alexander, and U.S. Congressman Steve Cohen.[2023] Using coded language, he claimed that there were two "snakes" who had been "crawling in the grass," and one "finally raised his head."[2024] The other, according to Herenton with a veiled threat, is still "in our midst, crawling on his belly, low in the grass, and I'm going to put him on notice, when he raises his head, when he raises his head—you complete the rest of it."[2025]

One local blogger asked the logical question of whether A C Wharton was the second snake referred to by Herenton, in that business leaders had been trying to recruit him to run for city mayor.[2026] Wharton had been holding $1,000 a plate fundraisers even though he was in his last term as county mayor.[2027] The blogger warned that if Wharton did run, he would be looked upon as a pawn of the power brokers used to destroy Herenton and perceived as the black candidate of white Republicans.[2028] He cautioned A C to lay his head low if he were the snake, or else he might lose it.[2029] Both Herenton's press conference and the blogger's follow-up caused quite a stir.

Wanting the voters to have the truth, I called upon Herenton to reveal the names of people he claimed were involved in the alleged conspiracy so they could answer the charges.[2030] Morris and Councilman Lowery called the story "bizarre." [2031] Regardless of whatever the true facts were about the alleged sex-plot, the allegations totally distracted from the issues that needed to be addressed for the citizens.

3

After the alleged sex-plot conspiracy splash, Memphis Networx made the news again. New questions were raised about whether the company's proposed purchaser had ties with the Networx Chief Operating Officer since they both lived in Denver.[2032] Reports that the Networx website hadn't been updated since 2005 and that it appeared to have little marketing effort or sales force caused speculation about whether a touted purpose of expanding fiber optic to underserved areas had been a real objective of the public-private venture.[2033] Facing a $30 million loss of ratepayer funds if sold, along with monies invested by wealthy prominent businessmen, some warned that more transparency was needed before an $11 million sale was approved to a company that was not even the highest bidder.[2034] The news reports generated even more questions about what had transpired.

Nick Clark, MLGW board commissioner and one of those accused by Herenton in the sex-plot controversy, was also the point person to the press in support of the sale of Networx.[2035] I wondered how he could be in an alleged sex-plot conspiracy involving the mayor and continue to serve on the MLGW board as a mayoral appointee without Herenton asking for his resignation? In the past, Clark always had been a straight arrow in my dealings with him as a councilmember.

Financial questions were raised about overspending by Networx, lack of oversight by MLGW, and a lack of transparency.[2036] None of it added up.

Herman Morris maintained his position that if properly funded, Memphis Networx might be more profitable over time.[2037] I simply asked for an explanation of why the city council was repeatedly told that Networx was about to start making money, and now it was being proposed to be sold at a huge loss. The ratepayers deserved a return of their money with interest.[2038]

The MLGW board approved the sale anyway, reporting that the Memphis Networx entity only had enough cash on hand to operate another six weeks before going bankrupt or losing value.[2039] The council eventually voted for an independent audit, and one of the higher bidders filed a lawsuit to block the sale.[2040] This was a huge loss of taxpayer money.

4

Meanwhile, my campaign continued, with my top three issues of stopping "crime, cronyism, and corruption." I pledged to get answers on the Memphis Networx lost monies, give the police a well-deserved pay raise after a two-year freeze, keep the Mid-South Coliseum, and make the Pyramid a classy venue. In a short profile, Baker with the *Memphis Flyer*, devoted several paragraphs to whether I could work with others as mayor, and the city council, to get things done. [2041] It sounded to me like just more of the same old stereotype that a woman who speaks her mind is disagreeable.

My response was that I had worked with my colleagues in the state legislature for years getting things done.[2042] There was push-back at City Hall related to my opposition to waste of public monies, especially concerning the twelve-year pension for elected and appointed officials. I was often the only one who confronted the issue initially, or at all, which made some others mad. However, I believed that the people of Memphis were going to elect a new mayor and a new city council that would work with me as the new mayor. Did the people want results or someone who would check their brain at the door of City Hall when reporting to work?

In fact, a big turnover on the city council was in the works, with Jack Sammons and Tom Marshall announcing they would not seek reelection, and half the council seats expected to be occupied by new members (including those of retiring members Brent Taylor, E.C. Jones, Dederick Brittenum and Edmund Ford Sr.).[2043] Since I was running for mayor, I could not seek reelection to the council.

Moving forward with the campaign, my more formal announcement for mayor was made on the Memphis Showboat on July 3, just in time for over a hundred supporters to watch fireworks after a beautiful sunset on the Mississippi River.[2044] As the crowd on the riverboat cheered, I reminded them that for seventeen years, I'd been a good steward of their money, stood up for them, cared about them, and never sold out. I pledged to stop crime, corruption, and cronyism and clean up the city once and for all. I would read the contracts to ensure that the city did not suffer other fiascos such as omitting to build an entire floor in the FedExForum parking garage and forfeiting $6 million in grant funds. I would negotiate agreements in the best interest of the citizens, instead of hogtying the public's ability to fully utilize public facilities such as the Pyramid due to the right of first refusal on concerts given to the Grizzlies with no solid mechanism in place to ensure the use of both facilities to the taxpayers' benefit. Our campaign continued at various Fourth of July neighborhood picnics.

Herenton also filed for reelection. Former Mayor Dick Hackett, who had been beaten by him in 1991, said that the race was his to lose.[2045] While Herenton had a significant war chest of half a million dollars, he had raised only $1,650 in the first quarter of 2007 as a testament to his beleaguered status as mayor.[2046] And reports were to the effect that nearly half the monies he raised in 2006 were from nonresidents who could not vote in the election.[2047] At the next reporting period, Morris had raised nearly $170,000. Strickland, who was still considering a mayoral bid, had over $100,000 leftover in his city council campaign account. And my campaign had about half that.[2048]

Fundraising was difficult against an incumbent Mayor who would retaliate if angered. Many contributed to my campaign amounts less than the reporting name disclosure limit to avoid retribution.

Ironically, Herenton now himself played the race card, calling out the "white-controlled media" for "playing the race card" with a news story about MLGW board member Nick Clark. [2049] Clark discounted the mayor's statements as designed to get votes but admitted that he had paid the former waitress cash through Fields to visit strip clubs to obtain the dancers' addresses. [2050] The waitress had met with an FBI agent at Clark's home. [2051] Clark, a wealthy real estate developer, was also involved with a local group that worked to save strippers from the business by helping them find jobs. [2052]

Richard Fields claimed he went with the waitress for her to tell the FBI that Herenton partied with strippers provided by the strip club owner. [2053] Fields was the waitress's lawyer in a criminal case and said she was cooperating to help her boyfriend get a reduced sentence. [2054] The waitress claimed to have been paid $6,000 thus far to visit clubs to find any strippers who had had sexual relations with the mayor. [2055] Fields, however, called the claims of a Herenton sex-plot sting ludicrous in that the mayor already had a sexually tarnished reputation with the prior lawsuit that was settled when he was superintendent of the schools, and with recent reports of fathering a child out of wedlock. [2056] He made a good point.

Herenton called this the devil's work, saying that God had revealed the plot to him through the waitress coming forward. [2057] However, the club owner was also reported by the *Commercial Appeal* to be a contributor to his campaign and a sponsor of the charity boxing match held the prior year, with Joe Frazier and Herenton as the boxers. [2058] With strong language, Herenton drew comparisons between Clark's claims that his actions were fueled by his strong Christian faith, with the mayor's belief it was the same reasoning used by "self-righteous bigots" who were members of the Ku Klux Klan that supported segregation. [2059] But then again, if Herenton believed Clark to be a bigot, why had he nominated him to the MLGW board?

The following week, a *Commercial Appeal* poll revealed that 42% of those polled did not believe Herenton's account of the sex-plot, with three-fourths of those white. [2060] My Harrison, the special agent in charge of the Memphis area, also denied any FBI involvement in a sex-plot. [2061] The story dominated the press and media and diverted attention from our campaign. Herenton now played the victim, and the election for the time being became more of a contest between him and the "white-controlled" media, Clark and Fields, rather than the other candidates.

5

Speculation continued as to whether or not A C Wharton would enter the city mayoral election, with some saying that he feared being "mauled" by Herenton, who was known for his ability to turn out the vote.[2062] I remained steadfast to stay in the race whether Wharton entered the field or not. Two high profile preachers, both African American, who had helped Herenton win his first election in 1991, along with former Shelby County Mayor Bill Morris, and restauranteur Thomas Boggs, began a "Draft A C" campaign.[2063] Wharton said he would listen.[2064] Pundits referred to prior polls that placed A C before me, and then Herenton, as further support for the Draft A C effort.[2065]

One prominent preacher, Lasimba Gray, expressed his disappointment with Herenton for failing to expand economic opportunity for black citizens, failing to appoint more African Americans in his administration, only playing the race card for his own benefit, and "all kinds of scandals, suspicions, allegations and investigations."[2066] However, another famous preacher, Rev. Billy Kyles, discouraged an A C candidacy.[2067] County Commissioner Sidney Chism was blunter, saying that it would divide the black community for years.[2068]

Herenton fired back, calling the pastors seeking to draft Wharton "self-serving preachers."[2069] Bill Adkins, one of the preachers, reminded that he had helped Herenton get into office as mayor and also helped him fight off the effort to terminate him as the Memphis City Schools superintendent.[2070] At that time, Adkins had threatened a student boycott, with A C Wharton and Richards Fields serving as Herenton's legal counsel.[2071] Both Bill Morris and Thomas Boggs responded that the city needed uniting due to Herenton's divisive statements.[2072] In my view, what the city needed was less ego, and leadership that was not beholden to special interests and truly focused on results for the greater public good.

A political cartoon of A C as a snake with a forked tongue ran in the *Commercial Appeal*, with many letters to the editor against Herenton and some supporting an A C candidacy.[2073] Political writer Wendi Thomas observed that Wharton was a "nice guy," a "charmer" with a "gap-toothed smile," and "smooth," but added that very few people could recall anything concrete that he had ever accomplished.[2074] He benefited greatly from his stark contrast with Herenton, who had more than one sex scandal controversy, made racially divisive statements on occasion, and at times acted more like the back-yard bully than the mayor of a major metropolitan city. Would the voters be lulled into picking Wharton with a lackluster county mayoral record, simply because he was less controversial than Herenton?

Indeed, some criticized Wharton's indecisiveness, who was said to have "more style than substance."[2075] Their comments mirrored what I had said in the 2002 county mayor's campaign – that the community needed more than a mayor who "styles, smiles, and profiles."

For my part, I called for an end to the "soap opera" playing out over whether Wharton would abdicate his position as county mayor, along with the sex scandal and circus atmosphere at City Hall.[2076] Calling on Wharton to either "get in or get out" of the race, I observed that he had much unfinished business in the county mayor's job, such as saving the public hospital which was on life support, reducing crime in the county, and also improving air quality.[2077] I called for an end to "recycling" candidates and a new generation of leadership, vowing to stay in the race no matter what.[2078] Were some in Memphis so threatened by the possibility of an independent-minded female mayor that they ran to Wharton just to stop me? Or was it just an effort to keep the status quo by some with Wharton since Herenton was lagging in the polls?

The specter of a Wharton city mayoral candidacy led to questions as to whether he would try to hold both the county and city mayor jobs simultaneously, since he had just won reelection as county mayor in 2006.[2079] While Pastor Adkins mentioned the possibility of "instant consolidation," the fact remained that the county and city charters each required the mayor to devote full-time to that particular job and state law required a vote by the public for any merger.[2080]

Significantly, in the midst of the angst over who would run for mayor, the *Tri-State Defender* described a markedly different view of the state of the area.[2081] The editorial called for reforms given that 85% of those incarcerated in the county jail were black, vacant properties and blight were abundant, racial and economic division were growing, and there was a huge city and county debt, and high poverty.[2082]

Other reports painted a similar picture of Memphis. Forty-six percent of home purchase loans in 2006 were high-cost subprime loans, ranking second nationally for such loans and ninth for the number of foreclosures.[2083] Also, new U.S. Census Bureau reports showed the city had lost 12,000 in population in the past six years, despite several annexations. [2084] With these statistics, respectfully, one had to ask, even if they were doing their best, why would anyone want either incumbent man as the next Memphis mayor?

6

While the debate continued over whether Wharton would enter the city mayor's race, news spread about the federal indictment of former MLGW President Joseph Lee III and Councilman Edmund Ford Sr.[2085] The charges were bribery and extortion related to Ford's alleged outstanding funeral home utility bill, and Lee's approval by the city council as MLGW president.[2086] Lee pled not guilty, with his lawyer Robert Spence saying the failure to pay a utility bill did not constitute a crime.[2087] Spence called the charges "trumped-up," referencing that the allegations against Lee were first made by Richard Fields, "the same snake" said by a waitress to have tried to get her to set up the mayor in the sex-plot. [2088] In addition, Lee argued selective prosecution in that the funeral home landlord, Dennis Churchwell, had not been similarly charged.[2089] But, the court ruled against him on that issue because the landlord was not a public official and public monies were not involved as to him, among other things.[2090]

However, Edmund Ford Sr.'s funeral home's landlord was indicted on charges of giving false testimony under oath related to the FBI's investigation of whether the councilman was current on his rent for the lease of property for his funeral home at the end of 2005, among other things. [2091] The FBI had investigated whether there was a connection between forgiven rent payments by the landlord and Edmund Ford Sr.'s assistance in getting a special use permit approved by the city council for another property owned by the landlord's wife. [2092] Years later, the landlord pled guilty to one count of false declaration before a grand jury related to his questioning by the FBI, with the other charges dropped.[2093]

During the same week of the indictments of Lee III and Edmund Ford Sr., former state Sens. Ward Crutchfield, age seventy-eight, and Kathryn Bowers, age sixty-four, each pled guilty to bribery charges stemming from the Tennessee Waltz FBI sting.[2094]

Charles Brown

SGA President Carol Chumney (left) and committee chairman Catherine Hayes-Crawford (right) flank Gov. Lamar Alexander.

Photo with Governor Lamar Alexander at the Tennessee Governor's Mansion.
The Daily Helmsman March 8, 1983

U.S. Senator Al Gore at Carol Chumney for State Representative headquarters 1990-
from left Sen. Steve Cohen, Rev. Herman Powell, Jean Rae Bowers, Chumney, Gore

Carol hoping for a victory on primary election day, August 1990

Carol Chumney takes the oath of office as State Representative- January 1991

Carol Chumney meeting with Gov. Ned McWherter in his State Capitol office
about stopping a proposed extension of interstate in her legislative district

Carol Chumney presenting on floor of Tennessee General Assembly

Carol Chumney making a campaign speech at a rally event
before the 1994 general election for state house

Carol meeting with senior citizens at her town hall meeting

Garth Brooks gives Rep. Carol Chumney a hug after his presentation in support of her ticket-scalping bill to the House Judiciary Committee—1993

State Representative Carol Chumney presents at a bill-signing in Gov. McWherter's office

State Rep. Carol Chumney presenting in the well on the
Tennessee State House floor with women legislators, 1995

Rep. Carol Chumney and Hillary Clinton on 1996 Tennessee campaign bus tour

Rep. Carol Chumney, President Bill Clinton, Rev. Billy Kyles and Vice-President Al Gore
backstage at Memphis City Hall – 1996 U.S. Presidential campaign reelection event

President Bill Clinton, State Rep. Carol Chumney
and Sen. Steve Cohen at Memphis reception

Carol Chumney with campaign team kicking off Shelby County Mayor's race 2002

Mayor Willie Herenton backs his nominee for MLGW president, city finance director Joseph Lee (standing second from right). But "nagging concern" about Lee's lack of experience in the utility sector led the City council personnel committee on an 8-3 vote to put off action for four weeks. @ A.J. Wolfe- USA TODAY NETWORK, January 7, 2004

Councilmembers (from left) E. C. Jones, Scott McCormick, Rickey Peete
and Carol Chumney listen to Mayor Willie Herenton's plans Tuesday.
@ Karen Pulfer Focht- USA TODAY NETWORK, December 8, 2004

March 17, 2005; Memphis, TN, USA; Memphis Mayor Willie Herenton, left, and Shelby County
Mayor A.C. Wharton make their introductions during the first meeting of a task force on consolidated schools at the Botanic Gardens on Thursday. School board members were absent from the
meeting, despite being extended an invitation. @ Lance Murphey- USA TODAY NETWORK

Carol Chumney with Yohei Kono, Speaker of the House of
Representatives of the National Diet, Tokyo, Japan 2006

July 24, 2007; Memphis, TN, USA; City Council member and city
mayoral candidate Carol Chumney (cq) chairs the council's utilities committee.
She listens to council attorney Allan Wade (cq) (Right) discuss issues with legal
matters involving MLG&W. @ Dave Darnell-USA TODAY NETWORK

Sept. 30, 2007; Memphis, TN, USA; Mayoral candidate Carol Chumney, left, talks with Lessie Hall during a visit to Columbus Missionary Baptist Church Sunday morning. @Jim Weber- USA TODAY NETWORK

Sept. 30, 2007; Memphis, TN, USA; Mayoral candidate Herman Morris waves to the congregations at New Sardis Baptist Church during the Sunday service. By 12:30 in the afternoon Morris and his team had visited seven churches through out the Memphis metro area and where [sic] going strong. @Mike Brown- USA TODAY NETWORK

Sept. 19, 2007; Memphis, TN, USA; Mayor Willie Herenton speaks to local media about what the Mayor's office calls an early voting machine problem at Bishop Byrne during a press conference outside City Hall. @ Mark Weber- USA TODAY NETWORK

Sept. 1, 2007; Memphis, TN, USA; Candidate for the Memphis Mayor's position Carol Chumney (cq) shakes hands with University of Memphis tailgaters before the start of the Memphis Ole Miss game at the Liberty Bowl. @ Matthew Craig- USA TODAY NETWORK

Oct. 4, 2007; Memphis, TN, USA; Mayoral Candidate Carol Chumney gives her concession speech at the Peabody Hotel. @ Mark Weber- USA TODAY NETWORK

Memphis Mayoral candidate Carol Chumney and Memphis
skyline 2009 - Photo by Keith Renard/Skipworth Photography

Carol Chumney kicks off 2009 Memphis Mayoral campaign at her headquarters

Carol campaigning for Memphis Mayor at backyard picnic 2009

Memphis, TN; USA; Memphis Police Department Director Michael Rallings (left)
and District Attorney General Amy Weirich (middle) listens [sic] as Memphis Mayor
Jim Strickland announces the /"Fed Up/" gun control campaign in July.
The campaign will bring tougher state penalties and possible federal prosecution
for violent criminals in possession of a gun. @ Mark Weber-USA TODAY NETWORK

Carol Chumney on a mission trip at the Olive Garden park in Meru, Kenya, 2013

President Jimmy & Rosalyn Carter and Carol Chumney at the
Maranatha Baptist Church in Plains, Georgia, September 2017

Joseph Weinberg, M.D., former Rep. Mike Kernell, Attorney Carol J. Chumney,
and Rep. Joe Towns Jr. outside the Sixth Circuit Court of Appeals courthouse.

Later, former state Sen. John Ford asked for leniency after his conviction in Memphis on one count of bribery involving federal programs.[2095] The obstruction charge of the indictment was dismissed, and he was found not guilty on the remaining counts of the indictment.[2096] The proof had shown payments of several thousand dollars to support the legislation in favor of the fictitious E-Cycle company set up by the FBI.[2097] There was also evidence of an agreement wherein the senator would receive benefits from the public stock offering by E-Cycle if the legislation passed.[2098]

The prosecutor wanted to include the $70,000 Rolex watch that Ford received from a local developer to increase his sentence, saying it was a bribe. The defense claimed that Ford had merely switched watches with the developer.[2099] John Ford was sentenced to over five years in prison. [2100] The Rolex watch, which had been seized by the government, was forfeited by court order when the accused failed to timely sign a claim for its return under penalty of perjury.[2101]

With the Lee III and Edmund Ford Sr. indictments, the MLGW board decided that Lee had forfeited his health insurance benefits because he had not returned and executed the separation agreement timely. [2102] Lee countered by filing suit against the utility for breach of contract, blaming the "politics of race" as the reason he was being denied the payment of his legal fees. [2103]

7

Amid the controversies, the mayoral field narrowed. Alternating views of the candidates' strengths and weaknesses were discussed by Baker in the *Memphis Flyer*, such as whether Herenton was "proud" or "reckless" and "haughty;" I was "determinedly independent" or "foolishly stubborn;" Herman Morris was elite or "reserved;" and Willingham was "respected" or an "eccentric."[2104] And there I was in a photo with supporters, with the typical caption "Mayoral candidate Carol Chumney: Joan of Arc of the disaffected?" [2105]

Robert "Prince Mongo" Hodges, a "perennial mayoral" candidate and restauranteur, whose garb was often a loincloth, beads, and bare feet, and who claimed to be an alien from the Planet Zambodia, thank heavens did not make the final cut due to an insufficient petition.[2106]

Now, commentator Blake Fontenay with the *Commercial Appeal* took a swipe at both me and Morris, claiming that we were losing support to

Wharton as the Draft A C movement grew.[2107] He referenced the Joseph Lee vote as purely "symbolic." Still, he reported the same allegations by some that my vote against Sammons's proposal was in retaliation for his failure to support mine (when nothing was further from the truth). [2108] Fontenay even mentioned my political consultant, John Bakke, as "abruptly" ceasing work for me when he heard Wharton might run, and quoted him as saying voters would "rush toward him" if he entered the race. [2109] Predictably, no shortcomings of A C Wharton were mentioned.

A pollster, Ethridge, also claimed I was losing support because I did not call Herenton out for his "racist" remarks about the "white-controlled" media.[2110] However, I knew that the press and media were fully capable of defending themselves. A response by me would only further polarize the community.

No mention was made by the pollster similarly of Herman Morris, although he did not call Herenton out for the same remarks. According to the commentary, the criticism of him was that he was not "dynamic" or "well-known." [2111]

Noting that the racial divide was growing, the *Commercial Appeal* editorialized against race-based campaigning.[2112] Yet, Herenton had already gained eleven points in the polls with some voters using such tactics. [2113] The editors, apparently leaning towards Wharton, also argued that the voters were sophisticated enough to distinguish between two or more black candidates, such as Wharton and Herenton.[2114]

Herenton sat on his campaign cash through the second quarter, coyly waiting for the fight.[2115] Morris raised about $160,000 but spent three-fourths of that. [2116] As the little engine that could, I had raised about $61,000 despite the hyped "Draft A C" campaign, with half left in the account. Wharton was still being discussed as a possible candidate. My days were spent at events around the city and in a small room at the back of my campaign headquarters dialing for dollars. I also had to work on my clients' legal cases and appear for them in court. Every minute mattered.

Finally, the saga of whether Wharton would enter the race came to a head. The media caught Herenton and Wharton at a *tete-a-tete* at a local wine bar named *Le Chardonnay*. Rumors of a backroom deal spread. Shortly after that, in mid-July, Wharton declined to run. He sent a statement while out of town, citing family, timing, "the impact on the community," and his county mayor obligations. [2117] Branston, with the *Memphis Flyer*, wrote that now Wharton's supporters would have to look for other solutions than "Mr. Agreeable as the stop-gap Answer to Everything."[2118]

Apparently, Wharton's decision also impacted the decisions of Councilmen Marshall and Sammons not to run for mayor, according to one news story. The speculation was that one or the other had planned to enter the race if both Herenton and Wharton were candidates.[2119] This left me in a dead heat tied at twenty-four to twenty-four with Herenton, and Herman Morris lagging way behind. [2120] Nearly half of those polled said they would not vote for Herenton no matter what. [2121] We had a chance.

29

The People's Mayor

1

With the election only a couple of months away, Blake Fontenay with the *Commercial Appeal* began to spin the possibility that Herenton might win a fifth term due to Wharton's decision not to run and the entry into the race of Sharon Webb.[2122] Webb, an African American female pastor, was not a household name, although serving as a commissioner of the Memphis Board of Education and the Memphis Charter Commission.[2123] Fontenay began to cast doubt on my candidacy, contending that Webb could be "especially damaging for Chumney" in that she could garner the women's vote, which is 60% of the electorate. [2124] Unexplained is why he believed she was more likely than me to get the women's vote since I am a woman too.

Fontenay added that if Herenton "beats" me in the mayor's race, then he "kills two birds with one stone" in that I could not run for both mayor and reelection to the council at the same time. [2125] Also, he opined that Herenton's power would grow with a weaker newly elected city council due to the retirement of many veteran members. [2126] That was a possible scenario, but why was Fontenay poo-poohing my candidacy when my polling was strong?

Baker with the *Memphis Flyer* called me "a maverick's maverick."[2127] I guess you can't get more unbranded than that! He admitted that my position on the Lee vote was "technically correct" in that he had already resigned and that my reform stances drew "cheers" from conservative groups, even though a Democrat.[2128] He deemed me the "Joan of Arc of the disaffected" by virtue of my "leading role in exposing and correcting child-care abuses" as a state legislator, my "damn-the-torpedoes positions" at City Hall, including my effort to repeal the twelve-year pension for elected and appointed officials, and my uncovering of the city's bond rating drop and inflated revenue projections.[2129] Would the general public have preferred that I had looked the other way and left babies to die in daycare and city appointees to keep the twelve-year pension? If taking action to save lives and stop public pension abuses made me Joan of Arc in his eyes, so be it. But, unlike Joan, I was still alive and kicking.

Jackson Baker acknowledged my strong grassroots support, but he missed the mark in contending that my campaign was "cash-poor" and questioning my ability to attract African American voters.[2130] In the end, my campaign raised over $200,000, and several polls had already demonstrated sufficient black support to defeat Herenton.[2131]

Memphis Magazine, owned by the same company as the *Memphis Flyer*, selected me, and Wharton, among its "Who's Who" of Memphis in August 2007.[2132] The bio of me sounded similar to the one in April 2007 in the *Memphis Flyer*, with some of the facts and my credentials marginalized and distorted. Among other things, the bio said my city council district was "basically Midtown," a progressive area, when in fact it also contained most of the more conservative East Memphis. [2133] The profile further said that during my thirteen years in the state legislature, I "briefly held a position in the Democratic leadership." In fact, I held leadership positions during eleven years of my entire tenure, as an officer on the House Judiciary and Children & Family Affairs Committees, respectively, and as House Majority Whip. [2134]

And my former role as the only female chairing any standing committee in the state legislature was diminished to being chair "of a special Children's Services committee" as a "watchdog." [2135] The fact that I built coalitions over and over again to pass a substantial number of reform measures in the state house was never mentioned. Instead, I was said to be a "go-it-alone" politician in the state house and city council. [2136] In addition, the bio labeled me as "controversial and outspoken" as a city council member, who was mostly a "critic" and a "long-shot" candidate for mayor even though I was leading in the polls. [2137]

Other male politicians, on the other hand, were given substantial bios. Sen. Jim Kyle's past chairmanship of the Senate Rules Committee was called "influential."[2138] Senator Mark Norris was recognized for his work on raising issues regarding the county's debt, when in fact, we both prime-sponsored and passed the state law in each respective chamber.[2139] A C Wharton was deemed an "ideal political candidate" with a "genial manner" and "air of competence." [2140] And as controversial as he was, nowhere in Herenton's bio was he called such, with only issues about his record mentioned and the fact that he had not been indicted in the Tennessee Waltz sting. [2141]

My credentials fared better in the *Memphis Health & Fitness Sports Magazine*, which called me a "health advocate" running for mayor and reported on my address to the Tennessee Nurses Association. [2142] The story recognized my "accomplishments in health care reform," including selection as a recipient of the UT Health Science Center Leadership Award. [2143] And, the *Commercial Appeal* Memphis' Most Magazine's readership poll listed me as a finalist for the most praiseworthy politician along with Cohen and Ford Jr., with A C Wharton voted that and the Most Likable Local. [2144] At least those magazines recognized my solid record, unlike the author of the bios in the *Memphis Magazine*.

Meanwhile, according to Baker, Herman Morris was dubbed by some as a member of "the black bourgeoisie" due to his private school degrees, mansion in Midtown, and large retirement package given when he was unceremoniously *dis*appointed by Herenton in 2003 as the president of MLGW.[2145]Although he had numerous wealthy supporters to raise a campaign war chest and a good reputation as an attorney, his downside included the Memphis Networx boondoggle, reserved nature, and questions that dogged him about why he refused to accept help from another utility during the "disastrous" 2003 windstorm. [2146] Morris dismissed the Networx debacle as due to the "short-sightedness of the profit-focused private investors," the elite of Memphis. [2147] But the deal had been put together on his watch as MLGW president, and the public lost millions!

The *Memphis Flyer's* Jackson Baker said Willingham was known for his efforts to expose and bring to justice those responsible for the missing floor in the FedExForum parking garage, wanting to turn the Memphis Pyramid into a casino and to turn a local large urban park into an Olympic Village.[2148] He secured the local Republican party endorsement by a narrow margin.[2149] However, Willingham was just a blip in the polls, with little chance of winning but possibly taking votes away from me.

Seeing that Herenton was in trouble with the recent poll, some of his detractors said that he had not dealt with the crime problem and had helped his African American friends, but not black citizens in the inner city. [2150] Councilman Lowery criticized Herenton's "attitude" and "mixed signals" during his most recent term when he told those who did not agree with his approach to pick up and move out of the city. [2151] Lowery further called out the mayor for his recent child born out of wedlock as failing to set a good example, and for the sex-plot believing that the alleged conspirators would not have tried it if they didn't think it would pan out. [2152] As Lowery pointed out in the column by Fontenay with the *Commercial Appeal*, Herenton had a lot of baggage.

Perhaps as a response to the criticisms on high crime, Herenton now made a show of holding a press conference with the Shelby County D.A. Bill Gibbons, after sending the police to shut down several crack houses.[2153] They touted the increased drug indictments, with the mayor promising greater visibility. [2154] He was promptly called out by the *Commercial Appeal* editors as holding a "dog and pony show." [2155] Statistics showing crime had significantly dropped would have been more credible, but it hadn't.

2

In late July, my pollster released new results showing me in the lead now at 33%, with Herenton second at 29%, and Morris lagging behind at 14%.[2156] Despite all the brouhaha over my position on the Joseph Lee votes and predictions by various pundits that I had lost support after that, even Baker with the *Memphis Flyer* backtracked. Now, he mused if my votes seemed more an indication of being "steadfast" in a "Churchillian" way, rather than the accused "go-it-alone stubbornness."[2157] And he further acknowledged in a long discourse that the poll suggested either I had "rebounded" from a prior lapse, or there never was a dip in my support as others contended after the votes.[2158] But the lack of evidence of a dip in my support hadn't stopped some in the press and media from trying to convince the voters otherwise after the Lee vote.

As the debates began to be scheduled, Herenton declined to participate, with his campaign manager Charles Carpenter calling them a "beauty contest."[2159] This certainly was a disservice to the public (and perhaps another subtle sexist innuendo)? My response in a letter to Herenton was that "debates are the best forum for an honest and substantive exchange of ideas." "Please don't duck the debates."

Morris agreed to debate and was boosted by the endorsement of former "Draft A C" supporters, Pastors Gray and Adkins.[2160] The move raised eyebrows due to their contrasting positions on gay rights. For example, Morris had appeared at the Mid-South Pride Festival. [2161] Yet, Pastor Gray was a vocal opponent of the federal hate crime bill that included sexual orientation. [2162]

Herenton's refusal to debate was a disappointment. The *Memphis Flyer* ran a cartoon by Mike Niblock, with a giant Herenton and a tiny me trying to pick up a ball four times my size bearing the words "Joe Lee, MLGW and Crime." [2163] The cartoon had words coming from my mouth, "Too Heavy, can't pick up," and was named "Chumney vs. Goliath." [2164] Sometimes, it felt that way.

At this time, some of the other candidates had very low visibility. Fontenay with the *Commercial Appeal*, however, unabashedly continued to push Webb as a potential spoiler in the mayoral race. [2165] As he acknowledged, Webb had not raised any money, had no campaign materials or yard signs, and few articulated solutions to specific problems. [2166] His playbook was that the votes would be so split up that if Herenton got 30% with Morris and me splitting the bulk of the remaining votes and Webb in the race as well, then Herenton would win. [2167] This was not the newspaper's last attempt to convince voters that Morris was an equal contender with me, despite the many polls showing me as the only candidate capable of beating Herenton.

As the campaign intensified, I unveiled an MLGW reform plan that would require greater transparency and improve customer service. [2168] In my view, the top executives at the utility had lost sight of the fact that the people owned it.

As to crime, Herenton continued to say that a mayor could not do anything to reduce crime but added that he could provide the necessary manpower and equipment. [2169] I pledged better coordination between the city police and the county sheriff's officers as crime-fighting measures and strengthening code enforcement and neighborhood watch groups. Morris pushed for more neighborhood policing. [2170] Willingham said he would start entirely new, calling the methods used at the present time for fighting crime insane and not working. [2171]

Getting my message out included my attendance at various church services across Memphis to worship and listen to voters regarding their community needs. I loved visiting the Pentecostal, Baptist, Methodist Episcopal, COGIC churches, Temple Israel, and other religious institutions because of the inspiring sermons, wise words, and warm hearts behind the doors. Often, I was asked to speak to the congregation and share with them about my faith. As a result, some of the pastors became my friends, even trusting me to be their legal counsel on various church or personal matters over the years. Pastor Dwight Montgomery, head of the local Southern Christian Leadership Conference, welcomed me with open arms at Annesdale Cherokee Missionary Baptist Church for this campaign.[2172] Not every church welcomed us—but as the saying goes, we simply shook the dust off our feet and moved on.[2173]

Another constituency was the youth vote, although it was almost non-existent. My campaign team was young, including my campaign manager, Charles Blumenthal, and scheduler Will Beatty. One young eighteen-year-old candidate for the city council, an African American, was criticized for his age. I came to his defense, saying in a media interview that he had a right to run.[2174] George Monger would lose the election but go on to be featured in a national documentary about young candidates running for office. He later was appointed a Shelby County Election Commissioner and worked for legendary musician David Porter's consortium.

In late August, with a heatwave underway, Herman Morris went on the offense. News reporters asked about the ownership of the small townhouse where I had resided for many years. The story broke the day before my closing to buy the property. I had rented the property instead of purchasing a home primarily because my state legislative work had required me to work in Nashville several months of the year. It was easier to have a landlord be responsible for maintenance on the property. When the property came up for sale during the mayor's race, I bought it.

I had spent thousands of hours out of town devoted to my public service at the lower-paying $16,500 state legislative job, and then substantial time on my city council responsibilities. I could have earned a lot more money during those years in my private practice as an attorney if it weren't for my public service. The claim that as a renter, I had never paid property taxes was misleading and disrespectful of many hard-working renters since landlords factor the property taxes into the monthly rental amount. In any event, I was now a homeowner.

On the other hand, Herman Morris was well-off. He earned over $50,000 a year, along with stock options, just as a corporate board member for a pharmaceutical manufacturer.[2175] The former public utility president had also benefited from the lump sum of over two hundred thousand dollars in a severance payment from MLGW criticized by Herenton as "vulgar."[2176] Councilman Tom Marshall deemed some of the MLGW executive benefits as "absolutely excessive," with Morris "caught up in a culture of entitlement within the top brass of Memphis Light, Gas, and Water."[2177] Marshall's comments were correct in that the perks were out of touch with the average citizen's way of life.

Just a few days after the Morris campaign's attack, I drew a contrast between my opponents and me before several hundred supporters, including labor leaders Paul Shaffer, Melvin McCoy, Kermit Moore, and others, rallied in the parking lot in front of our modest campaign headquarters.[2178] I reminded them that "my opponents—they love to walk you through their humble beginnings." "Their actions both in political office and as executives, demonstrate that they have long forgotten where they came from." "It's rather difficult for someone living in a half-a-million-dollar home or a million-dollar mansion and only socializing with the elite and powerful to remember those of us who get up and go to work every single day to make a living."

In the sweltering heat shaded by a large open-sided tent, I went on the offense, saying that my opponents had a record of giving special service to the elite, the powerful, and the privileged at the expense of regular citizens. I shared my values, learned from my parents, of hard work, honesty, and fairness. My remarks called for leadership and not showmanship.

Applause thundered with my announcement that it was time for a "People's Mayor" and "when I'm Mayor, everyone's going to be a VIP," pledging to give attention to all areas of the city and all of its people and making it safe for children who walk to school. I called for their help and urged the public to hold me accountable to work daily to bring down crime and make the city better once elected. The rally benefited from several endorsements by labor leaders, County Commissioner Steve Mulroy, Republican former County Commissioner Ed Williams, State Rep. Mike Kernell, and others. I was grateful for their support.

Herenton continued to duck community forums and debates. Billboards began to appear, along with T-shirts from his campaign emblazoned with the words "shake the haters off." The slogan implied that anyone who opposed him was a "hater" as opposed to merely having a different view on who was best to lead city government. One citizen wrote a letter to the editor explaining that the term was from a rap song with profane lyrics.[2179] Herenton later claimed the song was not the origin of his campaign slogan but rather a preacher's remarks.[2180] He went around inner-city neighborhoods autographing T-shirts, holding rallies, and, as Baker with the *Memphis Flyer* reported, dancing the "Cupid Shuffle."[2181]

Remarkably, he continued to completely disavow a mayor's ability to do anything to prevent crime and blamed the state legislature for not passing strict enough criminal laws.[2182] Again on the offense, I replied, "A mayor who says he can't cut crime is just as ridiculous as a pilot who says he can't land a plane. It's part of the job, plain and simple. Mayors all across the country have cut crime." Mayor Herenton needed to show up and start answering why he had been unable to do the same.

Herenton had gotten into the ring with heavyweight champion "Smokin' Joe" Frazier but wouldn't even debate me on the issues. Bill Dries with the *Daily News* commented that I had been a "tenacious debater" in the 2002 county mayor's race.[2183] In 1991, Herenton had been on the other side of the debate fence when Mayor Dick Hackett refused to debate him.[2184] Yet in 2007, Herenton continued only to show up where he could give remarks and leave without answering questions.

Willingham pressed for cutting patronage positions and limiting the mayor's contracting authority. Morris pushed for hiring not based "just on diversity" and demanded that all candidates take a drug test, which all promptly refused as a campaign gimmick.[2185] Herenton touted his claimed accomplishments in reducing blight, providing diversity in the city workforce, increasing downtown development, and the FedExForum. And now Jackson Baker in the *Memphis Flyer*, dubbed me the "avenger" of "everything that was wrong with city government," as I continued to call for safer streets, schools and neighborhoods, more accountability, public-private partnerships, and even review of moonlighting practices at City Hall.[2186] Indeed, the plethora of issues needing solutions might call for a super-heroine—whether it be Joan of Arc, Carol Danvers (Captain Marvel) – if not the very human woman dedicated to the people—Carol Chumney.

3

As Election Day neared, I proceeded to roll out my crime plan as my top priority.[2187] The police chief, and others appointed by Herenton, would have to reapply for their jobs so I could evaluate all candidates to select the best applicants. My plan included getting more officers from behind desks and onto the streets, offering signing bonuses, additional street cameras in high crime areas, working with neighborhoods by providing tax incentives for blighted areas, aiding neighborhood groups with administrative help, and several initiatives to keep at-risk youth off the streets, such as weekend activities, summer camps, and summer jobs.

Herman Morris, trying to out-tough me on crime, vowed if elected mayor he would cut crime by 10% a year for four years (which Herenton and I branded as another campaign gimmick).[2188] Morris advocated for a nationwide search to bring top crime-fighting experts to Memphis.[2189] My response was that no further research was needed. Because of my experience, I already knew what to do. We both criticized Herenton for saying he could do nothing about the high crime.[2190] While police reports claimed a drop of 5.7% for serious crimes from the last year, nobody believed them, and the more independent FBI stats often differed substantially. [2191]

Some called for Morris and me to draw straws with the one getting the shorter stick to drop out of the race. [2192] Another called on me to drop out even though I was in the lead, saying I could not win if Morris dropped out because I am white.[2193] Obviously, a white could win since Memphis had elected Steve Cohen to Congress in 2006 in a majority-black district. Yet there still had been some African American ministers calling for his defeat due to his race, while others disagreed, saying that race-based voting is contrary to Dr. King's dream. [2194] In any event, the polls showed that I was well ahead of Morris and the only candidate that could defeat Herenton.

Some political pundits couldn't believe that a white woman could be elected to lead a southern majority African American city. Letters to the editor abounded, alternatively saying that only I, or only Morris, could beat Herenton.[2195] One urged breaking the gender barrier and voting me in; another wrote that only Morris could beat Herenton, in essence, because he is black.[2196] One writer praised my specifics on how I would address city problems, while another argued that the white candidates should drop out of the race and get behind Morris. [2197]

The high-pressure tactics to get one of us to drop out weren't the only aggravations. Part of being in the political arena is sometimes being the butt of jokes. *Fox 13 Memphis News* didn't hold back. Morris had made the mistake as MLGW president of having bobble heads made in his likeness, which were featured on the station's website.[2198] Also, a cartoon image of me with "Her Magic Mirror" was posted where the viewer could control my eye blink rate (making fun of my excessive blinking in a debate due to my yet then undiagnosed dry eyes medical condition).[2199] An unflattering shirtless photo appeared of the slightly hefty Willingham, taken after he had auctioned his pacemaker on eBay. And Herenton was pictured boxing.[2200]

As we rounded the bend toward early voting, Morris began flooding the airwaves with television ads, and my commercials were filmed. Herenton claimed that he intentionally waited until the end to campaign with "intensity," with the *Commercial Appeal* comparing it to a horse race, where most folks don't pay attention until the horses are out of the gate.[2201] Herman Morris politicked from the jury duty pool, where he had been called to serve, and also attended a $1,000 a couple fundraising dinner.[2202] And, even though some argued that I could not win due to my race, the workers of the historic and primarily African American membered American Federation of State, County and Municipal Employees local union for the sanitation workers gave me its endorsement. [2203]

My campaign had a diverse team, with long-time friends of all races going to the mat for me. One such friend, Phronda Burks, hosted a soul food dinner fundraiser at her home for me—and cooked the entire meal herself. Phronda, her mother, and her family had helped me in my first state legislative race. We call each other sisters, having become friends while volunteering in various campaigns over the years.

In the final weeks, the live televised debates also were scheduled. Live debates can be nerve-racking, as the candidates do not get the questions in advance—at least I never did. In the days leading up to the first televised debate, some voters said they would vote for whoever could defeat Herenton.[2204]

Morris touted his management experience and called me a career politician, despite my 21 years of private practice as an attorney.[2205] I pointed out my record fighting for reforms while Morris had been AWOL on the key issues the last four years. Rhodes professor Pohlmann, once again, despite the polls, opined that Herenton might win if Morris and I split the anti-Herenton vote. [2206]

Herenton was a no show for the *WREG News* Channel 3 live debate, so only I, Morris, and Willingham took the stage. I continued to go on the offense about Herenton's refusal to debate, despite former Mayor Hackett's remarks that it was a smart political move by the mayor.[2207] Hackett had refused to debate Herenton in 1991 and said it was to avoid dividing the city racially or helping his opponent get out the vote.[2208] Regardless of whether or not it was a smart political move, the public deserved to hear in the debates from any top mayoral candidate who wanted their vote.

My candidacy was boosted by the AFL-CIO labor group's endorsement, and I led in the polls. However, *WREG News* long-time venerable political commentator, Norman Brewer, still asked me in the debate if I would withdraw from the race to get behind Herman Morris as a consensus candidate against Herenton. [2209] The Memphis mayor's race is winner takes all. The federal court enjoined Memphis mayoral runoffs in 1991 after a DOJ lawsuit. Since then, the city had grown from 55% to 60% African American.[2210]

Brewer's question was *deja vu* for me, having been asked to drop out of the 2002 Shelby County mayor's race when I was ahead of Byrd in the Democratic primary, and in my first race for elected office as state representative in 1990. As in the past, I followed Barbara Lawing's advice and refused to drop out. Moreover, my own polls showed me as the only candidate who could defeat Herenton. And in my view, based upon his track record at MLGW as a Herenton appointee, Morris was not a real change agent.

During the first televised debate, Willingham criticized Morris for the Memphis Networx loss, which Morris defended as a good investment sold too soon.[2211] Morris struggled to try to answer my query as to why his own family was on the MLGW VIP list if he created it to be notified if jails, hospitals, airports, and other public facilities had power-outages.[2212] Near the end, I called out Herenton for failing to appear and answer the voters' questions, saying that he couldn't defend the fact that people were afraid to go to their mailboxes due to the high crime.

Many questions remained unanswered about Herenton's positions on critical issues facing the city due to his failure to debate.[2213] In the end, Herenton only showed up to answer questions at a community forum in a school gym with a sound system and acoustics that rebounded so badly that no one could understand what anyone said.[2214] I suppose that's why.

In addition to debates, community events were prime campaign ground for the mayoral election. The Orange Mound Parade, in one of the historic African American communities of the city, involved a parade of cars with dignitaries, various marching bands, and candy. Thousands of folks lined the streets for the annual festivity that preceded the cherished Southern Heritage Classic football game between Tennessee State University and Jackson State University. My team gathered to attend with a friend's convertible.

Unfortunately, our campaign underestimated the amount of candy needed for the event. I smiled and waved to the crowd walking in the parade at the front of our group. When the candy-throwers at the back ran out, an inexperienced volunteer in desperation threw a supporter's donated bars of soap to some kids. The bars contained the words "Clean Up Memphis" with my campaign logo on the label.

Later, in the last days of the campaign, a conservative local radio station talk show host had a field day claiming that the soap-throwing to a few children in the crowd was racist. While I had known nothing of it and replied that only candy was authorized to be given to the crowd by the campaign, the damage was done.

30

It's a Man's World

1

As we neared the home stretch in the mayoral campaign, the Memphis Liberty Bowl stadium that adjoins the Orange Mound area again made the news. Herenton's refusal to share with the public and press a consultant's report on the proposed new football stadium aggravated his detractors.[2215]

The *Commercial Appeal* editors called for Herenton's retirement, denouncing his "2007 Political Conspiracy" claims, criticism of the "white-controlled media," divisive rhetoric, his administration's unreliable budget projections, the city's unstable bond ratings, and lack of progress on development projects.[2216] Also mentioned was his refusal to take responsibility to solve the city's crime problems, instead simply calling out those who opposed him as "haters" and telling them to leave the city. The editors deemed this to have become a "drag on the city's progress."[2217] In my view, the high crime, divisive rhetoric, and financial mismanagement were more than a drag on progress; it was moving the city in the opposite direction.

Both Morris and I announced support in March for a new football stadium on the campus of the University of Memphis as long as no city funds were used.[2218] In an opinion editorial to *Main Street Journal*, I had previously explained that the city was still reeling from two bond rating drops in the past two years for the failure to comply with its debt policy, with the one billion dollars of debt exceeding that of comparable cities.[2219]

If the city provided funds for a new football stadium, then needed repairs would be delayed for senior citizen and neighborhood centers and possibly result in a third bond rating drop. In my view, a better plan was to find a quality tenant or buyer for the Pyramid, rehab and reuse the Mid-South Coliseum, and allow the University of Memphis Tigers to take the lead on any proposed new football stadium without city funds in the mix.[2220]

After that, the *Commercial Appeal* editors endorsed Herman Morris, contending he had the executive skills for the job.[2221] The editors, however, admitted I was "well-prepared," "an effective legislator," "a successful attorney," "with a wealth of ideas," and "potentially" a "strong mayor." [2222] They excused Morris's role in the multi-million dollar loss of public funds in Memphis Networx on the basis that other business investors were optimistic about the venture.[2223] The editors added that he "acknowledges his mistakes" and supported tax breaks for businesses to invest in downtown. [2224] However, their professed reasons did not square with some of the blatantly sexist questions asked of me in my editorial endorsement interview, such as "who are you dating," which prompted my campaign manager to urge me to get up and leave.

Ultimately, Herenton decided to release the $140,000 taxpayer paid consultant's report on the cost of building a new football stadium.[2225] The city officials tried to justify the failure to do so earlier on the need to correct alleged flaws in the report, although the national consultant stood by its work. [2226] The *Commercial Appeal*, which had been denied a copy in prior open records requests, penned a blistering editorial calling the mayor's slow response a sign of "dysfunction."[2227] When the report was finally released, the cost estimate of a new stadium was an approximate whopping $200 million. [2228]

The push for the new stadium fit in with Herenton's in-depth profile in the *Commercial Appeal*. The mayor predictably listed among his accomplishments downtown redevelopment, replacement of some public housing with affordable homes, and increased private capital investment in the city. [2229] He also mentioned the FedExForum, Auto Zone Ball Park, the Grizzlies, and future biomedical jobs in the pipeline. [2230]

Interestingly, Herenton spoke about the successful effort to stop the "tiny towns," which I had led on as well. The mayor said, "there would be no Memphis as we know it today had we lost that fight." [2231] He believed that historically it would be one of his greatest accomplishments, with no mention of my role in the successful effort to undo Lieutenant Governor Wilder's "tiny towns" law. [2232]

Jacinthia Jones, the reporter, reviewed the litany of problems that had plagued Herenton in more recent years. She cited the high crime, a child out of wedlock, and his subpoena to testify in the Atlanta Mayor Bill Campbell's corruption and tax evasion trial. They also included the financial crisis where the city's reserves were virtually depleted with corresponding bond rating drops, and the Joseph Lee/MLGW saga. [2233] The alleged sex-plot and his lashing out at the "dominantly controlled white media" were duly noted. [2234]

Yet, Herenton made no apologies for his style, admitting that he is not a "consensus builder."[2235]Instead, the mayor argued that he was a "leader" that had the right "style" to move Memphis ahead. [2236] Jack Sammons, said by the newspaper also to have mayoral aspirations, thought Herenton had lost interest in being mayor. [2237] And Tom Marshall, also noted by the reporter to have mayoral ambitions, believed the mayor was tired. [2238] Others, such as Commissioner Sidney Chism, urged folks to look at Herenton's record instead of his style. [2239] But, the plain facts, as ably set out in the article, were that different leadership was sorely needed.

In his column, John Branston with the *Memphis Flyer*, drew interesting comparisons between Herenton and former Memphis Mayor Wyeth Chandler, another bachelor. Chandler was said to have succeeded in keeping the mayoralty for ten years in the 1970s and early 80s by utilizing the often-duplicated Memphis model of winning elections by rallying primarily one race to the polls—albeit his model was the white voters. [2240]

Herenton said he wanted another term to work to consolidate the city and county governments and complete riverfront development among other things. [2241] But the polls indicated that his support was lower even than in 1991 when he won with 49.44% of the vote, and 1999 with only 45.7% of the vote. [2242] According to the *Commercial Appeal*, the mayor had lost nearly all white voters' support, and was relying on older African American voters for a victory. [2243] Besides, he had been in office for 16 years—if he hadn't gotten it done yet, why would anyone believe he could in another four years?

Zack McMillan with the *Commercial Appeal* called me "Memphis to the bone," having been "devoted to public service" from a young age.[2244] The profile went back to my junior high days when I penned the student government constitution, to my election as president of the SGA at the University of Memphis, selection as Editor-in-Chief of my law review, and election to the state legislature before the age of thirty. [2245] It even properly stated my credentials as having served as chair of the Shelby County state legislative delegation, Tennessee House Majority Whip, and Chair of the Tennessee House Children & Family Affairs Committee. [2246] My devotion to the church and my family were duly mentioned. [2247]

My campaigns as the "people's candidate" were discussed, with the comment that Wharton had won the county mayor Democratic primary in 2002 with 80% of the vote to my 17%, with a substantial fund-raising advantage.[2248] However, there was no mention that the demographics in that countywide primary were markedly different than that of this city-wide mayoral election.[2249] Less than 13% of voters who identified themselves as white voted in that Democratic county mayoral primary in 2002. That election was also just as the area's racial voting preferences began gradually to relax.

And, despite the hundreds of bills I had sponsored and passed in the state legislature, the reporter cited the contention of some that I was not a consensus builder.[2250] The article even craftily quoted my unsuspecting father with a story from kindergarten about how I wouldn't climb into a playhouse.[2251] The newspaper also relied upon city council colleagues' statements to make its case, the same ones who were angered by my efforts to repeal the twelve-year city pension for elected and appointed officials.[2252] Missing was the prior *Tennessean's* editorial in 2003 upon my resignation from the state house, opining that I "had a bipartisan ability to bridge the gaps on important issues."[2253] That was after observing 13 years of my work as a state legislator at the State Capitol.

Republican Councilman Jack Sammons piled on. He claimed that even though I appropriately sounded alarms about the city's problems, I was "greedy to receive credit" on the Lee vote.[2254] His own motive, as to his refusal to support my Lee resolution as a possible mayoral candidate, was given a complete pass by the press, as well as the fact that my position was correct as to the removal process for Lee.[2255]

Councilman Tom Marshall, more conciliatory, said that I would be a "decisive" and "very fair-minded" mayor whose "motives would be pure," but added that I needed to work harder at consensus building.[2256] This was not the first time my motives have been described as pure—such as by the *Commercial Appeal* editors in the 2002 county mayor's race[2257] – and this was a compliment. In my view, when motives are pure, and fairness is the guiding principle for all involved, consensus should be easy to achieve. And, while I am always open to constructive criticism or improving negotiation skills, perhaps others at City Hall had some work to do as to motives in light of their prior support of the twelve-year pension that was not in the public's best interest.

The newspaper reprinted the whole unsubstantiated staff dispute when I was first elected to the council but did not correlate it with the fact that some colleagues were upset about my work to repeal the twelve-year pension.[2258] My proposal to apply the pension repeal more broadly was cast as an example of the failure to compromise. There was no mention of the possibility that

McCormick's version simply passed because it included protection for several current councilmembers or that the newspaper had even editorialized at the time in support of my position. [2259] My retort pointed to successfully handling the budget process as chair of that council committee, as well as other unreported accomplishments such as passing the resolution to save the Carousel and famous Zippin Pippin at the Fairgrounds that Elvis Presley loved to ride.

Republican former county mayoral candidate Larry Scroggs suggested that my strong ideas about what should be done sometimes were formulated before hearing "from everybody who might have a thought or assessment about the proper thing to do."[2260] While hearing from others is an integral part of leadership, as a former state legislator, Scroggs should have been aware that my child care reform bills would not have become law without my assertive advocacy. Another former colleague, Rep. Mike Kernell, a Democrat, countered that the city needed a "fighter for the people" and not a backslapper. [2261] My final words were that the consensus that I sought was for change.

How often are women labeled "aggressive" and "difficult" when expressing a different opinion, but men are deemed leaders, confident, assertive, and decisive? I asked, "do you want someone who is really going to push the right agenda that we need for the city and lead us in the right direction? Or do you want someone who is just going to be part of the club?"[2262]

The insanity of the campaign cycle continued, with each day filled with fundraising calls, media interviews, public appearances, and forums. My young campaign team worked extremely hard, and we attended most forums. However, the ball was dropped on occasion, such as not being able to participate in a Midtown neighborhood forum because the questionnaire was not timely returned. Instead, I ended up shaking hands outside, while Morris was inside. On another occasion, I was shaking the hands of parents dropping their kids off out front of a public school. From my car radio through an open window, I heard a disc jockey announce me as a guest on the air that morning—a candidate's worst nightmare. I promptly called, and the disc jockey was kind enough to schedule me for another day.

The second live televised debate on *WMC Action News 5* once again had Herenton represented by an empty stool.[2263] Voting began.

Then, Herenton abruptly called for the early voting to cease contending that the electronic voting machines were faulty. [2264] Alleging possible voting machine fraud, Herenton called for federal monitors. [2265] He claimed that early voters were trying to cast votes for him, yet it registered as a vote for

Morris or me.[2266] It was later reported that the city attorney, Elbert Jefferson, sought to have the election commission "reprogram" the voting machines. [2267]

Herenton had barely won by about 142 votes in 1991 in a show-stopper election when some ballot boxes were found long after the polls had closed. [2268] He referenced "contaminated" past elections and implied that Morris, who "mathematically cannot win," was the candidate that would benefit from the "irregularities." [2269] Herenton now said that the race was "between Willie Herenton and Carol Chumney" and wondered why Morris believed he could win. [2270] At the time, his claims were discounted as merely a desperate effort to rally the troops. In hindsight, based upon the long Memphis history of challenged elections and voting irregularities, one wonders – what did Herenton know that we didn't?

2

As the city's work continued even though we were are all campaigning madly, the Police Director Larry Godwin emailed Tom Marshall that the investigation into the KKK robe sent to Councilman Edmund Ford Sr. was closed. [2271] Godwin reported that the package was mailed by a white woman wearing nurse's scrubs from a post office in the northeast part of the city. [2272] The police claimed that they could not identify the woman because the nearby hospital would not provide photos of the nurses on staff, and there were no fingerprints on the package. [2273] Edmund Ford Sr. replied that the FBI should handle the investigation.[2274] The councilman also questioned why city council staff had opened the package addressed to him that contained the robe and an anonymous note with comments calling him a hypocrite and coward. [2275]

The atmosphere at the city council was also tense when I objected to rescheduling Councilman Edmund Ford Sr.'s motion to delay reconsideration of a pay raise for the mayor until after the October election.[2276] The raise needed to be defeated without delay. Republican Councilman Brent Taylor, although agreeing with my position, went on the offense. He proceeded to rehash the entire Lee vote, resulting in a news report of a "cold war" between the council and me, as the "maverick" councilmember. [2277] This appeared timed as an effort to harm my mayoral campaign since the Lee discussion had nothing to do with the pay raise issue on the agenda.

It was interesting to see years later, Taylor's colleagues on the Shelby County Commission, where he then served, criticize him for referring to his service on the city council.[2278] He had been critical of me in the city council meetings for referring to my service as a state legislator. Apparently, Taylor could get by exhibiting the exact same methods without being called a "maverick" or difficult by the press.

As Election Day neared, letters to the editor abounded. Some in my support called for an end to mediocrity and asked why the *Commercial Appeal* did not report on my detailed plans for community revitalization, reform of MLGW, and my endorsement by the Memphis Police Association. [2279] Another wrote that my intelligence, integrity, dignity, honesty, hard-work, and well-preparedness were the needed change for the city to benefit the many instead of "catering to the few" on the "VIP lists."[2280] The writer pointedly noted that my gender might be "disconcerting" to the "nonproductive status quo" who were used to "comfort and rarely challenged." [2281]

Another wrote that a vote for Morris would be to elect a "yes, massa," and a vote for me would be a vote to go back to the 1960s.[2282] While Morris could speak for himself, that analogy was certainly false as to me since no woman had ever been elected mayor of Memphis and due to my years of progressive leadership.

My campaign's new poll showed Herenton at 30.2%, Chumney 28.4%, and Morris at 20.5%, with the race too close to call.[2283] Morris claimed, with easily manipulated automated polls, to be ahead of me (which was quickly debunked by our campaign).[2284] With voter apathy high, more than half the registered voters did not participate in municipal elections.[2285] *Memphis Flyer* columnist John Branston correctly projected that only 70,000 votes (or about 21% of the registered voters) were needed to win the election. [2286] Even the *Memphis Flyer's* Baker now admitted that I claimed a "significant fraction" of the African American vote.[2287]

Yet, Baker gave in to the outdated "cosmetic" commentary on the mayoral candidates' appearances, referring to Herenton's "Marlboro Man" image, my purported "visage" which he said ranged from "bland" to "radiant," and saying Morris looking like the board game's "Mr. Monopoly." [2288] While this might be amusing to some, it also seemed to fall into the gender bias motif with Herenton's masculinity accentuated by the rugged cowboy comparison to my purported degree of glow.

As a city councilmember, juggling my work as an attorney and on the campaign trail was no easy feat with live TV interviews, speaking appearances, fundraising calls, court appearances, and constituent calls for assistance. As "the only serious female mayoral candidate Memphis has seen in years," Bianca Phillips with the *Memphis Flyer* shadowed me.[2289] She reported on the jeers made at my supporters by one Herenton poll worker before I arrived at a poll, who yelled "It's a man's world. It's a man's world." [2290] Obviously, Herenton's supporter had forgotten the rest of the famous James Brown song about how none of it would matter without a woman. [2291]

Even that progressive well-respected female reporter, although remarking on the fact that gender barriers still existed where some in the press and media commented on Hillary Clinton's attire, fell into the same trap by asking me about my fashion wardrobe. [2292] I politely steered the interview back to my platform.

My new commercials began to run featuring poll results showing Herenton and me in a dead heat, with Morris lagging. Morris had raised about $400,000 to my over $200,000, but I was still ahead in the polls. [2293] Herenton spent nearly $400,000 in the third quarter, but none on television advertising. [2294] His volunteers were reported to be handing out a Memphis Democratic Club ballot with the city seal in violation of city policy. [2295]

3

On the Sunday before Election Day, despite numerous other polls showing me as the only candidate within reach of defeating Herenton, the *Commercial Appeal* released a new poll claiming that Herenton was at 24%, with Morris and myself each tied at 19%, and 22% undecided. [2296] This brought back memories of the 2002 county mayor primary when the Byrd campaign asked me to drop out of the race claiming its poll showed Wharton at 41%, with Byrd and me tied at 22% when my own poll had shown me well ahead of Byrd. The news article, written by Jacinthia Jones, now claimed that "as the leading female contender in the race," I had not "been able to garner a significant female voter support which comprises the largest block of voters in the city." [2297] Although the *Commercial Appeal* editors had endorsed Morris, they had no ethical qualms whatsoever about attempting to persuade undecided voters by having the newspaper's own paid pollster conclude on Election eve that it was now more of a race between Herenton and Morris, as opposed to me.

[2298] And, to boot, they allowed their own female reporter to play the gender card, albeit to my detriment and not my advantage.

In conjunction with the poll, the *Commercial Appeal* also ran an opinion piece by Fontenay, fearmongering that the election might cause the city to be racially polarized, similar to the 1991 mayoral election when Herenton narrowly beat Dick Hackett. [2299] Sammons was quoted as saying this may be a "pivotal" election in the city's history due to the low morale and likening it to the city's prior 1870s yellow fever crisis. [2300] However, Marshall called the changeover for the city council a good thing in that "we're dead in the water" in the aftermath of two councilmembers' indictments. [2301] My former law partner, Jim Gilliland, had served as Herenton's transition team co-chair in 1991. He now was quoted describing how they had organized issue-oriented focus groups to help Herenton reach out to citizens from all walks of life after the highly polarized election. [2302] And fortunately some, such as Johnnie Turner, executive director of the Memphis NAACP, were optimistic that whoever won, the city would unite. [2303]

Continuing the push for Morris, the next day, Fontenay wrote another opinion editorial, theorizing that Morris was Herenton's real competitor because, according to the *Commercial Appeal's* poll, he was gaining support, while I had lost support. [2304] His thinking was that Morris was more of a threat to Herenton in that he is black, which is why Herenton called him a "boy" and said he could not win. [2305] So, now the newspaper had played the race card as well against me, trying to convince the voters that Morris would be the stronger candidate because he was black. Fontenay ended the piece saying that it is a "sprint to the finish" for the top three candidates, to push the narrative that Morris had the edge by reminding the voters that Morris was a former athlete at Rhodes College holding the best record in the 100-yard dash. [2306]

After the *Commercial Appeal's* last-minute all-out unabashed push for Morris with the misleading poll and other tactics, I had to ask myself, while there is supposed to be journalistic integrity, who monitors the press? The public should know whether a reporter or news entity has taken a pay-off, has a financial interest that conflicts with the news reporting, or even whether a columnist plays golf regularly with a candidate (as was told to me about one high-ranking editor and Morris). Rumors abounded in the past that one editor's family member was employed with a local official whose sexual harassment scandal was not disclosed in the press until shortly after his reelection. Whether or not there was any familial connection for the delay in the scandal's report, these potential conflicts should be fully disclosed to the public on the front end.

The possibility of employment after the election is also an issue. Often, the political reporters who write favorable articles about a particular candidate suddenly end up with a coveted higher-paying government job as public relations director after the election. While that is not saying there is a *quid pro quo*, the public can not ensure that they receive an unbiased news story when post-election jobs are sought during the campaign season. A journalistic ethics policy of a one year ban on political appointments for press members post-employment, similar to post-government service lobbying bans, might further the public trust in news reporting.

For those newspapers that do not disclose owners,[2307] certainly one hopes that the reporters are shielded from efforts to sway their journalistic integrity. But how can the readers evaluate whether that is the case without full disclosure? For example, a Memphis newspaper should disclose in its publications and on social media that a local developer is the president of its parent company. Are advertisers afforded better coverage? Are there other business connections by the newspaper owners, editors, or reporters with local politicians; or, as alleged before as to a former newspaper editor, different treatment afforded concerning his personal public utility payments? A reporter should not switch watches with a developer, get special help in financing for a house or business pursuit, or accept a gift from a politician. Early in my career, one reporter even asked me for a "loan" after a praiseworthy story. I declined but wondered if this were a momentary lapse in judgment. If not, and it were a modus operandi, then others may have acquiesced and accordingly received more favorable coverage.

These questions are not to disparage any newspaper, media outlet or the vast majority of honest, diligent journalists, reporters, editors, publishers, and station owners. Full disclosure would simply allow the public to filter what they read and judge for themselves. At least then, a newspaper's push poll could be given a proper frame of reference by the citizens.

In a more balanced report, Michael Erskine, with the *Commercial Appeal*, mentioned that Morris's corporate background made it difficult for him to sway poor and less educated black voters.[2308] In fact, despite their spin, the newspaper's own polls over the course of the campaign showed Herenton gaining African American support, with Morris having lost black voter support since the spring.[2309]

On the same day, the newspaper ran an article about the candidates appearing at various churches, with the election too close to call. [2310] Herenton spoke with congregations about his childhood chopping cotton; Morris bragged on his wife; I reminded the congregants of my track-record standing up to the entitled culture at City Hall.[2311] One pastor, an African American, urged his congregation to vote for character and not on race.[2312] He said that the city needed someone like me to bring jobs and who does not "bow down."[2313] The pastor added that "there are some progressive blacks who believe a white female can be mayor of this city" and were supporting me "under the radar." [2314] I was thankful for his supportive and gender-unbiased remarks.

Nearing Election Day, the *Commercial Appeal* now, in a headline about the mayoral election, declared "gender" a "nonissue."[2315] This was even though the article's contents, written by Zack McMillan, noted I would join Herenton in making electoral history if elected. Herenton was the city's first elected mayor of the black race. If elected, I would be the first female Memphis mayor and one of only six women leading U.S. municipalities of 400,000 population or greater. [2316] Like most women running for higher office, I downplayed the issue – caught between the proverbial rock of alienating some voters by acknowledging that gender was an issue, or the hard place of not calling out stereotypes at play that might sway inattentive voters. The headline was misleading in that history would be made if I were to win. In that sense, gender was an issue. But, obviously, the editors who were for Morris wanted the voters to think otherwise.

Women were about 60% of the voters. However, the Center for American Women in Politics at Rutgers cited statistics that in 2006 only 14.4% of the 243 mayors of U.S. cities with populations exceeding 100,000 were female, with only nine female governors in office nationally in 2007. [2317] And the disparity in numbers was a disadvantage to women according to one University of Memphis political science college professor, Doug Imig, because issues affecting females, children, and families often get greater attention when women are in power.[2318] Why weren't more women in these positions when they are the majority of the voters? Would this pattern repeat itself in this mayoral election, or would there be a breakthrough?

Herenton now pulled out all the stops to win. His campaign announced that former Congressman and GOTV king Harold Ford Sr. (dubbed "long time don-at-large of Memphis's most powerful political family" by the *Commercial Appeal)* would appear at the mayor's scheduled "unity" rally. [2319]

Ford Sr. had helped Herenton pull out the win in 1991 but later backed his own brother against the mayor in 1999. [2320]

When asked about the rally announcement, I simply replied my surprise because others said Harold Ford Sr. now resided in Florida, not Tennessee. Lo and behold, the press investigated and reported that the former congressman had, in fact, early voted in Memphis, although he had previously declared his two and a half million dollar home in Miami Beach as his legal residence (for a tax break).[2321] However, he had not registered to vote in Florida. [2322] In any event, Harold Ford Sr. was a no-show at the rally. Instead, he had to secure legal counsel to resolve the mess.[2323] He declined to say whom he voted for as Memphis mayor.

After the front page Sunday edition poll inaccurately claimed that Morris and I were tied, the *Commercial Appeal* tucked away on an inside page a short article with the *Fox 13 Memphis News* poll released the next day showing Herenton to only have a one-point lead over me, 35 to 34 %, with Morris at 22%.[2324] The placement of the news story in conjunction with the front-page splash for Morris showed a lack of journalistic integrity in my view.

In another small article on Election Day, Steven Ethridge, the *Commercial Appeal* pollster back peddled in light of the *Fox 13 Memphis News* poll, saying that the race was "volatile," and he did not discount that Chumney might surge (although it was downplayed in the Sunday front page story about his poll). [2325]

Other last-minute campaign antics abounded, including Herenton's endorsement by the same controversial blogger who had led his recall effort the year before.[2326] And, new yard signs for the Morris campaign sprouted up with the misleading message "Only Herman Can Win!" [2327]

4

Election Day arrived with the usual appearances by various candidates at polls around the city, TV interviews, robocalls, and sign-waving at local intersections by volunteers. Early in the day, we were optimistic while campaigning in Whitehaven, Elvis Presley's Graceland neighborhood. I told a volunteer, "we're working so hard, even Elvis is going to vote for me today." At the next poll stop, a man told me he had voted for me and said, "My name is Elvis," which seemed an auspicious sign.[2328] I spent the day shaking hands at grocery stores, bus stops, and calling into radio shows urging citizens to vote.[2329]

The *Commercial Appeal* predictably continued to reinforce the theme that Morris could win, with a front-page story on Election Day saying, "It's anybody's game."[2330] The story reiterated the paper's poll claiming that Herenton was five points ahead, with Morris and myself tied despite the many other polls showing that the race was a dead heat only between Herenton and me. [2331] The newspaper also reported Herenton's endorsement by several breakaway police officers who bucked the union's endorsement of me. [2332]

My campaign rented a Memphis Peabody ballroom for election night, with a large stage and a private suite upstairs to await the returns. Confident of a victory, after the early vote came in with Herenton in the lead, we still hoped for the best. When the media reported that Herenton won with 42% of the vote to my 35%, with Herman Morris lagging behind at 21% and no other candidate above 1%, it was time to go downstairs and address the public.[2333]

Since we had written only a victory speech, I hastily scribbled a few notes on a piece of paper and joined my parents and key supporters on the stage, which now seemed more like gallows than a victory platform. Years later, when Hillary Clinton scheduled her 2016 projected presidential victory party for the New York's Javits Center featuring a glass ceiling, I thought back to my speech on the Peabody stage in 2007. I privately told friends that Clinton's venue with the symbolic glass ceiling, was a bad idea. My sentiments turned out to be well-founded when she did not appear on election night, and the public was left instead with the view of a large crowd, no candidate, and a glass ceiling firmly in place.

In 2007, on my election night, I understood the disappointment of so many Memphians who wanted change. So, I gave what was reported as a "feisty" concession speech before my diverse crowd of supporters.[2334] "I love the city of Memphis so much, and that's why I ran for the office of Mayor of Memphis because this city has so much potential. There is so much we can do for the city of Memphis. I think we have won something tonight. We have sent a message that Memphis deserves better. It deserves safe streets, safe schools. We don't need a corrupt government. We need a clean city."[2335] Saying that we made a "really good showing" but needed "more votes to get change," my final words were, "Let's come together."[2336]

In post-speech election night media interviews, I blamed the loss squarely on the *Commercial Appeal* poll, which misled some voters to believe that

Morris and I were tied on the Sunday before Election Day. Instead, I had a substantial lead over Morris, and the newspaper's actions were a "disservice to the public."[2337] At age forty-six, I came within seven points of being elected the first female mayor of Memphis. I patiently and professionally gave media interviews throughout the election evening. I then bid my supporters goodnight, soon to be only a private citizen after seventeen years of public service. Later, I couldn't hold back my tears at the lost opportunity to bring change to our city in the cab ride home by myself.

On the other side of downtown at the Cannon Convention Center, Herenton gave credit for his victory to the Lord before a nearly entirely African American crowd as supporters danced and shouted.[2338] His remarks about "some mean-spirited people in Memphis" angered many, with his calling them "haters" and the crowd yelling "shake 'em off."[2339] Ominously, but typical for Memphis, voting cartridges from four precincts were left at polling places over two and half hours after the polls had closed.[2340]

Morris seemed unperturbed by the loss, dancing with his wife at the Holiday Inn where my campaign had begun.[2341] Oddly, he was reported to repeatedly say, "It's a great day for Memphis" in conceding.[2342] Despite their endorsement of him, only one day after the election, the *Commercial Appeal* editors came clean and called the Memphis Networx loss of $28 million a "mess" that needed investigation.[2343]

It wasn't easy in the days that immediately followed either, knowing how close we had come to victory and a new direction for Memphis. While I didn't take long walks in the woods like Hillary Clinton did in 2016, I would go over to the campaign headquarters to help pack up, and then take a break to go home and lay down for an hour or so. And, then go back to the headquarters to pack up; and then go back home for a while.

In the post-election wrap-up, John Branston with the *Memphis Flyer* justifiably wrote a viewpoint about the inaccuracy of polls, featuring those done in the Memphis mayoral election.[2344] He called the poll, which was published by the *Commercial Appeal* the Sunday before the election, "outrageous."[2345] Branston noted that the poll "played neatly" into the newspaper's endorsement of Morris and that candidate's claim on his yard signs that only he could win (which he sarcastically said was only true if the other candidate was Prince Mongo).[2346] Branston added that the *Commercial Appeal* should be "ashamed and disgraced" because they, in essence, promoted a "highly dubious piece of partisan polling as big news knowing full well it would be seized upon by the Morris campaign." [2347] It was good to see a credible reporter call the practice out.

Shortly after the election, even the *Commercial Appeal's* Blake Fontenay acknowledged that the paper's own commissioned poll played a part in confusing the voters.[2348] Fontenay was still talking about it a year later. In an opinion piece, he questioned the validity of polls after seeing that the newspaper's own poll published a few days before the mayoral election reporting that Morris was "surging in popularity and had the best chance of unseating Mayor Willie Herenton" was not what happened. [2349] Fontenay wrote that although Herenton finished first, "his closest rival was actually Carol Chumney, with Morris a not-so-close third." [2350] Even Rhodes College's Dr. Polhmann acknowledged that I might have won in a two-way race with Herenton. [2351] The post-election admissions were welcome, but the failure by some to tell the voters the truth before the election appeared to be a disguised effort to put Morris in or tip the race to Herenton. The public deserved better from their major daily newspaper. So did I, having spent years serving the public, with a solid record and as a female candidate who only asked for fair coverage.

Post-election reports also noted the populist and grassroots nature of my campaign.[2352] Derek Haire writing for the *Memphis Flyer*, called it "remarkable" for relying so heavily on volunteers and regular people for support, instead of endorsements from elected officials. [2353] Baker with the *Memphis Flyer* noted my "bulldog" determination, calling it "gallant" and "even impressive," and speculated whether I would have become "an instant cynosure for the national media" if elected. [2354] I deeply appreciated my hard-working supporters who stood with me in a tough election. As to a national profile, my goal was to make Memphis the talk of the nation in a positive way—not myself.

Herenton now saw Harold Ford Sr.'s abandonment of the proposed election eve rally and failure to render an endorsement as a conspiracy. [2355] And, after the election, the mayor showed a prior drug test result to *Memphis Flyer* reporter Jackson Baker claiming he was in good health. [2356]

Many voters were still upset that Herenton's election night remarks were "defiant," without accepting any responsibility to help heal the city's racial divide post-election. [2357] Herenton replied that he didn't separate the races. [2358] Memphis needed healing, but it was their "problem," and the "onus" should not be on him to unite the city. [2359] Although having lost the election, my remarks the same night were "to come together." This was another example of the contrast in our leadership styles.

He further talked about how "hurt" he was to be booed at a University of Memphis basketball game by some white citizens, and at another large event televised on national TV with Justin Timberlake present. [2360] Herenton also spoke about the betrayal of some former supporters, who were now his enemies.[2361]

The *Commercial Appeal* editors called upon him to stop the "divisive rhetoric," be a "statesman," and begin to address the city's serious problems in order to stop the exodus of citizens and to attract needed commercial investment for the city to survive. [2362] Angry letters to the editor were printed in the newspaper for days after Herenton's election night remarks, with many saying they were taking the mayor at his word and sadly moving out of the city.[2363] Others pled with him to do something to make the city safer. One had to admire him for breaking the racial barrier to be the city's first elected African American mayor; however, he had lost a great deal of goodwill previously earned by his own more recent actions and inactions.

Memphis struggled with the highest property taxes in the state, highest violent crime in the nation, declining property values and city revenues due to the departure of many citizens, high foreclosure rates, and high poverty. [2364] The fact that Herenton called his detractors racist and haters when the city was in such lousy shape under his tenure was mentioned in many letters as an example of his inability to take ownership of the real cause of the loss of his support.[2365] Fifty-eight percent of the voters had chosen another candidate. [2366] A few blamed Morris and me for not dropping out of the race and endorsing the other. Another said we had the right to run and attributed the real cause of Herenton's reelection as apathy, with only 40% turnout.[2367]

One writer suggested the mayoral race was not about Herenton playing the race card, but instead a play of the gender card. [2368] Perhaps so, with a University of Iowa poll of the Obama/Clinton presidential race showing over 90% of those democratic caucus goers polled saying race or gender would not affect their choice.[2369] But, 40% admitted race could hurt Obama's chances, and 51% said gender could hurt Hillary Clinton's chances in a general election. [2370] David Redlawsk, the pollster, was quoted by the *McClatchy* newspaper as saying, "we've reached a time when social convention suggests it's not appropriate to express these concerns openly," adding "but in the privacy of the voting booth?" [2371] If his analysis were accurate, that would explain a lot in the 2007 Memphis mayoral election.

5

The task left before me was to complete my council term, which would end on December 31, 2007. I pledged to continue to fight for Memphis because I love the city, albeit soon to be out of public office.

Only ten days after the election, I was back at work on the council opposing a gas and water rate increase for MLGW. [2372] With the election over, the council now reversed itself and voted Herenton an $11,500 pay raise effective on New Year's Day.[2373] I cast a no vote, along with four others.[2374] Marshall voted yes, saying the raise was part of the "healing" process post-election.[2375]

One of my last actions as a member of the Memphis City Council was to push for Memphis Networx to open its books for an auditor authorized by the council at my request.[2376] The councilmembers were not getting some of their questions answered by Networx.[2377] With the proposed sale, the taxpayers would lose all but about $1 million of the huge public investment.[2378] Calls for the state Attorney General to investigate and the possibility of a lawsuit were mentioned as leverage to get Networx to cooperate.[2379]

Later in 2009, after acquired by another company, Networx would be in court with the City of Memphis over a contractual dispute.[2380] Allan Wade, as the attorney for the city, claimed to the court in a brief that the audited financial statements for Networx for the period ending December 31, 2003, reflected that the agreed contributions by MLGW and the private joint venture members of 53% and 47%, respectively, had not occurred.[2381] As of December 31, 2004, MLGW had funded $25 million of the company's losses, which represented 84% [rather than 53%] of capital contributions by the joint venture's members.[2382] In the brief, the city admitted that "by all standards, Memphis Networx was a dismal failure, which wasted over $30 million in taxpayer funds."[2383]

And, only 14 years later, in 2021, the city leaders were developing plans to spend another $36 million dollars of the public's monies for a broadband plan to serve parts of the city that lacked access – just as had been the impetus for Memphis Networx.[2384] Sadly, others in the private sector had gained the benefits of the fiber optic network paid for with millions of the taxpayers' money when Memphis Networx had been sold in a firesale – with no proper investigation or accountability to the public for the loss. Now, the city was proposing that the public pay again for the same thing.

As the year ended in 2007, Fontenay with the *Commercial Appeal* acknowledged that I had come closer to defeating Herenton than any politician since

Hackett in 1991. [2385] He pitched me for Shelby County mayor in three years since Wharton was term-limited. [2386] Other exiting councilmembers said they were interested in various other offices, with Sammons suggested also for county mayor but saying that his political career was probably over.[2387] Still wanting to move Memphis ahead, I certainly wasn't ruling out a future run for public office.

At the last council meeting for the year, Tom Marshall joked that a voice vote would be needed for the perfunctory complimentary resolution for me as a departing council member in order to ensure its passage.[2388] But, regardless of the jest, I stayed true to the public service principles that had guided me for years as a member of the council. My last act was to try to get the council to adjourn briefly and take action so as to avoid the huge pay raise for the mayor. They declined.

And, with that, after seventeen years in public office, I returned to life as a private citizen.

PART SEVEN

Memphis Mayor's Race II

31

Cracks in the Glass Ceiling

1

The 2008 New Year kicked off. Branston with the *Memphis Flyer*, either having a premonition or inside information, queried whether Herenton was one of four possible high-profile Memphians likely to leave his job. [2389] While my candidacy for mayor of Memphis in 2007 did not prevail, the gender barrier was becoming visible with more cracks in the glass ceiling due to my effort. And Herenton's tenure as mayor still appeared to be up in the air.

Meanwhile, Herenton pitched state legislation to allow one vote countywide for consolidation as opposed to separate votes by urban and suburbanites.[2390] He then characteristically dropped the issue only a month later.[2391]

Herenton's close working relationship with County Mayor Wharton again caused some to wonder whether a backroom deal had been made at *Le Chardonnay* in 2007 when Wharton thereafter dissed the "Draft AC" campaign. [2392] On the *WMC Action News 5* local news station, Jackson Baker commented that many thought an agreement had been made between Herenton and Wharton for "some kind of handover of power midway in this term of Mayor Herenton," along with a push for consolidation so "if A C became mayor, he'd become mayor of everything." [2393] Wharton countered, denying any conversation at *Le Chardonnay* "about our political futures" or any plot for him to consolidate the city and the county, to succeed Herenton and serve as mayor for the whole area. [2394]

The FBI probe of Herenton was reported to continue, now regarding computer-related contracts with seven companies, including a million dollars in no-bid subcontracts to a company headed by a former Herenton city director. [2395] Perhaps to distract attention from the probe, Herenton hinted at plans for expanding the Cook Convention Center and building a new football stadium.[2396] With the recent renovations for the convention center exceeding $92 million, twice the projections, many were concerned about the cost in light of the city's ongoing budget problems.[2397] It made no sense for the city to fund a brand new football stadium when Memphis had not gotten its bond rating back up, given its workers pay raises for two years, or even paid for the Pyramid arena or FedExForum.[2398]

John Branston with the *Memphis Flyer* editorialized that the city was in disarray. He noted the ongoing federal investigations, the weak economy, high rental vacancy rate, and foreclosures. Also, he mentioned lower tax collections due to falling property values, profits down for most of the area's largest employers such as Federal Express and several banks, and possible loss of the Memphis airport hub due to the Delta and Northwest airlines merger. Moreover, Branston pointed out the stalled public developments and aging leadership. [2399] However, he still expressed optimism that new leaders and solutions would emerge by 2011 or sooner. [2400] I hoped there would be a chance to bring the new leadership and to be the one to make it happen.

Even though out of political office, I stayed involved. U.S. Sen. Hillary Clinton came through town running for U.S. President, having just lost South Carolina to Obama. I was invited to meet her at a private morning event at the Peabody Hotel.

As we chatted briefly, Clinton told me that she had heard of my strong showing in the mayoral election and asked for my endorsement.[2401] I agreed, and understanding how tough the effort to achieve higher office can be for a woman, told her to "Hang in There." A few days later, despite being opponents in the 2007 mayoral contest, Herenton and I agreed to a joint press conference to announce our endorsement of Clinton for President. [2402] In my remarks, I endorsed her based upon her experience, adding that "women deserve a chance to lead." [2403]

Some in the press wanted to find a place for me to serve, just not as mayor. Maybe it was a tweak of their conscience about the unfair coverage and push-polling that impacted the mayoral election outcome. So, when the long-serving County Trustee Bob Patterson unexpectedly died, rumors began to spread that I was interested in the position.[2404]

My mother had worked in the trustee's office during Patterson's tenure. Some friends called and asked me to consider it. However, I decided it only would be part of the same practice of steering me away from the mayor's job.

And I was not too far off track. A newspaper report was published shortly after that about a purported conversation between anonymous county commissioners and me about the position, with one wondering if I would forgo a county mayoral bid if appointed county trustee. [2405] Apparently, it was an offer of a deal by someone since the conversations never took place. I promptly denied the story with a courteous note to the reporter that I was not interested in the job and wanted no part of any backroom deal-making.[2406]

Nevertheless, Baker with the *Memphis Flyer* continued to report that I had meetings with two county commissioners about the trustee opening where the county mayor's race was discussed – which never occurred. [2407] Baker further reported that County Commissioner Deidre Malone wanted an assurance that I would not run for county mayor if appointed county trustee. [2408]However, the *Commercial Appeal* got it right when it reported that some constituents approached me to consider running for the post, but I had not given up my dream to be Memphis mayor.[2409] After researching the trustee position, I was not interested.

2

With the 2007 mayoral election barely over, the press began to speculate on who would be a candidate for the 2011 Memphis mayoral election. Wharton was identified as a candidate, along with me. Now that he was looking at a city mayoral race, Wharton called for city/county consolidation, something he wouldn't touch in the 2002 county mayoral primary – or during the years he had served as county mayor for that matter. [2410]

Baker with the *Memphis Flyer* speculated that I would consider the county mayor's race in 2010, but the primary would include Deidre Malone, a female African American county commissioner. [2411] However, I would not be steered to a different mayoral position that might preclude me from running for Memphis mayor in the next election. He was correct in opining that I saw myself as representing not only reform but also "the political aspirations of her gender." [2412] Memphis had never elected a woman mayor. Yet, women with a solid record are equally capable of doing the job as the guys, including myself.

Having left politics for the first time in seventeen years, I felt like a fish out of water. Suddenly my days, evenings, and weekends were free of community meetings, campaigning, and working on public policy efforts, apart from my law firm practice. I likened the experience in a radio interview to the movie *Groundhog Day* where the newscaster played by actor Bill Murray relived the same day over and over again until he got it right with his romantic interest. Every day I woke up, punched the alarm clock, and then remembered that Herenton was still the mayor and wanted to roll over and go back to sleep.

So, to bridge the transition back to solely private life, I proposed and was approved to teach an undergraduate class at the University of Memphis political science department titled "American Political Leadership." The class focused on the upcoming presidential election.[2413] By reading books by the top presidential candidates Obama, Hillary Clinton, Romney, and Giuliani, we explored racism, sexism, religion, and leadership in politics. Since my father was a history professor at the university, it was fun to be on campus in the building next door. My dad kindly told the student newspaper that my "experience in the public arena" and "passion for politics" had always made him proud. [2414]

Class assignments included writing an opinion essay for submission to the local press or volunteering in a campaign and writing a paper on the experience. I asked provocative questions, such as how the "first husband" duties would resemble the current "first lady" duties in the White House. Would he pick out china, host parties and million-dollar galas, "all while explaining how he supports his wife at the end of a long hard day?" The students responded with their own views. Some women commented on how they wanted to be taken seriously as leaders, but also to enjoy their femininity by picking out a party dress or new china patterns. Certainly, leadership and femininity should not be considered mutually exclusive.

At the national level, Hillary Clinton's 2008 campaign struggled. Reports of internal conflict distracted from her strong TV commercial, implying that she was the better prepared Democratic candidate to handle an early morning crisis telephone call at the White House.[2415] The endorsement of Obama by Ted Kennedy, and some of her husband's impromptu comments on the campaign trail (although well-meaning), also made Clinton's effort more difficult.[2416]

Her challenge to break the political gender barrier, and my own, gave me pause to reflect when I was asked to author a chapter for the *Memphis Profiles in Courage (2008)* book. [2417]After experiencing the double standard myself first hand in the 2002 and 2007 mayoral elections, I decided to profile four women who had run for either Shelby County or Memphis Mayor before my own attempts. I interviewed and researched the candidacies of Mary Rose McCormick, Minerva Johnican, Pat Vander Scaaf, and Carolyn Gates, and wrote about their successes and challenges. They were Republicans and Democrats, black and white, of different generations, who each had tried to shatter a very thick glass ceiling. I detailed their difficulties raising money, sexist coverage about their appearance, marginalization of often superior credentials, and gender stereotypes made about their personalities that often depicted them as angry while the male candidates were glorified.

As a younger woman interested in politics, I had watched all of their campaigns. I remembered when City Councilwoman Pat Vander Schaaf appeared on my college campus with other male Memphis mayoral candidates. And, I recalled her provocative television ad where a male voice asked would it make her record of public service any more significant if the male voice were, in fact, her real voice? Then, the answer in her own voice that it wouldn't change her record at all, and she just happened to be a female in Memphis who could get things done.

The former mayoral candidates also noted the lack of support by women generally, remarking on a double standard by their own gender. From my research, it appeared that the press had piled on blaming the lack of female support for their losses, just as they had done in my 2007 mayoral election.

Those profiled also said that they did not receive prominent business leaders' support due to their gender. And it certainly didn't surprise me given my own experiences of pressure to drop out of races, that three of these women faced the same test with promises of financial support or other positions, which they declined.

3

Near the end of March, only five months after the October 2007 mayoral election, Herenton suddenly and to the shock of all, announced his resignation for July 31, 2008. [2418] Herenton was reported to believe that under the city charter, his CAO, Keith McGee, would become the mayor and serve until 2010 if the council deadlocked on the interim mayor replacement. [2419] Herenton claimed that the resignation only was because he wanted to be the new Memphis City Schools superintendent and not because of a federal investigation. [2420]

He also was reported to say that he never intended to complete this mayoral term, which would expire on December 31, 2011. [2421] I was flabbergasted that he had misled the public with his candidacy for a job he didn't even want.

According to the *Commercial Appeal,* the federal grand jury was still investigating Herenton's dealings with a businessman related to the transfer of a vacant lot and city contracts to see if there were a connection. [2422] Also under investigation were dealings in 2006 regarding an engineering contract award to the businessman by the local public transit authority. [2423]Both denied any improprieties. Herenton attributed the investigation to racial bias in that they both are African American. [2424] Although he denied a connection, many wondered if his resignation was due to the federal investigations.

John Willingham, who had been a mayoral candidate in 2007, said that the FBI met with him about the building of the FedExForum, and Herenton. In particular, Willingham revealed that he spoke with the agents regarding whether or not the mayor and other city officials misled authorities and the public in accepting a $20 million federal grant purportedly to construct an intermodal bus transfer at the FedExForum but then never built the station. [2425] It was clear that the Herenton administration was under serious scrutiny by the feds.

The *Commercial Appeal* editors expressed their disappointment that Herenton caused "a nasty and racially divisive election" in 2007 to "satisfy his own ego."[2426] Interestingly, the editors also contended there should be a "caretaker" interim mayor until there could be a special election and that the council should not try to appoint an interim mayor "they deem worthy of the full-time job" or allow Herenton to "hand-pick" the interim mayor. [2427] I agreed that Herenton should not have run merely to prove he could win and that he should not select the interim mayor. But why shouldn't the council select as interim mayor the woman who had nearly won the election since the people supported the choice?

Speculation immediately began on the possible field of mayoral candidates to replace Herenton. Blake Fontenay, a commentator with the *Commercial Appeal,* called Wharton an "early favorite" if he ran, but wondered if he might appear "hypocritical" having said that he was committed to completing his term as county mayor the year before. [2428] While he didn't draw the comparison, wouldn't Wharton running for Memphis mayor now be a lot like Herenton quitting only half a year into his fifth term? The columnist predicted a crowded field, with a possible winner garnering only a fourth or less of the vote. [2429] He then pitched the possibility of another "Draft A C" movement, with Wharton being a consensus candidate for both the black and white communities. [2430]

Amazingly, school board member Kenneth Whalum Jr. said that he was glad that Herenton did not step aside before he was reelected in 2007 and was now "free" to be the school superintendent. [2431] This statement baffled me. Another Herenton supporter said that the mayor just wanted to prove that he could win. Some claimed that many African Americans voted for Herenton only because they did not want the first elected black mayor to be discredited with a loss.

My response was, as I had said on election night, given the high crime, high taxes, and continuing federal investigations, Memphis deserved better.[2432] I asked who knew what and when, and was there a backroom deal?[2433] Were the powerbrokers trying to handpick the mayoral successor?[2434] Despite the defeat, I was still committed to Memphis and believed that we could turn things around.[2435]

The next day, Herenton incredibly responded at a crime summit that he ran for reelection just to protect Memphis from "Chumney" and "Morris" because they could not "take this city to the next level." [2436] He contended that he had no choice but to run for reelection to protect *his* investment in the city from his sixteen years as mayor. [2437] He added that he would not leave the mayor's office if he did not become school superintendent in July. [2438]

Was he using the desire of many that he step down as leverage to gain the superintendent's job? It was preposterous that he had run for reelection in 2007 to protect Memphis from me - an honest, experienced, capable change-agent for the better, while he had brought the city to the brink of bankruptcy during his last term.

While Morris laughed at the remarks saying the mayor needed prayers, I dryly responded "I guess *he's* not planning on taking Memphis to the next level" since he was applying for another job.[2439] While the public was left to wonder whether Herenton was even doing his job as Memphis mayor with his focus elsewhere, he proclaimed that "when I go to work every day, the citizens of Memphis get a day's work out of Willie Herenton...." [2440]

Herenton reiterated that he would not resign as mayor if he were not appointed school superintendent. [2441] The *Commercial Appeal* reported that Herenton already had met privately with some Memphis City School board members at the first of the year. [2442] So, this idea of switching jobs had been in the works only a few months after the election, if not sooner. He had obviously deceived the public as to his intentions.

The *Commercial Appeal* editors justifiably chastised Herenton's pronouncements as "outrageous and downright laughable." [2443] They pointed out that the statements were "disingenuous" in that Morris and I could run again for mayor after he resigned, suggesting that he was really job-hopping due to the problematic budget mess. [2444] Or was this merely a contrived effort to save Wharton a place for the city mayor-ship and make Herenton the superintendent?

The specter of a backroom deal between Herenton and Wharton swirled again in the wake of Herenton's surprise announcement. Wharton continued to deny that the *tete-a-tete* at *Le Chardonnay* in 2007 included any discussion of the "Draft A C" movement, his announcement immediately thereafter that he was not running, or the announced resignation of Herenton shortly after the election. [2445] However, Wharton now expressed interest in the job if Herenton resigned, which fueled the debate as to whether this was the plan all along. [2446]

Baker with the *Memphis Flyer* opined that Wharton slickly might have been the "prime mover" for Herenton's decision to resign and seek the school superintendent position. [2447] Wharton claimed to have been consulting with Herenton about saving the Memphis "troubled schools" before the 2007 election, during the same time some business leaders were drafting him to run for Memphis mayor. [2448] Obviously, Wharton had considered entering the 2007 Memphis mayoral election when he didn't immediately shut down the "Draft AC" movement. Perhaps he wanted Herenton out of the mayoral race and pitched the superintendent's job to appeal to that mayor's ego. Perhaps, he was secretly behind the "Draft AC" movement to begin with. Ultimately, Wharton stayed on the sidelines after the *Le Chardonnay* meeting, in what Jackson Baker called a "bruising three-way battle" between MLGW head Herman Morris, Herenton, and me.[2449]

Herenton later explained the *Le Chardonnay* meeting with Wharton as not a backroom deal, but a discussion in which he told the county mayor his consideration of entering the Memphis mayoral race against him was divisive.[2450] Herenton called it a "character flaw" on Wharton's part.[2451] He added that Wharton was falling into the trap of "divide and conquer," apparently a reference to splitting the black vote if he had run. [2452] It would have been great for Baker to have been a fly on the wall to report what was actually said by each mayor.

Based upon Baker's sources, Herenton was told by Wharton at the meeting that he was "divisive."[2453] Herenton responded that he was being himself. [2454] Herenton told Baker that if Wharton had entered the 2007 mayoral race, he would have lost, and it would have been "ugly" in that he would have "described him."[2455] What the description would be was unclear, but certainly not good.

According to Baker with the *Memphis Flyer*, Wharton had discussions with business leaders about the need to have a leader of the schools independent of the white business community to spearhead the schools' consolidation.[2456] With Herenton being so independent, he reasoned that no one could say he was doing their "bidding" in some sort of "imperialistic plantation style."[2457] Wharton at the time supported a unified system of the Memphis and Shelby County Schools, but with two separate school districts.[2458] Apparently, Herenton believed he could resign as mayor and be appointed school superintendent, work towards consolidation of the schools, and continue to run the city through his CAO (former county jailor) whom he thought would become the interim mayor through 2010.[2459] Yet, some speculated that the pitch to Herenton was merely a guise designed to get him to vacate the mayoral seat.

Whalum Jr., the cheerleader now for Herenton, said that there was no need for a national search for school superintendent if Herenton applied. [2460] Others warned that if Herenton sought the position, other qualified applicants might not apply.[2461] Herenton taking the bait, boasted to the *New York Times*, "When you are good, you don't seek positions, they seek you."[2462]

4

With Herenton's surprise announcement that he was resigning, I was hopeful that there would be another chance to become the mayor of Memphis and the first woman to hold the position as well. On the 40th anniversary of the death of Dr. Martin Luther King Jr., there I was outside the National Civil Rights Museum in the rain, reflecting on his civil rights battle.

Traveling to town for the ceremonies were Jesse Jackson Sr., Hillary Clinton, John McCain, Al Sharpton, Martin Luther King III, and a slew of national media and press reporters.[2463] Jacqueline Smith, a former worker and resident at the Lorraine Motel, continued her long-standing picket out front, advocating for the museum to be used to serve the poor with job training, housing, education, or a medical clinic in keeping with King's message of equality.

In many respects, she was right as to the need for action. Fewer and fewer citizens were voting in local elections, the area's violent crime and infant mortality rates were the highest in the nation, with poverty also high. [2464] And Shelby County had the third-highest jail incarceration rate in the country, with many poor nonviolent offenders unable to make bail. [2465] As *Memphis Flyer* columnist John Branston pointed out, the city in some respects was still stuck in 1968 in terms of progress in tackling these issues. [2466] Others tended to focus instead on the progress made with sports, music, and successful business ventures in hopes of presenting a more positive image for the city.[2467]

But in my opinion, the real battle for the city is a spiritual one. Resentment smolders in some citizens who are African American, who lived through segregation and struggle economically, with financial power still firmly in the hands of the area's white elite. And on the other hand, some white citizens resent race being used as leverage to gain an advantage in contracting, college admission, or government funding of certain projects. Others, black and white, just want the community to unite and move forward.

Meanwhile, inner-city poverty increased, temp jobs with no benefits grew, and more middle class white and black citizens exited the city to escape crime and racial tension. But there in the rain at the civil rights museum, I heeded the advice of a man who shared his umbrella with me. I decided not to give up on serving the people and pressed forward.

5

2008 was a tough year for all. Inapposite with his push for a new convention center and football stadium was Herenton's proposed "austerity" budget, with five libraries and four community centers slated to be closed and a tax hike.[2468] The nation was entering the worst recession since the Great Depression of the 1930s. The council balked at a property tax hike since Memphis already had the highest rate in the state. Wendi Thomas, with the *Commercial Appeal*, pointed out that the city government had incredibly proposed increasing the number of positions by some 27% since 2006. [2469]

Also, staying on the offense despite the federal investigations, Herenton pressured the special state prosecutor in the "sex-plot" blackmail controversy to keep that investigation open and charge the alleged perpetrators. [2470] The special prosecutor replied that the waitress may have been asked to gather incriminating information on Herenton, but never intended to take any action and there was no evidence of a "plan to extort" the mayor. [2471] Nick Clark added his view that the alleged conspiracy was a reelection gimmick.[2472] The bizarre tale ended with no charges being brought.

However, one investigation did come to an end. Michael Hooks Jr., a school board member and bit actor in the Craig Brewer *Hustle & Flow* film, pled guilty to converting another's property to his own use related to dealings with Tim Willis in the juvenile court clerk's office.[2473] Hooks Jr., a smart young man, had been snagged in the investigation but was sentenced to only thirty days in jail. [2474] Former County Commissioner Bruce Thompson also pled guilty to mail fraud related to his work brokering a school construction contract as a consultant for a construction company, resulting in a six-month jail sentence and a $10,000 fine. [2475] Each later reinvented himself in the real estate construction industry.

Others, who might have been charged in the stings, had taken prompt action to amend financial disclosure forms to reflect monies received as campaign contributions.[2476] Questions still lingered as to why those accused were primarily black Democrats and why the federal agents did not equally target business persons.[2477] Obviously, if taking payoffs or abuse in contracting was the modus operandi of certain elected officials, someone other than just the FBI was making the payments.

Remaining were the charges against Councilman Edmund Ford Sr. related to his interactions with lobbyist Joe Cooper. After a trial, the jury came back with Edmund Ford Sr. fully acquitted on all charges.[2478] Edmund Ford Sr. had taken the stand in his own defense. Completely vindicated, he gave the credit to God.[2479]

6

Now just as abruptly as he had announced that he would resign as mayor, Herenton decided not to apply for the open school superintendent position after all. [2480] The *Commercial Appeal* lost no time in editorializing that he would have been the wrong choice in light of the recent problems at City Hall. [2481] The cause of his fickleness was a mystery.

With it clear there was not going to be a special mayoral election after all, the press turned back to the issue of whether Memphis would ever become a metropolitan government by combining with the county. Comparisons were made to Nashville, which had formed a metro government in 1962, while a merger had been defeated more than once for the Memphis area. [2482]

When asked, I told the *Commercial Appeal* that having championed consolidated government against Wharton in the 2002 county mayoral election, I would gladly work with him on the issue if the people elected me Memphis mayor should Herenton resign. [2483] As I said, "If folks in the business community have this light bulb come on and think it's important to the community, they need to get somebody in there who's going to fight for it."[2484] It still seemed to me that Memphis and the county united could better leverage their resources to create a much greater economic engine that would benefit all.

Wharton was doing his typical hedging on the hot-button issue after suburban mayors rallied against it, with former County Mayor Rout saying that a popular leader would be needed to make it a reality.[2485] Rout likened it to Louisville, which had consolidated with united support from city, county, and business leaders, as well as the leadership of popular Mayor Jerry Abramson.[2486]

I had met Mayor Abramson in Louisville years earlier at a workshop on consolidation as a newly elected Memphis city councilmember. Somewhat ironically, the only other person at the workshop from Memphis was Wharton. Despite our differences, I invited him to join me for dinner with my sister, Mary, and her husband (Louisville residents). He declined. If I had been elected Memphis mayor in 2007, we could have worked on it together, built support for it, and gotten it done.

Surprisingly, another former county mayor candidate from 2002, Republican Larry Scroggs, now sounded more positive on the issue of consolidation, saying that it would give suburban citizens a greater voice in how Memphis is run. [2487] Former County Mayor Bill Morris opined that one day the Memphis City Council would just vote to surrender the charter to the county. Former Memphis Mayor Dick Hackett believed that both the city and county residents would ultimately have to do it out of financial necessity. [2488] However, under state law, the city could not just vote to surrender the charter.[2489] So, the county and city governments continue today as separate entities, perhaps as a testament of how the citizens still can not truly unite.

Although consolidation was not underway, a wrinkle in the city charter still needed addressing should Herenton actually resign. Though no longer in public office, I proposed a charter amendment to the newly formed Memphis Charter Commission that required a special election within two months should a mayor resign.[2490] Under the charter at that time, the city council chairman would become the mayor if that office were vacated. Then the city council could appoint a mayor to serve until the next municipal or general election. [2491]However, if the councilmembers could not agree on an interim mayor within the twenty days, then the CAO served until the council acted or the next such election.[2492] My primary concern was that if Herenton resigned, the council might stalemate. Then, Herenton's CAO would become the interim mayor for possibly two years without a vote by the people.

In 1982, Memphis Mayor Wyeth Chandler resigned to become a judge, making Council Chairman J. O. Patterson Jr. the first African American mayor of Memphis for twenty days.[2493] Then, the council appointed Wallace Madewall, the former CAO, as interim mayor until Dick Hackett was elected shortly thereafter.[2494] During his tenure, Madewell made the most of his brief time as mayor by entering the city into a thirty-two-year lease with Beale Street Development Corporation to develop the area, followed by two ten year options.[2495] Madewell would have continued as mayor if three attorneys had not filed a lawsuit to force an election on the November ballot. [2496] After the lawsuit, an election was held with only three weeks for candidates to raise money and get their message out to the voters. [2497] The city charter needed amending to clarify the successor and election process where a mayor resigns in order to avoid another similar lawsuit.

City Councilman Lowery proposed for the council chair to serve as interim mayor for ninety days until a special election if a regular election was not scheduled during that time-period. [2498] Should Herenton resign, the proposal might benefit the council chair in the special election by allowing him or her to become an incumbent of sorts as interim mayor. However, although it might give the interim mayor an edge if Herenton resigned, my civic duty was to push a charter amendment. I couldn't fathom Memphis having a mayoral vacancy filled with an interim CAO, not elected by the people, for two years or more (absent another successful lawsuit similar to that in 1982). [2499]

7

Having said he would not resign as mayor after all, Herenton apparently still coveted the superintendent's job and name-called all of the candidates for the open position as "third-rate."[2500] Some worried that his about-face on using city funds usually allocated to the city schools for other purposes was not calculated to force consolidation but instead to push his own appointment for the post, which paid substantially more. One editorial in the *Commercial Appeal* called it a "desperation bid" by the mayor, reminding the public of the prior scandal which precipitated his resignation in 1991 from the school system. [2501] Yet despite the same, he still had some supporters on the school board.

In fact, the schools did not fare well in the city budget process. A majority of the city council, led by newly elected Councilmen Edmund Ford Jr. and Bill Morrison, decided to fund only about $20 million of the $93.5 million city funds requested by the public schools.[2502] They also adopted an eighteen cent per hundred dollars accessed property tax reduction. [2503] However, an advisory opinion of the Tennessee Attorney General warned that cutting the school funds violated state law, which prohibits governments from reducing funding for schools.[2504] City Council Attorney Allan Wade and City Attorney Sara Hall disagreed with that portion of the opinion by Paul Summers. [2505]

I emailed a local reporter that Mayor Herenton had delivered a bloated budget in conjunction with a request for a hefty fifty-eight cent property tax increase.[2506] Although my views were not reported, I shared with him that the council could cut the budget substantially more and avoid taking the funds from public education altogether. In my view, with the high poverty in Memphis, public education needed to be supported to help the young children and level the playing field. While I felt there was some wasteful spending in both the city schools and at City Hall, I also advocated that the council should identify on the record what cuts should take place in the schools' budget (i.e., administration and not programs for children).

My concern was that the council might be unwittingly playing into Herenton's agenda to either force the school board to select him as school superintendent or punish the school board by cutting their budget in retaliation for not selecting him for the job. In my view, most folks in Memphis were tired of this gamesmanship and bullying.

As I explained to Amos Maki with the *Commercial Appeal*, the mayor gave the council a budget padded with patronage positions. There was probably not another city in America where the credential for a city directorship was whether you were the mayor's former bodyguard. Did the council factor into their decision to cut taxes the expenses of pay raises over the next four years, increased gas costs, and the increased amounts needed to fund the city's health care and pension costs in light of Councilman Morrison's statement that the lowered tax rate would fund the city's budget for the next four years?

As I pointed out, if the council's analysis were based upon the monies the city would keep with a proposed phase out of city schools funding, then how would the members respond if they lost the legal battle in court on their power to cut such funding? What would the impact be on the precarious county budget if it later had to pick up the tab for the schools from the amounts the city cut?

Otis Sanford, an editor with the *Commercial Appeal,* deemed the situation at City Hall as "chaos."[2507] He referred to Herenton's saying cutting the millions in city school funding would be a way to force "drastic reform," and then his flip-flop to say that it would be wrong and "have a devastating effect on the school system."[2508] Sanford likened the statement that taxes would not be raised for four years by the "gang" of ten council members who voted for the school cuts to an offer to buy some "swampland in Mississippi.[2509] In this instance, I thought he was right.

Ultimately, the city council cut millions of the city's share of public school funds, increased city operating expenses by millions, and cut the property tax rate. And the body made no effort to make any line-item budget cuts. [2510] Later, the public would pay the price.

Since Herenton apparently still wanted the superintendent position, speculation began in the press as to who might run for mayor of Memphis should he resign.[2511] Councilman Lowery was mentioned as interested. And so was Wharton, who fessed up to talking with Herenton about applying for the school superintendent position – again leading to speculation that they made a deal at the *Le Chardonnay* meeting in 2007. [2512]

Baker with the *Memphis Flyer* also mentioned me as a possible candidate. He analyzed the race saying that if the field was crowded with African American candidates, including Whalum Jr. and others, my chances were better.[2513] Of course, until Herenton actually resigned, the field would not be certain.

In any event, it appeared that the next election might be much sooner than expected. There would be another chance to bring real change to Memphis, and a woman to the mayor's office!

32

Winds of Change

1

While the winds of change were growing more evident, Herenton, now amazingly said that he had never actually resigned as mayor. [2514] I guess he didn't accept his own resignation!

The school system finally hired a new superintendent, Dr. Kriner Cash. Herenton apologized and greeted him with a basketball game of hoops to show that he was a good sport. Cash inherited a system that only graduated about 70% of the students, was fighting violent crime and guns being brought by youth to the schools, and with 85% of the students economically challenged. [2515] To top it off, the schools were now in a lawsuit with the City of Memphis about the cut in funds.[2516] State officials threatened to withhold $400 million from the city schools' $1.2 billion budget if the city funding issue was not resolved. [2517] This was a crisis.

Herenton distanced himself from the school's lawsuit with the city over funding. His outrageous antics caused the *Memphis Flyer's* Baker to name him a "tease."[2518] Cited in support of the label were the alleged sex-plot exposé on the eve of the last mayoral election, his claims of being ordained by God to lead the city, trying to step outside to fight with one councilmember, and actually doing it in a charity bout with Joe Frazier. [2519] The drama never ceased.

As to his letter in March to his CAO expressing his intent to resign effective July 31, 2008, Herenton said it was subject to unmet conditions.[2520] Now, he claimed never to have sought the school superintendent position. [2521] Baker speculated that Herenton was organizing support to fend off "a rumored future indictment relating to city contracts awarded to mayoral associates."[2522] While the status of the FBI investigations was uncertain, Baker was correct that many citizens desired Herenton to resign. They saw his flip-flopping as toying with their emotions and contrary to the well-being of the city.

2

The summer of 2008 also brought the end to Hillary Clinton's first presidential campaign, after Obama began taking the country by storm. However, as she historically said, "Although we were not able to shatter that highest and hardest glass ceiling this time, thanks to you it's got about 18 million cracks in it, and the light is shining through like never before, filling us all with the hope and the sure knowledge that the path will be a little easier next time...."[2523]

I had been excited about the national candidacies of both Democrat Hillary Clinton and Republican Sarah Palin. Finally, women were permitted to be serious contenders for the highest offices of the land. However, when running for president, Clinton reportedly experienced boorish sexist remarks on the campaign trail, much as I had when running for mayor.[2524]

And, a *Commercial Appeal* reporter even wrote a story mentioning the hairstyle of vice-presidential candidate Sarah Palin when she had worked years earlier as a reporter in Anchorage, Alaska. [2525] Playing off a comment she made, Geoff Calkins called it "from the Beaver Roundup to the Republican Roundup." [2526] With a tongue in cheek comparison of Palin's credentials as a former small-town mayor to Biden's service on the Senate Foreign Relations Committee, Calkins fell into the gender bias trap. He sarcastically observed that Palin did her job "while wearing hair spray and pantyhose." [2527] Whatever her qualifications, the unabashed Palin defined herself as a "pit bull fighting good ole boy politics." [2528] Now, I can relate to that.

And, despite it all, Clinton's line resonated that "My mother was born before women could vote;" "My daughter got to vote for her mother for President." [2529] I thought about my grandmothers and my own mother and how times had changed, but still not enough.

Similarly to Clinton's recent effort, my hopes of election to higher office had not panned out. Speculation was rampant that I would run for city council when Scott McCormick decided to vacate his seat for a nonprofit position. I considered my options.[2530] After prayerful consideration, I held a press conference and declined to be a candidate for the open seat.[2531] I love the city and wanted to serve the people. When the right opportunity presented itself, I would be ready again to offer my platform for positive change, as well as my passion, drive, and dedication to making Memphis a world class-city.

My philosophy is to walk by faith and not by sight.[2532] Even though Herenton now said he was not resigning—he might change his mind again. If I were back on the council, and only a few months later, Herenton actually did resign, then it would be difficult for me to run for mayor after just returning to the city council. Would the voters think they could get a "twofer" by electing another candidate mayor and keeping me on the city council? This had been pitched by Strickland in the 2003 city council election- for the people to keep me as a state legislator and elect him to the council job.

Also, I wondered if a return to the council would typecast me as a legislator as opposed to a potential mayor, with my gender being a factor in that respect. And I didn't want to send the wrong message to young girls that a woman can only be a councilmember, not the mayor, by going back to a council position. Plus, I wanted to serve in a greater way, always loving a challenge. I had done the council job already and done it well. I wanted to take the city to the next level and could only do that as mayor. Therefore, I decided to keep my name in the hat for mayor—not the council.[2533]

3

The Herenton saga continued, as he now updated official disclosures to show the monies received from a businessman for the real estate as a loan. [2534] He also disclosed investments related to his investment company and a joint venture limited liability company. [2535] Once again, some felt that the FBI was unfairly targeting minority contractors in its investigations, while others called for more oversight of city contracts by the city council. [2536] But would the city council stand up to the mayor and not back down?

Taking heed, the council considered proposals to require its approval of deputy director appointees and city contracts exceeding $100,000.[2537] Some citizens were upset that Herenton nominated three of his former bodyguards to top positions. [2538] One nominee was controversial for having served time for helping to conceal proceeds from a drug deal related to a friend. [2539] In a compromise, the council decided to delay the ordinance, with Herenton promising to provide appointee resumes in advance.[2540] And, the council instead considered a resolution to require the mayor to provide quarterly updates on reoccurring contracts exceeding $100,000 and long-term contracts.[2541] The frequent dance between the council and the mayor continued, with the council often making bold statements and then backing down like a whooped pup.

With the millions in monies usually allocated to city schools retained in the city budget, a $16 million surplus and bond rating upgrades were reported.[2542] The council tried to give some of the excess funds to the police budget to help with overtime costs, but the Police Director Godwin refused to accept the monies. Instead, he wanted more officers. [2543] With teachers being laid off due to the city funding cuts, some reasoned that the monies should go to the schools instead because crime increases when the quality of education decreases. [2544] But the die was already cast to solve the city's budget problems at the school system's expense.

4

Besides the city budget controversy, other matters were concluded as well.[2545] The U.S. Attorney now dropped the charges against Joseph Lee III and Edmund Ford Sr. regarding allegations of special treatment related to payment of utility services for Ford Sr.'s funeral home.[2546] Hence, the MLGW public utility voted to pay Lee's legal fees of nearly half a million dollars.[2547]

The *Commercial Appeal* editorialized against the large bill for Lee's legal fees. [2548] The editors called for a reduction in the total bill, saying that the ratepayers should not pay for the attorney's time advising his client not to answer questions by their elected representatives on the council. [2549] The Herman Morris VIP list also reared its head again, with reported billings by Spence the same week that he had provided proof that it was indeed the brainchild of Morris. [2550] The fallout continued.

However, City Attorney Elbert Jefferson espoused the longstanding practice that the city would reimburse legal fees at the approved hourly rate if the indicted employee prevailed.[2551] Thereafter, the bill was cut some $62,000 for a clerical error, with the MLGW board finally approving the reduced payment of about $425,000.[2552] But, some of the public were outraged.

With Lee's legal battle with the federal prosecutors behind him, Herenton brought him back to City Hall as deputy director of parks.[2553] Lee was now employed at a significant salary reduction of about $110,000 less than he had made as MLGW president.[2554] Some were critical of the appointment, in light of his past actions and the prior controversy regarding Nick Clark (the developer and MLGW board member).[2555] Like it or not, he was back on the Herenton team.

5

In the fall, rumors resurfaced about Herenton's possible resignation, with reports that Wharton was in the process of appointing a campaign treasurer to run for city mayor in 2011.[2556] The *Memphis Flyer* predictably called Wharton "well-liked."[2557] The *Commercial Appeal* quoted their favorite political science professor, Marcus Pohlmann, saying that he believed Wharton would win in 2011 if Herenton did not seek reelection, starting the bandwagon effect.[2558] Some in the press openly wondered why the election was beginning three years early.[2559] That was a good question. More importantly, how could a Wharton candidacy and efficacy be evaluated without any idea as to his platform?

While there was no pronouncement from Herenton regarding the renewed rumors of his possible resignation, it was only the calm before the storm. In September 2008, the stock market plunged, with the country falling into a deep recession. A reported $700 billion in investments disappeared overnight due to the market correction.[2560] Retirement portfolios dropped in value, and financial institutions were in jeopardy.[2561]

With the new financial crisis, Herenton now denied "wild speculations" that plans were underway to replace the city's convention center built in 1973 for a new multi-million dollar convention center to be located near Beale Street and the FedExForum.[2562] Of course, Memphis leaders were keenly aware that Nashville was building a billion-dollar convention center and expansion of Opryland, which would provide an advantage in competition with Memphis as a destination for various conferences.[2563] In light of the economic hardship faced by many in the recession, Herenton's denial was good news. Publicly funding a new convention center when folks were filing bankruptcy right and left would make no sense.

Mayor Herenton was also on the hot seat with reports that the FBI was investigating the plans to move the downtown Greyhound bus station south to the airport.[2564] Rumors of a proposed new convention center adjacent to the downtown bus station property again raised questions about an option held by the mayor's business friend.[2565] According to the *Commercial Appeal,* the option to buy the Greyhound downtown bus station property had been granted a few years earlier, over a major hotel group and another developer. [2566] Transparency was needed as to the option, business relations, and convention plans in light of the investigation.

While the *Commercial Appeal* editors called the dealings a "foul odor," Herenton replied that it was a "private matter." [2567] Beale Street merchants were also concerned about an audit of its businesses by the city, with rumors of secret meetings where the mayor expressed an interest in using the city-owned properties as collateral for a convention center loan. [2568] Whatever the mayor's intentions, his focus was needed on running the city and addressing the economic crisis, instead of funneling millions of public monies into a new convention center.

6

Perhaps to change the subject, Herenton again called for consolidation of the city and county governments and offered to surrender the city charter.[2569] Because of his controversial image, the mayor urged others to take up the banner and lead on the issue. [2570] In support were Councilmen Strickland and Morrison, although they worried that surrendering the city charter might result in suburban cities within the county cherry-picking to annex the more profitable portions of what now lay within the Memphis city limits. [2571] However, their fears were a red herring as a charter surrender was not possible.

Memphis does not have a charter surrender clause. Therefore, the people inside Memphis and the people in the suburban areas would have to vote in favor separately to effect a merger.[2572] Also, a plan would need to address taxation and annexation post-merger. Now that he was a candidate for Memphis mayor, Shelby County Mayor Wharton had no problem saying he supported the consolidation of the governments, but not the schools at that time. [2573] But, if that were the case, then why hadn't he done anything about it during the six years he had served as county mayor?

Although Herenton offered to step down as city mayor in order to achieve a metro government, some feared he would simply run for the new combined mayoral position only to enhance his power. [2574] In any event, there definitely was not majority support for consolidation by suburban voters who paid lower property taxes.[2575] However, a lower-taxed suburban zone could be part of the merger plan if fewer services were designated to be provided by the metropolitan government in that area.

The fact that Herenton had angered suburban leaders with his plans to push state legislation to obviate the separate consolidation vote led some to say that he had too much baggage to lead such a campaign. [2576] John Branston with the *Memphis Flyer* even opined that the real change needed was not consolidation but new leadership in the mayor's office where Herenton had served for seventeen years. [2577] In any event, Herenton moved forward, telling the press that he and Wharton had met on the issue.[2578] He called for an exploratory committee and the formation of a charter commission to draft a charter for a metro government. [2579] He was still trying to lead the effort despite his controversial persona.

Part of the impetus for pushing consolidation by city leaders was the continued eastward shift of development to the suburban areas in Shelby County and adjacent counties in Tennessee and Mississippi.[2580] With the extension of a highway to the county's southeastern part, areas closer inside Memphis, such as Hickory Hill, were now struggling with a loss of retail businesses and high foreclosures.[2581] As one developer said, Memphis was not growing but just moving the same people around the area.[2582] This was the cost of nonstrategic development, and it harmed the city.

Both Herenton and Wharton now said they were working on combining the engineering, fire, and tax collection departments. [2583] Wharton claimed that the plans were moving forward, with the county CAO estimating a savings of $20 to $25 million a year due to increased efficiencies if a metro government was formed. [2584] Some advocated for the entities to contract with each other for services as opposed to an actual merger. [2585] The fear of giving up control by some leaders and the need for equalization of city and county worker pay and benefits were also impediments to merging the governmental workforces into one entity.[2586] But, whether Wharton would stay put in his county mayoral position to work through the details and make the merger a reality remained to be seen.

7

The merger issue did not distract the press from Herenton's other problems. With the rumors of an FBI investigation continuing, the *Commercial Appeal* again ran stories regarding the sale of homes from Herenton Investment Company to four or more city workers or appointees. [2587] Needless to say, many of the public were upset.

Some letters to the editor recited the litany of problems in the past years with the Tennessee Waltz indictments, convictions and guilty pleas, city budget crisis, Joseph Lee saga with the nearly half a million dollars in legal fees paid by the ratepayers, and now questions about Herenton's business dealings while serving as mayor.[2588] The editors of the *Commercial Appeal* lost no time in calling for him to sell his real estate business and cease private deal-making or step down as mayor in order to comply with the charter provision that the mayor must devote his entire time and attention to the duties of his office. [2589] Indeed, the city business needed his full attention.

Wendi Thomas, a columnist for the paper, even wrote a scathing opinion. [2590] She called the mayor's interest in the sale of property to appointees a "side hustle" in that he could *dis*appoint them from their appointed positions if they didn't go along with the purchase.[2591] Thomas ended sarcastically that she knew he was "not going to act right," "but a girl can dream, can't she?"[2592] While Herenton might have convinced himself that all were willing participants, the lack of an arms-length relationship due to his power to *dis*appoint was the elephant in the room. In essence, Thomas nailed it.

8

Still, the winds of change were great in 2008 with the possible Herenton resignation, federal investigations, and the election of Barack Obama, the first African American president in the nation's history. And, in Tennessee, the Republicans gained control of the state house. The Republicans now controlled both chambers, also the first time since 1869.[2593]

The state legislature's change came about after middle Tennessee Sen. Rosalyn Kurita sought the Democratic nomination for U.S. Senate in 2006. Congressman Harold Ford Jr. also was running. Democratic Party leaders asked Kurita to drop out of the race.[2594] Sound familiar?

Kurita eventually did end her candidacy but was not rewarded with any substantial leadership position by Lt. Governor Wilder after that. Hence her pay-back the next year. In 2007, she single-handedly changed the party leadership majority in the state senate to Republican by voting against long-serving

Democrat John Wilder, and in favor of Republican Ron Ramsey, for lieutenant governor.[2595] Kurita was then rewarded by the new Lt. Governor Ramsey with her appointment as Speaker Pro Tempore. The timing of the change in power was bad for the Democrats because the ten year redistricting was slated for 2010. The Republicans now controlled the leadership that would draw the new senate district boundaries. [2596]

At stake was the possibility that the majority Republican state legislature would pass a law to authorize special school districts for Shelby County, thus blocking annexation of county schools by Memphis in developed suburban areas.[2597] With the Great Recession underway, losing the power to annex higher-income areas was of concern to the city leaders, and of course, annexed areas need schools.

The fiscal concerns about the annexation issue weren't the only headache for city leaders. Herenton also warned of declining tax revenues and increasing costs, including health and retirement benefit contributions for employees. [2598]

Herenton was also still under investigation. His special assistant, Pete Aviotti, testified before the federal grand jury regarding the Greyhound contract. [2599] The mayor denied that he ever tried to influence a city contract.[2600] According to the *Commercial Appeal,* the MATA documents included handwritten notes showing Aviotti was involved in the discussions with Greyhound. [2601] The newspaper also questioned Aviotti's private business dealings for Herenton, including managing zoning requests for Herenton Investment Company while also being paid by the city to advise the mayor (with an office at City Hall). [2602] Once again, the issue of conflicts of interest surfaced.

Perhaps seeing the winds of change, or inside information, County Mayor Wharton moved ahead with a $500 a person fundraiser for the 2011 Memphis mayoral election. [2603] Not to be outdone, I announced my candidacy as well. I blasted Wharton as out of touch for hosting the high dollar event when "people are losing their jobs, companies are going bankrupt, and banks are going out of business," and the election was three years off. [2604]

Digging in, I called upon him to "come clean" if he knew something that had not been revealed to the general public about a possible early city mayoral vacancy. If there was a private scheme cooked up for Herenton to transfer power to an anointed successor, it was very disrespectful to the voters, in my view.

Calling again for change, I stated my intentions to begin organizing my campaign for Memphis mayor as well. Andy Meek, with the *Daily News,* noted that it had been barely a year since I stood before supporters at The Peabody Hotel on election night and "unapologetic and unshaken by the outcome" declared that "Memphis deserves better." [2605] My platform for the next mayoral race was again for change, with my focus on making Memphis a world-class city, ending corruption, and giving young people hope and a future. Maybe the winds of change would sweep me into the Memphis mayor's office this time.

33

Flying Saucers?

1

Memphis politics often seems out of this world, such as the crazy machinations as to whether or not Herenton would resign as mayor. As 2009 began, the *Memphis Flyer* ran Baker's predictions of who would be the next city and the next county mayor.[2606] He predicted that Wharton would be the next city mayor, opining his close association with Herenton did not tarnish him. [2607] Baker believed that either Republican Sheriff Mark Luttrell or County Commissioner Deidre Malone would be the next county mayor.[2608] Why he so opined in the article was a mystery, especially since I had a close second-place finish for Memphis mayor in 2007.

With an "intensifying federal investigation that threatens his legacy," the *Commercial Appeal* did a series profiling Herenton over the years.[2609] The first story by veteran reporter Marc Perrusquia dealt with his early hardships, having grown up in a poor neighborhood with segregated schools and rising to become a Golden Gloves champion. [2610] It also described his style of politics as "brawling." [2611] His selection as the first African American school superintendent in 1979 was controversial. [2612] The series adeptly set out the conflicting sides of the man who came from humble beginnings to rise to the city's top government position.

As superintendent, he did not always adhere to protocol. As reported by the series, Herenton questioned Memphis Mayor Chandler's intelligence, called the city council out as Chandler's "puppets," and refused to apologize. [2613] Even then, he referred to himself in the third person as "Willie Herenton." [2614] Over the years, the propensity to name call opponents never waned but grew.

However, Herenton's advocacy for education was recognized by job offers from Atlanta and other metropolitan areas. There were kudos for his optional schools, remedial courses, and innovative educational programs. [2615] Some teachers and parents were pleased with his service. As I graduated from the public schools the same year he became superintendent, I had no frame of reference as to his effectiveness.

A mar on the record was the breach of promise lawsuit by a fifth-grade teacher.[2616] The lawsuit was settled.[2617] The accuser attributed the end of the alleged relationship to the superintendent's mayoral aspirations. [2618] When pressured by conservative County Commissioner Pete Sisson, Herenton took a buy-out calling the allegations "all about politics, race, power, jealousy, envy, even bigotry." [2619] But it didn't stop his ascendancy to the mayor's office.

Later as mayor, controversy continued to surround Herenton, such as when he rehired and then promoted the female bodyguard previously assigned to his personal security detail. She had pled guilty and served time for three felony counts for concealing a drug dealer's $70,000 in cash, giving notice of a possible search to a minor to prevent the authorized seizing and securing of the money, and defrauding the government.[2620] The bodyguard was ultimately paid over $100,000 a year for a top position and served on the police conduct review board.[2621]

Herenton's disappearance in the aftermath of the major 2003 storm to attend a campaign fundraiser in Little Rock;[2622] calling out city councilmembers on New Year's day in 2004 telling them "don't bring me no mess;"[2623] fathering a child out of wedlock in 2005 at the age of sixty-four;[2624] and being subpoenaed to testify in the Atlanta federal corruption and tax evasion trial of former Atlanta Mayor Bill Campbell in 2006 added to his notoriety.[2625]

His macho tendencies were on display when he challenged Councilman Taylor to meet him outside as to a council dispute, and issued another warning to a TV news anchor that "I'm going to drop him." [2626] And the alleged sex-plot against him purportedly involving a local businessman, an attorney, and a waitress provided more controversial twists to his story. [2627]

Herenton's detractors often called him "King Willie" for his prideful statements and autocratic behavior or "Slick Willie" for his inconsistent positions.[2628] Herenton's supporters pointed to his down to earth and personable private side. They agreed with his rhetoric that the feds were persecuting him for being an African American mayor with too much power.[2629] Perhaps there were some truthful aspects to both views, but it was still clear that the city had suffered under his more recent erratic leadership.

Mayor Herenton's abrupt announcement of his resignation only five months after his reelection and during the federal investigations was another oddity in his unique history.[2630] His resignation letter quoted the Bible, saying that he was called then to another purpose.[2631] Thereafter, he reneged on resigning as mayor when he did not get the support needed for appointment as Memphis City Schools' superintendent. This was just another example of his unpredictable behavior.

Questions still lurked about the motives behind the Greyhound bus station's proposed relocation from its valuable downtown location directly near the Peabody Hotel and the new AutoZone [Redbirds'] ballpark. The *Commercial Appeal* reported that Herenton defended himself on the land dealings by saying that he was only trying to increase minority investment and was being subjected to a double-standard (quoting Theodore Roosevelt's "Man in the Arena" speech).[2632] He compared himself to the wealthy New York Mayor Bloomberg, who had many investments. Indeed, increasing minority investment was a very worthy cause, but some wondered if his intentions were self-serving. Was he the man in the arena fighting for the people or his own interest?

Meanwhile, Council Chair Myron Lowery asked for legal opinions on whether there was a violation of the mayor's oath of office.[2633] Sensing legal trouble, Herenton also took steps to secure affidavits from city officials to the effect that he had not interfered in the city contracting process.[2634] Yet, the local press still called him out for inappropriately involving himself in the deal that involved millions of the city's monies.[2635] The jury of public opinion was not in his favor.

Otis Sanford with the *Commercial Appeal* noted Herenton's skillful ability to handle the two divides in the city—the poor (mostly African American) citizenry and the better-off (primarily white male) business community.[2636] He knew how to use the language and hype of a street fighter to galvanize support in the inner city but also made calm speeches and concessions to the developers and business elite who funded his reelection campaigns over the years.[2637] While the mayor said he wanted to be a consensus builder, he also recognized that he did not have the temperament to be the one to unite the city and the county.[2638] The *Commercial Appeal's* Editor Chris Peck noted Herenton's "emotional tirades" to inner-city supporters in the 2007 mayor's race, blasting the same "white power establishment" that he charmed at a local Rotary luncheon.[2639] Why either group succumbed to the duplicitous behavior over the years was unknown.

On the plus side, Herenton had succeeded in using federal grants to replace several public housing developments and to build new mixed-income developments. Two of them, Hurt Village and Dixie Homes, were public housing developments that had been in my state legislative district in my early years of service. I had spent a good deal of time meeting and talking with constituents who resided in the apartments. Many of those residents were now scattered elsewhere in the city, having been displaced and given Section 8 vouchers to use in other neighborhoods, high rises, or apartments.[2640]

Herenton's alleged interests related to the Greyhound station, as well as other properties where his investment company had just built homes, were now under scrutiny.[2641] A massive proposed redevelopment of twenty city blocks downtown was called Triangle Noir.[2642] Plans were to expand the Beale Street district to add housing, a luxury hotel, and over a billion dollars in public and private investment.[2643] While Herenton said that his vision for Triangle Noir was to pay tribute to African American historical figures and promote minority development opportunities, others saw it differently due to his company's real estate holdings near the area.[2644] Calls were made for him to either devote full time to being mayor or resign and focus on his business endeavors.[2645] He was trying to have it both ways—be the mayor and a developer. But, sometimes, the interests intertwined, which left things murky as to putting the public interest first and paramount.

A city attorney had advised Herenton as far back as 1993 that he could lawfully conduct a private real estate development business and serve as mayor. She also later opined that his use of a local car dealership's Cadillac sedan free of charge, only for city business, did not violate the city charter's prohibition of gifts to the mayor.[2646] This was also the appointed employee who bought real property from Herenton's company during her tenure as city attorney and obtained a loan from his investment company.[2647] The interrelatedness of some private business dealings with government positions raised a red flag.

The FBI made the rounds, even interviewing me and at least three other councilmembers over whether Herenton had ever disclosed any personal involvement in the Greyhound bus station redevelopment.[2648] Obviously,

I knew nothing about it. Allan Wade, city council attorney, opined that Herenton had done nothing improper in the land deal. [2649] One of Herenton's sons, a successful investment banker, was called before the federal grand jury to testify, along with the Memphis Area Transit Authority general manager. [2650] Of course, being called to testify as a witness as the grand jury conducts fact-finding is not an indication of the guilt of any crime.

Questions were also raised as to business dealings regarding Beale Street properties. A judge ordered property manager Elkington (for Performa) to turn over records regarding the district's proceeds.[2651] Elkington claimed that Herenton had plans to gain control of the street and let a national developer connected to Justin Timberlake take over.[2652] The leases for the district were held by the Beale Street Development Corporation, who hired Performa to manage and help develop the area.[2653] Robert Lipscomb, a Herenton administration appointee, denied he had discussed Beale Street with Timberlake's representatives. [2654] However, a lawsuit was filed by the merchant association, which included emails between him and a representative of Timberlake's record label.[2655] The claims were intriguing. Timberlake had a connection to Memphis, having been raised in the area.

The FBI and IRS also began inquiries about the annual swank Christmas party for Herenton put together by his special assistant Pete Aviotti.[2656] Herenton's former city attorney, Robert Spence, issued a statement that it was not a campaign event and that the leftover monies kept by Herenton after the event were gifts which he treated as income and reported on his tax returns.[2657] City stationery was once used, and sometimes the RSVP for the event was Aviotti's City Hall telephone number.[2658] However, he said that he personally paid for the stationery and postage. Herenton thanked the donors on campaign stationery in 2001, with an invitation to a dinner at an expensive steakhouse in town.[2659] But the state officials did not find a state law violation.[2660] Several prominent developers were interviewed by the agents as part of the investigation, with questions about how any excess funds were handled.[2661]

In the wake of all of the investigations, *Forbes.com* piled on naming Memphis the second most miserable city in the country.[2662] It would have been nice if the holiday party had been for the public to make things seem less miserable, as opposed to the elite of Memphis. Then, perhaps there would be fewer questions about who, if anyone, benefited from the event.

2

With the high unemployment rate growing in conjunction with the national economic crisis, Herenton warned of additional lay-offs and budget cuts ahead.[2663] He projected a $25 million city shortfall for the next fiscal year and a deficit for the current fiscal year as well.[2664] The city budget crisis worsened when the chancellor ruled that the city had illegally withheld over $57 million in Memphis city school funding.[2665] The city appealed.[2666] Chancellor Kenny Armstrong held that the city owed the city schools over $84 million for the last fiscal year and had paid only $27 million.[2667] The school system was over $40 million in the red and at risk of losing some state funding.[2668] The city needed to find $57.2 million to pay the school system.[2669] The repercussions were now apparent from the city council's 2008 city schools money grab.

These were not the city's only budget problems, with the county claiming that it was owed $125 million from payments made by the public utility in lieu of taxes (which is subject to a fee-sharing agreement).[2670] And the U.S. Department of Justice gave the city notice that $40 million in ADA improvements to the Liberty Bowl must be completed within sixteen months.[2671] The heat to solve the budget problems was on!

The budget crisis renewed calls for the consolidation of county and city government to eliminate duplicate costs in services. Although he had been in office now since 2002 with plenty of time to work on consolidation, Wharton had now only seriously pushed the issue.[2672] One commentator observed to the *Commercial Appeal* that he had "kept quiet" on the subject while running for county mayor but now was leading the parade.[2673] Suburban leaders were distrustful despite Wharton's personal promises that any savings from consolidation would be used to avoid tax increases.[2674] With a separate vote required in the county on the measure and the lack of a merger plan that could sway suburban voters, there was not much likelihood it would pass at this time despite the new-founded all-out push from Wharton or County Commissioner Chair Deidre Malone's listening tours around the county.[2675] If there had been more work to merge county and city departments during his tenure, then a favorable merger vote would be more likely, to only reaffirm and finish up the process.

In the midst of the budget problems, speculation began as to whether Herenton would resign as mayor to run against incumbent Steve Cohen for Congress. If he did resign, City Council Chair Myron Lowery would serve as interim mayor under the new charter provision until a special election was held within at least 180 days. Sidney Chism, a Teamsters union leader and long-time Herenton supporter, said the mayor wanted to replace Cohen so a politician who was African American could represent the majority-black 9th congressional district. [2676] Apparently, Herenton was also motivated by his aggravation over the support for Cohen's reelection by former Congressman Harold Ford Sr.

However, Herenton's problems continued. There were new grumblings that a waste collection company had gained an unfair advantage in city contracting by making large donations to a gala for the Mike Tyson-Lenox Lewis heavy-weight boxing fight in Memphis in 2002. [2677] The city's "negotiating memo" with the company noted past charitable contributions to the city. [2678] As Amos Maki with the *Commercial Appeal* reported, the city's former public works director acknowledged that the entity pledged to contribute $225,000 to local organizations. [2679]

Donations over the years by the company included those for the city's barbeque tent at the Memphis in May festival and to the Beale Street Merchants' Association (which Councilman Peete headed).[2680] The Tyson-Lewis pre-fight gala had been held at the Peabody Hotel with 850 people, an ice sculpture of the Pyramid, and a large replica of boxing gloves. [2681] The city contended that the contributions were offered by the company voluntarily, with no enforceable contractual requirement. [2682] So, it wasn't clear that the letter of the law had been violated.

But the fix was in with the *Memphis Flyer* declaring Wharton the next mayor in January 2009, before Herenton even announced he was resigning again or a special election was even called.[2683] Despite their close relationship over the years, for some reason, Herenton's high negatives did not translate to Wharton in the minds of many voters. [2684] But would Wharton assertively push the agenda Memphis needed? His more passive pleasing manner might be a relief in the wake of Herenton's bull in the china shop style, but was it any more effective in the long run?

At this point, Wharton, term-limited for county mayor, was predicting a successful city/county consolidation referendum in the 2010 county elections.[2685] Wharton announced that the business community was behind consolidated governments, which was separate from the issue of a single source of funding and consolidation of the schools.[2686] However, his private plans to run for city mayor would possibly take him out of the county mayor bully-pulpit, where he could advocate for a merger countywide. Would the new county mayor lead the county effort if he departed?

Herenton confirmed the rumors that he wanted to run for Congress with a bombshell announcement through an aide at the budget presentation to the city council.[2687] Some councilmembers found the timing to be suspicious and merely an effort to deflect attention from the city's financial crisis and the federal investigations. [2688] Sidney Chism said that Herenton was tired of being mayor, with Councilman Lowery wondering if Herenton would change his mind again the next year. [2689] Many questioned his motives. Wendi Thomas, editorial columnist, with the *Commercial Appeal,* compared him to a "toddler" with his claims that he only ran for the fifth term because he thought the other candidates inadequate, and then shortly thereafter losing interest in doing the job himself. [2690] His double-mindedness confused the public, keeping the city in disarray.

In any event, the congressional endeavor did not appear auspicious for Herenton, with a new poll by the Cohen camp showing him well in the lead for reelection to Congress at 65%, with Herenton lagging at 14%. [2691] It did appear that since the 2007 mayoral election, he was just looking for another position – first the superintendent of the schools and now Congress. In my view, the people would have been better off electing a mayor who had a passion for the job and was sincere about moving the city forward.

As to Wharton's interest to switch mayor-ships, not everyone was on board. Some county commissioners warned that despite the spin, he lacked the skills needed to build a consensus as was held by the prior two county mayors. [2692] But the press and media did not label him in this regard as they had done me in the 2007 mayor's race – either another gender stereotype in play or merely because he was now the one anointed by those in power.

The field of potential candidates was growing, including Councilman Lowery, County Commissioner Harvey, and me. Jackson Baker with the *Memphis Flyer* noted that I was "certain-to-run" and had not really stopped running since the mayoral race of 2007. [2693] He was right in that a suspected backroom deal would not punk me from trying again. Besides, Wharton would not bring the reform needed, as evident from his county mayor record. Instead, I would place my name on the ballot to give Wharton a run for his money.

3

While the public wondered if Herenton would resign again, more troubling news came from the city's Rape Crisis Center of a nursing staff shortage.[2694] Delays in testing for sexual assault victims were at a crisis level, with one pre-teen unable to be tested on a weekend because no one was available at the center. [2695] The center served the region, and employees were reluctant to talk on the record about why so many of the nursing staff had departed. [2696] The center handled victims of all ages, including babies, and a delay could jeopardize the collection of evidence needed to prosecute the perpetrator. [2697] The mismanagement of the center by city leaders was a tragedy.

Revelations that the city may have used state reimbursements for the sexual assault exams for other purposes raised additional concerns. [2698] The county district attorney, Bill Gibbons, assigned the investigation to the White Collar Crime Prosecutors' Unit after reports that the state reimbursements were hundreds of thousands of dollars over the city's budgeted line item of $100,000. [2699] The reimbursements should have been used to maintain sufficient staffing at the center.

During the crisis, LeBonheur Children's Hospital agreed to handle future forensic exams for juveniles. Some city councilmembers voted to eliminate all funding should the county or a third party take over the rape crisis services.[2700] With only half of the 368 forcible rape crimes reported in Memphis in 2008 cleared, and only fifty-six arrests, some rightfully wondered why the rape prosecution rates in Memphis were so low. [2701]

One Memphis police officer with the sex crimes unit attributed the low prosecution rates of sex crimes in the area to the victims' reluctance to go to the rape crisis center for an exam or because the victims declined to prosecute or lied.[2702] Years later the horrible truth was revealed as to the low rape prosecution rate. The DNA in thousands of victim rape kits was never tested. Instead, they were left to gather dust on the shelves with the accused rapists walking around free to strike again.

4

During this time, the federal grand jury proceedings continued with Charles Carpenter, Herenton's former campaign manager and the principal in a joint venture, testifying regarding the option to buy the Greyhound downtown bus terminal property. [2703] The *Commercial Appeal* also reported that the FBI was investigating whether or not some $50,000 in excess cash from the annual holiday party was unreported personal income for Herenton.[2704] The press raised more questions than the reporters could answer due to the proceedings' secrecy.

And, nearly simultaneous with the unexpected death of the pop king Michael Jackson, Herenton decided once again to announce that he was resigning as mayor—this time effective July 10, 2009. [2705] According to the *Commercial Appeal* editors, the mayor "signaled" that his congressional election strategy would be similar to his 2007 mayoral campaign - -"an appeal to the city's African American voters to remain united behind a candidate of their own race." [2706] Cohen was white, and the congressional district had a majority of black voters. Apparently, Herenton was going to "beat it" from the mayor's office with hopes of also beating Cohen for Congress. [2707]

While noting Herenton's achievements, such as becoming the city's first elected African American mayor, improvements to public housing, and a revitalization of downtown, the *Commercial Appeal* editors also reminded the public of his short-comings such as the high crime, high poverty, the several directors who had moved up from bodyguard positions, and the continuing federal investigations.[2708] Although acknowledging having met with the federal prosecutors, his attorney denied as "a fantasy thing" that any deal was cut that they would not pursue an indictment if Herenton resigned.[2709] The timing did raise questions by some as to the reason for Herenton's resignation announcement, but he passionately denied all allegations. [2710] It remained to be seen whether his stepping down as mayor was a fantasy or for real this time.

Speculation grew as to the major candidates who would seek to succeed Herenton. Wharton, Lowery and I were mentioned, with me dubbed by the *Commercial Appeal* as "the woman who has been running for mayor of some sort for most of the decade."[2711] Maybe so, but why not if I believed myself the "person" that could bring needed reforms if elected? Also, first-term councilmembers' Strickland and Kemp Conrad were considering entering the race, and Charles Carpenter.[2712] Bringing up Wharton's private meeting with Herenton at *Le Chardonnay* in the 2007 mayoral race, I once again called for real change.[2713]

The *Commercial Appeal's* Otis Sanford lost no time in bemoaning the "chaos" that lay ahead and lauding Wharton's candidacy for Memphis mayor.[2714] Gushing, Sanford called him "the antithesis of Herenton," "likeable," with "a calming public demeanor."[2715] Former Mayor Dick Hackett chimed in drawing analogies to his mayoral election in 1982 after Chandler resigned, with similar sign-waving on city streets by Wharton supporters after the Herenton announcement.[2716]

Lowery spoke about the advantage he would have as a candidate because of his brief tenure as interim mayor. After Herenton departed, Lowery would hold the interim mayor position until the special election due to the city charter amendment initiatives.[2717] Otis Sanford found it "astounding" that Herenton would resign and allow Lowery to take the interim post when only a few years earlier, the mayor had called Lowery, me, and the news media part of an "array of evil."[2718] Apparently, Herenton's urge to quit overcame any aversion he had for Lowery becoming interim mayor, which made it that much more remarkable.

Now serving as a councilmember, Strickland contemplated a mayoral bid and claimed he represented generational change (only two years younger than me). [2719] The *Commercial Appeal* questioned his limited support in the black community, as well as his ability to raise money and become better known outside the council district. [2720] Also interested was Jack Sammons, saying he had spoken to Strickland to talk about a consensus candidate. [2721] What the "consensus" platform would be was unclear, with Strickland claiming to be a Democrat and Sammons a Republican.

Columnist Otis Sanford mentioned that I was a "good campaigner."[2722] Zack McMillan with the *Commercial Appeal* reported that I had previously defeated Strickland for the city council, lost "badly" to Wharton in 2002, and "nobody believes she will drop out of the race."[2723] The article further noted my second place close showing to Herenton in 2007, despite a "huge funding disadvantage," and my belief that my loyal followers would elect me the first female Memphis mayor.[2724] As I replied, "Elections are never about money. Elections are about people." I hoped that the people would not be fooled this time and would rally behind the woman who had their best interest at heart.

Political science professor Marcus Pohlmann predicted that Wharton would be tough to beat.[2725] Wharton said he was prepared to defend against attacks regarding his friendship with Herenton and lack of accomplishments as county mayor.[2726] At least he was not dubbed "unbeatable" at this point as had been said in the 2002 county mayor primary, with the field of contenders still undecided.

Herenton moved forward with his plans, announcing he would join his son's investment firm. [2727] It appeared he was serious as to stepping down this time. An exodus of City Hall directors and appointees began, including the relatively youthful CAO whose career started as a deputy jailor. Many, although relatively young, would draw the twelve-year pension.

Herenton touted the number of African American hires at City Hall during his administration. At a press conference, he stood in front of the forty-three portraits of all-male mayors at City Hall—with the only diverse photo being of 1982 interim mayor J. O. Patterson (an African American). [2728]He pronounced that the congressional race would be a "beat-down." [2729] While accomplishments of having rebuilt the city's reserves after the last financial crisis were duly noted by him, the problem was the many black and white middle-class citizens that had fled the city for the suburbs in recent years.[2730] And, also noticeably absent from his remarks was mention of the unwise debt refinancing and that the reserves were rebuilt by illegally withholding the public school funds (now required to be repaid by court order).

Thomas with the *Commercial Appeal* wasted no time in blasting Herenton as arrogant, unavailable at critical times when the city needed him, a race-baiter and full of conspiracy theories. [2731] But *Commercial Appeal* Editor Chris Peck was kinder. He reminded the citizens that Herenton was the first elected African American mayor for a city with a prior history of segregation, grew up poor, and had broken down many barriers by his years in public office. [2732]

Meanwhile, the *Memphis Flyer's* Jackson Baker claimed that Strickland was boosted with the backing of his mayoral candidacy by Democrat Councilman Shea Flinn (Republican George Flinn's son). [2733] However, he observed that Strickland's main political supporters were all white males like himself. [2734] The lack of diversity would be a negative if he entered the race.

Baker discounted my candidacy, even though noting that women had fared better at the polls lately.[2735] It was interesting that implicit in his analysis was an acknowledgment of past gender bias toward female candidates. Mentioning my "impressive second-place finish" in the 2007 mayoral election, Baker questioned, without explanation, how much of my support was attributable to "anti-Herenton sentiment."[2736] Did he mean some voted for me despite my gender just because they didn't like Herenton? He further commented that I had been "largely out of the public eye" since the last election.[2737] Apparently, the columnist was unaware that I had continued to make appearances around the city's neighborhoods and other events. Again, Baker proclaimed Wharton the favorite but acknowledged that he might have a challenge after all due to the number of contenders.[2738]

Pastor Kenneth Whalum Jr. also decided to throw his hat into the mayoral ring, claiming that his good showing in a recent citywide school board election made him a strong candidate. [2739] Whalum Jr. opposed consolidation of the governments, supported corporal punishment in the schools, and was said by Zack McMillan with the *Commercial Appeal* to be known for his "forceful and often controversial stands." [2740] That was true, but I welcomed Whalum Jr. to the race. The Whalum family was well-known, with his father a pastor and former politician as well. The family also included American jazz saxophonist and songwriter Kirk Whalum who had toured with Whitney Houston, and Kameron Whalum, who performs with Bruno Mars. Besides, Whalum Jr.'s addition to the field would raise the level of debate.

5

The field for mayor continued to grow. Herenton predicted a low turnout. Staying true to character, he contended that there would be less public interest because the candidates running were not at the same level of "leadership capabilities" as he had shown during his tenure as mayor. [2741]

After acknowledging that Lowery and I had sufficient name recognition to contend against the touted "front-runner" Wharton, [2742] Baker with the *Memphis Flyer* began the familiar process of what seemed to me discounting, discrediting, and debunking my candidacy for mayor. An example was his response to my report of two grass fires seen while campaigning at a downtown outdoors 4th of July celebration at Tom Lee Park on the river. A band of about one hundred youth shot off firecrackers that ignited the grass fires.

I had never seen anything like it in Memphis, with the teenage youth chanting and swarming out of control. One lone police officer on a motorcycle impotently waited for back-up. Moms with babies scrambled to get out of the way. A campaign volunteer caught the video on her cell phone, which my campaign manager, Rick Maynard, prepared for release to the press and media.

But, Baker, without waiting for the video, wrote an entire column online for the *Memphis Flyer*, likening my report to that of seeing flying saucers.[2743] The article relied upon terms such as "political maverick," "would-be reformer," "never a strong fundraiser," and "out of the public eye" for two years. [2744] My prior call for an independent investigation of the failure of Wharton's car to be inspected for licensure in a scandal involving preferential treatment by some at the county clerk's office was now said to be "largely ignored" and "even privately ridiculed in some media quarters." [2745] Adding to the cajoling was this reporter's musings (attributed to others' comments) as to whether my claim of the gang-related grass fires was "opportunism," merely an effort to advance my own political agenda, or like U.S. Presidential candidate Dennis Kucinich's claims of having seen a flying saucer. [2746] What a hit piece.

My campaign provided the video proof of the grass fires set by the youth and set the record straight with an email reminding the columnist: (1) in 2007, my campaign for mayor raised over $200,000; (2) the *Commercial Appeal* had editorialized in favor of my call for an independent investigation of Wharton's car licensing; (3) of my seventeen years of prior public service; (4) of my accomplishments of getting things done, including statewide child care reform, the Memphis Plan which provides medical care for thousands of working poor, laws to protect victims, and ethics reform.

I asked why he painted me in the article as some airhead female seeing flying saucers in a manner that appeared to me to be sexist and totally unacceptable. I pointed out that he might disagree with my candidacy and favor another candidate, but that did not give him license to use one standard for a female candidate and a totally different one for the male candidates. Generally, I tried to avoid making an issue of gender bias. However, as both a professional attorney and a veteran public servant, I added my hope for the sake of his readers that he would provide fair and more balanced reporting in the upcoming election.

Baker defended himself, saying that a female police officer had not confirmed my report and that his reference to a flying saucer was not gender-specific. [2747] He added that he was "impressed" by my "determination to forge ahead" as a candidate "despite the obvious obstacles." [2748] Then, he updated his column, calling me a "friend." Now he acknowledged that after having viewed the video, the reports made by me, a campaign worker, and others of "vandalism and aggressive behavior by bands of roaming juveniles, possibly gang members, were substantially correct."[2749] He now added that I had the right to bring up the charge of insufficient police presence. [2750] Of course I did. Thank heavens for the video! Otherwise, his flying saucer story would have stood with my report from my own observations inexplicably deemed uncredible for no good reason.

The police said they felt powerless to stop the youths' actions.[2751] Sadly, years later, reports continued of a large group of teens daily roaming downtown, robbing people at Tom Lee Park on the Memphis riverfront and breaking into cars.[2752] Maybe this was something that the city just wanted to be kept under wraps. But, obviously, action was needed to protect the citizens and tourists.

Continuing in his column, Baker wrote that my candidacy "has aroused a good deal of skepticism in the media—some of it published, more of it private" and that he was only the "messenger."[2753] He vehemently denied any gender bias saying that he warned in the article against prejudging my motives or the public's view.[2754] Baker added that he did not think the race "hinges in any way whatsoever on the fact of gender...," and that I should not use it as a "shield against criticism."[2755] Again, he remarked that it was admirable that I would "forge ahead in the face of odds that would prove daunting to almost anybody else."[2756] But, if there were no gender biases, then why such skepticism about my candidacy now, when I had nearly won in 2007? Why the mantra that my chances of winning were nearly impossible? And, while gender shouldn't be used as a shield against legitimate criticism, it also shouldn't be used as a weapon by others to stereotypically discredit me either.

Baker wielded a lot of power as one of the top political columnists in the city. On occasion, he wrote positive columns about me and seemed supportive of my leadership ability. Other times I felt marginalized in certain columns (whether by his intention or not), or even worse, like he was my nemesis. Yet, we always managed to maintain a cordial relationship.

Looking back, I wish some of the columnists and media reporters had harbingered the #MeToo movement, with more balanced coverage of women candidates seeking higher office (even if the candidate was not the choice of the status quo). Baker and others did advocate for women and progressive issues many times and gave me positive coverage in many of my races for public office. However, I felt news coverage by many in the mayoral races reflected the cultural climate oppressive to female leadership's advancement to the mayor's office.

For example, my call for an independent investigation of how Wharton's family car obtained tags by a county employee without inspection was valid.[2757] Later in the year, some former employees of the county clerk's office, along with others, pled guilty in state court related to charges they took money to pass vehicles without an inspection, registered vehicles without proper identification and proof of residence, and participated in a scheme that allowed illegal immigrants to obtain vehicle registrations. [2758] The *Commercial Appeal* editors queried whether the irregularities as to licensing vehicles (in what the county attorney termed a "pervasive culture of political and familial entitlement") included the county mayor and why bribers were not prosecuted as well as the clerks. [2759]

Why the county mayor would not be subject to independent scrutiny was a fair question in my view. The *Commercial Appeal* editorial wholeheartedly agreed, saying my proposal for a special prosecutor to investigate, as opposed to a county attorney who could be *dis*appointed by the county mayor, made a lot of sense.[2760] So regardless of the "ridicule" of me by some media reporters as reported by Baker, the major daily newspaper editors found it to be a credible demand.

In any event, it seemed that some were rattled by my mayoral candidacy and continued efforts to speak truth to power and bring reform. The thought of an independent-minded female mayor of Memphis was so alien to their frame of reference, it was like a ship from outer space trying to land at City Hall.

34

What Message for Young Girls?

1

As the election for mayor began, I was cognizant of the many eyes on me, especially of young girls, just as Gaia had been a role model for me in high school. I recalled the words of Barbara Lawing, who had encouraged me in my early career with her advice that money doesn't vote; people do. But it seemed difficult to convince the people of that in light of the consistent media coverage about how much money the candidates had raised. The stories had a chilling effect on fundraising for a female candidate where the status quo had never backed a woman.

One news station "rumored" that Wharton had already raised $250,000. [2761] My response was that the frontrunner did not win the Kentucky Derby that year. And, in the Belmont horserace, the female won.

The first mayoral forum went on without Wharton and Lowery. Carpenter, Whalum Jr., Conrad, Strickland, and I appeared before the West Tennessee Chapter of Associated Builders and Contractors, Inc. [2762] Professional wrestler Jerry Lawler, who also entered the race, was not invited because the organizer Mike Carpenter did not consider him a "serious candidate, only a spoiler." [2763] Lawler retorted that "We're all pretty much tired of politicians, and that was nothing more than a meeting of politicians, probably trying to put their heads together and continue the circus. Who is going to be the ringmaster?" [2764] With so many candidates, that was the question indeed.

I advocated for change and mentioned my record of fighting for the people for seventeen years as a state legislator and city councilwoman. I would not give lip-service to ethics but would apply them to myself. I told the crowd that I had the brains, heart, and guts to do the job. Strickland and Whalum

Jr. took shots at Wharton's no-show.[2765] Wharton was also criticized for running for city mayor when his county mayor term had another year to go.[2766] Perhaps instead of a circus, the process was more like the children's game of musical chairs. Wharton simply was seeking to have a different chair when the election was over.

Whalum Jr. pointed out that Carpenter would have a hard time distancing himself from his twenty-year association with Herenton.[2767] Carpenter had managed Herenton's campaign in 2007, in which the mayor refused to debate Herman Morris Jr. or me. Now, only a year and a half later, Carpenter said he was running due to the "lack of leadership" at City Hall. [2768]Strickland, also taking a shot at Wharton, chimed in that "We cannot change Memphis for the next generation with leaders from the last generation." [2769] While I agreed that new leadership was needed at City Hall, Carpenter had never held elective office and Strickland only barely. My credentials were much stronger.

In July, my campaign team organized a backyard party at a Midtown home with about 100 supporters. We invited the press to see first-hand my diverse support from around the city. I called it a "new day" in politics and a "clean break from the past."

But would Herenton ever quit? He now announced that he would delay his resignation until July 30, 2009. [2770] The county election commission chair stopped any planning for the special election and called out the mayor's behavior as "bizarre." [2771]

The editor of the *Memphis Flyer* worried that with a crowded field, professional wrestler Jerry Lawler might actually win. [2772] Bruce Vanwyngarden opined his concerns about several of the candidates, including Wharton's chuckling while interviewed on a controversial radio show as the African American host "threw all manner of racist crap in his face." [2773] He likened a debate of the candidates to a *Jerry Springer* show. [2774] It sometimes seemed that way.

On the other hand, it was nice to be called "kind" by a ten-year-old African American girl and endorsed by her to be the first female mayor of Memphis in the *Tri-State Defender*. [2775] In fact, all the candidates embraced youth involvement as important to the process and recognized their superior social media skills. Larry Moore, a college professor and political analyst, commented that both adults and youth were "disconnected from the political process." [2776] Whether the youths who had helped propel Obama to victory would be similarly heavily engaged in electing the next mayor of Memphis remained to be seen.

2

As Herenton prepared to step down, the *Commercial Appeal* reminisced over his long tenure dating from 1991 when he won only 2% of the white vote.[2777] That turned around with the city's elite supporting him financially to win in 1995 with 74% of the vote, and by nearly 40% in several almost 100% white precincts. [2778] As reporter Zack McMillan noted, downtown had boomed.[2779] But in the 1999 mayoral election against Joe Ford, there were complaints that low-income neighborhoods were being ignored. [2780] The difficulty in appeasing two masters—the mostly white business elite versus the poor—had become more apparent for Herenton in recent years.

Both Herenton and I had worked to stop the "toy towns" law and prevent the formation of tiny suburban towns that would harm the city and metro area. But the rampant financial problems and mismanagement at City Hall during his recent administrations now had made us adversaries.

The 2007 mayor's race had been the turning point for Herenton when he received only 42% of the vote against my 35%. As observed by the newspaper, that election was in the wake of middle-class citizens leaving for the suburbs, reports of cronyism at City Hall with bodyguards gaining directorships outside their areas of expertise, and aggrandizing remarks by the mayor about being anointed to lead the city.[2781] Others pointed to the city's lack of progress reusing the Pyramid and the Fairgrounds, the inadequate staffing of the Rape Crisis Center, and ongoing federal investigations into his business dealings. [2782] Whatever his administration's past successes, it had seriously faltered in many respects. It was time for him to move on.

At this juncture, Alex Doniach with the *Commercial Appeal* reported the view of some that Wharton and Lowery were the frontrunners due to their power of incumbency - one about to become the interim Memphis mayor, and the county mayor now running for Memphis mayor. [2783] Political analyst Larry Moore, however, saw an opportunity for me to win in the crowded field if my former state legislative and city council districts turned out in large numbers due to the anticipated low turnout for the special election. [2784] Finally, a college professor commentator said outright that a woman could win.

Lowery was sworn in as interim mayor, appointed former City Councilman Jack Sammons as his CAO, and began his brief term with an evenly divided city council in racial composition due to his seat's vacancy.[2785] Despite Herenton's warning that it was ill-advised to make many personnel changes until the interim mayor learned the job, the drama now unfolded between Lowery and City Attorney Jefferson. [2786] Jefferson had resigned, but Herenton did not accept his resignation before the mayor resigned himself. [2787] Doesn't this sound familiar when considering the past controversy over Joseph Lee's proffered resignation as MLGW president?

Just after his swearing-in, Lowery announced in a press conference that he had asked for Jefferson's resignation. The interim mayor was replacing him with former U.S. Attorney Veronica Coleman Davis and said he was concerned about several new employees hired in the legal department. [2788] Lowery even had Jefferson unceremoniously escorted from the building during the swearing-in ceremony. [2789] This was quite a first day on the job for the interim mayor.

Some councilmembers, including the new chair Harold Collins, balked at the departure of Jefferson.[2790] Jefferson, himself, obtained a temporary Chancery Court injunction preventing his termination. [2791] Lowery was left with appointing Coleman Davis as Deputy City Attorney instead. [2792] As the lead attorney is critical to the mayor's success, this was a setback for the interim Lowery administration.

In the wake of the City Hall drama, Jackson Baker with the *Memphis Flyer*, wrote about the city electorate's fragmentation in the 2009 mayor's race, with so many candidates splitting up the vote. [2793] And Wharton also was said to worry about the divided field and the possibility that a longshot candidate might slip through to win. [2794] It remained to be seen whom the divided field might favor.

City Councilwoman Wanda Halbert entered the race. [2795] And wrestler Jerry Lawler remained in the field, having received 12% of the vote in the 1999 mayoral race. [2796] Herenton saw Lawler as a serious candidate despite his scripted wrestling persona. [2797] Whalum Jr. continued to be viewed as entertaining and so adept at the use of social media that Baker also artfully deemed it his "guerrilla warfare."[2798] Others initially entering the race included Edmund Ford Sr. and Thomas Long, city court clerk.[2799] I wondered at this juncture how many would join the fray.

Some still presumed Wharton the frontrunner, due in part to his large war chest.[2800] Reports of another poll showed Lowery in the single digits. [2801]County Commissioner James Harvey, however, expressed his belief that I was in the lead after my team helped to provide emergency supplies to victims of the recent tornado, and by also being one of the few white candidates in the field. [2802] The jumble of candidates and more than likely low-turn-out for the special election made the race unpredictable.

Baker protected Wharton in his column, naming my call for an independent investigation of his car registration "verbal ambush." [2803] Even Wharton's forceful response to a county commissioner's complaint that he purposefully did not notify the commission of an appointment—that he resented "the implication" that he "was sneaking around here" —somehow resulted in him being described as normally amiable, and "mild-mannered." [2804] The article even went so far as to express concerns that Wharton might "have to endure" criticism in the months ahead, just as the other candidates. [2805] Why he would be entitled to special treatment was unclear, except that the status quo favored him.

My campaign slogan returned to "Count on Carol" and my message centered on bringing racial reconciliation and healing to Memphis. In my view, the wound to the city's spirit from the death of Dr. Martin Luther King Jr. festered. Also, noting "chaos" from Herenton's administration, I asserted that Memphis needed less drama and more results. [2806] Since the last election, I also was invigorated and prepared for the battle, having come in twelfth in my age category in the St. Jude Firecracker 5k run.[2807]

The mayoral field was fluid, with Strickland, Conrad, and Edmund Ford Sr. still undecided about the race.[2808] Wharton said he was worried about a crowded field that might weaken the eventual winner and wanted to meet with other candidates (presumably to get some of them out of the race). [2809] Strickland said he would meet with Wharton. [2810]

The conversations with Wharton and Strickland paid off. Strickland dropped out after a poll. [2811] And Wharton announced Strickland as a campaign co-chair. [2812] Apparently, Strickland had changed his mind that only a generational change could provide the leadership the city needed (or perhaps just thought it in his own best interest, after all, to be on the status quo team).

Wharton benefited from the volatile and erratic actions of Herenton. Now, after resigning as Memphis mayor, Herenton brazenly pulled a petition to run in the special election – *for Memphis mayor*—something supporter Sidney Chism had predicted earlier. [2813] Not long after that while on a controversial blogger's radio show, Herenton opined that Wharton would get 65% of the vote. But he also called Wharton neither a leader nor a real mayor. [2814] Incredibly, Herenton added that he ran for a fifth term in 2007 because "Carol Chumney, had I not been in that race, would have been your mayor, and I felt that would have been disastrous for Memphis." [2815] The absurdity of his statements about me were self-explanatory, especially in light of his antics of pulling a petition to run for a seat he had just resigned.

Apparently a fan of Wharton, Jackson Baker argued that my traction in the 2007 mayor's race as a "maverick" city councilwoman was only due to my role as Herenton's "chief nemesis." [2816] He understated my 35% of the vote by 3%, albeit acknowledging that I might have achieved a majority of the votes if Herman Morris had not been the third candidate in the race. [2817] After describing Wharton only a few weeks earlier as "mild-mannered," I was deemed "defiant" and "somewhat abstract" for insisting on change. [2818] Now, Wharton was termed "smooth" and "popular." [2819] Obviously, the status quo advocates were working the press.

Once again, I was called Joan of Arc by Baker because Herenton pronounced that he ran for reelection in 2007 to stop me from being elected mayor. [2820] Lowery was deemed to have received a boost as well from Herenton's comments that he had pulled a petition to run in the special election to challenge Lowery but would not file. [2821] The columnist claimed that Herenton's remarks "rejuvenated" my stature and "enlarged" me at a time when I had been less visible. [2822] He wrote his view that Herenton's singling us out was like a "grudge" wrestling match that might help counteract the "professional good-guy" Wharton (whom Herenton also declined to endorse). [2823] What was never explained by Baker was why Herenton thought my serving as mayor would harm the city—was it my gender, my race, something in my platform, or simply because I was my own woman?

Lowery took a shot at Wharton for being on a controversial radio show a few weeks previously and sitting quietly, while the African American host used the racist "N" word. [2824] Unperturbed, Wharton proceeded to pull and file his petition for city mayor and open a campaign headquarters in predominately white East Memphis. [2825] Herenton moved forward with "Keeping it Real" campaign T-shirts for his congressional race, with attorney Ricky Wilkins at the helm. [2826]

As Election Day neared, campaigning intensified. I shook hands and handed out bottled water and candy outside of factory gates, participated in a televised debate, and talked with voters at local cafeterias all over town. The historic *Tri-State Defender* ran an article focusing on my passion for community service with compassionate politics. [2827] The reporter, Wiley Henry, wrote that I am known for my "willingness and readiness to fight for causes she believes in." [2828] That meant bringing reforms to Memphis for the betterment of all.

In the *WMC Action News 5* televised live debate, I contended that the city and county leaders were not responsive enough in the June tornado storm's aftermath. I had worked for a full week as a volunteer to provide aid to victims from Boxtown to Hickory Hill.[2829] Wharton took offense, saying, "You don't just pop up while the cameras are there," which had not been the case. [2830] His vehement response gave credence to my assertions that he was nowhere to be found during that time, as well as his failure to answer my query – "And when did *you* pop up?" [2831]

The debate was challenging for some, with well-intentioned candidate Sharon Webb freezing up on the question of what two things she could do to make Memphis a better city. She was only able to articulate her goal to improve education. [2832] Also present was Robert "Prince Mongo" Hodges, who wore goggles and proposed "flushing most politicians along with the 'rest of the crooks' down the toilet." [2833]

3

After the beat-down by Herenton and some in the press, it was a blessing to have the supportive words of Frederick De Wayne Tappan Sr. (pastor of Eureka True Vine Baptist Church) in the *Tri-State Defender*. Pastor Tappan, an African American, called me "smart, articulate and community-oriented," having the "right skill set for mayor: administrative acumen, an understanding of political history, knowledge of government operations, and the ability to work with diverse stakeholders and groups." [2834] Having taken a college history class from my father, the pastor added that because of the wisdom learned from my dad, I was "uniquely" qualified for "whatever position she undertakes in public service—including mayor." [2835] I was so grateful for his words of respect and that the historic newspaper published his comments in an article by veteran reporter Wiley Henry.

That heritage the pastor referenced, passed on by my parents, includes my faith. Herenton had often said that God anointed him to be mayor. One of my campaign supporters took me to a large church service with a mostly African American congregation. Imagine my surprise when the pastor (whom I had never met before) called me up to sit on the platform. I did, honored at the request. Then, the pastor stopped during his sermon, called me over to the pulpit with him, and anointed me to lead the city. He then asked the entire congregation to point to me and affirm the anointing, which they did. What a powerful experience!

After that, I was anointed at two other African American church congregations during the campaign. I felt empowered! But, unlike Herenton, I did not announce that God anointed me to be mayor. As the verse goes, "you do not know what a day may bring forth."[2836] Instead, I prayed for the victory.

Even though campaigning was underway, I also had to attend to my duties as an attorney, including a federal court jury trial in August. But, once that verdict was in with a victory, I was able to spend more time on the campaign trail and lease a headquarters.

Our campaign was grassroots. We ventured all over the city. I even walked the runway in a fashion show at the Eureka True Vine Church in South Memphis, which was fun.[2837]

On one occasion, we visited a high rise tower to help the low-income disabled and senior citizen residents address some issues regarding their care. An elderly pastor in a wheelchair invited me to attend his church the next Sunday. It was a tiny church, with only about ten people present (not including myself and my campaign volunteer). While some candidates would run through several churches the Sunday mornings preceding Election Day, it was generally frowned upon as disingenuous because they rarely returned after the election to worship. We stayed the entire service.

As we clapped and sang, visions popped in my mind about my main opponent, Wharton, breezing through several huge churches while we spent about two hours at the one small church. Some of the primarily white church congregations had also allowed him to address their men's Sunday school classes as a guest speaker (although not an official campaign appearance), with no similar venue offered for my campaign. I felt discouraged. But finally, the men's group at Calvary Episcopal Church who heard of the disparity graciously invited me.

Then the most amazing thing happened! The guest preacher for the tiny African American church congregation happened to be a leader in the entire Pentecostal organization for the area. As a result of faithfully attending that one service, we were now invited to several large Pentecostal churches, recognized, and given a chance for their members' support. And, as a result, I built friendships with several of the pastors. As they say, God works in mysterious ways.

During the campaign, my key message was that it had been forty years since the death of Dr. Martin Luther King Jr., and it was time to come together and heal.[2838] I likened Memphis to the Israelites wandering in the wilderness about to enter the Promised Land and conquer the giants. The giants in Memphis were crime, poverty, youth needing hope and a future, and a mechanism to attract good-paying jobs. As I said, after forty years of wandering, it was time for the people of Memphis to come together, cross over and conquer those giants.

My platform was for real change and to end the backroom politics that had plagued Memphis for so long. Reducing crime and increasing school funding for more certified teachers were my top issues, as well as bringing jobs.[2839] I spoke of my admiration for Dr. Martin Luther King Jr.'s dream of equality and belief that it was meant to include everyone—boy, girl – regardless of race, gender, or religion. [2840]

I also shared my view that President Barack Obama's historic win was proof that people were tired of folks playing the race card. As I said, Obama was elected president in a majority white nation, Cohen was elected to Congress in a predominately black congressional district, and I almost was elected the first woman mayor of Memphis in 2007. My work fighting for the oppressed, values of being fair, and standing up for people, would result in a city administration that genuinely reflected the real populace. I pledged to include all races, such as African American, Latino, and Asian, on my team.

With the press and media efforts to anoint Wharton, I reminded the voters that the mayor's office is not a monarchy. And just as I hit the ground running when first elected to the state legislature at the age of twenty-nine, if given a chance, I would do everything possible as mayor to leave Memphis stronger after taking the oath of office.

4

Campaigning continued through the Labor Day weekend. Wharton and I agreed on the correlation between crime and jobs, with a different twist. Wharton pitched bringing jobs to reduce crime; I said that we had to move down the list as the worst crime capital in the nation to get more companies to look at Memphis.[2841]

Wharton was a no show again at a debate hosted by women business owners at a café. He said his absence was because Robert "Prince" Mongo, a self-proclaimed space alien, was allowed to participate.[2842] Yet, there were plenty of other candidates in attendance, including Webb, Willingham, Halbert, Lawler, and me. Mongo wore his usual attire of a white wig, goggles and held a plastic chicken. At one point, when asked what the city's biggest fear was, he answered that it was "thinking I could be your next mayor." [2843] At least he was entertaining.

Herenton, not to be left out, took the opportunity at the Young Republicans gathering to defend a $55,000 city payment to Robert Spence for legal representation for the ongoing grand jury investigation into the Greyhound bus station deal. [2844] Herenton, now described as "amiable" and "relaxed" by reporter Alex Doniach with the *Commercial Appeal*, predicted that Wharton would win with 60% of the vote because he "smiles a lot," "wears nice suits" and "rules by committees."[2845] Herenton described himself as "the man: King Willie" and "arrogant." [2846] He also criticized Lowery for attempting to terminate Jefferson as city attorney and not keeping attorney Ricky Wilkins on the Beale Street litigation. [2847] The speech was typical of his direct, no apologies, rhetoric.

As early voting was about to begin, the *WREG News, Commercial Appeal*, MPACT Memphis televised debate allowed only Wharton, Lowery, Carpenter, and me to participate from the field of twenty-five candidates, based upon a recent poll.[2848] Whalum Jr., who finished fifth in the poll, protested outside with his supporters, and Jerry Lawler, who was in 6th place, threatened to sue the news station. [2849] In the debate, Lowery put Wharton and Carpenter on the hot seat, asking if a controversial political operative had or was working in their campaigns. [2850] Both admitted he had, but neither said he was currently involved in their campaigns. [2851] The heat was on.

Again, I emphasized my platform as a change candidate and questioned Wharton's refusal to have an independent prosecutor review the legality of his car registration. I pledged that as mayor, if a similar question came up, I would send it to an outside prosecutor to review. The county mayoral aide who had handled the car registration was reprimanded for not following the inspection process. [2852] Wharton claimed he had followed the procedure under the county's ethics ordinance for the investigation. [2853]

The report for the administrative investigation for the Mercedes titled in the name of Mayor Wharton stated that the aide volunteered to take the car, "primarily" driven by the county mayor's wife, to renew the motor vehicle registration and did so during work hours.[2854] The aide claimed to have received a "waiver" in the past sometimes to avoid taking his own vehicle and the Wharton Mercedes through inspection.[2855] However, the aide claimed that he had never told the mayor or his wife about the waiver (which he admitted violated a city ordinance).[2856] In 2009, the clerk's office advised that the mayor would have to appear to get the renewal. Wharton took the paperwork. In the report, he claimed that the aide told him the vehicle had been inspected.[2857] Wharton denied knowing that the car had not been inspected and had his own appointed county attorney (who could be fired by him), to conduct the investigation about the special treatment.[2858] Even though the attorney was well-respected, in my view, it was a bad protocol for the county mayor.

Lowery questioned why Wharton was now running on "One Memphis" when he didn't run on "One Shelby" for county mayor in 2002, referring to the decades-old merger issue. [2859] As a county mayor candidate in that race, I had run on the city-county consolidation platform. Wharton dodged the question claiming that he did negotiate a joint ambulance services contract. [2860]

Keeping the heat on, I called for Wharton to drop out of the race because he wasn't devoting full time to his job as county mayor as required by the county charter.[2861] Wharton declined to respond. I pressed on, pointing out that there had been insufficient progress in reducing the infant mortality rate in the past seven years. The public hospital needed help, and nothing had been accomplished during his tenure on consolidation. Others accused him of being a "fence-sitter" or "moving too slowly" on reforms. [2862] Taking offense, Wharton refused to shake my hand at the debate.

It is ironic that in the 2002 county mayoral election, Wharton was on the fence on consolidation. Throughout his tenure as county mayor, he did not accomplish much working towards the merger of city and county governments. Now running for Memphis mayor, he was *for* discussing consolidation. [2863] My position remained consistent regardless of what office I sought.

Continuing on the offense, we officially opened our campaign office. Even Jackson Baker, with the *Memphis Flyer*, often one of the most critical reporters over my career, admitted that my headquarters opening speech was one of my best. [2864] My remarks brought up the fact that Wharton was "jumping ship" from the county mayor challenges, such as addressing serious problems at the Regional Medical Center where the area's poor receive health care services. My platform included addressing blight, improvements to the police department, and avoiding the bureaucratic nightmare that Wharton proposed with his new forty point plan to add new positions (apparently doubled from his 20 point plan in the 2002 county mayor's race).

Carpenter, meanwhile, was proposing to tear down the empty Pyramid for new development. [2865] He had run three of Herenton's mayoral campaigns in 1991, 2003, and 2007, with Wharton heading them up in 1995 and 1999. [2866] Yet somehow, they each were running on platforms of change and better government than during the Herenton administration.

The next mayoral forum, unfortunately, included not only Mongo but also another nominal candidate who was white and made outrageous statements about conspiracies with racial references.[2867] The issue of taxes, usually a hot topic, seemed a welcome respite. Carpenter and Halbert endorsed a payroll tax, and Wharton suggested a tax on cell phones. [2868]

Wharton was now identified as a chief proponent of consolidated government in a national state and local government magazine.[2869] Yet, the *Commercial Appeal* accurately reported me as the candidate who had actually supported it, with Wharton and Lowery only encouraging discussion of the idea. [2870]

A *Commercial Appeal* and *WREG News* 3 poll was released reporting Wharton with 45% of the vote, 21% undecided, me second with 11%, Lowery with 10%, and Carpenter with 5% with a plus or minus 5% margin of error. [2871] I reminded the voters of the flawed prior *Commercial Appeal* poll in 2007 reported on the weekend before the election and called upon them to turn out in mass numbers to elect a new mayor independent of the status quo. Lowery said he would campaign harder, and Carpenter discounted the poll numbers contending that he would close strong. [2872]

What bothered me more than the poll was the news station commentators' prediction that ultimately Lowery would come in second, and myself third in the election. What basis did they have for making a prediction that contradicted their own poll?

Another forum by a business group at a local private college was attended by candidates Wharton, Carpenter, and me.[2873] Carpenter criticized Wharton as having been a "miserable" county mayor, who had "gotten a pass because he's always been compared to Willie Herenton."[2874] He called on him to resign as county mayor while campaigning for city mayor. [2875] Wharton squirmed.

My platform was simply to cut crime, give kids something positive to do, revitalize neighborhoods, clean-up government, and find a reuse for the

Pyramid. Wharton pledged to be "nondivisive" and ethical. [2876] Carpenter complained that the *Commercial Appeal* was "very opinionated" and did not always draw the necessary distinctions between editorializing and news reporting. [2877] Echoing his concerns, I again reminded voters of the newspaper's push poll that impacted Herenton's victory and my defeat in the close 2007 mayoral election.

Although often contrasted in their leadership style, Wharton had a long association with Herenton. He had represented the then superintendent when he was accused of breach of promise by a teacher as far back as 1989. [2878] But, for some unfathomable reason, many voters ignored the close connection. Once again, he was deemed "affable" by the local press "known more for his pressed suits" than his affiliation with Herenton. [2879]

Even though I reminded the voters of the backroom meeting between Herenton and Wharton in 2007, he still got a pass. He benefited from his mild-mannered demeanor in comparison with Herenton, who was controversial, blunt, and aggressive. And, Republican County Sheriff Mark Luttrell's dutiful Wharton endorsement, although he previously had told me that he would stay out of the race, kept with the good ole boy tradition benefiting Wharton's candidacy.[2880]

My critique of Wharton is not intended to be personal (*he* was the one who refused to shake my hand at the debate). But the plain facts are that somehow the voters did not focus on the lack of progress in his seven years as county mayor in areas such as consolidation of governments, getting the debt under control, or adequate support for the Memphis Regional Medical Center.[2881] And, some of the programs he took credit for were not even funded by the county. [2882] He certainly had the right to run. However, I wish some in the press and media had focused more on his record instead of adopting a façade of fairness that, in reality, actually favored his candidacy.

Wharton finally acknowledged that the county debt incurred to build the suburban schools and infrastructure was a huge impediment to the area's growth, as I had said in the 2002 campaign for county mayor. [2883]It had grown under his administration from $1.4 billion to $1.8 billion in 2006. [2884] He also was criticized by some for not making more gains on job growth for minorities. [2885] Wharton conversely claimed that he had made some gains with early childhood education, improved emergency services, and preserved the Shelby Farms Park. [2886] But the considerable county debt overshadowed everything.

In my *Commercial Appeal* profile, I drew a distinction from Wharton. I was the true change agent due to my lack of ties with the recent administrations, my proven track record of getting results, and my commitment to bringing Memphians together to be a world-class city. [2887] I wasn't afraid to rock the boat or fight to build a consensus for what was best for Memphis. I wasn't just a show horse. I was also a workhorse. In my view, I had both style and substance.

5

With reports of Memphis being held back by "crushing poverty and instability," the *Commercial Appeal* editors endorsed Wharton.[2888] They hoped Wharton would move the city up from its economic ranking of 52d of the metro areas of a million people or more and reverse the trend that had increased vacant housing by 45% over the past three years according to the U.S. Census Bureau. [2889] Overlooked was that he had done none of that so far as county mayor. Yet, Wharton was touted as the best consensus builder and "vigorous" despite his sixty-five years. [2890]

The editors referred to me as "experienced, honest and sincere, with a strong work ethic and an understanding of what this community has gone through over the past forty years." [2891] Yet, the editorial summarily dismissed my candidacy with the statement that "[t]he community would be better off if she returned to public service in some capacity." [2892] That was appreciated, but the editors appeared to be clueless that the lack of support provided qualified female candidates for higher office significantly reduces which jobs they can do. And, reforms were needed at the top, with my solid record as a reformer undisputed.

The *Commercial Appeal* editorial was also complimentary of Lowery and Carpenter and acknowledged that Wharton's attributes might not be "radical enough for Memphis or even real." [2893] The editors believed that Wharton would need to make a "clean break from the past," be transparent, and frugal to succeed. [2894] Their concerns about his ability to bring far-reaching change and get things done were justified, but they still went with the status quo.

Wharton was now described by Baker with the *Memphis Flyer* as "well-liked" and said to be playing "rope-a-dope" by skipping forums and debates where he would have to respond to attacks from his opponents. [2895] Even he had to admit, however, that Wharton was "cranky and ad hominem once or twice" in the *WREG News* debate after attacks by Lowery and Carpenter. [2896] Apparently, some of the punches were hitting their mark.

Wharton waffled on his record, such as the consolidation issue. He claimed to have gotten control of the county debt during his tenure when, in fact, it increased. Yet, while former Mayor Hackett spoke well of Lowery as interim mayor, he predicted Wharton would win regardless of his inconsistent positions. [2897] One had to ask, was this an election about who could best lead the city and his or her platform, or a personality contest? If a personality contest, then how did preconceived notions as to gender factor into the mix?

Once again, I was described by Jackson Baker as a "civic crusader," with some who believed that my pledge to "fight for you" more appropriate for a legislative race than that of the mayor. [2898] Hadn't Wharton described himself as a "friendly fighter" when running for county mayor in 2002?

Carpenter continued to attack Wharton, now for using former aides in his campaign after their ethical lapses related to "pension-gate." [2899] Lowery attacked Wharton and Carpenter, and they defended their use of another controversial former Herenton aide in their campaigns. [2900] Lowery explained his "fist bump" with the Dali Lama in September when he had greeted the Buddhist leader during a Memphis visit; Carpenter defended his close association with Herenton (including millions in payments from the city for legal work); and Wharton denied my claim that he was jumping ship as county mayor.

At the Rotary forum, I reminded the audience that I was the only candidate who could bring true change. After having come in second place in the Democratic primary in 2002 for county mayor, and second place in the nonpartisan 2007 city mayor's race, I also asked the question at the forum: "what message does it send if someone like me doesn't get to be mayor, ever? What message does it send to young girls?" Perhaps as a comment on what felt like a spectacle to me, Prince Mongo watched from the audience, wearing his goggles and a white wig with a rubber chicken attached to his overcoat.

As Election Day approached, all of the candidates escalated their efforts. Councilman Jim Strickland, who was previously critical of Wharton, now appeared in an endorsement video as his campaign co-chair. [2901] Lowery attacked Wharton alleging a *Le Chardonnay* backroom deal with Herenton and that the county mayor had begun campaigning for Memphis mayor shortly after that meeting. [2902] Carpenter blasted Wharton for ducking forums and debates, and I agreed that he couldn't "just run off and be in an ivory tower."[2903]

The polling was less certain due to the anticipated low turnout for the special election. A new Mason Dixon Research poll just before Election Day showed me second behind Wharton, albeit trailing thirty-four points. [2904]

My election effort was spirited, although we were short on money and volunteers due to Wharton's anointing by the press and media. The campaign took me all over the city. I visited sanitation workers as they left the bus barn for the day, beauty shops, and nightclubs with primarily African American patrons, where I was introduced and invited to say a word on the stage. I only hoped it would translate into more votes. It was hard to counter the false rumors spread about me, such as that I supported privatizing the sanitation workers when precisely the opposite was true.

As Election Day drew near, I hoped that this time the right message would be sent to young girls—that a woman can be the mayor!

35

Will There Ever Be
a Wonder Woman?

1

The mayoral forums relentlessly continued with three scheduled on one day in early October.[2905] The city council delayed action until after the election on how to pay back the city school system the millions owed to it after winning suit for the funds.[2906] At the forums, I called for interim mayor Lowery to address the issue now since he had voted for the city to keep the school monies while on the council. Despite a good relationship and agreement on many issues, we respectfully disagreed on that prior vote. Lowery replied that he would work to find cuts in an effort to avoid a special tax by the council, although a few months earlier, he said a loss in the courts on the school funding issue would necessitate a tax increase.[2907]

Strickland, now co-chairing Wharton's campaign, and Wharton both said the court-ordered payment of school funds could be handled without raising taxes.[2908] I reiterated my view that the council should not have cut the school funds.

Carpenter and I both criticized Wharton for skipping several community events, including a "green" forum at the University of Memphis.[2909] In my view, it was important for the voters to know this was an election, not a coronation, and the people's voices matter.[2910] Plus, the voters deserved to know where he stood on environmental issues.

Carpenter blasted Wharton's claims that county debt had decreased during his county mayor term when according to Carpenter, it had increased a half-billion dollars.[2911] Wharton retorted that Carpenter had made money as an attorney in doing some of the county government bond deals.[2912] Both were relevant issues.

Citizens debated who they were for, with some angry that Wharton had sheriffs' deputies always parked out front to guard his home and about the nearly $2 billion in county debt. Others called him a "nice man in nice suits" but wanted more decisive leadership to move the area forward.[2913] Some criticized the *Commercial Appeal's* "glowing" coverage of Wharton as "disgraceful," "embarrassing," and "push-polling." [2914] This sounded familiar to the 2007 mayor's race with its coverage as to the *Commercial Appeal*- endorsed Herman Morris. Certainly, Wharton had some good qualities, but we fundamentally disagreed on the best way to move Memphis forward and who could best do that.

Interim Mayor Lowery now disclosed that Herenton was paid a large sum of money upon his retirement for unused vacation time and claimed that the records had been hidden in former city attorney Jefferson's office. [2915] When asked if we would seek to recover some $200,000 in unused vacation time paid to Herenton, Wharton and I said yes. [2916] However, Lowery wanted to consult with the city council and lawyers, and Carpenter hedged. [2917] The amount was about the same that Herenton had criticized Morris for receiving as his severance package from MLGW. Evidently, Herenton saw his own situation differently.

My platform included creating a safe learning environment for children and providing positive and recreational opportunities after school.[2918] Also, I pledged to hire the fully authorized complement of police officers, review internal security to ensure that their deployment locations were a surprise to criminals, and tear down vacant houses and buildings that were havens for criminals to operate so new development could occur.[2919]

Wharton pledged to strengthen sentencing for illegal guns, enhance special intervention programs for juvenile offenders, and rehabilitation programs for former prisoners. [2920] He further said he would appoint an "auxiliary police chief" in each neighborhood as liaison to the MPD. [2921] He also planned on starting a police car take-home policy.[2922]

A new *WREG News* poll reported Wharton well ahead at 53%, with Lowery 2nd at 16% and me now 3rd at 9%.[2923] I wondered whether their pollster's prior speculation that Lowery and I would switch places was correct or if this might be just another example of push-polling to achieve the desired result. Whalum Jr. brought up the rear, with 5%, Lawler 4%, Carpenter 3%

and, 7% undecided. [2924] Wharton, as might be expected, attributed his lead to the voters' weariness of drama and criticism of his past performance. [2925] However, the power of incumbency as county mayor and the press and media's anointing played a large part in his support.

In light of the musical chairs underway, I asked, "Isn't it time that we gave someone else a chance to have some leadership in this city?" [2926] I continued with my message of healing and change. The *Commercial Appeal* went to former councilmember colleague and conservative Brent Taylor, who said that I had to present myself "as an alternative to her formidable opponents." [2927] Despite the fundraising disparity and the polls that showed Wharton well ahead, I stood strong contending that "the dynamics of this race are even more compelling because the economy is in the tank," "people are hurting more," "they want change."

Herman Morris, who might benefit with a Wharton victory, piled on, saying that he didn't think I had a winning strategy. [2928] The issue of whether a loss for me would be a "curtain call" was actually reported on in the *Commercial Appeal*.[2929] I was grateful that this time political scientist Marcus Polhmann was on my side, saying each of my mayoral races involved strong and hard to beat opponents.[2930] He saw me as a viable candidate for a 2010 county mayor open seat race without a high-profile incumbent, even if losing the 2009 city mayor special election. [2931] The discussion only highlighted how difficult it was to break the cultural barriers in place as a female candidate for mayor.

While Whalum Jr. hoped to capitalize on the youth vote, the voting trends did not support the effort. The election administrator stated that senior citizens and government employees decide elections. [2932] The early vote numbers seemed to support his hypothesis, with those aged sixty-five and older representing 37% of all early voters and only 7% voting between ages eighteen to thirty-four. [2933] Whalum Jr. legitimately questioned why he was one of the youngest candidates running at the age of fifty-two—myself being forty-eight; Carpenter fifty-seven; Lawler fifty-nine; Lowery sixty-two; and Wharton sixty-five. [2934]

Otis Sanford, the *Commercial Appeal* editor, jokingly referred to Whalum Jr. as "Sir-Text-A Lot," noting his effectiveness in working to give youth a voice. [2935] Sanford agreed that most people in charge of government are from the "old school" and opined that the voters usually pass on the chance to elect more youthful leaders and probably would this time as well. [2936] He also commented that I spoke the most "passionately" about youth, primarily women leaving the city for lack of perceived opportunities. [2937] As a candidate who was female, I had a good reason.

The creative class that Memphis, and all large cities, hoped to attract and keep were primarily single professional women in their twenties to forties. The failure to promote a female mayoral candidate sends the wrong message to the very women and young professionals that the city needs to thrive.

One last televised debate was scheduled by *WREG News* Channel 3 for October 14, with Wharton, Lowery, Whalum Jr., and me participating. Whalum Jr. had edged Carpenter out for fourth place in the recent poll out of a field of twenty-five candidates.[2938] All of the top four professed to be ready to hit the ground running, with only about ten days between the election results, certification, and swearing-in to start the job. Lowery said he would keep Jack Sammons as CAO if elected.[2939] Wharton claimed he could juggle the county mayor job, campaign for city mayor, and handle the transition after the election. [2940] I had prepared my law office for the transition as well.

As reported, the only "real sparks" during the hour-long debate were between Wharton and me. I asked how much money he would make as city mayor while also drawing a county pension.[2941] Wharton fired back, unfairly blaming me for not stopping Herenton's pay raise (although I had opposed and voted against it).[2942]

Wharton also claimed that I was too independent to lead the city because my push to repeal the twelve-year pension was instead passed with McCormick's resolution (even though the press acknowledged my leading role in getting it repealed).[2943] I had fought to repeal an outrageous public pension for elected and appointed officials, while McCormick's was watered down to the benefit of newer council members and appointees. In fact, during Wharton's tenure as county mayor, the former mayor Rout's top aide who had served time for misuse of a county credit card, had been taken back on the payroll in order to boost his pension (although the pension increase was later revoked after public outcry).[2944] Apparently, the Wharton administration's role in "pension gate" was conveniently forgotten by the press, powers that be, and public. Under the circumstances, my independence was a sorely needed virtue, as opposed to being a mayor that looked the other way for pension abuses until brought to the spotlight.

In my closing remarks, I asked voters not to elect Wharton, which would only create a new "dynasty" immediately after the end of Herenton's reign.[2945]

Whalum Jr. compared Wharton to Goliath from biblical times, asking voters to be the slingshot.[2946]

In its last issue before the election, *Memphis Flyer* reporter Jackson Baker analyzed the candidates, calling me a "veteran" in public service and reformer.[2947] He also commented that as the "would-be leading lady of change," I was "more fashionable in appearance" than the 2007 campaign.[2948] While this was an unusual comment, I suppose it wasn't much different than all of the remarks about Wharton's nice suits.

Baker appropriately credited me for being the first to challenge the twelve-year pension that was subsequently repealed.[2949] He found me "icon-oclasm" on issues (apparently he meant at challenging the status quo) and good at "finding the flaws" with Herenton as an "admirable foil."[2950] Yet, he again called my campaign message to "fight for you" as "retro" and more befitting a legislator as opposed to an executive position.[2951]

I appreciated Baker's positive remarks but disagreed with his analysis of my campaign slogan and platform. I had a robust positive reform platform that went well beyond just throwing rocks at the other candidates. And, as a county mayoral candidate in 2002, Wharton had advertised himself as a "friendly fighter" with no objection. Hillary Clinton, who won the popular vote for president in 2016, used the slogan "she will fight for us."[2952] Maybe it was just hard for some in the local press to envision a woman as the mayor whatever her slogan or platform.

Wharton, according to Baker, was "calm," reassuring, and "amiable" in contrast to Herenton's "Alpha male" persona.[2953] He had been considered as a candidate by the African American People's Convention organizers in 1991, who ultimately picked Herenton to run on a platform of being the city's first black elected mayor.[2954] Baker also described Wharton as bland and "able."[2955] While Wharton's more passive demeanor seemed a plus in contrast to the past chaos from the Herenton administration drama, in my view, it lacked the edge needed to get things done.

The columnist called Lowery the "anti-Willie" of the field due to his attempt to fire Herenton's city attorney on the day he was sworn in as interim mayor.[2956] However, that was called a "stumble" due to the failure to garner the city council's support for the action.[2957] The event did show independence, although overshadowing the interim mayor's first days in office. However, Lowery's pledge to keep Sammons as CAO was evidence of a status quo mentality when a real change was needed.

Otis Sanford, with the *Commercial Appeal*, actually said on the local news that it would take a miracle for anyone other than Wharton to be elected as Memphis mayor.[2958] Perhaps I had read the *Little Engine that Could*[2959] book too many times as a child, but I doubled down. My telephone voicemail to voters asked them to make a miracle on Election Day by voting me into office.

My last literature mailed to the voters compared and contrasted my record with Wharton and Lowery. In the piece urging voters to "Vote for the Change Memphis Needs," I reminded voters that Lowery had voted for the twelve-year pension for elected and appointed officials and also had to sign an apology to the Iraqi delegation banned from City Hall. The mailer further warned that Wharton had raised property taxes 24% in seven years as county mayor and of his meeting with Herenton at *Le Chardonnay*, which some suggested was a backroom deal between the two. In contrast, I had worked to repeal the twelve-year pension, consistently voted against property tax increases, diplomatically welcomed Iraqi delegation members sponsored by the U.S. State Department and stood against the Herenton administration's harmful policies.

Another mailer by my campaign mentioned that 60% of the voters in Memphis were women, and asked, "Why has no woman ever been Mayor of Memphis?" The piece added that "Every vote for Carol Chumney is another crack in the glass ceiling. It is a vote that gives hope to our daughters and tells them that the highest office in this city is within their reach if they work hard enough." I hand-wrote notes on thousands of the mailers, humbly asking for the recipients' votes.

On Election Day, the *Commercial Appeal* editors reminded the voters that the newspaper supported Wharton, asking them to turnout for him if they agreed after his "'One Memphis' campaign."[2960] They referred to Lowery as having "energy," "bold," and "confident," and more open than the prior administrations.[2961] I was described as youthful, brash, and appealing for a new direction.[2962] The editors considerately urged the voters supporting Lowery or myself to turn-out as well.[2963] The editorial reminded the voters that Memphis was the nation's highest poverty metro area of a million people or more, of the budgetary problems, and "perception" of high crime, calling Wharton a "unifying" and "stabilizing force" for the area.[2964] However, the fact that this was the status despite his tenure as county mayor was disregarded.

With a turnout of less than one in four voters, Wharton was elected with 60% of the vote. The *Commercial Appeal* editors opined that A C's victory was a "spanking" for the other candidates, but no mandate due to the low voter turn-out. [2965] Lowery came in second with 18%, and I followed third with 10% of the vote. [2966] Carpenter was fourth with only 5% of the vote, despite spending over $120,000.[2967]Wharton had spent close to half a million dollars on the campaign, more than any other candidate had raised combined. [2968] Whether it was a political spanking or not for me, at least he had been given a run for his money.

After Lowery conceded on TV, I did so as well amongst my supporters at a local restaurant. I politely acknowledged that Wharton was a "formidable opponent." I also expressed my hopes that someday a woman can be the mayor of Memphis.[2969]

Although, we could have run a stronger race with more funds, I attributed my loss primarily to a "glass ceiling" for female candidates.[2970] How else can you explain that America was able to break through and historically elect the first African American U.S. President when whites constituted 72% of the electorate, but there still has never been a female president even though women are the majority of the voters? How else can you explain that there are no portraits of women mayors on the wall at Memphis City Hall even though women have had the right to vote since 1920?

Wharton said he saw the sun shining on Memphis in his victory speech.[2971] A cartoon ran the next day in the *Commercial Appeal* of a smiling sun over the Memphis bridge across the Mississippi River. In the cartoon, Wharton was now the one with his own Superman cape and gap-toothed smile (as opposed to Herenton's Superman emblazoned chest in the 2003 cartoon). [2972] One of my favorite childhood shows was *Wonder Woman*. Surely one day that Memphis sun will shine on her too, with her red boots standing tall above the city. Or maybe there will be a victory cartoon of a determined woman named Carol standing on top of City Hall – with Captain Marvel's red photon blasts ablaze, ready to fight for Memphis.

Next on the agenda was Wharton's resignation as county mayor, with County Commissioner Chair Joyce Avery to serve as interim county mayor— the first woman to ever hold the post (and still the only one as of this book's publication in 2021).[2973] At least one barrier was broken after all for the county mayor's job, although only for a brief period of time and because another man stepped aside in the middle of his term.

After the election, Wharton was hit with criticism from County Commissioner Joe Ford that his administration had mismanaged the county budget. [2974] Ford was in a stand-off with another commissioner to fill the remainder of the county mayor term. [2975] Wharton brushed it off since he was on the way to City Hall. [2976] Ultimately, Joe Ford was elected interim mayor by the county commission and began working with the Metropolitan Government Charter Commission on drafting a proposed charter, chasing that ever just out of reach goal of combining the governments.[2977]

Having campaigned for mayor pledging he would explore cuts to help fund the millions in school funding ordered to be paid back by the court, less than two months after the election, Wharton proposed a thirty-one cent property tax increase. [2978] The measure, which would raise about $31 million, was rejected by the city council. [2979] Councilman Strickland wanted to take most of the money to pay the debt from the city's reserve fund. [2980] In response, the city finance director warned that taking more than $16 million from the reserves might result in a drop in the bond rating and leave the city unprepared for any unexpected natural disasters. [2981] The Strickland proposal was deemed "poaching from the city's reserve fund" by the *Memphis Flyer* editors. They also criticized the failure to identify specific cuts that would not compromise public services. [2982] It appeared that the professed promises to find budget cuts to free up funds to pay the schools back had gone to the wayside.

The year ended with the *Memphis Flyer's* John Branston writing in his column that he missed me in public office. [2983] He added, "bash public officials all you want, but at least they [myself and two others] own up to their comments and do battle face to face." [2984] I missed serving the people too.

PART EIGHT

Election Security and Other Reform Efforts

36

It Will Take a Miracle

1

After the special city mayoral election, Wharton appointed Herman Morris as city attorney. This completed what many believed to be a backroom deal made during the 2007 mayor's race.

Having been defeated a second time for Memphis mayor, I decided to focus on my private law practice and stay active in the community. That glass ceiling was still firmly in place. Would it take a miracle for an experienced woman to be elected mayor of Memphis or Shelby County?

In August of 2010, city leaders held a women's suffrage celebration in the City Hall of Mayors. Remembering the 75th anniversary in 1995 at the State Capitol, I attended. Wharton gave remarks at the event. The women present all clapped, seemingly oblivious to the mayoral disparity of gender, which the all-male mayoral portraits on the walls surrounding and staring down at them demonstrated. At this point, American women had exercised the right to vote for ninety years, but no woman had ever served as the mayor of Memphis.

Since being shut out of being the mayor, I did not challenge Wharton again in the regular 2011 Memphis mayoral election. Instead, I spent several months training for a one hundred mile bike ride. Although my bike was not built for racing, I frugally had it souped-up with thinner tires and special peddles. I spent my summer after work and on weekends riding through area neighborhoods and parks, including the Shelby Farms large urban park with the buffalos staring as our group of bikers peddled by. As a result of my slower bike, I usually was one of the last team members to cross the finish line in the training rides. However, I stuck with it, and on the day of the century ride, was able to complete the route on time before 5 pm by starting with a few others an hour early (around 7 am). Peddling during that long day, I reflected on the last mayoral elections. Who knows, maybe one day, the tortoise instead of the hare would win the race.

At another event, my friend and local businessman Jack Morris was honored for his years of service for the Methodist Hospital. The luncheon room was packed with business and civic leaders, including several former Memphis and Shelby County mayors seated at one of the tables. The coordinators sat me at the same table as the former mayors. A prominent developer gave remarks honoring Jack Morris. After recognizing the many former mayors seated at the table, in an off-hand way, he looked around and asked, "has anyone here not been the Mayor?" *He paused.* Then I slowly raised my hand, with the entire room roaring with laughter.

The current Memphis Mayor AC Wharton usually ignored me whenever we crossed paths and made no effort whatsoever in his mayoral position to reach out to include my skills and knowledge for the citizens of Memphis in any capacity. I know they say to the victor belong the spoils, but President Obama set a much better example when he made Hillary Clinton part of his team after the 2008 presidential election. It created a win-win, where both of their knowledge and skills were put to use to benefit all Americans.

A friend of mine knew Wharton. We were at dinner one evening in Cooper-Young—an eclectic midtown hip, artsy neighborhood with cool shops, trendy bars, and the independent Burke's bookstore. The tiny restaurant had one room with only a few tables. Wharton sauntered in with his security guard and was seated at a table. My friend, Marc Kullman, went over to say hello to the mayor. I remained seated. He came back and said that Wharton was going to come over and say hello at his request. I didn't believe it. It didn't happen.

My friend went back over to Wharton again and asked him to say hello to me. Finally, Wharton got up, and walked over in slow motion in what seemed like an eternity. I rose to shake his hand, and instead, he kissed it, then returned to his table. We reminisced about this for months—that my friend could get Wharton to do this, and how incredible it was since Wharton wouldn't even shake my hand at the mayoral debate.

I was taking a break from politics at the time but did note the defeat of another vote to consolidate Memphis and Shelby County governments in 2010. [2985] While those in the city narrowly favored the merger, it was defeated overwhelmingly by the county voters that did not reside in Memphis. [2986] As

Mark Luttrell, the Shelby County mayor, opposed the measure, he made no joint effort with Wharton to push it through. [2987] A federal court lawsuit had been filed by eight Memphians before the election, challenging the constitutionality of the separate city/county votes.[2988] In 2014, the district court judge summarily denied the plaintiffs' claims and dismissed the lawsuit in favor of the state, its election officials, and the intervening suburban cities. [2989] The separate city/county governments remained firmly intact.

And I further noted the 4.6% salary cut for city employees made in August 2011.[2990] The salary cut was said by city officials to prevent laying off about 500 employees.[2991] This was a precursor to more problems ahead. The city unions fought back by filing a federal court lawsuit.[2992] And, the police union put up billboards around the city that read, "Danger: enter at your own risk. This city does not support public safety."[2993] However, Wharton was still easily reelected for a full term as Memphis mayor in the fall of 2011, with his closest opponent the exonerated former city council member Edmund Ford Sr.[2994]

2

In 2012, not only was the presidential primary heating up, but the local Democratic Party also recruited me to run for Shelby County District Attorney. Republican Bill Gibbons had vacated his seat and was now the state's homeland security commissioner.[2995] Republican Governor Haslam had appointed Amy Weirich to the position, and she was unopposed in the Republican primary. [2996] I still felt I could best make a difference for the people as mayor. But I decided to enter the race in that the doors for those of the female gender for the mayor-ship were still closed.

One day while out at a restaurant, I mentioned to a local developer who happened also to be waiting for a table that I was entering the race. I'll never forget his flippant response—"why don't you just go sit down and shut up?" Stunned at the somewhat hostile remark after seventeen years of solid dedicated public service, I ended the conversation grateful that the hostess appeared. Would he have said that to a man?

In May, a fundraiser held for Weirich received headlines with the connection made between certain hosts implicated by informants and not charged, and the indicted former mayor of the suburban town of Millington. [2997] The investigation related to alleged corruption, with charges of gambling at the

Millington City Hall. [2998] While Weirich was a competent prosecutor, this would not be the first time her ethical judgment was called into question.

News also broke of the U.S. Department of Justice findings, based upon a review of four years of data, that the Shelby County juvenile justice system had failed to ensure constitutionally required due process to all children appearing for delinquency proceedings.[2999] The report also found that the court's administration of justice discriminated against African American children and that its detention center violated the substantive due process rights of detained youth by not providing them with reasonably safe conditions of confinement. [3000] Among other things, the study found that black youth, compared to white juveniles, were twice as likely to be detained and transferred to adult court. [3001] A third less of the black youth were likely to receive only a warning for the same violations. [3002] The Shelby County D.A.'s office had some responsibility here, and it was a compelling campaign issue. All children deserve equal treatment under the law.

Summer also brought the opening of the local Democratic party headquarters. At the event, I was photographed with Memphis Mayor AC Wharton, Congressman Cohen, the state Democratic party chair, and even Wharton's grandson.[3003] It was duly noted by reporter Jackson Baker in his column that the local Democratic party was hoping to perform better than the 2010 countywide elections where the GOP had defeated its entire slate of candidates. [3004]

The GOP had held a majority solid lock on the Tennessee Senate and House of Representatives since 2008, and more so after redistricting in 2010.[3005] After the change in power, the election reform law mandating counties to upgrade their voting machines with a verifiable paper trail was inexplicably amended in 2011 by the state legislature to make it optional.[3006] The paper trail was essential to audit the election results properly.

Thereafter, new claims of election abuse arose in the spring of 2012, with allegations that some African American voter histories had been erased from the Shelby County election commission records.[3007] A pollster, Berje Yacoubian, called for an investigation by the U.S. Department of Justice. [3008] State Sen. Jim Kyle assured that the state election commission would investigate the large purge, with similar allegations in Nashville ending up in federal court. [3009]

When asked to explain the erased voter histories for 488 African American voters (according to an election activist), the Shelby County election administrator attributed it to a "computer glitch" related to a special report for an election runoff.[3010] Jackson Baker with the *Memphis Flyer* retorted that "public confidence is eroded by too many glitches," likening it to "a shell game," with the "whoopsie" explanations beginning to appear "disingenuous." [3011] He was right.

Higher Republican voter turnout was expected in the August county elections due to a referendum pushed by Republican state Sen. Mark Norris allowing the suburbs to vote on establishing special school districts under certain circumstances.[3012] In 2011, the senator had passed the Norris-Todd law that lifted the ban on new municipal and special school districts. This was after many years of often heated debates between Memphis urban and Shelby County suburban state legislators on the house floor about school funding and organization (while others from across the state were scratching their heads).[3013] The law established a Transitional Planning Commission and Unified School interim board in the aftermath of the controversial 2010 surrender of the Memphis City Schools charter, which had disbanded the Memphis school board.[3014] The series of events had turned the community on its ear as both sides struggled to either keep the county school system intact or siphon off students in special school districts set up in suburban towns.

A volatile issue for the August 2nd primaries was the seven permanent Unified School Board members' election, with the appointment of the new county school superintendent for the merged school systems at stake.[3015] The Shelby County Board of Education had sued the Memphis City Board of Education, city council, and county commission. They asked for a declaratory judgment that the Memphis City School's actions in surrendering its charter in 2010 were unconstitutional.[3016] The citizens of Memphis had approved the surrender in March 2011.[3017] The constitutionality of the new law sponsored by Sen. Mark Norris was in question (providing that where a surrender occurs under such circumstances, the suburban municipalities could create their own school districts). [3018]

Former chief of staff for Republican Governor Don Sundquist, Hardy Mays, was now the U.S. District federal court judge to decide the schools' lawsuit. He let the suburban special school district referendum go forward on the August ballot, despite not having ruled yet whether the process had been legal.[3019] The referendum substantially increased suburban conservative voter turnout in the countywide elections.[3020] This had an impact on countywide races.

The city and county were in virtual chaos due to the uncertainties of whether there would be one unified school district or whether the suburban cities would break off and form their own schools.[3021] This was all prompted by the fateful decision of the Memphis City Council to substantially reduce the annual millions contributed to the former Memphis city school system, the change in power in the state legislature creating fear by some of suburban special school district authorization, and the Memphis school board's decision to surrender the city schools charter in 2010 (which was agreed to by the city council).[3022]

Apart from the thorny educational issues, the city's budget was challenging in 2012. The *Commercial Appeal* reported a loss of 27,000 residents and scores of businesses since the 2008 economic crisis.[3023] But the city's spending was said to have increased some 24% over the same time-period. [3024] A rating agency reported that the debt levels were high for the city, with only about $200 million left in capacity to borrow.[3025] One apparent miscalculation by a municipal consultant was that Memphis had plenty of time to add $600 million to the municipal pension fund.[3026] That would soon become a new crisis.

3

As the county general election candidates jockeyed for votes, Otis Sanford with the *Commercial Appeal* wasted no time dismissing my district attorney campaign. [3027] His column featured my mayoral losses to Wharton and Herenton, arguing that African Americans would not support me against Weirich because I ran "aggressive" and "bitter" campaigns "against those guys." [3028] To make his case, he overlooked the fact that I had been unchallenged in the Democratic primary for district attorney, with solid votes on primary Election Day from the overwhelmingly African American electorate. Or that I had diverse support in the 2007 and 2009 mayoral campaigns.

Sanford even craftily quoted local Democratic Party Chair Van Turner, who had recruited me to run for district attorney, as saying this election would be "challenging" for me and that some of my supporters might suffer from "fatigue." [3029] Turner was reported to say that the party's focus would be on electing the nominees for Assessor and General Sessions Court Clerk as the winnable candidates. [3030]

The Sanford narrative was questionable based upon past voting patterns in the county, which was about equally split between white and black voters.

I am white, and the other Democratic nominees, Stanton Sr. and Johnson, who were dubbed "winnable" candidates, were black. Under traditional voting patterns, my chances of winning should be at least equal to theirs in our respective races due to the solid Democratic base of voters and my additional base of independent and some Republican supporters from my past many years of public service (including the East Memphis area I represented on the city council).

Elaborating further, Sanford sarcastically compared Weirich to Warren Buffet and me to Harry Hippie regarding fundraising. [3031] Actually, Harry Hippie was a song about a lazy, carefree singer who had nothing whatsoever similar to my record, work ethic, or lifestyle. Perhaps by calling me a hippie, this was an attempt to typecast me negatively and alienate moderate and conservative voters who had supported me previously.

This same editor, who previously had opined that it would take a miracle for me to be elected mayor against Wharton in the 2009 special election, ended his column pronouncing Weirich "invincible" and predicting that I would suffer "another embarrassing defeat" despite my prior "productive" record of service in elective office and "household name." [3032] If so, why kick me while down – as the saying goes? Whatever my chances of raising money were before the article, suffice it to say they were greatly diminished after that.

A better story aired by Les Smith, a television reporter with the local *Fox 13 Memphis News*. He called me "politically bloodied but unbowed."[3033] Likening me to Scarlett O'Hara in my willingness to face adversity, Smith opined that I needed a "knock-out punch" to beat Weirich due to her large war chest.[3034] The story drew a contrast between my approach of "compassionate justice" based upon calls for reform in the juvenile offender system by the Department of Justice, with the "law and order" platform of the incumbent.[3035] Smith understood the tough battle, what was at stake, and the fact that serious reforms were needed.

With the talk now that the Democratic party was not supporting me even though it had recruited me and nominated me, I secured Turner for a press conference. It did seem that the table allocated to my campaign at the party headquarters kept being appropriated to other uses. At the press conference, Turner did dutifully assure the press, media, and public that the party was squarely behind my candidacy.

Also, my press conference focused on the recent Department of Justice report that found racial disparities and that constitutional reforms were needed with regard to the handling of alleged offenders in the juvenile court system in Memphis. [3036] Weirich played it off as merely evidence of incomplete reports by arresting officers and claimed that reforms had already been completed to come into compliance. [3037]

I pushed forward, appearing in neighborhoods throughout the county and even knocking on some doors with a campaign supporter. In one economically challenged area, I met a ninety-year old African American man called "Popcorn." We sat on his porch and chatted about the needs of the community. In another neighborhood, I met a former drug dealer named "Cold Cash." He had a grave marker in his front yard that read "Cold Cash Pimp or Die" and apologetically explained that the livelihood had been the only way he was able to survive.

One day I was in a low-income residential neighborhood knocking on some doors with a volunteer when we came across a tiny church. The African American pastor invited us inside, and we talked in his study. He then played the organ for us in the small sanctuary. When we stepped out on the porch to leave, he said a prayer and anointed me with holy oil. Then, he stopped, and recognizing me for the first time, said, "you're Carol Chumney." While Weirich had been anointed by most in the press and media, I preferred my anointing by this humble pastor.

There were also some strange occurrences related to the campaign that made me wonder if someone was trying to set me up. An attorney asked me to meet with a potential client. When I found out that the person had connections to the gambling industry, I declined the case. After telling a colleague that I had sent the retainer check back uncashed, my cell phone abruptly went dead as if it had been wire-tapped.

Another constituent said he had a great billboard sign location for me. When I researched who owned the property, I discovered it was a man in the topless dancing industry. The campaign decided to skip that location.

And, by an unusual turn of events, I detected that a former FBI agent was one of my campaign's independent contractors. I had to wonder whether the opposition, or someone else, was doing surveillance, or was it just a coincidence. Either way, I followed the sage advice from Machiavelli's *The Prince*,[3038] and kept him close on the campaign team. Besides, I had nothing to hide anyway.

With Election Day approaching, I prepared for a debate hosted by the local League of Women Voters. Baker with the *Memphis Flyer* expressed surprise at how well I performed, calling it an even match. [3039] Weirich, in her opening remarks, lauded herself as the first female district attorney in the county (appointed), which Jackson Baker reported took the issue of the "glass ceiling" off the table. [3040] Obviously, it wasn't on the table anyway, since a woman would be elected regardless with only the two of us on the ballot for the position in the general election.

However, I was thankful that Baker opined that the election could be a race, even with Weirich's large war chest and bipartisan support.[3041] Republican nominee Weirich inexplicably boosted support from local Democrats Mike Cody (a renowned former Tennessee Attorney General), Councilmen Jim Strickland, Shea Flinn, and Harold Collins, among others.[3042] Thus, it was disappointing that the party label and my platform of equal justice were not the deciding factor for some Democrat officials in Memphis.

On the heels of the Baker article, the *Commercial Appeal* ran a headline "Chumney fundraising lacking." [3043] The article compared my minimal funds raised to Weirich's of about $260,000, with her campaign account remaining balance of $110,000. [3044] After the publicity favoring Weirich, fundraising had dried up. Weirich's ads were running on TV, with my advertising focused on free social media. [3045] But, I was proud of my YouTube video, featuring former State Rep. Rufus Jones attesting to my "boundless energy," and work for female leadership as a fighter for the people, who also can "take a licking and keep on ticking." [3046] At least he stood for the candidate who had the track record and ability to ensure equal justice.

Republican strategist Susan Adler Thorp predicted in the article that the high conservative suburban turnout for the schools' referendum would boost Weirich's chances.[3047] Mike Lollar, the reporter, noted that the local Democratic party had offered "meager support," even though I had asked for help. [3048] Political scientist Marcus Pohlmann now jumped on saying that the prior mayoral losses would hurt me. [3049]

Not giving up, I set out my platform to make our community one of the safest in the U.S.; to be tough on crime, bring the highest ethics to the job; and bring equal justice, especially for crime victims. I pledged to work to stop crime before it started, with my two decades of experience as an attorney and public servant. I would join with citizens, law enforcement, and leaders to fight crime, including even Wharton's youth initiatives.[3050] Weirich's platform was basically to prosecute violent criminals with scant mention of ethics, although she tritely pledged that no one would be above or below the law. [3051]

During the campaign, I raised issues regarding ethical lapses by the local district attorney's office in several cases. One involved conduct by Weirich herself with improper comments in closing arguments, and another prosecutor's withholding of evidence that should have been produced to the defense.[3052] The national *CBS TV* show, *48 Hours Mystery,* ran over and over again a story about the Noura Jackson trial for the alleged murder of her mother.[3053] In the televised trial, Weirich shrieked at Jackson to tell the jury where she was on the night of the murder, which violated her constitutional right to remain silent.[3054] However, the show's repeated coverage gave Weirich free press during the heat of the campaign.

Trying to be a kingmaker, Cohen came forth with various endorsements for his election ballot handout, including countywide Democratic nominees Stanton Sr. (the father of the U.S. Attorney for the area), and Cheyenne Johnson.[3055] When asked about an endorsement in the district attorney's race, he mentioned the "experience" of Weirich and then incredibly remarked that he "gave birth" to me in 1990.[3056] He did not endorse me, although I was the Democratic nominee for district attorney and had endorsed him more than once for Congress (as one of the few elected officials to appear at the local election commission *at his personal request* when he filed his petition in 2006). The endorsement would have furthered the administration of justice by helping elect the reform candidate in the wake of the DOJ Report on the county's juvenile justice system.

Thereafter a hit email went out by the Republican party of Shelby County bragging that Cohen and Wharton "have pointedly refused to endorse their Democratic counterpart, Chumney, and offered words of high praise for Amy Weirich and the work she has done. Several other elected Democrats and former Democrat party chairs have publicly endorsed Amy...." But, regardless of the party affiliation of any who endorsed or gave implicit support to Weirich, they all betrayed my platform to uphold the constitutional rights of all, where the current regime had ignored them in some instances.

Perhaps Cohen and the others had forgotten my seventeen years in public office that included enacting criminal laws, my twenty-six years at the time as a practicing trial attorney during which I had earned a partnership at a major Memphis law firm, and my having sat as a special judge in the General Sessions Criminal and Civil Courts at the request of elected judges of both parties. My experience was more broad-ranging than Weirich's, gave me greater insight into the community, and my ethical record was solid.

While I respected Cohen's progressive agenda in many respects as a congressman, in this instance, his tacit support of Weirich was contrary to those values. There was no good reason for him not to endorse me, especially when I had endorsed him for Congress more than once at his request. In fact, he had endorsed Wharton over me in the county mayoral race, but I still endorsed him for Congress after that.

I was called out as not a "team player" in the past, but these Democratic officeholders were given a pass when supporting Republican nominee Weirich. Even if they didn't like me because I wouldn't bow down to them, I had an exemplary record, and the district attorney's office needed reform. The duplicity of some astounded me.

To counter the slight, I promptly announced and was grateful for endorsements by Councilman Myron Lowery, the Memphis Labor Council, AFSCME, and the IBEW.[3057] They all stepped up to the plate to stand for equal justice, when others did not.

Weirich took full advantage of every opportunity for a photo op or press conference due to her incumbent status, including the brand new Multi-Agency Gang Unit partnership announced only a few days before the August 2nd primary Election Day.[3058] She ran television ads featuring her appointment as the first woman to hold the office and about her role as a mother. [3059]While that was admirable, I had broken gender barriers in the state legislature myself. And, I had spent years traveling back and forth to the State Capitol to help protect everyone's kids, including through my own arduous task of birthing child care reform.

Despite being *dissed* by some Democratic leaders and some in the press and media, I was able to run a few TV ads and continued to reach out to voters on social media and campaign at neighborhood events. Every day I spent several early morning hours before my law work posting campaign videos on various Facebook pages, with endorsements by Councilman Myron Lowery and former State Rep. Rufus Jones—two whom to their credit had the integrity to stick with the equal justice platform.

Weirich had a huge fundraising advantage fueled by support from the Republican governor. I did not attack her record with TV ads because she had money to bury me with false and misleading commercials that I did not have the funds to refute. That didn't stop a local Republican party operative from sending out a nasty email comparing me to the perennial candidate Prince Mongo because I had run for higher office more than once. The email did not mention that I came in second or third each time against formidable male opponents. Apparently, she forgot the illustrious career of Abraham Lincoln, who lost several races and was ultimately elected U.S. President. Or how about Mitch Landrieu defeated twice for New Orleans mayor and finally elected in 2010? Or yet to happen at that time, Joe Biden, who in 2020 won his third race for U.S. president, after losing badly in 1988 and 2008. They came back after defeats to win big. No, I was no Mongo—I was a serious, credible candidate.

Before Election Day, Weirich sent a mailer highlighting her *Commercial Appeal* and other endorsements, with Wharton's photo. Wharton, supposedly a Democrat, was quoted saying she is "a woman of character and integrity" who would not let "politics" exist in the D.A.'s office and that he knew her and trusted "her to make the right decisions for Memphis and Shelby County." That sounded like an endorsement to me. Later Weirich would use her position to endorse an arch-conservative Republican gubernatorial candidate, Diane Black, contrary to Wharton's promise of her non-politicizing the office.[3060]

In fact, Wharton's duplicity in aiding Weirich, as well as his support of other Republicans over the years, didn't cost him. He received an award from the board of directors of the Democratic Municipal Officials at the Democratic National Convention in 2012. [3061] One writer to the *Memphis Flyer* expressed his view of the award as "This must be the same group that picks the candidates for 'Hell's Kitchen," apparently alluding to the New York City neighborhood that was historically known for high crime and poor living conditions, and the popular cooking television show.[3062]

Weirich also sent a mailer to Democratic voters featuring photos of Jim Strickland asking voters to join him "in voting to keep Amy Weirich as our DA." On the mailer, Strickland identified himself as a city councilman and *former Chair of the Shelby County Democratic Party*. Also, on the mailer was Shea Flinn's photo, endorsing Weirich with his titles identified as a city councilman and *former Democratic State Senator*. The unauthorized use of the party label to endorse Weirich did more than just betray those Democrats who had voted for these men for those positions. The betrayal was also of the equal justice principles they claimed to support.

After the defections by them and others to Weirich, I was concerned. Now, as Election Day neared, I called one of the Pentecostal pastors to tell him what was happening. He suggested lunch with Diane, an evangelist from one of the churches. When we met up at Whole Foods, she predicted that

I would win in the final count. Whether that was metaphorically or literally remained to be seen.

4

Early voting brought claims of thousands of early voters being given the wrong ballot. The editor of the *Memphis Flyer* deemed this to "undermine the very integrity of the electoral system." [3063] The newspaper confirmed reports that several thousand voters had been given the wrong ballot to date.[3064] As a result, the election was a debacle.

The Tennessee Secretary of State Tre Hargett wrote the Tennessee Comptroller of the Treasury on July 26, 2012, that "These recent issues are just the latest in a series of errors in the Shelby County [Memphis area] Election Commission stretching back at least a decade. Nearly every election cycle in the county in recent memory has been plagued by a myriad of errors and complaints of wrongdoing." Hargett stated that these "indicate a troubling pattern of errors that cannot go unnoticed. These errors have eroded public confidence in the Shelby County Election Commission."

Election Day results came in with reports that Weirich had won with about 65% of the vote to my 35%. [3065] Somehow, Democratic candidates Ed Stanton Sr. and Cheyanne Johnson were able to narrowly win their respective county-wide elections by similar margins of error in their general elections, but I did not. This statistical result, along with election irregularities, raised questions in my mind, despite the fundraising disparity and Democratic leader defectors in my race.

The *Commercial Appeal's* Mike Lollar reported that Weirich benefited from the "strong support from some of the most high-profile Democrats in the city" who were "heavy-weights." [3066] Obviously, they would not have ganged up on me, and Weirich would not have spent over $212,000 on the campaign if I had not been within reach of winning. The reporter called me "gracious in defeat."[3067]

I issued a statement that "We ran a positive campaign based upon a platform of bringing equal justice and the highest ethics to the job. I am so thankful for all of those who stood with us in that effort. While there were overwhelming odds against us in being outspent ten to one, we made a strong showing. I am returning to the practice of law and serving my clients and wish Amy Weirich the very best in her position as district attorney."

Marcus Pohlmann, Rhodes college professor, was kind enough to comment now that I have a "kind of earthy, every-person" approach as a supporter "of the little person." [3068] The newspaper also noted Weirich's advantage with press conferences about "high profile arrests leading up to the election" and raising over a quarter of a million dollars. [3069] Also, a factor cited in the result was the "landslide approval" by the six suburban cities of referendums establishing their own school districts, all of which had spurred huge Republican suburban turnout. [3070] But, I had other questions about the results as well.

On election night, I watched the televised returns come in with my family, friends, and supporters. What troubled me was the statistical correlation between the early vote and Election Day numbers in my race and that of the assessor and general sessions court clerk candidates. However, I chatted with my team and thanked them for their loyal support. None of the television news crews stopped by, but Jackson Baker with the *Memphis Flyer* did. And, he managed to take a shot at writing my political obituary in his next column.

Jackson Baker had to acknowledge in the *Memphis Flyer* that I was in "good cheer." Yet, he wrote that "It was hard not to feel Chumney's pain – and that of her ever supportive parents – after a one-sided loss, the fourth in succession, that all three of them knew would mean the end of her political ambitions." [3071] Yet, it wasn't the fourth in succession, only the third loss, and having won sixteen elections out of twenty times on the ballot from 1990 through 2012. In fact, the loss in 2007 was second place as Memphis Mayor coming within seven points of defeating Herenton, a sixteen-year incumbent. The other was to Wharton in 2009, who was a seven-year incumbent county mayor. Before those elections, I had won the city council race in 2003 against better-funded opponents. I had informed Baker of this in an email before Election Day. Yet, for some reason, he disregarded it and misquoted me as saying that I would never run for public office again. [3072] While I did not know if I would or not, I certainly wouldn't rule a future candidacy out.

In fact, I had sent Baker a courteous note thanking him for stopping by on election night and stating my admiration for his way with words and ability to express himself as a journalist. I was taken aback the next day when he posted the misinformation about whether I would ever run for office again. We went back and forth that day with several emails asking him to correct the error and reforwarding my formal statement, which expressed no such sentiments.

He refused to run a "correction" but said he would note my position in the next print edition, and ultimately did two weeks later. [3073]However, the article reiterated the entire prior story.[3074]

Baker did mention the "conspicuous failure of certain Democrats to support" me, as well as those who endorsed Weirich. [3075] Dragging my sweet parents into it, he talked about how my father accepted the loss, while my mother was "less forgiving" due to the media bias, turncoat Democrats, and large financial donations to Weirich. [3076] But, if his prior professed friendship (which he expressed in the 2009 back-track from the flying saucer story) was genuine, I did not appreciate Baker trying to close the door on a possible future Chumney run.

With the election over, now my platform to not only put the bad guys away but also to stop the revolving door for youth in our county's criminal justice system would not be realized. The "progressive" *Memphis Flyer* missed a chance to write about that. With Weirich's election, the status quo was once again preserved.

Apart from trying to get the record straight with Baker, I wondered if there had been more election "glitches" after having watched the election returns and learning thousands of voters received the wrong ballot. On election night and the next morning, I visited several key precincts to review poll tapes posted on the outside doors as required by state law.

Only a few days after election night, I went with State Rep. Mike Kernell (who had lost his Democratic state legislative primary after thirty-seven years in that position) and a supporter of his who was given the wrong ballot to meet with FBI agents, report election irregularities, and request an investigation. We provided statements from voters who were given the wrong ballots and who had tried to vote for me, and Weirich's name popped up instead. One man reported that his wife, who was living at and registered at the same home, was given a congressional ballot for a different district.

The next day, I wrote the DOJ Public Integrity Section in Washington, D.C., asking for an investigation and disclosed an irregularity never made public. On the August 2012 Election eve, 132 poll workers drove to the east election commission offices to be trained and pick up microchips for insertion in electronic poll books. This voided any chain of custody to ensure that the voter data was not compromised.

The state election coordinator told me that he did not rule out that the Shelby County Election Commission's continued problems might be intentional. I asked for an investigation and told him of the election results, which never varied more than one or two points on the TV news reports the entire night regardless of the percentage of polls reporting or of the areas reporting. He assured me that the Tennessee comptroller would do a thorough performance audit.

In December, news was reported that the FBI was investigating unnamed irregularities at the Shelby County Election Commission. [3077] Accordingly, the Shelby County Commission adopted a bipartisan no-confidence resolution regarding the Administrator Richard Holden. [3078] In the end, it was proven that more than 3,000 wrong ballots were issued in the August 2nd elections, as uncovered by local Democratic activists Dr. Joseph Weinberg and Steve Ross, and resulting in a six-month probation for the election administrator. [3079]

Although my miracle did not materialize for this election, I decided to take a closer look at the local election process.

37

On the Mountaintop

1

"Memphis is a dream killer," said the deep male voice when I picked up the phone one Saturday morning. He identified himself as Doug from inner-city Memphis. Although trying to keep a stiff upper lip, I found myself expressing my feelings with Doug—a man I did not know.

"Carol, please don't give up. Please continue to help us. We need you."

Doug was disappointed that some local male Democratic party leaders did not support me as the Democratic nominee for district attorney. How come we "little people" vote the party line, and the mayor and congressman don't have to, he asks?

As we spoke, I thought back to the words of the evangelist Diane Norwood when we met just before the election, "Carol, remember it's about your purpose—not the position." Perplexed, I had pushed forward with the district attorney election.

After my defeat in the race, I realized they were right. Doug and Diane each had brought me back to my purpose in seeking public office in the first place. I still should try to help the people regardless of the announced election results—and get to the truth.

Doug told me that we had met before—once at the Malco movie theater near my home, where I went by myself on occasion to unwind. Another time at the National Civil Rights Museum, where he remembered me confidently joking as a candidate about picking out the drapes for the mayor's office. In my years in public life, I have attended many events, marches, and celebrations at the museum. And I do recall talking with a tall African American man in 2008 who may have been Doug.

We were standing in the rain facing the famous balcony where Dr. King was killed. The man shared his umbrella and commented that it was the 40th year after the tragic death of Dr. Martin Luther King. We were, in a sense, on hallowed ground and at a significant time in history. That man in the rain encouraged and inspired me to press forward.

After the 2012 D.A. election loss, I had returned to full-time private law practice. After seventeen years of successful public service, I was baffled that there appeared to be no opportunities for me to contribute even more in higher office. Being female, progressive, and "nobody's shoeshine girl" (as called by the press in 1991) appeared to be prohibitive to serving in certain public offices in Memphis. This was another time for soul searching on my part, trying to figure out why God put the dream in my heart to serve the people in public office, and pastors had anointed me four different times, but the doors to move up did not open.

On one occasion, I pulled through a church's public prayer drive-through. A middle-aged African American woman asked me what to pray about. I told her a shortlist of requests, including that God would open the way for my promotion to higher office. When she prayed holding my hand, she left that request off. I brought it to her attention. She *paused* – and instead of adding it to her prayer, abruptly responded, "he heard it." I guess she wasn't a fan!

At lunch one day with a friend from college, we discussed racial politics in Memphis. He explained to me that Memphis is all about white and black. Then, in analyzing the 2007 city mayoral election, he referenced my abstention vote on Sammons's Joseph Lee resolution as a factor in Herenton's reelection. My friend, who is African American, explained that the white voters had thought I was "white" due to my skin color, but then my Lee vote reminded them I am really "black."

2

On occasion, I was interviewed by the press or media about various issues. For example, in June 2013, the state comptroller reported that Memphis was in serious financial trouble.[3080] The 1.46 billion dollar debt due to the past scoop and toss refinancing and continued funding of large development projects had led to a financial crisis. [3081] Councilman Strickland and Memphis Mayor Wharton took shots at each other in the press, with Wharton pointing out that the councilman had quietly voted against the refinancing without leading "any sustained opposition."[3082]I reminded my social media friends of my resolution as a councilmember in 2006 for an audit of the city's books and my objection to using debt service funds to pay operating expenses.

As the days wore on, I still felt stymied, unable to use my years of political experience for the public good due to the good ole boy network in my hometown. Some of my time was now devoted to researching and writing this book. When Al Gore came through town for his own book signing, it was nice to get a hug. I told him about this book in progress and the barriers for women in the political arena. I also wished him well on his post-election journey after his own problems with the electoral voting system.

Maybe it was time for me to contribute in a different way. Some friends had previously invited me to join their Methodist church's annual mission trip to Kenya, which at the time I had not seriously considered. Somehow that resonated with me now. Even though attending another church, I decided to participate in their July 2013 trip.

Part of the required process was to raise money for the projects we would do for the children and families in Kenya. I was worried about raising enough money but sent out letters to about 100 people who had been campaign supporters over the years. Ultimately, as a tribute to the power of God, just enough money came in to meet the trip requirements, along with my own contribution.

God also inspired me with a fundraising idea for a prayer breakfast. It would be an interdenominational event, racially diverse, with traditional Kenyan fare for the buffet and music. Monies for the event would be raised primarily with ad sales for a program book. The event's centerpiece would be displaying artwork by children in Memphis to be hand delivered by the mission team to children at the E.C. Clark Pre-school in Maua, Kenya. The group would then bring back artwork from the children in Maua, Kenya, to share with the children in Memphis. Ed Clark suggested that the children at Coleman Avenue Elementary School participate, where the church members were volunteer tutors.

The event went well with the hard work of the mission team. We raised over $5,000 for the projects we did on the journey. Several black and white pastors participated. Some were my friends from my experiences worshipping at their various congregations over the years. They included pastors from Methodist, Baptist, Church of Christ, and Pentecostal churches.

The Memphis children's artwork was precious, with color crayoned depictions of what they wanted to be when they grew up — police officers, teachers, pilots, and even an FBI agent. The breakfast was timed to occur during the same week as the Africa in April annual celebration in the city, which featured events in recognition of a selected country in Africa. Several political leaders attended, and the prayer breakfast was featured in local media and the press.

Taking the trip was challenging since I am a self-employed attorney. Only a week before the trip, I won a jury trial case for a client as her sole attorney—which was quite an undertaking with five attorneys on the other side. After that, I arranged for my friend and attorney, Mike Gatlin, to take any calls to my law office while I was out of town. However, one client, unaware of the difference in time-zones, still called me at 3 am one morning in Kenya.

Our work on the trip included volunteering at the Maua Methodist Hospital, and visiting the E.C. Clark pre-school. Some of us spent a day painting a hospital apartment that would be used by a resident doctor. We also visited the patients, including a young mother whose newborn child had suffered severe burns when a lantern was knocked over. An anonymous good Samaritan later provided funds for the baby to travel to the U.S. for surgery.

On a mountaintop, the team also worked to hammer together a small one-room house, that would be the new home for a single mother, daughter, and son. Getting up and down the mountain was tough for me due to a recent knee injury. We had to scale a narrow dirt path and cross a wooden footbridge over a river. At one point, I stumbled, and my oranges bought earlier rolled down the mountainside.

Children watched from a perch above as we worked to build the house. Other children watched us from the surrounding forest. We took breaks and sang songs with the children. One team member played "London Bridge is Falling Down" with the group of kids, which they loved even though they knew little English.

Although the weather was cool, I was worried about sunburn due to the high elevation on top of the mountain and replenished my sunscreen. Unfortunately, some got in my eyes. I was concerned that it was sun damage instead, since we were near the equator, and sat down to wipe my eyes. A large rooster walked right up beside me. But, in the narrow area where we were working, it was the best place to sit down without risking falling down the mountain. One young girl, who did not respond to our earlier questions, watched. Now, she surprised me by asking in English if I was ok. I told her, "yes," and then got up and continued working.

We returned to the mountain a few days later for the house dedication ceremony. The mountain inhabitants greeted us at the bottom singing and chanting to us on the way up to the top in their own language. There was shouting and clapping. At the top of the mountain, a preacher from the hospital blessed the new house. Stanley Gitari, the communications officer from the hospital, spoke about how vital the new home was for the family.

The mother was present, with her son, and the same young girl who had asked me if I was ok. That was her daughter, who would also live in the house. Since her mother did not speak English, the young girl had a turn to speak. She thanked God and then embarrassed at the large crowd giving her our full attention, turned and shyly ducked her head. We all laughed and clapped to encourage her.

One older woman, a mountain inhabitant, grabbed my arm and helped me get down the mountain. I might not have made it without her help. She told some of the other women when we got to the bottom that I was her friend. It was a powerful experience altogether.

At the E.C. Clark pre-school on another day, we played with the children. For the first time, I found out that Ed Clark, one of the mission team members, had provided funds to help keep the school open.

Because of the many people who contributed to our prayer breakfast, made donations, and participated in other fundraising projects, we now were able to add to Clark's support by sponsoring a health clinic in the outback of Maua. We drove on an extremely bumpy dirt road to an empty school building in the countryside. A doctor and resident from the hospital came, as well as our mission team medical members. People were lined up outside the small school when we arrived. Transportation to town and the hospital was difficult due to the lack of paved roads or public transport. Most people walked to get places and even to fetch the day's water or drove motorcycles.

The trip reminded me of so many things we often take for granted in America, such as the health care system and even medical records. One boy came to the clinic with a serious cut on his knee, which might not have received medical care without our one-day clinic. Another elderly gap-toothed woman brought in her own medical records, which were notations on a scrap of paper. She was so happy to get some basic treatment and medicine from the doctor.

Back in the town, we visited a tiny beauty shop and small goods huts to learn how the youth are given nonprofit seed money to start their own businesses. At a regular meeting of a youth group, they told us how they helped teach each other skills. One member of our team took Polaroid photographs of the youth as gifts. From their expressions, it was evident that they treasured the images due to the lack of electronic equipment in their community, having few cell phones, cameras, and limited access to the internet.

The next part of our journey was to take a youth group to Meru, Kenya, for training in better farming techniques. Many of the youth had responsibilities to provide for their younger siblings due to the AIDs epidemic that took many parents' lives. They were very excited about the trip, although rather shy at first.

In Meru, we stayed at the training facility in small houses. We spent time with the youth, played volleyball and games, and did projects to help the facility during the time they were in class. Our work included preparing the food to eat and even painting a pigsty.

On Sunday, we walked to a church to worship in the small town nearby called Kagaa. Thinking back to my first trip to Japan, I wondered what were the odds that in my life, I would visit two places in the world called Kagaa—one in Kaga, Japan, and the other in Kenya?

One morning, Mount Kenya was visible in the distance out front of the training facility. I had hoped for a mountaintop experience on the trip. Even though we did build a house on a mountaintop in Maua and the celebration was inspiring, I still desired a personal spiritual mountaintop experience. But the group was not scheduled to go to Mount Kenya. The mountain beckoned me, but I could not break the team's rules and slip away. On a call to a friend in the United States, I told him about wanting the mountaintop experience, but we were not going to Mount Kenya. My friend reminded me that God can do anything.

Only a day or so later, we visited Meru University. After the presentations, our host decided to find us a place to sit down on the ground and eat the sack lunches we had brought with us. She took us to an urban park called the Olive Garden. Having eaten my lunch in the car, I walked around to see what was in the park.

There were various mediation paths, one called Mount Sinai. I walked up the hill for that mediation path. At the top were a chair and a plaque. On the plaque was the Bible verse, "Forget the past things... see am doing a new thing... making a way in wastelands." Isaiah 43:18. This moment was when

I knew once and for all the true power of God. Not only did He give me a mountaintop experience, but He also took me to the top of Mount Sinai, albeit in Kenya, not Egypt. And He gave me a special message and hope for the future.

Back at the training center, we sang, prayed, and shared words of gratitude with the youth who were excited for their graduation from the training program. They were overjoyed at having the learning and social experience at the facility. The next morning, we bid them farewell as they boarded their bus back home. They would go back and teach many other youths what they had learned.

Our next stop was Sweetwaters Serena Camp for a safari, which was paid for by our own personal funds. We saw elephants, giraffes, rhino, all kinds of birds, and moose, among other animals in the wild. The large tents where we stayed were on the other side of an electric fence in front of a pond, and the animals came and drank water only yards away. One afternoon while exploring, we saw cheetahs. One of the safari buses got stuck. The guys nervously got out of the bus to push it out of the hole and were fortunate that the animals didn't make a run for them!

Our last stop was back in Nairobi, where we had a celebratory dinner at the Tamambo Karen Blixen restaurant, which had been a farmhouse. The property was formerly owned by Danish author Baroness Karen von Blixen in the early 1900s. Her memoir about her experiences in Kenya, "*Out of Africa*,"[3083] became a feature film.[3084] When I had watched the movie featuring Robert Redford and Meryl Streep years before the mission trip, I never thought I would actually see Kenya. What a tremendous experience!

While in Kenya, we were careful to adhere to safety protocols. Shortly after our return, we were surprised to hear that much of the Nairobi airport we had flown into and out of had burned down.[3085] Also, it was a shock only a few months later, when more than sixty foreigners were tragically massacred in a Nairobi mall due to their faith.[3086] Even a year later, the Peace Corps ceased its program in Kenya due to dozens of terror attacks during the past two years.[3087] The U.S. embassy was fortified with armed Marines on the roof.[3088] We were fortunate to have returned safely.

Inspired by my mountaintop experience, I began work to create a documentary with musician Richard Hervey about the art exchange between the children in Kenya and Memphis. Maybe this was another way I could make a difference in my capacity as a private citizen.

3

Although not in the mayor's office to bring needed reforms, there were other ways for me to prompt change at City Hall. After my trip, I prepared for a federal court trial in September against the City of Memphis. My client was a woman appointed the public records coordinator for the city by Mayor Herenton in 2007. Her appointment continued after Mayor A C Wharton was sworn in as Memphis mayor in 2009. His first order of business was to issue a proclamation requiring more transparency in government, including open records' requests.[3089] My client's job was to process those requests.

At issue in the lawsuit was why she was terminated after she submitted her own open records requests. Among other things, she sought records related to her boss, City Attorney Herman Morris. Herman Morris had been appointed by Wharton and approved by the city council as city attorney in the fall of 2009. So, Morris was one of the defendants in the lawsuit since he had initiated her termination. While he was respected as an attorney, in this matter his judgment was justifiably challenged.

My client, Bridgett Handy Clay, had complained to Morris early on about favoritism in the office and other problems and disparities.[3090] Part of her complaint was that some employees were not monitored for timekeeping, while the office manager did monitor others.[3091] Ultimately, she submitted her own open records requests, asking for time and leave records for all city attorney's office employees for the past year, including those of her boss Morris.[3092] Subsequently, Morris personally drafted Handy Clay's termination letter, which Wharton approved the next morning.[3093]

When he first was appointed city attorney, Morris did not yet qualify for vacation time. [3094]But, the documents and deposition testimony showed that he was paid by the city when he traveled on personal business in Israel for a week, on another trip to Italy for a week, for several other days at corporate board meetings not related to city business, and even a day to give his son a tour of a college.[3095] Emails sent to the CAO indicated he would take leave or that if allowed, he would "true-up" at the end of the year by selling vacation time (if and when it accrued.)[3096] While some later vacation and bonus days were credited by the time of his deposition, they did not equal the number of days taken off the job for which he was paid.[3097] He had a deer caught in headlights look on his face in his deposition when confronted with the evidence.

In their depositions, Wharton and CAO George Little did not confirm that they expressly approved Morris's plan to later "true-up" the advance in his paid time. [3098] Morris was paid, but Little only approved uncompensated leave for many of the dates in question.[3099] However, another new hire did not fare as well when she asked Morris to approve advance vacation leave for a doctor's appointment.[3100] She was referred to human resources, and her pay was docked.[3101]

The lawsuit initially had several claims. After the U.S. Sixth Circuit Court of Appeals overturned an order dismissing the case, in the end, a single free speech retaliation claim remained.[3102] The Court found that Handy Clay alleged sufficient facts to justify an inference that she spoke on city policy absence, leave and pay violations as a concerned citizen "addressing an issue of public corruption." Because Handy Clay's job duties did not include reporting on government corruption or misuse of public funds, the Sixth Circuit found that her speech "alleging corruption and mismanagement by public employees must be construed at this stage of the litigation as speech on a matter of public concern."[3103] It reversed the dismissal and remanded back to the district court for further action.[3104]

I had taken several deposition transcripts from the case to Kenya to review in my spare time at night since a brief was due on a motion for summary judgment shortly after my return. I hoped the mission trip spiritual experience would be to our benefit in the case. Handy Clay was a woman of faith and brave to take on the system. Also, I brought back a grass-skirted angel figurine and told my client that it was our angel for the case.

After we filed our briefs in 2013, the federal district court decided that Handy Clay's case could proceed upon her protected complaints about "violations of city policies related to absences, leave, and pay." [3105] It found her complaint of "misuse of city time" to be protected activity. [3106] The Judge further held that Handy Clay's filing of open records requests constituted a protected speech activity under her *First Amendment* retaliation claim.[3107] The defendants that remained in the case were the City of Memphis and Morris in his individual capacity.[3108] Thereafter, the city settled the lawsuit. It was a sweet victory, indeed!

In 2015, Wharton asked Mike Carpenter, a former city-appointed official, to study the city's open records policy due to citizen complaints about delayed responses. [3109] One animal rights activist who had submitted open records requests was reported to say that Wharton had known about the problems for years and was only taking action that year because he was up for reelection.[3110] Even the *Commercial Appeal* editors opined that the city had an "abysmal record" on the timely response to open records based upon the newspaper's own request experiences.[3111] Certainly, after the Handy Clay lawsuit in 2013, the city should have fixed the problems.

My law work during this time also involved submitting my own open records requests. Dr. Joseph Weinberg (a retired physician), Mike Kernell, and I began meeting to develop a plan of action. In November 2013, we submitted our first open records requests to the Shelby County Election Commission. We hoped to find out why there were so many election night "glitches."

And my law practice had expanded to include representing indigent children and parents in the juvenile courts. While I thought knocking on thousands of doors as a candidate over the years in economically diverse neighborhoods had given me insight into the challenges of the poor, this legal work opened my eyes to a greater degree. I visited families in homes, apartments, schools, and daycares all over the county, learning first hand of the tragedies of drug use, neglect, abandonment, and abuse.

The work also enabled me to have the joy of seeing babies and young children loved and protected by relatives and foster parents, who stepped up to help in times of crisis. I often recall the look in the teenage boy's eyes in Kenya who was so impressed that we had a foster care system in the U.S. And, I will never forget one young girl in Memphis who will never walk or talk. However, she laughed in glee at school whenever a young disabled boy danced for her after making the only movement she could, by swinging her arm to hit a toy drum. It was a year of coming home to what is really important in life.

38

Truths and Injustices

1

2014 was kicked off with another prayer breakfast by Myron Lowery. He graciously sat me at the same table with Memphis Mayor Wharton and Shelby County Mayor Luttrell in the packed ballroom. Somehow, I was worthy of always being seated at the mayors' table but never given a chance actually to be the mayor.

In his remarks, Wharton pledged to try harder to resolve disputes with the city council over pension reform.[3112] Congressman Cohen also called for Election Administrator Richard Holden's removal to restore faith in the election process. [3113] A new audit showed a failure to process some voter registration applications over a nine-month period, among other irregularities. [3114]

The city council followed the example of the county commission, with its own vote of no confidence in Holden.[3115] The *Commercial Appeal* editorialized that the Shelby County Election Commission "bungled" the 2012 general election with an audit uncovering additional problems.[3116] The editors even went so far as to say that Holden "should have been fired months ago," but was not due to partisan politics.[3117] The editors' acknowledgment of the serious irregularities was welcome, but a full investigation was also needed.

Baker, with the *Memphis Flyer*, compared the voting machines to slot machines, calling the past twenty-five years of election commission snafus a "fact of life."[3118] The continued reports of vote-flipping did make one wonder if the "house" was rigged. Steve Mulroy, county commissioner and law professor, called for replacing the county's electronic voting machines with an "optical scan" voting system with a paper trail of the votes cast. [3119] Mulroy reasoned that the lines would be shorter, the results better ensured as accurate, and the funds were available by the state from the federal "Help America Vote Act." [3120] While the local election commission officials talked about getting optical scan voting machines in time for the 2014 elections with available federal funds, it didn't happen.[3121] However, I, Dr. Weinberg, and Mike Kernell, pressed forward with open records requests to the election commission to search for the truth about the disenfranchisement of many voters.

2

In addition to calls for the election administrator to resign, D.A. Weirich was also under fire when the Tennessee Supreme Court censured a top prosecutor in her office for failing to reveal evidence in a death penalty case. [3122] The *Commercial Appeal* editorialized that he had "tainted the credibility of the District Attorney General's office" and called on Weirich to remove her office from the case. [3123] It was a logical and well-justified request.

The *Memphis Flyer*'s Toby Sells wrote that some insiders believed the prosecutor's reprimand "has shaken faith in Weirich's leadership," as well as the office and the county's justice system.[3124] But, Weirich defended the top prosecutor, issuing a statement that the court had ordered a new trial for the accused solely because the defendant's attorneys were ineffective as opposed to any actions or inactions by the district attorney's office.[3125] She further went so far as to praise the prosecutor for his dedication and work performance. [3126] There was no announced effort to address the cause of the censure so as to avoid reoccurrences in other cases.

The *Commercial Appeal* editors promptly called her out for overlooking the fact that the censured prosecutor had "cheated," where "honesty, integrity and a strict adherence to the rules of court procedures are sacred." [3127] And Toby Sells in the *Memphis Flyer* wondered why Weirich would not answer why, as his boss, she had not reprimanded him.[3128] Soon, the pattern of skirting the rules by some in the office would become even more apparent.

Some judges and attorneys were said to privately disagree with the prosecutor and Weirich's claim that the failure to produce the statement was merely an oversight. [3129] Bowing to pressure, Weirich finally called a press conference and announced that she was removing her office from the case and asking for the appointment of a special prosecutor.[3130] The administration of justice required no less.

3

In another shocking revelation, a Jane Doe filed a class action lawsuit alleging that thousands of rape victim DNA kits had not been tested in Memphis over the past twenty-five years or more. [3131] The failure to take sexual assault seriously was a slap in the face to the victims who had been brave enough to undergo the kit collection process after a traumatic experience of rape.

The fact that over 12,000 rape victim kits had never been tested for DNA evidence caused public outrage. [3132] Weirich reported that her office was "trying to piece together its participation" as to why only half a million of a 3.4 million dollar 2003 federal grant was utilized for testing but claimed they could not determine "whether anyone dropped the ball." [3133] Of course, no one wanted to take responsibility for such an omission, but they owed the victims no less.

Rape victims spoke out. They decried that for years they had been ignored or treated differently than other victims. [3134] One survivor, raped at age sixteen, publicly stated that her rape kit was not tested for nine years during which time the same rapist raped other women. [3135] She only found out that her kit had not been tested after news of an attacker who used a mask and similar tactics on another victim. [3136] The failure to test the kits left the victims without protection or justice and the public at risk for more attacks.

National experts now admitted the need to test and upload DNA evidence as paramount to catch and stop serial rapists. [3137] More than one lawsuit was filed against local governments and officials by victims, naming as parties, among others, the former police director, past district attorney, the current MPD chief, and incumbent District Attorney Amy Weirich. [3138]

From more open records requests, I had learned that the district attorney had to sign off on each rape kit for it to be DNA tested. Weirich, who first took office in 2011, appeared to push the blame onto the Memphis police, claiming that her office had signed off on every police request to test rape kits. [3139] As the *Commercial Appeal* editorialized, it was not disclosed who in the police department decided not to submit the kits for testing, or "who in the Shelby County District Attorney General's Office acquiesced...." [3140] They also criticized the law enforcement officials' "blame-the-victim" mentality as "shameful," but added that Police Director Tony Armstrong had quickly moved to begin testing when the backlog was brought to his attention. [3141]

After a statewide count, it was determined that Memphis's untested rape kits were 77% of the entire state backlog. [3142] The huge Memphis backlog evidenced the lack of respect for the victims by those in the criminal justice system who had either failed to act or looked the other way. It was a gross injustice!

At a press conference, Memphis Mayor Wharton admitted that the failure to test the rape kits was a "systemic failure" of justice. [3143] Even if it was a systematic failure of justice—the system is composed of people. If responsibility were never determined, it might happen again.

Although other cities now identified large quantities of untested rape kits (nationally estimated at 400,000), Memphis had the largest backlog in the entire country. [3144] While the city administration promptly pledged to fund the testing of the kits, some asked whether the problem would reoccur with the same people in charge. [3145] Wharton predicted that it would take five years and six and a half million dollars to get the backlog of rape kits tested, while statutes of limitations to bring charges continued to expire in the meantime.[3146]

After testing the massive number of backlogged kits slowly began, fourteen indictments came down, with ninety-one investigations open just two years later. [3147]Some cases were barred by the statute of limitations despite a hastily passed state law to lengthen it in the spring of 2014. [3148] City officials were so ashamed that they built a special climate-controlled storage room for the kits.

In 2018, according to Deborah Clubb, Executive Director for the Memphis Women's Council, nearly 700 cases were being pursued by the Memphis police from the testing of the backlogged rape kits, with 312 requested indictments.[3149] Clubb reported in the *Commercial Appeal* that fifty-one persons were implicated in multiple rape cases, and there had been fifty-two guilty pleas or verdicts, with more kits in the pipeline to be tested. [3150]One man pled guilty in 2018 for rapes in 2000 and 2002 of three different women when the rape kits were not tested until after the backlog discovery. [3151] Another was convicted in 2018 for a rape in 2000 after the DNA was finally tested.[3152] The negligence of those who did not process the kits and of the local officials who did not require appropriate procedures to flag the failure quickly was a travesty.

Despite the new aggressive efforts, the questions lingered as to why the kits were not tested in a timely manner.[3153] In 2021, proposed class action lawsuits against the City of Memphis were still being litigated in state and federal courts, with the county government also a defendant in the state court.[3154] The injustice of ignoring the thousands of victims' evidence and jeopardizing other citizens due to the failure to act was inexcusable.

4

In early 2014 shortly after the rape-kit backlog was exposed, the local county Democratic Party annual banquet featured a panel of female elected officials. Special guest U.S. Rep. Barbara Lee (D-Calif.) gave the keynote address. [3155] After the panel discussion, questions were allowed from the audience. To continue to advocate for the equal administration of justice, I stood from the floor and called out the male leaders who gave direct or tacit support of Amy Weirich. I had been the candidate for equal justice. Now, we knew that thousands of rape kits had never been tested while she was D.A. and during the prior administration. Baker, with the *Memphis Flyer,* found my remarks "jarring and curiously rousing."[3156] I was only speaking the truth.

Some of those male party leaders ran on the Democratic platform of equal justice or served as Democratic Party officials, and then used those Democratic credentials to support Republican Weirich despite my equal justice platform. In my view, the truth was that regardless of the party of the candidates, the defections by these leaders had harmed the cause for equal justice reform for youth and rape victims by keeping in office the status quo district attorney. [3157] Frankly, their lack of support for me was also an injustice given my long record of public service as a reformer.

I also pointed out the need for more support for female candidates in the Democratic party. Republican women at that time had made greater gains. Sara Palin had been nominated for vice-president. Beth Harwell was elected the first female Tennessee House Speaker. Weirich was elected as Shelby County D.A. Joyce Avery had served briefly as interim county mayor when Wharton resigned to become Memphis mayor.

My remarks ended on a positive note encouraging the "team" to "stick together."[3158] Wharton and Cohen, at the front, shuffled nervously looking for the nearest exit, which was way in the back of the large banquet room.

I continued my theme of equal justice, equality, and unity at the next local party meeting. To bring the point home, I did a show and tell with the Weirich campaign literature featuring endorsements by Strickland and Shea Flinn and her mailer with Wharton's words of support.

The issue was featured in the *Tri-State Defender*, the historic African American-focused newspaper. [3159] My ardent equal justice reform campaign platform in the D.A.'s race was undermined when some of the Democratic leaders endorsed or "cozied up" for "photo-ops" with the candidate who made excuses and downplayed the need for reforms. [3160]

Cohen, who has a long and accomplished public service record, claimed he had never endorsed Weirich (although he had referenced her as more experienced at a press conference that gave implicit support). [3161] He and I had spent years working on legislation together in the state legislature. I wish he had stepped up this time if not based upon past friendship, but to enable local reforms in the criminal justice system.

Strickland was quoted as saying that being the party nominee did not mean the person was "qualified" to be the district attorney, apparently a jab at me although he had supported me for state representative previously.[3162] Yet, Strickland previously had no qualms about supporting Republican and former county commissioner Bill Gibbons for D.A., who had been a private attorney, like me, before his appointment to an unexpired term.

Obviously, I had been disappointed with the actions of these leaders who knew beforehand the cost to equal justice by their direct or tacit support of my opponent. And the missed opportunity to bring reform was even more apparent after the election. For example, Weirich was in the news again later that year when the Tennessee Supreme Court rendered an opinion in the Noura Jackson case that the prosecutor had made inappropriate statements in closing argument.[3163] During the jury trial, Weirich had asked the accused to "just tell us where you were" on the night of her mother's murder.[3164] Jackson's defense attorney, Valerie Corder, objected on the grounds that the statement violated her client's *Fifth Amendment* right not to testify or to have her silence used against her in the trial.[3165]

The Court, referring to three other cases, noted a pattern, where appellate courts had criticized Weirich for inappropriate arguments to the jury.[3166] The Court further rebuked the prosecutors on the case for failing to turn over evidence that could have been used to impeach one of the state's key witnesses.[3167] They found this to be a violation of Jackson's constitutional rights and material because the state's case was based upon circumstantial evidence.[3168] With the Noura Jackson decision overturned, Weirich eventually asked to be removed from the case after defense attorneys sought to have the entire Shelby County district attorney's office disqualified for the new trial.[3169]

Only two months later, Weirich was again in the news in another case. There were allegations by attorneys of a defendant convicted of second-degree murder that the prosecutor, at the direction of Weirich, intentionally withheld a sealed envelope of evidence during a 2005 trial. [3170] Weirich had been a prosecutor on the case. The post-conviction prosecutor and defense attorney who discovered the envelope said it bore a sticky note with Weirich's initials and was marked to the effect that it not be produced to the defense attorneys.[3171] The prosecutor did not allow the defense attorney to open the envelope at that time, wanting first to ask permission from his superiors. [3172] He never unsealed it to review the contents. [3173] That prosecutor was later reassigned to another unit. [3174]

After that, when he was asked about it and reviewed the file, there was now a note on a different envelope in the file saying, "I am NOT giving these items in discovery 8-22-05 APW," and then below it "12-6-05 (Investigator Jencks' STMTS) of witnesses who testified were turned over at the appropriate time." [3175] The change in notes raised questions.

In another case involving two other Shelby County prosecutors, the Tennessee Court of Appeals overturned the verdict because the jury was told about an uncharged rape allegation against the defendant and a prosecutor improperly made a prediction as to the consequences of the jury's verdict. [3176] The appellate court wrote that one prosecutor appeared to have the intent to "inflame the passions and prejudices of the jury." [3177] The "win at all costs" philosophy of some in the local D.A.'s office was duly noted by local reporter Les Smith as not only being contrary to justice but costing the taxpayers money for the many retrials after the reversal of the convictions on appeal.[3178]

Later, in 2016 Weirich was in the hot seat again when the Tennessee Board of Professional Responsibility filed charges for her and another prosecutor's censure by the Tennessee Supreme Court related to the overturned Noura Jackson case.[3179] A family friend of Jackson had filed the complaint with the board, arguing that her constitutional right not to testify against herself had been violated.[3180] The other prosecutor's failure to provide a piece of evidence to the defense about an important witness was also questioned.[3181] Weirich announced that she would fight the charges, and there would be a trial before a hearing panel.[3182] But, in 2017, on the eve of trial, she publicly announced a negotiated private reprimand while the charges against her co-counsel were cleared. [3183]

5

Although the new local Democratic party chief asked me to consider running for district attorney again in 2014, a petition was pulled from the election commission for celebrity TV "Judge" Joe Brown, an African American.[3184] The *Commercial Appeal*, despite that about half of the county voters were black and traditionally voted Democratic, downplayed Brown's chances on the reasoning that the seat had been Republican since 1974.[3185]

Baker with the *Memphis Flyer* observed that Brown had "an impulse to implode," and was mistaken in making scandalous personal claims against Weirich without any evidence. [3186] Baker believed that the status quo Weirich would win despite Brown's celebrity.[3187] He did note that some saw her "more interested in winning cases than seeking justice." [3188] When justice is not the primary objective, the administration of equal justice fails.

With the upcoming elections, local election reform activist Dr. Joseph Weinberg sounded the alarm again about the use of what he called "outdated" and as a result "easily hacked" Diebold voting machines.[3189] Weinberg argued that other states had decertified the machines or requested software changes, the updates had not been applied to the local machines, and audit procedures were inadequate.[3190]

On the August 7, 2014, primary day, I was asked by the local Democratic party to be the attorney on call should there be any issues raised about election irregularities. I took the opportunity to submit a letter to the DOJ's Public Integrity Section, local U.S. Attorney, and FBI about what our open records requests had uncovered.

More particularly, the election commission emails we obtained for the August 2012 election referenced a problem with one precinct, COR-09, which caused the precinct file to fail. One email sent on August 20, 2012, from a local election official, reported that one of the election's databases was downloaded and contained no results. Another email referenced that the vendor was sending the database to its Canada office to research. Yet, that same night the local election commission still voted to certify. The next afternoon, another email was sent from the vendor's representative to the effect that they could not get the file to work without rewriting the code and were looking to see what else could be done. It appeared that the vote been had certified without counting all the votes cast, and some of the results were sent out of the country!

We reviewed the upload precinct report for that election's voting machines. Each voting machine has a memory card that records the vote tallies which are then uploaded from the memory to the tabulator. The upload report showed what time the memory card with votes for each voting machine was uploaded.

With the help of my paralegal, Scarlett Boswell, we found that the COR-09 poll reported thirty memory cards carrying votes uploaded into the system. However, only nine voting machines were assigned to that poll, and it was not an early vote site. There should have been only one memory card per voting machine. The votes from the majority of those memory cards were uploaded to the tabulator *before* the polls were even closed, which was contrary to the state regulations. This was the same precinct that was flagged by the vendor. The unexplained extra memory card uploads could contain thousands of votes. What had happened at that precinct?

We obtained the election night video from a local station's news coverage. My paralegal charted the times and reported election return numbers periodically scrolled across the bottom of the news screen in the three countywide races which had troubled me on election night in August 2012. We then compared those televised reported votes per candidate and times with official election reports that documented in military time each voting machine's vote upload to the tabulator. There were significant discrepancies in results reported on TV and the actual vote returns uploaded at the election commission at those points in time. Why would the votes for candidates reported on the evening news at a specific time (as shown on the bottom of the TV screen) differ markedly from the total actual votes uploaded into the tabulator at the same time?

Federal monitors from the U.S. DOJ were present in Memphis. My faxed letter requested an audit and investigation and that the machines be inspected by a computer elections security expert—especially with regard to the tabulator issues. I also sought an investigation of the 2012 elections (which had included federal congressional primaries). My letter asked that the review be coordinated by the DOJ Washington office to avoid any issues of conflict of interest since the local U.S. Attorney's father had been on the ballot in that election as a candidate for a court clerk position.

On August 27, 2014, I followed up again, asking in a letter for an investigation. Despite my prior letter to the DOJ, the Shelby County Election Commission chairman was quoted in the *Commercial Appeal* saying that they had invited federal monitors present in Memphis to observe the tabulation process on August 7th, but none did.[3191] Why not, especially after my letter specifically requested the same and explained why?

In August 2014, the D.A. general election came to an end. Weirich was reported to defeat Joe Brown with 65% of the vote.[3192] Brown blamed the *Commercial Appeal's* coverage for racially polarizing the community and also filed an election lawsuit with several other candidates alleging fraud and willful, deliberate and continuous dereliction of duty.[3193] While many truths and injustices had been revealed, our election commission open records requests continued in order to find out the rest.

39

Broken Promises

1

While working on election security reform, I also followed the Wharton administration's actions and inactions. Wharton was at odds with some city councilmembers for poor communication and handling of financial issues, although he had sailed into office pitched as the candidate able to build coalitions and work with others.[3194]

A significant issue for the city was how to fund its pension liability and future health care benefits.[3195] Wharton was quoted in the *Commercial Appeal* as saying that his proposal for pension and health care reform cuts would enable the city to have the funds for projects such as clearing space for an industrial park to attract an automobile manufacturer.[3196] The area's chamber of commerce actively lobbied council members for the benefit reductions, with some union leaders questioning the motives for the group's involvement in the issue.[3197] Were they merely trying to shift the monies to new projects in disregard of commitments made to city workers?

A proposed state law by Sen. Mark Norris would require the cities to develop a five-year plan to fund the pension liabilities, with a six-year deadline for 100% funding.[3198] Norris claimed he worked on it with Wharton and Strickland, but Wharton now expressed concern.[3199] One retiree who was opposed to Wharton's proposed cuts, noted that the city paid less into the pension fund than it would for social security (or than the pension contributions of fifty major U.S. cities).[3200] Most city workers, except AFSCME and some other employees, were not within the social security system.[3201] Thus, a fully funded city pension was critical to their livelihood in retirement, which the Norris bill sought to address.

However, Wharton sent shockwaves, proposing that the city "get out of retiree health care." [3202] His plan was to stop the 70% subsidy the city paid for the monthly premium for about 4,000 retirees. [3203] Under his proposal, the city would then use the savings to fund the pension liability without a property tax increase. [3204] Ultimately, Wharton also proposed a 57% health insurance premium increase for both current workers and retirees, as well as ending coverage for employee spouses who had other coverage. [3205]

Basically, the idea was to make the city insurance premium cost so high that most retirees would choose other available health care insurance options such as Medigap or through a subsequent employer. If his plan were adopted, all on the city's health insurance would pay a great deal more each month. Many retirees would face unaffordable premiums, might not qualify for supplemental Medicare policies (although the city later came forward with its own Medigap plan),[3206] or face high deductibles with an Obamacare plan.[3207] Although in support, the *Commercial Appeal* editors acknowledged the proposals might seem "political suicide." [3208] These certainly were unusual proposals in light of the mayor's claim to be a Democrat, which party supported expanding and making health care more affordable – not the opposite.

Wharton also proposed converting the city's pension plan from a defined-benefit model to a 401k type defined-contribution plan for new city employees and those with less than ten years of service. [3209] The city's expert claimed that the fund was short some seven hundred million dollars due to the failure to make adequate city contributions.[3210]

City workers and retirees were facing benefit cuts while large property tax breaks were still awarded to corporations. A news report by Daniel Connolly with the *Commercial Appeal* bolstered the positions of angry workers and retirees on the public cost of tax abatements to businesses.[3211] The newspaper reported that the total cost was in the range of $60 million annually lost to the city and county together. [3212] But business leaders argued that Memphis would lose thousands of jobs without the tax abatements, over a billion dollars in capital investment, along with half a billion in new sales tax and other revenues. [3213] Even with the tax abatements, metro Memphis had an estimated 40,000 fewer employees as of June 2014 than seven years earlier. [3214] In essence, Memphis needed to expand the economic base but not unfairly benefit corporations in the process to the detriment of city workers and retirees.

When my city council term had ended on December 31, 2007, the city's pension fund was fully funded.[3215] Then, in 2008, the Great Recession hit, and the over two billion dollar fund lost millions.[3216] As the *Memphis Flyer's* Toby Sells reported, many cities made higher pension fund payments when the economy rebounded, but Memphis didn't. [3217] According to Wharton's own chart, contributions to the fund by the city were short about $335 million from 2008 to 2013.[3218] Councilman Kemp Conrad sheepishly called it a "multi-year Ponzi scheme" between the mayor and the council that was "dishonest." [3219] In 2013, the city was still only contributing less than a fourth of the required annual amount. [3220] The failure by the Wharton administration as well as the council to adopt honest budgets during the time-period had created a financial calamity.

With the budget issues dominating news, Wharton gave a state of the city address at the beginning of 2014. He pledged that his administration would focus on five "Ps" in the year ahead: public safety, poverty, potholes, pensions, and a future plan.[3221] After serving as county mayor for seven years and city mayor for five, combating poverty and a future plan were finally on Wharton's agenda.

Pushing forward, Wharton announced a ten-year plan to reduce poverty by 10%.[3222] The mayor decided to address poverty, according to newspaper reports, after an incident when he rode in a convertible in the South Memphis Whitehaven Parade while throwing candy at the crowd. [3223] Wharton said a woman retorted that she wanted a job, not candy.[3224] After years as mayor, apparently only now did he realize that the people wanted jobs and not a handout. [3225]

Wharton's plan was called a "bucket of solutions" in a "sea" of poverty by the *Commercial Appeal* editors.[3226] The *Commercial Appeal* had endorsed him in 2009 over me, claiming that he was the one who could reduce poverty.[3227] Yet, Memphis reclaimed the nation's top spots as the poorest MSA overall and in child poverty in 2016.[3228] Wharton admitted that he should have addressed poverty sooner, remembering Dr. Martin Luther King Jr.'s admonition that it is a curse.[3229] However, the incongruity in professing to begin to tackle poverty in 2014, while at the same time drastically cutting the benefits of retirees on fixed incomes, appeared to escape him.

Also, it was a non sequitur that one of his "Ps" was public safety. The anti-crime initiative, Operation: Safe Community, proposed increasing police officers to 2,600 in the city, while at the same time, the city's proposed cuts in officer benefits would result in the departure of hundreds of officers.[3230]

2

In the summer of 2014, city worker protests of the proposed benefit cuts dominated the news. Hundreds of police officers and firefighters called in sick to work. This led to speculation that the absences were a silent protest of the health care benefit cuts that the council had passed on June 18, 2014, by a vote of seven to five, with the support of Councilmen Strickland, Conrad, Flinn, Edmund Ford Jr., Hedgepeth, Lowery, and Morrison. [3231] The phenomenon was dubbed "Blue Flu" and "Red Rash," and the practice created more budget problems for the city due to increased overtime.[3232]

Police Chief Tony Armstrong called it a "crisis," but also reassured that actions had been taken to ensure that public safety was not at risk. [3233] Eventually, Mayor Wharton canceled the sick leave policy as the numbers of officers out ill continued to rise, with all vacation days canceled as well. [3234] The firefighter absences resulted in browning out (taking out of service) four trucks. [3235] It was clear the city workers were going to continue to fight to restore the benefits.

At a press conference on the crisis, Wharton looked dwarfed by his much larger and taller CAO, George Little, as they faced the protestors.[3236] Governor Haslam offered to send state troopers if necessary.[3237] Protest rallies continued outside of City Hall. City leaders pondered whether any legal action was possible, as there was no identified leader of the "Blue Flu" or "Red Rash" movement. Firing so many workers could result in lawsuits by any worker who could document an illness, which would cost the city legal fees and back pay. [3238] The number of workers out sick gradually subsided a few weeks later, although the unions continued billboard and television advertising against the cuts. [3239]

The city council announced that it would seek suggestions from the public on funding the $55 million annual pension liability gap without the health care benefit reductions.[3240] A former Memphis police officer and the mayor of a suburban town, as well as some union leaders, proposed a sales tax increase. If adopted, this would raise about $50 million a year, but a public referendum to increase the sales tax for pre-k programs had been recently defeated. [3241] My former city council colleague, Tajuan Stout Mitchell, and I teamed up. We called for all parties to come back to the bargaining table. As private citizens, we presented our own proposed solution to the budget and benefit impasse. [3242]

Our four-point plan was for: (1) 10% across the board cuts for each city department (generating approximately $60 million); (2) a modest property tax increase to generate about $25 million and costing a middle-income home-owner less than $100 a year; (3) negotiating permission from state officials to extend the five-year deadline to replenish the unfunded pension liability to seven years; and (4) a review of commercial property tax freeze incentives (which the state comptroller had flagged). [3243]We pointed out that the proposed property tax increase, in essence, restored the council's property tax cuts from the past few years. We believed that both our proposed cuts and the small property tax increase would ensure public safety was not compromised and prevent a windfall should the Memphis economy pick up steam in the next few years. If it improved, then the across the board cuts could be restored or property taxes lowered.

I argued that the risk of corruption increases when public safety workers are not paid reasonable wages and benefits. Also, some risk their lives for the public. Our proposed budget would enable the city to move forward on a sound financial footing, better protect the citizens, and honor its promises to the workers and their families.

Like Stout Mitchell and me, many former councilmembers were upset at the administration's proposed benefit cuts. Previously often bumping heads while serving on the city council, Stout Mitchell and I were now allies in the effort to bring a better solution where the mayor had not. Wharton was taking a lot of heat on the issue, with his luster now fading. Yet, the council committee and Wharton ignored our proposal, as well as the calls from others for a sales tax increase and to review the PILOTS (corporate tax breaks).

Some of the public argued that city worker benefits should be cut because private-sector workers were suffering from the rising health insurance premiums and loss of value of their retirement plans. Yet, most private sector workers had social security for their retirement, in addition to any 401k or other private-sector retirement benefit. Most city workers did not.

The full council vote raised insurance premiums 24% for current and retired city workers, with some retirees now responsible for the entire premium amount due with no city subsidy.[3244] The result was that their monthly payments would be five times what they paid before the changes in some instances, which would be unaffordable for many. [3245]

At the emotional meeting approving these measures, Councilwoman Janis Fullilove called Wharton a "coward" for not appearing to defend his proposed budget before the vote. [3246] Many in the overflow crowd spoke of broken promises by the administration, wondered out loud how they would afford health insurance with the increase, and threatened a lawsuit. [3247] While some health insurance reforms might have been needed, the ones enacted were extreme.

The heated confrontations continued a few days later at Fullilove's town hall meeting, where union leaders contended that Wharton had mismanaged the city's spending. [3248] The fire union president, Thomas Malone, blamed PILOT corporate tax breaks as the cause of the city's worker benefit funding problems, citing a study from a think tank that found over $42 million was "siphoned off" the city's tax base annually from the incentives. [3249] Malone argued that many of the companies receiving the tax breaks did not reach the employment and investment requirements for the incentive. [3250] The city workers had been forced to shoulder all of the burdens of the city's financial problems, with the issues raised by Malone as to mismanagement of the corporate tax breaks disregarded.

As columnist Ted Evanoff with the *Commercial Appeal* noted, the trio of the drop in the value of the pension fund due to the recession, the council's action cutting taxes afterward, and the decision to use borrowed funds to repay the city schools the monies wrongly withheld from them, created a budget mess for the years ahead. [3251] While that was true, the newspaper unfortunately also ran a cartoon that played upon some members of the public's fears and prejudices. The cartoon depicted white and black police officers calling in sick and a young black male robbing an elderly white woman at gunpoint saying, "I don't take sick days."[3252]

The *Commercial Appeal* editorialized that the city had "borrowed too much money" for years and failed to adequately fund the pension plan, with both the "administration" and the council to "share in the blame" "having kicked the debt problem down the road."[3253] Ted Evanoff lamented that the city had no definite vision and plan for the future.[3254] Yet, if Wharton as the leader of the city had articulated no vision, why had the newspaper editors endorsed him for election as city mayor in 2009 and thereafter?

There was a backlash to the health care cuts, with the mayor's own appointed police director, Tony Armstrong, publicly critical. [3255] He spoke out that the cuts would harm police morale and hurt recruitment efforts, especially since there had been no pay increase in several years. [3256] Councilman Strickland called Armstrong out for not speaking out before the vote. [3257] But everyone knew the adverse consequences before the vote. City workers, including police officers, had spoken out and engaged in nonviolent protest since the cuts were first announced.

Hundreds of protestors began showing up at City Hall again, saying they had been betrayed by the city leaders who had reneged on their benefits promises.[3258] And, the union leaders' arguments that the pension unfunded liability projection made by the city's expert was too high was substantiated. The same expert in the summer lowered his own projections another $78 million to $474.2 million due to market gains.[3259] Even the city's own expert called the Wharton proposal "a little extreme."[3260] This admission and the lowered pension liability projection gave credence to the arguments of the protestors and their leaders.

As David Waters with the *Commercial Appeal* reported, several ministers met with city and union leaders in an effort to get the city officials to back off of the benefit cuts and advocate for a sales tax increase instead.[3261] They called it a moral obligation to honor prior promises made to workers.[3262] But the city leaders did not back down on the cuts.

Not giving up, in the fall of 2014, the firefighters' union proposed an alternative high-deductible health care plan that they claimed would save the city more than $24 million.[3263] The city's benefits consultant foresaw smaller savings from the proposal but deemed them still substantial if half of the city's workers signed up for the higher deductible plan.[3264] As the union's proposal was considered by the council, protests continued over the health care cuts. Bumper stickers cropped up around town blasting the mayor with the symbols: "FU A C."

A majority of councilmembers were reluctant to adopt the union proposal, with Kemp Conrad arguing that another change in the plan would increase taxes, reduce services or force mass lay-offs.[3265] While he appeared to be exaggerating, the arguments fed into the fears of some that Memphis would go the way of Detroit which was in the throes of bankruptcy.[3266]

So, in the end, the council's only significant conciliatory changes were the restoration of health care subsidies for a year to about 300 retirees under the age of sixty-five who were uninsured, with some disabled retaining subsidies longer.[3267] According to Strickland, that measure passed due to emails from some of those affected who had stage three or four cancer and could not get health insurance.[3268] The emails only underscored the grave consequences to many from the health care cuts.

Wharton, in the meantime, made much-a-do about opening a free minor health care clinic for city workers. He then did an about-face, unilaterally deciding to keep 1,200 working spouses of city employees on the city's plan.

[3269] He claimed to have consulted with "key" councilmembers and that another council vote was unnecessary.[3270] This ruffled the feathers of those on the council left out of the loop.[3271] They had taken the heat on the prior cuts when perhaps the mayor could have implemented many, if not all of them, without a council vote as he just did in restoring some to the plan.

With the budget problems still looming despite the health care cuts, the city council also voted on pension reform. The compromise allowed city employees with seven and a half years of service or longer to remain in the pension fund and moved the other current and new employees to a 401k type plan. [3272] Councilman Lowery's proposal to apply the changes only to new hires (which would keep about 2,400 workers with less than ten years on the job in the current pension plan) ultimately was shelved. [3273]

Shortly before the vote, the new plan's effective date was changed by the council from January 2016 to July 2016, which favored a new councilmember, among other city employees. [3274] And the seven and a half years of service, as opposed to the ten years, allowed nine council members a chance to stay with the traditional pension. [3275]This was similar to 2005 when the council passed a repeal of the twelve-year pension for elected and appointed officials but did not include my broader proposal that would have included some current councilmembers and many more appointees.[3276] In any event, the union leaders now promised they would take the matter to court, and did. [3277]

Sadly, a few short years later, the 2016 budget made it apparent that the workers had borne the brunt of the city's fiscal problems. No major cuts were proposed, and spending was increased, including several new hires at salaries in the $140,000 range.[3278] But, the broken promises were not forgotten or forgiven.

40

Musical Chairs 1

1

During this time, I researched this book and submitted open records to the election commission. It increasingly grew apparent that something different was needed to bring real change to the city. Maybe my book would help the people see the patterns over the years that held the city back.

In 2014, some supporters tried to draft me to be the local Democratic party nominee for the vacated state senate seat of Jim Kyle.[3279] Reluctantly, I agreed to be a consensus candidate for the senate position if the Democratic caucus, which would nominate its candidate, reached an impasse. My reluctance was because I had already served in the state legislature, accomplished child care and other reforms, and still wanted to bring reforms to the local level arena.

Former Tennessee Regulatory Commissioner Sara Kyle and former state Sen. Beverly Marrero entered the race for the Democratic nomination.[3280] On the Republican side, my former council opponent, George Flinn, sought the nomination.

When the day arrived for the Democratic caucus vote, I was seated with Kyle and Marrero at the head table before the local county Democratic executive committee. When my turn came, I stood and spoke about my record. I talked about the glass ceiling and how it was time for women to be allowed to lead in higher office in Memphis, Tennessee, and nationally.[3281] Then, because there were two other well-qualified candidates for that position, I withdrew from the selection process.

Yet, another election was on the horizon. The 2015 mayoral race was approaching. I was identified in the *Commercial Appeal* as a possible candidate by reporter Kyle Veazey, along with Wharton, Strickland, City Councilman

Harold Collins, and police union chief Mike Williams.[3282] It was reported that a recent poll showed Wharton's favorable rating at 43%, just ahead of his unfavorable rating of 41% (after losing a great deal of support in the African American community).[3283]

Strickland claimed to be interested only in running for reelection to the city council but held a fundraiser where he conveniently did not specify the office sought on the invitation —merely asking for donations to "Friends of Jim Strickland."[3284] I explored my options with supporters. One concern of mine was whether the election results would be accurate if I ran. Our election research had uncovered serious problems with the county's voting machines, methods, and audit processes, including the 21 unexplained extra memory cards uploaded in the 2012 August elections.

Wharton was vulnerable due to a 50% increase in the number of police officers retiring or resigning and the lack of adequate replacements.[3285] And it was difficult to understand how the city that had Herenton as mayor for eighteen years, and Wharton for five years, both African Americans, could only muster less than 2% of minority firm business receipts in the Mid-South.[3286] However, Otis Sanford with the *Commercial Appeal*, and Rhodes professor Marcus Pohlmann, both still deemed Wharton the man to beat for city mayor in 2015, purportedly having fully recovered from his prior political problems.[3287]

2

Wharton's bad press had continued throughout 2014, with a public outcry over his giving a controversial rapper the key to the city. The rapper had appeared in support of a job creation franchise. But several women complained that the rapper had a song with lyrics that glorified drugging women to have sex.[3288] New reports showed crime on an upswing in the city for the first half of 2014, including a 10% increase in reported rapes.[3289] That, along with the huge rape kit backlog scandal, made the gesture by the mayor appear disrespectful and out of touch.[3290]

On the heel of that controversy, Memphians debated about the Ferguson, Missouri protest and police reforms after a white police officer fatally shot an African American citizen.[3291] And, then a mob of youth in Memphis attacked two Kroger grocery store employees and a third person only a few blocks from my home.[3292] The video, posted online, outraged many citizens in the area and nationwide.

During the same week, youth leaving a high school football game beat up on two moving cars out of anger when a driver honked at them for blocking the street. [3293] And it was reported that there were now over 9,000 gang members in the Memphis area.[3294] We had come a long way since my town hall meeting on gangs in 1995, and not in the right direction. Wharton's proposal to stop evening sporting events to create a curfew was widely panned.[3295] Why punish all of the parents and youth for the actions of a few?

Earlier in the year, a twenty-two year old man had been shot by another twenty year old inside a shopping mall in an upscale eastern area of the city. [3296] On social media, some angry citizens commented that they would start packing weapons for self-protection.[3297] Violent crime for the past six months had increased by nearly 6% in the city. [3298] And, Wharton's emergency forum to address youth violence was deemed by the *Commercial Appeal* editors as the same-ole same-ole, not producing any new ideas on how to address the issue. [3299] Despite their prior heralding of Wharton as the savior of the city, they were now openly critical of his leadership.

Better received were the mayor's plans for the city to purchase dash cameras for police cars, which he later expanded to include pricing of body cams for police officers. [3300] But, with violent crime rising, many worried that the lack of sufficient commissioned officers would only increase the negative trend.[3301] The need to recruit and train over 265 such officers did not square with the city's drastic health care and pension benefit cuts. [3302]

With Memphis in the top five of the *Forbes* annual list of highest crime cities for the past five years, there were fears that economic development and tourism would now be adversely impacted. [3303] Some called for stronger law enforcement measures on youth. But others bemoaned the cuts in social services, high unemployment, the governor's failure to allow the state to participate in Obamacare, and the city's reductions in school funding, as all destroying the youth's hope for a future out of poverty. [3304] Obviously, enough had not been done as to the youth, and some decisions had worsened their situation.

Taking a shot at Wharton, the *Commercial Appeal* editorialized that the city leaders and the chamber of commerce had not coalesced to solve issues of blight, poverty and high crime or been able to get the buy-in of the public to a "common vision." [3305] The editors noted that the city was "losing its creative people" due to a lack of opportunity and long-standing racial and class conflict. [3306] This brought back to mind my plea in the 2009 mayoral election about the need to afford women more opportunities as well, so as to attract and keep the creative class.

3

On New Year's Day 2015, Wharton appeared at Councilman Lowery's prayer breakfast pushing a proposed tax break for an IKEA retail store, pay raises for city workers, and a $43 million payment to settle the $57 million owed by the city to the county school system (now merged with the former Memphis system).[3307] But the shocker were the remarks by Lowery. He asked Strickland not to depart the breakfast early because he was going to praise him.[3308] At the end of the program, Lowery asked Strickland to stand. He praised his work as chairman of the council for the past year, saying he had the "potential" to be the mayor one day.[3309] Then, the zinger. Lowery added, "just not this year," and proceeded to endorse Wharton.[3310] A stunned Strickland angrily left.

The *Commercial Appeal* editors called out Wharton's proposal for pay raises for city workers as "absolute lunacy" due to the budget problems and possibly "an election-year ploy."[3311] Later in the year, the editors also advocated for a thorough review of the EDGE entity that approved PILOT corporate tax breaks. [3312] A study would allow an evaluation of the costs and benefits of the tax breaks where the city was said to be "under severe financial strain" with an eroding tax base. [3313] The practice of looking the other way as to the efficacy of some of the breaks was taking its toll.

Shortly after the prayer breakfast, Wharton wrote an opinion editorial in the *Commercial Appeal*. He opined that if Dr. King were alive, he probably would have participated in protests related to the Ferguson, Missouri shooting of a youth by a police officer by lying down on the Selma bridge where civil rights protestors had marched in the 1960s. [3314] Wharton pitched a pay raise for workers and showed up to honor the remaining nine living sanitation strikers from 1968, and others, at the historic Mason Temple where Dr. King delivered his last speech. However, he had just been the leader to reduce worker benefits drastically. Hence, my question was – would Dr. King have stood with city workers in 2014 against Wharton and the majority of the city council's huge health insurance and pension benefit cuts? I think so.

4

Strickland, campaigning for mayor, claimed that he would get the job done on crime where Wharton had failed.[3315] He pointed out that the city was more violent than a few years earlier. [3316] His crime plan was for aggressive policing, stronger state criminal laws, and getting government and community groups to come together to intervene in the lives of children. [3317] However, his plan for aggressive policing was inconsistent with the vote he had cast to cut police benefits.

Reporter Veazey wrote that Councilman Harold Collins was still considering entry into the race and had said that a new mayor was needed "whether it be somebody else or me." [3318] This led to speculation that Collins might endorse Strickland if he did not run for mayor. [3319] Collins had served as a special assistant to Weirich in the D.A.'s office for many years. [3320] Once again, the interconnectedness of Memphis political players was evident.

It was interesting to see another "fake poll" run by the *Commercial Appeal*, where people could vote for their candidate for mayor. The online poll's problem was that a person could vote as many times as they wanted for their candidate of choice. Certainly, this was an unscientific way of measuring the support of the electorate.

As the potential mayoral candidates considered the race, part of the public debate was the city's serious financial problems. The *Commercial Appeal* in an editorial pronounced that the city was "badly in debt," even though employee benefits had been cut. [3321] The editorial further noted that the metropolitan area at this point had lost over 33,000 jobs as of early 2015 since just before the Great Recession. While the recovery was underway, lower taxes were needed to spur job growth. [3322] How to get the city out of debt while also lowering taxes would need to be a topic for mayoral candidates.

In 2015, Wharton again proposed restructuring the city's debt so as to flatten the annual debt repayments and to borrow another $75 million. [3323] This was reminiscent of his and the council's restructuring in 2009. [3324] Strickland had opposed that measure, albeit the council's poor fiscal decisions had prompted the action by the mayor. [3325] The state comptroller in 2010 had been critical of the refinancing known as "scoop and toss" due to the city's rising debt being pushed off to later administrations. [3326] Yet, a similar method was proposed again.

The council, not trusting Wharton, delayed the vote to obtain a separate financial review. But they later approved the refinancing, with only four "no" votes. [3327] Strickland argued that it would only "kick the can down the road" in terms of solving the unfunded pension liability. [3328] The *Commercial Appeal* placed the blame for the financial "mess" squarely on the mayor and the city council. [3329] The pattern of refinancing and borrowing more money to escape addressing the city's financial problems was merely an expensive way of pass-ing the buck to later administrations.

Apart from the budget problems, Wharton's administration was also crit-icized for appearing indifferent in February 2015, when a homeless man froze to death outside in less than 10-degree weather. [3330] And the proliferation of gaping potholes after several freezing winter days aggravated citizens, who had to pay for car repairs and swerve to try to avoid them while driving down major city streets.[3331]

Apparently trying to get an edge in the mayoral election, Wharton announced that he was moving the current CAO, George Little, to the posi-tion of special assistant to the mayor. He offered the CAO job to former city council member and Republican Jack Sammons. Sammons at the time was also chairman of the Memphis-Shelby County Airport Authority and had served briefly as CAO during the interim mayoral term of Myron Lowery in 2009.[3332]

Questions were immediately raised as to how Sammons could hold posi-tions with the airport and the city and run a private company, especially in light of a state law prohibition on holding both the airport and city jobs. Harold Collins declared that Sammons needed to choose one job over the other to get his vote.[3333] Even Republican County Mayor Mark Luttrell said both jobs were too much for one person to handle.[3334]

Recalling my days on the council serving with Sammons, I expressed my view to the press that while he was capable, qualified, and well-connected, he was not the best choice if the goal was for a more progressive city for all of the people.[3335] Sammons did have powerful connections by virtue of his marriage to a relative of FedEx's founder, Fred Smith.[3336] I speculated that Wharton was merely trying to shore up Republican and corporate support.[3337]

According to Little, part of the plan was for the deputy CAO to take on more daily management responsibility.[3338] Unexplained was why the deputy would have more duties after the addition of Sammons? Was Wharton pro-posing that the CAO position become a part-time position for Sammons at the full-time pay?

Wharton defended Sammons's plan to keep both jobs, saying the pro-posed CAO would give up his private-sector job running a hair-care products company. [3339] One heavy hitter, a former airport official, came out in strong opposition to the proposal. He worried that the city administration would try to take over the airport's contracting authority.[3340]

Even veteran news reporter Les Smith said in the *Memphis Flyer* what many thought, but wouldn't say aloud—why did Memphis "recycle the same people through the meat grinder of government?"[3341] He wasn't critical of Sammons, but of Wharton, who he said had a tank that "is nearly running on empty" in terms of getting things done. [3342] Smith also wondered why Sammons wanted to work for Wharton when he had not even appointed him to stay on as CAO after the 2009 special election?[3343] Les Smith nailed it when he called the plan to have Sammons do both government jobs a "backroom deal" and "political musical chairs," lamenting the practice of continually using "career bureaucrats" and "political cronies." [3344] This practice perpetuated the status quo.

Finally, Sammons agreed to resign his position as chairman of the airport authority board and take a leave of absence from his business until after the city mayoral election (contingent upon his approval as CAO by the Memphis City Council).[3345] Sammons was pitched as someone who could help smooth over relations between Wharton and the city council and actually get things done.[3346] Wharton admitted complaints of a lack of follow-through on ideas and programs.[3347] This propensity had been raised by some county commissioners when he first ran for Memphis Mayor in 2009 but was ignored by the press, media, and editors who endorsed him for the job.

An example of Wharton's procrastination on issues was his revelation that he had been "frustrated" with CAO Little's performance since 2010. [3348] It was now five years later that he was making a change. However, some saw the move as just evidence of the business community's control over Wharton. [3349] In fact, one reliable source told me that several prominent business leaders had met privately with Wharton and demanded that he let their designated person run the city or they would not support him for reelection. But, some wondered whether Sammons was being pushed as CAO to save Wharton or instead to set him up?

Some councilmembers were critical of perceived flip-flops and misinformation from the Wharton administration, the lack of consistent leadership, and the perception that he was throwing African American George Little "under the bus" with the Sammons nomination.[3350] Others grumbled that Sammons's annual pension would double a year after taking the CAO job.[3351] His approval as CAO by the council continued the musical chairs practice, leaving little room for a fresh perspective to solve the city's financial and other problems.

41

Musical Chairs 2

1

April 4, 2015, marked the 47th year since the assassination of Dr. Martin Luther King Jr. Despite having led the way to cut city worker benefits, Wharton campaigned around town, showing up at commemorative events.[3352] Harold Collins officially entered the mayoral field, saying that Wharton had his ear to "big business" as opposed to "people who live in neighborhoods." [3353] Collins also attacked Wharton and Strickland on the city worker and retiree benefit cuts. [3354] It was a compelling issue in light of the city's history.

The mayoral candidate field that included Wharton led me to ask myself why the same male players were recycled instead of promoting an experienced woman? Even on the national level, the new U.S. Senate and House of Representatives had only about 20% female members—still not anywhere comparable to the female 51% of the adult population. [3355] The Tennessee state legislature began its business in 2015 with only 17% female members. [3356] About two-thirds of those bodies were white male Republicans. [3357] In the spring of 2018, there were only five Democrats out of thirty-three in the state senate and twenty-six out of ninety-nine in the house. [3358] Certainly, things had changed since my years of service in the Democratic-controlled body, but not so much as to the low number of women serving.

Meanwhile, with the filing deadline looming, I contemplated whether to enter the Memphis mayoral race. It was amusing to see a cartoon in the *Commercial Appeal,* showing six men, and a caricature of me getting out of a car, with onlookers identifying us as mayoral candidates.[3359] The others appeared to be Wharton, Strickland, and four other African American men. [3360] All of the men wore business suits, with some carrying briefcases. I was depicted carrying a purse, with only a top and skirt as opposed to a business suit. [3361]

While one might think being the only female would be an advantage in a crowded field, both Wharton and Strickland had a head start on fundraising.[3362] And just this simple cartoon showed the sometimes subtle gender bias culture in Memphis, with me dressed less professionally than the other men.

But history was in the making with the announcement of Hillary Clinton for President on April 12, 2015. [3363] With the titles first lady of Arkansas and the White House, U.S. Senator and U.S. Secretary of State under her belt, she had a wealth of experience to bring to the job.

2

Unexpectedly, a new crisis emerged. Under consideration in the state legislature was a de-annexation bill. The measure would allow certain areas that had been annexed by municipalities to vote to de-annex themselves by referendum (such as the affluent Southwind/Windyke area previously annexed by Memphis).[3364] The *Commercial Appeal* editors likened it to the "tiny towns" law in 1997.[3365] That was the law that I had sounded the alarm about as a state legislator, and which had been struck down by the Tennessee Supreme Court as unconstitutional due to bill caption problems.

Some argued that the city would be better off financially without the area. The risk was that other higher-income areas would vote to de-annex, leaving the city with only low-income citizens to foot the expense of city amenities that all in the metropolitan area enjoyed.[3366] Not considered was the issue of whether certain areas could constitutionally be given the right to de-annex without allowing other poor neighborhoods the same right—and then essentially pushing expensive city services altogether onto the county government.

The issue prompted the *Commercial Appeal* to run a series on the city's "financial mess," placing blame on the past city spending and borrowing. [3367] Cited was the 70% increase in city operating costs since 1973 adjusted for inflation; 0% population growth during the past thirty years despite heavy annexation since 1960; high administrative salaries; over 500 city-pensioned retirees with 15 or fewer years of service; debt tripled since 1997; and 92% of borrowing capacity under the city's debt policy used.[3368] These were all indicators that the city's financial condition would be challenging in the years ahead. [3369] The facts were bleak.

In 2008, the city council's action had withheld $57 million usually allocated for the schools, using it instead to give pay raises and cut property taxes.[3370] Then later, the city was ordered to pay the school system back, effectuated with a Wharton backed refinancing that only delayed debt payments and adding to the financial mess "famously."[3371] (In all fairness, Wharton initially proposed a thirty-one cent property tax increase, which the city council rejected). [3372] There were no easy choices now.

The series also blamed the city's financial problems on annexation practices that increased expenditures for services and the Herenton administration's borrowing and spending practices up to the 2008 Great Recession.[3373] This had doubled the city's general obligation debt to over a billion dollars. [3374] It was refreshing to see the *Commercial Appeal* editors acknowledge that they also had some responsibility, having editorialized in support of several annexations. [3375] They also now called for a bold vision on how to attract people back to the city. [3376] There had been opportunities for that in the past, but the editors and many of those in the voting public had settled instead for the status quo leadership.

Newly announced CAO Jack Sammons had served on the council during at least five of the annexations. He now described them as "building our own coffin" due to the increased costs to provide services to the new areas.[3377] In addition, more than 250 companies had garnered tax breaks over the past decade, and there was a shrinking population to pay taxes.[3378] Some advocated for spending cuts.[3379] Others supported tax increases, although the city's property tax was already the highest in the state. [3380] The poor decision-making of the past two administrations was now glaringly apparent.

Some citizens argued that annexations over the years had cost Memphis more than revenues collected. The land size had grown, which they contended made it difficult to provide necessary services without more manpower. But there was also some evidence that annexations at least initially brought in needed revenues. City revenues increased over 11% after the Hickory Hill annexation in 1998, according to Marc Perrusquia and Grant Smith with the *Commercial Appeal.* [3381] Perhaps, this was one reason the Herenton administration had forestalled larger property tax increases during his early tenure as mayor.[3382]

However, it was difficult to analyze whether the city's increased revenues after that were greater than the cost over time to serve the newly annexed

Hickory Hill.[3383] Years later, despite new schools, a police station, and parks, Hickory Hill had declined.[3384] There had been an exodus of the middle class from the area, many foreclosures, and an influx of people renting apartments and houses using Section 8 vouchers (presumably some relocated from downtown redeveloped housing projects).[3385] The attorney for the citizens who had fought the annexation attributed the decline to the fact that parents wanted to pick their schools and moved over the state line to escape the anticipated annexation. [3386] It was speculative whether that could have been avoided with more concessions to those residents since they had already left.

Even though the city aggressively annexed, the *Commercial Appeal* series reported that the property tax base was about the same since 2000 due to declining property values.[3387] Some inner-city neighborhoods suffered from the loss of manufacturing jobs in the area. The medium income of city residents fell over that time-period with growing blight.[3388]

The "leap-frogging" practices of sprawl development, which I had opposed when running for county mayor in 2002, were now cited by expert Phyllis Betts as a reason Memphis was suffering from population loss.[3389] Some owners had abandoned their city properties to tax foreclosure due to the loss in value, creating more blight.[3390] Efforts were now underway to create livable communities to attract millennial professionals into the city.[3391] If the city and county leaders had addressed these issues in 2002, perhaps the city could have avoided the financial mess in 2015.

The city's debt was increased substantially during Herenton's tenure, although he defended it as an investment in infrastructure for the inner-city.[3392] In the *Commercial Appeal* series, he explained that the city's extension of the sewers beyond city limits, was an effort to stimulate regional growth.[3393] The former mayor had believed that ultimately the city and county governments would consolidate to a metro government (which did not happen).[3394]

Herenton blamed the inability to merge on both African American urbanites and white suburbanites, who each feared a loss of political power. [3395] Herenton had pushed the issue over the years but couldn't get it done. Would conditioning the sewer expansion on merger within a specified time period, with an annual financial penalty to the county if it did not occur, have gotten it done? That would have protected the city's financial investment and made more sense than just acquiescing to development interests and hoping things would work out in the long run.

In the early 1970s, Mayor Chandler had adhered to the same path (but for inner-city development), substantially increasing the city's debt obligation after investing in downtown and other improvements.[3396] While bond ratings were still sound, the city's financial picture now was difficult overall due to the heavy borrowing over the past forty-five years.[3397] As a councilmember, I had pushed to cut capital project expenditures, but the mayor and most of the council had moved forward with the multi-million RDC projects and others.

In addition, the full twelve-year pension for elected and appointed officials, regardless of their age, which I had led the charge to repeal in 2004, was back in the news. My former colleague Councilman Brent Taylor admitted that he began drawing $9,411 a year from the city pension at the age of thirty-nine.[3398] Taylor acknowledged that there is "just something fundamentally wrong" with a thirty-nine year old drawing a pension for life, reminding that he had voted against the measure. [3399] According to reporters Marc Perrusquia and Daniel Connolly with the *Commercial Appeal,* some city retirees were drawing between $60,000 to even $95,000 a year in pension payments.[3400] However, most rank and file workers drew about $36,000 annually.[3401] The firefighter union chief, Thomas Malone, pointed out that the pension was less costly to the city than if it paid into social security for the workers.[3402] But the prior rule set in place, allowing a pension for elected and appointed officials of any age after serving only twelve years, was poor fiscal policy.

When I had pushed the repeal of the twelve-year pension rule, most of the council got angry. Some had argued the rule was put in place to help retain needed talent at City Hall. In reality, it created a revolving door where many left after twelve years of service to draw the pension and earn other income at the same time elsewhere.[3403] Because the council repeal in 2004 did not include my broader version, some city appointees remained in the twelve-year pension benefit after the vote who could have been excluded and the fund bolstered.[3404] In 2009, Strickland pushed a measure to close the loophole that allowed lower-ranking appointees to benefit from the twelve-year pension rule when they moved up.[3405] Years later, the rank and file city workers' pension was altered for those serving less than seven and a half years, despite the arguments made by others in 2004 that it couldn't be lawfully done as to some already-serving elected and appointed officials.

It was ironic that I spent some of my own funds from my law firm 401k in the 2002 county mayor's campaign to seek to stop the disastrous growth policies. Later, I suffered the wrath of some of my city council colleagues by pushing to repeal the twelve-year pension. Then, instead of seeking reelections to a safe council seat (which ultimately would have qualified me for a twelve-year city pension myself), I instead took the political risk of challenging Herenton and his harmful fiscal policies. Maybe I cared more about the future of Memphis and Shelby County than some voters did. But I stayed true to my beliefs as to what was best for the citizens regardless of the personal consequences. I only wish more people had stood with me so as to avoid the fiscal problems down the road.

After the "financial mess" *Commercial Appeal* exposé, Wharton wasted no time in proposing a budget that would increase the city's spending over $12 million to pave streets and for law enforcement.[3406] Strickland was quoted as saying that he agreed with many of the programs.[3407] Certainly, the streets needed paving and crime needed to be addressed, but it also did not appear that enough belt-tightening had been done elsewhere.

The city's failure to use more civilians for law enforcement, like other cities, was also questioned in the series.[3408] Once again, this had been part of my platform for Memphis Mayor in 2007 and 2009. According to Beth Warren with the *Commercial Appeal*, in 2015 Memphis still used about half the number of civilians in law enforcement compared to other cities.[3409] Wharton jumped on, beginning the hiring process for public service technicians ("PSTs") in later 2015.[3410] If I had been elected in 2007, the city could have saved money over those past eight years with my proposed reform measure.[3411]

3

Although I had not announced my intentions yet and had been mentioned as a possible mayoral candidate several times in the press, Jackson Baker now asked if it would be a "two-man" race between Wharton and Strickland.[3412] One citizen wrote a letter to the *Memphis Flyer* about the column, observing the lack of difference between the two candidates in that they were "both backed by the same power players."[3413] The writer noted that Strickland's prior endorsement of Wharton as one of his campaign co-chairs was evidence of the "incestuous political wheel" in Memphis.[3414] Strickland apparently had either supported Wharton then on political expediency grounds or had used poor judgment in doing so in that he now opposed him. Strickland's emergence as a mayoral candidate reminded me from my state legislative days of the never-ending polite but ingratiating males, next in line to move up the ladder for political appointments. They were groomed and waiting in the wings to be the next state constitutional officer, thus precluding a woman's chance for appointment to one of those positions.

Wharton was busy with his usual mayoral public appearances, which gave him an edge in earned media. One such event was the Sexual Assault Kit Taskforce to bring public awareness to the need to speak out against rape and domestic violence. [3415] Advocate Meaghan Ybos, however, blasted the press conference by Wharton. [3416] Ybos was quoted by Bianca Phillips with the *Memphis Flyer* as saying that public service announcements are "nice," but the real problem in Memphis was the lack of prosecution—hence the 12,300 backlogged rape kits. [3417] The reality check by her about what really needed to be done was a breath of fresh air in contrast to an orchestrated public relations media op.

With the election filing deadline at hand, I issued a press release declining to be a candidate for Memphis mayor in 2015. In my view, the city needed progressive leadership, especially with regard to the challenges of bringing and growing jobs for the 45,000 youth who were unemployed and not in school; making our city safer for our citizens, businesses, and to protect our tourism industry; solving our budgetary problems without undue hardship on citizens, workers, or businesses; and unifying our diverse citizenry with one common vision. Yet, from my research, not enough Memphians were ready to elect an independent-minded, experienced woman as mayor – or to elect any woman for that matter.

I also believed that this book would be a better way for the time-being to prompt real change, having gone up against the status quo in more than one mayoral election. I already knew the playbook. For real change, a shift in attitudes is needed by the voters and a recognition that the insanity of continuing to elect the same type of leadership will not bring different results.

I thanked my supporters for their words of encouragement and stood by my message for change. Although I was not entering the mayoral race, I pledged to continue serving the people as an attorney, volunteer, and citizen dedicated to the city. My heart is always with the people of Memphis. With that announcement, I went back to work to prepare for a client's federal court jury trial in August. I also continued to write this book and investigate the local election commission in order to make a public service contribution, albeit as a private citizen.

After I issued the statement, Whalum Jr. opted out of the mayor's race as well. Perhaps he sensed that the field would be too crowded. [3418] But, despite efforts that had been made by myself and others to build support for a consensus change candidate (either me or another), the usual practice of divide and conquer in Memphis politics was still at play. For example, the mayoral candidates included Mike Williams (the police union chief), and Councilman Harold Collins, who both had similar positions on worker benefits. This resulted in a divided labor vote with the firefighters' union endorsing Collins.[3419]

Thereafter, the Memphis mayor's race took an ugly turn, with the four major candidates Wharton, Strickland, Mike Williams, and Harold Collins vying for the votes. Strickland called out Wharton's "slick maneuvers."[3420] Wharton blamed Strickland, Collins, and the council for the budget problems, while Strickland attacked the mayor's debt refinancing.[3421] In an analysis in the *Commercial Appeal* by Kyle Veazey, it was interesting to see myself now referenced as having been a "formidable" candidate in 2009 against Wharton.[3422] Otis Sanford, a *Commercial Appeal* columnist, had portrayed Wharton as virtually unbeatable during that campaign.[3423] If he had used Veazey's terminology about me in his column in 2009, perhaps more of my supporters would have turned out, or more voters given me a chance with their vote.

As the election contest moved forward and in the wake of controversy about personal allegations against his director of housing, Wharton now benefited from the endorsement of Congressman Steve Cohen.[3424] A new poll commissioned by the *Commercial Appeal* showed him five points ahead of Strickland.[3425] The poll showed Williams and Collins tied for third place, each at 12%.[3426] Strickland now gained the "recommendation" of the Shelby County Republican party even though he was a former local Democratic party chair.[3427] Apparently, the Sammons CAO appointment had not cemented Wharton's Republican support in the nonpartisan election. The four men jockeyed for the mayoral prize.

A Strickland supporter invited me to lunch, asking me to endorse his candidate. He previously had been a candidate himself for the city council. We met at a local restaurant not far from the National Civil Rights Museum. I brought to his attention that Strickland had been the campaign co-chair for Wharton in the 2009 mayoral election against me *and* had endorsed Weirich against me in 2012. The supporter commiserated how much harder it was for candidates like us, who speak truth to power, to get elected.

My reply was that sometimes those who speak truth to power are the measuring stick for others. If everyone sells out, then who is left to measure against as to the truth? After a long discussion, my position was that I would consider an endorsement of Strickland if he announced a plan for the city workers. I never heard back.

The mayoral race labored on with new revelations that a private marketing group was the beneficiary of a lucrative $880,000 public relations subcontract related to the purchase by the city of police body cams. [3428] An owner of the marketing group was Wharton's campaign manager. The firm promptly canceled the subcontract. [3429] Wharton was asked about it on a conservative radio talk show and incredibly claimed that he did not know the group had won the public relations subcontract.[3430] The mayor said it was a private subcontract entered into after the city contract award. [3431] He gamely explained that Deidre Malone was still acting as his campaign manager, but this was despite his "displeasure" with the subcontract situation. [3432] Most of the public didn't buy his explanation.

On Election eve, Strickland was elected the new mayor of Memphis with only about 41,000 votes (16,000 less than I had mustered against Herenton in 2007).[3433] Perhaps there had been one too many controversies for Wharton with the scandal involving his housing director, the campaign manager's body cam contract misstep, and the pension and healthcare benefit cut issues. However, it appeared to me in the campaign's final days that Strickland was blitzing the airwaves with prime time television commercials, while Wharton, with a similar war chest, kept a low profile. Rumor had it that more damaging city contracts were to be revealed. Perhaps Wharton chose to avoid any further embarrassment.

After the election, Wharton's beleaguered campaign manager had her say in the *Tri-State Defender*. Malone, who had a solid record of prior public service as a county commissioner, remained loyal to Wharton despite the perception that he had thrown her under the bus on local radio in the last days of the campaign. [3434]She attributed Wharton's loss, in part, to the health care and pension benefit cuts but opined that if he didn't do them, then the state comptroller would have taken action. [3435] Malone also regretted not notifying the vendor of her role as Wharton's campaign manager when she sought the body cam public relations subcontract. [3436] She later became the Executive Director of the local NAACP chapter, continued her successful public relations career, and eventually became a board member of the company that owns the *Tri-State Defender* newspaper as well.[3437]

While Wharton was now out of office, the musical chairs continued with Strickland deciding to keep his predecessor's director of the finance division as CFO and making the prior administration's innovation delivery team director his COO.[3438] Surely, these were all capable men. But, once again, the precious status quo was preserved.

42

—

Sexism in the City

1

Leading up to the October 2015 election, John Branston had written a column in *Memphis Magazine* opining that Memphis had "erectile dysfunction" because of the continued low voter turnout patterns.[3439] He blamed low voter turnout, in part, on the addition of early voting, which he said took the "climax" out of Election Day. [3440] Indeed, things had changed.

Branston also observed that I had over 57,000 votes in the 2007 mayor's race against Herenton, while Wharton mustered only 48,600 votes to win the 2011 mayoral contest.[3441] Strickland won in 2015 with fewer votes than Wharton had in 2011. Branston attributed the declining voter turnout also to the Memphis habit of reelecting incumbent mayors repeatedly—such as Wharton who had served as either county or city mayor for thirteen years. [3442] Amen, although Strickland broke that pattern by defeating Wharton in 2015.

The columnist also noted the irony that the 1991 federal court ruling eliminating a runoff for Memphis elections in order to bring racial equities later harmed my candidacy in the 2007 mayor's race.[3443] He observed that I might have been elected the first woman mayor by winning a runoff with Herenton (or if Morris had not run). [3444] Also, the lack of a runoff helped Strickland, the only leading white candidate in the 2015 mayoral election with a divided field of African American candidates. [3445]

For my interview for the article, Branston had sent me several provocative written questions to review in advance. One was whether a woman could be elected mayor of Memphis, with me, "the only one who's even come close."

After the 2015 mayoral election, the *Tri-State Defender's* editor, Bernal Smith II, also called for change at the Shelby County Election Commission.[3446] The newspaper mentioned a 2014 FBI inquiry, a DOJ-monitored election, and the fact that the Administrator Richard Holden had a prior three-day suspension. [3447] In the October 2015 municipal election, there had been new "glitches." Smith appropriately demanded that in light of the "well-documented vulnerabilities with the Diebold voting machines," they be replaced with a new voting system.[3448]

Dr. Joseph Weinberg commented as well in the *Commercial Appeal* about the "strange delay in producing results" on election night until 12:30 am the next morning. According to him, city court clerk candidate Wanda Halbert's vote total appeared to switch with another candidate before her very eyes on the news television screen.[3449] Weinberg said that the election commission officials admitted that the switch occurred, without explaining why.[3450]

Also, others were given the wrong ballot in split precincts, with the exact number of voters affected unknown.[3451] Weinberg called for the state election commission to appoint an outside consultant to recommend reforms and supervise upcoming elections.[3452] Discrepancies noted included over one hundred vote variances up or down in some races from election night and the audited results. [3453] Noone could be certain their votes were properly cast and counted in the correct electoral contests with the continuing irregularities.

The election night delays were explained by the election vendor and the local election commission as due to the use of two election databases. They claimed that the initial one had to be updated.[3454] A second database had been used in the August 2012 election as well, where the twenty-one unexplained cards were uploaded for precinct COR-09. This pattern and practice raised another red flag.

I, Dr. Weinberg, Shelby County School Boardmember Mike Kernell, and others decided to submit more open records requests in light of the reoccurring problems. Our team, including Mary Wilder (a former state legislator and city council candidate), poured over data and documents produced, with several trips to the election commission to review original poll tapes and voter sign-in sheets. Among other things, we found (as first reported by private citizen and computer expert Bennie Smith) that some machine memory cards that contained votes from urban polls were not uploaded into the system on Election night in the 2015 municipal election. Candidate Wanda Halbert, an articulate and hard-working city councilwoman, filed a lawsuit based upon the discovery. [3455] It did not appear that any investigation was ever made of the cause of these irregularities by the election officials, although one manager notified the administrator.

In addition, a 2013 Shelby County Election Process Final Report ("2013 *SCEPF Report*") had found that the tabulation server room could be "accessed by many people, which makes it difficult to defend against allegations of tampering."[3456] The report stated that the server "is also plugged into the county's network which exposes the server to the potential for external penetration, even if the server is only on the network for a few hours."[3457] The report added that with the current configuration, "when the server is plugged into the county network, it was vulnerable to hacking, virus, and malware."[3458] This was very disturbing.

We also reviewed a state agency report by the Tennessee Advisory Commission on Intergovernmental Relations ("*TACIR*").[3459] It noted a critical security breach in 2006 in Shelby County. Not only was the central tabulator for the local election commission plugged into a county government network switch, but unauthorized software had been installed.[3460] The *TACIR* report stated that the PC Anywhere software would allow "unfettered remote access to the central tabulator to anyone connected to the county government network or the Internet."[3461] Also, the Microsoft Office Professional installed program would "allow manual editing of the Diebold GEMS database file," with the "AuditLog" table able to be "easily" edited.[3462] Why would there be such lax security, and why would an audit log need editing?

The *TACIR* report found that "Vote totals can be altered in the 'CandidateCounter' table much like editing a spreadsheet.[3463] Or, the candidate names can simply be switched in the "'Candidate' table."[3464] It further found that the HTML editor software installed indicated that "someone was attempting to edit saved Diebold election summary reports, perhaps to agree with altered vote totals in the Diebold Microsoft Access database file."[3465] In essence, the report said that the election winner's name could be simply switched with the loser's and that there was circumstantial evidence of fraud.

The *TACIR* report concluded that "unless Shelby County election officials can be seen as conducting a good faith investigation as to who had access to this central tabulator PC and the above unauthorized software and who actually did the illegal install, voters in this county (and ultimately the state) can have no confidence in the integrity of the November 2006 election."[3466]

Incredibly, the 2007 *TACIR* recommendation had not been followed. The 2013 *SCEPF Report* stated that the tabulator was still being plugged into the county network and not properly secured. Obviously, there never was an investigation and security procedures added, because the practice was continuing.

In addition, as in the August 2012 primary, records produced by the local election commission indicated that it voted to certify the October 2015 election without having all of the data.[3467] And the local election commission's practice to audit only a sample of precinct results, contrary to state regulations, was uncovered by Dr. Weinberg.[3468]

We dug in. Kernell and I even traveled to Nashville to review poll tapes at the Tennessee Election Coordinator's office, along with another volunteer Nashville attorney Steve Nunn. A client of mine once sent me a set of *Nancy Drew* books, a childhood favorite. The character Drew is a young girl sleuth who solved mysteries. My client likened me to Drew because I had solved his legal case. So, I put my best Nancy Drew skills to the effort of uncovering the reason for so many "glitches" over the years at our local election commission.

2

In addition to his call for new election machines, Editor Bernel Smith of the *Tri-State Defender* mentioned that Strickland would be the first white mayor of Memphis to serve in twenty-four years. He noted that despite the quarter of a century of African American mayors, there was still "significant work" needed to "advance Memphis as a whole."[3469] Interestingly, Editor Smith added that if Strickland did not act quickly to solve the city's problems, then "2019 will probably mark the return of an African American to the mayor's office" or possibly the election of the first woman to serve in that position. [3470]

My friend Steve Steffens, a local blogger, published a provocative piece for the *Memphis Flyer* about why there has never been a woman elected mayor of Memphis or Shelby County. [3471] Steffens pointed out that Nashville had just elected its first woman mayor, following Knoxville's first woman mayor elected in 2011 and Clarksville's in 2010 (which are three of Tennessee's five largest cities). [3472] With numerous qualified female candidates, both black and white, over the years, he asked why can't a woman be elected mayor of Memphis or Shelby County?

Steffens wondered if African American women's more conservative religious beliefs prevented them from supporting a woman, believing that a man should be in charge?[3473] He ended the article by saying that in 2015, he was "mystified" at the disparity.[3474] Whatever the reason, so am I.

And now, some twenty-five years after my first race for public office, Linda Moore with the *Commercial Appeal,* wrote about the shortage of female leaders in top positions in public office in the area.[3475] In late November 2015, only one woman served on the thirteen-member Shelby County Commission, with three elected to serve on the thirteen-member Memphis City Council. Still, no woman had ever been elected Memphis or Shelby County mayor.[3476] The wall at City Hall still showed only male portraits of former mayors. All were white men, and four African American men having served in elected or interim mayoral positions. Now, Strickland, another white male, would eventually add his portrait to the wall.

As the article pointed out, some small suburban towns in the Memphis metro area had elected women mayors who served well and were reelected.[3477] With women comprising about 60% of those who regularly vote, it was hard to understand why more had not been elected to the larger local legislative bodies and for the executive positions of Shelby County and Memphis mayor.

Here Dr. Pohlmann of Rhodes College admitted that he was baffled by the gender disparity.[3478] He wondered if the bias was taught in the schools.[3479] At one point, he speculated whether the numbers just meant that African American men were progressing faster than African American women.[3480] But if this were so, it does not explain the lack of more white female leadership in positions, including in the Memphis mayor's job.

In the article, longtime councilmember Janis Fullilove complained about male colleagues' disrespect towards her and the few other female Memphis city councilmembers.[3481] County Commissioner Heidi Shafer, Republican, called the difference in treatment more marked in the political world than in business.[3482] Shafer said that she was called by her first name more often than her male colleagues, and she had to monitor more carefully how she expressed her viewpoint than the men.[3483] It was good to hear the bias finally brought to light in the newspaper.

I offered my view, saying that in the Memphis area, race still dominated the discussion so much that gender disparities were rarely considered. With the 100th anniversary of women's suffrage fast approaching in 2020, I lamented the low use of female talent in the area. The continued and open disrespect of women politicians over time by some colleagues, the press and media, had deterred other qualified women from placing their names on the ballot. Since women had broken through and were serving well in many other parts of the country, I expressed my hope that one day Memphis and Tennessee would follow suit.[3484]

And I didn't just talk. I walked the talk. I had put my name on the mayoral ballot more than once. I also had supported other female candidates. And, in 2016, I volunteered at the Hillary Clinton for President's local headquarters. It was good to see Congressman Cohen and others endorse her and give active support. It was also interesting to read in the *Tri-State Defender* how a mother brought her third-grade daughter to hear Hillary Clinton speak at the Lemoyne Owen College in Memphis.[3485] The mother told the girl that her dreams to lead could come true one day. [3486]I paused to consider how my own mother had told me the same thing nearly fifty years earlier.

A few months later, when Bill Clinton was in Memphis to campaign for his spouse, I was there to shake his hand again. He gave a rousing speech. Much to my surprise, I was included in a campaign internet video of the event on his Facebook page, nodding my head in agreement at his words to the effect that his spouse should be given a chance to lead.

3

After twenty-five years of being involved in politics, I had come to realize how the same political dynamics often reappeared. After the Tennessee Supreme Court resolved the "tiny towns" crisis in 1997, the de-annexation bill had begun working its way through the state legislature years later. Here we were again. Various areas annexed into Memphis after the ruling now were trying to pass a law that would allow them to gather signatures on a petition and then vote to leave Memphis.

It was easy to understand why some annexed areas wanted to leave the city to avoid higher taxes. Without the resultant cost-efficiencies and reductions in expenses, the lack of a consolidated government prevented the leveling out of the tax burden. However, if the city's wealthier areas left, it would only add to the burden on those citizens remaining to pay for the necessary services. In a sense, this was an economic class issue since economically challenged areas would not similarly be allowed to de-annex and escape the city's heavier tax burden.

Later in 2018, Strickland himself would propose de-annexing a portion of the affluent Southwind and another area despite Memphis's resultant estimated $4 million revenue loss.[3487] Maybe he did it under duress to avoid losing other areas with the proposed legislative permission. But, by supporting de-annexation of the designated area of Southwind with an affirmative vote by the council later in the year, Strickland left himself open to charges that he was simply trying to appease wealthy residents and corporations at the expense of the rest of the taxpaying Memphians.[3488]

In fact, the Strickland administration was off to a rocky start. Although the new mayor seemed sincere in wanting to get control of crime, he did not have a police director hired until seven months after taking the oath of office. Then, despite a national search, he appointed the same interim director to do the job.[3489] Murders skyrocketed to rates unseen since 1993.[3490]

Despite campaign promises, Mayor Strickland was initially short on female appointments. After criticism from local women's advocate, Deborah Clubb, he quickly added a female fire chief and other appointments.[3491] However, the top spots of COO and CFO were given to the same white men who, although very qualified, had served in Wharton's administration.[3492] Later in 2018, he appointed a female CFO, but the same man continued to hold both the COO and CAO positions.[3493]

Strickland also appointed the same man as Special Assistant to the Mayor for Community Affairs, who served as Division Director of Public Services and Neighborhoods in Wharton's administration.[3494] His prior position had oversight of the Memphis Sexual Assault Resource Center.[3495] During his tenure, the center was taken over by the county due to failure to have adequate staff to gather evidence for rape victim kits promptly.[3496] The musical chairs continued.

Similarly, Strickland's pledge of improving the open records process was right out of the Wharton playbook that the Handy Clay lawsuit had exposed as more show than substance.[3497] Not long after that, the *Commercial Appeal* filed an open records lawsuit when the city administration refused to release the names of applicants and records related to the police director search. This occurred despite promises of transparency by the new mayor upon taking office.

And Strickland's new media policy caused an uproar in the press, with city employees no longer allowed to comment on city business to the press without notifying their boss. My opinion editorial published in the *Commercial Appeal* discussed the unconstitutional restraint of free speech of possible whistleblowers and referenced the Handy Clay case that the prior administration had been forced to settle.[3498]

Besides those issues, Strickland, originally from Indiana and not moving to Memphis until age twelve, appeared not to appreciate the rich Memphis musical heritage.[3499] Upon taking office, he disbanded the Memphis Music Commission and used the monies to fund his own C-Suite staff, including some large communication staff salaries.[3500]

In addition, Strickland's administration had supported charging a fee during certain hours for the public to gain access to the Beale Street Historic District. The fee had begun during the Wharton administration. A "Beale Street Bucks" payment receipt could be used as a coupon for food and drink purchased at participating clubs on the street for a partial refund of the fee. As the Executive Director of the Beale Street Development Corporation, Lucille Catron initiated a lawsuit against the city and the Downtown Memphis Commission (DMC) to stop the fee. Thereafter, I was retained, in my capacity as an attorney, to represent the plaintiff corporation and some individuals who opposed the fee. The amended lawsuit alleged constitutional violations, including race discrimination.[3501] Ultimately, the defendants decided to settle the case and stop the Beale Street Bucks fee. After the DMC paid the settlement, in 2018, they incredibly sought to bring the fee back again, now without a partial refund coupon.

Several African American city council members spoke out against the fee as discriminatory since their own expert report showed that more black citizens frequented the street on late Saturday nights when the fee was usually levied.[3502] Eventually, the council authorized a Strickland backed lower security fee, on an as-needed basis, during the 2019 summer months.[3503] The city leaders claim the fee is needed for street security, but club leases require security to be paid by the street merchants.[3504] The fee merely passes the "buck" from the merchants to the citizens.

The "Beale Street Bucks" fee, which denies public street access to those who can not afford to pay it, is also contrary to Beale Street's civil rights musical heritage. It brings a new meaning to the W. C. Handy song, *Beale Street Blues*.[3505] Memphis appears to be the only city in the entire nation that charges such a fee to enter a music entertainment district on a public street. While the pandemic obviated the practice due to a resultant significant drop in tourism, the fee was reinstated in the summer of 2021.

In addition to disregarding the musical heritage of Beale Street, the Strickland administration also has not taken sufficient action concerning another Memphis historical musical venue. During the 2015 election, Strickland had courted the Mid-South Coliseum Coalition with an appearance at the Roundhouse Revival at the fairgrounds. The coalition wants the historic facility, known for its musical concerts and professional wrestling events, to be renovated for public use. The Strickland administration subsequently proposed and secured state approval of $100 million in projected Tourism Development Zone funds to build a sports plex complex at the fairgrounds site.[3506] The coalition supporters, including leaders Roy Barnes, and filmographer Mike McCarthy, were relieved that the coliseum was not slated for demolition in the plan and pleased that the city has granted limited access to show potential investors.[3507] However, the coliseum is still mothballed, without any funds allocated explicitly by the Strickland administration for its redevelopment.[3508]

There has also been a controversy between the Strickland administration and those who manage Graceland, Elvis's prior home. The Elvis Presley Enterprises (EPE) wanted to add a concert arena to the luxurious Guest House hotel that features Elvis impersonators playing the piano in the lobby and his favorite foods such as peanut butter and banana sandwiches. The hotel EPE manager, Joel Weinshanker, publicly complained that the Strickland administration was not supportive of the plans to expand the popular tourist attraction.[3509] He even claimed that there were offers on the table worldwide to move the state's largest tourist attraction out of Memphis.[3510] At one point, he threatened to run a mayoral candidate against Strickland.[3511] Both the Mid-South Coliseum and the Graceland arena proposals were subjugated by the administration to its support of the Memphis Grizzlies and that team's lock on the city's concert hall venues due to a first right of refusal clause related to the FedExForum. Litigation ensued by EPE against the City of Memphis seeking a declaratory judgment that the incentives and tax breaks sought for its proposed concert arena would not violate the non-compete agreement for the FedExForum, and in 2021 the Tennessee Supreme Court reversed the trial court's dismissal and remanded for further action.[3512]

Besides push-back for not wholeheartedly supporting Memphis music, the Strickland administration encountered resistance when protestors with the Black Lives Matter group shut down the Memphis I-40 bridge over the Mississippi River to Arkansas for several hours. Strickland remained in his office, never even showing his face.[3513] The protest lasted until late in the evening.[3514]

It was disturbing to see police officers in riot gear with shields and billy clubs lined up on the bridge facing protestors, while the mayor did not address the public, even from the safety of the Hall of Mayors. All were grateful that the police handled the matter with no casualties or injuries, but many were angry that interstate traffic had been shut down for hours. Others were upset that more had not been done to address poverty in the city, with the protestors advocating for change. Although Strickland made some audio comments later that night, he was publicly criticized for lack of leadership.[3515]

Not long after that, Strickland put himself in a position to be booed and ridiculed in a public Black Lives Matter meeting.[3516] And, after a nonviolent "die-in" protest over poverty, crime, and police relations by a few citizens on his front yard, he authorized over $200,000 in overtime for 24-hour security for his personal residence.[3517] This was roundly criticized by some as protecting the mayor's personal family in a safer part of the city when more funds were needed to protect citizens in areas riddled with gangs and violence.[3518]

While Strickland claimed to have received death threats on social media from some of the supporters of the die-in protestors, as well as confederate statue supporters, it didn't help that he approved a "blacklist" requiring an escort at City Hall for specific persons with no criminal record.[3519] Included were some who merely had exercised free speech rights in protests.[3520] On the list was an ordained minister and graduate of the city's clergy police academy.[3521] This prompted a lawsuit by the ACLU and a ruling by a federal judge that the city had violated a 1978 Consent Decree with its political surveillance.[3522]

Moreover, Strickland had to eat crow over his campaign promise of getting crime "drastically" down when 2016 yielded 228 homicides, the worst count in twenty-three years.[3523] Perhaps to deflect attention, he invited Herenton to be the keynote speaker at his 2017 New Year's Day prayer breakfast. Herenton, who had served as school superintendent for twelve years, and Mayor of Memphis for seventeen years, now proposed a solution to the city's crime problems, calling it a "black" problem.[3524] He wanted to raise funds to start a mentoring and tutoring program and blamed Shelby County District Attorney Weirich, in part, for the high crime.[3525] More musical chairs—more recycling of status quo politicians—and amnesia apparently by Strickland as to how Herenton had brought the city to the brink of bankruptcy in the prior decade.

4

On August 26, 2016, I felt bittersweet when the Tennessee Women's Suffrage statue was dedicated by the female mayors of Nashville, Knoxville, and Clarksville.

Yes, progress had been made, but I still had to wonder when Memphis will elect an experienced woman as mayor; when our state will elect a woman governor, appoint a female as the state treasurer or comptroller; when our nation will elect a woman president.

When asked to be on a panel by the senior pastor at my church to discuss how the congregation could better serve our community, even I was surprised at the passion that welled up in my voice when describing my public service. The appearance made me wonder again why the doors had not opened for myself and many other women to serve in a greater way.

The barriers were brought home to me more intensely a few months later, when I mentored a white female youth as a volunteer at the local Youth Court hearing. The program helps teenagers learn about the judicial system in juvenile court. Some teenagers with a first-time minor offense are given a second chance after a trial by their peers and restorative justice. The girl who was serving as one of the peer youth lawyers told me that she was interested in attending law school but would probably leave the city for college. She explained that where you go to college is where you usually end up living. The teenager expressed an interest in politics and even said she wanted to be the mayor of Memphis. Next, the zinger. *She paused.* Then, she said, "but it would be hard for me ever to get elected mayor of Memphis." How many other girls and women of any race feel this way about opportunities?

In encouragement, I told her about my second place close finish for mayor of Memphis in 2007. She seemed surprised. Here I was face to face with a young girl whose dreams were the very same that mine had been forty years earlier. Forty years later, we both wondered if either of our dreams would ever be fulfilled. It seemed time had stood still.

Should I tell her to count the cost before jumping into the fray? Because of the time I devoted to public service over the years, there was substantially less time for my personal life. Even, my campaign manager once explained to a group of senior citizens that I wasn't single but married to *Memphis!*

Yes, I was there when constituents called needing help. I was there to protect thousands of children from a corrupt and negligent daycare system. I was there to pass the Memphis Plan for thousands to receive medical care. I was there to help pregnant women get the medical care they needed and to stop the system from throwing moms out of the hospital too soon after the delivery of their babies. I was there to help victims of domestic violence, rape victims, and women and men who were sexually harassed. I was there to fight for decent housing, better education, and job training. I was there.

The list includes helping a law professor get approved by the state for experimental cancer treatment that helped save her life and convincing a doctor to treat another constituent when a special experimental program was her last hope. Calling about potholes, problems at schools, attending PTA meetings, visiting the elderly in retirement homes and senior citizen centers, venturing to high school football and basketball games around the city, neighborhood parades and picnics, sitting in folks' back yards and on their front porches, stopping by fire stations and police stations, and hospitals. I gave 100% to the job.

My friend Mike Kernell always says that Memphis is a spiritual assignment. Being a white, progressive *female* independent-minded politician in Memphis sometimes seems like no man's—*or rather woman's* land.

My feelings for the city, which sometimes seems in a time warp, are like a love-hate relationship. I love the down-to-earthiness of the city; the barbeque at the Rendezvous, Corky's, and the One and Only; the soul food at the Four Way Restaurant in South Memphis where civil rights activists frequented; the huge Huey's burger and blowing toothpicks into the locally-owned restaurant's ceiling; the beautiful riverfront with gorgeous sunsets; the blues, jazz and rock music on Beale Street downtown and at the Overton Park Levitt Shell where Elvis played; musicals at the Orpheum; and the strong expressions of faith at the many religious institutions. I hate the underlying and sometimes overt racial tension, backwardness in terms of the lack of empowerment of women, high crime, lack of inclusiveness, marginalization on occasion by the press, and the practices of some pundits, politicians, and business leaders who gang up to keep control. A lot of talent is wasted simply because some are not the right race, gender, too honest, or just not part of the club. But, at the end of the day—Memphis does have *soul!*

It's a shame that perhaps the only prototypes allowed to me in this culture as a female politician so far are Joan of Arc, That Girl, the devil, or Scarlett O'Hara (as compared to by *Fox 13 Memphis News* reporter Les Smith). If so, then I go with Scarlett's toughness *after* the war, where she held onto the dirt and survived, albeit for my entirely different reasons.

The fact that metropolitan Memphis continually struggles with coming together causes me often to contemplate how Dr. King Jr. himself got caught in the spiritual trap. His death is a wound that festers and won't heal, perhaps until the entire truth of the circumstances is known, if ever. But, in the meantime, King Jr.'s dream of equality for all lives on. That includes women, too. Maybe one day, sexism in the city will be a thing of the past.

As part of my own effort to foster healing, in the summer of 2016, I volunteered for the Orange Mound parade committee. Instead of walking in front or riding in a car as a politician throwing candy to the crowd, I arrived at 7 am and spent the morning in the hot sun directing participants to their proper locations. Perhaps in humbling myself, it would help erase any doubts about the fact that the soap thrown by a campaign volunteer in 2007's parade was truly an innocent and unauthorized mistake. It felt good.

43

Musical Chairs 3

1

As the city geared up to honor Memphis sanitation workers and commemorate the fiftieth anniversary of Dr. King Jr.'s death, Memphis Mayor Strickland was blindsided by the remarks of *CNN* news political commentator Angela Rye about the city's lack of progress.[3526] As reported by veteran opinion columnist Wendi Thomas, now head of the *MLK50* economic justice project, Rye had met with Black Lives Matter and other activists before the speech. She had also agreed to donate funds from her city-paid appearance fee to some of their causes.[3527] At the "#I Am Memphis" event at the Orpheum, Rye blasted the city for high poverty, Strickland's City Hall "blacklist," and insufficient funding of education.[3528] The *MLK50* successfully brought its message to the nation's attention with the Rye remarks, to the current mayor's chagrin.

And, lo and behold, in the spring of 2018, former Mayor W. W. Herenton, age seventy-seven, unexpectedly announced that *he* would run for Mayor of Memphis in the 2019 election. Herenton said he wanted to make history again with a campaign theme of "Let's Do it Again."[3529]

Perhaps the possible closing of two charter schools of the consortium of which he was the superintendent impacted his decision?[3530] The schools had ranked in the bottom 5% in Tennessee the prior year. Herenton claimed on his campaign website that the ranking was due to flawed testing data.[3531] Then again, as *Commercial Appeal* reporter Ryan Poe postulated, maybe Herenton was simply doing Strickland "a favor" by announcing his candidacy.[3532] As Poe said, it "effectively cleared the field" for the incumbent.[3533] Or was it merely more musical chairs?

Otis Sanford, a *Commercial Appeal* columnist, wasted no time calling Herenton a serious contender for the 2019 mayoral contest.[3534] But, in the same article Lexie Carter, a long-time Democratic party official, expressed her belief that perhaps the voters this time would prefer a woman candidate.[3535] Now that would be something!

Many positives were happening in Memphis with the redevelopment of the vast Sears warehouse into a bustling Crosstown Concourse; the long-awaited opening of the Bass Pro Shop in the Pyramid with the elevator to the top finally built, along with a hotel, and fish ponds containing alligators; the revitalized Overton Square midtown neighborhood shopping and restaurant area; the opening of the Guest House at Graceland Hotel in Whitehaven; the new locally-owned Novel bookstore; as well as the move of ServiceMaster's headquarters to a vacant retail building downtown (although in 2021 it announced that the ServiceMaster Brand's headquarters would move to Altanta leaving only Terminix). However, Herenton cited the city's continuing problems with housing, deteriorating communities, crime, and poverty. [3536]

He was right in that despite Strickland's pledge in 2015 to "drastically reduce violent crime," saying he was the "man" with "the sense of urgency to fix" the problems, Memphis was still ranked third on the FBI's major city violent crime list.[3537] Even Memphis Police Deputy Ryall had admitted that the city was short over 600 police officers out of the needed complement of 2500.[3538] The officer defections due to benefit cuts had taken a toll on the city, and bitter resentment remained against all who had supported them (including prior councilmember Strickland). While Strickland now contended that gun crime was trending down in the summer of 2018, property crimes had increased. [3539] Moreover, crime was not "drastically" down as he had promised, now back peddling and calling it a "decades-old" "problem."[3540]

In the summer of 2018, Herenton reiterated that he was very earnest about his candidacy, citing his main goal of addressing economic inequality. [3541] He often exuded sincere passion when talking about helping the impoverished. He did not explain why he thought he could solve poverty now, after having had over seventeen years as Memphis mayor from 1991-2009 to tackle the problem.

Herenton did explain that his resignation as mayor in 2009 was not due to a desire to run for Congress. Instead, his campaign website stated that he resigned because he needed to devote time to defending against the FBI investigation, calling it "unfounded" and "ultimately unsuccessful." This left unanswered why he didn't run for mayor in 2011 or 2015.

And, even though low-key Strickland had promised to be "brilliant at the basics" as mayor, the proliferation of potholes in the city was so dangerous that it spawned a 3,000 plus member Facebook group devoted solely to advocate for repairs.[3542] I can attest to the problem, having reported one on a major street that wasn't fixed for more than a year.

More significant, while development was booming, Memphis Chamber of Commerce Chairman Richard Smith (son of Memphis-based Federal Express founder Fred Smith) sounded the alarm that the city's growth had stalled since 2001.[3543] This was during the Herenton, Wharton, and Strickland administrations. Ted Evanoff with the *Commercial Appeal* quoted Smith to say that no one has held the mayors accountable for the stagnant growth.[3544] The lack of enough good-paying jobs had left nearly 27% of the city's population struggling in poverty.[3545] Interestingly, Smith, who took some criticism for raising the growth issue, as a child was given a poster from his father of the famous Theodore Roosevelt "Man in the Arena" speech.[3546] Whether his call to action in Evanoff's column, as a respected business leader, would result in the needed reforms to jumpstart economic growth in the city was the subject of considerable debate.

Memphis is the nation's poorest large city.[3547] The county is one of the highest in persons working temp jobs at minimum wage with no benefits.[3548] Unfortunately, the tenures of Herenton and Wharton, both long-serving mayors, had not been able to reverse the plight of the poor, many of whom are African American. Nor, had Strickland, a white male, since his election in 2015, which some say was the impetus for the Black Lives Matter Memphis protests.

The data supported Smith's statements, with reported fewer employers in the entire Memphis metropolitan region than twenty years ago.[3549] Although there had been increased private sector investment, experts cited by Evanoff found that the metro area's gross domestic product adjusted for inflation had decreased after the Great Recession of 2008 ended.[3550] This was during the Wharton and now Strickland tenures as mayor.

Strickland blamed the decline on insufficient workforce development. However, he agreed that unlike most of the nation's metropolitan areas, the Memphis area GDP had not grown.[3551] And, Memphis had not recruited a major out-of-town corporation in the past six years.[3552] In the aftermath of Smith's pronouncements, finger-pointing followed as to whether the lack of leadership was attributable to the Chamber of Commerce or the EDGE board that recruited major corporations and manufacturers (as Smith contended).[3553]

It appeared from the statistics that none of the mayors since 2001 had taken the city to the next level.

Over the years, questions had been raised about whether there was proper oversight to ensure that companies awarded tax abatements produced the jobs promised and met other requirements. Some believed that the EDGE board gave tax breaks to some companies that might stay in the area regardless, thus unnecessarily reducing government revenues.[3554] They argued that the application process did not properly consider whether the corporate property tax breaks for the applicants justified the resulting cost-shifting of the tax burden more heavily onto the citizens.[3555] Certainly, these were important considerations.

Weathersbee of the *Commercial Appeal* also pointed out that from 2010 to 2016, metro Memphis had one of the highest outward migrations in the nation of fifty major cities.[3556] The area was losing the race to attract and keep enough millennial and Gen Z workers.[3557] Since a "culture of inclusion" is one of the top factors in attracting and retaining such talent, the failure to include a woman in the mayor's office and other key positions detracted from the area's long-term economic development goals.[3558] Studies show that these generations want a society free of gender bias.[3559]

It was refreshing to hear new voices stepping up to bring out the truth about what our city needs, instead of the usual submission to "groupthink." Yet, the seemingly never-ending musical chairs continued, with Herenton pushing forward against Strickland for the October 2019 mayor's race. Strickland boosted a million-dollar war chest, and Herenton the loyal support of his base of older citizens.

Another entry into the race was articulate Tami Sawyer, a newly elected thirty-six-year-old county commissioner. She garnered the support of a new People's Convention organized by local ministers and civil rights advocates.[3560] Strickland, deemed "no progressive" by *Commercial Appeal* columnist Tonyaa Weathersbee, had skipped the convention.[3561] He claimed a convener, Pastor Earle Fisher, was biased in Sawyer's favor.[3562]

Fisher relayed that the hot topics for the meeting included the "tale of two cities."[3563] The pastor contrasted booming downtown development with "South Memphis which showcases the results of years of economic disinvestment and exploitation."[3564] The irony was that the first People's Convention of 1991 catapulted Herenton into office with a similar agenda, which still had not been fully accomplished. Now 28 years later, he was on the ballot again with the same plan.

As to his record, once again, Strickland's goal of getting crime down had not been achieved. As the local *Fox 13 Memphis News* reported in August 2019, a net increase of only three police officers had been added to the 2,064 employed when he took office.[3565] At that point, his target complement of officers was 2,400, with some calling him "weak on crime."[3566] Violent juvenile crime was up nearly 65% in 2019 from the prior year, and homicides increased as well during that time period (although the total violent crime rate had decreased from the preceding year).[3567] It was obvious that his pledge to get crime drastically down whether by additional law enforcement measures, or intervening in the lives of children, had not materialized.

Strickland did boost increased development in Memphis, improving 911 call response times and expanding pre-K, with no increased property taxes.[3568] But, Herenton challenged him on failing to reduce the crime rate and the proliferation of gaping potholes.[3569] Strickland retorted with the same tactics he had used against Wharton in 2015, criticizing Herenton as having failed by leaving office with high poverty, crime, and poor-performing schools.[3570] But, he hadn't made a dent solving the problems either.

The *Commercial Appeal* endorsed Strickland based, in part, upon the economic development progress (although admitting that City Hall might not have much to do with that success).[3571] Mentioning Richard Smith's arguments that the region had stalled for twenty years, the editors observed that the recent job growth was still below national gains since the recession and even the 1999 figures.[3572] Moreover, some parts of the city had been ignored.[3573] It clearly was not a ringing endorsement as to the city's progress during his tenure.

Earlier, Strickland had claimed to double the city's minority and women-owned business contracting. His embarrassed administration had to back-track after the *Memphis Business Journal* reported substantial errors in the data (although noting it was still higher than the year he took office).[3574]

Moreover, Memphis has the highest rate of youth between the ages of 16 to 24 who are not in school and are unemployed.[3575] While the city had added some activities, the *Commercial Appeal* editors agreed with Sawyer that much was needed to be done.[3576]

It was refreshing that those editors now said that Sawyer, a female, spoke: "with authority on equity, inclusion and the need to focus on education."[3577] This was after an outcry that caused *Memphis Magazine* to pull its September cartoon cover.[3578] The cartoon had exaggerated Sawyer's features and her size and depicted Herenton's hands positioned as if making a gang sign (both candidates are African American).[3579] Republican Mark Billingsley, the new chair of the Shelby County Commission, and others spoke out that the cartoon perpetuated racial stereotypes.[3580] The CEO of the parent company for the magazine issued a public apology on behalf of the magazine.[3581] Obviously, there was still work needed to eliminate racial and gender stereotypes by some in the press and media.

The *Commercial Appeal* editors also panned Herenton, age 78, for his refusal to debate (just as he had done in 2007).[3582] While some thought Herenton had an organized GOTV effort, he did little advertising and kept a low profile most of the campaign. It was fair to wonder if he was sincerely seeking to do the job, or (as in 2007) running with another agenda.

Ultimately, Strickland won with 59,904 votes (about the same number of votes cast for me in the 2007 mayor's race against Herenton). [3583] Herenton could only muster 27,702 votes in the 2019 mayoral election, with Sawyer coming in a distant third with 6,669 votes. [3584] Interestingly, Prince Mongo had made an appearance garnering 471 votes, with Sharon Webb receiving 445 votes.

There had been some name-calling in the race, with Herenton dismissing Sawyer as a "distraction."[3585] Sawyer had reciprocated, claiming Herenton was a "misogynist."[3586] She was related to the legendary civil rights leader Benjamin Hooks. However, her campaign suffered some embarrassment over her old tweets. [3587] But, after the election, she retained her respected status as a county commissioner.[3588] Thus, the musical chairs continued, with Strickland retaining his position as mayor this time.

As the coronavirus raged in 2020, a study by consultants to the city indicated that 2,800 police officers are the real compliment needed to protect the citizens.[3589] The mayor's own human resource chief, Alex Smith, even called the city's complement of about 2,100 police officers in place in the summer of 2020 as a "personnel crisis."[3590] Strickland's push for a referendum to allow officers to live outside the county as a recruitment strategy failed later in the summer with insufficient city council support.[3591] The Memphis Crime Commission and the Public Safety Institute at the University of Memphis reported huge jumps in violent crime and murders from the prior year. [3592] The city broke its homicide record, with 323 murders as of December 21, 2020.[3593]

The need to retain experienced officers and recruit others should have been considered before the fateful vote by Strickland and others to cut benefits in 2014, which prompted many officers to retire early, and others to depart to greener pastures. As a result of the successful referendum pushed by the city police and fire workers to increase the sales tax by a half-cent, in 2020 the Strickland administration was reluctantly discerning how to restore pension and health care benefit cuts for police officers and firefighters hired from 2009 through the middle of 2016.[3594] The grand experiment in making the cuts had failed, with the public left at risk due to the officer shortage.

Later, MPD Police Director Rallings announced his retirement. As this book goes to publication in 2021, Strickland attempted to rebound on the policing fiasco by nominating the first female for the position (who also was from out-of-state). Perhaps, she will be able to get the job done on reducing crime where others have not succeeded.[3595]

44

Working to Save Democracy

1

After the 2016 presidential election, there had been a renewed interest in election security. My open records requests had continued with Kernell and Weinberg, as we learned that some poll tapes from 2012 had been inexplicably lost or destroyed by the election commission. Hundreds of hours were spent reviewing documents. Our work was even mentioned in the *Bloomberg Businessweek* magazine and reported across the nation by the Associated Press.[3596]

We dug further for the truth and submitted our forty-nine-page *Voting on Thin Ice: How systematic voting failures are a real threat to our democracy* report to U.S. Sen. Mark Warner, ranking member, and the U.S. Select Senate and House Congressional Intelligence and Judiciary Committees in the fall of 2017. Included with the report were three huge notebooks full of over 1,000 pages of supporting exhibits. And I personally hand-delivered our *Voting on Thin Ice* report to former President Jimmy Carter at his Sunday school class in Plains, Georgia, and to the Carter Center Foundation. Our report was sent to experts, leaders, and attorneys involved in the recount effort after the 2016 presidential election.

It was mind-boggling to hear reporters nationwide say over and over again that the voting machines are not connected to the internet. Our report documented that our system *was* connected to our county network and the internet in at least two different years.[3597] In fact, each voting machine in our county sports a modem, and the results are remotely transmitted on election night from different satellite zones to the tabulator.

In 2016, the former Tennessee Attorney General, Mike Cody, reported that his vote cast for a candidate flipped to another in a congressional election. And a local election commissioner exclaimed that on numerous occasions, the voter's choice for Hillary Clinton flipped to Donald Trump, and votes for Trump disappeared. A Memphis city councilwoman even called for an investigation due to machines rendering voters the wrong electronic ballot.

In 2017, unencrypted data of 650,000 Shelby County voters was exposed at the DEF CON international hackers' convention from an electronic poll book sold on eBay. Poll book data can be used on Election Day to disenfranchise thousands of voters by incorrectly marking some voters as having already voted.

In 2018, over 6,000 voters were not found in the county electronic poll books, resulting in long lines to try to address the problems. And those who needed larger type on the voting machine were provided an electronic ballot that bumped one major party's gubernatorial nominee onto the second page. One local election commissioner stated in an email her belief that "manipulation" occurs inside the election operations, either at satellite zones during reconciliation or possibly during tabulation. She reported that the daily early vote totals did not balance and rumors that ballots had been backed out.

Despite the repeated serious irregularities, there has been no disclosure of any forensic audit. The local election administrator has refused to produce the system's audit logs, claiming they are proprietary to the vendor. She even stalled giving the logs to new election commissioner and IT expert, Bennie Smith, forcing a legal opinion. Although it was determined that as a commissioner he was entitled to receive the information, months have gone by still without it forthcoming as of the publication of this book.

Shelby County has the largest African American voting population in the state. The county has enough voters to impact statewide election results. In 2018, the NAACP alleged voter suppression as to the reduction of early voting sites in predominately black neighborhoods.[3598] And, the Tennessee Black Voter Project filed a lawsuit when the county election commission rejected approximately half of 36,000 voter registration applications.[3599]

Our research found, among other things, that system passwords were insecurely emailed to state officials, and databases remotely transferred to the out-of-state election vendor "to fix." A county audit reported that 29 unauthorized users had system access that would allow them to change the system security and coding. [3600] The chain of custody of memory cards from the precincts carrying thousands of votes was not adequately documented. And election vendor technicians and others had unsupervised access to the tabulation server on more than one occasion.

We discovered that the 21 extra memory cards uploaded to the system for COR-09 before the August 2012 Election Day polls closed was not the first time irregularities were reported related to that precinct. In a 2010 post-election lawsuit by various candidates, the plaintiffs' cybersecurity expert reported that thousands of "phantom" votes were uploaded the day before Election Day for five precincts, including COR-09. [3601] In that election, the wrong database was uploaded to the system, impacting over five thousand voters. And, the early vote poll tapes, as had been the case for the August 2012 election, were mysteriously missing from the state and local archives.

When we submitted open records requests to find out who uploaded the 21 extra cards in 2012, a piece of paper was produced with a note that an election worker had done so with the election vendor's knowledge. However, we could not ask him what happened because he drowned in a private lake, reported as a fishing accident. The death occurred only one week after my letter was faxed to the DOJ, U.S. Attorney, and FBI reporting the 21 extra cards in August 2014. Thereafter, our volunteer veteran private investigator, Nate Lenow, dug in to attempt to find out what had transpired.

While we had been working together on election security reform since 2012, news of Russian interference in the U.S. elections now had become an international issue. Former CIA Director Woolsley warned that the most serious threat to election security is that about 25% of America's voting machines do not have a paper trail.[3602] Weinberg, Kernell and I had warned of the vulnerabilities of DREs for years, with Kernell quoted in the *New York Times* as far back as 2003.[3603]

Despite contacting numerous federal, state, and local authorities, including the election officials, nothing was done. So, in October, 2018, in my capacity as an attorney, I filed a federal district court election security civil rights lawsuit on behalf of the Shelby Advocates for Valid Elections (a nonprofit).[3604] After the complaint was amended, the plaintiffs were the SAVE nonprofit, Mike Kernell, State Rep. Joe Towns Jr., Britney Thornton, and Ann Scott [the "SAVE plaintiffs"]. The claims were constitutional violations related to due process and equal protection.

The SAVE plaintiffs asked the district court to enjoin and require decertification of the Shelby County election system and implement hand-marked paper ballots that can be optically scanned. The lawsuit sought cybersecurity protections, a ban on remote transmission, and the use of voting machines and systems with no wireless communication capability. The SAVE plaintiffs asked to observe all stages of election processing, to be notified of any irregularities, for accurate audits, and the appointment of an Independent Master. The SAVE lawsuit asked that the court order a forensic audit of the software, voting machines, tabulators, and the production of the audit logs. The SAVE plaintiffs demanded criminal background checks of workers, vendors, and volunteers; preservation of all digital ballot images; and retention of the current voting systems until the expert examination.

Investigations and hearings were held during this time by the U.S. Select Senate Intelligence Committee. The committee's report (the "*SSIC Report*") issued in the summer of 2019, found election systems in all fifty states were targeted by the Russians in 2016.[3605] The interference was ongoing, continuing in 2018.[3606]

The *SSIC Report* discusses the motive for the attacks as to sow chaos on Election Day and undermine confidence in the results. [3607] An example of possible methods used by the hackers is changing voter data in the voter registration database.[3608] The result sought is to disenfranchise or impede voters who seek to cast a ballot. [3609] Certainly, this might explain the thousands of voters in Shelby County rendered the wrong ballots on Election Day in repeated years. A forensic audit could shed light, but our state and local election officials have refused to answer the request.

The *SSIC Report* notes the ES & S vendor's admission that it had installed remote-access software on election equipment sold in the mid-2000s. [3610] The remote access is documented in our *Voting on Thin Ice* report. When questioned by U.S. Senator Wyden, the company admitted that over 300 jurisdictions had the software which allowed remote access. [3611] ES & S testified that the software was only installed on election management systems, not voting machines.[3612]

However, the *SSIC Report* also found many DRE voting machines to be internet-enabled.[3613] It further observed that the voting machines were often programmed for Election Day by downloading software to them from a computer connected to a local network computer or by using removable media with a thumb-drive.[3614] The *SSIC Report* stated that if the computer used to write or distribute the program is compromised, so are the voting machines.[3615] As documented in the *Voting on Thin Ice* report, the Shelby County voting system still in use in 2021 was connected to the county IT department and the internet.

Moreover, the *SSIC Report* described the 2017 DEF CON Voting Village Hacker's Convention findings that voting machines could be infiltrated through USB ports.[3616] And, election security expert, Dr. Alex Halderman, testified that once injected, a virus can spread to the other voting machines.[3617]

The *SSIC Report* further ominously finds that "machines can be programmed to show one result to the voter while recording a different result in the tabulation. Without a paper backup, a 'recount' would use the same faulty software to re-tabulate the same results, because the primary records of the vote are stored in computer memory."[3618] Our concerns set out in the lawsuit and the *Voting on Thin Ice* report were confirmed by the *SSIC Report's* findings.

The bipartisan *SSIC Report* recommends optical scanners with paper ballots as the "least vulnerable to cyber attack."[3619] It further advocates for states to ensure that the supply chain for vendors is secure, to utilize the highest cybersecurity protections, to develop strong chain of custody protocols for the paper ballots with timestamps when scanned, and to adopt risk-limiting audits that check a statistically accurate sample of paper ballots for each precinct after the election.[3620]

Senator Ron Wyden issued a blistering Minority View for the *SSIC Report*, wherein he urged that Congress take immediate action to protect the U.S. voting systems. He pointed out that the committee had heard expert testimony about "successful Russian exfiltration of databases of tens of thousands of voters."[3621] Among other things, he recommended that Congress adopt mandatory rules for voter database security.[3622] Consider that the Shelby County electronic poll book, containing the data of 650,000 votes, was sold on eBay. Wyden is right.

Wyden further observed that the claim of government experts that foreign actors had not changed any votes was speculation.[3623] He pointed out that the U.S. Department of Homeland Security admitted that it did not conduct forensic audits of any voting machines.[3624] Moreover, its assessment of whether any votes were changed did not apply to state or local elections.[3625] Sen. Wyden further noted the lack of information about whether state and local election commissions had forensically audited voter registration databases.[3626] And he reminded the committee about the documented foreign infiltration of an election technology company.[3627]

Despite the reports, in September 2019, the district court dismissed the SAVE plaintiffs' lawsuit without prejudice after oral arguments of the attorneys. Present for the plaintiffs were Mike Kernell, Dr. Joseph Weinberg, myself as counsel, and my bright college student assistant Jack Zheng. Judge Tommy Parker opined that the plaintiffs could not show injury sufficient to bring the case (standing).[3628] The SAVE plaintiffs appealed to the Sixth Circuit Court of Appeals. Amici Curiae briefs from current and former election officials from 13 states (bipartisan) and cybersecurity experts were submitted on behalf of the plaintiffs.[3629] Their respective counsel, the Brennan Center, Troutman Pepper Hamilton Sanders, Covington Burling, Andrew Gross Law Firm, and Free Speech for People succinctly set forth the realistic danger that the nation's voting systems have become prey to nefarious interests.[3630]

I argued the SAVE appeal before the Sixth Circuit in December 2019. Present for the oral arguments for the plaintiffs in Cincinnati were Mike Kernell, Dr. Joseph Weinberg, State Rep. Joe Towns Jr., and my sister Mary. On expedited review, the panel affirmed the district court's dismissal on January 24, 2020.[3631] A petition for rehearing en banc was denied on March 10, 2020.

Not giving up, the SAVE plaintiffs filed a petition for writ of certiorari with the U.S. Supreme Court in June 2020.[3632] An Amici Curiae Brief in support was filed again for the bipartisan individual election security experts by the Free Speech for People and Covington & Burling LLP law firm.[3633] The defendant state and local election commissions and officials decided not to file any response. However, only one week after Justice Ruth Bader Ginsburg died, the Court operating with only eight justices denied the petition on September 29, 2020.

The SAVE plaintiffs, and I, respectfully disagree with the lower court opinions that held there was no standing to bring the lawsuit. On August 15, 2019, Georgia's entire state was enjoined by a federal district judge from using the same type voting system used in Shelby County, Tennessee, due to its proven vulnerabilities.[3634] That Judge had allowed expert testimony on the jurisdictional issue of standing in that case. But the SAVE plaintiffs were not given the same opportunity in the Tennessee federal district court, with the case dismissed after briefs and oral arguments of counsel. Nor was the SAVE plaintiffs' expert, Mathew Bernhard, allowed to testify.

In the SAVE lawsuit, the Sixth Circuit incredibly held there was no imminence of injury in fact such as to constitute standing to bring the lawsuit. The panel ruled that the same exact voting system hacked anywhere in the United States, such as in Georgia, did not suffice to show the imminence of injury in fact for standing. SAVE's position is that the same system known to be insecure and hacked in another state should constitute sufficient injury to bring a lawsuit for redress.[3635] And, in the SAVE lawsuit, the facts as to the breach of the system are even more egregious than in the *Curling, etal v. Kemp, etal*, Georgia district court decision.

In the *Curling* case, two cybersecurity experts could access the system online.[3636] In the SAVE case, the *TACIR Report* documents a *critical security breach* where the voting system was found to be exposed to the internet and to have *unauthorized editing software.* The *TACIR* further found that *someone was attempting to edit saved election summary reports, perhaps to agree with altered vote totals* in the database file.

In *Curling*, cybersecurity experts found voter data exposed online. [3637] In the SAVE case, the individual plaintiffs' voter data *was exhibited at an international hackers' conference* when an unwiped poll book was sold on eBay.

In *Curling*, the experts accessed system passwords. [3638] In the SAVE case, passwords were insecurely emailed, *and 29 unauthorized users were given access.*

In *Curling*, the plaintiffs alleged that their votes could be manipulated by remote transmission from satellite zones on election night. In the SAVE case, the plaintiffs allege the same.

In *Curling* the cybersecurity experts promptly reported the data and system exposure to state and federal authorities. Yet, the *TACIR Report* warned of *fraud* and urged a good faith investigation by the Shelby County Election Commission as to who had access to the central tabulator, the unauthorized software, and who *did the illegal install.* Thus, the harm alleged by the SAVE plaintiffs *has occurred.* There is no evidence that a forensic audit was ever done to remove the unauthorized editing software, malware from the internet exposure, or any coding changes from unauthorized users. There is a real and immediate threat of repeated injuries due to the continuing adverse effects of the corrupted server, tabulator, and system.

Moreover, equal protection has been denied to SAVE plaintiffs, two of whom are black. On the other side of Tennessee, Hamilton County uses optical scan machines. Under state law, such machines have mandated safeguards, including a ban on the machines having any capacity, enabled or disabled, for wireless communication of any sort.[3639] But, the law does not include the DRE-type machines used in Shelby County. Thus, plaintiffs Towns Jr. and Thornton's votes are diluted due to the vulnerabilities of the system used in Shelby County and less likely to be counted than those of voters in Hamilton County.

In 2006, the Sixth Circuit held in the famous *Stewart v. Blackwell* decision that the punch card voting machines used in Ohio violated equal protection where there was an *increased risk* that the individual plaintiffs' votes would be improperly discounted. [3640]

Yet, the circuit panel chaired by Judge Julia Gibbons in 2020 held that the

SAVE plaintiffs would have to prove that it was "inevitable" that their voting rights would be denied.[3641] The circuit panel, without the district court having heard any expert proof, opined that all of the facts of election irregularities raised by the SAVE plaintiffs were "human error" or "mistakes."[3642]

The heightened "inevitable" injury standard for imminence now set by the Sixth Circuit disregards the realistic danger of undetectable hacking or internal manipulation of the voting system. It ignores that the SAVE expert opined there was circumstantial evidence of the same. It also departs from prior precedent that excuses definitive proof where the injury is impossible to show with absolute certainty or cannot be specifically identified in advance.[3643] Because the defendants control the local election system and refuse inspection, definitive proof of the piracy of the plaintiffs' votes should be excused until the courts order a forensic audit.

Clearly, there is more than one kind of virus that threatens us. The continued use of paperless, unauditable electronic voting machines in many jurisdictions jeopardizes democracy. It opens the door for sophisticated hackers to insert viruses or internal operators to manipulate votes without detection. The close 2020 presidential election in conjunction with the 2016 findings of international election interference bring home the point that this is not a partisan issue—it is an American issue.

A hand-marked paper ballot system should be required, so there is always a back-up to ensure that all votes are correctly counted. A paper receipt is not sufficient. There have been instances where races have been left off the ballot that the voter can catch with a hand-marked paper ballot—but not with a receipt after the vote is cast. Also, a bar code scan of votes can not be read by the human eye. Tried and true hand-marked paper ballots that can be scanned are the gold standard for election security.

We joined with other election security advocates to push for reforms, including U.M. Law professor Steve Mulroy, Erica Sugarmon and her daughter, libertarian Mitchell Morrison, college professor Sara Freeman, and activist Marlene Strube, civil rights leader Rome Withers, long-time election security advocate "Yahweh," Free the Speech operative Susan Greenhalgh, John Brakey, Susan Pychon and others affiliated with Audit USA, and many others around the country.

As I told Columbia Law students in early 2020 as a panelist for the American Constitution Society, we will continue to fight for the truth and secure fair elections. This is essential to preserve our democracy.

45

——

What's Ahead

1

Since being out of public office, I have used my spare time to help the LINCS domestic violence shelter run by survivor Wanda Taylor in northwest Memphis, volunteer for Youth Court, regularly guest host "Let's Talk Law" with host Cleveland on the historic *WLOK* radio station, and fight for election truth and other reforms. I even scored three first-place wins with my talented ballroom dance instructor Arman Sahakyan at the 2018 Tennessee Volunteer Dance Competition, and traveled to Buenos Aires, Argentina in 2019 with him and his other students to tango! Life goes on.

An activist, who is African American, encouraged me at church with her observation that I have *been* the mayor of Memphis for the past many years, even though unpaid and without an official position. It was a huge compliment. I have continued to attend community events, volunteer, and speak up long after leaving public office in 2007. Many constituents still call me for help. One even left a voice mail recently about how I was "unstoppable, incorruptible, and a real gem."

Yet, I reflect that women have been presidents and the top leader in many cultures and countries, but not here.[3644] When will America join the ranks? When will Tennessee? When will Memphis? Of course, not just to elect any woman, but those who are experienced, qualified, tested, and ready to lead.

A harbinger may be the #MeToo movement clearing out the worst gender-bias offenders in the press and media. Women holding top positions in the press and media also matters, as evidenced by the *Tennessean*'s endorsement in 2015 of that city's first woman elected as Nashville mayor (although she later resigned).[3645] The newspaper's publisher and president, and its vice-president, and executive editor at the time of the endorsement, were female. [3646]

Some good news came with a "pink wave" in the August 2018 Shelby County elections, in which women won nine of thirteen overall countywide races.[3647] But, despite the female voting majority, only three women were elected to the thirteen-member Shelby County Commission.

The *Commercial Appeal's* editors found the female victories "encouraging and instructive."[3648] Yet, the newspaper yielded again to gender stereotypes by writing that the women candidates focused more on family issues, health care, education, and gun violence, while male candidates talked about more "distant" issues such as immigration, taxes, budgets and bringing jobs.[3649] Thinking back to the article years ago in the same newspaper stereotyping the "personalities" of women leaders such as Janet Reno and Madeline Albright, I know we discuss all genres of issues. Certainly, the woman who was elected Shelby County Trustee, for example, focused on finances in her electoral contest.

After the elections in August 2018, I celebrated with the victorious newly elected officials at their swearing-in ceremony. Democratic state senator and law professor Lee Harris was sworn in as the newly elected Shelby County mayor. In part, I was prompted to help him in his election due to a published review he had authored about Otis Sanford's new book on Memphis racial politics.[3650] In the review, he noted the absence of any substantial coverage of black women leaders in Sanford's book, such as of former mayoral candidate Minerva Johnican.[3651] Although it was only a few paragraphs in his overall positive review of the book, Harris had brought to light the obscuration of women leaders in our city's culture.

Many I have mentioned in this book were at the county swearing-in ceremonies. There was Myron Lowery with his wife, attending for his son who was newly elected to the Shelby County Commission. There was Edmund Ford Sr., with his son who was now leaving the Memphis City Council to serve on the Shelby County Commission. There was one son of A C Wharton, a bright attorney. I even shook hands with Joseph Lee III (who had lost a bid in the Democratic primary for county trustee) and utility and energy law attorney Herman Morris.

On another occasion, Tajuan Stout Mitchell organized a former city councilmember reunion dinner. We all sat around the table enjoying barbeque and old stories at the famous Rendezvous restaurant. It was easier to chat, no longer encumbered with the open meetings act, or pitted against each other by some in the press or media. While serving on the city council, some in the press had seemed like a lion that prowled—looking for a story, or else you would be their raw meat for the night.

At the dinner, E. C. Jones handed out gifts of bottled mineral water, Edmund Ford Sr. offered to pay for everyone's dinner, and some Republicans grumbled about the potholes and tall uncut grass on city right of ways. Rickey Peete, always displaying his best communication skills, called me *Senator.* There were hugs all around. Some had faced serious health issues, which brought them a different perspective in conjunction with a few additional years. Perhaps the wisest thing said the entire night was by Michael Hooks Sr. In response to being asked how he was doing, Hooks replied that he finally learned how to get out of his own way. Good advice for us all!

Afterwards, we posted photos on social media of us all sitting at the table smiling. I noted in my post how hard those years on the city council had been between 2003-2007 and that maybe healing for our city had begun. I wondered if those who had written in the press about the past disagreements between different members would notice or write about the friendly reunion. They didn't.

And, shortly after that, I ended up back at the city council at City Hall for a client. Waiting and watching for hours brought back memories of heated debates and long nights. Peace was even made with Councilman Joe Brown, who recognized me in the audience, said, "we used to be adversaries," and then graciously added, "no, she's good people." It's amazing what a few years can do.

I even happened to sit next to reporter Jackson Baker at a baseball game event, trading stories about days gone by. At another event, he asked if it has been difficult to write about the mayoral elections. I explained that the reason for my book is that it has been one hundred years since women's suffrage in the USA, and Memphis has never had a woman mayor, Tennessee a governor, or the USA a president. I told him that this is a cultural problem, but the culture is changing.

With the changing times, who knows, maybe Baker will be the one who uses his award-winning journalistic skills to write the story that propels the first woman to win the Memphis mayor's election. Perhaps author and Tennessee Journalistic Hall of Fame political columnist Otis Sanford, now with the *Daily Memphian,* will be the one to predict a female victory for the Memphis mayorship, or at least that a woman can win.

In early 2020, Sanford did write his opinion that Tennessee has a "man problem," with many leaders having "a paternalistic and chauvinistic attitude toward women."[3652] The article pointed out that a woman has never been elected Memphis or Shelby County mayor.[3653] And, that women only held 8 of the 33 senate seats, and 12 of the 99 in the state house (less than there were during my first year of service in 1991).[3654] Now, Sanford said he could hardly wait for the day when women have more significant leadership roles. I couldn't resist commenting below the article that it would have been nice if an opinion piece like that one had been penned by him years ago when I ran for mayor. I added my hopes that his column now was a sign of good things ahead for fairer coverage of women candidates.

And, when Kamala Harris was picked as a vice-presidential running mate by Joe Biden, Sanford acknowledged the "sexist attitudes" that women trying to move up face, such as being deemed "too ambitious," or with references to their disposition. [3655] Certainly, that happened to me. Maybe more of the press and media will become harbingers of the much needed cultural change to include female leadership at the highest levels.

In the end, it is merely a question of wanting basic respect. The truth is that it is not so much about electing women but about ceasing *not* to elect women who are more qualified and better able to do what is needed. It's about giving women a fair shake.

Sadly, the 100th anniversary of women's suffrage demonstrated how little progress has been made in Tennessee since my speech on the house floor in 1995. As reported by Natalie Allison in the *USA Today's Commercial Appeal* in August 2020, there are only 14 women of 99 state representatives and 8 of 33 in the state senate. [3656] Keep in mind that there were 13 female state house members for my first term as a state legislator in 1991. More than half of the Tennessee population is female.[3657] It is hard to understand why the state is 49th in the nation as to the proportion of women serving in the state legislature, according to the Rutgers University's Center for American Women and Politics for 2020.[3658]

Yet, some progress has been made. Nationally a woman was nominated for president of the USA by a major party in 2016, and another is the newly elected vice president in 2020. We are approaching watershed years ahead. Maybe electing a woman president of the USA, governor of Tennessee, or mayor of Memphis will cease to be the impossible dream and actually be achieved.

As I spoke at a local Girl Scouts Career Day, two young girls each told me they want to be president of the USA one day. A second-grader was disappointed that Hillary Clinton lost, but also expressed natural feelings of wanting to be the first woman president herself. I encouraged her to focus instead on growing up to be the *best* president of the USA.

Yes, I am hopeful.

I paid my dues, traveled the roads late at night to Nashville and back, and answered the phone at 3 am when constituents needed help. I worked hard and played by the rules (well – sometimes I did make some new rules and even broke a few). I won many big elections. And although not victorious in the mayoral contests, I competed against powerful well-funded men, and even came very close to winning in 2007. Despite the knocks and blows, false rumors, cheap shots, election irregularities, and sometimes biased coverage, I stayed true to my purpose. I have been a bold "woman" in the arena and dared greatly.

And who knows. Now that times are finally changing with a growing cultural shift and greater election security, – maybe I will dare greatly once again and God-willing triumph, winning the final count in the end.

Notes

1 Alisha Haridasani Gupta, "A Ground-breaking election for Women in Congress? Kind of," *New York Times*, November 5, 2020.

2 "Memphis State elects woman chief," *Memphis Press-Scimitar*, May 6, 1982.

3 Editorial, "Sound check," *Daily Helmsman* (Memphis, TN), February 24, 1983; "SGA chief vetoes Greek fund bill," *Daily Helmsman* (Memphis, TN), February 22, 1983.

4 "Attempted rape spurs petition drive," *Daily Helmsman* (Memphis, TN), December 2, 1982.

5 "SGA plans no role in Liddy funds," *Daily Helmsman* (Memphis, TN), November 19, 1982.

6 "Big Names on Campus," *Daily Helmsman* (Memphis, TN), December 3, 1982.

7 Charles Brown, "Praise Given for Funding of Education," *Daily Helmsman* (Memphis, TN), March 8, 1983.

8 Ibid.

9 Dave Hirschman, "Gaia's act comes as surprise," *Commercial Appeal* (Memphis, TN), May 17, 1990.

10 Joey Senat, "Dual role questioned in Gurley House bid," *Commercial Appeal* (Memphis, TN), June 15, 1990.

11 Jackson Baker, "Flaks, Flakes, and Flaps," *Memphis Flyer*, June 21-27, 1990.

12 Ibid.

13 Bob Bernstein, "District 89 Promises Action for Political Observers," *Memphis Business Journal*, July 23-27, 1990.

14 Ibid.

15 "Prize Your Right to Vote!" [Ad], *Memphis Flyer*, July 26-August 1, 1990.

16 Ibid.

17 Attributed to former U.S. President Harry S Truman.

18 Jackson Baker, "Strange Bedfellows: A between-the-sheets look at the odds and ends of this summer's campaign trail," *Memphis Flyer*, August 2-8, 1990.

19 "Harold Ford Sr.," *Wikipedia.*

20 Editorial, "Home alone at Justice?" *New York Times*, February 25, 1993; Jackson Baker, "Politics, Bush League," *Memphis Flyer*, September 13-19, 1990; Chris Conley, "Nominee says Rep. Ford Case to be Pursued," *Commercial Appeal* (Memphis, TN), September 5, 1991.

21 John Branston, "Flyer Flashback," *Memphis Flyer*, January 29-February 4, 2009.

22 Jackson Baker, "Road Warriors," *Memphis Flyer*, September 27-October 3, 1990.

23 Terry Keeter, "McWherter says budget impasse could cut agencies' workweek," *Commercial Appeal* (Memphis, TN), October 20, 1990.

24 Dave Hirschman, "Chumney wins seat in House," *Commercial Appeal* (Memphis, TN), November 7, 1990; Paula Wade, "Gore in Memphis pulpits, on TV for finale," *Commercial Appeal* (Memphis, TN), November 4, 1990.

25 Editorial, "Our picks for Nov. 6," *Memphis Business Journal*, October 29, 1990.

26 Dave Hirschman, "Months of work drawing to close in District 89 race," *Commercial Appeal* (Memphis, TN), November 1, 1990.

27 Christine Tracey, "Chumney mulls constituents' needs during legislative recess," *Daily News* (Memphis, TN), January 1991.

28 Terry Keeter, "Legislators blast I-40 proposal," *Commercial Appeal* (Memphis, TN), January 25, 1991.

29 Jackson Baker, "Future Tense," *Memphis Flyer,* December 27, 1990-January 2, 1991.

30 "Business Briefcase," *Memphis Business Journal,* February 4, 1991.

31 Wayne Risher, "Corridor talks will take a broader avenue," *Commercial Appeal* (Memphis, TN), December 23, 1999.

32 Jackson Baker, "Swing Shift," *Memphis Flyer,* April 4, 1991.

33 "Chumney to hold town meetings," *Mid-South Senior* (Memphis, TN), April 1991.

34 Paula Wade, "Novice legislator Chumney passes bills, breaks the rules," *Commercial Appeal* (Memphis, TN), April 30, 1991.

35 Ibid.

36 Ibid.

37 Ibid.; Paula Wade, "Health Center bill," *Commercial Appeal* (Memphis, TN), April 4, 1991; *See also,* Wayne Risher, "Church health center growing up," *Commercial Appeal,* March 14, 1991.

38 Bill Lewis, "Memphis Plan Scheduled to Go into Operation by Mid-July with Governor's Blessing," *Memphis Business Journal,* May 20-24, 1991.

39 Ibid.; "Winning the Game," *Memphis Health Care News,* May 24, 1991.

40 Kevin McKenzie, "World's Experts Take Notice of Church Health Center," *Commercial Appeal* (Memphis, TN), November 23, 2014; Viewpoint, "Study defines Church Health Center's value," *Commercial Appeal,* November 25, 2014; Email from Andreana Smith, Director of Clinical Administration, Church Health Center, August 27, 2020.

41 Kevin McKenzie, "World's Experts Take Notice of Church Health Center," *Commercial Appeal* (Memphis, TN), November 23, 2014; Church Health Center website, August 16, 2020.

42 Paula Wade; "Novice Legislator Chumney passes bills, breaks the rules," *Commercial Appeal* (Memphis, TN), April 30, 1991.

43 Ibid.

44 Ibid.

45 Ibid.

46 John Branston and Jackson Baker, "The State of Abortion," *Memphis Flyer,* July 9-15, 1992.

47 Richard Locker and Paula Wade, "House poised on bill; Senate lags," *Commercial Appeal* (Memphis, TN), May 16, 1991.

48 Ibid.

49 Bill Lewis, "Legislators Get Mixed Tax Signals from Constituents," *Memphis Business Journal,* May 27-31, 1991.

50 Bill Lewis, "Dobbs, FedEx Tutor State Agency in Lessons on Quality," *Memphis Business Journal,* September 30-October 4, 1991.

51 Ibid.

52 Ibid.

53 Paula Wade, "Panel: Time at other jobs won't boost teacher pay," *Commercial Appeal* (Memphis, TN), September 5, 1991.

54 Ibid.

55 *Tennessee Journal,* July 22, 1991.

56 Jackson Baker, "Race of Clubs," *Memphis Flyer,* August 8-15, 1992; Jackson Baker, "Trouble In and Out of School: Beginning a Series on Superintendent Willie Herenton's Departure from the MCS," *Memphis Flyer,* March 23, 2008.

57 Ibid.

58 Ibid.

59 Trevor Aaronson, "'89 study examined system—Then-Supt. Herenton faced suit, sex allegations," *Commercial Appeal* (Memphis, TN), April 20, 2008.

60 Marc Perrusquia, "First Black Mayor," *Commercial Appeal* (Memphis, TN), January 4, 2009.

61 Ibid.

62 Ibid.

63 Jackson Baker, "Race of Clubs," *Memphis Flyer,* August 8-1, 1992.

64 Calvin L. Burns, "Dr. Herenton moves into City Hall as his own man," *Tri-State Defender* (Memphis, TN), January 4, 1992.

65 Marc Perrusquia, "Willie Herenton: Always a Fighter," *Commercial Appeal* (Memphis, TN), January 4, 2009.

66 Kriste Goad, "Herenton campaign has spent a record $825,000," *Commercial Appeal* (Memphis, TN), October 5, 1999; "Mid-South Memories Nov. 22," *Commercial Appeal* (Memphis, TN), November 22, 2016.

67 Patti Patterson, "Breakfast hails a need to hug, Herenton ascent," *Commercial Appeal* (Memphis, TN), January 2, 1992.

68 Ibid.

69 Ibid.

70 Glen Yaun, "Black History Making Events," *Tri-State Defender* (Memphis, TN), January 4, 1992.

71 Calvin L. Burns, "Dr. Herenton moves into City Hall as his own man," *Tri-State Defender* (Memphis, TN), January 4, 1992.

72 "Three state legislators will hold a joint town meeting," *Commercial Appeal* (Memphis, TN), January 31, 1992.

73 Dave Hirschman, "Highway work in limbo," *Commercial Appeal* (Memphis, TN), January 2, 1992.

74 Michael Kelley, "A Day in the Life of a Tennessee Lawmaker," *Commercial Appeal* (Memphis, TN), January 31, 1992.

75 Ibid.; Bill Rawlins, Associated Press, "Official is Second Suicide During Federal probe in Tennessee," December 21, 1989; *Wikipedia Encyclopedia,* "Gentry Crowell, December 5, 2019.

76 "Operation Rocky Top," *Wikipedia Encyclopedia,* October 3, 2020.

77 Paula Wade, "Legislative flurry marks final day," *Commercial Appeal* (Memphis, TN), April 30, 1992.

78 Michael Kelley, "A Day in the Life of a Tennessee Lawmaker," *Commercial Appeal* (Memphis, TN), January 31, 1992.

79 Ibid.

80 Ibid.

81 Gail B. Stahl, Editor, "House assistant majority leader's predisposition is to make it hard for criminals," *Tennessee Town & City,* May 15, 1995.

82 Terry Keeter, "Endorsements flow at visit by Hillary Clinton," *Commercial Appeal* (Memphis, TN), March 7, 1992.

83 Ibid.

84 Ibid.

85 Jackson Baker, "The Year of the Woman," *Memphis Flyer,* May 7, 1992.

86 Ibid.

87 Lee Elder, "Legislators' High Jinks Condemned," *Leaf-Chronicle* (Clarksville, TN), May 5, 1992; Duran Cheek,

"Lawmakers object to pantie prank," *Tennessean* (Nashville, TN), May 5, 1992.

88 Lee Elder, "Legislators' High Jinks Condemned," *Leaf-Chronicle* (Clarksville, TN), May 5, 1992.

89 Duran Cheek, "Lawmakers object to pantie prank," *Tennessean* (Nashville, TN), May 5, 1992.

90 Ibid.

91 Ibid.

92 Ibid.

93 Jackson Baker, "The Year of the Woman," *Memphis Flyer,* May 7, 1992.

94 Ibid.

95 Jackson Baker, "Going with the Flow," *Memphis Flyer,* April 9, 1992.

96 Paula Wade, "Bids to alter tax by Constitution come up empty," *Commercial Appeal* (Memphis, TN), May 2, 1992.

97 Editorial, "Last chance to plan ahead," *Commercial Appeal* (Memphis, TN), April 28, 1992.

98 Paula Wade, "Cohen's 'insult' of House risks tax, lottery plan," *Commercial Appeal* (Memphis, TN), April 19, 1992.

99 Ibid.

100 Ibid.

101 Ibid.

102 Ibid.

103 Ibid.

104 Quintin Robinson, "Tax picketers target senator's residence," *Commercial Appeal* (Memphis, TN), April 19, 1992.

105 Paula Wade, "Cohen's 'insult' of House risks tax, lottery plan," *Commercial Appeal* (Memphis, TN), April 19, 1992.

106 Editorial, "Last Chance to plan ahead," *Commercial Appeal* (Memphis, TN), April 28, 1992.

107 Ibid.

108 Paula Wade, "Bids to alter tax by Constitution come up empty," *Commercial Appeal* (Memphis, TN), May 2, 1992.

109 Ibid.

110 Paula Wade, "Legislative flurry marks final day," *Commercial Appeal* (Memphis, TN), April 30, 1992; Paula Wade, "Bids to alter tax by Constitution come up empty," *Commercial Appeal,* May 2, 1992.

111 Paula Wade, "Bids to alter tax by Constitution come up empty," *Commercial Appeal* (Memphis, TN), May 2, 1992.

112 Ibid.

113 Ibid.

114 Paula Wade, "Unsolved big issues await next session," *Commercial Appeal* (Memphis, TN), May 10, 1992.

115 Tenn. Code Ann. 39-17-315.

116 Dennis Freeland, "Political Clout and Mental Health Facilities," *Memphis Flyer*, August 13, 1992.

117 Ibid.

118 "Tenn. Lawmakers win 5k road race," *Commercial Appeal* (Memphis, TN), July 18, 1992.

119 "Takako Doi," *Wikipedia Encyclopedia*, October 3, 2020.

120 Yuri Kageyama, A.P., "Emotional robot set for sale in Japan," *Commercial Appeal* (Memphis, TN), June 6, 2014.

121 Ibid.

122 Jackson Baker, "Crystal Balling," *Memphis Flyer*, 1992.

123 Ibid.

124 Ibid.

125 Jackson Baker, "For What It's Worth," *Memphis Flyer*, January 27, 1993.

126 Ibid; Laurel Campbell, "Tenn. Ban on games of chance keeping boats from Memphis," *Commercial Appeal* (Memphis, TN), April 25, 1993.

127 Jackson Baker, "For What It's Worth," *Memphis Flyer*, January 27, 1993.

128 Ibid.

129 Editorial, "Harassment policy fails," "Legislative, judicial branches should be covered," *Tennessean* (Nashville, TN), February 4, 1993.

130 Reed Branson, "Chumney files bill on sexual harassing," *Commercial Appeal* (Memphis, TN), January 15, 1993.

131 Ibid; Duran Cheek, "Quit or face ouster, convicted judge to be told," *Tennessean* (Nashville, TN), February 23, 1993; "The case of the sexual predator," *U.S. News & World Report*, April 19, 1993; *USA v. Lanier*, Case No. 2:92-cr-20172-BBD, ECF 343 (W.D. Tenn.), *U.S. v. Lanier*, 520 U.S. 259 (1997).

132 Paula Wade, "A bill lawmakers should take to heart," *Commercial Appeal* (Memphis, TN), February 14, 1993.

133 Ibid.

134 Ibid.

135 Ibid.

136 Ibid.

137 Ibid.; Editorial, "Sex Harassment, Tennessee needs a law that defines violations," *Commercial Appeal* (Memphis, TN), March 21, 1993.

138 Paula Wade, "A bill lawmakers should take to heart," *Commercial Appeal* (Memphis, TN), February 14, 1993.

139 Ibid.

140 Ibid.

141 Rebecca Ferrar, "Sexual harassment on legislative agenda," *Knoxville News-Sentinel*, February 14, 1993.

142 Ibid.

143 Ibid.

144 Ibid.

145 Ibid.

146 Duran Cheek, "Quit or face ouster, convicted judge to be told," *Tennessean* (Nashville, TN), February 23, 1993.

147 Ibid.

148 Ibid; "The case of the sexual predator," *U.S. News & World Report*, April 19, 1993; *U.S. v. Lanier*, 520 U.S. 259, 260 (1997).

149 "The case of the sexual predator," *U.S. News & World Report*, April 19, 1993.

150 Chris Conley, "Prosecutors want Judge's Bond Ended Lanier's Dyersburg Visits called Improper," *Commercial Appeal* (Memphis, TN), August 11, 1992; Lawrence Buser, "Judge Cancels Bond, Has Lanier Jailed for Pressing Witnesses," *Commercial Appeal* (Memphis, TN), February 6, 1993.

151 Bill Hiles, "Cole: wait for Court of the Judiciary ruling," *Dyersburg Gazette*, March 1, 1993.

152 Ibid.

153 Donna White, "Chumney, Cohen to proceed at 'full speed,'" *Dyersburg Gazette*, March 1, 1993.

154 Ibid.

155 Ibid.

156 Ibid.

157 Ibid; Reed Branson, "Two seek speedy ouster of Lanier," *Commercial Appeal* (Memphis, TN), March 16, 1993.

158 Reed Branson, "Capitol Chronicle" "Tenn. House joins Senate in extending sales tax increase," *Commercial Appeal* (Memphis, TN), March 4, 1993.

159 Ibid.

160 Richard Locker, "Cohen Withdraws Tenn. Lottery Bill While Blaming Casino Issue," *Commercial Appeal* (Memphis, TN), March 4, 1993.

161 Ibid.

162 Editorial, "Some potty training for Senator Ford," *Tennessean* (Nashville, TN), March 26, 1993.

163 Ibid.

164 Ibid.

165 Gail McKnight, "Harper flushes Sen. Ford for his potty parity remarks," *Tennessean* (Nashville, TN), March 26, 1993.

166 Ibid.

167 Duran Cheek, "Ban scalping, Brooks urges legislators," *Tennessean* (Nashville, TN), March 25, 1993.

168 Ibid.

169 Reed Branson, "House revives bill on ticket scalping," *Commercial Appeal* (Memphis, TN), May 6, 1993.

170 Pat Halloran, Guest Column, "Make scalpers accountable in ticket fairness," *Commercial Appeal* (Memphis, TN), February 22, 2013.

171 Ibid.

172 Marilyn Edwards, "Chumney bill will help define what sexual harassment is and isn't," *Tennessee Town & City*, March 8, 1993.

173 Bob Johnson, "Legislator Uses BNAC Videos to Help Pass New Sexual Harassment Law," *BNA Commissioner*, Fall 1993.

174 Ed Cromer, "House approves sex harassment bill," *Nashville Banner*, April 22, 1993.

175 Gail McKnight, "Lawmakers OK bill outlawing sex harassment," *Tennessean* (Nashville, TN), April 29, 1993.

176 Ibid.

177 Ibid.

178 "House Votes to Expand Sexual Harassment Training for Members," *Talking Points Memo*, May 1, 2014; "Process for reporting sexual misconduct in Congress," *Ballotpedia, citing* "How Congress plays by different rules on sexual harassment and misconduct," *Washington Post*, October 27, 2017.

179 Editorial, "No more guessing," *Tennessean* (Nashville, TN), May 3, 1993.

180 Judy Walton, "Tennessee Georgia taking steps to address sexual harassment," *Chattanooga Times Free Press*, January 22, 2018; Joel Ebert, "Despite misconduct allegations, Tennessee lawmakers remain confident of safe environment, experts concerned," *Tennessean* (Nashville, TN), April 11, 2019.

181 Dave Boucher and Kirk A. Bado, "Harwell Ramsey approve new sex harassment policy," *Tennessean* (Nashville, TN), July 14, 2016.

182 Joel Ebert and Natalie Allison, "Glen Casada to resign as speaker in coming weeks," *Tennessean* (Nashville, TN), May 21, 2019.

183 Ed Cromer and Lyda Phillips, "Lawmakers revoke Lanier judgeship," *Nashville Banner*, April 22, 1993; Paula Wade, "Legislative votes oust Lanier as Tenn. Judge," *Commercial Appeal* (Memphis, TN), April 22, 1993.

184 Editorial, "Stop the secret voting," *Tennessean* (Nashville TN), April 15, 1993. Other House and Senate sponsors were Rep. Frank Buck (D-Dowelltown), Sen. Joe Haynes (D-Nashville), and Sen. Bud Gilbert (R-Knoxville).

185 Editorial, "A chance to shed light," *Tennessean* (Nashville, TN), April 21, 1993.

186 Paula Wade, "Panel Ok's sex quota on education boards, *Commercial Appeal* (Memphis, TN), March 9, 1994; Ed Cromer, "Wanted: women to serve education," *Nashville Banner*, March 3, 1994.

187 Paula Wade, "Panel Ok's sex quota on education boards," *Commercial Appeal* (Memphis, TN), March 9, 1994.

188 Ibid.

189 Ibid.

190 Ibid.

191 Ed Cromer, "Wanted: women to serve education," *Nashville Banner,* March 3, 1994.

192 Robert Houk, "Lawmaker continues her crusade for women," *Johnson City Press,* January 19, 1994.

193 Photo by Marilyn Edwards, *Tennessee Town & City,* January 18, 1994.

194 Wendi Watts, "Assembly honors female members," *Daily News Journal* (Rutherford County, TN), April 18, 1995.

195 Ibid.

196 Associated Press, "Women may soon have potty parity," *Jackson Sun,* April 14, 1994.

197 Paula Wade, "House Ok's Chumney's 'potty parity' bill," *Commercial Appeal* (Memphis, TN), April 20, 1994.

198 Paula Wade, "Lawmakers brace for battle on merit selection of judges," *Commercial Appeal* (Memphis, TN), April 7, 1994.

199 Ibid.

200 Ibid.

201 Jackson Baker, "Systems Go, Says Sammons," *Memphis Flyer,* May 18, 1994.

202 Ibid.

203 "Political Women," *Women's News of the Mid-South,* August 4, 1994.

204 Leilani Rector, "Sasser, Chumney update seniors on crime bill, health care legislation," *Daily News* (Memphis, TN), August 31, 1994.

205 "Chumney tells seniors she will push TennCare changes," *Commercial Appeal* (Memphis, TN), August 31, 1994.

206 Michael Kelley, "Abuse" "He could kill me," *Commercial Appeal* (Memphis, TN), June 22, 1994.

207 Ibid.

208 Patti Patterson, "Loser in city radio bid pleads case," *Commercial Appeal* (Memphis, TN), June 30, 1994.

209 Ibid.

210 Tony Jones, "Herenton unveils his 'business'," *Tri-State Defender* (Memphis, TN), August 27-31, 1994.

211 Ibid.

212 "Representation that 'Can Do' for You!" *Mid-Memphian,* September 10, 1994.

213 Tenn. Code Ann. 53-13-102.

214 Peter Schutt, "Deer hunters to help feed hungry," *Daily News,* (Memphis, TN), August 23, 1995.

215 Tennessee Wildlife Federation, "About Hunters for Hungry," August 13, 2020.

216 Editorial, "Bredesen for Governor," *Memphis Business Journal,* October 31, 1994.

217 Editorial, "Re-elect Ford, Byrd, Chumney and Kernell," *Commercial Appeal* (Memphis, TN), November 3, 1994.

218 Ibid.

219 Ibid. "Politics" *Memphis Flyer,* October 27, 1994.

220 Christina Connor, "Women's Suffrage anniversary panel has rocky launch," *Commercial Appeal* (Memphis, TN), October 19, 1994.

221 Ibid; Paula Wade, "Tennessee Suffrage panel vows to end bickering, do job," *Commercial Appeal* (Memphis, TN), November 21, 1994.

222 Paula Wade, "Tennessee Suffrage panel vows to end bickering, do job," *Commercial Appeal* (Memphis, TN), November 21, 1994.

223 Nate Hobbs, "Low-key Shelby legislative races pit mostly well-known candidates," *Commercial Appeal* (Memphis, TN), November 6, 1994.

224 Emily Yellin, "Not There Yet" "Women candidates are vastly underrepresented in state and local elections," *Memphis Flyer,* August 1994.

225 Ibid.

226 Ibid.

227 Ibid.

228 Editorial, "Cabinet Cloud," "Are Sundquist choices as diverse as pledged?" *Commercial Appeal* (Memphis, TN), December 18, 1994.

229 Jerry Markon, "Gingrich's mom says he can't stand Hillary," *Nashville Banner,* January 4, 1995.

230 Kriste Goad, "Number of women in office swells," *Nashville Banner,* January 4, 1995.

231 Ibid.

232 Ibid.

233 Ibid.

234 Kriste Goad, "'Sensitized' Republicans close gender gap," *Nashville Banner,* January 4, 1995.

235 Ibid.

236 Rebecca Ferrar, "Women's health bill is proposed," *Knoxville News-Sentinel,* February 2, 1995.

237 Tim Sewell, "Chumney Backs Women's Health Center for Memphis," *Memphis Business Journal,* March 20, 1995.

238 Ibid.

239 Paula Wade, "Hotel-tax bill for Pyramid projects hits wall in House," *Commercial Appeal* (Memphis, TN), April 7, 1995.

240 Rebecca Ferrar, "House Oks Senate amendments on total gift ban," *Knoxville News-Sentinel,* May 18, 1995.

241 Associated Press, "Lawmakers, Sundquist Have Been Like Newlyweds This Year: Kisber," *Citizen Tribune* (Morristown, TN), May 22, 1995.

242 Ed Cromer, "Underage drivers face mandatory road course," *Nashville Banner,* May 18, 1995.

243 Ibid.

244 Ed Cromer, "House passes bill to require licenses for massage workers," *Nashville Banner,* April 28, 1995; "House approves massage-licensing bill," *Knoxville News-Sentinel,* May 1, 1995.

245 Ed Cromer, "House passes bill to require licenses for massage workers," *Nashville Banner,* April 28, 1995.

246 Ron Maxey, "Kingsbury parents worry about gangs and violence," *Commercial Appeal* (Memphis, TN), April 21, 1995.

247 Beth Warren, "The Big Picture: MPD Spending," *Commercial Appeal* (Memphis, TN), April 23, 2015.

248 Editorial, "Campaign against domestic violence," *Chattanooga Times,* April 25, 1995.

249 Ibid.

250 Ibid.

251 Ibid.

252 Bill Snyder, "Health reform risk to infants, panel warns," *Nashville Banner,* May 19, 1995.

253 Richard Locker and Paula Wade, "State reform of adoption, ethics laws hit late snags," *Commercial Appeal* (Memphis, TN), May 26, 1995; Paula Wade, "Bill defining rape heads to Sundquist despite arguments," *Commercial Appeal,* May 26, 1995.

254 Editorial, "Legislature should slow down audit bill," *Tennessean* (Nashville, TN), May 14, 1995.

255 Elizabeth Murray, "Bicentennial brouhaha brewing," *Nashville Business Journal,* April 3-7, 1995.

256 Ibid.

257 Ibid.

258 Ibid.

259 "Sundquist, Ingram patch up squabble," *Commercial Appeal* (Memphis, TN), July 19, 1995.

260 Rebecca Ferrar, "State lawmaker probed in sex case," *Knoxville News-Sentinel,* June 2, 1995; Duren Cheek and Larry Daughtrey, "Rep. Bell accused of harassment," *Tennessean* (Nashville, TN), June 21, 1995.

261 Larry Daughtrey, "Rep. Bell accused of harassment," *Tennessean* (Nashville, TN), June 21, 1995.

262 Ibid.; Rebecca Ferrar, "State lawmaker probed in sex case," *Knoxville News-Sentinel,* June 2, 1995.

263 Kriste Goad, "Secretary accuses lawmaker of harassment," *Nashville Banner,* June 20, 1995.

264 Duren Cheek and Larry Daughtrey, "Rep. Bell accused of harassment," *Tennessean* (Nashville, TN), June 21, 1995.

265 Kriste Goad, "Accuser's mom slams Bell," *Nashville Banner,* June 22, 1995.

266 Ibid.

267 Ibid.

268 Ibid.

269 Paula Wade, "Speaker hands harsh penalty to Rep. Bell for harassment," *Commercial Appeal* (Memphis, TN), June 23, 1995; Kriste Goad, "Bell, secretary swap charges of untruths," *Nashville Banner,* June 23, 1995.

270 Paula Wade, "Speaker hands harsh penalty to Rep. Bell for harassment," *Commercial Appeal* (Memphis, TN), June 23, 1995.

271 Rebecca Ferrar, "Bell paid per diem while being probed in sex harass case," *Knoxville News-Sentinel,* June 22, 1995.

272 Duren Cheek and Larry Daughtrey, "Rep. Bell loses leadership spot over harassment charge," *Tennessean* (Nashville, TN), June 23, 1995.

273 Karin Miller, "Bell's Punishment 'Doesn't Matter to Him,' Gibson says," *Wilson County News,* June 26, 1995.

274 Larry Daughtrey and Duren Cheek, "How rare is sexual harassment on the Hill?" *Tennessean* (Nashville, TN), June 25, 1995.

275 Nashville Banner, Editorial, "New day for legislature," *Nashville Banner,* June 28, 1995.

276 Larry Daughtrey and Duren Cheek, "How rare is sexual harassment on the Hill?" *Tennessean* (Nashville, TN), June 25, 1995.

277 Ibid.

278 Larry Daughtrey, "Tipper Gore joining suffrage celebration," *Tennessean* (Nashville, TN), August 3, 1995.

279 Rebecca Ferrar, "Mother's push decided suffrage vote," *Plain Dealer,* (Lenoir City, TN), August 18, 1995.

280 Ibid. (attributed to Carol Lynn Yellin).

281 Ibid.

282 Ronald Smothers, "One Small Vote for a Man Brought One Giant Leap for Women," *New York Times,* August 18, 1995.

283 Rebecca Ferrar, "Mother's push decided suffrage vote," *Plain Dealer,* (Lenoir City, TN), August 18, 1995.

284 Ibid.

285 Ibid.; "Harry T. Burn," *Wikipedia Encyclopedia,* October 3, 2020.

286 Ibid. (attributed to Carol Lynn Yellin & others' reports).

287 Ibid.

288 Ronald Smothers, "One Small Vote for a Man Brought One Giant Leap for Women," *New York Times,* August 18, 1995.

289 Rebecca Ferrar, *Plain Dealer* (Lenoir City, TN), August 18, 1995.

290 Ronald Smothers, "One Small Vote for a Man Brought One Giant Leap for Women," *New York Times,* August 18, 1995.

291 Rebecca Ferrar, *Plain Dealer* (Lenoir City, TN), August 18, 1995.

292 Ricky Rogers photo, "Past and future vote," *Tennessean* (Nashville, TN), August 20, 1995.

293 Jim "Spider" Dumas, "State's suffrage vote re-enacted," *Post-Intelligencer* (Paris, TN), August 21, 1995.

294 Tamar Levin, "Women are becoming Equal Providers," *New York Times,* May 11, 1995.

295 Ibid.

296 Andy Sher, "Suffrage victory marked," *Chattanooga Times,* August 19, 1995.

297 James Brooke, "3 Suffragists (in Marble) To Move Up in the Capitol," *New York Times,* September 27, 1996.

298 Ibid.

299 Jackson Baker, "Ground Control to Major Don," *Memphis Flyer,* October 26, 1995.

300 Terry Keeter, "Governor sees GOP taking House," *Commercial Appeal* (Memphis, TN), October 16, 1995.

301 Editorial, "A prescription for women," *Tennessean* (Nashville, TN), November 3, 1995.

302 Ibid.

303 Ibid.

304 Stephanie Plaisance, "Chumney to brief women's convention on TennCare," *Daily News* (Memphis, TN), July 28, 1995.

305 Editorial, "State v. David Lanier," *Tennessean* (Nashville, TN), January 25, 1996.

306 Chris Conley, "Dyersburg ex-judge Lanier gets early exit from jail," *Commercial Appeal* (Memphis, TN), June 16, 1995; *U.S. v. David Lanier,* 73 F. 3d 1380 (1996).

307 Ibid; *USA v. David Lanier,* Case No. 2:92-cr-20172-BBD, ECF 343 (W.D. Tenn, April 19, 1993), *"Judgment in a Criminal Case."*

308 Ibid.

309 Ibid.

310 Editorial, "State v. David Lanier," *Tennessean* (Nashville, TN), January 25, 1996.

311 Warren Duzak, "'Think ahead' on stadium bathrooms," *Tennessean* (Nashville, TN), January 13, 1996.

312 Warren Duzak, "Arena restrooms pose problem," *Tennessean* (Nashville, TN), July 27, 1995.

313 Ibid.

314 Editorial, "Another restroom wait," *Tennessean* (Nashville, TN), July 30, 1995.

315 Warren Duzak, "'Think ahead' on stadium bathrooms," *Tennessean* (Nashville, TN), January 13, 1996.

316 Ibid.

317 Kathryn H. Anthony and Meghan Dufresne, "Potty Parity in Perspective: Gender and Family Issues in Planning and Designing Public & Restrooms," *Journal of Planning Literature*, 2007.

318 Alisa LaPolt and Bill Snyder, "TennCare decision gets kudos from cancer patients, legislators," *Nashville Banner*, January 24, 1996.

319 Ibid.

320 Richard Locker, "Breast cancer patients get break on high-risk treatment," *Commercial Appeal* (Memphis, TN), January 24, 1996.

321 Associated Press, "Proposed Bill Protects Mother's Hospital Stay," *Citizen Tribune* (Morristown, TN), January 21, 1996.

322 Ibid.

323 Paula Wade, "Abuse victims supported," *Commercial Appeal* (Memphis, TN), November 3, 1995; Associated Press, "House Passes Domestic Abuse Insurance Bill," *Citizen Tribune* (Morristown, TN), May 12, 1996.

324 Tammie Smith "Rise in infant mortality 'raises red flag'," *Tennessean* (Nashville, TN), September 21, 1996.

325 Ibid.

326 Paula Wade, "Bills to lure Oilers advance," *Commercial Appeal* (Memphis, TN), February 21, 1996.

327 Rebecca Ferrar, "Homosexual marriage ban cleared by panel," *Knoxville News-Sentinel*, February 21, 1996.

328 Paula Wade, "Bills to lure Oilers advance," *Commercial Appeal* (Memphis, TN), February 21, 1996.

329 Patrick Graham, "Chumney says Oilers deal bad," *Nashville Business Journal*, February 26-March 1, 1996.

330 Paula Wade, "Bills to lure Oilers advance," *Commercial Appeal* (Memphis, TN), . February 21, 1996.

331 Rob Moritz and Alisa LaPolt, "Council asks for Sports Authority residency rule," *Nashville Banner*, February 21, 1996.

332 Richard Locker, "Liberty Bowl rebates freed," *Commercial Appeal* (Memphis, TN), May 29, 1997; Jackson Baker, "Adjusting the Scale," *Memphis Flyer*, May 29-June 4, 1997.

333 Richard Locker, "Liberty Bowl rebates freed," *Commercial Appeal* (Memphis, TN), May 29, 1997.

334 Andy Sher and Aliza LaPolt, "Religious right ends year with mixed bag," *Nashville Banner*, April 29, 1996.

335 Susan Adler Thorp, "GOP turning stones for runners, money," *Commercial Appeal* (Memphis, TN), March 31, 1996.

336 Nate Hobbs, "Herenton backs Rufus Jones for Congress," *Commercial Appeal* (Memphis, TN), June 26, 1996.

337 Ibid.

338 Ibid.

339 Susan Adler Thorp, "GOP turning stones for runners, money," *Commercial Appeal* (Memphis, TN), March 31, 1996.

340 The Bible, Book of Luke *17:11-19*.

341 Ad, *Memphis Flyer*, October 31-November 6, 1996.

342 Bill Carey, "Pity the poor golf course owner who must pay this tax," *Tennessean* (Nashville, TN), April 13, 1997.

343 Karin Miller, "Pregnant TennCare recipients denied care," *Tennessean* (Nashville, TN), April 25, 1997.

344 Ibid.

345 Duran Cheek, "More jail time sought for use of date-rape drug," *Tennessean* (Nashville, TN), February 1, 1997; Rebecca Ferrar, "Bills seek harsher penalties against use, possession of 'date-rape drug'," *Knoxville News-Sentinel*, April 12, 1997.

346 Duran Cheek, "More jail time sought for use of date-rape drug," *Tennessean* (Nashville, TN), February 1, 1997.

347 Richard Locker, "Memphis police jolt lawmakers with report on gang initiations," *Commercial Appeal* (Memphis, TN), March 20, 1997.

348 Brian Hicks, "Family panel gets off to impressive start," *Chattanooga Times*, April 28, 1997.

349 Editorial, "Life in Hell," *Memphis Flyer*, May 29-June 4, 1997.

350 Phil Campbell, "Public Reckoning for a Private Mayor," *Memphis Flyer,* May 29-June 4, 1997.

351 Ibid.

352 Ibid.

353 Marc Perrusquia, "Shining City on the Bluff," *Commercial Appeal* (Memphis, TN), January 4, 2009.

354 Editorial, "One for silly season," *Commercial Appeal* (Memphis, TN), July 13, 1997.

355 Marc Perrusquia, "Shining City on the Bluff," *Commercial Appeal* (Memphis, TN), January 4, 2009.

356 Jackson Baker, "Defender of the City," *Memphis Flyer,* July 17-23, 1997.

357 Ibid.

358 Ibid.

359 Ibid.

360 Ibid.

361 Carol Chumney, "It's about leadership," *Commercial Appeal* (Memphis, TN), July 20, 1997.

362 Ibid.

363 Cornell Christian, "New Town Loss of LG &W Service Proposed," *Commercial Appeal* (Memphis, TN), July 22, 1997.

364 "Bullies of the town," *Commercial Appeal* (Memphis, TN), July 27, 1997.

365 Ibid.

366 Ibid.; Edith Chumney Russell, Letter to the Editor, *Commercial Appeal* (Memphis, TN), July 27, 1997.

367 Editorial, "Right on Chumney, TSD supports suggested boycott," *Tri-State Defender* (Memphis, TN), July 26-30, 1997.

368 Ibid.

369 Ibid.

370 Ibid.

371 Ibid.

372 Ibid.

373 Editorial, "Wilder's Whim: Conspiracy theories all involve speaker," *Commercial Appeal* (Memphis, TN), July 27, 1997.

374 Ibid.

375 *Tennessee Municipal League, et al v. Brook Thompson in His Official Capacity as State Election Coordinator, et al,* 958 S.W. 2d 333 (Tenn. 1997).

376 Ibid.

377 Paula Wade, "Memphis won't bail out of TML in protest," *Commercial Appeal* (Memphis, TN), August 9, 1997.

378 Ibid.

379 Louis Graham, "Politicians come and go; Wilder endures," *Commercial Appeal* (Memphis, TN), August 10, 1997; Jerry Markon, "Ford won more than case, say local observers," *Commercial Appeal* (Memphis, TN), June 10, 1991; Jeffrey M. Fleming, "Sen. Ford Trial Set June" "Charges filed Against Texan," *Commercial Appeal,* April 10, 1991.

380 Louis Graham, "Politicians come and go; Wilder endures," *Commercial Appeal* (Memphis, TN), August 10, 1997.

381 Ibid.

382 Letter to Editor, Chris B. Morgan, "Fayette languishes despite Wilder's state power," *Commercial Appeal* (Memphis, TN), August 17, 1997.

383 Editorial "Cities Alone" "Legislature avoids stand on annexation," *Commercial Appeal* (Memphis, TN), August 17, 1997.

384 Paula Wade, "Legislature's novel idea: Give people light," *Commercial Appeal* (Memphis, TN), August 17, 1997.

385 Ibid.

386 Editorial, "Cities Alone," "Legislature avoids stand on annexation," *Commercial Appeal* (Memphis, TN), August 17, 1997.

387 Ibid.

388 Editorial, "Needed: A Special Session— Now!" *Memphis Flyer,* 1997.

389 Ibid.

390 Patti Patterson and Richard Locker, "Petition asks for session to Revise Annex Law," *Commercial Appeal* (Memphis, TN), July 11, 1997.

391 Kriste Goad, "New Towns Could Face Business-tax Sharing," *Commercial Appeal* (Memphis, TN), September 20, 1997.

392 Carol Chumney "Future rides on incorporation issue," *Commercial Appeal* (Memphis, TN), October 26, 1997.

393 Ibid.

394 Ibid.

395 Ibid.

396 Ibid.

397 Ibid.

398 Ibid.

399 Jonathan Scott, "Boycott, Annexation Were Hot Spots in Local Politics," *Memphis Business Journal,* December 28, 1997.

400 Ibid.

401 Ibid.

402 *Tennessee Municipal League v. Thompson,* 958 S.W. 2d 333 (Tenn. 1997).

403 Richard Locker, "4.9 million women's health center eyed for UT," *Commercial Appeal* (Memphis, TN), December 8, 1997.

404 Ibid.

405 Rickard Locker, "Democrats raise 11th hour funds," *Commercial Appeal* (Memphis, TN), January 13, 1998.

406 As noted by the *Commercial Appeal,* the incorporation law approved the year before and later held unconstitutional as a caption bill, was an amendment that was added to the bill "with virtually no notice" on the floors of the respective legislative bodies after the original bill had passed through the committee process. Richard Locker, "Democrats raise 11th hour funds," *Commercial Appeal* (Memphis, TN), January 13, 1998.

407 John Semien, with contributions by Larry Taylor in Dyersburg, "Lanier on the lam: A warrant is issued for fugitive ex-judge," *Commercial Appeal* (Memphis, TN), August 23, 1997.

408 Ibid; *USA v. David Lanier,* 520 U.S. 259 (1997).

409 Ibid; Ibid *USA v. David Lanier,* Case No. 2:97-mj-00171-dkv, Doc. 2, (W.D. Tenn August 22, 1997).

410 Darcy O'Brien, *Power to Hurt, Inside a Judge's Chambers: Sexual Assault, Corruption, and the Ultimate Reversal of Justice for Women,* Harper Collins, March 1, 1997.

411 Because of his failure to appear, the Sixth Circuit Court of Appeals dismissed Lanier's appeal with prejudice on October 10, 1997. *U.S. v. Lanier,* Case No. 93-5608 Doc. 248, (Sixth Cir, October 10, 1997). His conviction and sentence was affirmed by the Sixth Circuit. *U.S. v. Lanier,* Case No. 98-5447, (January 24, 2000.)

412 Wayne Risher, "VECA dedicates park tractor to Chumney," *Commercial Appeal* (Memphis, TN), September 28, 2000.

413 Kriste Goad, "Mayor Rout and Prince Mongo planets apart," *Commercial Appeal* (Memphis, TN), August 4, 1998.

414 Ibid.

415 Ibid.

416 Editorial, "State House, Shelby delegation can use continuity, change," *Commercial Appeal* (Memphis, TN), October 19, 1998.

417 Ibid.

418 Rob Johnson, "Pleasant wins trip back to Nashville," *Commercial Appeal* (Memphis, TN), November 4, 1998.

419 John Commins, "Move Afoot to Oust Chairman Turner," *Chattanooga Times,* January 14, 1999.

420 Ibid.

421 Ibid.

422 Duren Cheek, "Naifeh takes leader off panel, citing complaints," *Tennessean* (Nashville, TN), January 15, 1999.

423 Ibid; Richard Locker, "Chumney gets a chairmanship as Naifeh doles out key roles," *Commercial Appeal* (Memphis, TN), January 15, 1999.

424 "Committee Chairs Picked for '101st' Senate, House Standing Committees," *Tennessee County News,* Jan. Feb. 1999.

425 Richard Locker, "Chumney gets a chairmanship as Naifeh doles out key roles," *Commercial Appeal* (Memphis, TN), January 15, 1999.

426 Paula Wade, "Sundquist tax proposal confounds both parties," *Commercial Appeal* (Memphis, TN), February 12, 1999.

427 Ibid.

428 Richard Locker, "House OKs bill targeting adults for school guns," *Commercial Appeal* (Memphis, TN), May 14, 1999.

429 Marc Perrusquia, "Bill aims to keep guns off campus, make parents vigilant," *Commercial Appeal* (Memphis, TN), March 2, 1999.

430 Richard Locker, "House OKs bill targeting adults for school guns," *Commercial Appeal* (Memphis, TN), May 14, 1999; Associated Press, "House approves bill punishing adults who don't report students' guns," May 14, 1999.

431 Duren Cheek, "Bill forbids silence when student has gun," *Tennessean* (Nashville, TN), April 29, 1999.

432 Associated Press, "House approves bill punishing adults who don't report students' guns," May 14, 1999.

433 Ibid.

434 Marc Perrusquia, "Bill aims to keep guns off campus, make parents vigilant," *Commercial Appeal* (Memphis, TN), March 2, 1999.

435 Associated Press, "House Oks bill targeting adults for school guns," *Commercial Appeal* (Memphis, TN), May 14, 1999.

436 Editorial, "Gun Caution," *Commercial Appeal* (Memphis, TN), May 17, 1999.

437 Associated Press, "Pro-gun lobby stalls in state," *Herald-Citizen* (Cookeville, TN), June 1, 1999.

438 Sharon H. Fitzgerald, "Ned McWherter and Tax Reform: An Inseparable Pair," *Tennessee County News,* July Aug. 1999.

439 Ibid.

440 Ibid.

441 "Clinton extols 'energy' in dispelling lame duck," *New York Times News Service,* July 22, 1999.

442 Bill Dries, "Lawler appears on CNBC, talks of 'stealing' win," *Commercial Appeal* (Memphis, TN), July 22, 1999.

443 Ibid.

444 Kriste Goad, "Herenton's Poll Puts Him Ahead, But Foes Skeptical," *Commercial Appeal* (Memphis, TN), July 29, 1999.

445 Ibid.

446 *Tennessee Alumnus,* Spring 1999.

447 While the Methodist Endowed Professorship for Women's Health is still identified on the UT Medical website, it is listed as currently vacant. And the Women's Health Center later ran into funding problems and is no longer in existence.

448 Bill Dries and Michael Erskine, "2 forgotten toddlers die in stifling day-care vans," *Commercial Appeal* (Memphis, TN), July 22, 1999.

449 Ibid.; Yolanda Jones and Tom Bailey Jr., "Toddlers' Families, Care Centers Struggle with 'Why'," *Commercial Appeal* (Memphis, TN), July 23, 1999.

450 Yolanda Jones and Tom Bailey Jr., "Toddlers' Families Care Centers Struggle with 'Why'," *Commercial Appeal* (Memphis, TN), July 23, 1999.

451 Ibid.

452 Ibid.

453 Kimberly Edwards, "Grieving Remember Toddler as 'God's Angel'," *Commercial Appeal* (Memphis, TN), July 25, 1999.

454 Kriste Goad, "Herenton Day Care Ordinance Goes to Council," *Commercial Appeal* (Memphis TN), August 3, 1999.

455 Editorial, "Tragedies justify rules on childcare," *Tennessean* (Nashville, TN), August 14, 1999; Jacinthia Jones, "Day care hearings will put problems before lawmakers," *Commercial Appeal* (Memphis, TN), September 1, 1999.

456 "Tennessee: Memphis," *USA Today,* September 3, 1999.

457 Kriste Goad, "Ford lists $531,000 in mayor race costs," *Commercial Appeal* (Memphis, TN), October 2, 1999; Kriste Goad, "Up to 50% turnout expected," *Commercial Appeal,* October 7, 1999.

458 Kriste Goad, "Herenton Asks State to Back Up City's Steps to Monitor Centers," *Commercial Appeal* (Memphis, TN), July 24, 1999.

459 Ibid.; Yolanda Jones, "Day-Care Aid Program Launched," *Commercial Appeal* (Memphis, TN), August 10, 1999; Jacinthia Jones, "Herenton Wants Day Care Centers Accredited; State Lifts License of Latest Offender," *Commercial Appeal,* August 11, 1999.

460 Kriste Goad, "Herenton Asks State to Back Up City's Steps to Monitor Centers," *Commercial Appeal* (Memphis, TN), July 24, 1999.

461 Ibid.

462 Ibid.

463 Ibid.

464 Ibid.

465 Ibid.

466 Ibid.

467 Jacinthia Jones and Chris Conley, "Day Care Owner Charged with DUI; Stopped While Driving 7 Kids; Complaint Last Week Voided," *Commercial Appeal*

(Memphis, TN), August 4, 1999; Jacinthia Jones, "DUI Charge a Setup, Day Care Owner Says," *Commercial Appeal,* August 12, 1999.

468 *State of Tennessee v. Gillard,* No. 99139821-01, Shelby County Criminal Court, February 17, 2000.

469 Editorial, "Cost-Quality Link Must Be Strengthened," *Commercial Appeal* (Memphis, TN), August 12, 1999.

470 Yolanda Jones and Jacinthia Jones, "Girl Left in Day Care Van, Gets Out by Herself," *Commercial Appeal* (Memphis, TN), August 10, 1999; Jacinthia Jones, "Herenton Wants Day Care Centers Accredited; State Lifts License of Latest Offender," *Commercial Appeal,* August 11, 1999.

471 John Commins, "State Will Review Day-Care Statutes After Heat Deaths," *Chattanooga Times,* August 9, 1999.

472 Jacinthia Jones, "Pall over van deaths inspires committee to push for change," *Commercial Appeal* (Memphis, TN), July 29, 1999.

473 Anna Byrd Davis, "Day cares' food money scrutinized," *Commercial Appeal* (Memphis, TN), October 25, 1999.

474 Ibid.

475 Editorial, "Tragedies justify rules on child-care," *Tennessean* (Nashville, TN), August 14, 1999.

476 Ibid.

477 Ibid.

478 Jacinthia Jones, "Day care hearings will put problems before lawmakers," *Commercial Appeal* (Memphis, TN), September 1, 1999; Jacinthia Jones, "Stricter day care rules promised," *Commercial Appeal,* September 3, 1999.

479 Jacinthia Jones, "Stricter day care rules promised," *Commercial Appeal* (Memphis, TN), September 3, 1999.

480 Ibid.

481 Ibid.

482 Ibid.

483 Ibid.

484 Anna Byrd Davis, "Childcare committee hears day care ideas," *Commercial Appeal* (Memphis, TN), September 23, 1999.

485 Ibid.

486 Marc Perrusquia, Anna Byrd Davis and Jacinthia Jones, "Nonprofit day care execs get top pay," *Commercial Appeal,* (Memphis, TN), October 24, 1999.

487 Ibid.

488 *In Re Estate of James W. Ford, M.D.,* W2005-01194-COA-R3-CV (Tenn. App. May 5, 2006).

489 Ibid.

490 Marc Perrusquia, "Millions poured in day care barely show on pay stub," *Commercial Appeal* (Memphis, TN), October 25, 1999.

491 Ibid.

492 Ibid.

493 Ibid.

494 In an award-winning series, reporters Anna Byrd Davis, Jacinthia Jones, and Marc Perrusquia with the *Commercial Appeal* combed through financial records; "About this Project," *Commercial Appeal* (Memphis, TN), October 24, 1999.

495 Marc Perrusquia, "Unfiled tax returns no barrier to day care," *Commercial Appeal* (Memphis, TN), October 31, 1999.

496 Ibid.

497 Ibid.

498 Ibid.

499 Ibid.

500 Jacinthia Jones, "Cherokee keeps state contract; legislators will probe day care," *Commercial Appeal* (Memphis, TN), November 2, 1999.

501 Ibid.

502 Marc Perrusquia, "Day Care dollars enrich Memphis couple," *Commercial Appeal* (Memphis, TN), October 24, 1999.

503 Ibid.

504 Ibid.

505 *Rayborn, et al v. John Ford, et al,* No. 2:99-cv-02941-jsg, U.S. District Court ECF 53 (W.D. Tenn. July 10, 2000).

506 Ibid

507 Jacinthia Jones, "Cherokee keeps state contract; legislators will probe day care," *Commercial Appeal* (Memphis, TN), November 2, 1999.

508 Marc Perrusquia, "Sen. Ford Cozy with Day Care Insurers Not Illegal, But Renews Conflict, Favoritism Issues," *Commercial Appeal* (Memphis, TN), December 19, 1999.

509 Ibid.

510 Ibid.

511 Ibid.

512 Ibid.

513 Ibid.

514 Ibid.

515 Paula Wade, "Cruise with kin will keep Person far from gavel," *Commercial Appeal* (Memphis, TN), November 6, 1999.

516 *Mark A. Mayhew, et al v. John Wilder*, Case No. M2000-01948-COA-R10-CV, Tenn. Court of Appeals at Nashville, January 11, 2011.

517 Paula Wade, "Irate tax opponents daunt Capitol staff," *Commercial Appeal* (Memphis, TN), November 6, 1999.

518 *Mark A. Mayhew, et al v. John Wilder*, Case No. M2000-01948-COA-R10-CV, Tenn. Court of Appeals at Nashville, January 11, 2011.

519 Richard Locker, "DHS Commissioner Promises Tougher Child Care Licensing," *Commercial Appeal* (Memphis, TN), January 13, 2000.

520 Marc Perrusquia, and Anna Byrd Davis, "Day care license suspended under no-tolerance rule," *Commercial Appeal* (Memphis, TN), January 7, 2000.

521 Ibid.

522 Ibid.

523 Associated Press Wire, Karin Miller, "Lawmakers demand quick improvements to care centers in wake of Memphis toddlers' deaths," January 13, 2000.

524 Ibid; Associated Press, "Make child care top priority, lawmakers urge," *Tennessean* (Nashville, TN), January 13, 2000.

525 Marc Perrusquia, "Chumney pushes day care reforms," *Commercial Appeal* (Memphis, TN), January 17, 2000.

526 Ibid.

527 Ibid.; Associated Press Wire, "Get tough, check backgrounds of day care workers: lawmaker," January 18, 2000; Editorial, "Day Care, Children's needs must come before providers," *Commercial Appeal* (Memphis, TN), February 22, 2000.

528 Editorial, "Day Care, Children's needs must come before providers," *Commercial Appeal* (Memphis, TN), February 22, 2000.

529 Marc Perrusquia, "Chumney pushes day care reforms," *Commercial Appeal* (Memphis, TN), January 17, 2000.

530 Blake Fontenay, "City may bid for day care broker contract," *Commercial Appeal* (Memphis, TN), January 20, 2000.

531 Blake Fontenay, "Mayor's takeover plan stirs education debate," *Commercial Appeal* (Memphis, TN), January 28, 2000.

532 Ibid; *Rayborn, etal v. John Ford, etal*, No. 2:99-cv-02941-jsg, U.S. District Court, (W.D. Tenn.), ECF 53 (July 10, 2000), *"Order Granting in Part and Denying in Part Defendants' Motions to Dismiss."*

533 Blake Fontenay, "Mayor's takeover plan stirs education debate," *Commercial Appeal* (Memphis, TN), January 28, 2000.

534 *Rayborn, etal v. John Ford*, et al, No. 2:99-cv-02941-jsg, U.S. District Court, (W. D. Tenn.), ECF 53 (July 10, 2000).

535 Ibid, Doc. 94 (November 22, 2000) & Doc. 114, (February 8, 2001).

536 Marc Perrusquia, "Chumney adds 10 proposals to reform day care," *Commercial Appeal* (Memphis, TN), January 27, 2000.

537 Ibid.

538 Marc Perrusquia, "Bill allows fines against day cares," *Commercial Appeal* (Memphis, TN), January 29, 2000.

539 Marc Perrusquia, "Chumney adds 10 proposals to reform day care," *Commercial Appeal* (Memphis, TN), January 27, 2000.

540 Vicki Brown, "Tougher child care standards recommended," *Jackson Sun*, January 27, 2000.

541 *Tennessee Municipal League v. Thompson*, 958 S.W. 2d 333 (Tenn. 1997); Tom Sharp, "Appeal of 'tiny towns' law denied," *Commercial Appeal* (Memphis, TN), January 28, 2000.

542 Tom Sharp, "Appeal of 'tiny towns' law denied," *Commercial Appeal* (Memphis, TN), January 28, 2000.

543 Editorial, "Too much talk, Rep. Chumney's rhetoric on day care just opportunism," *Jackson Sun*, January 18, 2000.

544 Ibid.

545 Ibid.

546 Ibid.

547 Marc Perrusquia, "Sundquist proposes extensive child care reform," *Commercial Appeal* (Memphis, TN), February 3, 2000.

548 Ibid.

549 Marc Perrusquia, "Tennessee proposes stricter regulations for day care centers," *Commercial Appeal* (Memphis, TN), February 4, 2000.

550 Ibid.; Marc Perrusquia, "Sundquist proposes extensive child care reform," *Commercial Appeal* (Memphis, TN), February 3, 2000.

551 Marc Perrusquia, "Tennessee proposes stricter regulations for day care centers," *Commercial Appeal* (Memphis, TN), February 4, 2000.

552 Marc Perrusquia, "Sundquist proposes extensive child care reform," *Commercial Appeal* (Memphis, TN), February 3, 2000.

553 *In Re Estate of James W. Ford, M.D.,* No. W2005-01194-COA-R3-CV (Tenn. App. May 5, 2006).

554 Ibid.

555 "The Clinton Administration and Child Care," October 23, 1997.

556 Ibid.

557 Marc Perrusquia, "Ford blasts day care reforms," "Rep. Chumney sponsor of 10 bills, defends them," *Commercial Appeal* (Memphis, TN), February 11, 2000; Marc Perrusquia, "Naifeh to support day care reform," *Commercial Appeal,* February 25, 2000.

558 Marc Perrusquia, "Ford blasts day care reforms," "Rep. Chumney sponsor of 10 bills, defends them," *Commercial Appeal* (Memphis, TN), February 11, 2000.

559 Ibid.

560 Ibid.

561 Ibid.

562 Ibid.

563 Ibid.

564 Ibid.

565 Ibid.

566 Ibid.

567 Editorial, "Day Care, Ford mustn't be allowed to block needed change," *Commercial Appeal* (Memphis, TN), February 12, 2000.

568 Ibid.

569 Ibid.

570 Ibid.

571 Marc Perrusquia, "Child care providers thick as gun lobby at Capitol," *Commercial Appeal* (Memphis, TN), February 20, 2000.

572 Ibid.

573 Ibid.

574 Ibid.

575 Marc Perrusquia, "Naifeh to support day care reform," *Commercial Appeal* (Memphis, TN), February 25, 2000.

576 Richard Locker and Paula Wade, "Reform called 'knee-jerk' act" "Herenton pushes delegation for day care changes," *Commercial Appeal* (Memphis, TN), February 24, 2000.

577 Ibid.

578 Ibid.

579 Marc Perrusquia, "Grand jury pores over Cherokee records," *Commercial Appeal* (Memphis, TN), March 5, 2000.

580 Marc Perrusquia, "John Ford, Cherokee link shown," *Commercial Appeal* (Memphis, TN), March 5, 2000.

581 Editorial, "Day Care" "Children, taxpayers must come first in Nashville," *Commercial Appeal* (Memphis, TN), March 7, 2000.

582 Ibid.

583 Ibid.

584 Bill Day, *Commercial Appeal* (Memphis, TN), March 7, 2000.

585 Editorial, "Butt Out, John Ford!" *Memphis Flyer,* March 9, 2000.

586 Ibid.

587 Ibid.

588 "The Read House Hotel," *Wikipedia.*

589 "The Read House Hotel," *Wikipedia.*

590 Robert Houk, "Toddlers' deaths spur child care law revision," *Johnson City Press,* March 13, 2000.

591 Ibid.

592 Bill Dries, "Day care reforms face vote," "Baby's parents join rally," *Commercial Appeal* (Memphis, TN), April 16, 2000.

593 Ibid; *State v. Tammy Hobson*, Case No. 97-08895-97626179, Shelby County Criminal Court, (Memphis, TN).

594 Ibid.

595 Ibid.

596 Paula Wade, "Panel agrees on day care issues," *Commercial Appeal* (Memphis, TN), April 19, 2000.

597 Bonna M. de la Cruz, "Hearings take on day-care reforms," *Tennessean* (Nashville, TN), April 19, 2000.

598 Ibid.

599 Associated Press, Karin Miller, "State changes for overseeing day care may take time, broker says," April 26, 2000.

600 Paula Wade and Richard Locker, "Ford panel Oks day care bill," *Commercial Appeal* (Memphis, TN), April 27, 2000.

601 Ibid.

602 Editorial, "Day Care, Eliminating brokers could serve interest in reform," *Commercial Appeal* (Memphis, TN), April 27, 2000.

603 Ibid.; Paula Wade, "Legislators discuss cost of lower children-to-adults day care ratios," *Commercial Appeal* (Memphis, TN), April 28, 2000.

604 Associated Press, Karin Miller, "Lowering ratios would hurt poor, working families: Herron," April 28, 2000.

605 Ibid.

606 Ibid.

607 Paula Wade, "Legislators discuss cost of lower children-to-adults day care ratios," *Commercial Appeal* (Memphis, TN), April 28, 2000.

608 Ibid.

609 Bob Gary, Jr., "More Counselors Boost Child Care," *Chattanooga Times Free Press,* May 3, 2000.

610 Paula Wade, "Bill waters down child care ratios," *Commercial Appeal* (Memphis, TN), May 2, 2000.

611 Ibid.

612 Ibid; Jon Yates, "A rally cry for worthy day-care wages," *Tennessean* (Nashville, TN), May 2, 2000.

613 Bob Gary, Jr., "More Counselors Boost Child Care," *Chattanooga Times Free Press,* May 3, 2000.

614 Ibid.

615 Ibid.

616 Richard Locker, "Day care reforms debated, on hold," *Commercial Appeal* (Memphis, TN), May 4, 2000; Vicki Brown, Associated Press, "Chumney: Changes dilute child care bill," May 9, 2000.

617 Paula Wade, "Day care financial reporting cut," "House panel backs limiting audits," *Commercial Appeal* (Memphis, TN), May 10, 2000.

618 Vicki Brown, Associated Press, "Chumney: Changes dilute child care bill," May 9, 2000.

619 Ibid.; Paula Wade, "Day care financial reporting cut" "House panels backs limiting audits," *Commercial Appeal* (Memphis, TN), May 10, 2000.

620 Ibid.

621 Ibid.

622 Richard Locker, "Senators ax day care ratio plan," *Commercial Appeal* (Memphis, TN), May 11, 2000.

623 Ibid.

624 Ibid.

625 Ibid; Vicki Brown, Associated Press, "Amendment would require audits of centers taking more than $500,000," May 16, 2000; Paula Wade, "Revision seeks new day care disclosure," *Commercial Appeal* (Memphis, TN), May 17, 2000.

626 Karin Miller, Associated Press, "House committee approves child care reform bill, set stage for battle," May 22, 2000; Richard Locker, "House panel OK's day care bill, with rare applause," *Commercial Appeal* (Memphis, TN), May 23, 2000.

627 Richard Locker, "House panel OK's day care bill, with rare applause," *Commercial Appeal* (Memphis TN), May 23, 2000.

628 Ibid.

629 Marc Perrusquia, "Real estate buy followed rent hike for Cherokee" "Buildings resold to director's sister, board chairman," *Commercial Appeal* (Memphis, TN), May 23, 2000; *United States v. WillieAnn D. Madison and John A. Madison,* Case No. 2:02-cr-20448-BBD, Doc. 498, pg. 2, (6th Cir. April 23, 2007).

630 Marc Perrusquia, "Real estate buy followed rent hike for Cherokee" "Buildings resold to director's sister, board chairman," *Commercial Appeal* (Memphis, TN), May 23, 2000.

631 Ibid.

632 Ibid.

633 Ibid.

634 Ibid.; Marc Perrusquia, "Cherokee office space half of what lease says," *Commercial Appeal* (Memphis, TN), May 25, 2000.

635 Marc Perrusquia, "Real estate buy followed rent hike for Cherokee" "Buildings resold to director's sister, board chairman," *Commercial Appeal* (Memphis, TN), May 23, 2000.

636 Ibid.; Marc Perrusquia, "Cherokee's tax-exempt status in jeopardy, auditors warn," *Commercial Appeal* (Memphis, TN), May 23, 2000.

637 Marc Perrusquia, "Cherokee office space half of what lease says," *Commercial Appeal* (Memphis, TN), May 25, 2000.

638 Bill Day, *Commercial Appeal* (Memphis, TN), May 31, 2000.

639 Richard Locker, "Panel OK's day care reform," *Commercial Appeal* (Memphis, TN), May 31, 2000.

640 Ibid.

641 Phil West, Associated Press, "House child care overhaul differs from senate version," June 6, 2000.

642 Paula Wade, "House approves massive reform of day care rules," *Commercial Appeal* (Memphis, TN), June 7, 2000.

643 Marc Perrusquia, "Cherokee will repay state rent; subpoenas issued by grand jury," *Commercial Appeal* (Memphis, TN), June 7, 2000.

644 Ibid.

645 *Memphis Publishing Co., et al v. Cherokee Children & Family Services, Inc.,* No. CT-002141-00, Shelby County Circuit Court.

646 Ibid, *"Findings of Fact & Conclusions of Law,"* June 6, 2000.

647 *Memphis Publishing Co., etal v. Cherokee Children & Family Service, Inc., etal, and John Morgan v. Cherokee Children & Family Services, Inc.,* 87 S.W. 3d 67 (Tenn. September 05, 2002).

648 Marc Perrusquia, "Cherokee will repay state rent; subpoenas issued by grand jury," *Commercial Appeal* (Memphis, TN), June 7, 2000.

649 Editorial, "Day Care," "Lawmakers must cross reform finish line," *Commercial Appeal* (Memphis, TN), June 9, 2000.

650 Paula Wade, "Legislature OK's comprehensive day care reform," *Commercial Appeal* (Memphis, TN), June 10, 2000.

651 Ibid.

652 Paula Wade, "Day care reform bill becomes law with governor's signature," *Commercial Appeal* (Memphis, TN), June 27, 2000.

653 Bonna M. de la Cruz and Duren Cheek, "Income tax on the ropes; pivotal session tomorrow," *Tennessean* (Nashville, TN), June 11, 2000.

654 Ibid.

655 Richard Locker, "Legislators await Sundquist's budget move," *Commercial Appeal* (Memphis, TN), June 27, 2000; *Mark A. Mayhew, etal v. John Wilder,* 46 S.W. 3d 760 (Tenn. App. 2001).

656 *Mark A. Mayhew, et al v. John Wilder,* 46 S.W. 3d 760, (Tenn. App. 2001).

657 Andrew Goldstein, "It Took Three Dead Babies," *TIME Magazine,* July 10, 2000.

658 Ibid.

659 Ibid.

660 Ibid.

661 Associated Press, "Day-care worker involved in van death says education records were faked," *Commercial Appeal* (Memphis, TN), July 27, 2000; Marc Perrusquia, "Day care laws come too late for tot's family," *Commercial Appeal,* July 30, 2000; *State v. Laverne Long,* No. 99-10023-9964 1330, Shelby County Criminal Court, November 1, 2000; *State v. Higghus,* No. 99-10023-9964 1333, Shelby County Criminal Court, November 2, 2000.

662 Associated Press, "Day-care worker involved in van death says education records were faked," *Commercial Appeal* (Memphis, TN), July 20, 2000.

663 Marc Perrusquia, "Day care laws come too late for tot's family," *Commercial Appeal* (Memphis, TN), July 30, 2000.

664 Associated Press, "DHS won't look into claim that day care faked records," *Commercial Appeal* (Memphis, TN), July 27, 2000.

665 Marc Perrusquia, "Day care laws come too late for tot's family," *Commercial Appeal* (Memphis, TN), July 30, 2000.

666 Ibid.

667 Marc Perrusquia, "Tot's family sues day care and owner Ford," *Commercial Appeal* (Memphis, TN), September 1, 1999; *Sheita Mann, et al v. Vivian Braxton, et al*, No. 303509-4 T.D., Shelby County Circuit Court, June 17, 2002, "*Consent Order of Dismissal with Prejudice*," (due to settlement).

668 DLC Idea of the Week: Child Care Report Cards, July 2000.

669 Ibid.

670 Ibid.

671 Ibid.

672 Ibid.

673 Associated Press, Karin Miller, "Chumney gets child care accountability added to platform draft," August 15, 2000.

674 Ibid.

675 Editorial, "Spread word on child care," *Tennessean* (Nashville, TN), August 18, 2000.

676 Ibid.

677 Ibid.

678 Richard Locker, "Improved day care standard delayed," *Commercial Appeal* (Memphis, TN), July 1, 2001.

679 Ibid.

680 Ibid.

681 Ibid.

682 Ibid.

683 Editorial, "Day care accountability under attack," *Commercial Appeal* (Memphis, TN), July 20, 2001; *Tennessee Quality Child Care v. Donald Sunquest* [sic], No. CT-004292-01, Shelby County Circuit Court; Marc Perrusquia, "Group Files Suit to Kill New Day Care Audit Law," *Commercial Appeal*, July 14, 2001.

684 *Tennessee Quality Child Care v. Donald Sunquest* [sic], CT-004292-01, Shelby County Circuit Court; Marc Perrusquia, "Judge won't halt day-care audit rules," *Commercial Appeal* (Memphis, TN), July 17, 2001.

685 Marc Perrusquia, "Judge won't halt day-care audit rules," *Commercial Appeal* (Memphis, TN), July 17, 2001.

686 Ibid.

687 Marc Perrusquia, "Suit targets Memphis owners of 4 day cares," *Commercial Appeal* (Memphis, TN), January 21, 2002.

688 Ibid.

689 Ibid.

690 Marc Perrusquia, "State's 4th suit claims woman looted day care," *Commercial Appeal* (Memphis, TN), February 20, 2002.

691 Ibid.

692 Ibid; *State, ex rel, Little People's Child Development Center, Inc. v. Little People's Child Development Center*, No. M2007-00345-COA-R3-CV, (Tenn. App. Sept. 9, 2009), "*Opinion.*"

693 Marc Perrusquia, "State's 4th suit claims woman looted day care," *Commercial Appeal* (Memphis, TN), February 20, 2002.

694 Ibid; *Summers v. Cherokee Children Family Servs., Inc., et al*, No. 00-2988-1 (Tenn. Ch. April 11, 2001), *aff'd*, 112 S.W. 3d 486 (Tenn. App. 2002).

695 Ibid; Ibid.

696 Richard Locker, "Bill seeks rollback in day care ratios," *Commercial Appeal* (Memphis, TN), January 24, 2002.

697 Ibid.

698 Editorial, "Children left behind in lawmakers' retreat," *Commercial Appeal* (Memphis, TN), February 16, 2002.

699 Richard Locker, "Bill seeks rollback in day care ratios," *Commercial Appeal* (Memphis, TN), January 24, 2002.

700 Ibid.

701 Shirley Downing, "Day Care Felon Checks Find Doozies," "Day Care," *Commercial Appeal* (Memphis, TN), February 3, 2002.

702 Ibid.

703 Editorial, "Case builds for tougher day care rules," *Commercial Appeal* (Memphis, TN), February 7, 2002.

704 Shirley Downing, "Day Care Felon Checks Find Doozies," "Day Care," *Commercial Appeal* (Memphis, TN), February 3, 2002.

705 Bonna de la Cruz, "Lawmakers lash out about day care," *Tennessean* (Nashville, TN), April 9, 2002.

706 Editorial, "Lawmakers strike a pose on day care," *Commercial Appeal* (Memphis, TN), April 10, 2002.

707 Bonna de la Cruz, "Lawmakers lash out about day care," *Tennessean* (Nashville, TN), April 9, 2002; *State v. Wesley B. Hudson,* No. 00656966-01, Shelby County Criminal Court, January 31, 2001.

708 Shirley Downing, "Chumney urges registry for operators of day cares," *Commercial Appeal* (Memphis, TN), April 17, 2002.

709 Ibid.

710 Ibid.; Bonna de la Cruz, "Lawmakers lash out about day care," *Tennessean* (Nashville, TN), April 9, 2002; *USA v. Shintri Gibson,* No. 2:00-cr-200011-BBD, (W.D. Tenn April 26, 2000), ECF 30, "*Order on Change of Guilty Plea";* (Oct. 30, 2001), ECF 56, "*Order Dismissing Indictment;*" (May 26, 2000), ECF 34, "*Order Continuance and Specifying Period of Excusable Delay."*

711 Shirley Downing, "Drug raid cost day care figure her license," *Commercial Appeal* (Memphis, TN), April 16, 2002.

712 Ibid.

713 Ibid; *USA v. Robert K. Simpson aka Robert Gibson, aka Willie Gibbs,* Case No. 4:96-cr-00089-MPM-EMB, Doc. 49, (N.D. Miss., October 5, 1999), "*Amended Judgment."*

714 Anna Byrd Davis, "Day care job on hold for counterfeit inquiry," *Commercial Appeal* (Memphis, TN), January 11, 2000.

715 David Halbfinger, "Deaths in Memphis Day Care Expose Lax Oversight," *New York Times,* April 22, 2002.

716 Shirley Downing, "Drug raid cost day care figure her license," *Commercial Appeal* (Memphis, TN), April 16, 2002.

717 Shirley Downing, "Chumney urges registry for operators of day cares," *Commercial Appeal* (Memphis, TN), April 17, 2002.

718 Marc Perrusquia, "Cherokee check fans rent fraud allegation," *Commercial Appeal* (Memphis, TN), October 16, 2002; *United States v. WillieAnn Madison and John A. Madison,* Case No. 2:02-cr-20448-BBD, Doc. 498, pg. 2, (6th Cir. April 23, 2007).

719 Marc Perrusquia, "Cherokee check fans rent fraud allegation," *Commercial Appeal* (Memphis, TN), October 16, 2002;

720 *Summers v. Cherokee Children & Family Serv.,* 112 S.W. 3d 486 (Tenn. App. 2002).

720 *Summers v. Cherokee Children & Family Serv.,* 112 S.W. 3d 486, 516 (Tenn. App. 2002).

721 Ibid. at 517; *United States v. WillieAnn Madison and John A. Madison,* Case No. 2:02-cr-20448-BBD, Doc. 498, pg. 5, (6th Cir. April 23, 2007).

722 *Summers v. Cherokee Children & Family Serv.,* 112 S.W. 3d 486, 517 (Tenn. App. 2002).

723 Ibid. at 517.

724 Ibid. at 525.

725 Ibid. at 519-520.

726 Ibid.

727 *United States v. WillieAnn Madison and John A. Madison,* Case No. 2:02-cr-20448-BBD, Doc. 498, (6th Cir. April 23, 2007).

728 Ibid., Doc. 511, (June 29, 2007), "*Redacted Amended Judgment in a Criminal Case."*

729 Ibid.

730 Ibid., Doc. 498, pg. 5.

731 Ibid. Doc., 498, pg. 5.

732 Ibid. Doc. 498, pg. 2.

733 Editorial, "Don't back down from day care reform," *Commercial Appeal* (Memphis, TN), April 22, 2003.

734 Ibid.

735 Ibid.

736 Ibid.

737 Editorial, "Expect an assault on day care reforms," *Commercial Appeal* (Memphis, TN), March 30, 2003.

738 Sam Youngman, "Accord targets day care ratios," *Commercial Appeal* (Memphis, TN), April 23, 2003.

739 Richard Locker, "Senators cut lower ratios for child care," *Commercial Appeal* (Memphis, TN), April 29, 2003.

740 Editorial, "Opponents take aim at day care reform," *Commercial Appeal* (Memphis, TN), May 1, 2003.

741 Jackson Baker, "AC's Purgatory," *Memphis Flyer,* May 22, 2003.

742 Richard Locker, "Delay of tax reform could cause sales tax hike, Sundquist warns," *Commercial Appeal* (Memphis, TN), March 21, 2001.

743 Ibid.

744 Richard Locker, "Leaders see clock running out on tax plan," *Commercial Appeal* (Memphis, TN), May 17, 2001; Tom Humphrey, "House in for better schools-debate still fiery," *Knoxville News-Sentinel*, May 17, 2001.

745 Richard Locker, "Legal view pans budget-cut 'options'," *Commercial Appeal* (Memphis TN), May 23, 2001.

746 Editorial, "Neglect of mentally disabled is a scandal," *Commercial Appeal* (Memphis, TN) May 30, 2001.

747 Ibid.

748 Paula Wade, "Senators say 'no' to income tax: conferees get message during budget work," *Commercial Appeal* (Memphis, TN), May 30, 2001.

749 Ibid.

750 Lewis Donelson, Commentary, "State's future hinges on tax reform now," *Commercial Appeal* (Memphis, TN), May 30, 2001.

751 Paula Wade, "Lawmakers eye business tax tweaks," *Commercial Appeal* (Memphis, TN), June 5, 2001.

752 Paula Wade, "Budget 'patch' is same old quick fix," *Commercial Appeal* (Memphis, TN), June 7, 2001.

753 Russ Oates, "Lawmakers 'passing the buck', Sundquist tells local officials," *Commercial Appeal* (Memphis, TN), June 13, 2001.

754 Paula Wade and Richard Locker, "Sales tax backers try ½-, ¾ cent hikes" "Votes to end budget impasse unclear," *Commercial Appeal* (Memphis, TN), June 22, 2001.

755 Richard Locker, "Sundquist signs education bill, calls for financing," *Commercial Appeal* (Memphis, TN), June 5, 2001.

756 Karin Miller, Associated Press, "Trooper assigned to desk duty during investigation of protest confrontation," July 19, 2001.

757 Brian Kelsey, Special to Viewpoint, "'Yes' on Amendment 3= 'no' to tax," *Commercial Appeal* (Memphis, TN), October 22, 2014.

758 Ibid.

759 Associated Press, "Tennessee Officials Drop Tax Plan After Protest," *New York Times*, July 13, 2001.

760 Ibid.

761 Ibid.

762 "Weak franchise and excise taxes keep deficit on track to be $300 million," *Nashville Post*, March 13, 2002.

763 Ibid.

764 Paula Wade, "Collapse of Temporary Sales Tax Hike Leaves House in Dark," *Commercial Appeal* (Memphis, TN), March 15, 2002.

765 Paula Wade, "Naifeh Ready to Bring 4.5% Income Tax Plan to Vote," *Commercial Appeal* (Memphis, TN), May 22, 2002.

766 "Income tax not dead yet," *Nashville Post*, May 22, 2002.

767 Ibid.

768 Ibid.

769 Ibid.

770 Bartholomew Sullivan, "Westmoreland widow declines House seat," *Commercial Appeal* (Memphis, TN), July 3, 2002.

771 Ibid.

772 Jackson Baker, "Meltdown in Nashville," *Memphis Flyer*, July 12, 2002.

773 Richard Locker, "Deadline tax plan inching closer," *Commercial Appeal* (Memphis, TN), June 25, 2002.

774 Ibid.

775 Jackson Baker, "Meltdown in Nashville," *Memphis Flyer*, July 12, 2002.

776 Ibid.

777 John Gerome, "State employees cheer on income tax," *Commercial Appeal* (Memphis, TN), June 27, 2002.

778 Paula Wade and Richard Locker, "6% income tax plan 'promising," *Commercial Appeal* (Memphis, TN), June 27, 2002.

779 Ibid.

780 Ibid.

781 Bonna de la Cruz, "Sales Tax Plan Rejected, Proponent may take idea to Senate floor," *Tennessean* (Nashville, TN), June 28, 2002.

782 Ibid.

783 Ibid.

784 Paula Wade, "House rejects CATS budget plan," *Commercial Appeal* (Memphis, TN), July 3, 2002.

785 Ibid.

786 Michael Wilson, "Sales Tax Defeats Income Tax in Tennessee Battle," *New York Times,* July 4, 2002.

787 Ibid.

788 Ibid.

789 Richard Locker, "Budget ills have been feverish since 1998," *Commercial Appeal* (Memphis, TN), July 3, 2002.

790 Ibid.

791 Michael Wilson, "Sales Tax Defeats Income Tax in Tennessee Battle," *New York Times,* July 4, 2002.

792 Ibid.

793 "Here's how Tennessee lawmakers voted on the sales tax bill Wednesday," *Commercial Appeal* (Memphis, TN), July 4, 2002.

794 Tenn. Const. XI-3 (2014).

795 Jackson Baker, "Tennessee Politics" "Chumney Joins Kyle in '02 County Mayor's Race," *Memphis Flyer,* May 5, 2001; Susan Adler Thorp, Commentary, "Suddenly, local politics is competitive," *Commercial Appeal* (Memphis, TN), March 7, 2001.

796 Jackson Baker, "Tennessee Politics" "Chumney joins Kyle in '02 County Mayor's Race," *Memphis Flyer,* May 5, 2001.

797 Susan Adler Thorp, Commentary, "Suddenly, local politics is competitive," *Commercial Appeal* (Memphis, TN), March 7, 2001.

798 Drew Pitt, "Alumna plans to run for Shelby County Mayor," *Daily Helmsman* (Memphis, TN), March 8, 2001.

799 Ibid.

800 Mickie Anderson, "Judge to rule in May on jail fine," *Commercial Appeal* (Memphis TN), April 25, 2001.

801 Ibid.

802 Ibid.; Mickie Anderson, "Jail's Troubled History Continues to Haunt County," *Commercial Appeal* (Memphis, TN), June 24, 2001.

803 Ibid; Ibid.

804 Editorial, "Fix, don't ignore, county jail's problems," *Commercial Appeal* (Memphis, TN), April 26, 2001.

805 Jimmie Covington, "Legislation tells Shelby to curb rising debt," *Commercial Appeal* (Memphis, TN), February 16, 2001.

806 Ibid.

807 David Williams, "Fed Ex aggressively woos NBA Grizzlies, wants rights to name team and arena," "Heisley says proposal 'looks very attractive'," *Commercial Appeal* (Memphis, TN), March 21, 2001.

808 Ibid.

809 Ibid; Blake Fontenay, "Public would pay just about all of arena's cost," *Commercial Appeal* (Memphis, TN), March 21, 2001.

810 David Williams "Grizzlies best bet for move, adviser says," *Commercial Appeal* (Memphis, TN), March 28, 2001.

811 Bonna de la Cruz, "Memphis NBA boosters unveil funding plan," *Tennessean* (Nashville, TN), April 10, 2001.

812 Ibid.

813 Ibid.

814 Rob Johnson, "Pyramid 'passe' as professional sports venue," *Tennessean* (Nashville, TN), April 10, 2001.

815 Ibid.

816 Ibid.

817 Richard Locker, "Mayors ask Shelby legislators to support arena plan," *Commercial Appeal* (Memphis, TN), April 11, 2001.

818 Ibid.

819 Jackson Baker, "Rout's Out," *Memphis Flyer,* July 25, 2001.

820 Rebekah Gleaves, "What AC stands for," *Memphis Flyer,* July 26-August 1, 2001.

821 Ibid; *USA v. WillieAnn Madison,* No. 2:99-cv-02941-jsg, (W.D. Tenn); Marc Perrusquia, "Memphis DayCare Scandal: As Madisons answer changes, more loom," *Commercial Appeal* (Memphis, TN), November 22, 2002; Miriam DeCosta-Willis, *Notable Black Memphians,* Cambria Press, Amherst, N.Y 2008, pg. 332.

822 Rebekah Gleaves, "What AC stands for," *Memphis Flyer,* July 26-August 1, 2001.

823 Ibid.

824 Ibid.

825 Ibid.

826 Ibid.

827 Ibid.

828 A Flyer Bonus, "Jim Kyle's County Mayor Poll," *Memphis Flyer,* September 6, 2001.
829 Ibid.
830 Ibid.
831 Photo, "Community," *Germantown News,* September 19, 2001.
832 Bill Dries, "Chism works to close ranks of Byrd backers," *Commercial Appeal* (Memphis, TN), September 28 2001.
833 Ibid.
834 Susan Adler Thorp, "Don't doubt that Rout is GOP all the way," *Commercial Appeal* (Memphis, TN), October 3, 2001.
835 Bill Dries, "Chism works to close ranks of Byrd backers," *Commercial Appeal* (Memphis, TN), September 28, 2001.
836 Jackson Baker, "AC Is In!," *Memphis Flyer,* October 18-24, 2001.
837 Jackson Baker, "Flinn vs. Wharton," *Memphis Flyer,* July 25-31, 2002.
838 Ibid.
839 David Kushma, Editorial, "Load table with facts in county mayor contest," *Commercial Appeal* (Memphis, TN), November 11, 2001.
840 Ibid.
841 Ibid.
842 Jackson Baker, "Bakke Poll Shows Wharton with Big Lead," *Memphis Flyer,* January 4, 2002.
843 Ibid.
844 Tom Bailey Jr., "Herenton envisions city, county united," *Commercial Appeal* (Memphis, TN), January 2, 2002; Bill Dries, "County Slate Faces Merger Debate," *Commercial Appeal,* January 21, 2002.
845 Tom Bailey Jr., "Herenton envisions city, county united," *Commercial Appeal* (Memphis, TN), January 2, 2002.
846 Ibid.
847 Editorial, Susan Adler Thorp, "Byrd's in mayor race to stay, backers say," *Commercial Appeal* (Memphis, TN), January 23, 2002.
848 Ibid.
849 Jackson Baker, "Hanging in There," *Memphis Flyer,* January 31-February 6, 2002.
850 Ibid.; Bill Dries, "Kyle Endorses Wharton in Primary," *Commercial Appeal* (Memphis, TN), January 26, 2002.
851 Jackson Baker, "Hanging in There," *Memphis Flyer,* January 31-February 6, 2002.
852 Ibid.
853 Ibid.
854 Ibid.
855 Ibid.
856 Thomas Jordan, "Merger joins mayoral contest," *Commercial Appeal* (Memphis, TN), February 3, 2002.
857 Ibid.
858 Jackson Baker, "Sources of Support," *Memphis Flyer,* February 7-13, 2002.
859 Ibid.
860 Ibid.
861 Ibid.
862 Ibid.
863 Ibid.
864 Ibid.
865 Ibid.
866 Wiley Henry, "Chumney stumps for mayor; alleges bias against realtor," *Tri-State Defender* (Memphis, TN), February 9-13, 2002.
867 John Branston, "Unbalanced Growth," *Memphis Flyer,* February 7-13, 2002.
868 Ibid.
869 Susan Adler Thorp, "Wharton gets two big boosts," *Commercial Appeal* (Memphis, TN), February 17, 2002.
870 Ibid.
871 Jackson Baker, "Herenton 'Disappointed' in Wharton," *Memphis Flyer,* March 4, 2002.
872 Ibid.
873 Jackson Baker, "On Their Mark," *Memphis Flyer,* February 28-March 6, 2002.
874 Ibid.
875 Ibid.
876 Ibid.
877 Jackson Baker, "After the Fact," *Memphis Flyer,* March 7-13, 2002.
878 Ibid.
879 Thomas Jordan and Bill Dries, "Byrd abandons bid to be county mayor," *Commercial Appeal* (Memphis, TN), March 1, 2002.
880 Ibid; Jackson Baker, "Byrd Exits Mayor's Race!" *Memphis Flyer,* February 28, 2002.

881 Thomas Jordan and Bill Dries, "Byrd abandons bid to be county mayor," *Commercial Appeal* (Memphis, TN), March 1, 2002.

882 Ibid.

883 Jackson Baker, "Byrd exits Mayor's Race!" *Memphis Flyer,* February 28, 2002.

884 Ibid.

885 Thomas Jordan and Bill Dries, "Byrd abandons bid to be county mayor," *Commercial Appeal* (Memphis, TN), March 1, 2002.

886 Jackson Baker, "After the Fact," *Memphis Flyer,* March 7-13, 2002.

887 Ibid.

888 "Ford labels Shelby County mayoral candidate A.C. Wharton 'a republican puppet'," *Tri-State Defender* (Memphis, TN), March 30-April 3, 2002.

889 Ibid.

890 Ibid.

891 Bill Dries, "Wharton poses jail consolidation," *Commercial Appeal* (Memphis, TN), March 10, 2002.

892 Ibid.

893 Ibid.

894 Blake Fontenay, "Herenton Touting Merger in New Climate," *Commercial Appeal* (Memphis, TN), March 10, 2002.

895 Ibid.

896 Bill Dries, "Democratic Rivals for County Mayor Trade Accusations," *Commercial Appeal* (Memphis, TN), March 24, 2002.

897 Ibid.

898 George Mayo, "Shelby County Mayor Candidates Forum," *North Shelby Times* (Memphis, TN), March 20, 2002.

899 Bill Dries, "Wharton wants Summit on Growth, Debt Issues," "County," *Commercial Appeal* (Memphis, TN), March 23, 2002.

900 Ibid.

901 Bill Dries, "Tax Freeze an Option, Chumney Tells Forum," *Commercial Appeal* (Memphis, TN), May 15, 2002.

902 Ibid.

903 Thomas Jordan, "Wharton defends both low and mighty," *Commercial Appeal* (Memphis, TN), April 3, 2002.

904 Ibid.

905 Bill Dries, reporters Paula Wade, Mickie Anderson and Thomas Jordan contributed to this story, "Legislator Chumney is focused, fearless," *Commercial Appeal* (Memphis, TN), April 3, 2002.

906 Ibid.

907 Ibid.

908 Ibid.

909 Ibid.

910 Ibid.

911 Bill Dries, "Chumney vows day care action, faults Wharton's connections," *Commercial Appeal* (Memphis, TN), April 20, 2002.

912 Blake Fontenay, contributors Jody Callahan, Lela Garlington and John Guinozzo, Viewpoint, "Chumney thinking in terms of 'Her Honor'," *Commercial Appeal* (Memphis, TN), April 6, 2002.

913 Ibid.

914 Jackson Baker, "GOP Optimism Growing Locally," *Memphis Flyer,* April 8, 2002.

915 Ibid.

916 Ibid.; Jackson Baker, "War on All Fronts," *Memphis Flyer,* April 11-17, 2002.

917 Jody Callahan, "Development is Key, agree 4 candidates," *Commercial Appeal* (Memphis, TN), April 14, 2002.

918 Ibid.

919 Ibid.

920 Tom Charlier "Elected officials face economic, environmental, esthetic issues," *Commercial Appeal* (Memphis, TN), April 14, 2002.

921 Ibid; Editorial, "Sprawl is urgent issue in county elections," *Commercial Appeal* (Memphis TN), April 16, 2002.

922 Tom Charlier, "Elected officials face economic, environmental, esthetic issues," *Commercial Appeal* (Memphis, TN), April 14, 2002.

923 Editorial, "Sprawl is urgent issue in county elections," *Commercial Appeal* (Memphis, TN), April 16, 2002.

924 Ibid.

925 Ibid.

926 Jackson Baker, "The Air War," *Memphis Flyer,* April 25-May 1, 2002.

927 Ibid.

928 David B. Halbfinger, "Deaths in Memphis Day Care Expose Lax Oversight," *New York Times,* April 22, 2002.

929 Ibid.

930 Ibid.

931 Thomas Jordan and Bill Dries, "School Funding at Fore of Debate," *Commercial Appeal* (Memphis, TN), April 24, 2002.

932 Editorial, "Wharton, Scroggs Best Picks for County Mayor," *Commercial Appeal* (Memphis, TN), April 28, 2002.

933 Ibid.

934 Ibid.

935 Ibid.

936 Ibid.

937 Ibid.

938 Ibid.; Thomas Jordan and Bill Dries, "Eager to Hold First Elected Post, Flinn, Wharton Take on Issues," *Commercial Appeal* (Memphis, TN), July 12, 2002.

939 Jackson Baker, "The Air War," *Memphis Flyer,* April 25-May 1, 2002.

940 Ad, *Tri-State Defender* (Memphis, TN), April 28, 2002.

941 Ad, *Memphis Flyer,* April 25, 2002.

942 Jackson Baker, "Election 2002: Who's on First?" *Memphis Flyer,* May 2-8, 2002.

943 Ibid.

944 Ibid.

945 Ibid.

946 Ibid.

947 Ibid.

948 Jackson Baker, "Defender of the City," *Memphis Flyer,* July 17-23, 1997.

949 Jackson Baker, "Election 2002: Who's on First?" *Memphis Flyer,* May 2-8, 2002.

950 Ibid.

951 Ibid.

952 Thomas Jordan, "90% of voters not primarily interested in Tuesday's balloting," *Commercial Appeal* (Memphis, TN), May 5, 2002.

953 Ibid.

954 Ibid.

955 Thomas Jordan, "Tactics, tiffs eclipse weighty mayoral issues," *Commercial Appeal* (Memphis, TN), May 5, 2002.

956 Ibid.

957 Ibid.

958 Jackson Baker, "Sound & Fury," *Memphis Flyer,* October 31-November 6, 2002.

959 Wiley Henry, "Wharton: A 20-point plan," *Tri-State Defender* (Memphis, TN), May 4-8, 2002.

960 Ibid.

961 Wiley Henry "Chumney: Making a difference," *Tri-State Defender* (Memphis, TN), May 4-8, 2002.

962 Ibid.

963 Ibid.

964 Ibid.

965 Ibid.

966 Ibid.

967 Editorial, "Tri-State Defender choices for May 7 Primary Election," *Tri-State Defender* (Memphis, TN), May 4-8, 2002.

968 Wiley Henry, "A new sense of pride seen in Wharton victory," *Tri-State Defender* (Memphis TN), May 11-15, 2002.

969 Ibid; Thomas Jordan, "Flinn v. Wharton for mayor," *Commercial Appeal* (Memphis, TN), May 8, 2002.

970 Wiley Henry, "A new sense of pride seen in Wharton victory," *Tri-State Defender* (Memphis, TN), May 11-15, 2002.

971 Editorial, Paula Wade, "Not all anti-income taxers do nothing," *Commercial Appeal* (Memphis, TN), May 21, 2002.

972 Thomas Jordan, "Flinn vs. Wharton for mayor," *Tri-State Defender* (Memphis, TN), May 8, 2002.

973 Van Pritchartt, Editor, "How Flinn Might Penetrate Wharton's Memphis Stronghold," *Collierville Herald,* May 16, 2002.

974 Ibid.

975 Jackson Baker, "Taken at the Flood," *Memphis Flyer,* May 9-15, 2002.

976 Ibid; Jackson Baker, "Flinn vs. Wharton," *Memphis Flyer,* July 25-31, 2002.

977 Ibid.

978 Jackson Baker, "Taken at the Flood," *Memphis Flyer,* May 9-15, 2002.

979 Ibid.

980 Ibid.

981 Jackson Baker, "AC Sizes it Up," *Memphis Flyer,* May 16-22, 2002.

982 Ibid.

983 Ibid.

984 Ibid.

985 Ibid.

986 Ibid.

987 Ibid.

988 Bill Dries, reporters Paula Wade, Mickie Anderson and Thomas Jordan contributed to the story, "Legislator Chumney is Focused, Fearless," *Commercial Appeal* (Memphis, TN), April 3, 2002.

989 Ibid.

990 John Semien, "Budget, Issues Top Candidates' Lists," *Commercial Appeal* (Memphis, TN), July 4, 2002.

991 Mickie Anderson, "No-tax stance sets Flinn apart from Wharton," *Commercial Appeal* (Memphis, TN), June 25, 2002.

992 Ibid.

993 Thomas Jordan, "Mayoral debate off as Flinn declines," *Commercial Appeal* (Memphis, TN), July 6, 2002.

994 Thomas Jordan and Bill Dries, "Eager to Hold First Elected Post, Flinn, Wharton Take on Issues," *Commercial Appeal* (Memphis, TN), July 12, 2002.

995 Jackson Baker, "Signs of Change," *Memphis Flyer*, October 8-14, 2009.

996 Michael Kelley, "What do women want? Can we talk?" *Commercial Appeal* (Memphis, TN), August 4, 2002.

997 Ibid.

998 Ibid.

999 Ibid.

1000 Ibid.

1001 Carol Chumney, Letter to the Editor, *Commercial Appeal* (Memphis, TN), August 2002.

1002 Ibid.

1003 Ibid.

1004 Mark Watson, "Money & Business Section," "Region's women 'worst off'" "Study puts Mississippi, Ark., Tenn. in Bottom 5," *Commercial Appeal* (Memphis, TN), December 29, 2002.

1005 Ibid.

1006 Thomas Jordan and Bill Dries, "Eager to Hold First Elected Post, Flinn, Wharton Take on Issues," *Commercial Appeal* (Memphis, TN), July 12, 2002.

1007 Ibid.

1008 Ibid.

1009 Ad, *Commercial Appeal*, July 12, 2002.

1010 Michael Erskine and Thomas Jordan, "Wharton Wins," *Commercial Appeal* (Memphis, TN), August 2, 2002.

1011 David Kushma, Editorial, "County's voters picked, ...chose well with spit-ticket tactic," *Commercial Appeal* (Memphis, TN), August 4, 2002.

1012 Jackson Baker, "Flinn v. Wharton," *Memphis Flyer*, July 25-31, 2002; Jackson Baker, "At the Crossroads," *Memphis Flyer*, August 1-8, 2002.

1013 Ibid; Ibid.; Michael Erskine and Thomas Jordan, "County Mayor-elect gets 62% over Flinn," *Commercial Appeal* (Memphis, TN), August 2, 2002.

1014 Jackson Baker, "At the Crossroads," *Memphis Flyer*, August 1-8, 2002.

1015 Ibid.

1016 Michael Erskine and Thomas Jordan, "County mayor-elect gets 62% over Flinn," *Commercial Appeal* (Memphis, TN), August 2, 2002.

1017 Ibid.

1018 Ibid.

1019 Editorial, "For Tennessee General Assembly," *Commercial Appeal* (Memphis, TN), October 19, 2002.

1020 Marc Perrusquia, "Cherokee check fans rent fraud allegations," *Commercial Appeal* (Memphis, TN), October 16, 2002; *Summers, et al v. Cherokee Children & Family Services, Inc.*, 112 S.W. 3d 486, 523 (Tenn. App. 2002).

1021 Jackson Baker, "Sound & Fury," *Memphis Flyer*, October 31-November 6, 2002.

1022 Ibid.; Letter to David Kushma, October 28, 2002.

1023 Jackson Baker, "Sound & Fury," *Memphis Flyer*, October 31- November 6, 2002.

1024 Ad, *North Shelby Times* (Memphis, TN), October 16, 2002.

1025 Jackson Baker, "Sound & Fury," *Memphis Flyer*, October 31-November 6, 2002.

1026 Ibid.

1027 "Chumney elected to chair delegation," *Memphis Business Journal*, January 16, 2003.

1028 Richard Locker, "Shelby delegation may take a metro focus, aimed at clout," *Commercial Appeal* (Memphis, TN), January 22, 2003.

1029 Jackson Baker, "Short Bread," *Memphis Flyer,* January 30-February 5, 2003.

1030 Duren Cheek and Anne Paine, "Budget: Bredesen unveils 'painful choices,'" *Tennessean* (Nashville, TN), March 11, 2003.

1031 Jackson Baker, "Short Bread," *Memphis Flyer,* January 30-February 5, 2003; John Branston, "Do Something!" *Memphis Flyer,* January 30-February 5, 2003.

1032 Jackson Baker, "Short Bread," *Memphis Flyer,* January 31-February 5, 2003.

1033 AC Wharton Jr., "Growing out, growing smart," *Commercial Appeal* (Memphis, TN), March 9, 2003.

1034 Carol Chumney, "Before fixing schools, do the math," *Commercial Appeal* (Memphis, TN), March 2, 2003.

1035 Blake Fontenay, "School merger talk still just talk," *Commercial Appeal* (Memphis, TN), April 15, 2003.

1036 Blake Fontenay, "Legal opinion goes against Herenton on school merger," *Commercial Appeal* (Memphis, TN), April 4, 2003; TN Attorney General Opinion, No. 03-037, April 2, 2003.

1037 Ibid.

1038 Michael Erskine, "Mayor spurs merger meeting," *Commercial Appeal* (Memphis, TN), April 22, 2003.

1039 Ibid.

1040 Ibid.

1041 Ibid.

1042 Editorial, "The city mayor and the county budget," *Commercial Appeal* (Memphis, TN), April 23, 2003.

1043 Deborah M. Clubb, "Development tax brings warnings," *Commercial Appeal* (Memphis, TN), April 23, 2003.

1044 Editorial, "A Useful Respite," *Memphis Flyer,* May 8-14, 2003.

1045 Ibid.

1046 Michael Erskine, "Developer tax capped at 1% gets go-ahead," *Commercial Appeal* (Memphis, TN), May 6, 2003.

1047 Ibid.

1048 Editorial, "A Useful Respite," *Memphis Flyer,* May 8-14, 2003.

1049 Jackson Baker, "AC's Purgatory," *Memphis Flyer,* May 22, 2003; John Branston, "No Way Out?" *Memphis Flyer,* July 10-16, 2003.

1050 John Branston, "No Way Out?" *Memphis Flyer,* July 10-16, 2003.

1051 Ibid.; Jackson Baker, "AC's Purgatory," *Memphis Flyer,* May 22, 2003.

1052 Brenda Hughes, Letter to Editor, *Commercial Appeal* (Memphis, TN), April 29, 2003.

1053 Michael Erskine, "Shelby County Property Taxes Hiked 25 Cents Countywide-Non-Memphians to Pay Extra 5 Cents for New School," *Commercial Appeal* (Memphis, TN), July 31, 2003.

1054 Jackson Baker, "Taking Turns," *Memphis Flyer,* May 8-14, 2003.

1055 "George Flinn Endorsed by Republican Party for City Council," *Shelby GOP News* (Memphis, TN), May 14, 2003.

1056 Jackson Baker, "Chumney's Hat in Ring for District 5 Council Seat," *Memphis Flyer,* May 27, 2003.

1057 Blake Fontenay, "Chumney running for City Council," *Commercial Appeal* (Memphis, TN), May 28, 2003.

1058 Blake Fontenay, "Vergos joins pols backing Strickland," *Commercial Appeal* (Memphis, TN), May 28, 2003.

1059 Ibid.; Jackson Baker, "No Kustoff-Marsha Rematch," *Memphis Flyer,* June 1, 2003.

1060 Jackson Baker, "Political Snapshot," *Memphis Flyer,* July 3-9, 2003.

1061 Ibid.

1062 Jackson Baker, "Did Chumney try to pressure the Council?" *Memphis Flyer,* June 18, 2003.

1063 Ibid.; Jackson Baker, "Political Snapshot," *Memphis Flyer,* July 3-9, 2003.

1064 Ibid.

1065 Ibid.

1066 Marc Perrusquia, "Child center suspends transportation," *Commercial Appeal* (Memphis, TN), July 12, 2003.

1067 Ibid.; Almee Edmondson, Kevin McKenzie and Chris Conley, "Tot dies in day care van," *Commercial Appeal* (Memphis, TN), June 26, 2003.

1068 Ibid.

1069 Editorial, "Money isn't the only issue with day care vans," *Commercial Appeal* (Memphis, TN), June 30, 2003.

1070 Ibid.

1071 Editorial, "Keeping an eye on day care books," *Commercial Appeal* (Memphis, TN), August 25, 2003.

1072 Richard Locker, "End child care abuse, mother begs lawmakers," *Commercial Appeal* (Memphis, TN), August 21, 2003.

1073 Ibid.; Aimee Edmondson and Chris Conley, "Day care worker abused 3 kids, police say," *Commercial Appeal* (Memphis, TN), August 13, 2003.

1074 Aimee Edmondson and Chris Conley, "Day care worker abused 3 kids, police say," *Commercial Appeal* (Memphis, TN), August 13, 2003.

1075 *State v. Ivan Ward,* No. 10400036-0312249, Shelby County Criminal Court (October 27, 2004).

1076 Richard Locker, "End child care abuse, mother begs lawmakers," *Commercial Appeal* (Memphis, TN), August 21, 2003.

1077 Janel Davis, "Taking Responsibility," *Memphis Flyer,* August 14-20, 2003.

1078 Editorial, "Day care reform: beyond criminal charges," *Commercial Appeal* (Memphis, TN), August 10, 2003.

1079 Ibid.

1080 Ibid.

1081 Ibid.; Jackson Baker, "Storm-tossed," *Memphis Flyer,* July 31-August 5, 2003.

1082 Jackson Baker, "Storm-tossed," *Memphis Flyer,* July 31-August 5, 2003.

1083 Ibid.

1084 Ibid.

1085 Ibid.

1086 Ibid .

1087 Sharon Overman, Letters to Editor, "Those with power and without speak out," *Commercial Appeal* (Memphis, TN), July 30, 2003.

1088 Nick R. Swan, Letters to Editor, "Those with power and without speak out," *Commercial Appeal* (Memphis, TN), July 30, 2003.

1089 Jackson Baker, "Map or Trap?" *Memphis Flyer,* August 21-27, 2003.

1090 Editorial "For Memphis City Council (I)," *Commercial Appeal* (Memphis, TN), September 19, 2003.

1091 Ibid.

1092 Ibid.

1093 Ibid.

1094 Jackson Baker, "A Proper Challenger," *Memphis Flyer,* October 2-8, 2003.

1095 Blake Fontenay, "District 5 council foes pack them in," *Commercial Appeal* (Memphis, TN), September 23, 2003.

1096 Ibid.

1097 Jackson Baker, "Gloves Off," *Memphis Flyer,* September 25-October 1, 2003.

1098 Ibid.

1099 Blake Fontenay, "Schools grist for council races," *Commercial Appeal* (Memphis, TN), September 28, 2003.

1100 Ibid.

1101 Michael Kelly, "Herenton's aura of invincibility," *Commercial Appeal* (Memphis, TN), October 5, 2003.

1102 Ibid.

1103 Jason Terrell, cartoon, *Commercial Appeal* (Memphis, TN), October 5, 2003.

1104 Michael Kelly, "How big will Herenton's margin be?" *Commercial Appeal* (Memphis, TN), October 5, 2003.

1105 Ibid.

1106 Ibid.

1107 Michael Kelly, "Herenton's aura of invincibility," *Commercial Appeal* (Memphis, TN), October 5, 2003.

1108 Editorial, "TSD choices in the Oct. 9 Municipal election," *Tri-State Defender* (Memphis, TN), October 4, 2003.

1109 Ibid.

1110 Senate Joint Resolution 0060 (June 19, 2002).

1111 Michael Erskine, "District 5 Goes to OT," *Commercial Appeal* (Memphis, TN), October 10, 2003.

1112 Ibid.

1113 Martha Brown, Letter to Editor, *Commercial Appeal* (Memphis, TN), October 18, 2003.

1114 Blake Fontenay, "Flinn, Chumney brace for battle," *Commercial Appeal* (Memphis, TN), October 11, 2003; Jackson Baker, " An Open Seat" "Council hopeful Chumney quits the legislature as her runoff with Flinn continues," *Memphis Flyer*, October 23-29, 2003.

1115 John Branston, "City Beat" "Lots of pending appointments and some new faces will get the mayor's attention," *Memphis Flyer*, October 16, 2003.

1116 Ibid.

1117 Jackson Baker, "Council hopeful Chumney quits the legislature as her runoff with Flinn continues," *Memphis Flyer*, October 23, 2003.

1118 Wiley Henry, "Chumney resigns House seat to focus on council race," *Tri-State Defender* (Memphis, TN), October 29, 2003; Blake Fontenay, "Chumney resigns from legislature," *Commercial Appeal* (Memphis, TN), October 21, 2003.

1119 Blake Fontenay, "Chumney resigns from legislature," *Commercial Appeal* (Memphis, TN), October 21, 2003.

1120 Ibid; Jackson Baker, "An Open Seat" "Council hopeful Chumney quits the legislature as her runoff with Flinn continues," *Memphis Flyer*, October 23-29, 2003.

1121 John Cicala, Letter to the Editor, "Chumney shows integrity with her resignation," *Commercial Appeal* (Memphis, TN), October 25, 2003.

1122 Editorial, "A champion for children," *Tennessean* (Nashville, TN), October 28, 2003.

1123 Ibid.

1124 Ibid.

1125 Ibid.

1126 Editorial, "Chumney, Brooks best bets in city runoff," *Commercial Appeal* (Memphis TN), October 24, 2003.

1127 Ibid.

1128 Ibid.

1129 Blake Fontenay, "Chumney says Flinn ducking debate," *Commercial Appeal* (Memphis, TN), October 24, 2003.

1130 Tracy Adams, "Campus debate between City Council candidates cancelled," *Daily Helmsman* (Memphis, TN), October 30, 2003.

1131 Kelly McCarthy, "Citizen Carol" "Carol Chumney eager to bring experience, new ideas to Council in November 13 Runoff," *Democrat* (Memphis, TN), November 2003.

1132 Jackson Baker, "Poles Apart," *Memphis Flyer*, November 6-12, 2003.

1133 Blake Fontenay, "Rivals vie for edge in runoff," *Commercial Appeal* (Memphis, TN), November 10, 2003.

1134 Ibid.

1135 Blake Fontenay, "Flinn, Chumney have similar views on some issues," *Commercial Appeal* (Memphis, TN), November 11, 2003.

1136 Jackson Baker, "Upset in District 5," *Memphis Flyer*, November 13-19, 2003.

1137 Ibid.

1138 Ibid.

1139 Blake Fontenay, "Chumney, Brooks win in runoffs," *Commercial Appeal* (Memphis, TN), November 14, 2003.

1140 Ibid.

1141 Ibid.

1142 "Citizen Carol becomes Councilwoman Carol," *Democrat* (Memphis, TN), December 2003.

1143 Ibid.

1144 Ibid.

1145 Jackson Baker, "It Ain't Beanbag," *Memphis Flyer*, January 1-7, 2004.

1146 Blake Fontenay, "Mayor's top picks face hard questions," *Commercial Appeal* (Memphis, TN), December 31, 2003.

1147 Ibid.

1148 Ibid.

1149 Ibid.

1150 Jackson Baker, "The Testament of Willie Herenton," *Memphis Flyer*, January 15-21, 2004.

1151 Tom Bailey Jr., "'Steadfast' Mayor Sworn in for 4th Consecutive Term," *Commercial Appeal* (Memphis, TN), January 2, 2004.

1152 Jackson Baker, "News Cycle," *Memphis Flyer*, December 30-January 5, 2005; *see also*, Editorial, "Time for Herenton, Council to reconcile," *Commercial Appeal* (Memphis, TN), February 9, 2004.

1153 Jackson Baker, "News Cycle," *Memphis Flyer*, December 30-January 5, 2005.

1154 Tom Bailey Jr., "'Steadfast' Mayor Sworn in for 4th Consecutive Term," *Commercial Appeal* (Memphis, TN), January 2, 2004.

1155 Mary Cashiola, "Mayor of the Council," *Memphis Flyer,* January 15, 2004.

1156 Jackson Baker, "News Cycle," *Memphis Flyer,* December 31, 2004.

1157 Mary Cashiola, "Mayor of the Council," *Memphis Flyer,* January 15, 2004.

1158 Ibid.

1159 Ibid.

1160 Ibid.

1161 Ibid.

1162 Ibid.; Tom Bailey Jr., "'Steadfast' Mayor Sworn in for 4th Consecutive Term," *Commercial Appeal* (Memphis, TN), January 2, 2004.

1163 Tom Bailey Jr., "'Steadfast' Mayor Sworn in for 4th Consecutive Term," *Commercial Appeal* (Memphis, TN), January 2, 2004.

1164 Blake Fontenay, "4 Herenton picks rejected," *Commercial Appeal* (Memphis, TN), January 7, 2004.

1165 Ibid.

1166 Tom Charlier, "Panel cites Lee's inexperience, opens MLGW search," *Commercial Appeal* (Memphis, TN), January 7, 2004.

1167 Ibid.

1168 Blake Fontenay, "Council takes slap at mayor," *Commercial Appeal* (Memphis, TN), January 7, 2004.

1169 Jackson Baker, "Down from the Mountaintop" "The Testament of Willie Herenton," *Memphis Flyer,* January 15-21, 2004.

1170 Ibid.

1171 Ibid.

1172 Ibid.

1173 Ibid.

1174 Ibid.

1175 Ibid.

1176 Ibid.

1177 Ibid.

1178 Ibid.

1179 Ibid.

1180 Ibid.

1181 Blake Fontenay, "MLGW Bond deal questioned—Fundraiser for mayor was hired," *Commercial Appeal* (Memphis, TN), January 15, 2004; "MLGW Bond Probe,"

WREG News Channel 3 (Memphis, TN), January 15, 2004; John Branston, "Men of Many Hats," *Memphis Flyer,* February 12, 2004.

1182 Editorial "MLGW bond issue raises questions," *Commercial Appeal* (Memphis, TN), February 3, 2004.

1183 "MLGW Bond Probe," *WREG News Channel 3* (Memphis, TN), January 15, 2004; Blake Fontenay, "Council to look into bond deal," *Commercial Appeal* (Memphis, TN), January 21, 2004.

1184 "MLGW Bond Probe," *WREG News Channel 3* (Memphis, TN), January 15, 2004.

1185 Ibid.

1186 Blake Fontenay, "Council to look into bond deal," *Commercial Appeal* (Memphis, TN), January 21, 2004.

1187 Ibid.

1188 Ibid.

1189 Ibid.

1190 Blake Fontenay, "Interim pay ends at 45 days," *Commercial Appeal* (Memphis, TN), January 23, 2004; Blake Fontenay, "Herenton vetoes ordinance on interim appointee pay," *Commercial Appeal,* February 5, 2004.

1191 Blake Fontenay, "Interim pay ends at 45 days," *Commercial Appeal* (Memphis, TN), January 23, 2004.

1192 Ibid.

1193 Blake Fontenay, "Herenton vetoes ordinance on interim appointee pay," *Commercial Appeal* (Memphis, TN), February 5, 2004.

1194 Ibid.

1195 Blake Fontenay, "Mayor urged to dump nominee," *Commercial Appeal* (Memphis, TN), January 31, 2004.

1196 Ibid.

1197 Ibid.

1198 Editorial, "MLGW bond issue raises questions," *Commercial Appeal* (Memphis, TN), February 3, 2004.

1199 Ibid.

1200 Clay Bailey, "Herenton, suburban mayors amicably discuss joint concerns," *Commercial Appeal* (Memphis, TN), February 5, 2004.

1201 Editorial, "Challenges loom for public schools," *Commercial Appeal* (Memphis, TN), June 6, 2004.

1202 Editorial, "Shelby Farms road plan taking shape," *Commercial Appeal* (Memphis, TN), September 7, 2004.

1203 Editorial, "Challenges loom for public schools," *Commercial Appeal* (Memphis, TN), June 6, 2004.

1204 Ibid.

1205 Clay Bailey, "Herenton, suburban mayors amicably discuss joint concerns," *Commercial Appeal* (Memphis, TN), February 5, 2004.

1206 Tom Charlier, "A World Apart," *Commercial Appeal* (Memphis, TN), December 14, 2014.

1207 John Branston, "Men of Many Hats," *Memphis Flyer,* February 12, 2004.

1208 Ibid.

1209 Ibid.

1210 Norm Brewer, Commentary, *WREG News Channel 3* (Memphis, TN), February 18, 2004.

1211 Jackson Baker, "News Cycle," *Memphis Flyer,* December 31, 2004.

1212 Norm Brewer, Commentary, *WREG News Channel 3* (Memphis, TN), February 18, 2004.

1213 Editorial, "Wild Goose Chase," *Memphis Flyer,* June 21, 2012.

1214 Mary Cashiola, "Power Struggle," "Mayor says no to national search for MLGW president," *Memphis Flyer,* February 19-25, 2004.

1215 Ibid.

1216 Blake Fontenay, "Tigers' subsidy nixed," *Commercial Appeal* (Memphis, TN), February 18, 2004.

1217 Ibid.

1218 David Williams, "Council Acts – Council Ok's Tigers' Move From Pyramid to Forum—Private Funds will pay for locker room," *Commercial Appeal* (Memphis, TN), April 14, 2004.

1219 Carol Chumney, "My Olive Branch," *Memphis Flyer,* March 5, 2004.

1220 Ibid.

1221 Ibid.

1222 Jackson Baker, "Shattered Front," "Chumney opts out of the struggle between her council mates and Mayor Herenton," *Memphis Flyer,* March 5, 2004.

1223 Editorial, "Time to close easy exit to pensions?" *Commercial Appeal* (Memphis, TN), March 9, 2004.

1224 Ibid.

1225 Ibid.

1226 Ibid.

1227 Ibid.

1228 Blake Fontenay, "Chumney hits 'rich' pensions," *Commercial Appeal* (Memphis, TN), March 18, 2004.

1229 Ibid.

1230 Ibid; Blake Fontenay, "Council members wrangle over use of shared staffers," *Commercial Appeal* (Memphis, TN), March 10, 2004; Jackson Baker, "Chumney Agonistes" "The City Council's newest member finds herself at the center of a firestorm," *Memphis Flyer,* March 11, 2004.

1231 Jackson Baker, "Chumney Agonistes" "The City Council's newest member finds herself at the center of a firestorm," *Memphis Flyer,* March 11, 2004.

1232 Ibid.

1233 Ibid; Blake Fontenay, "Council members wrangle over use of shared staffers," *Commercial Appeal* (Memphis, TN), March 10, 2004; Ann Perry, contributing editor, "Memphis City Council is All Shook Up Over Newest Member, Carol Chumney— an interview with Carol," *Democrat* (Memphis, TN), June 2004.

1234 Jackson Baker, "Chumney Agonistes" "The City's newest member finds herself at the center of a firestorm," *Memphis Flyer,* March 11, 2004.

1235 George Brown, "A war of words is raging within the Memphis City Council," *WMC Action News 5* (Memphis, TN), March 16, 2004; Blake Fontenay, "Council members berate Chumney," *Commercial Appeal* (Memphis, TN), March 17, 2004.

1236 George Brown, "A war of words is raging within the Memphis City Council," *WMC Action News 5* (Memphis, TN), March 16, 2004.

1237 Ibid.

1238 Letters to the Editor, "As the Council Turns" "Council should follow Chumney's example" *Commercial Appeal* (Memphis, TN), March 21, 2004; Ann Perry, contributing editor, "Memphis City Council Is All Shook Up Over Newest Member, Carol Chumney—An Interview with Carol," *Democrat* (Memphis, TN), June 2004.

1239 Julia E. Tate, Letters to the Editor, *Commercial Appeal* (Memphis TN), March 21, 2004.

1240 Carole Kimbrell Gillespie, Letters to the Editor, *Commercial Appeal* (Memphis, TN), March 21, 2004.

1241 Billy Ross, Letters to the Editor, *Commercial Appeal* (Memphis, TN), March 21, 2004.

1242 Elbert Rich Jr. and Jody Cohen, Letters to the Editor, "Officials Have Bottomless Source of Revenue," *Commercial Appeal* (Memphis, TN), March 21, 2004.

1243 Ann Perry, contributing editor, "Memphis City Council Is All Shook Up Over Newest Member, Carol Chumney— an Interview with Carol," *Democrat* (Memphis, TN), June 2004.

1244 Blake Fontenay, "Chumney hits 'rich' pensions," *Commercial Appeal* (Memphis, TN), March 18, 2004.

1245 Editorial, "City's retirement system needs fixing yesterday," *Tri-State Defender* (Memphis, TN), April 24-28, 2004.

1246 Ibid.

1247 Ibid.

1248 Ibid.

1249 Editorial, "Word to the Wise," *Memphis Flyer,* March 25, 2004.

1250 Ibid.

1251 Ibid.

1252 Ibid.

1253 Carol Chumney, "A Public Walloping?" *Memphis Flyer,* April 1-7, 2004.

1254 Ibid.

1255 Ibid.

1256 Ibid.

1257 Ibid.

1258 Ibid.

1259 Ibid.

1260 Blake Fontenay, "Chumney hosting forum on MLGW," *Commercial Appeal* (Memphis TN), March 31, 2004.

1261 Blake Fontenay, "Residents urge veteran at MLGW," *Commercial Appeal* (Memphis, TN), April 4, 2004.

1262 Ibid; Tom Charlier, "MLGW CEO finalists down to 4," *Commercial Appeal* (Memphis, TN), April 13, 2004.

1263 Ibid.

1264 Ibid.

1265 Allan Wade, "Pension proposal no help to taxpayers," *Commercial Appeal* (Memphis, TN), April 13, 2004.

1266 Ibid.

1267 Ibid.

1268 Ibid.

1269 Ibid.

1270 Ibid.

1271 Ibid.

1272 Blake Fontenay, "Tougher pension rules not going anywhere," *Commercial Appeal* (Memphis, TN), April 14, 2004.

1273 Editorial, "Council skirts pair of important issues," *Commercial Appeal* (Memphis, TN), April 18, 2004.

1274 Blake Fontenay, "Tougher pension rules not going anywhere," *Commercial Appeal* (Memphis, TN), April 14, 2004.

1275 "On the Wall" "Chum in the Water," *Memphis Flyer,* April 15-21, 2004.

1276 Ibid.

1277 Ibid.

1278 Ibid.

1279 Ibid.

1280 Ibid.

1281 Bill Day, Cartoon, *Commercial Appeal* (Memphis, TN), April 16, 2004.

1282 Ibid.

1283 Editorial, "Council skirts pair of important issues," *Commercial Appeal* (Memphis, TN), April 18, 2004.

1284 Ibid.

1285 Ibid.

1286 Ibid.

1287 Ibid.

1288 Ibid.

1289 Ibid.

1290 Ibid.

1291 Mary George Beggs, "Chumney is following her constituents' wishes," *Commercial Appeal* (Memphis, TN), April 22, 2004.

1292 Charles S. Peete Jr., "Chumney is following her constituents' wishes," *Commercial Appeal* (Memphis, TN), April 22, 2004.

1293 Richard Massey, "Chumney is following her constituents' wishes," *Commercial Appeal* (Memphis, TN), April 22, 2004.

1294 Felicia D. Boyd, "Chumney is following her constituents' wishes," *Commercial Appeal* (Memphis, TN), April 22, 2004.

1295 Blake Fontenay, "Chumney not giving up on pension reform," *Commercial Appeal* (Memphis, TN), May 4, 2004; Blake Fontenay, "Required residency may go to vote," *Commercial Appeal,* May 5, 2004.

1296 Carol Chumney, "City administration used covert revenue projections," *Memphis Business Journal,* September 24-30, 2004.

1297 Jacinthia Jones, "Group submits retirement referendum," *Commercial Appeal* (Memphis, TN), July 30, 2004.

1298 Ibid.

1299 Arthur L. Webb, "Council belatedly proposes salary increase for MLGW chief's position," *Tri-State Defender* (Memphis, TN), May 8-12, 2004.

1300 Editorial, "MLGW bond probe progresses," *Commercial Appeal* (Memphis, TN), May 15, 2004.

1301 Ibid.

1302 Ann Perry, "Memphis City Council is All Shook Up Over Newest Member, Carol Chumney—an interview with Carol," *Democrat* (Memphis, TN), June 2004.

1303 Ibid.

1304 Jackson Baker, "Main Men" "Watch Out Willie!" *Memphis Flyer,* May 19, 2004.

1305 Ibid.

1306 Tom Charlier "Critics: Lee's re-entry harms MLGW search," *Commercial Appeal* (Memphis, TN), June 3, 2004; Wendi C. Thomas, Editorial, "God hath spoken on utility czar," *Commercial Appeal* (Memphis, TN), June 6, 2004.

1307 Tom Charlier, "Critics: Lee's re-entry harms MLGW search," *Commercial Appeal* (Memphis, TN), June 3, 2004.

1308 Wendi C. Thomas, Editorial, "God hath spoken on utility czar," *Commercial Appeal,* June 6, 2004.

1309 Editorial, "The nomination that wouldn't go away," *Commercial Appeal* (Memphis, TN), June 9, 2004.

1310 Tom Charlier, "Critics: Lee's re-entry harms MLGW search," *Commercial Appeal* (Memphis, TN), June 3, 2004.

1311 Ibid.

1312 R. Brian Skelton, Letter to Editor, "Lee's reentry, MLGW pay hike no coincidence," *Commercial Appeal* (Memphis, TN), June 6, 2004.

1313 Editorial, "The nomination that wouldn't go away," *Commercial Appeal* (Memphis, TN), June 9, 2004.

1314 Jacinthia Jones, "Lee wins approval as CEO of utility," *Commercial Appeal* (Memphis, TN), June 16, 2004.

1315 Ibid; Blake Fontenay, "Herenton Demands Changes," *Commercial Appeal* (Memphis, TN), June 16, 2004.

1316 Jacinthia Jones, "Lee wins approval as CEO of utility," *Commercial Appeal* (Memphis, TN), June 16, 2004.

1317 Blake Fontenay, "Herenton Demands Changes," *Commercial Appeal* (Memphis, TN), June 16, 2004.

1318 Jody Callahan, "Lee gets nod at MLGW," *Commercial Appeal* (Memphis, TN), June 15, 2004.

1319 Arthur L. Webb, "Lee: Out of the oven and into the fire?" *Tri-State Defender* (Memphis, TN), June 19-23, 2004.

1320 Blake Fontenay, "Herenton Demands Changes," *Commercial Appeal* (Memphis, TN), June 16, 2004; Arthur L. Webb, "Lee, Out of the oven and into the fire?" *Tri-State Defender* (Memphis, TN), June 19-23, 2004; Jackson Baker, "News Cycle," *Memphis Flyer,* December 31, 2004.

1321 Carol Chumney, "Council member taking a stand," *Tri-State Defender* (Memphis, TN), June 26-30, 2004.

1322 Ibid.

1323 Ibid.

1324 Ibid.

1325 Ibid.

1326 "New Information: Investigation into Memphis Mayor Willie Herenton," *ABC Eyewitness News 24* (Memphis, TN), July 2, 2004.

1327 Ibid.; Tony McNary, "Council member wants inquiries into the mayor's actions stopped," *WMC Action News 5* (Memphis, TN), July 2, 2004.

1328 Jacinthia Jones, "Council May Suspend Inquiry of Bond Deal-Marshall wants to Yield to FBI in Herenton Probe," *Commercial Appeal* (Memphis, TN), July 3, 2004.

1329 "New Information: Investigation into Memphis Mayor Willie Herenton," *ABC Eyewitness News 24* (Memphis, TN), July 2, 2004.

1330 Ibid.; Tony McNary, "Council member wants inquiries into the mayor's actions stopped," *WMC Action News 5* (Memphis, TN), July 2, 2004.

1331 "MLG & W under FBI Investigation," *ABC Eyewitness News 24* (Memphis, TN), July 2, 2004.

1332 Jacinthia Jones, "Council: Talks needed on cuts," *Commercial Appeal* (Memphis, TN), July 22, 2004.

1333 Ibid.

1334 Jacinthia Jones, "Group submits retirement referendum," *Commercial Appeal* (Memphis, TN), July 30, 2004.

1335 Jacinthia Jones, "Pension eligibility petition rejected," *Commercial Appeal* (Memphis, TN), July 31, 2004.

1336 Ibid.

1337 Ibid.

1338 Jessica Garrison and Zeke Minaya, "Iraqi Group Gets a Taste of Local Politics," *Los Angeles Times,* August 6, 2004.

1339 Associated Press, "Iraqis on tour, banned from Memphis hall," August 3, 2004.

1340 Jody Callahan, "Welcome mat yanked from under visiting Iraqi leaders," *Commercial Appeal* (Memphis, TN), August 3, 2004.

1341 Ibid; Associated Press, "Iraqis on tour, banned from Memphis hall," August 3, 2004; Mary Cashiola, "Operation Iraqi Freedom," *Memphis Flyer,* August 12-18, 2004.

1342 Mary Cashiola, "Operation Iraqi Freedom" "Joe Brown's refusal to allow Iraqi visitors into City Hall shocked and awed the world," *Memphis Flyer,* August 12-18, 2004.

1343 Associated Press, "Iraqis on tour, banned from Memphis Hall," August 3, 2004.

1344 Jody Callahan, "Welcome mat yanked from under visiting Iraqi leaders," *Commercial Appeal* (Memphis, TN), August 3, 2004.

1345 Ibid.; Editorial, "Iraqis hang tough in Memphis," *Commercial Appeal* (Memphis, TN), August 5, 2004.

1346 Editorial, "Iraqis hang tough in Memphis," *Commercial Appeal* (Memphis, TN), August 5, 2004.

1347 Associated Press, "Iraqis on tour, banned from Memphis hall," August 3, 2004.

1348 Editorial, "Iraqis hang tough in Memphis," *Commercial Appeal* (Memphis, TN), August 5, 2004.

1349 "Iraqi tour group barred from city hall," *USA Today,* August 4, 2004; "Visiting Iraqis unwelcome at Memphis City Hall," *Tulsa World,* August 4, 2004; Associated Press, "Memphis Bars Iraqis' Visit," *Philadelphia Daily News,* August 4, 2004.

1350 Editorial, "'Apology' to Iraqis Admits no Mistakes," *Commercial Appeal* (Memphis, TN), August 10, 2004; Mary Cashiola, "Operation Iraqi Freedom" "Joe Brown's refusal to allow Iraqi visitors into City Hall shocked and awed the world," *Memphis Flyer,* August 12-18, 2004.

1351 Terry Kirby, Letter to Editor, "City of good abode? Iraqis have reason for skepticism," *Commercial Appeal* (Memphis, TN), August 4, 2004.

1352 Ibid; Editorial, "Iraqis hang tough in Memphis," *Commercial Appeal* (Memphis, TN), August 5, 2004.

1353 Terry R. Kirby and Jim Dorman, Letters to Editor, "City of good abode? Iraqis have reason for skepticism," *Commercial Appeal* (Memphis, TN), August 4, 2004.

1354 Tammy Braithwaite, Letter to Editor, "City of good abode? Iraqis have reason for skepticism," *Commercial Appeal* (Memphis, TN), August 4, 2004.

1355 James A. Carraway Jr., Letter to Editor, "City of good abode? Iraqis have reason for skepticism," *Commercial Appeal* (Memphis, TN), August 4, 2004.

1356 George Linder, "City of good abode? Iraqis have reason for skepticism," *Commercial Appeal* (Memphis, TN), August 4, 2004.

1357 George Linder, and Pastor Emeritus Nicholas L. Vieron, Annunciation Church, Letters to Editor, "City of good abode? Iraqis have reason for skepticism," *Commercial Appeal* (Memphis, TN), August 4, 2004.

1358 Tammy Stupp, Letter to Editor, "City of good abode? Iraqis have reason for skepticism," *Commercial Appeal* (Memphis, TN), August 4, 2004.

1359 Clark Smeltzer Jr., Letter to Editor, "City of good abode? Iraqis have reason for skepticism," *Commercial Appeal* (Memphis, TN), August 4, 2004.

1360 Bill Day, "Viewpoint," *Commercial Appeal* (Memphis, TN), August 6, 2004.

1361 Clark Smeltzer Jr., Letter to Editor, "City of good abode? Iraqis have reason for skepticism," *Commercial Appeal* (Memphis, TN), August 4, 2004.

1362 Ibid.

1363 Jessica Garrison and Zeke Minaya, "Iraqi Group Gets a Taste of Local Politics," *Los Angeles Times,* August 6, 2004.

1364 Ibid.

1365 Editorial, "Iraqis hang tough in Memphis," *Commercial Appeal* (Memphis, TN), August 5, 2004.

1366 Mary Cashiola, "Operation Iraqi Freedom," *Memphis Flyer,* August 12-18, 2004.

1367 Jessica Garrison and Zeke Minaya, "Iraqi Group Gets a Taste of Local Politics," *Los Angeles Times,* August 6, 2004.

1368 Ibid.

1369 Ibid.; "Amplifications and Corrections," *Commercial Appeal* (Memphis, TN), August 6, 2004; Mary Cashiola, "Operation Iraqi Freedom," *Memphis Flyer,* August 12-18, 2004.

1370 Jackson Baker, "Politics" "For better or for worse, the council maverick is widening her circle of support," *Memphis Flyer,* August 25, 2004.

1371 Associated Press, "Official Apologizes to Iraqi Delegation," *Commercial Appeal* (Memphis, TN), August 9, 2004.

1372 Ibid.

1373 Editorial, "'Apology' to Iraqis Admits no Mistakes," *Commercial Appeal* (Memphis, TN), August 10, 2004.

1374 Ibid.

1375 Editorial, "Welcome, Ya'll. Now, Git!" *Los Angeles Times,* August 6, 2004; Mary Cashiola, "Operation Iraqi Freedom," *Memphis Flyer,* August 12-18, 2004.

1376 Mary Cashiola, "Operation Iraqi Freedom," *Memphis Flyer,* August 12-18, 2004.

1377 Chris Davis, "Entitlement and the Jones Affair," *Memphis Flyer,* August 12, 2004.

1378 Don Swogger, Letters to Editor, "Half-hearted apology compounds snub," *Commercial Appeal* (Memphis, TN), August 11, 2004.

1379 Jody Hurt Patterson, Letters to the Editor, "Half-hearted apology compounds snub," *Commercial Appeal* (Memphis, TN), August 11, 2004.

1380 Mary Cashiola, "Operation Iraqi Freedom," *Memphis Flyer,* August 12-18, 2004.

1381 Chris Davis, "Entitlement and the Jones Affair," *Memphis Flyer,* August 12, 2004.

1382 Ibid.; John Branston, "[City Beat] Was Wharton out of the loop?" *Memphis Flyer,* August 13, 2004; Jackson Baker, "Tom Jones departs, leaving shockwaves," *Memphis Flyer,* August 18, 2004.

1383 Ibid.; Ibid.

1384 John Branston, "[City Beat] Was Wharton out of the loop?" *Memphis Flyer,* August 13, 2004.

1385 Ibid.

1386 Ibid.

1387 Ibid.; Jackson Baker, "Tom Jones departs, leaving shockwaves," *Memphis Flyer,* August 12-18, 2004; Chris Davis, "Entitlement and the Jones Affair," *Memphis Flyer,* August 12, 2004.

1388 Chris Davis, "Entitlement and the Jones Affair," *Memphis Flyer,* August 12, 2004.

1389 Ibid.

1390 Ibid.

1391 Jackson Baker, "Hatful of Names," *Memphis Flyer,* September 10, 2004.

1392 Jackson Baker, "Some Republicans Claim State Rep. John Deberry others covet, er, Willie Herenton?" *Memphis Flyer,* August 11, 2004.

1393 Ibid.

1394 Jane Davis, "Passing Through," *Memphis Flyer,* August 20, 2004.

1395 Ibid.

1396 John Branston, "Political Power Then and Now" "The last true dictator of Memphis died 50 years ago," *Memphis Flyer,* September 3, 2004.

1397 Ibid.

1398 Jackson Baker, "Politics" "For better or worse, the council maverick is widening her circle of support," *Memphis Flyer,* August 25, 2004.

1399 Ibid.

1400 Ibid.

1401 Ibid.

1402 Ibid.

1403 Editorial, "Generous pensions: MLGW and beyond," *Commercial Appeal* (Memphis, TN), August 13, 2004.

1404 Ibid.

1405 Ibid.

1406 Ibid.

1407 Ibid.

1408 Editorial, "Changing pension rule is a good move," *Commercial Appeal* (Memphis, TN), August 19, 2004.

1409 Ibid.

1410 Ibid.

1411 Ibid.

1412 Jacinthia Jones, "City council scrutinizes budget," "Warns mayor's team against more surprises," *Commercial Appeal* (Memphis, TN), September 17, 2004.

1413 *City of Memphis v. Shelby County Election Commission, etal,* Shelby County Chancery Court, No. CH-04-1736-II, September 8, 2004, *"Final Judgment";* Jacinthia Jones, "City sues for payroll tax vote," *Commercial Appeal* (Memphis, TN), August 28, 2004.

1414 Carol Chumney, "Play it straight with Memphians about budget," *Commercial Appeal* (Memphis, TN), October 27, 2004.

1415 George Metaxas, "Herenton warns city budget in bad shape," *WMC Action News 5* (Memphis, TN), September 7, 2004; Editorial, "Devil's still in payroll tax details," *Commercial Appeal* (Memphis, TN), September 17, 2004; Carol Chumney, "City administration used covert revenue projections," *Memphis Business Journal,* September 24-30, 2004.

1416 George Metaxas, "Herenton warns city budget in bad shape," *WMC Action News 5* (Memphis, TN), September 7, 2004; Editorial, "Budget candor shouldn't wait," *Commercial Appeal* (Memphis, TN), September 9, 2004.

1417 George Metaxes, "Herenton warns city budget in bad shape," *WMC Action News 5* (Memphis, TN), September 7, 2004.

1418 Editorial "Budget candor shouldn't wait," *Commercial Appeal* (Memphis, TN), September 9, 2004; Jacinthia Jones, "City council scrutinizes budget," *Commercial Appeal* (Memphis, TN), September 17, 2004.

1419 Editorial, "Budget candor shouldn't wait," *Commercial Appeal* (Memphis, TN), September 9, 2004.

1420 Ibid.

1421 Jacinthia Jones, "City council scrutinizes budget," *Commercial Appeal* (Memphis, TN), September 17, 2004.

1422 Ibid.

1423 Carol Chumney, "Play it straight with Memphians about budget," *Commercial Appeal* (Memphis, TN), October 27, 2004.

1424 Ibid.

1425 Janel Davis, "Digging Deeper" "Chumney does her own budget searching," *Memphis Flyer,* September 23-24, 2004.

1426 Ibid.

1427 Wendi C. Thomas, "Herenton adds Fuel to the Fire," *Commercial Appeal* (Memphis, TN), September 23, 2004.

1428 Ibid.

1429 Carol Chumney, "City administration used covert revenue projections," *Memphis Business Journal,* September 24-30, 2004.

1430 Ibid.

1431 Carol Chumney, "Play it straight with Memphians about budget," *Commercial Appeal* (Memphis, TN), October 27, 2004.

1432 Editorial, "Less fighting, more fixing at City Hall," *Commercial Appeal* (Memphis, TN), September 26, 2004.

1433 Bill Day Cartoon, "Viewpoint," *Commercial Appeal* (Memphis, TN), September 26, 2004.

1434 Ibid.

1435 Michael Erskine, "Council cuts retirement plan," *Commercial Appeal* (Memphis, TN), September 22, 2004.

1436 Ibid.; Editorial, "Scrapping bad rule required a tradeoff," *Commercial Appeal* (Memphis, TN), September 24, 2004.

1437 Jacinthia Jones, "Council kills pension rule," *Commercial Appeal* (Memphis, TN), October 8, 2004.

1438 Editorial, "Scrapping bad rule required a tradeoff," *Commercial Appeal* (Memphis, TN), September 24, 2004.

1439 Ibid.

1440 Ibid.

1441 Jacinthia Jones, "Council kills pension rule," *Commercial Appeal* (Memphis, TN), October 7, 2004.

1442 Ibid.

1443 Ibid.

1444 Ibid.

1445 Ibid.

1446 Ibid.

1447 Janel Davis, "Digging Deeper," "Chumney does her own budget searching," *Memphis Flyer,* September 23-29, 2004.

1448 Carol Chumney, "Play it straight with Memphians about budget," *Commercial Appeal* (Memphis, TN), October 27, 2004.

1449 Andy Meek, "Facing Budget Woes, City Leaders Seek New Cuts," *Daily News* (Memphis, TN), October 15, 2004.

1450 George Metaxas, "Eliminating the perks of power at MLGW," *WMC Action News 5* (Memphis, TN), September 21 2004.

1451 Ibid.

1452 Ibid.

1453 Editorial, "Trying to halt MLGW exodus," *Commercial Appeal* (Memphis, TN), October 8, 2004.

1454 Ibid.

1455 Tom Charlier, "MLGW delays halt to policies" "Board wants to study financial impact first," *Commercial Appeal* (Memphis, TN), October 8, 2004.

1456 Mike Matthews, "Joe and the Power Company," *WREG News Channel 3* (Memphis, TN), November 5, 2004; George Metaxas, "Council members say MLGW is cutting too many jobs," *WMC Action News 5* (Memphis, TN), November 5, 2004.

1457 "Memphis Councilman Says Bond Firm Subpoenaed," *ABC Eyewitness News 24* (Memphis, TN), November 9, 2004; George Metaxas, City – owned utility division being probed by feds," *WMC Action News 5* (Memphis, TN), November 9, 2004; Tedra DeSue, "Investigation of Memphis Mayor's Deals with Certain Firms Heats Up," *Bond Buyer online,* November 19, 2004.

1458 George Metaxas, "Mayor Herenton says changes are coming for the City of Memphis," *WMC Action News 5* (Memphis, TN), November 9, 2004.

1459 Ibid.

1460 George Metaxas, "Council waits for answers to questions in the MLGW bond investigation," *WMC Action News 5* (Memphis, TN), November 12, 2004.

1461 Ibid.

1462 Ibid.

1463 Ibid.

1464 John Branston, "From Wall Street to Front Street," *Memphis Flyer,* November 18-24, 2004.

1465 Ibid.; Jacinthia Jones, "City Council considers using subpoena power," *Commercial Appeal* (Memphis, TN), November 23, 2004.

1466 John Branston, "From Wall Street to Front Street," *Memphis Flyer,* November 18-24, 2004.

1467 Ibid.

1468 Jacinthia Jones, "City council closes investigation into mayor's bond role," *Commercial Appeal* (Memphis, TN), October 20, 2004.

1469 Ibid.

1470 John Branston, "On Further Review" "Second Thoughts: Rodney Herenton, the lottery, runoffs, and Jeopardy," *Memphis Flyer,* December 2-8, 2004.

1471 Ibid.; Jacinthia Jones, "City Council halts bond-deal probe," *Commercial Appeal* (Memphis, TN), November 24, 2004.

1472 Jacinthia Jones, "Herenton says bond probe 'personal'," *Commercial Appeal* (Memphis, TN), November 24, 2004.

1473 Ibid.

1474 Jacinthia Jones, "City Council halts bond-deal probe," *Commercial Appeal* (Memphis, TN), November 24, 2004.

1475 Jackson Baker, "The Last Ditch," "Whether victim or aggressor, Chumney keeps the pressure on about MLGW," *Memphis Flyer,* December 2-8, 2004.

1476 Ibid.

1477 Tom Charlier, "Herenton urges city to do some MLGW tasks" "Move could mean layoffs, utility has 'enriched itself'," *Commercial Appeal* (Memphis, TN), December 3, 2004.

1478 Jacinthia Jones, "Mayor wants tax hike," *Commercial Appeal* (Memphis, TN), December 8, 2004.

1479 Ibid.; Tom Charlier, "Herenton urges city to do some MLGW tasks," *Commercial Appeal* (Memphis, TN), December 3, 2004.

1480 Ibid.

1481 Tom Charlier, "TVA may not allow rate plan," *Commercial Appeal* (Memphis, TN), December 12, 2004.

1482 Jacinthia Jones, "Dinner for Herenton: $70,000," *Commercial Appeal* (Memphis, TN), October 5, 2004.

1483 Ibid.

1484 Jackson Baker, "Yule Tides," *Memphis Flyer,* December 16-22, 2004.

1485 Ibid.

1486 Carol Chumney, "What Does City Hall Need?" *North Shelby Times* (Memphis, TN), December 15, 2004.

1487 Editorial, "Less fighting, more fixing at City Hall," *Commercial Appeal* (Memphis, TN), September 26, 2004.

1488 Jackson Baker, "News Cycle," *Memphis Flyer,* December 31, 2004.

1489 Carol Chumney, "What Does City Hall Need?" *North Shelby Times* (Memphis, TN), December 15, 2004.

1490 Ibid.

1491 Ibid.

1492 Ibid.

1493 Ibid.

1494 Editorial, "Mostly good news at MLGW," *Commercial Appeal* (Memphis, TN), December 19, 2004.

1495 Roswell Encina, "Big Raises for City Council Assistants," *WREG News Channel 3* (Memphis, TN), December 21, 2004; Jacinthia Jones, "Memphis council staffers get big raises," *Commercial Appeal* (Memphis, TN), December 22, 2004.

1496 Roswell Encina, "Big Raises for City Council Assistants," *WREG News Channel 3* (Memphis, TN), December 21, 2004.

1497 Ibid.; Jacinthia Jones, "Memphis council staffers get big raises," *Commercial Appeal* (Memphis, TN), December 22, 2004.

1498 Jacinthia Jones, "Memphis council staffers get big raises," *Commercial Appeal* (Memphis, TN), December 22, 2004.

1499 Ibid.

1500 Jacinthia Jones, "Herenton outlines 4 options to fix Budget," *Commercial Appeal* (Memphis, TN), December 22, 2004.

1501 Ibid.

1502 "Balancing the Budget in 2005," *ABC Eyewitness News 24* (Memphis, TN), December 31, 2004.

1503 Tom Bailey, Jr., "Herenton will set tone for the new year," *Commercial Appeal* (Memphis, TN), December 30, 2004.

1504 Ibid.

1505 "Et Cetera" "Results From 'And the Best'," *Memphis Flyer,* September 30-October 6, 2004.

1506 Ibid.

1507 Ibid.

1508 Editorial, "Pam Gaia," *Commercial Appeal* (Memphis, TN), September 24, 2004.

1509 Ibid.

1510 Jackson Baker "For 2005, Willie Herenton speaks more softly," *Memphis Flyer,* January 2, 2005.

1511 Ibid.

1512 Ibid.

1513 Ibid.

1514 Ibid.; Mary Powers, "Mayor pushes consolidation," "City, county must find ways to save cash, Herenton says," *Commercial Appeal* (Memphis, TN), January 2, 2005.

1515 Jackson Baker, "For 2005, Willie Herenton speaks more softly," *Memphis Flyer,* January 2, 2005.

1516 John Branston, "Are You Following Me?" *Memphis Flyer,* December 30, 2004-January 5, 2005.

1517 Ibid.

1518 Ibid.

1519 Jacinthia Jones, "City's financial image takes hit""Bond rating agencies' red flags reflect budget gap, bad planning," *Commercial Appeal* (Memphis, TN), January 4, 2005.

1520 Ibid.

1521 Ibid.

1522 Ibid.

1523 Ibid.

1524 Ibid.

1525 "Norm Brewer Commentary," *WREG News Channel 3* (Memphis, TN), January 4, 2005.

1526 Ibid.

1527 Editorial, "Be candid about city finances," *Commercial Appeal* (Memphis, TN), January 9, 2005.

1528 Bill Dries, "Mayor in '07: Any takers?" *Commercial Appeal* (Memphis, TN), April 24, 2005.

1529 Jacinthia Jones, "Council staff's pay hike snagged""Committee votes 8-3 that decision made by Brown, Ford is out of line," *Commercial Appeal* (Memphis, TN), January 5, 2005.

1530 Jacinthia Jones, "Council cuts big raises," *Commercial Appeal* (Memphis, TN), January 19, 2005.

1531 Ibid.

1532 R. J. Tutko, Letter to Editor, "'Joe Blow citizens' are pretty sharp," *Commercial Appeal* (Memphis, TN), January 6, 2005; Johanna Ellis, Letter to Editor, "Expectations have already hit bottom," *Commercial Appeal,* January 6, 2005.

1533 R. J. Tutko, Letter to Editor, "'Joe Blow citizens' are pretty sharp," *Commercial Appeal* (Memphis TN), January 6, 2005.

1534 Ibid.

1535 Dorethea Laughlin, Letter to Editor, "Unintended consequences," *Commercial Appeal* (Memphis, TN), January 6, 2005.

1536 Clay Bailey, "Herenton snubs mayors again" "Doesn't brief suburban leaders about new remarks on uniting Memphis, Shelby County," *Commercial Appeal* (Memphis, TN), January 4, 2005.

1537 Douglas Gordon, Letter to Editor, "Sorry mayor, you can't give us less," *Commercial Appeal* (Memphis, TN), January 4, 2005.

1538 Jacinthia Jones, reporters Ruma Banerji Kumar and Michael Erskine contributed, "A clarion call from Herenton—Let's go metro""Consolidate and I'll resign in the bargain, mayor says," *Commercial Appeal* (Memphis, TN), February 10, 2005.

1539 Ibid; George Metaxas, "Mayor Herenton has a plan to fund your child's education," *WMC Action News 5* (Memphis, TN), February 9, 2005.

1540 Jacinthia Jones, reporters Ruma Banerji Kumar and Michael Erskine contributed, "A clarion call from Herenton—Let's go metro""Consolidate and I'll resign in the bargain, mayor says," *Commercial Appeal* (Memphis, TN), February 10, 2005.

1541 Ibid.; Bill Dries, "Consolidation dream isn't dying," *Commercial Appeal* (Memphis, TN), March 9, 2005.

1542 George Metaxas, "Mayor Herenton has a plan to fund your child's education," *WMC Action News 5* (Memphis, TN), February 9, 2005.

1543 Jacinthia Jones, reporters Ruma Banerji Kumar and Michael Erskine contributed, "A clarion call from Herenton—Let's go metro""Consolidate and I'll resign in the bargain, mayor says," *Commercial Appeal* (Memphis, TN), February 10, 2005.

1544 Ibid.

1545 Ibid.; George Metaxas, "Mayor Herenton has a plan to fund your child's education," *WMC Action News 5* (Memphis, TN), February 9, 2005.

1546 George Metaxas, "Mayor Herenton has a plan to fund your child's education," *WMC Action News 5* (Memphis, TN), February 9, 2005.

1547 Jacinthia Jones, reporters Ruma Banerji Kumar and Michael Erskine contributed, "A clarion call from Herenton—Let's go metro""Consolidate and I'll resign in the bargain, mayor says," *Commercial Appeal* (Memphis, TN), February 10, 2005.

1548 Ibid.; "Norm Brewer Commentary," *WREG News Channel 3* (Memphis, TN), February 13, 2005.

1549 Bill Dries, "Herenton concedes message getting lost" "Asks PR pros if charm would help," *Commercial Appeal* (Memphis, TN), March 10, 2005.

1550 Editorial, "What would happen if Memphis seceded from Shelby County?" *Tri-State Defender* (Memphis, TN), October 22-26, 2005.

1551 Jacinthia Jones, "Council mulls layoff alternatives," *Commercial Appeal* (Memphis, TN), March 2, 2005.

1552 Ibid.

1553 Ibid.; Jacinthia Jones, "54-cent tax hike to keep jobs?" "Herenton says cuts could be short-term if solution adopted," *Commercial Appeal* (Memphis, TN), March 9, 2005.

1554 Jacinthia Jones, "54-cent tax hike to keep jobs?" "Herenton says cuts could be short-term if solution adopted," *Commercial Appeal* (Memphis, TN), March 9, 2005; Editorial, "Council's ideas are worth a look," *Commercial Appeal* (Memphis, TN), March 4, 2005.

1555 Jacinthia Jones, "54-cent tax hike to keep jobs?" "Herenton says cuts could be short-term if solution adopted," *Commercial Appeal* (Memphis, TN), March 9, 2005.

1556 Carol Chumney, "Making the responsible choices," *Commercial Appeal* (Memphis, TN), March 8, 2005.

1557 Ibid.

1558 Bill Dries, "Council to examine spending before considering tax increase," *Commercial Appeal* (Memphis, TN), March 16, 2005.

1559 Jackson Baker, "Making Believe" "Chumney's mayoral campaign was presented as a virtual reality in the Gridiron show," *Memphis Flyer*, April 7-13, 2005.

1560 Ibid.

1561 Editorial, "No sacred cows in city budget," *Commercial Appeal* (Memphis, TN), April 10, 2005.

1562 Janel Davis, "Too Many Projects" "City must cut capital spending or face same problems next year," *Memphis Flyer*, June 30-July 6, 2005.

1563 Editorial, "A bridge better left uncrossed," *Commercial Appeal* (Memphis, TN), October 19, 2005.

1564 Editorial, "Land bridge going nowhere," *Commercial Appeal* (Memphis, TN), December 5, 2005.

1565 Jacinthia Jones, "Mayor thinks citizens will support tax increase to restore services," *Commercial Appeal* (Memphis, TN), April 20, 2005.

1566 "Norm Brewer Commentary," *WREG News Channel 3* (Memphis, TN), April 20, 2005.

1567 Ibid.; Mary Cashiola, "Hello, Goodbye," *Memphis Flyer*, April 28-May 4, 2005; Jacinthia Jones, "Mayor thinks citizens will support tax increase to restore services," *Commercial Appeal* (Memphis, TN), April 20, 2005.

1568 Mary Cashiola, "Hello, Goodbye," *Memphis Flyer*, April 28-May 4, 2005.

1569 Ibid.

1570 Ibid.

1571 Ibid.

1572 "MLGW board concerned about merger plan," *WMC Action News 5* (Memphis, TN), April 14, 2005.

1573 Ibid.

1574 Ibid.; Bill Dries, "Council committee kills MLGW-city merger plan," *Commercial Appeal* (Memphis, TN), April 20, 2005.

1575 Editorial, "MLGW reforms failed smell test" "Reassure City Council members-Herenton's unclear position about selling MLGW probably contributed to the defeat of a restructuring plan," *Commercial Appeal* (Memphis, TN), April 22, 2005.

1576 Ibid.

1577 Ibid.; Bill Dries, "Council committee kills MLGW-city merger plan," *Commercial Appeal* (Memphis, TN), April 20, 2005.

1578 "Chumney: Yo! Red flags weren't shared," *Commercial Appeal* (Memphis, TN), May 18, 2005; Jacinthia Jones, "Youth jobs program survives audit" "Chumney: 'Wasted money..spent legitimately'" *Commercial Appeal*, October 10, 2005.

1579 Roswell Encina, "Where did Yo! Memphis money go?" *WREG News Channel 3* (Memphis, TN), May 3, 2005.

1580 Jacinthia Jones, "Youth jobs program survives audit" "Chumney: 'Wasted money... spent legitimately'," *Commercial Appeal* (Memphis, TN), October 10, 2005.

1581 Bill Dries, "For Yo! The bell tolls— Parents, students lament school's closing; failed to meet math benchmarks," *Commercial Appeal* (Memphis, TN), August 16, 2007.

1582 Bill Dries, "Yo! Memphis Files Suit Against City Schools," *Daily News* (Memphis, TN), March 26, 2008.

1583 *Yo! Memphis Foundation, Inc. v. Dan Ward, etal,* No. CT-001385-08, Div. IX, Shelby County Circuit Court, (May 13, 2010).

1584 Bill Dries, "Council douses 911 spending," *Commercial Appeal* (Memphis, TN), May 19, 2005.

1585 Editorial, "A good first step on spending cuts," *Commercial Appeal* (Memphis, TN), May 24, 2005.

1586 Ibid.

1587 Ibid.

1588 Ibid.

1589 Ibid.

1590 Jacinthia Jones, "Biting the bullet," *Commercial Appeal* (Memphis, TN), June 8, 2005.

1591 Ibid.

1592 Ibid.

1593 Ibid.

1594 Bill Dries, "Political warrior in fight of his life," *Commercial Appeal* (Memphis, TN), May 30, 2005.

1595 Ibid; *USA v. Roscoe Dixon,* Case No. 2:05-cv-20202-JPM, Doc. 95, (W. D. Tenn., May 18, 2006), *"Order Denying Motion to Remove Surplus Language from Indictment."*

1596 *U.S. v. One Men's Rolex Pearl Master Watch,* Case No. 08-6524, Doc. 56, (6th Cir. December 16, 2009), *"Opinion."*

1597 John Branston, "The Last Waltz," *Memphis Flyer,* April 17-23, 2008.

1598 Ibid.

1599 Ibid.

1600 "'Willis' name pops up again in E-cycle sting," *WMC Action News 5* (Memphis, TN), June 1, 2005.

1601 Jackson Baker, "John Ford's J-ACCUSE!" *Memphis Flyer,* March 22, 2014.

1602 Bill Dries, "Political warrior in fight of his life," *Commercial Appeal* (Memphis, TN), May 30, 2005.

1603 *USA v. Edwards,* No. 3:98-cr-00165-RET-1 (M.D. La).

1604 Jackson Baker, "Political Cool," *Memphis Flyer,* June 16, 2005.

1605 Ibid.

1606 Ibid.

1607 Carol Chumney, "She is *NOT* Uncool!" *Memphis Flyer,* June 23-29, 2005.

1608 Ibid.

1609 Ibid.

1610 Ibid.

1611 Tara Milligan, "Readers make choices for the Best in Business," *Memphis Business Journal,* June 24-30, 2005.

1612 Tom Charlier, "Networx asking for $3 million more," *Commercial Appeal* (Memphis, TN), February 5, 2005.

1613 Chris Davis, "Networx Down," *Memphis Flyer,* June 21, 2007.

1614 Ibid.

1615 Ibid.

1616 Ibid.

1617 Ibid.

1618 Tom Charlier, "Networx asking for $3 million more," *Commercial Appeal* (Memphis, TN), February 5, 2005.

1619 Bill Dries, "Boost sought for Networx" "MLGW board OK's $6 million," *Commercial Appeal* (Memphis, TN), April 22, 2005; Editorial, "Pulling the plug on Networx deal," *Commercial Appeal* (Memphis, TN), May 22, 2005.

1620 Editorial, "Pulling the plug on Networx deal," *Commercial Appeal* (Memphis, TN), May 22, 2005.

1621 Press Release, "Chumney's Proposal for Memphis Networx would have Disclosed Cable Plans and Protected City Investors," June 15, 2005.

1622 Bill Dries, "Networx vote challenged," *Commercial Appeal* (Memphis, TN), May 20, 2005.

1623 Ibid.

1624 Ibid.

1625 "MLGW isn't done fighting for Networx," *WMC Action News 5* (Memphis, TN), June 16, 2005.

1626 Ibid.

1627 Andy Wise, "City Council Reinstates Vehicle Allowance for City Employees," *WREG News Channel 3* (Memphis, TN), July 5, 2005; Michael Erskine, "Car policy still on radar," *Commercial Appeal* (Memphis, TN), July 6, 2005.

1628 Andy Wise, "City Council Reinstates Vehicle Allowance for City Employees," *WREG News Channel 3* (Memphis, TN), July 5, 2005; "Memphis council members ready to put brakes on car allowances," *WMC Action News 5* (Memphis, TN), July 5, 2005.

1629 "Memphis council members ready to put brakes on car allowances," *WMC Action News 5* (Memphis, TN), July 5, 2005.

1630 Andy Wise, "City Council Reinstates Vehicle Allowance for City Employees," *WREG News Channel 3* (Memphis, TN), July 5, 2005.

1631 Ibid.

1632 Ibid.

1633 Michael Erskine, "Car policy still on radar," *Commercial Appeal* (Memphis, TN), July 6, 2005.

1634 Michael Erskine, "MLGW to study car stipend," *Commercial Appeal* (Memphis, TN), July 8, 2005.

1635 Ibid.

1636 David Parker and Dot Truitt Walk, Letters to Editor, "When city turns a profit, then we'll talk car allowances," *Commercial Appeal* (Memphis, TN), July 10, 2005.

1637 David Parker, Letter to Editor, "When city turns a profit, then we'll talk car allowances," *Commercial Appeal* (Memphis, TN), July 10, 2005.

1638 Editorial, "Pay city travel by the mileage," *Commercial Appeal* (Memphis, TN), July 11, 2005.

1639 Ibid.

1640 Ibid.

1641 Jacinthia Jones, "Council cancels vehicle perking—City officials lose car cash; fleet office OK'd," *Commercial Appeal* (Memphis, TN), July 20, 2005.

1642 Ibid.

1643 Ibid.

1644 Ibid.

1645 Ibid.

1646 Ibid.

1647 Editorial, "Getting better mileage," *Commercial Appeal* (Memphis, TN), August 8, 2005.

1648 Ibid.; Tom Charlier, "Car allowance stripped, base pay increased," *Commercial Appeal* (Memphis, TN), August 19, 2005.

1649 Tom Charlier, "Car allowances stripped, base pay increased," Commercial *Appeal* (Memphis, TN), August 19, 2005.

1650 Editorial, "Time for Lee to earn his pay," *Commercial Appeal* (Memphis, TN), October 27, 2005.

1651 Robert Fitting and Barbara Plummer, Letters to Editor, "Tighter reins needed at MLGW," *Commercial Appeal* (Memphis, TN), October 31, 2005.

1652 Doug Holloway, Letter to Editor, "Tighter reins needed at MLGW," *Commercial Appeal* (Memphis, TN), October 31, 2005.

1653 Jacinthia Jones, "MLGW cuts worker raises to 2 percent," *Commercial Appeal* (Memphis, TN), November 30, 2005; Michael Erskine, "LGW reverses on union raise, cites finances," *Commercial Appeal* (Memphis, TN), November 16, 2005.

1654 Michael Erskine, "MLGW, union near wages deal" "New pact would save $1.5 million," *Commercial Appeal* (Memphis, TN), December 3, 2005; Editorial, "MLGW accord helps ratepayers," *Commercial Appeal,* December 3, 2005.

1655 Jacinthia Jones, "Lee, Brown letters turn up the heat" "Utility chief says council is hostile, but councilman says no, just thorough," *Commercial Appeal* (Memphis, TN), December 10, 2005.

1656 Michael Erskine, "Lee to give up $12,600 benefit" "MLGW chief would forgo political issue," *Commercial Appeal* (Memphis, TN), December 15, 2005.

1657 Ibid; Editorial, "Every little bit helps," *Commercial Appeal* (Memphis, TN), December 17 2005.

1658 Jacinthia Jones, "Belt not tightened enough for city," *Commercial Appeal* (Memphis, TN), August 16, 2005.

1659 Ibid.; "City's $10 mil shortfall manageable," *Tri-State Defender* (Memphis, TN), August 20-24, 2005.

1660 Jacinthia Jones, "Belt not tightened enough for city," *Commercial Appeal* (Memphis, TN), August 16, 2005.

1661 Jacinthia Jones, "City says it can fill the gap," *Commercial Appeal* (Memphis, TN), August 17, 2005.

1662 Ibid.

1663 Ibid.

1664 Ibid.

1665 Michael Erskine, "Mayor offers fiscal plan," *Commercial Appeal* (Memphis, TN), September 21, 2005.

1666 Carol Chumney, Guest Column, "City Council, and citizens, need budget truth," *Commercial Appeal* (Memphis, TN), October 7, 2005.

1667 Ibid.

1668 Michael Erskine, "Mayor offers fiscal plan," *Commercial Appeal* (Memphis, TN), September 21, 2005.

1669 Ibid.; Carol Chumney, Guest Column, "City Council, and citizens, need budget truth," *Commercial Appeal* (Memphis, TN), October 7, 2005.

1670 Carol Chumney, Guest Column, "City Council, and citizens need budget truth," *Commercial Appeal* (Memphis, TN), October 7, 2005.

1671 Jacinthia Jones, "Moratorium being sought on PILOTS," *Commercial Appeal* (Memphis, TN), October 12, 2005.

1672 Norm Brewer, Commentary, *WREG News Channel 3* (Memphis, TN), October 31, 2005.

1673 Ibid.

1674 Jacinthia Jones, "Moratorium being sought on PILOTS," *Commercial Appeal* (Memphis, TN), October 12, 2005.

1675 Ibid.

1676 Ibid.

1677 "The Fly-by," *Memphis Flyer,* October 20-26, 2005.

1678 Editorial, "Same old story on city spending," *Commercial Appeal* (Memphis, TN), October 15, 2005.

1679 Ibid.

1680 Ibid.

1681 Jacinthia Jones, "On tour: Is a park worth keeping?" "Mayor wants savings; some neighbors balk," *Commercial Appeal* (Memphis, TN), October 19, 2005.

1682 Leon Gray, Letter to Editor, "City of Bad Abode," *Memphis Flyer,* November 2, 2005.

1683 Virginia Leonard, Letter to Editor, "Independent eyes for city's books," *Commercial Appeal* (Memphis, TN), October 27, 2005.

1684 Jonathan Page, Letter to Editor, "Independent eyes for city's books," *Commercial Appeal* (Memphis, TN), October 27, 2005.

1685 Michael Erskine, "Bond rating takes it on chin," *Commercial Appeal* (Memphis, TN), October 30, 2005.

1686 Ibid.

1687 Ibid.

1688 Sarah Mullis and Pamela Cate and Amy Blackwell, Letters to Editor, *Commercial Appeal* (Memphis, TN), October 31, 2005.

1689 Bob Williams, Letter to Editor, "Tighten PILOT standards," *Commercial Appeal* (Memphis, TN), October 27, 2005.

1690 Ibid.

1691 Mary Cashiola, "No Taxation Location?" *Memphis Flyer,* October 27, 2005.

1692 Ibid.

1693 Jacinthia Jones, "How did city get in this mess?" *Commercial Appeal* (Memphis, TN), October 30, 2005.

1694 Ibid.

1695 Ibid.

1696 Ibid.

1697 Michael Erskine, "Budget news rekindles bid to oust Herenton," *Commercial Appeal* (Memphis, TN), October 30, 2005.

1698 Jacinthia Jones, "No new public projects for now" "Council Oks moratorium on capital improvement works," *Commercial Appeal* (Memphis, TN), November 2, 2005.

1699 Ibid.

1700 Ibid.

1701 Editorial, "Same old story on city spending" "More Discipline Needed" "Memphis City Council members haven't shown that they are ready to make really tough choices to reduce the city's spending," *Commercial Appeal* (Memphis, TN), October 15, 2005.

1702 Tom Charlier, "Beale project starts" "$500,000 earmarked for landing," *Commercial Appeal* (Memphis, TN), November 10, 2005.

1703 Ibid.

1704 Ibid.

1705 Ibid.

1706 Jacinthia Jones, "Surplus seen, but fees, OT put city out of kilter," *Commercial Appeal* (Memphis, TN), November 16, 2005.

1707 Jacinthia Jones, "No new public projects for now" "Council Oks moratorium on capital improvement works," *Commercial Appeal* (Memphis, TN), November 2, 2005.

1708 Ibid.

1709 Editorial, "A sharp focus on spending," *Commercial Appeal* (Memphis, TN), December 16, 2005.

1710 Jacinthia Jones, "Surplus seen, but fees, OT put city out of kilter," *Commercial Appeal* (Memphis, TN), November 16, 2005.

1711 Ibid.

1712 Norm Brewer, Commentary, *WREG News Channel 3* (Memphis, TN), November 16, 2005.

1713 Ibid.

1714 Ibid.

1715 "Council member says division puts taxpayers at risk," *WMC Action News 5* (Memphis, TN), November 16, 2005.

1716 Blake Fontenay, Viewpoint, "Bloom's Off Rosy Outlook" "Budgeteers for city discover value of looking at doughnut hole," *Commercial Appeal* (Memphis, TN), November 27, 2005.

1717 Ibid.

1718 Ibid.

1719 Ibid.

1720 Tom Charlier and Jimmie Covington, "Median income sinks in Shelby County" "Migration to surrounding counties sucking out wealth," *Commercial Appeal* (Memphis, TN), November 30, 2005.

1721 Ibid.

1722 John Branston, "The Last Waltz," *Memphis Flyer,* April 17-23, 2008; *USA v. Barry Myers,* Case No. 2:05-cr-20203-JPM, U.S. District Court, Doc. 86 (W.D. Tenn. December 21, 2007), *"Judgment in a Criminal Case," Barry Myers,* Case No. 2:05-cr-20202-JPM, Doc. 184, (W.D. Tenn. December 21, 2007), *"Judgment in a Criminal Case," USA v. Ward Crutchfield,* No. 2:05CR20204-01-B, ECF 117 (W.D. Tenn. January 18, 2008), *"Judgment in a Criminal Case," USA v. Charles Love,* No. 2:05-cr-20205-JDB, ECF 76 (W.D. Tenn. August 3, 2007); "Dishonor Roll," *Commercial Appeal* (Memphis, TN), December 1, 2006.

1723 Michael Erskine and Jacinthia Jones, "Local leaders to feel new ethics restraints" "State reforms after Waltz order city, county rules," *Commercial Appeal* (Memphis, TN), December 4, 2005.

1724 Ibid.

1725 Ibid.

1726 Ibid.

1727 John Branston, "Mayor for the Millennium" "Another holiday season and another party honoring Mayor Herenton," *Memphis Flyer,* December 8-14, 2005.

1728 Ibid.

1729 Ibid.

1730 Ibid.

1731 Ibid.; Amos Maki, "Downtown luring retailers," *Commercial Appeal* (Memphis, TN), December 23, 2005.

1732 Jackson Baker, "Final Notice," *Memphis Flyer,* December 29, 2005-January 4, 2006.

1733 Ibid.

1734 Ibid.

1735 Ibid.

1736 Jacinthia Jones, "Upbeat Herenton assures a surplus," *Commercial Appeal* (Memphis, TN), January 5, 2006.

1737 Ibid.

1738 Jacinthia Jones, "City reveals plan to cut debt," *Commercial Appeal* (Memphis, TN), January 18, 2006.

1739 Ibid.

1740 Ibid.

1741 Editorial, "It's time to shape Memphis' future," *Commercial Appeal* (Memphis, TN), April 28, 2015.

1742 Jacinthia Jones, "Herenton in Atlanta, not on stand," *Commercial Appeal* (Memphis, TN), February 14, 2006; Jeffry Scott and

Beth Warren, "Campbell's defense still in wings," *Atlanta Journal-Constitution*, February 12, 2006.

1743 Ibid; Ibid.

1744 *USA v. William Campbell*, No. 1:04-cr-00424-RWS-ECS, ECF 423 *aff'd*, (11th Cir. August 15, 2007).

1745 Editorial, "'No comment' isn't satisfactory," *Commercial Appeal* (Memphis, TN), March 14, 2006.

1746 Jacinthia Jones, "City's credit rating sinks," *Commercial Appeal* (Memphis, TN), February 8, 2006; Editorial, "Recovery road won't be short," *Commercial Appeal* (Memphis, TN), February 10, 2006.

1747 Jacinthia Jones, "City's credit rating sinks," *Commercial Appeal* (Memphis, TN), February 8, 2006.

1748 Ibid.

1749 Editorial, "Recovery road won't be short," *Commercial Appeal* (Memphis, TN), February 10, 2006.

1750 Ibid.

1751 Andy Meek, "Budget Figures Show Huge Gap Between Governments," *Daily News* (Memphis, TN), March 3, 2006.

1752 Ibid.

1753 Marc Perrusquia, "Waltz tapes show how cash was dished out" "Video backs charges against lawmakers," *Commercial Appeal* (Memphis, TN), March 5, 2006.

1754 Ibid.

1755 Ibid.

1756 *USA v. Roscoe Dixon*, Case No. 2:05-cr-20202-JPM, Doc 92, (W.D. Tenn., May 11, 2006), "*Order Denying Motion to Dismiss Based on Selective Prosecution and Order Denying Motion to Continue.*"

1757 Ibid.

1758 *USA v. Roscoe Dixon*, Case No. 2:05-cr-20202-01-MI, Doc. 145, (W.D. Tenn., October 13, 2006), "*Judgment in a Criminal Case.*"

1759 Ibid.; John Branston and Jackson Baker, "The Last Waltz," *Memphis Flyer*, April 17-23, 2008.

1760 *USA v. Hooks, Sr.*, Case No. 2:05-cr-20329-JDB, Doc. 57, (W.D. Tenn., August 21, 2006), "*Memorandum of Plea Agreement;*"

Doc. 62, December 8, 2006, "*Judgment in a Criminal Case.*"

1761 Jackson Baker, "Bad Moon Rising," *Memphis Flyer*, March 2, 2006.

1762 Jacinthia Jones, "Recall will be a hard sell for Tennessee" "Effort to oust Herenton, if successful, would be a rarity," *Commercial Appeal* (Memphis, TN), March 21, 2006.

1763 Ibid.

1764 Thaddeus Mathews Dot Com, May 7, 2006.

1765 Ibid; comments.

1766 Jackson Baker, "Mayor Agonistes," *Memphis Flyer*, March 16-22, 2006.

1767 Ibid.

1768 Ibid.

1769 Ibid.

1770 Ibid.

1771 Editorial, "Herenton paints a rosy picture," *Commercial Appeal* (Memphis, TN), April 26, 2006.

1772 Ibid.

1773 Ibid.

1774 Ibid.

1775 Michael Erskine, "Keep Coliseum as venue for community: Chumney," *Commercial Appeal* (Memphis, TN), May 16, 2006.

1776 David Williams, "Coliseum needs a comeback—with redo of fairgrounds, some say it's one arena too many," *Commercial Appeal* (Memphis, TN), November 14, 2005.

1777 Laura Moore "Crime" "A Community Problem," *Tri-State Defender* (Memphis, TN), June 10-14, 2006.

1778 "Memphis councilwoman wants fewer officers on desk jobs," *Dyersburg State Gazette*, June 12, 2006.

1779 Ibid.

1780 Carol Chumney, "A Real Crime Fix," *Memphis Flyer*, July 6, 2006.

1781 John Branston, "Mayor Meets with Council on FedExForum Parking Garage," *Memphis Flyer*, June 20, 2006.

1782 David Williams and Michael Erskine, "Forum garage gets FBI attention," *Commercial Appeal* (Memphis, TN), July 6, 2006.

1783 Ibid.

1784 Ibid.

1785 John Branston, "Mayor Meets with Council on FedExForum Parking Garage," *Memphis Flyer,* June 20, 2006.

1786 Ibid.; David Williams and Michael Erskine, "Forum garage gets FBI attention," *Commercial Appeal* (Memphis, TN), July 6, 2006.

1787 John Branston, "Mayor Meets with Council on FedExForum Parking Garage," *Memphis Flyer,* June 20, 2006.

1788 Ibid.

1789 Ibid.

1790 David Williams and Michael Erskine, "Forum garage gets FBI attention," *Commercial Appeal* (Memphis, TN), July 6, 2006.

1791 Ibid.

1792 Jacinthia Jones, "Race on for city mayor," *Commercial Appeal* (Memphis, TN), August 22, 2006.

1793 Einat Paz-Frankel, "Business Pulse results: Memphians call for leadership change," *Memphis Business Journal,* August 28, 2006.

1794 Jacinthia Jones, "Crime plan adds 650 police," *Commercial Appeal* (Memphis, TN), September 29, 2006.

1795 Ibid.

1796 Ibid.

1797 John Branston "Criminal Confusion," *Memphis Flyer,* October 19-25, 2006.

1798 Ibid.

1799 Ibid.

1800 Ibid.

1801 Jacinthia Jones, "Mayor defends not asking more police," *Commercial Appeal* (Memphis, TN), October 24, 2006.

1802 Jacinthia Jones, "Annex bounty: $100 million," *Commercial Appeal* (Memphis, TN), November 17, 2006.

1803 "the cheat sheet," *Memphis Flyer,* December 7, 2006.

1804 Ibid; *USA v. Rickey Peete,* Case No. 2:06-cr-20466-SHM, Doc. 16, (W.D. Tenn. December 16, 2006), *"Indictment;" USA v. Edmund H. Ford,* Case No. 2:06-cr-20467-SHM, Doc. 12, (W.D. Tenn. December 19, 2006), *"Indictment."*

1805 John Branston, "Joe Cooper's Revenge," *Memphis Flyer,* December 7, 2006; *USA v. Joseph Glenn Cooper,*

No. 2:07-20036-01-B, ECF 24-1 (W.D. Tenn. June 24, 2008), *"Redacted Judgment in a Criminal Case."*

1806 *USA v. Joseph Glenn Cooper,* No. 2:07-cr-20036-JDG, ECF 17, (W.D. Tenn. May 22, 2008), *"Government's Motion and Memorandum for a Departure from the Sentencing Guidelines."*

1807 Jacinthia Jones, "In City Council Voting-0-9 against turned to 9-2—Peete moved that project be approved," *Commercial Appeal* (Memphis, TN), December 2, 2006.

1808 Ibid.; John Branston, "City Council members Rickey Peete and Edmund Ford indicted," *Memphis Flyer,* December 19, 2006; John Branston, "Joe Cooper may have overplayed his hand," *Memphis Flyer,* December 20, 2006; *USA v. Rickey Peete,* Case No. 2:06-cr-20466-SHM, Doc. 16, (W.D. Tenn. December 16, 2006), *"Indictment;" USA v. Edmund H. Ford,* Case No. 2:06-cr-20467-SHM, Doc. 12, (W.D. Tenn. December 19, 2006), *"Indictment."*

1809 John Branston, "Edmund Ford Takes the Witness Stand," *Memphis Flyer,* May 19, 2008.

1810 Marc Perrusquia, "Ford defends Welch loan," *Commercial Appeal* (Memphis, TN), December 13, 2006.

1811 John Branston, "Joe Cooper's Revenge," *Memphis Flyer,* December 7, 2006.

1812 Ibid; *USA v. Peete,* 919 F. 2d 1168 (6th Cir. 1990).

1813 Ibid.

1814 Jackson Baker, "Peete's Last Take," *Memphis Flyer,* December 7, 2006.

1815 *USA v. Rickey Peete,* Case No. 2:06-cr-20466-SHM, Doc. 16, (W.D. Tenn. December 19, 2006), *"Indictment."*

1816 Ibid., Doc. 34, June 20, 2007, *"Memorandum of Plea Agreement,"* Doc. 43, November 23, 2007, *"Redacted Judgment in a Criminal Case;"* Laurence Buser, "Peete faces sentencing today," *Commercial Appeal* (Memphis, TN), November 14, 2007; Laurence Buser, "51 months for Peete," *Commercial Appeal* (Memphis, TN), November 15, 2007; Laurence Buser, "Peete admits bribes," *Commercial Appeal* (Memphis, TN), June 21, 2007.

1817 Laurence Buser, "51 months for Peete," *Commercial Appeal* (Memphis, TN), November 15, 2007; Laurence Buser, "Peete admits bribes," *Commercial Appeal* (Memphis, TN), June 21, 2007.

1818 Laurence Buser, "Peete admits bribes," *Commercial Appeal* (Memphis, TN), June 21, 2007.

1819 Marc Perrusquia, "Squeeze scheme," *Commercial Appeal* (Memphis, TN), November 14, 2007.

1820 Ibid.

1821 Ibid.

1822 Ibid.

1823 John Branston, "A Down and Dirty Year," *Memphis Flyer,* December 28, 2006.

1824 Andy Meek, "It's Official" "Chumney commits to October mayoral run," *Daily News* (Memphis, TN), January 19, 2007; *Main Street Journal,* April 2007.

1825 Andy Meek, "It's Official" "Chumney commits to October mayoral run," *Daily News* (Memphis, TN), January 19, 2007.

1826 Mary Cashiola, "Royal Flush?" *Memphis Flyer,* January 11-17, 2007.

1827 Don Wade, "Build case, then stadium?" *Commercial Appeal* (Memphis, TN), January 2, 2007.

1828 Halimah Abdullah, "Herenton may win without a punch," *Commercial Appeal* (Memphis, TN), January 9, 2007.

1829 Jacinthia Jones, "Herenton tells Wharton he'll run again, asks for his support," *Commercial Appeal* (Memphis, TN), May 1, 2007.

1830 Amy O. Williams, "Mayoral Candidate Chumney Shares Plans and Aspirations for -07," *Daily News* (Memphis, TN), January 11, 2007.

1831 Ibid.

1832 Andy Meeks, "It's Official" "Chumney commits to October mayoral run," *Daily News* (Memphis, TN), January 19, 2007.

1833 Ibid.

1834 Ibid.

1835 James Robert Chumney, "The Pink Palace: Clarence Saunders and the Memphis Museum," *Tennessee Historical Quarterly,* Vol. 32, No. 1, Spring 1973.

1836 Jackson Baker, "Ready or Not," *Memphis Flyer,* February 15-17, 2007.

1837 Editorial, "Hope for debate in mayoral race," *Commercial Appeal* (Memphis, TN), February 11, 2007.

1838 Ibid.

1839 Ibid.

1840 Ibid.

1841 Editorial, Commentary, "Doughty pair make early move against mayor," *Commercial Appeal* (Memphis, TN), February 12, 2007.

1842 Ibid.

1843 Ibid.

1844 Ibid.

1845 Ibid.

1846 Ibid.

1847 Jackson Baker, "Two More for Mayoralty," *Memphis Flyer,* February 8-14, 2007.

1848 Ibid.

1849 The Flyer Staff, "MLGW: The Fallout," *Memphis Flyer,* March 1, 2007.

1850 James T. Hall, Chris Allen, Gloria Kahn, Perry Steele, Kelly Calder, Robert T. Baker, Patricia Parris, Letters to Editor, *Commercial Appeal* (Memphis, TN), February 18, 2007.

1851 Mary Cupp, John Aquadro, Tom Weker, Letter to Editor, *Commercial Appeal* (Memphis, TN), February 18, 2007.

1852 Jacinthia Jones, "Probe urged on Ford billing," *Commercial Appeal* (Memphis, TN), February 21, 2007.

1853 Ibid.

1854 Ibid.; Trevor Aaronson & Michael Erskine, "Exec notified if Ford faced cutoff," *Commercial Appeal* (Memphis, TN), February 24, 2007.

1855 Trevor Aaronson & Michael Erskine, "Exec. Notified if Ford faced cutoff," *Commercial Appeal* (Memphis, TN), February 24, 2007; Trevor Aaronson and Michael Erskine, "MLGW let Ford's delinquent bills slide," *Commercial Appeal* (Memphis, TN), February 23, 2007.

1856 Jacinthia Jones, "Probe urged on Ford billing," *Commercial Appeal* (Memphis, TN), February 21, 2007; Trevor Aaronson & Michael Erskine, " MLGW let Ford's delinquent bills slide," *Commercial Appeal* (Memphis, TN), February 23, 2007.

1857 Trevor Aaronson & Michael Erskine, "MLGW let Ford's delinquent bills slide," *Commercial Appeal* (Memphis, TN), February 23, 2007; *USA v. Edmund H. Ford, Joseph Lee, III,* Case No. 2:06-cr-20467-SHM, Doc. 30, (W.D. Tenn. July 11, 2007), "*Superseding Indictment.*"

1858 Ibid.

1859 Ibid.; Trevor Aaronson & Michael Erskine, "Exec notified if Ford faced cutoff," *Commercial Appeal* (Memphis, TN), February 24, 2007.

1860 Trevor Aaronson & Michael Erskine, "Exec notified if Ford faced cutoff," *Commercial Appeal* (Memphis, TN), February 24, 2007.

1861 Ibid.

1862 Trevor Aaraonson, "Media Witch Hunt," *Commercial Appeal* (Memphis, TN), March 2, 2007.

1863 Trevor Aaronson & Michael Erskine, "Exec notified if Ford faced cutoff," *Commercial Appeal* (Memphis, TN), February 24, 2007.

1864 Ibid.

1865 Jackson Baker, "It's Official—Herman Morris Enters Mayor's Race," *Memphis Flyer,* February 28, 2007; Jacinthia Jones, "Morris challenges for mayor," *Commercial Appeal* (Memphis, TN), March 1, 2007.

1866 Ibid.; Ibid.

1867 Jacinthia Jones, "Morris challenges for mayor," *Commercial Appeal* (Memphis, TN), March 1, 2007.

1868 Ibid.

1869 Ibid.

1870 Bernard Watson, "Councilmen want MLGW President to Quit," *Fox 13 Memphis News,* February 28, 2007; Michael Erskine, "MLGW president urged to resign," *Commercial Appeal* (Memphis, TN), March 1, 2007.

1871 Michael Erskine, "MLGW president urged to resign," *Commercial Appeal* (Memphis, TN), March 1, 2007.

1872 Jacinthia Jones, "Option for ouster," *Commercial Appeal* (Memphis, TN), March 2, 2007.

1873 Preston Lauterbach, "Power Play" "The mayor and the 'Array of Evil'" *Memphis Flyer,* March 8-14, 2007.

1874 Michael Erskine, Trevor Aaronson and Jacinthia Jones contributed to this story, "'Media witch hunt'" "Rejecting Lee's resignation from MLGW, mayor rails at 'array of evil'," *Commercial Appeal* (Memphis, TN), March 2, 2007.

1875 John Branston, "From Rotan Lee to Joseph Lee," *Memphis Flyer,* March 8-14, 2007.

1876 Ibid.

1877 Ibid.

1878 Les Smith, "Councilmen React to Herenton's Comments," *Fox 13 Memphis News* (Memphis, TN), March 1, 2007; Michael Erskine, Trevor Aaronson and Jacinthia Jones contributed to this story, "Utility chairman says board willing to wait until all the facts are in," *Commercial Appeal* (Memphis, TN), March 2, 2007; Preston Lauterbach, "Power Play" "The Mayor and the 'Array of Evil'," *Memphis Flyer,* March 8-14, 2007.

1879 Michael Erskine, Trevor Aaronson and Jacinthia Jones contributed to this story, "Media witch hunt" "Rejecting Lee's resignation from MLGW, mayor rails at 'array of evil'," *Commercial Appeal* (Memphis, TN), March 2, 2007; Preston Lauterbach, "Power Play" "The Mayor and the 'Array of Evil'," *Memphis Flyer,* March 8-14, 2007.

1880 Ibid.; Ibid.

1881 Ibid.; Ibid.

1882 Michael Erskine, Trevor Aaronson and Jacinthia Jones contributed to this story, "Utility chairman says board willing to wait until all the facts are in" *Commercial Appeal* (Memphis, TN), March 2, 2007.

1883 Editorial, "A missed chance to regain trust," *Commercial Appeal* (Memphis, TN), March 2, 2007.

1884 Ibid.

1885 Jacinthia Jones, "Herenton suspects sabotage at MLGW," *Commercial Appeal* (Memphis, TN), March 3, 2007; Preston Lauterbach, "Power Play" "The Mayor and the 'Array of Evil'," *Memphis Flyer,* March 8-14, 2007.

1886 "Herenton sounds off," *Commercial Appeal* (Memphis, TN), March 3, 2007.

1887 Jacinthia Jones, "Herenton suspects sabotage at MLGW," *Commercial Appeal* (Memphis, TN), March 3, 2007.

1888 Ibid.

1889 Ibid.

1890 Preston Lauterbach, "Power Play" "The Mayor and the 'Array of Evil'," *Memphis Flyer*, March 8-14, 2007.

1891 Bianca Phillips, "Thirty Days Late, Thousands of Dollars Short," *Memphis Flyer*, March 8-14, 2007.

1892 Ibid.

1893 Andrew Douglas, "Documents show Lee Doubled Retirement Benefits in Rarely Used Transfer," *WMC Action News 5* (Memphis, TN), March 6, 2007.

1894 Jason Miles, "Edmund Ford blows up over reports, scandal," *WMC Action News 5* (Memphis, TN), March 6, 2007.

1895 Jacinthia Jones, "Effort to oust Lee fails, 6-7, in Council—," *Commercial Appeal* (Memphis, TN), March 7, 2007.

1896 Adam Nossiter, "Uproar over Memphis Power Broker's Unpaid Utility Bills," *New York Times*, March 19, 2007.

1897 Janice Broach and Jason Miles, "Lee meets angry Council, answers questions, faces new call for resignation," *WMC Action News 5* (Memphis, TN), March 20, 2007.

1898 Ibid.

1899 Ibid.

1900 Jackson Baker, "Willie and 'the Dozens'," *Memphis Flyer*, March 8-14, 2007.

1901 Ibid.

1902 Ibid.

1903 Editorial, "A career choice for Herenton," *Commercial Appeal* (Memphis, TN), March 7, 2007.

1904 Ibid; Marc Perrusquia, "Mayor sells lot, pal gives it back—Herenton land deal raises questions," *Commercial Appeal* (Memphis, TN), March 4, 2007.

1905 Ibid; Ibid.

1906 Ibid; Ibid.

1907 Ibid; Ibid.

1908 Ibid; Ibid.

1909 Viewpoint, "Mayor's office up for grabs," *Commercial Appeal* (Memphis, TN), April 9, 2007.

1910 Ibid.

1911 Ibid.

1912 Jonathan Lindberg, "The Race for Memphis Mayor, Part II," *Main Street Journal*, Vol. IV, March 2007.

1913 "Herenton addresses 'boy' comment," *WMC Action News 5* (Memphis, TN), March 9, 2007.

1914 Andy Meek, "Herman Morris 'Going to the Mattresses' in Mayoral Race," *Daily News* (Memphis, TN), April 2, 2007.

1915 Jackson Baker, "Campus Stadium Gains," *Memphis Flyer*, March 15-21, 2007.

1916 Ibid.; Jonathan Lindberg, "The Race for Memphis Mayor Part III," *Main Street Journal*, April 2007.

1917 Jackson Baker, "Chumney Leads a Lagging Herenton, Say Two New Polls," *Memphis Flyer Online*, March 29, 2007.

1918 Jacinthia Jones, "Chumney early leader for mayor," *Commercial Appeal* (Memphis, TN), April 9, 2007.

1919 Ibid.

1920 Ibid.

1921 Ibid.

1922 Jackson Baker, "Bad News for the Mayor," *Memphis Flyer*, April 5-11, 2007.

1923 Jacinthia Jones, "Chumney early leader for mayor," *Commercial Appeal* (Memphis, TN), April 9, 2007.

1924 Ibid.

1925 Ibid.

1926 Editorial, "Mayor's office up for grabs," *Commercial Appeal* (Memphis, TN), April 9, 2007.

1927 Ibid.

1928 Jackson Baker, "Bad News for the Mayor," *Memphis Flyer*, April 5-11, 2007.

1929 Wendi C. Thomas, "Replace mayor? Don't get too hasty," *Commercial Appeal* (Memphis, TN), April 8, 2007.

1930 Ibid.

1931 Ibid.

1932 Ibid.

1933 Ruth Woodard, John Coker, Letters to the Editor, *Commercial Appeal* (Memphis, TN), April 15, 2007.

1934 John Coker, Letter to the Editor, *Commercial Appeal* (Memphis, TN), April 15, 2007.

1935 Michael Erskine, "Lee won't aid council probe," *Commercial Appeal* (Memphis, TN), March 17, 2007.

1936 Ibid.

1937 Michael Erskine, "Council fails to demand Lee quit," *Commercial Appeal* (Memphis, TN), April 11, 2007.

1938 Trevor Anderson, "Lee lashes at council-Utility boss backs lawyer's report: Facts twisted for 'nefarious goal'," *Commercial Appeal* (Memphis, TN), April 10, 2007.

1939 Michael Erskine, "Council fails to demand Lee quit," *Commercial Appeal* (Memphis, TN), April 11, 2007.

1940 Ibid.

1941 Associated Press, "KKK robe sent by mail to Memphis councilman," *Commercial Appeal* (Memphis, TN), April 14, 2007; Mary Cashiola, "Black, White, and Red," *Memphis Flyer*, April 19-25, 2007.

1942 Michael Erskine, "Council fails to demand Lee quit," *Commercial Appeal* (Memphis, TN), April 11, 2007.

1943 Ibid; Jacinthia Jones, "White robe to Ford: Case 'closed'," *Commercial Appeal* (Memphis, TN), September 19, 2007; Alex Doniach, "Klan robe to Ford sent along with note, prompts probe—after racial remarks," *Commercial Appeal* (Memphis, TN), April 15, 2007.

1944 Ibid.

1945 Ibid.

1946 Editorial, "Indecisiveness, division chaos," *Commercial Appeal* (Memphis, TN), April 12, 2007.

1947 Mary Cashiola, "Black, White, and Red," *Memphis Flyer*, April 19-25, 2007.

1948 Ibid.

1949 Michael Erskine, "Council fails to demand Lee quit," *Commercial Appeal* (Memphis, TN), April 11, 2007.

1950 Ibid.

1951 Jacinthia Jones, "Probes, scandals push council turnover," *Commercial Appeal* (Memphis, TN), July 19, 2007.

1952 Steve Steffens, *LeftWingCracker*, April 15, 2007.

1953 Finch was the fictional southern lawyer who represented black defendants in a highly publicized criminal trial (as played by the famed Gregory Peck in the 1962 movie *To Kill a Mockingbird* based upon Harper Lee's novel.)

1954 Jackson Baker, "Game On!" *Memphis Flyer*, April 12-18, 2007.

1955 Ibid.

1956 Jason Carter, "Is Chumney Losing Support in Mayor's Race?" *Fox 13 Memphis News* (Memphis, TN), April 12, 2007.

1957 Trevor Aaronson and Michael Erskine, "MLGW gets bill for Lee lawyer," *Commercial Appeal* (Memphis, TN), May 1, 2007; Trevor Aaronson & Michael Erskine, "MLGW shields Lee's legal records," *Commercial Appeal*, May 2, 2007.

1958 Trevor Aaronson and Michael Erskine, "MLGW shields Lee's legal records," *Commercial Appeal* (Memphis, TN), May 2, 2007.

1959 Trevor Aaronson and Michael Erskine, "MLGW gets bill for Lee lawyer," *Commercial Appeal* (Memphis, TN), May 1, 2007.

1960 Ibid.

1961 Trevor Aaronson and Michael Erskine, "MLGW shields Lee's legal records," *Commercial Appeal* (Memphis, TN), May 2, 2007.

1962 Ibid.

1963 Ibid.

1964 Michael Erskine, "MLGW turmoil getting personal-Board member accuses Lee of trying to blackmail him," *Commercial Appeal* (Memphis, TN), May 3, 2007.

1965 Ibid.

1966 Michael Erskine, "Solemn mayor hopes to restore customers' confidence in utility," *Commercial Appeal* (Memphis, TN), May 4, 2007.

1967 Ibid.; Michael Erskine, "MLGW shake-up-Masson becomes acting president today after Lee's resignation; Horton's also out," *Commercial Appeal* (Memphis, TN), May 4, 2007.

1968 "Morris on Filling MLGW Post: Wait until after the Election," *Memphis Flyer Online*, May 8-11, 2007.

1969 Thaddeus Mathews Dot Com, "Morris Takes His Fight to Herenton's Front Door without Landing a Single Blow," *Blog*, May 8, 2007.

1970 Carol Chumney, Letter to the Editor, *Memphis Flyer,* May 10, 2007.

1971 Andy Meek, "Can Carol Chumney Out-Shark 'King Willie' in Mayoral Race?" *Daily News* (Memphis, TN), May 4, 2007.

1972 Andy Meek, "City Budget an Issue in Mayor's Race," *Daily News* (Memphis, TN), May 11, 2007.

1973 Ibid.

1974 Jody Callahan, "Beale Street Landing dropped from city budget," *Commercial Appeal* (Memphis, TN), May 15, 2007; Andy Ashby, "City committee nixes Beale Street Landing," *Memphis Business Journal,* May 14, 2007.

1975 Ibid; Ibid.

1976 Jody Callahan, "Beale Street Landing dropped from city budget," *Commercial Appeal* (Memphis, TN), May 15, 2007.

1977 Andy Ashby, "City committee nixes Beale Street Landing," *Memphis Business Journal,* May 15, 2007.

1978 Jacinthia Jones, "Beale Street Landing still on deck," *Commercial Appeal* (Memphis, TN), May 23, 2007.

1979 Jacinthia Jones, "Beale Street Landing back," *Commercial Appeal* (Memphis, TN), May 25, 2007.

1980 John Branston, "Why Beale Street Landing is a Go," *Memphis Flyer,* June 6, 2007.

1981 Ibid.

1982 John Branston, "City Council Approves Beale Street Landing," *Memphis Flyer,* June 5, 2007.

1983 Editorial, "Landing project needs oversight," *Commercial Appeal* (Memphis, TN), June 27, 2007.

1984 Ibid.

1985 Daniel Connolly, "Long-delayed Beale site could be open by May, riverfront chief says," *Commercial Appeal* (Memphis, TN), March 18, 2014.

1986 Ibid.

1987 Tom Charlier, "RDC chews on Beale Landing eatery idea," *Commercial Appeal* (Memphis, TN), April 6, 2014.

1988 Ibid.; Editorial, "Riverfront dining," *Commercial Appeal* (Memphis, TN), April 8, 2014.

1989 Tom Charlier, "No Beale Street Landing Restaurant," *Commercial Appeal* (Memphis, TN), May 12, 2018.

1990 Ibid.

1991 Bill Dries, "Funding Questions Haunt Beale Street Landing Project," *The Daily News* (Memphis, TN), May 14, 2010.

1992 Daniel Connolly, "Private talks preceded council's vote," *Commercial Appeal* (Memphis, TN), November 19, 2014.

1993 Ibid.

1994 Ibid.; Editorial, "Council secrecy deals the public an open insult," *Commercial Appeal* (Memphis, TN), November 20, 2014; Daniel Connolly, "Council members private chats could violate Sunshine Law," *Commercial Appeal* (Memphis, TN), February 1, 2015.

1995 Editorial, "Council secrecy deals the public an open insult," *Commercial Appeal* (Memphis, TN), November 20, 2014; Editorial, "Public must see, hear leaders arrive at votes," *Commercial Appeal* (Memphis, TN), February 7, 2015.

1996 Daniel Connolly, "Council members' private chats could violate Sunshine law," *Commercial Appeal (*Memphis, TN), February 1, 2015.

1997 Ibid.

1998 John Branston, "On Polls and Votes" "Can traits that make Chumney unpopular with colleagues win over voters," *Memphis Flyer,* May 17, 2007.

1999 Ibid.

2000 Ibid.

2001 Ibid.

2002 Jackson Baker, "Still in the Game," *Memphis Flyer,* May 31- June 6, 2007.

2003 Ibid.

2004 Ibid.

2005 Marc Perrusquia, "Mayor says he snubbed buyouts" "Claims he was offered jobs to forgo 5th term," *Commercial Appeal* (Memphis, TN), June 10, 2007.

2006 Ibid.

2007 Ibid.

2008 Ibid.

2009 Jason Miles, "Sympathy for mayor could have impact on election," *WMC Action News 5* (Memphis, TN), June 14, 2007;

Marc Perrusquia, "War on sin lit fuse on 'plot'," *Commercial Appeal* (Memphis, TN), July 1, 2007.

2010 Marc Perrusquia, "War on sin lit fuse on 'plot'," *Commercial Appeal* (Memphis, TN), July 1, 2007.

2011 Ibid; Jacinthia Jones, "'Bizarre' charges weave knot of political confusion," *Commercial Appeal* (Memphis, TN), June 15, 2007.

2012 Ibid.; Ibid.

2013 Marc Perrusquia, "War on sin lit fuse on 'plot'," *Commercial Appeal* (Memphis, TN), July 1, 2007.

2014 Stephen Phillips, Letter to Editor, "It's easier to run as a victim," *Commercial Appeal* (Memphis, TN), June 18, 2007; Jeremy Boudivet, "Short on logic, long on desperation," *Commercial Appeal,* June 18, 2007; Fay Kruse, Letter to Editor, "A little truth in the fine print," *Commercial Appeal* (Memphis, TN), June 23, 2007.

2015 Jacinthia Jones, "Chumney files for Mayor," *Commercial Appeal* (Memphis, TN), June 13, 2007.

2016 "Transcript of Mayor Herenton's Press Conference," *Commercial Appeal* (Memphis, TN), June 14, 2007.

2017 Ibid.

2018 Ibid.

2019 Jacinthia Jones, "'Bizarre' charges weave knot of political confusion," *Commercial Appeal* (Memphis, TN), June 15, 2007.

2020 Ibid.

2021 "Transcript of Mayor Herenton's Press Conference," *Commercial Appeal* (Memphis, TN), June 14, 2007.

2022 Ibid.

2023 Ibid.

2024 Ibid.

2025 Ibid.

2026 Thaddeus Matthews, "Is AC a snake?" *Blog,* June 15, 2007.

2027 Ibid.

2028 Ibid.

2029 Ibid.

2030 Jacinthia Jones, "'Bizarre' charges weave knot of political confusion," *Commercial Appeal* (Memphis, TN), June 15, 2007.

2031 Ibid.

2032 Chris Davis, "Networx: Who Knows Who in This Deal?" *Memphis Flyer Online,* June 15, 2007.

2033 Ibid.

2034 Michael Erskine, reporter Trey Heath contributed, "MLGW Seeks to unload Networx," *Commercial Appeal* (Memphis, TN), June 10, 2007; Chris Davis, "Unplugged," *Memphis Flyer,* June 28-July 4, 2007; Tom Charlier, "Cash readiness tips Networx deal," *Commercial Appeal* (Memphis, TN), June 28, 2007.

2035 Chris Davis, "Unplugged," *Memphis Flyer,* June 28-July 4, 2007.

2036 Ibid.

2037 Michael Erskine, reporter Trey Heath contributed, "MLGW Seeks to unload Networx," *Commercial Appeal* (Memphis, TN), June 10, 2007.

2038 Ibid.

2039 Michael Erskine, "MLGW agrees to sell Networx," *Commercial Appeal* (Memphis, TN), June 6, 2007.

2040 Alex Doniach, "Council to audit MLGW's Networx," *Commercial Appeal* (Memphis, TN), July 11, 2007; *American Fiber System, Inc. v. MLGW, etal,* No. CH-07-1310-1, Shelby County Chancery Court.

2041 Jackson Baker "New Mayor, New Council?" *Memphis Flyer,* June 28-July 4, 2007.

2042 Ibid.

2043 Jody Callahan, "Sammons won't seek reelection," *Commercial Appeal* (Memphis, TN), July 16, 2007; Blake Fontenay, "Victory may be falling into place for Herenton," *Commercial Appeal,* June 23, 2007.

2044 Bill Dries, "Chumney Ups Ante on Mayoral Run," *Daily News* (Memphis, TN), July 3, 2007.

2045 Andy Meek, "Back in the Ring" *Daily News* (Memphis, TN), July 3, 2007.

2046 Ibid.

2047 Ibid.

2048 Zack McMillin, "Morris gathers funding, optimism," *Commercial Appeal* (Memphis, TN), July 11, 2007.

2049 Jacinthia Jones and Marc Perrusquia, "Herenton lashes out," *Commercial Appeal* (Memphis, TN), July 4, 2007.

2050 Ibid.; Marc Perrusquia, "War on sin lit fuse on 'plot'," *Commercial Appeal* (Memphis, TN), July 1, 2007.

2051 Marc Perrusquia, "War on sin lit fuse on 'plot'," *Commercial Appeal* (Memphis, TN), July 1, 2007.

2052 Ibid.

2053 Ibid.; Jacinthia Jones and Marc Perrusquia, "Herenton lashes out," *Commercial Appeal* (Memphis, TN), July 4, 2007.

2054 Marc Perrusquia, "War on sin lit fuse on 'plot'," *Commercial Appeal* (Memphis, TN), July 1, 2007.

2055 Ibid.

2056 Marc Perrusquia, "Mayor's backers point to Fields allegations," *Commercial Appeal* (Memphis, TN), July 1, 2007.

2057 Jacinthia Jones & Marc Perrusquia, "Herenton lashes out," *Commercial Appeal* (Memphis, TN), July 4, 2007.

2058 Ibid.; Marc Perrusquia, "War on sin lit fuse on 'plot'," *Commercial Appeal* (Memphis, TN), July 1, 2007.

2059. Jacinthia Jones and Marc Perrusquia, "Herenton lashes out," *Commercial Appeal* (Memphis TN), July 4, 2007.

2060 The CA Poll, *Commercial Appeal* (Memphis, TN), July 15, 2007.

2061 Marc Perrusquia, "War on sin lit fuse on 'plot'," *Commercial Appeal* (Memphis, TN), July 1, 2007.

2062 Jackson Baker, "One Mayor's In; What About the Other?" *Memphis Flyer,* July 3, 2007.

2063 Jacinthia Jones, "Wharton courted for city mayor seat," *Commercial Appeal* (Memphis, TN), July 9, 2007; Jackson Baker, "Coming to Shove," *Memphis Flyer,* July 12-18, 2007.

2064 Jacinthia Jones, "Wharton courted for city mayor seat," *Commercial Appeal* (Memphis, TN), July 9, 2007.

2065 Ibid.

2066 Ibid.

2067 Zack McMillan, "Both mayors still chummy," *Commercial Appeal* (Memphis, TN), July 13, 2007.

2068 Ibid.

2069 Jacinthia Jones, "Herenton digs in," *Commercial Appeal* (Memphis, TN), July 11, 2007.

2070 Ibid; Jackson Baker, "Coming to Shove," *Memphis Flyer,* July 12-18, 2007.

2071 Jacinthia Jones, "Herenton digs in," *Commercial Appeal* (Memphis, TN), July 11, 2007.

2072 Ibid.

2073 Bill Day, cartoon, "Snake in the Grass," *Commercial Appeal* (Memphis, TN), July 11, 2007.

2074 Wendi C. Thomas, "Is Memphis really calling for a gentleman?" *Commercial Appeal* (Memphis, TN), July 12, 2007.

2075 Editorial, "Stakes are high for Memphis," *Commercial Appeal* (Memphis, TN), July 13, 2007.

2076 Zack McMillan, "Both mayors still chummy," *Commercial Appeal* (Memphis, TN), July 13, 2007.

2077 Ibid; Bill Dries, "Push is on to Pull Wharton into Race Against Herenton," *Daily News* (Memphis, TN), July 12, 2007.

2078 Bill Dries, "Push is on to Pull Wharton into Race Against Herenton," *Daily News* (Memphis, TN), July 12, 2007.

2079 Ibid.

2080 Ibid.

2081 Editorial, "What Should the Ideal Candidate for Memphis Mayor be saying?" *Tri-State Defender* (Memphis, TN), July 12, 2007.

2082 Ibid.

2083 Ibid.; Eric Smith, "Real Estate Industry Adjusts to Changing Subprime Lending," *Memphis Daily News,* (Memphis, TN), May 15, 2007; "Memphis among cities with highest foreclosure rates," *Memphis Business Journal,* August 14, 2007.

2084 Editorial, "A warning sign in census data," *Commercial Appeal* (Memphis, TN), June 29, 2007; Blake Fontenay, "Talk Issues, Not Dirt," *Commercial Appeal* (Memphis, TN), July 15, 2007.

2085 *USA v. Edmund H. Ford, Joseph Lee III,* Case No. 06-20467-Ma, (W.D. Tenn. July 11, 2007), "*Superseding Indictment;*" Lawrence Buser, "Ruling reversed on MLGW ex-CEO," *Commercial Appeal* (Memphis, TN), July 13, 2007; Marc Perrusquia, "MLGW case to test limits of politics," *Commercial Appeal* (Memphis,

TN), July 13, 2007; Jacinthia Jones, "Draft AC' buzz grows," *Commercial Appeal* (Memphis, TN), July 16, 2007.

2086 Marc Perrusquia, "MLGW case to test limits of politics," *Commercial Appeal* (Memphis, TN), July 13, 2007; *USA v. Edmund H. Ford, Joseph Lee III*, Case No. 06-20467-Ma, (W.D. Tenn., July 11, 2007).

2087 Ibid; Ibid.

2088 "Lee, Spence Talk Back," *Commercial Appeal* (Memphis, TN), July 16, 2007.

2089 *USA v. Joseph Lee, III*, Case No. 2:08-cv-20001-SHM, Doc. 13, (W.D. Tenn., January 22, 2008), "*Order Denying Defendant's Motion to Dismiss for Selective Prosecution or, in the Alternative, for Discovery and Evidentiary Hearing.*"

2090 Ibid.

2091 Michael Erskine, "Landlord accused of lying when he said Ford's rent was current," *Commercial Appeal* (Memphis, TN), July 16, 2007; *USA v. Dennis Churchwell*, Case No. 2:07-cf-20212-BBD, Doc. 2, (W. D. Tenn. July 11, 2007), "*Indictment.*"

2092 Ibid; Ibid.

2093 Trevor Aaronson, "Ford's Landlord Admits he Lied: Pleads Guilty to Perjury in FBI Investigation," *Commercial Appeal* (Memphis, TN), April 10, 2008; *USA v. Dennis Churchwell*, Case No. 2:07CR20212-01-D, Doc. 41, (W. D. Tenn., October 10, 2008), "*Judgment in a Criminal Case.*"

2094 Lawrence Buser, "Bowers changing her plea to guilty," *Commercial Appeal* (Memphis, TN), July 13, 2007; *USA v. Bowers*, Case No. 2:05 -cr- 20203-01-B, Doc. 76, (W. D. Tenn.), July 16, 2007; *USA v. Ward Crutchfield*, No. 2:05-cr-20204-JDB, ECF 93 (W.D. Tenn., July 12, 2007), "*Memorandum of Plea Agreement.*"

2095 Marc Perrusquia, "A plea for mercy," *Commercial Appeal* (Memphis, TN), August 28, 2007; John Branston, "The Last Waltz," *Memphis Flyer*, April 17-23, 2008; *U.S. v. John Ford*, Case No. 07-6087, Doc. 180, (6th Cir. August 26, 2009).

2096 *U.S. v. John Ford*, Case No. 07-6087, Doc. 180, (6th Cir. August 26, 2009).

2097 Ibid.

2098 *U.S. v. John Ford*, Case No. 07-6087, Doc. 180, (6th Cir. August 26, 2009).

2099 Marc Perrusquia, " A plea for mercy," *Commercial Appeal* (Memphis, TN), August 28, 2007; Marc Perrusquia, "The Odd Man Out," *Commercial Appeal* (Memphis, TN), June 22, 2008.

2100 Marc Perrusquia, "A plea for mercy," *Commercial Appeal* (Memphis, TN), August 28, 2007; Marc Perrusquia, "Ford works angles on appeal," *Commercial Appeal* (Memphis, TN), August 30, 2007; *U.S. v. John Ford*, Case No. 07-6087, Doc. 180, (6th Cir. August 26, 2009) (affirming district court judgment).

2101 *U.S. v. One Men's Rolex Pearl Master Watch*, Case No. 08-6524, Doc. 56, (6th Cir. December 16, 2009), "*Opinion.*"

2102 Tom Charlier, "Lee lawsuit fires back at MLGW," *Commercial Appeal* (Memphis, TN), July 20, 2007; *Joseph Lee III v. City of Memphis*, No. CH-07-1404, Shelby County Chancery Court.

2103 Ibid; Ibid.

2104 Jackson Baker, "Four More Years?" *Memphis Flyer*, July 26-August 1, 2007.

2105 Ibid.

2106 Ibid.

2107 Blake Fontenay, "Chumney, Morris losing support to Wharton," *Commercial Appeal* (Memphis, TN), July 16, 2007.

2108 Ibid.

2109 Ibid.

2110 Ibid.

2111 Ibid.

2112 Editorial, "Racial divide emerges as issue," *Commercial Appeal* (Memphis, TN), July 16, 2007.

2113 Ibid.

2114 Ibid.

2115 Andy Meek, "Herenton Campaign Chest Large, But Not From '07 Fundraising," *Daily News* (Memphis, TN), July 17, 2007.

2116 Ibid.

2117 Jackson Baker, "A.C., in D.C., Says No," *Memphis Flyer*, July 19-25, 2007.

2118 John Branston, "Something's Gotta Give," *Memphis Flyer*, August 9-15, 2007.

2119 Jacinthia Jones, "Probes, scandals push council turnover," *Commercial Appeal* (Memphis, TN), July 19, 2007.

2120 Jackson Baker, "A.C. in D.C., Says No," *Memphis Flyer,* July 19-25, 2007; Blake Fontenay, "Back in, or Ex?" *Commercial Appeal* (Memphis, TN), July 22, 2007.

2121 Blake Fontenay, "Back in, or Ex?" *Commercial Appeal* (Memphis, TN), July 22, 2007.

2122 Blake Fontenay, "Victory may be falling into place for Herenton," *Commercial Appeal* (Memphis, TN), July 23, 2007.

2123 Ibid.

2124 Ibid.

2125 Ibid.

2126 Ibid.

2127 Jackson Baker, "Four More Years?" *Memphis Flyer,* July 26-August 1, 2007.

2128 Ibid.

2129 Ibid.

2130 Ibid.

2131 Ibid.

2132 "The City of Good Abode" "Who's Who," *Memphis Magazine,* Vol. XXXII, No. 5, August 2007, pg. 75.

2133 Ibid.

2134 Ibid.

2135 Ibid.

2136 Ibid.

2137 Ibid.

2138 Ibid., pg. 94.

2139 Ibid., pg. 95

2140 Ibid., pg. 160.

2141 Ibid., pg. 64.

2142 *Memphis Health & Fitness Sports Magazine,* September 2007.

2143 Ibid.

2144 *"Memphis Magazine Most,"* *Commercial Appeal,* August 12, 2007.

2145 Jackson Baker, "Four More Years?" *Memphis Flyer,* July 26-August 1, 2007.

2146 Ibid.; Michael Erskine, "Morris' mission: Unseat ex-boss," *Commercial Appeal* (Memphis, TN), September 18, 2007; John Branston, "Ten Inconvenient Truths," *Memphis Flyer,* September 27-October 3, 2007; Chris Davis, "The Man Behind the Moustache," *Memphis Flyer,* September 27-October 3, 2007.

2147 Jackson Baker, "Who's on First?" *Memphis Flyer,* August 2-8, 2007.

2148 Jackson Baker, "Four More Years?" *Memphis Flyer,* July 26-August 1, 2007.

2149 Jackson Baker, "The 'Ron Paul Revelation'," *Memphis Flyer,* August 9-15, 2007; Abby Cardwell, Letter to Editor, "Searching for someone to vote for," *Commercial Appeal* (Memphis, TN), July 22, 2009.

2150 Blake Fontenay, "Back in, or Ex?" *Commercial Appeal* (Memphis TN), July 22, 2007.

2151 Ibid.

2152 Ibid.

2153 Lawrence Buser, "Herenton touts closing crack houses," *Commercial Appeal* (Memphis, TN), July 24, 2007.

2154 Ibid.

2155 Editorial, "Willie Herenton: crime fighter," *Commercial Appeal* (Memphis, TN), July 25, 2007.

2156 Jackson Baker, "Chumney Re-Examined," *Memphis Flyer,* July 25, 2007; Jackson Baker, "Who's On First?" *Memphis Flyer,* August 2-8, 2007.

2157 Jackson Baker, "Chumney Re-Examined," *Memphis Flyer,* July 25, 2007.

2158 Ibid.

2159 Zack McMillan, "Herenton will forgo debates," *Commercial Appeal* (Memphis, TN), July 27, 2007.

2160 Jacinthia Jones, "New Support for Morris," *Commercial Appeal* (Memphis, TN), August 1, 2007.

2161 Jody Callahan, "Gay political event draws pols," *Commercial Appeal* (Memphis, TN), September 13, 2007; Jacinthia Jones, "Pastor's endorsement puzzles some," *Commercial Appeal,* August 16, 2007.

2162 Jacinthia Jones, "New Support for Morris," *Commercial Appeal* (Memphis, TN), August 1, 2007; Jacinthia Jones, "Pastor's endorsement puzzles some," *Commercial Appeal,* August 16, 2007.

2163 Mike Niblock, "Commentary," *Memphis Flyer,* August 2-8, 2007.

2164 Ibid.

2165 Blake Fontenay, "Webb may net enough to

stop Herenton's foes," *Commercial Appeal* (Memphis, TN), August 13, 2007.

2166 Ibid.

2167 Ibid.

2168 Michael Erskine, "MLGW enters race for mayor," *Commercial Appeal* (Memphis, TN), August 19, 2007.

2169 Jacinthia Jones, "Talking heads," *Commercial Appeal* (Memphis, TN), August 17, 2007.

2170 Ibid.

2171 Ibid.

2172 Alex Doniach, "Church visits seeking votes," *Commercial Appeal* (Memphis, TN), August 20, 2007.

2173 The Bible, Matthew 10:14.

2174 Blake Fontenay, "Commentary" "Teen says it's time for him to stand up for city," *Commercial Appeal* (Memphis, TN), August 20, 2007.

2175 Michael Erskine, "Morris' mission: Unseat ex-boss," *Commercial Appeal* (Memphis, TN), September 18, 2007.

2176 Ibid.

2177 Ibid.

2178 Bill Dries, "Chumney Touts 'Change' as Campaign Platform," *Daily News* (Memphis, TN), August 28, 2007; Jackson Baker, "Mayoral Shuffling," *Memphis Flyer,* August 30-September 5, 2007.

2179 Mary Dean, Letter to Editor, *Commercial Appeal* (Memphis, TN), August 24, 2007.

2180 "Excerpts from Mayor Herenton's Election-Night Victory Speech," *Commercial Appeal* (Memphis, TN), October 6, 2007.

2181 Jackson Baker, "Mayoral Shuffling," *Memphis Flyer,* August 30-September 5, 2007; Editorial Flyer staff, "Off Camera, Off Mike," *Memphis Flyer,* September 13-17, 2007.

2182 Bill Dries, "Chumney Touts 'Change' as Campaign Platform," *Daily News* (Memphis, TN), August 28, 2007.

2183 Ibid.

2184 Ibid.

2185 Jackson Baker, "Forum Fever," *Memphis Flyer,* August 23, 2007.

2186 Ibid.

2187 Jody Callahan, "Chumney lays out proposal for fighting crime," *Commercial Appeal* (Memphis, TN), September 10, 2007.

2188 Michael Erskine, "Hard Lines on crime," *Commercial Appeal* (Memphis, TN), September 5, 2007.

2189 Ibid.

2190 Ibid.

2191 Ibid.; Alex Doniach, "Crime panel hears of revolving door," *Commercial Appeal* (Memphis, TN), September 6, 2007.

2192 Teresa Polzin, Letter to Editor, "Draw Straws to oppose Herenton," *Commercial Appeal* (Memphis, TN), August 24, 2007.

2193 Lynn Strickland, Letter to Editor, "In defeating Herenton, we all win," *Commercial Appeal* (Memphis, TN), August 30, 2007.

2194 James Dowd, "Cohen: Race is 'wedge'," *Commercial Appeal* (Memphis, TN), August 30, 2007; James Dowd, "Be blind to race says SCLC leader," *Commercial Appeal,* September 6, 2007.

2195 William T. Mitchell, Letter to Editor, "Only Chumney can beat Herenton," *Commercial Appeal* (Memphis, TN), September 13, 2007; John C. Sheffield, Letter to Editor, "Want a winner? Choose Morris," *Commercial Appeal,* September 13, 2007.

2196 Ibid.; Ibid.

2197 Zenia Revitz, "Want specifics? Chumney's got them," *Commercial Appeal* (Memphis, TN), September 13, 2007; Oliver Doughtie, "Split the vote, and Herenton wins," *Commercial Appeal,* September 13, 2007.

2198 Chris Davis, "Fly on the wall" "Big Heads," *Memphis Flyer,* September 27, 2007.

2199 Ibid.

2200 Ibid.

2201 Zack McMillan, "Mayoral race begins to sizzle," *Commercial Appeal* (Memphis, TN), September 6, 2007.

2202 Ibid.

2203 Jacinthia Jones, "Morris outscores foes in new rating," *Commercial Appeal* (Memphis, TN), August 30, 2007.

2204 Zack McMillan, "Can 'ABH' spell Oct. surprise?" *Commercial Appeal* (Memphis, TN), September 9, 2007.

2205 Zack McMillan, "Challengers want to be 'anybody'," *Commercial Appeal* (Memphis, TN), September 9, 2007.

2206 Ibid.

2207 Otis Sanford, "View's different from the inside looking out," *Commercial Appeal* (Memphis, TN), September 9, 2007.

2208 Ibid.

2209 Jackson Baker, "In the spotlight," *Memphis Flyer*, September 13-17, 2007.

2210 Blake Fontenay, "Some voters may want to return to city runoffs," *Commercial Appeal* (Memphis, TN), September 17, 2007.

2211 Jody Callahan, "Candidates dig in," *Commercial Appeal* (Memphis, TN), September 11, 2007.

2212 Ibid.

2213 Otis Sanford, "View's different from the inside looking out," *Commercial Appeal* (Memphis, TN), September 9, 2007.

2214 Editorial, Flyer Staff, "Off Camera, Off Mike," *Memphis Flyer*, September 13-17, 2007.

2215 Editorial, "Memphis stalls under Herenton," *Commercial Appeal* (Memphis, TN), September 13, 2007.

2216 Ibid.

2217 Ibid.

2218 Jackson Baker, "Campus Stadium Gains," *Memphis Flyer*, March 15-21, 2007.

2219 "Carol Chumney on Proposed Stadium," *Main Street Journal*, April 2007.

2220 Ibid.

2221 Editorial, "For mayor: Herman Morris," *Commercial Appeal* (Memphis, TN), September 14, 2007.

2222 Ibid.

2223 Ibid.

2224 Ibid.

2225 David Williams, "Council to see controversial stadium report," *Commercial Appeal* (Memphis, TN), September 15, 2007.

2226 Ibid.

2227 Editorial, "Mayor's tactic: Make 'em guess," *Commercial Appeal* (Memphis, TN), September 15, 2007.

2228 David Williams, "Report favors new stadium," *Commercial Appeal* (Memphis, TN), September 19, 2007.

2229 Jacinthia Jones, "Mayor's legacy a matter of style—Herenton touts brash manner; others recoil," *Commercial Appeal* (Memphis, TN), September 16, 2007.

2230 Ibid.

2231 Ibid.

2232 Ibid.

2233 Ibid.

2234 Ibid.

2235 Ibid.

2236 Ibid.

2237 Ibid.

2238 Ibid.

2239 Ibid.

2240 John Branston, "Ten Inconvenient Truths," *Memphis Flyer*, September 20, 2007.

2241 Jacinthia Jones, "Mayor's legacy a matter of style—Herenton touts brash manner; others recoil," *Commercial Appeal* (Memphis, TN), September 16, 2007.

2242 Ibid.

2243 Ibid.

2244 Zack McMillan, "Chumney banks on political dossier," *Commercial Appeal* (Memphis, TN), September 17, 2007.

2245 Ibid.

2246 Ibid.

2247 Ibid.

2248 Ibid.

2249 Ibid.

2250 Ibid.

2251 Ibid.

2252 Ibid.

2253 Editorial, "A champion for children," *Tennessean* (Nashville, TN), October 28, 2003.

2254 Zack McMillan, "Chumney banks on political dossier," *Commercial Appeal* (Memphis, TN), September 17, 2007.

2255 Ibid.

2256 Ibid.

2257 Editorial, "Sprawl is urgent issue in county elections," *Commercial Appeal* (Memphis, TN), April 16, 2002.

2258 Zack McMillan, "Chumney banks on political dossier," *Commercial Appeal* (Memphis, TN), September 17, 2007.

2259 Editorial, "Changing pension rules is a good move," *Commercial Appeal* (Memphis, TN), August 19, 2004.

2260 Zack McMillan, "Chumney banks on political dossier," *Commercial Appeal* (Memphis, TN), September 17, 2007.

2261 Ibid.

2262 Ibid.

2263 Trey Heath, "Herenton skips 2d debate," *Commercial Appeal* (Memphis, TN), September 22, 2007.

2264 Alex Doniach, "Mayor wants vote halted," *Commercial Appeal* (Memphis, TN), September 19, 2007.

2265 Editorial, "Less talk more action," *Commercial Appeal* (Memphis, TN), September 21, 2007; Zack McMillan "Mayor cites irregularities with early voting machines," *Commercial Appeal*, September 20, 2007.

2266 Editorial, "Less talk more action," *Commercial Appeal* (Memphis, TN), September 21, 2007; Alex Doniach, "Mayor wants vote halted," *Commercial Appeal* (Memphis, TN), September 19, 2007.

2267 Editorial, Jackson Baker & Staff "Down the Stretch!" *Memphis Flyer,* September 27, 2007.

2268 Ibid.

2269 Zack McMillan, "Mayor cites irregularities with early voting machines," *Commercial Appeal* (Memphis, TN), September 20, 2007.

2270 Ibid.

2271 Jacinthia Jones, "White robe to Ford: Case 'closed'," *Commercial Appeal* (Memphis, TN), September 19, 2007.

2272 Ibid.

2273 Ibid.

2274 Ibid.

2275 Ibid.

2276 Jacinthia Jones, "Council will reconsider proposed raise for mayor," *Commercial Appeal* (Memphis, TN), September 1, 2007.

2277 Andy Meek, "Mayoral Pay Could be Current Council's Last Battle," *Daily News* (Memphis, TN), September 24, 2007.

2278 Jackson Baker, "It's Always Something," *Memphis Flyer,* May 10, 2012.

2279 Joan K. Solomon, Letters to Editor, "This candidate will end the mediocrity," *Commercial Appeal* (Memphis, TN),

September 22, 2007.

2280 Randi Guigui, Letter to Editor, "Vote for Chumney is a vote for change," *Commercial Appeal* (Memphis, TN), September 22, 2007.

2281 Ibid.

2282 John Setler, Letter to Editor, "This candidate has a backbone," *Commercial Appeal* (Memphis, TN), September 22, 2007.

2283 Zack McMillan & Michael Erskine, "Candidates say polls show race too close to call," *Commercial Appeal* (Memphis, TN), September 27, 2007.

2284 Ibid.

2285 John Branston, "Election Day Countdown," *Memphis Flyer,* September 27, 2007.

2286 Ibid.

2287 Jackson Baker & Staff, "Down the Stretch," *Memphis Flyer,* September 27, 2007.

2288 Ibid.

2289 Bianca Phillips, "Working 9-to-9," *Memphis Flyer,* September 27, 2007.

2290 Ibid.

2291 James Brown, "It's a man's world" (1991).

2292 Bianca Phillips, "Working 9-to-9," *Memphis Flyer,* September 27, 2007.

2293 Ibid.; Michael Erskine & Zack McMillan, "Herenton spends $378,675," *Commercial Appeal* (Memphis, TN), September 28, 2007.

2294 Michael Erskine & Zack McMillan, "Herenton spends $378,675," *Commercial Appeal* (Memphis, TN), September 28, 2007.

2295 John Branston, "Election Day Countdown," *Memphis Flyer,* September 27, 2007.

2296 Jacinthia Jones, "Too close to call," *Commercial Appeal* (Memphis, TN), September 30, 2007.

2297 Ibid.

2298 Ibid.

2299 Blake Fontenay, "Viewpoint" "Coming apart at the polls," *Commercial Appeal* (Memphis, TN), September 30, 2007.

2300 Ibid.

2301 Ibid.

2302 Ibid.

2303 Ibid.

2304 Blake Fontenay, "Comment" "Mayor's words on Morris aimed to shape vote?" *Commercial Appeal* (Memphis, TN), October 1, 2007.

2305 Ibid.

2306 Ibid.

2307 The public does not often know who even owns or controls the newspapers and media outlets. For example, the *Memphis Flyer,* is published by Contemporary Media, Inc. whose President, according to the Better Business Bureau, is the local developer Henry Turley, although this is not disclosed on the *Memphis Flyer's* social media sites, or in the publication. In 2013, the *Tri-State Defender* (Memphis, TN), was purchased by BEST Media Properties, Inc., a privately owned company, from Real Times Media Inc. Its board of directors were disclosed in the newspaper, including politician Deidre Malone. TSD Newsroom, "The way forward: A message from the board of directors of TSD's parent company," *Tri-State Defender,* December 19, 2017. *The Daily Memphian* is a privately held newspaper that has received funding from several foundations to the Memphis Fourth Estate, Inc., a 501(c)(3) that owns and operates the newspaper. It solicits direct donations, paid sponsorships, and advertisements. "About Us," *Daily Memphian.*

2308 Michael Erskine, "Morris struggles to sway black voters," *Commercial Appeal* (Memphis, TN), October 10, 2007.

2309 Ibid.

2310 Jacinthia Jones, Michael Erskine, and Alex Doniach, "Sunday blitz," *Commercial Appeal* (Memphis, TN), October 1, 2007.

2311 Ibid.

2312 Ibid.

2313 Ibid.

2314 Ibid.

2315 Zack McMillan, "Gender's a notable 'nonissue'," *Commercial Appeal* (Memphis, TN), October 2, 2007.

2316 Ibid.

2317 Ibid.

2318 Ibid.

2319 Trevor Aaronson, "Ford Sr.'s vote raises questions on residency," *Commercial Appeal* (Memphis, TN), October 3, 2007; Jacinthia Jones, "Ford Sr. may lend a hand," *Commercial Appeal* (Memphis, TN), October 2, 2007.

2320 Jacinthia Jones, "Ford Sr. may lend a hand," *Commercial Appeal* (Memphis, TN), October 2, 2007.

2321 Trevor Aaronson, "Ford Sr.'s vote raises questions on residency," *Commercial Appeal* (Memphis, TN), October 3, 2007.

2322 Ibid.

2323 Jacinthia Jones, "Ford Sr., skips 'unity rally' for Herenton," *Commercial Appeal* (Memphis, TN), October 3, 2007; Jackson Baker, "The Shell-Game Election," *Memphis Flyer,* October 4-10, 2007; Jacinthia Jones, "It's anybody's game," *Commercial Appeal* (Memphis, TN), October 4, 2007.

2324 Zack McMillan, "Poll: Herenton and Chumney in dead heat," *Commercial Appeal* (Memphis, TN), October 3, 2007; Zack McMillan, "Poll results can change over-night," *Commercial Appeal* (Memphis, TN), October 4, 2007.

2325 Zack McMillan, "Poll results can change overnight," *Commercial Appeal* (Memphis, TN), October 4, 2007.

2326 Michael Erskine, "Recall leader backs Herenton," *Commercial Appeal* (Memphis, TN), October 3, 2007.

2327 Michael Erskine, "Signs target the unde-cided," *Commercial Appeal* (Memphis, TN), October 3, 2007.

2328 Zack McMillan, "Early turnout excites councilwoman," *Commercial Appeal* (Memphis, TN), October 5, 2007.

2329 Zack McMillan, "Election Notebook" "Shoppers seem to like Chumney," *Commercial Appeal* (Memphis, TN), October 4, 2007.

2330 Jacinthia Jones, "It's anybody's game," *Commercial Appeal* (Memphis, TN), October 4, 2007.

2331 Ibid.

2332 Chris Conley, "Police officers rally for mayor," *Commercial Appeal* (Memphis, TN), October 4, 2007.

2333 Tom Charlier, "Mayor seeks unity, calls out 'haters'," *Commercial Appeal* (Memphis, TN), October 5, 2007.

2334 Zack McMillan, "Early turn out excites councilwoman," *Commercial Appeal* (Memphis, TN), October 5, 2007.

2335 Ibid.

2336 Ibid.; Zack McMillan, "Chumney likely won't stay out of sight from public eye," *Commercial Appeal* (Memphis, TN), October 6, 2007; Tom Charlier, "Mayor seeks unity, calls out 'haters'," *Commercial Appeal*, October 5, 2007.

2337 Tom Charlier, staff reporters Alex Doniach, Michael Erskine, Zack McMillan, and Marc Perrusquia, "Mayor seeks unity, calls out haters," *Commercial Appeal* (Memphis, TN), October 5, 2007; Zack McMillan, "Early turnout excites councilwoman," *Commercial Appeal*, October 5, 2007.

2338 Alex Doniach, "Mayor lauds the loyal, hits detractors," *Commercial Appeal* (Memphis, TN), October 5, 2007.

2339 Ibid.

2340 Tom Charlier, with contributions from Alex Doniach, Michael Erskine, Zack McMillan, and Marc Perrusquia, "Mayor seeks unity, calls out haters," *Commercial Appeal* (Memphis, TN), October 5, 2007.

2341 Michael Erskine, "Ex-MLGW chief falls short of challengers," *Commercial Appeal* (Memphis, TN), October 5, 2007.

2342 Bruce Van Wyngarden, "Herman Morris' Last Dance," *Memphis Flyer*, October 11-17, 2007.

2343 Editorial, "Learning from a mess," *Commercial Appeal* (Memphis, TN), October 5, 2007.

2344 John Branston, "Polls: The Dark Side," *Memphis Flyer*, October 11-17, 2007.

2345 Ibid.

2346 Ibid.

2347 Ibid.

2348 Blake Fontenay, "Comment" "Chumney, Morris didn't have vote-for-me mojo," *Commercial Appeal* (Memphis, TN), October 8, 2007.

2349 Blake Fontenay, "Viewpoint" "Pollsters are not oracles foreseeing future," *Commercial Appeal* (Memphis, TN), November 3, 2008.

2350 Ibid.

2351 Jacinthia Jones, "Three-way race provides plurality for incumbent," *Commercial Appeal* (Memphis, TN), October 5, 2007.

2352 Derek Haire, "Chez Chumney," *Memphis Flyer*, October 11-17, 2007.

2353 Ibid.

2354 Jackson Baker, "Something for Everybody," *Memphis Flyer*, October 11-17, 2007.

2355 Jackson Baker, "What's Next?" *Memphis Flyer*, October 11-17, 2007.

2356 Ibid.

2357 Jacinthia Jones, "Herenton defiant in his victory address," *Commercial Appeal* (Memphis, TN), October 6, 2007.

2358 Ibid.

2359 Ibid.; "Excerpts from Mayor Herenton's Election-Night Victory Speech," *Commercial Appeal* (Memphis, TN), October 6, 2007.

2360 "Excerpts from Mayor Herenton's Election-Night Victory Speech," *Commercial Appeal* (Memphis, TN), October 6, 2007.

2361 Ibid.

2362 Editorial, "A crossroads for Mayor Herenton," *Commercial Appeal* (Memphis, TN), October 6, 2007.

2363 Charles C. Lambert, Letters to Editor, "Now the exodus begins," *Commercial Appeal* (Memphis, TN), October 8, 2007.

2364 John Branston, "Auctioning Memphis," *Memphis Flyer*, December 5, 2007.

2365 David Moinestar, Letters to Editor, "Long on invective, short on ideas," *Commercial Appeal* (Memphis, TN), October 9, 2007.

2366 Ibid.

2367 Fred Hidaji, Letters to Editor, "Apathy, ignorance keep Memphis down!" *Commercial Appeal* (Memphis, TN), October 12, 2007.

2368 Letter to Editor, Julia Young, "Silent sexism at work in mayor's race," *Commercial Appeal* (Memphis, TN), October 6, 2007.

2369 McClatchy newspapers, "Truth in the Booth," *Commercial Appeal* (Memphis, TN), October 14, 2007.

2370 Matt Stearns & Margaret Taley, "Do gender, race still matter? Many voters say they don't," *Commercial Appeal* (Memphis, TN), October 14, 2007.

2371 McClatchy newspapers, "Truth in the Booth," *Commercial Appeal* (Memphis, TN), October 14, 2007.

2372 Michael Erskine, "MLGW seeks gas, water rate hikes," *Commercial Appeal* (Memphis, TN), October 12, 2007.

2373 Jacinthia Jones, "Herenton will get $11,500 pay hike," *Commercial Appeal* (Memphis, TN), October 17, 2007.

2374 Ibid.

2375 Ibid.

2376 Bill Dries, "Memphis Networx Sale Receives 'Contested Case' Label," *Daily News* (Memphis, TN), December 10, 2007.

2377 Ibid; Editorial, "Learning from a mess," *Commercial Appeal* (Memphis, TN), October 5, 2007.

2378 Bill Dries, "Memphis Networx Sale Receives 'Contested Case' Label," *Daily News* (Memphis, TN), December 10, 2007.

2379 Ibid; Kontji Anthony, "Committee wants state to investigate Memphis Networx," *WMC Action News 5,* December 18, 2007.

2380 *City of Memphis v. Zayo Bandwith Tennessee, LLC aka Memphis Networx, LLC,* No. 2:09-cv-2205-SHM-cgc, ECF 24 (W.D. Tenn.), *"Memorandum of City of Memphis in Opposition to Defendants' Motion for Judgment on the Pleadings."*

2381 Ibid., pg. 7, fn. 5.

2382 Ibid., pg. 7, fn. 5.

2383 Ibid., pgs. 27-28.

2384 Bill Dries, "City budget vision still blurry as first federal funds arrive," *Daily Memphian,* June 1, 2021.

2385 Blake Fontenay, "Outgoing council members may not be done," *Commercial Appeal* (Memphis, TN), December 31, 2007.

2386 Ibid.

2387 Ibid.

2388 Blake Fontenay, "True to character, right to the end," "Blake's Blog," *Commercial Appeal* (Memphis, TN), December 19, 2007.

2389 John Branston, "Predictions for 2008: A Quiz," *Memphis Flyer,* January 1, 2008.

2390 Richard Locker, "Big talk, but no action—Herenton won't seek change in voting," *Commercial Appeal* (Memphis, TN), February 12, 2008; Blake Fontenay, "Mayors mapping out political exit strategy?" *Commercial Appeal,* February 25, 2008.

2391 Ibid; Ibid.

2392 Blake Fontenay, "Mayors mapping out political exit strategy?" *Commercial Appeal* (Memphis, TN), February 25, 2008.

2393 Kontji Anthony, "Nashville meeting on consolidation," *WMC Action News 5* (Memphis, TN), January 16, 2008.

2394 Kontji Anthony, "Wharton speaks out against rumors," *WMC Action News 5* (Memphis, TN), January 17, 2008.

2395 Marc Perrusquia, "FBI probes pacts by city," *Commercial Appeal* (Memphis, TN), January 11, 2008.

2396 David Flaum, "Herenton brews big ideas," *Commercial Appeal* (Memphis, TN), January 16, 2008; Lori Brown, "Herenton plans Liberty Bowl announcement," *WMC Action News 5,* January 28, 2008.

2397 Ibid; Ibid.

2398 Lori Brown, "Herenton plans Liberty Bowl announcement," *WMC Action News 5,* January 28, 2008.

2399 John Branston, "Disarray and Memphis... Times are tough now, but new leaders will move Memphis forward," *Memphis Flyer,* January 18, 2008.

2400 Ibid.

2401 Andy Meek, "Morris, Chumney Reinvent Themselves in Private Sector," *Daily News* (Memphis, TN), February 13, 2008.

2402 Associated Press, "Herenton, Chumney to endorse Clinton for president," *WMC Action News 5* (Memphis, TN), January 27, 2008.

2403 Sarah Buduson, "Mayor Herenton Endorses Sen. Clinton," *ABC Eyewitness TV News 24* (Memphis, TN), January 29, 2008.

2404 Jackson Baker, "Matilla, Chumney Eye Trustee's Job," *Memphis Flyer,* January 31, 2008.

2405 Ibid.

2406 "Response to story on Matilla," *Memphis Flyer,* January 31, 2008; Jackson Baker, "Choosing Sides," *Memphis Flyer,* February 7, 2008.

2407 "Response to story on Matilla," *Memphis Flyer,* January 31, 2008.

2408 Jackson Baker, "Choosing Sides," *Memphis Flyer,* February 7, 2008.

2409 Alex Doniach, staff reporter Lindsay Melvin contributed, "Commission searches for Patterson successor," *Commercial Appeal* (Memphis, TN), February 5, 2008.

2410 Jackson Baker, "Raising the Bar," *Memphis Flyer,* February 28, 2008.

2411 Ibid.

2412 Ibid.

2413 Andy Meek, "Morris, Chumney Reinvent Themselves in Private Sector," *Daily News* (Memphis, TN), February 13, 2008.

2414 Meghan Harris, "Former councilwoman teaches political science," *Daily Helmsman* (Memphis, TN), February 28, 2008.

2415 Peter Baker and Anne E. Kornblut, "Even in Victory, Clinton Team is Battling Itself," *Washington Post,* March 6, 2008.

2416 Ibid.

2417 Jonathan Lindberg, General Editor, "Memphis Profiles in Courage," *Main Street Journal, Main Street Publications* (Memphis, TN), 2008.

2418 Alex Doniach, "Puzzle remains on date for vote," *Commercial Appeal* (Memphis, TN), March 22, 2008.

2419 Ibid.; Editorial, "Mayor's exit no cause for alarm," *Commercial Appeal,* March 22, 2008.

2420 Marc Perrusquia, reporter Kristina Goetz contributed, "Willie Herenton resigns" "Mayor: It's about schools—Denies grand jury probe influenced his decision," *Commercial Appeal* (Memphis, TN), March 23, 2008.

2421 Ibid.

2422 Ibid.; Marc Perrusquia, "Feds probe doubles down on Moon- MATA contract, e-mails, land deal get scrutiny," *Commercial Appeal* (Memphis, TN), January 23, 2008.

2423 Ibid; Ibid.

2424 Marc Perrusquia, reporter Kristina Goetz contributed, "Mayor: It's about schools," *Commercial Appeal* (Memphis, TN), March 23, 2008.

2425 Ibid.

2426 Editorial, "Mayor's exit no cause for alarm," *Commercial Appeal* (Memphis, TN), March 22, 2008.

2427 Ibid.

2428 Blake Fontenay, "Comment" "Mayoral election likely to be political free-for-all,"

Commercial Appeal (Memphis, TN), March 24, 2008.

2429 Ibid.

2430 Ibid.

2431 Newsroom, "Bombshell: The 'Doc' is stepping aside," *Tri-State Defender* (Memphis, TN), March 20, 2008.

2432 Ibid.

2433 Ibid.

2434 Ibid.

2435 Ibid.

2436 Amos Maki, "Herenton said he ran for reelection to protect Memphis from Chumney, Morris," *Commercial Appeal* (Memphis, TN), March 25, 2008.

2437 Ibid.

2438 Ibid.

2439 Amos Maki, "Ran to 'protect' city says Herenton," *Commercial Appeal* (Memphis, TN), March 26, 2008.

2440 Ibid.

2441 Amos Maki, "Herenton said he ran for reelection to protect Memphis from Chumney, Morris," *Commercial Appeal* (Memphis, TN), March 25, 2008.

2442 Ibid.

2443 Editorial, "Reluctant mayor can't help city," *Commercial Appeal* (Memphis, TN), March 26, 2008.

2444 Ibid.

2445 Jackson Baker, "Viewpoint" "Constructive Confusion," *Memphis Flyer,* April 3, 2008.

2446 Ibid.

2447 Jackson Baker, "The Mayor's Gambit..How AC Wharton played a major background role in a plan to enlarge Willie Herenton's power," *Memphis Flyer,* April 3-9, 2008.

2448 Ibid.

2449 Ibid.

2450 Jackson Baker, "Willie Herenton: The Exit Interview," *Memphis Flyer,* July 2, 2009.

2451 Ibid.

2452 Ibid.

2453 Ibid.

2454 Ibid.

2455 Ibid.

2456 Jackson Baker, "The Mayor's Gambit, How AC Wharton played a major background role in a plan to enlarge Willie Herenton's power," *Memphis Flyer,* April 3-9, 2008.

2457 Ibid.

2458 Ibid.

2459 Ibid.

2460 Preston Lauterbach and Chris Davis, "The mayor and the superintendent search," *Memphis Flyer*, April 3-9, 2008.

2461 Ibid.

2462 Shaila Dewan, "Mayor seeks job switch, but response is lukewarm," *New York Times*, March 30, 2008.

2463 John Branston, "Past and Present," *Memphis Flyer*, April 10, 2008.

2464 Ibid.

2465 Bartholomew Sullivan, "Shelby County has nation's third-highest jail incarceration rate, study finds," *Commercial Appeal* (Memphis, TN), April 11, 2008.

2466 John Branston, "Past and Present," *Memphis Flyer*, April 10, 2008.

2467 Editorial, "Spotlight shines on Bluff City," *Commercial Appeal* (Memphis, TN), April 1, 2008.

2468 Bill Dries, "'Austerity' to Be Central to Today's Budget Proposal," *Daily News* (Memphis, TN), April 15, 2008.

2469 Amos Maki, "Council reviews growing payroll-Questions posed to administration about employee expenses," *Commercial Appeal* (Memphis, TN), May 2, 2008; Wendi Thomas, "Mayor's decisions make no sense," *Commercial Appeal* (Memphis, TN), May 4, 2008.

2470 Amos Maki, "Mayor: Keep probe open," *Commercial Appeal* (Memphis, TN), April 12, 2008.

2471 Ibid.

2472 Ibid.

2473 *USA v. Michael Hooks Jr.*, Case No. 2:06-cr-20223-JDB, Doc. 39, (W.D. Tenn., January 10, 2008), "*Plea Agreement*."

2474 Ibid., Doc. 46, April 14, 2008, "*Judgment in a Criminal Case*;" John Branston, "The Last Waltz," *Memphis Flyer*, April 17-23, 2008; Hooks Jr. later reinvented himself as a successful public contractor. Marc Perrusquia, "Hooks legacy rises again as confederate statues fall," *Commercial Appeal* (Memphis, TN), May 27, 2018.

2475 *USA v. Robert Bruce Thompson*, Case No.

2:07-cr-20350-JPM, Doc. 26, (W.D. Tenn., February 27, 2008), "*Plea Agreement*," Doc. 54, (December 18, 2008), "*Judgment in a Criminal Case*;" Jackson Baker, "Bruce Thompson Gets Light Sentence in Fraud Case," *Memphis Flyer*, December 17, 2008.

2476 John Branston, "The Last Waltz," *Memphis Flyer*, April 17-23, 2008.

2477 Ibid.

2478 Newsroom, "Jury Acquits Former Councilman Edmund Ford, Sr.," *Tri-State Defender* (Memphis, TN), May 22, 2008.

2479 Ibid.

2480 Editorial, "Herenton's hat out of the ring," *Commercial Appeal* (Memphis, TN), April 19, 2008.

2481 Ibid.

2482 Richard Locker, "Nashville reaped benefits of plan eyed for Memphis," *Commercial Appeal* (Memphis, TN), May 4, 2008.

2483 Michael Kelley, "Can we get together?" *Commercial Appeal* (Memphis, TN), May 4, 2008.

2484 Ibid.

2485 Ibid.

2486 Ibid.

2487 Ibid.

2488 Ibid.

2489 Tennessee Attorney General Opinion, No. 02-028 (March 14, 2002).

2490 Amos Maki, "Voters to decide on instant runoff," *Commercial Appeal* (Memphis, TN), May 17, 2008.

2491 Ibid.

2492 Ibid.

2493 Jody Callahan, "Simplifying mayoral succession," *Commercial Appeal* (Memphis, TN), May 30, 2008.

2494 Ibid.

2495 Patti Patterson, "Beale Street Panel Votes to dismiss Elkington's Firm," *Commercial Appeal* (Memphis, TN), December 25, 1991.

2496 Alex Doniach, "Willie Herenton Resigns—Puzzle remains on date for vote," *Commercial Appeal* (Memphis, TN), March 22, 2008; Otis Sanford, "Chaos just getting warmed up," *Commercial Appeal* (Memphis, TN), June 26, 2009.

2497 Otis Sanford, "Chaos just getting warmed up," *Commercial Appeal* (Memphis, TN), June 26, 2009.

2498 Amos Maki, "Voters to decide on instant runoff," *Commercial Appeal* (Memphis, TN), May 17, 2008.

2499 Blake Fontenay, "Ballot breakdown – expect to spend some time perusing the host of city, county charter amendments" "Amendments can bewilder voter," *Commercial Appeal* (Memphis, TN), October 26, 2008.

2500 Viewpoint, "Candidates calm in MCS storm," *Commercial Appeal* (Memphis, TN), June 7 2008; Amos Maki, "School cuts may fuel reform," *Commercial Appeal* (Memphis, TN), May 30, 2008.

2501 Editorial, "Desperation bid by the mayor," *Commercial Appeal* (Memphis, TN), May 30, 2008.

2502 Amos Maki, "New Council…; School funding, tax rate trimmed—council helps property owners, hits education," *Commercial Appeal* (Memphis, TN), June 4, 2008.

2503 Amos Maki, "New council proves to be no pushover" "Freshman leaders tackle big issues in first six months," *Commercial Appeal* (Memphis, TN), June 8, 2008; Zack McMillan, "Can Memphis schools be fixed?" *Commercial Appeal,* June 29, 2008.

2504 Tennessee Attorney General Opinion, No. 05-021 (March 10, 2005); Amos Maki, "School cuts may fuel reform," *Commercial Appeal* (Memphis, TN), May 30, 2008.

2505 Amos Maki, "School cuts may fuel reform," *Commercial Appeal* (Memphis, TN), May 30, 2008.

2506 Email to Amos Maki, reporter with *Commercial Appeal* (Memphis, TN), June 8, 2008; Kontji Anthony, "Herenton proposes tax increase," *WMC Action News 5* (Memphis, TN), April 15, 2008.

2507 Otis Sanford, "Finding Mayor's inconsistencies is like shooting fish in a barrel," *Commercial Appeal* (Memphis, TN), June 22, 2008.

2508 Ibid.

2509 Otis Sanford, "OK, Gang of 10, take a look at your handiwork," *Commercial Appeal* (Memphis, TN), August 31, 2008. The fateful vote was approved by council members Bill Boyd, Harold Collins, Shea Flinn, Edmund Ford Jr., Janis Fullilove, Wanda Halbert, Reid Hedgepeth, Myron Lowery, Scott McCormick, and Bill Morrison.

2510 Blake Fontenay, "Council's sharp budget pencil is dull to reality," *Commercial Appeal* (Memphis, TN), June 23, 2008.

2511 Jackson Baker, "Who Wants to be the Next Mayor? An Update," *Memphis Flyer,* June 1, 2008.

2512 Ibid.

2513 Ibid.

2514 Jackson Baker, "The Illusionist," *Memphis Flyer,* July 3-9, 2008.

2515 Shane McDermott, "Can Memphis schools be fixed?" "10 challenges facing Memphis City Schools," *Commercial Appeal* (Memphis, TN), June 29, 2008.

2516 *State of Tennessee, ex rel., the Board of Education of the Memphis City Schools, et al v. City of Memphis, et al,* 329 S.W. 3d 465 (Tenn. App. 2010).

2517 Ibid.

2518 Jackson Baker, "The Illusionist," *Memphis Flyer,* July 3-9, 2008.

2519 Ibid.

2520 Ibid.

2521 Ibid.

2522 Ibid.

2523 "Hillary Clinton, 2008: 18 million cracks in the glass ceiling," *Maclean's,* June 7, 2016.

2524 Ellen Goodman, "Year's hurdles for cause of women," *Commercial Appeal* (Memphis, TN), August 25, 2008 (bumper stickers "Life's a B_____, Don't Elect One").

2525 Geoff Calkins, "VP Palin? Let's go to the replay," *Commercial Appeal* (Memphis, TN), September 3, 2008.

2526 Ibid.

2527 Ibid.

2528 Brett J. Blackledge, "Palin got zoning aid, gifts—Investigation hints at small town politics as usual," *Commercial Appeal* (Memphis, TN), September 29, 2008.

2529 Ellen Goodman, "Still looking through glass ceiling," *Commercial Appeal* (Memphis, TN), August 31, 2008.

2530 Jackson Baker, "Now for Round Two," *Memphis Flyer*, August 14, 2008.

2531 Jackson Baker, "Field Grows: What Does Chumney Say About Council Race?" *Memphis Flyer*, August 20, 2008.

2532 The Bible, 2 Cor. 5:7.

2533 Amos Maki, "Seven file to run for open council seat," *Commercial Appeal* (Memphis, TN), August 21, 2008.

2534 Marc Perrusquia, "Herenton provides details of land deal," *Commercial Appeal* (Memphis, TN), August 16, 2008.

2535 Ibid.

2536 Ibid.; Editorial, "Put a limit on mayor's power," *Commercial Appeal* (Memphis, TN), August 19, 2008.

2537 Amos Maki, "Council to vote on two measures," *Commercial Appeal* (Memphis, TN), August 19, 2008.

2538 Ibid.

2539 Ibid.

2540 Amos Maki, "Power-limiting plan on hold" "City Council delays ordinance that could constrain Herenton," *Commercial Appeal* (Memphis, TN), August 20, 2008.

2541 Ibid.

2542 Amos Maki, "City expects large surplus," *Commercial Appeal* (Memphis, TN), August 20, 2008.

2543 Editorial, "Sorting out school funding," *Commercial Appeal* (Memphis, TN), September 15, 2008.

2544 Ibid.

2545 *USA v. Edmund H. Ford*, Case No. 06-20467-Ma, Doc. 106 (W.D. Tenn., May 21, 2008), *"Jury Verdict."*

2546 *USA v. Edmund H. Ford, Joseph Lee III*, Case No. 08-20001-Ma, Doc. 30, (W.D. Tenn., June 25, 2008), *"Order Granting Government's Motion to Dismiss Indictment."*

2547 Amos Maki, "MLGW board to pay Lee legal tab," *Commercial Appeal* (Memphis, TN), August 22, 2008.

2548 Editorial, "Sticker shock at MLGW," *Commercial Appeal* (Memphis, TN), August 23, 2008.

2549 Ibid.

2550 Editorial, "Hefty legal fee merits scrutiny," *Commercial Appeal* (Memphis, TN), August 29, 2008.

2551 Amos Maki, "MLGW to pay $64k less for Lee's legal bills," *Commercial Appeal* (Memphis, TN), August 28, 2008.

2552 Ibid.; Amos Maki, "MLGW Oks Lee's legal fee payment," *Commercial Appeal* (Memphis, TN), September 5, 2008.

2553 Alex Doniach, "Herenton taps Lee to parks position," *Commercial Appeal* (Memphis, TN), August 30, 2008.

2554 Ibid.

2555 Editorial, "Like it or not, Lee is back," *Commercial Appeal* (Memphis, TN), September 1, 2008.

2556 Editorial, "Be Prepared," *Memphis Flyer*, September 11, 2008.

2557 Ibid.

2558 Alex Doniach, "Wharton appears to plan campaign," *Commercial Appeal* (Memphis, TN), September 17, 2008.

2559 Blake Fontenay, "Advantages, risks in early Wharton bid," *Commercial Appeal* (Memphis, TN), September 22, 2008.

2560 Patrick Rizzo and Joe Bel Bruno, "Stocks Plummet as Woes Mount," *Commercial Appeal* (Memphis, TN), September 16, 2008; Editorial, Chris Peck, "Living in newsworthy time," *Commercial Appeal*, September 21, 2008.

2561 Patrick Rizzo and Joe Bel Bruno, "Stocks Plummet as Woes Mount," *Commercial Appeal* (Memphis, TN), September 16, 2008.

2562 Amos Maki, "Room to improve," *Commercial Appeal* (Memphis, TN), September 19, 2008.

2563 Ibid.

2564 Marc Perrusquia, "Mayor's bus site plans probed," *Commercial Appeal* (Memphis, TN), September 21, 2008.

2565 Ibid.

2566 Ibid.

2567 Editorial, "A foul odor at the depot," *Commercial Appeal* (Memphis, TN), September 23, 2008.

2568 Marc Perrusquia and Amos Maki, "Beale St. merchants worrying," *Commercial Appeal* (Memphis, TN), September 24, 2008; Editorial, "Murky moves on Beale Street," *Commercial Appeal*, September 25, 2008.

2569 Alex Doniach, "Mayor willing to cede charter," *Commercial Appeal* (Memphis, TN), October 4, 2008.

2570 Ibid.

2571 Ibid.

2572 Ibid.

2573 Ibid.

2574 Amos Maki, "City, county to talk consolidation," *Commercial Appeal* (Memphis TN), October 7, 2008.

2575 Ibid.

2576 Editorial, "Thanks, now it's time to talk," *Commercial Appeal* (Memphis, TN), October 7, 2008.

2577 John Branston, "On Not Moving On," *Memphis Flyer,* October 16-22, 2008.

2578 Amos Maki, staff reporter Alex Doniach contributed, "Consolidation on the table again," *Commercial Appeal* (Memphis, TN), October 8, 2008.

2579 Ibid.

2580 Jerome Wright, "Development shifts east," *Commercial Appeal* (Memphis, TN), October 5, 2008.

2581 Ibid.

2582 Ibid.

2583 Alex Doniach, "Merger resistance deeply rooted," *Commercial Appeal* (Memphis, TN), October 26, 2008.

2584 Ibid.

2585 Ibid.

2586 Ibid.

2587 Amos Maki, "Mayor's side job raises concern," *Commercial Appeal* (Memphis, TN), October 27, 2008.

2588 Letters to Editor, *Commercial Appeal* (Memphis, TN), October 27, 2008.

2589 Editorial, "Mayor is a full-time job," *Commercial Appeal* (Memphis, TN), October 28, 2008.

2590 Wendi Thomas, "Mayor if it looks untoward, leave it be," *Commercial Appeal* (Memphis, TN), October 30, 2008.

2591 Ibid.

2592 Ibid.

2593 Richard Locker, "Tenn. Republicans relish new clout," *Commercial Appeal* (Memphis, TN), November 6, 2008.

2594 Editorial, "Invalid election sets precedent," *Commercial Appeal* (Memphis, TN), September 21, 2008.

2595 "Party loyalists go after Kurita," *Commercial Appeal* (Memphis, TN), August 3, 2008; Associated Press, "Kurita to run as write-in candidate," *Commercial Appeal,* September 16, 2008.

2596 Ibid.; Ibid.

2597 Richard Locker, "Tenn. Republicans relish new clout," *Commercial Appeal* (Memphis, TN), November 6, 2008.

2598 Amos Maki, "Bleak decisions ahead for city," *Commercial Appeal* (Memphis, TN), November 9, 2008.

2599 Marc Perrusquia and Amos Maki, "Herenton seeks to counter inquiry," *Commercial Appeal* (Memphis, TN), November 15, 2008.

2600 Ibid.

2601 Ibid.

2602 Marc Perrusquia, "Aviotti duties enrich mayor," *Commercial Appeal* (Memphis, TN), November 16, 2008.

2603 Alex Doniach, "Wharton raising money for run," *Commercial Appeal* (Memphis, TN), November 11, 2008.

2604 Andy Meek, "Chumney Chimes in on Mayor's Race," *Daily News* (Memphis, TN), November 18, 2008.

2605 Ibid.

2606 Jackson Baker, "Who's Going to Be the Next Mayor—And When?" *Memphis Flyer,* January 1-7, 2009.

2607 Ibid.

2608 Ibid.

2609 Marc Perrusquia, "Man on a Mission," *Commercial Appeal* (Memphis, TN), January 4, 2009.

2610 Ibid.

2611 Ibid.

2612 Ibid.

2613 Ibid.

2614 Ibid.

2615 Ibid.; Marc Perrusquia, "The Sex Scandal," *Commercial Appeal* (Memphis, TN), January 4, 2009.

2616 Marc Perrusquia, "The Sex Scandal," *Commercial Appeal* (Memphis, TN), January 4, 2009.

2617 Ibid.

2618 Ibid.

2619 Ibid.

2620 *USA v. Yolanda McFagdon,* Case No. 2:98-cr-20271-JPM, Doc 6, (W. D. Tenn., December 10, 1998), "*Order on Guilty Plea;*" Marc Perrusquia, "The Lady in Blue," *Commercial Appeal* (Memphis, TN), January 5, 2009.

2621 Marc Perrusquia, "The Lady in Blue," *Commercial Appeal* (Memphis, TN), January 5, 2009.

2622 Marc Perrsuquia, "A Cold Wind Blows," *Commercial Appeal* (Memphis, TN), January 8, 2009.

2623 Marc Perrusquia, "Don't Bring Me No Mess," *Commercial Appeal* (Memphis, TN), January 7, 2009.

2624 Marc Perrusquia, "The Mayor's Baby," *Commercial Appeal* (Memphis, TN), January 10, 2009.

2625 Marc Perrusquia, "The French Connection," *Commercial Appeal* (Memphis, TN), January 9, 2009.

2626 Marc Perrusquia, "Don't Bring Me No Mess," *Commercial Appeal* (Memphis, TN), January 7, 2009.

2627 Marc Perrusquia, Viewpoint, "Willie W. Herenton: Always a Fighter," *Commercial Appeal* (Memphis, TN), January 11, 2009.

2628 Ibid.

2629 Ibid.

2630 Ibid.

2631 Ibid.

2632 Amos Maki, "Mayor: I didn't cross the line," *Commercial Appeal* (Memphis, TN), January 14, 2009.

2633 Ibid.

2634 Ibid.

2635 Editorial, "Herenton plea falls short," *Commercial Appeal* (Memphis, TN), January 15, 2009.

2636 Editorial, Otis Sanford, "Herenton seems resigned to fate as misunderstood," *Commercial Appeal* (Memphis, TN), January 11, 2009.

2637 Ibid.; Editorial, Chris Peck, "Mayor's words shift with audience," *Commercial Appeal* (Memphis, TN), January 18, 2009.

2638 Editorial, Otis Sanford, "Herenton seems resigned to fate as misunderstood," *Commercial Appeal* (Memphis, TN), January 11, 2009.

2639 Editorial, Chris Peck, "Mayor's words shift with audience," *Commercial Appeal* (Memphis, TN), January 18, 2009.

2640 Marc Perrusquia and Amos Maki, "Herenton touch: Midas or minus for Downtown?" *Commercial Appeal* (Memphis, TN), January 25, 2009.

2641 Ibid.

2642 Ibid.

2643 Ibid.

2644 Marc Perrusquia, "Willie Herenton: Always a Fighter," *Commercial Appeal* (Memphis, TN), January 11, 2009.

2645 Editorial, "Mayor clouds a worthy plan," *Commercial Appeal* (Memphis, TN), January 27, 2009.

2646 Marc Perrusquia, "Mayor's legal adviser later bought from him," *Commercial Appeal* (Memphis, TN), January 25, 2009.

2647 Ibid.

2648 Amos Maki and Marc Perrusquia, "Officials quizzed about Herenton," *Commercial Appeal* (Memphis, TN), January 21, 2009.

2649 Amos Maki, "Mayor OK in deal," *Commercial Appeal* (Memphis, TN), February 7, 2009.

2650 Marc Perrusquia and Amos Maki, "Mayor's son called before federal grand jury," *Commercial Appeal* (Memphis, TN), January 29, 2009.

2651 Amos Maki, "Battling over Beale- District Manager ordered to supply financial records," *Commercial Appeal* (Memphis, TN), January 26, 2009.

2652 Ibid.

2653 Ibid.

2654 Ibid.

2655 Bill Dries, "Why the struggle to control Beale Street continues," *Memphis Daily News,* June 1, 2009.

2656 Marc Perrusquia and Amos Maki "FBI, IRS inquire about parties," *Commercial Appeal* (Memphis, TN), February 1, 2009.

2657 Marc Perrusquia, "Herenton prospers from Yule generosity, FBI investigates mayor's receipt of party donations," *Commercial Appeal* (Memphis, TN), April 5, 2009.

2658 Marc Perrusquia and Amos Maki, "FBI, IRS inquire about parties," *Commercial Appeal* (Memphis, TN), February 1, 2009.

2659 Ibid.

2660 Ibid.

2661 Ibid.

2662 Jody Callahan, "Miserable Memphis? Well, not all think so," *Commercial Appeal* (Memphis, TN), February 10, 2009.

2663 Amos Maki, "City buyout plan seeks 100 takers—mayor's proposal would cost $7M, save $6.4 annually," *Commercial Appeal* (Memphis, TN), February 4, 2009.

2664 Amos Maki, "All about the budget for council" "As city faces shortfall, cuts loom for schools, health and other departments," *Commercial Appeal* (Memphis, TN), January 6, 2009.

2665 *State of Tenn., ex rel, the Board of Education of the Memphis City Schools v. City of Memphis,* 329 S.W. 3d 465 (Tenn. App. 2010).

2666 Ibid.; Editorial, "The school funding puzzle," *Commercial Appeal* (Memphis, TN), February 19, 2009.

2667 *State of Tenn., ex rel, the Board of Education of the Memphis City Schools v. City of Memphis,* 329 S.W. 3d 465 (Tenn. App. 2010); Amos Maki and Jane Roberts, "City faces $100 million hit" "Council appeals court order to return $57.4 M to MCS," *Commercial Appeal* (Memphis, TN), February 18, 2009.

2668 Editorial, "The school funding puzzle," *Commercial Appeal* (Memphis, TN), February 19, 2009.

2669 Amos Maki, "City has big job to find $100M," *Commercial Appeal* (Memphis, TN), February 19, 2009.

2670 Alex Doniach, "County claims city owes $125 M," *Commercial Appeal* (Memphis, TN), February 3, 2009.

2671 Jim Masilak, "City faces $100 million hit" "Liberty Bowl disability fixes due by 2010, to cost Memphis more than $40 million," *Commercial Appeal* (Memphis, TN), February 18, 2009.

2672 Mary Cashiola, "Flying United," *Memphis Flyer,* March 26, 2009.

2673 Viewpoint, *Commercial Appeal* (Memphis, TN), April 4, 2009.

2674 Daniel Connolly, "Suburban mayors oppose merger" "Leaders of city and county leery of government, tax," *Commercial Appeal* (Memphis, TN), April 17, 2009.

2675 Ibid.; Editorial, "Suburbs hope for the best," *Commercial Appeal* (Memphis, TN), April 20, 2009.

2676 Jackson Baker, "The Race Factor," *Memphis Flyer,* June 18, 2009.

2677 Amos Maki, "Memphis trash pact linked to donations—Questions raised over waste firm generosity," *Commercial Appeal* (Memphis, TN), February 22, 2009.

2678 Ibid.

2679 Ibid.

2680 Ibid.

2681 Ibid.

2682 Ibid.

2683 Jackson Baker, "Who's Going to Be the Next Mayor- and When?" *Memphis Flyer,* January 1-7, 2009.

2684 Ibid.

2685 Ibid.

2686 Bill Dries, "Wharton Not Giving Up on Consolidation," *Daily News* (Memphis, TN), March 6, 2009.

2687 Zack McMillan and Amos Maki, "Surprise amid smoke of Herenton bomb," *Commercial Appeal* (Memphis, TN), April 23, 2009.

2688 Ibid.

2689 Ibid.

2690 Wendi Thomas, "Let's just ignore his tantrums," *Commercial Appeal* (Memphis, TN), April 23, 2009.

2691 Zack McMillan, "Poll finds Cohen ahead of Herenton," *Commercial Appeal* (Memphis, TN), April 29, 2009.

2692 Jackson Baker, "Ford's Out-and In," *Memphis Flyer,* April 16-22, 2009.

2693 Ibid.

2694 Clay Bailey, "Staffing short at rape center," *Commercial Appeal* (Memphis, TN), April 29, 2009.

2695 Ibid.

2696 Ibid.

2697 Nina Sublette, Letter to the Editor, "MSARC staff not 'just nurses'," *Commercial Appeal* (Memphis, TN), May 6, 2009.

2698 Clay Bailey, "Payments to crisis center in question," *Commercial Appeal* (Memphis, TN), May 16, 2009.

2699 Amos Maki, "Crisis of confidence," *Commercial Appeal* (Memphis, TN), May 20, 2009.

2700 Ibid; Amos Maki, "Officials discuss MSARC funding," *Commercial Appeal* (Memphis, TN), June 5, 2009.

2701 Linda S. Wallace, "Justice often elusive when it comes to violence against women and girls," *Tri-State Defender* (Memphis, TN), June 18-24, 2009.

2702 Ibid.

2703 Marc Perrusquia, "Herenton allies appear at grand jury," *Commercial Appeal* (Memphis, TN), April 29, 2009.

2704 Ibid.

2705 Michael Lollar, "Memphians reminisce on king of pop's visits," *Commercial Appeal* (Memphis, TN), June 26, 2009; Editorial, "Springtime in Memphis," *Commercial Appeal,* June 26, 2009; Amos Maki, "Departing city hall with eye on congress," *Commercial Appeal,* June 26, 2009.

2706 Editorial, "Springtime in Memphis," *Commercial Appeal* (Memphis, TN), June 26, 2009.

2707 Michael Jackson (1982).

2708 Ibid.

2709 Marc Perrusquia, "Resignation won't deter probe," *Commercial Appeal* (Memphis, TN), June 26, 2009.

2710 Ibid.

2711 Zack McMillan, "Special Election" "Several potential candidates weigh mayoral chances," *Commercial Appeal* (Memphis, TN), June 26, 2009.

2712 Ibid.

2713 Ibid.

2714 Otis Sanford, "Chaos just getting warmed up," *Commercial Appeal* (Memphis, TN), June 26, 2009.

2715 Ibid.

2716 Zack McMillan, "Mayoral hopefuls consider the odds," *Commercial Appeal* (Memphis, TN), June 28, 2009.

2717 Zack McMillan, "Several potential candidates weigh mayoral chances," *Commercial Appeal* (Memphis, TN), June 26, 2009.

2718 Otis Sanford, "Chaos just getting warmed up," *Commercial Appeal* (Memphis, TN), June 26, 2009.

2719 Zack McMillan, "Mayoral hopefuls consider the odds," *Commercial Appeal* (Memphis, TN), June 28, 2009.

2720 Ibid.

2721 Ibid.

2722 Otis Sanford, "Chaos just getting warmed up," *Commercial Appeal* (Memphis, TN), June 26, 2009.

2723 Zack McMillan, "Mayoral hopefuls consider the odds," *Commercial Appeal* (Memphis, TN), June 28, 2009.

2724 Ibid.

2725 Ibid.

2726 Ibid.

2727 Marc Perrusquia, "Private citizen Herenton to join son's firm," *Commercial Appeal* (Memphis, TN), June 26, 2009.

2728 Amos Maki, "GONE...AGAIN— Herenton vows anew to step down" "Departing city hall with eye on congress," *Commercial Appeal* (Memphis, TN), June 26, 2009. Several of the mayors with portraits on the wall served more than one term. Not all of those who have led the city have portraits on the wall. For example, some men led the city when it had been disincorporated for a few years in the late 1890's during the yellow fever epidemic, and was a taxing district.

2729 Ibid.

2730 Ibid.

2731 Wendi Thomas "Herenton resigning? Don't plan party yet," *Commercial Appeal* (Memphis, TN), June 26, 2009.

2732 Chris Peck, "Herenton's legacy is pioneer's pride," *Commercial Appeal* (Memphis, TN), June 28, 2009.

2733 Jackson Baker, "Changing the Odds," *Memphis Flyer,* June 25-July 1, 2009.

2734 Ibid.

2735 Ibid.

2736 Ibid.

2737 Ibid.

2738 Ibid.

2739 Zack McMillan, "Whalum will run for mayor in special election," *Commercial Appeal* (Memphis, TN), June 30, 2009.

2740 Ibid.

2741 Jackson Baker, "Madhouse!" *Memphis Flyer,* July 2, 2009.

2742 Ibid.

2743 Jackson Baker, "Candidate Chumney's Conundrum," *Memphis Flyer,* July 6, 2009.

2744 Ibid.

2745 Ibid.

2746 Ibid.

2747 Jackson Baker, "Baker's Response," *Memphis Flyer,* July 6, 2009.

2748 Ibid.

2749 Jackson Baker, "Score One for Chumney," *Memphis Flyer,* July 6, 2009.

2750 Ibid.

2751 Ibid.

2752 Sabrina Hall, "Police say Teens Hard to Control in Mob Robberies," *WREG News Channel 3* (Memphis, TN), April 23, 2013.

2753 Jackson Baker, "Score One for Chumney," *Memphis Flyer,* July 6, 2009.

2754 Ibid.

2755 Ibid.

2756 Ibid.

2757 Editorial, "Fresh look at scandal," *Commercial Appeal* (Memphis, TN), June 25, 2009.

2758 Lawrence Buser, "4 plead guilty in auto-registration scam," *Commercial Appeal* (Memphis, TN), July 22, 2009.

2759 Editorial, "Fresh look at a scandal," *Commercial Appeal* (Memphis, TN), June 25, 2009.

2760 Ibid.

2761 Lacey Crisp, "Cost of Running for Memphis Mayor," *ABC Eyewitness News 24* (Memphis, TN), July 3, 2009.

2762 Zack McMillan, "Testing the Waters," *Commercial Appeal* (Memphis, TN), July 10, 2009.

2763 Ibid.

2764 Ibid.

2765 Ibid.

2766 Ibid.

2767 Ibid.; Jackson Baker, "Counting the Wounded," *Memphis Flyer,* July 16, 2009.

2768 Bill Dries, "Carpenter, Chumney Intensify Efforts to Become Memphis Mayor," *Daily News* (Memphis, TN), July 14, 2009.

2769 Jackson Baker, "Counting the Wounded," *Memphis Flyer,* July 16, 2009.

2770 Zack McMillan, "Testing the Waters," *Commercial Appeal* (Memphis, TN), July 10, 2009.

2771 Ibid.

2772 Bruce Vanwyngarden, Letter from the Editor, "So this is what we've come to," *Memphis Flyer,* July 16, 2009.

2773 Ibid.

2774 Ibid.

2775 Wiley Henry, "Candidates keep an eye on voters of the future," *Tri-State Defender* (Memphis, TN), July 23-29, 2009.

2776 Ibid.

2777 Zack McMillan, "Evaluating Herenton's legacy" "Loved and loathed, it may take city years to gain the proper outlook," *Commercial Appeal* (Memphis, TN), August 2, 2009.

2778 Ibid.

2779 Ibid.

2780 Ibid.

2781 Ibid.

2782 Ibid.

2783 Alex Doniach, "Crowded race has observers guessing" "Lowery, Wharton may hold advantage in large field of 9," *Commercial Appeal* (Memphis, TN), August 2, 2009.

2784 Ibid.

2785 Jackson Baker, "CONFUSION! Special Election 2009: With Herenton out of the picture, who will win this thing?" *Memphis Flyer,* August 6, 2009.

2786 Ibid.

2787 Ibid.

2788 Ibid.

2789 Ibid.

2790 Ibid.

2791 Ibid; *City of Memphis, etal v. Myron Lowery,* CH-09-1607, Shelby County Chancery Court, August 13, 2009.

2792 Jackson Baker, "CONFUSION! Special Election 2009: With Herenton out of the picture, who will win this thing?" *Memphis Flyer*, August 6, 2009.

2793 Ibid.

2794 Ibid.

2795 Ibid.

2796 Ibid.

2797 Ibid.

2798 Ibid.

2799 Ibid.

2800 Ibid.

2801 Ibid.

2802 Ibid.

2803 Ibid.

2804 Ibid.

2805 Ibid.

2806 April Thompson, "Profile of Carol Chumney in her second bid for Memphis Mayor," *WREG News Channel 3*, (Memphis, TN) August 11, 2009.

2807 "Get Lost!" *Health & Fitness Magazine*, August 2009.

2808 Zack McMillan, Alex Doniach and Amos Maki, "Mayoral aspirants position for spots," *Commercial Appeal* (Memphis, TN), July 15, 2009.

2809 Ibid.

2810 Ibid.

2811 Jackson Baker, "CONFUSION! Special Election 2009: With Herenton out of the picture, who will win this thing?" *Memphis Flyer*, August 6, 2009.

2812 Zack McMillan, "Wharton names co-chairmen," *Commercial Appeal* (Memphis, TN), August 23, 2009.

2813 Jackson Baker, "UPDATE—Official Statement from Herenton," *Memphis Flyer*, August 13, 2009.

2814 Jackson Baker, "A Knock Could Prove a Boost as Herenton Goes After Chumney, Lowery," *Memphis Flyer*, August 25, 2009.

2815 Ibid.

2816 Ibid.

2817 Ibid.

2818 Ibid.

2819 Ibid.

2820 Ibid

2821 Ibid.; Jackson Baker, "AC's Rollout: More or Less?" *Memphis Flyer*, August 27, 2009.

2822 Jackson Baker, "A Knock Could Prove a Boost as Herenton Goes After Chumney, Lowery," *Memphis Flyer*, August 25, 2009.

2823 Ibid.; Jackson Baker, "AC's Rollout More or Less?" *Memphis Flyer*, August 27, 2009.

2824 Jackson Baker, "'Underdog' Lowery Lashes Out at Wharton, Herenton, Thaddeus Matthews," *Memphis Flyer*, August 26, 2009.

2825 Jackson Baker, "AC's Rollout: More or Less?" *Memphis Flyer*, August 27, 2009.

2826 John Branston, "Six-Ticket Ride," *Memphis Flyer*, August 6-12, 2009.

2827 Wiley Henry, "Compassionate politics and service," *Tri-State Defender* (Memphis, TN), September 3, 2009.

2828 Ibid.

2829 Ibid; Michael Lollar, "Little heat when candidates meet," *Commercial Appeal* (Memphis, TN), August 28, 2009.

2830 Ibid.; Ibid.

2831 Ibid.; Ibid.

2832 Geoff Calkins, "Sizing the hopefuls: Nutty, not so much," *Commercial Appeal* (Memphis, TN), September 2, 2009.

2833 Michael Lollar, "Little heat when candidates meet," *Commercial Appeal* (Memphis, TN), August 28, 2009.

2834 Wiley Henry, "Compassionate politics and service," *Tri-State Defender* (Memphis, TN), September 3, 2009.

2835 Ibid.

2836 The Bible, Proverbs, 27:1.

2837 Andy Meek, "Chumney Readies 'Grassroots' Campaign for Mayor," *Daily News* (Memphis, TN), August 28, 2009.

2838 Ibid.

2839 Wiley Henry, "Compassionate politics and service," *Tri-State Defender* (Memphis, TN), September 3, 2009.

2840 Ibid.

2841 Alex Doniach, "Talk of jobs rules campaign trailway," *Commercial Appeal* (Memphis, TN), September 8, 2009.

2842 Jody Callahan, "Wharton Skips Mayoral Forum," *Commercial Appeal* (Memphis, TN), September 9, 2009.

2843 Ibid.

2844 Alex Doniach, "City Should Pay Legal Debt, Herenton Says," *Commercial Appeal* (Memphis, TN), September 9, 2009.

2845 Ibid.

2846 Ibid.

2847 Ibid.

2848 Alex Doniach, "Candidates Trade Blows in Debate" "Herenton associations, vehicle inspections are hot-button topics for four mayoral hopefuls," *Commercial Appeal* (Memphis, TN), September 27, 2009.

2849 Ibid.

2850 Ibid.

2851 Ibid.

2852 Ibid.

2853 Ibid.

2854 Shelby County Mayor's Office Administrative Investigation, File No. A5533-09, "*Memorandum,*" July 2, 2009.

2855 Ibid.

2856 Ibid.

2857 Ibid.

2858 Alex Doniach, "Candidates Trade Blows in Debate," *Commercial Appeal*, September 27, 2009.

2859 Ibid.

2860 Ibid.

2861 Janice Broach, "Chumney says Wharton should drop out of mayoral race," *WMC Action News 5,* (Memphis, TN), September 10, 2009.

2862 Alan Greenblatt, "In Memphis, a Plea for Regionalism," *Governing,* August 31, 2009.

2863 Ibid.

2864 Jackson Baker, "Still Swinging" "Repeat Candidate Carol Chumney bores in on front-runner AC Wharton," *Memphis Flyer,* September 17, 2009.

2865 Ibid.

2866 Ibid.

2867 Jody Callahan, "Mayoral hopefuls gather at forum," *Commercial Appeal* (Memphis, TN), September 15, 2009.

2868 Ibid.

2869 Alan Greenblatt, "In Memphis, a Plea for Regionalism," *Governing,* August 31, 2009.

2870 Jody Callahan, "Mayoral hopefuls gather at forum," *Commercial Appeal* (Memphis, TN), September 15, 2009.

2871 Zack McMillan, "Survey puts Wharton in lead," *Commercial Appeal* (Memphis, TN), September 18, 2009.

2872 Ibid.

2873 Jody Callahan, "Candidates promote abilities," *Commercial Appeal* (Memphis, TN), September 18, 2009.

2874 Ibid.

2875 Ibid.

2876 Ibid.

2877 Ibid.

2878 Alex Doniach, "Public's Image of Wharton powerful," *Commercial Appeal* (Memphis, TN), September 20, 2009.

2879 Ibid.

2880 Jackson Baker, "AC's Endorse-arama," *Memphis Flyer,* September 26, 2009.

2881 Alex Doniach, "Public's image of Wharton Powerful," *Commercial Appeal* (Memphis, TN), September 20, 2009.

2882 Ibid.

2883 Ibid.

2884 Ibid.

2885 Ibid.

2886 Ibid.

2887 "Meet the Candidates," *Commercial Appeal* (Memphis, TN), September 28, 2009.

2888 Editorial, "AC Wharton for mayor," *Commercial Appeal* (Memphis, TN), September 29, 2009.

2889 Ibid.

2890 Ibid.

2891 Ibid.

2892 Ibid.

2893 Ibid.

2894 Ibid.

2895 Jackson Baker, "Rope-a-Dope," *Memphis Flyer,* October 1, 2009.

2896 Ibid.

2897 Ibid.

2898 Ibid.

2899 Ibid.

2900 Ibid.

2901 Zack McMillan, "Wharton skeptical of own publicity-mayoral candidates using opposition to stay focused," *Commercial Appeal* (Memphis, TN), October 4, 2009.

2902 Ibid.

2903 Ibid.

2904 Ibid.

2905 Zack McMillan, "Debate forums on tap for mayoral candidates," *Commercial Appeal* (Memphis, TN), October 6, 2009.

2906 Zack McMillan, "Mayor to face funding problem," *Commercial Appeal* (Memphis, TN), October 6, 2009.

2907 Ibid.

2908 Ibid.

2909 Jackson Baker, "Signs of Change," *Memphis Flyer,* October 8-14, 2009.

2910 Zack McMillan, "Ex-mayor still on campaign radar-candidates discuss whether Herenton exit benefits legal," *Commercial Appeal* (Memphis, TN), October 7, 2009.

2911 Ibid.

2912 Ibid.

2913 "Public Image of Wharton Powerful," comments, *Commercial Appeal* (Memphis, TN), October 7, 2009.

2914 Ibid.

2915 Zack McMillan, "Candidates address controversy over vacation cash out," *Commercial Appeal* (Memphis, TN), October 8, 2009.

2916 Zack McMillan, "Ex-mayor still on campaign radar-candidates discuss whether Herenton exit benefits legal," *Commercial Appeal* (Memphis, TN), October 7, 2009.

2917 Ibid.

2918 Wiley Henry, "Candidates all have plans to take down crime," *Tri-State Defender* (Memphis, TN), October 8-14, 2009.

2919 Ibid.

2920 Ibid.

2921 Ibid.

2922 Ibid.

2923 "Memphis Mayoral Poll," *Commercial Appeal* (Memphis, TN), October 13, 2009.

2924 Ibid.

2925 Alex Doniach, "Wharton widens lead in new poll," *Commercial Appeal* (Memphis, TN), October 13, 2009.

2926 Alex Doniach, "Chumney touts message of change," *Commercial Appeal* (Memphis, TN), October 13, 2009.

2927 Ibid.

2928 Ibid.

2929 Ibid.

2930 Ibid.

2931 Ibid.

2932 Viewpoint, Otis Sanford, "Young people aren't invested in mayoral race," *Commercial Appeal* (Memphis, TN), October 11, 2009.

2933 Ibid.

2934 Ibid.

2935 Ibid.

2936 Ibid.

2937 Ibid.

2938 Zack McMillan, "Mayoral rivals make ready for City Hall—leading candidates starting to plan quick transition after election," *Commercial Appeal* (Memphis, TN), October 14, 2009; Zack McMillan, "Aiming at 'Goliath'," *Commercial Appeal* (Memphis, TN), October 15, 2009.

2939 Zack McMillan, "Mayoral rivals make ready for City Hall- leading candidates starting to plan quick transition after election," *Commercial Appeal* (Memphis, TN), October 14, 2009.

2940 Ibid.

2941 Zack McMillan, "Aiming at Goliath," *Commercial Appeal* (Memphis, TN), October 15, 2009.

2942 Ibid.

2943 Ibid.

2944 John Branston, "[City Beat] Was Wharton Out of the Loop?" *Memphis Flyer,* August 13, 2004; Jackson Baker, "Tom Jones Departs Leaving Shockwaves," *Memphis Flyer,* August 18, 2004.

2945 Zack McMillan, "Aiming at Goliath," *Commercial Appeal* (Memphis, TN), October 15, 2009.

2946 Ibid.

2947 Jackson Baker, "Signs of change," *Memphis Flyer,* October 8-14, 2009.

2948 Ibid.

2949 Ibid.

2950 Ibid.

2951 Ibid.

2952 "How 'Stronger Together' Became Clinton's Response to 'Making America Great Again'," *NPR,* August 8, 2016.

2953 Jackson Baker, "Signs of Change," *Memphis Flyer,* October 8-14, 2009.

2954 Ibid.

2955 Ibid.

2956 Ibid.

2957 Ibid.

2958 *WREG News, Channel 3,* (Memphis, TN) September 17, 2009, 10pm.

2959 Olive Beaupre' Miller, *The Book House for Children (1920).*

2960 Editorial, "The game's on; are you in?" *Commercial Appeal* (Memphis, TN), October 15, 2009.

2961 Ibid.

2962 Ibid.

2963 Ibid.

2964 Ibid.

2965 Alex Doniach, "Hot for AC," *Commercial Appeal* (Memphis, TN), October 16, 2009.

2966 Ibid.

2967 Zack McMillan, "Wharton's support eclipses polls," *Commercial Appeal* (Memphis, TN), October 16, 2009.

2968 Ibid.; "GOP ahead in local spending," *Commercial Appeal* (Memphis, TN), July 28, 2014.

2969 Alex Doniach, "Hot for AC," *Commercial Appeal* (Memphis, TN), October 16, 2009.

2970 Zack McMillan, "Wharton's support eclipses polls," *Commercial Appeal* (Memphis, TN), October 16, 2009.

2971 Ibid.

2972 Ibid.; Cartoon by Dale Crum, *Commercial Appeal* (Memphis, TN), October 16, 2009; Jason Terrell, Cartoon, *Commercial Appeal* (Memphis, TN), October 5, 2003.

2973 Daniel Connolly, "County mayor vacancy tips dominoes," *Commercial Appeal* (Memphis, TN), October 16, 2009.

2974 Jackson Baker, "Wharton Responds Testily to Joe Ford's Criticism of 'Former' County Administration," *Memphis Flyer,* November 12, 2009.

2975 Ibid.

2976 Ibid.

2977 Mary Cashiola, "An Education in Consolidation," *Memphis Flyer,* December 24-30, 2009.

2978 Ibid.

2979 Ibid.; Editorial, "Shooting Blanks," *Memphis Flyer,* December 24-30, 2009.

2980 Mary Cashiola, "An Education in Consolidation," *Memphis Flyer,* December 24-30, 2009.

2981 Ibid.

2982 Editorial, "Shooting Blanks," *Memphis Flyer,* December 24-30, 2009.

2983 John Branston, "Year in Review," *Memphis Flyer,* December 24-30, 2009.

2984 Ibid.

2985 "County voters send consolidation to defeat," *WMC Action News 5* (Memphis, TN), November 3, 2010.

2986 Ibid.

2987 Ibid.

2988 Bill Dries, "Federal court ruling ends consolidation quest," *Memphis Daily News,* March 24, 2014.

2989 Ibid; *Harrison Kerr Tigrett, etal v. Robert E. Cooper, in his official capacity as Attorney General for the State of Tennessee, etal.,* No. 2:10-cv-02724-STA-tmp, ECF 140, (W.D. Tenn. March 17, 2014), *"Order Granting Defendants' Motion for Summary Judgment, Granting Intervenor Defendants' Motion for Summary Judgment, and Denying Plaintiffs' Motion for Summary Judgment;"* dismissed on appeal as moot, Case No. 14-5473, ECF 148, (6th Cir., December 30, 2014), *"Opinion."*

2990 Amos Maki, "4.6 percent pay cut for Memphis city workers starts Aug. 5," *Commercial Appeal* (Memphis, TN), July 27, 2011.

2991 Ibid.

2992 Daniel Connolly, "Union lawsuit/Not on same page," *Commercial Appeal* (Memphis, TN), July 23, 2014; *American Federation of State, County, Municipal Employees Local 1733, et al v. City of Memphis,* Case No. 2:11-cv-02577-SHM-tmp, (W.D. Tenn.) (ultimately summary judgment granted for the Defendant).

2993 Viewpoint, "Police stunts cloud issue," *Commercial Appeal* (Memphis, TN), September 28, 2013.

2994 Kyle Veazey, "As Wharton turns 70, no plans to slow down," *Commercial Appeal* (Memphis, TN), August 17, 2014.

2995 Jackson Baker, "Super Tuesday in Tennessee," *Memphis Flyer,* March 1-7, 2012.

2996 Ibid.

2997 Clay Bailey, "DA fans deny tie to case," *Commercial Appeal* (Memphis, TN), April 4, 2012.

2998 Ibid.

2999 Beth Warren, "Juvenile probe cites rights, race," *Commercial Appeal* (Memphis, TN), April 27, 2012; "Investigation of the Shelby County Juvenile Court," U.S.DOJ Civil Rights Division, April 26, 2012, pg. 1.

3000 "Investigation of the Shelby County Juvenile Court," U.S. DOJ Civil Rights Division, April 26, 2012, pg. 2.

3001 Ibid, pg. 2.

3002 Ibid, pg. 2.

3003 Jackson Baker, "Party Lines," *Memphis Flyer,* May 3-9, 2012.

3004 Ibid.

3005 Ibid; Editorial, Check it Out," *Memphis Flyer,* May 31-June 6, 2012.

3006 Editorial, "Check it Out," *Memphis Flyer,* May 31- June 6, 2012.

3007 Ibid.

3008 Berje Yacoubian, "A Purge Too Far," *Memphis Flyer,* June 21, 2012.

3009 Jackson Baker, "Recount in Advance?" *Memphis Flyer,* June 21, 2012.

3010 Jackson Baker, "Clear as Mud," *Memphis Flyer,* June 28-July 4, 2012.

3011 Ibid.; Jackson Baker, "What We Got Here…," *Memphis Flyer,* July 5, 2012.

3012 Jackson Baker, "Party Lines," *Memphis Flyer,* May 3-9, 2012.

3013 Editorial, "Mark Norris, Orwellian," *Memphis Flyer,* May 3-9, 2012.

3014 Jackson Baker, "The Jones Factor," *Memphis Flyer,* May 31, 2012.

3015 Ibid.

3016 *Bd. of Education of Shelby County, TN. v. Memphis City Board of Education, etal,* , No. 2:11-cv-02101-SHM-cgc, ECF 1, (W.D. Tenn. February 11, 2011).

3017 Ibid., ECF 52.

3018 Ibid.

3019 Editorial, "The Lid's Off…," *Memphis Flyer,* July 19-25, 2012.

3020 Ibid.

3021 John Branston, "Creative Confusion," *Memphis Flyer,* August 20-September 5, 2012.

3022 Ibid; *Bd. of Education of Shelby County, TN v. Memphis City Board of Education, etal,* No. 2:11-cv-02101-SHM-cjc, ECF 52, (W.D. Tenn.).

3023 Ted Evanoff, "Financial hurdles loom for city-Mayor: 'Here's where it gets tight' in Memphis," *Commercial Appeal* (Memphis, TN), July 15, 2012.

3024 Ibid.

3025 Ibid.

3026 Ibid.

3027 Otis Sanford, "Chumney bid is 'quiet' for lots of reasons," *Commercial Appeal* (Memphis, TN), May 20, 2012.

3028 Ibid.

3029 Ibid.

3030 Ibid.

3031 Ibid.

3032 Ibid.

3033 "Chumney to Take on Weirich for DA," *Fox 13 Memphis News,* May 24, 2012.

3034 Ibid.

3035 Ibid.

3036 Jackson Baker, "Chumney Gets Party Boost in D.A.'s Race," *Memphis Flyer,* May 5, 2012.

3037 Jackson Baker, "No K.O. in first Weirich-Chumney Encounter," *Memphis Flyer,* June 7-13, 2012.

3038 Often attributed to *The Prince,* by Niccolo Machieveli, and said by the character Michael Corleane in *The Godfather, Part II* (1974).

3039 Jackson Baker, "Recount in Advance," *Memphis Flyer,* June 21, 2012.

3040 Ibid.

3041 Ibid.

3042 Michael Lollar, "Chumney fundraising lacking-D.A. candidate banks on name recognition," *Commercial Appeal* (Memphis, TN), July 15, 2012.

3043 Ibid.

3044 Ibid.

3045 Ibid.

3046 Ibid.

3047 Ibid.

3048 Ibid.

3049 Ibid.

3050 "Shelby County General Election 2012 Ballot Primer," *Commercial Appeal* (Memphis, TN), July 15, 2012.

3051 Ibid.

3052 *State v. Noura Jackson,* 444 S.W. 3d 554 (Tenn. 2014).

3053 Lawrence Buser, "High court to hear Jackson appeal," *Commercial Appeal* (Memphis, TN), April 12, 2013.

3054 *State v. Noura Jackson,* 444 S.W. 3d at 585, 598 (Tenn. 2014).

3055 Jackson Baker, "News from Huddleston," *Memphis Flyer,* July 19-25, 2012.

3056 Ibid.

3057 Ibid.

3058 Beth Warren, "New tactics target gangs—Task force of agencies to intensify fight," *Commercial Appeal* (Memphis, TN), July 24, 2012.

3059 Michael Lollar, "Weirich defeats Chumney for Dist. Atty position-crossover votes propel first-time politician past veteran campaigner," *Commercial Appeal* (Memphis, TN), August 3, 2012.

3060 "Sumner law enforcement officials join Diane Black's Law and Order Coalition," *Tennessean* (Nashville, TN), October 25, 2017.

3061 Jackson Baker, "Mayor Wharton to Get Burgess Award at DNC," *Memphis Flyer,* September 14, 2012.

3062 G.W. Carver, "What they said," *Memphis Flyer,* September 13-19, 2012; *Wikipedia,* "Hell's Kitchen, Manhattan," March 7, 2021.

3063 Editorial, "Time to Fix It," *Memphis Flyer,* August 2-8, 2016.

3064 Ibid.

3065 Michael Lollar, "Weirich defeats Chumney for Dist. Atty. Position-crossover votes propel first-time politician past veteran campaigner," *Commercial Appeal* (Memphis, TN), August 3, 2012.

3066 Ibid.

3067 Ibid.

3068 Ibid.

3069 Ibid.

3070 Clay Bailey, Sara Patterson and Cindy Wolff staff writers compiled by Tom Charlier, "Elections 2012/Suburban Schools: YES—Municipalities unanimously endorse separate districts, gird for legal hurdle," *Commercial Appeal* (Memphis, TN), August 3, 2012.

3071 Jackson Baker, "Post-election," *Memphis Flyer,* August 9-15, 2012.

3072 Ibid.

3073 Jackson Baker, "Updating the Scoreboard," *Memphis Flyer,* August 23, 2012.

3074 Ibid.

3075 Jackson Baker, "Post-election," *Memphis Flyer,* August 9-15, 2012.

3076 Ibid.

3077 Jackson Baker, "FBI Launches Investigation of Holden and SCEC," *Memphis Flyer,* December 20, 2013.

3078 Ibid.

3079 Jackson Baker, "Local and National Election Preview 2012," *Memphis Flyer,* November 1-7, 2012.

3080 Toby Sells, "In the red, Memphis debt load $1.46 billion," *Commercial Appeal* (Memphis, TN), June 17, 2013.

3081 Ibid.

3082 Ibid.

3083 Isak Dinesan, *G.P. Putnam Sons,* (1937).

3084 "Out of Africa," *Mirage Enterprises,* (1985).

3085 Khushbu Shah, "New fire at Nairobi airport after large parts destroyed in massive blaze," *CNN,* August 7, 2013.

3086 Jason Strazimso, "Peace Corps halts Kenya program," *Commercial Appeal* (Memphis, TN), July 25, 2014.

3087 Ibid.

3088 Ibid.

3089 Deposition of AC Wharton, pgs. 10-12 (April 20, 2013).

3090 *Bridgett Handy Clay v. City of Memphis, etal,* No. 2:10: cv-02927-STA-tmp, Dk. No. 165, page 7 (W.D. Tenn. September 9, 2013), *Order Granting in Part, Denying in Part Defendant City of Memphis' Motion for Summary Judgment; Order Granting Defendant Cathy Porter's Motion for Summary Judgment; and Order Denying Herman Morris, Jr.'s Motion for Summary Judgment,* (hereinafter "*Clay v. City,* Order 9/19/13").

3091 *Clay v. City,* Order, 9/19/13, pgs. 10-11.

3092 Ibid, pgs. 14-15.

3093 Ibid, pgs. 16-17.

3094 Deposition of Herman Morris, April 24, 2013, pgs. 39, 42.

3095 Ibid., pgs. 39, 42-43, 53-56, 67-70, 85-87.

3096 Ibid., pgs. 70, 83, 86, 88.

3097 Ibid, pgs. 60-61.

3098 Deposition of George Little, April 24, 2013, pgs. 1,15-29; Deposition of AC Wharton, April 20, 2013, pgs. 47-50.

3099 Deposition of George Little, April 24, 2013 pgs. 1-15, 29.

3100 Deposition of Herman Morris, April 24, 2013, pgs. 79-80.

3101 Ibid.

3102 *Clay v. City*, Order, 9/19/13, pg. 19; *Handy-Clay v. City of Memphis, etal*, 695 F. 3d 531, 541 (6th Cir. 2012).

3103 Ibid.

3104 Ibid.

3105 *Clay v. City*, Order, 9/19/13, pg. 20.

3106 Ibid. at 26-27.

3107 Ibid. at 27.

3108 Ibid. at 46.

3109 Jody Callahan, "Mayor seeks review of open-records process," *Commercial Appeal* (Memphis, TN), March 31, 2015.

3110 Ibid.

3111 "Editorial: City talks up transparency, but is abysmal in releasing public records in timely fashion," *Commercial Appeal* (Memphis, TN), March 24, 2015.

3112 Jackson Baker, "Area Officials Strive for Unity at Prayer Breakfast," *Memphis Flyer*, January 1, 2014.

3113 Clay Bailey, staff reporter Samatha Bailey contributed, "Cohen calls for removal of elections chief," *Commercial Appeal* (Memphis, TN), January 2, 2014.

3114 Ibid.; Marc Perrusquia, "Feds eye election operations," *Commercial Appeal* (Memphis, TN), January 17, 2014.

3115 Viewpoint, "No confidence in election officials," *Commercial Appeal* (Memphis, TN), January 11, 2014; Daniel Connolly and Christina Wright, 'No confidence in election czar," *Commercial Appeal*, January 22, 2014.

3116 Viewpoint, "No confidence in election officials," *Commercial Appeal* (Memphis, TN), January 11, 2014.

3117 Ibid.

3118 Jackson Baker, "Slot Machine Politics," *Memphis Flyer*, May 22-28, 2014.

3119 Steve Mulroy, "Getting the Vote Right," *Memphis Flyer*, May 22-28, 2014.

3120 Ibid.

3121 Zack McMillan, "Election Commission looking at problems," *Commercial Appeal* (Memphis, TN), January 20, 2013.

3122 Editorial, "Dishonesty hurts Shelby DA's office," *Commercial Appeal* (Memphis, TN), January 14, 2014; Beth Warren, "Censure issued to Shelby asst. DA," *Commercial Appeal*, January 11, 2014.

3123 Editorial, "Dishonesty hurts Shelby DA's office," *Commercial Appeal* (Memphis, TN), January 14, 2014.

3124 Toby Sells, "The Prosecution Rests," *Memphis Flyer*, January 30, 2014.

3125 Beth Warren, "Censure issued to Shelby asst. DA," *Commercial Appeal* (Memphis, TN), January 11, 2014.

3126 Ibid.

3127 Viewpoint, "Dishonesty hurts Shelby DA's office," *Commercial Appeal* (Memphis, TN), January 14, 2014.

3128 Toby Sells, "Public Rebuke," *Memphis Flyer*, January 16-22, 2014.

3129 Toby Sells, "The Prosecution Rests," *Memphis Flyer*, January 30-February 5, 2014.

3130 Beth Warren, "Rimmer trial gets special prosecutor," *Commercial Appeal* (Memphis, TN), January 18, 2014.

3131 Kerry Crawford, "Clear the Backlog!" *Memphis Flyer*, January 16-22, 2014.

3132 Marc Perrusquia, "Rape-kit backlog grew despite grant," *Commercial Appeal* (Memphis, TN), January 26, 2014.

3133 Ibid.

3134 Marian Bacon, Letter to Editor, "Stand up for women victimized by violence," *Commercial Appeal* (Memphis, TN), February 7, 2014.

3135 Carissa Shaw, Esq., Special to TSD, "Rape kit backlog a 'systemic failure,' says Wharton," *Tri-State Defender* (Memphis, TN), February 13-19, 2014; Bill Dries, "Backlog Backlash," *Memphis News*, March 21-27, 2014.

3136 Bill Dries, "Backlog Backlash," *Memphis News*, March 21-27, 2014.

3137 Marc Perrusquia, "CA Investigation: Untested Rape Kits/DID NOT ACT," *Commercial Appeal* (Memphis, TN), March 23, 2014.

3138 Editorial, "Rape-kit backlog triggers 2nd lawsuit," *Commercial Appeal* (Memphis, TN), March 28, 2014; *Meaghan Ybos, et al v. City of Memphis, et al*, Case No. 2:14-cv-02211-JTF-cjc, (W. D. Tenn.)

3139 Ibid.

3140 Editorial, "Rape kit fiasco is a sad chapter in crime fight," *Commercial Appeal* (Memphis, TN), March 23, 2014.

3141 Ibid.

3142 Richard Locker, "TBI: State storing 9,000 rape kits," *Commercial Appeal* (Memphis, TN), September 3, 2014.

3143 Carissa Shaw, Esq., Special to TSD, "Rape kit backlog a 'systemic failure,' says Wharton," *Tri-State Defender* (Memphis, TN), February 13-19, 2014; AC Wharton and Sarah Torfte, "Special to Viewpoint" "End to rape kit backlog will serve healing," *Commercial Appeal* (Memphis, TN), February 18, 2014.

3144 Carissa Shaw, Esq., Special to TSD, "Rape kit backlog a 'systemic failure,' says Wharton," *Tri-State Defender* (Memphis, TN), February 13-19, 2014; Michael Collins, reporter Daniel Connolly contributed, "City could get more funds for rape kits," *Commercial Appeal* (Memphis, TN), May 31, 2014; Marc Perrusquia, "Wharton to seek another $1M from council," *Commercial Appeal* (Memphis, TN), February 13, 2014.

3145 Letter to Editor, Peter White, "Rape kit fiasco calls for leadership upgrade," *Commercial Appeal* (Memphis, TN), February 20, 2014.

3146 Bill Dries, "Backlog Backlash," *Memphis News*, March 21-27, 2014; Marc Perrusquia, "Wharton to seek another $1M from council," *Commercial Appeal* (Memphis, TN), February 13, 2014.

3147 Samantha Bryson, staff reporter Christina M. Wright contributed, "MPD making strides in rape kit backlog," *Commercial Appeal* (Memphis,

TN), April 17, 2014.

3148 Ibid.; "State lawmakers remove statute of limitations on rape," *Commercial Appeal* (Memphis, TN), April 10, 2014.

3149 Deborah Clubb, "Facing Reality," *Commercial Appeal* (Memphis, TN), June 24, 2018.

3150 Ibid.

3151 Linda A. Moore, "Man pleads guilty to rapes after backlogged rape kits tested," *Commercial Appeal* (Memphis, TN), September 17, 2018.

3152 Phillip Jackson, "DNA ties Memphis man to unsolved rape," *Commercial Appeal* (Memphis, TN), October 17, 2018.

3153 Editorial, "Aggressively seeking justice," *Commercial Appeal* (Memphis TN), February 14, 2014.

3154 *Jane Doe, et al v. City of Memphis, et al*, Case No. CT-003516-14, Shelby County Circuit Court; *Doe v. City of Memphis*, Case No. 13-cv-3002, (W.D. Tenn.)

3155 Jackson Baker, "Ready to Rumble," *Memphis Flyer*, February 13-19, 2014.

3156 Ibid.

3157 Ibid.

3158 Ibid.

3159 Wiley Henry, "Caution: 'Dems' changing lanes," *Tri-State Defender* (Memphis, TN), February 13-19, 2014.

3160 Ibid.

3161 Ibid.

3162 Ibid.

3163 Samantha Bryson, "Trial & Error," *Commercial Appeal* (Memphis, TN), September 7, 2014; *State v. Noura Jackson*, 444 S.W. 3d 554 (Tenn. 2014).

3164 Ibid; Ibid. at 589.

3165 Samantha Bryson, "Trial & Error," *Commercial Appeal* (Memphis, TN), September 7, 2014.

3166 Ibid; *State v. Noura Jackson*, 444 S.W. 3d 554, fn. 49 (Tenn. 2014).

3167 Ibid; Ibid.

3168 Ibid; Ibid.

3169 Samantha Bryson, "D.A. wants off Jackson retrial," *Commercial Appeal* (Memphis, TN), January 13, 2015.

3170 Samantha Bryson, "Attys. Focus on lost

papers," *Commercial Appeal* (Memphis, TN), November 22, 2014; Toby Sells, "The Brady Bunch," *Memphis Flyer,* January 15-21, 2015; *State v. Braswell,* No. W2016-00912-CCA-R3-PC (Tenn. Crim. App. 2018).

3171 *State v. Braswell,* No. W2016-00912-CCA-R3-PC (Tenn. Crim. App. 2018).

3172 Ibid.

3173 Ibid.

3174 Toby Sells, "The Brady Bunch," *Memphis Flyer,* January 15-21, 2105.

3175 Samantha Bryson, "Attys. Focus on lost papers," *Commercial Appeal* (Memphis, TN), November 22, 2014; *State v. Braswell,* No. W2016-00912-CCA-R3-PC (Tenn. Crim. App. 2018).

3176 Samantha Bryson, "Improper closing negates sexual battery verdict," *Commercial Appeal* (Memphis, TN), November 25, 2014; *State v. Gossett,* No. W2013-011120-CCA-R3-CD (Tenn. Crim. App. 2014).

3177 Ibid; Ibid.

3178 Les Smith, "Dubious Justice," *Memphis Flyer,* October 6, 2014.

3179 Katie Fretland, "I have chosen to fight this," *Commercial Appeal* (Memphis, TN), January 30, 2016.

3180 Ibid.

3181 Ibid.

3182 Ibid.

3183 Katie Fretland, "Weirich takes reprimand," *Commercial Appeal* (Memphis, TN), March 21, 2017.

3184 Jody Callahan, "TV Judge Brown ponders run for DA," *Commercial Appeal* (Memphis, TN), February 11, 2014.

3185 Ibid.

3186 Jackson Baker, "Gripes, Groans, and Grudge Matches," *Memphis Flyer,* July 24-30, 2014.

3187 Ibid.

3188 Ibid.

3189 Joe Weinberg, "Time to replace Shelby County voting machines," *Memphis Flyer,* August 21, 2014.

3190 Ibid.

3191 Kyle Veazey, "Election panel certifies results from Aug. 7 voting," *Commercial*

Appeal (Memphis, TN), August 26, 2014.

3192 Ibid.; Kyle Veazey, "9 candidates claim election fraud in lawsuit," *Commercial Appeal* (Memphis, TN), September 5, 2014.

3193 Thomas Bailey, "Voters' verdict: Weirich over TV's Joe Brown," *Commercial Appeal* (Memphis, TN), August 8, 2014; Kyle Veazey, "Winners, losers appraise election," *Commercial Appeal,* August 9, 2014; *Joseph Brown, etal v. Shelby County Election Commission,* No. CH-14-1324-2, Shelby County Chancery Court, "*Complaint,*" September 2, 2014.

3194 Jackson Baker, "Poor Relations," *Memphis Flyer,* January 30-February 5, 2014.

3195 Toby Sells, "The Pension Crisis," *Memphis Flyer,* April 10, 2014.

3196 "Coffee Break" "City needs money to grow projects," *Commercial Appeal* (Memphis, TN), May 24, 2014.

3197 Kyle Veazey, "Chamber lobbies for pension reform," *Commercial Appeal* (Memphis, TN), April 28, 2014.

3198 Zack McMillan, "Norris balancing varied legislative interests," *Commercial Appeal* (Memphis, TN), February 8, 2014.

3199 Ibid.

3200 Danny Todd, Letter to Editor, "City created this mess," *Commercial Appeal* (Memphis, TN), February 9, 2014.

3201 Thomas Malone, Jr., Special to Viewpoint, "Pension politics threaten our public safety," *Commercial Appeal* (Memphis, TN), January 19, 2014.

3202 Daniel Connolly, "Mayor: 'Get out of retiree health care'," *Commercial Appeal* (Memphis, TN), April 12, 2014.

3203 Ibid.

3204 Ibid.; Daniel Connolly, "Tough choices," *Commercial Appeal* (Memphis, TN), April 16, 2014.

3205 Daniel Connolly, "Questions and answers about retiree health insurance," *Commercial Appeal* (Memphis, TN), May 19, 2014; Daniel Connolly, "Changes could cost retirees, employees," *Commercial Appeal,* May 18, 2014.

3206 Daniel Connolly, "City Council hears insurance details," *Commercial Appeal* (Memphis, TN), May 21, 2014; Daniel

Connolly, "Questions and answers about retiree health insurance," *Commercial Appeal,* May 19, 2014.

3207 Daniel Connolly, "Questions and answers about retiree health insurance," *Commercial Appeal* (Memphis, TN), May 19, 2014.

3208 Editorial, "Retirees will have viable health insurance options," *Commercial Appeal* (Memphis, TN), May 25, 2014.

3209 Editorial, "Different figures can't be used as an excuse not to fix pension plan," *Commercial Appeal* (Memphis, TN), May 11, 2014.

3210 Ibid.

3211 Daniel Connolly, "Price to 'play'," *Commercial Appeal* (Memphis, TN), July 7, 2014.

3212 Ibid.

3213 Ibid.

3214 Ted Evanoff, "Area job growth remains sluggish," *Commercial Appeal* (Memphis, TN), June 7, 2014.

3215 Toby Sells, "The Pension Crisis," *Memphis Flyer,* April 10-16, 2014; Timothy Martin, "Pension Fight Comes to a Head in Memphis," *Wall Street Journal,* March 15, 2015.

3216 Toby Sells, "The Pension Crisis," *Memphis Flyer,* April 10-16, 2014.

3217 Ibid.

3218 Ibid.

3219 Ibid.

3220 Ibid.

3221 Daniel Connolly and Christina M. Wright, "Potholes to poverty," *Commercial Appeal* (Memphis, TN), January 30, 2014.

3222 Wendi Thomas, "Great divide," *Commercial Appeal* (Memphis, TN), April 6, 2014.

3223 Editorial, "Sweet Adventures," *Memphis Flyer,* May 15-21, 2014; Wendi Thomas, "From Poverty to Possibility," *Commercial Appeal* (Memphis, TN), May 5, 2014.

3224 Ibid.; Ibid.

3225 Ibid.; Ibid.

3226 Editorial, "Tackling poverty at its enduring core," *Commercial Appeal* (Memphis, TN), May 8, 2014.

3227 Editorial, "AC Wharton for mayor," *Commercial Appeal* (Memphis, TN), September 29, 2009.

3228 "Memphis Poverty Fact Sheet," pg. 6, Updated 2017, Dr. Elena Delavega, Dept. of Social Work, University of Memphis.

3229 Wendi C. Thomas, "From Poverty to Possibility," *Commercial Appeal* (Memphis, TN), May 5, 2014.

3230 Editorial, "Partners against crime achieve success to build on," *Commercial Appeal* (Memphis, TN), May 11, 2015.

3231 Toby Sells, "Few Rebuked After Blue Flu, Red Rash," *Memphis Flyer,* August 21, 2014; Daniel Connolly and Kyle Veazey, "Council Approves Hard Budget Cuts," *Commercial Appeal* (Memphis, TN), June 18, 2014; Kyle Veazey, "Ford's confident council voted right," *Commercial Appeal,* June 19, 2014.

3232 Toby Sells, "Few Rebuked After Blue Flu, Red Rash," *Memphis Flyer,* August 21, 2014; Timberly Moore, "Sick calls stretch budget," *Commercial Appeal* (Memphis, TN), May 23, 2014; Jonathan Acapriel, "Blue flu? 181 police officers call in sick," *Commercial Appeal,* July 6, 2014.

3233 Jody Callahan, "More than 500 out; no time off allowed," *Commercial Appeal* (Memphis, TN), July 8, 2014; Dr Sybil Mitchell, "'Sick' police and a city on alert," *Tri-State Defender* (Memphis, TN), July 10-16, 2014.

3234 Jody Callahan, "City cancels police sick-leave policy," *Commercial Appeal* (Memphis, TN), July 9, 2014.

3235 Jody Callahan, "4 trucks idled as more firefighters call in sick," *Commercial Appeal* (Memphis, TN), July 13, 2014.

3236 Kyle Veazey, "Wharton's challenge toughest of his career," *Commercial Appeal* (Memphis, TN), July 9, 2014.

3237 Richard Locker, "Haslam offers extra state troopers," *Commercial Appeal* (Memphis, TN), July 9, 2014.

3238 Timberly Moore and Daniel Connolly, "In 'blue flu,' 'red rash' cases subside," *Commercial Appeal* (Memphis, TN), July 20, 2014.

3239 Ibid.

3240 Jody Callahan, "City Council seeks ideas," *Commercial Appeal* (Memphis, TN), July 7, 2014.

3241 Daniel Connolly, "Proposal: Raise sales tax to fund pension," *Commercial Appeal* (Memphis, TN), July 8, 2014; Daniel Connolly and Kyle Veazey, "Sales tax idea can end sick-out," *Commercial Appeal,* July 12, 2014.

3242 Daniel Connolly, "Open to suggestions," *Commercial Appeal* (Memphis, TN), July 16, 2014; Mike Matthews, "Proposals for Solving Health Care Crisis Presented to Council," *ABC Eyewitness News 24* (Memphis, TN), July 15, 2014.

3243 Jackson Baker, "Former Council Members Chumney and Stout-Mitchell Offer Plan to Resolve City Impasse," *Memphis Flyer,* July 9, 2014.

3244 Daniel Connolly, "Changes don't affect Wharton," *Commercial Appeal* (Memphis, TN), October 5, 2014; Daniel Connolly and Kyle Veazey, "Council Approves Hard budget Cuts," *Commercial Appeal* (Memphis, TN), June 18, 2014.

3245 Daniel Connolly, "Changes don't affect Wharton," *Commercial Appeal* (Memphis, TN), October 5, 2014.

3246 Daniel Connolly and Kyle Veazey, "Council Approves Hard Budget Cuts," *Commercial Appeal* (Memphis, TN), June 18, 2014.

3247 Ibid.

3248 Jody Callahan, "Crime forum turns against government," *Commercial Appeal* (Memphis, TN), June 20, 2014.

3249 Editorial, "Bad breaks?" *Commercial Appeal* (Memphis, TN), July 1, 2014.

3250 Ibid.

3251 Ted Evanoff, "City desperately needs a financial plan," *Commercial Appeal* (Memphis, TN), February 22, 2015; Editorial, "Pension fund's debt can't get lost in protests," *Commercial Appeal* (Memphis, TN), July 13, 2014.

3252 Robert Ariail, Viewpoint, *Commercial Appeal* (Memphis, TN), July 13, 2014.

3253 Editorial, "Bitter medicine proposed to cure the city's debt," *Commercial Appeal* (Memphis, TN), April 20, 2014; Editorial, "Raising taxes vs. preserving city benefits," *Commercial Appeal,* June 21, 2014.

3254 Ted Evanoff, "Memphis in need of a clear strategy," *Commercial Appeal* (Memphis, TN), September 21, 2014.

3255 Jane Roberts, "Armstrong critiques council vote," *Commercial Appeal* (Memphis, TN), June 21, 2014.

3256 Ibid.

3257 Ibid.

3258 Ibid; Katie Fretland and Kyle Veazey, "$2M 'safety net' OK'd," *Commercial Appeal* (Memphis, TN), July 2, 2014.

3259 Kyle Veazey, "Expert: No gain from 401(k)," *Commercial Appeal* (Memphis, TN), July 2, 2014.

3260 Kyle Veazey, "Council quizzes budget experts," *Commercial Appeal* (Memphis, TN), July 3, 2014.

3261 David Waters, columnist, "City's fiscal mess also is a moral obligation," *Commercial Appeal* (Memphis, TN), July 23, 2014.

3262 Ibid.

3263 Toby Sells, "The Battle Over Benefits," *Memphis Flyer,* September 11-17, 2014.

3264 Ibid.

3265 Daniel Connolly, "Council appears unlikely to reverse cuts," *Commercial Appeal* (Memphis, TN), September 11, 2014.

3266 Robert Reich, Commentary, "Detroit's a model of U.S. divide," *Commercial Appeal* (Memphis, TN), September 14, 2014.

3267 Daniel Connolly, "Vote restores some benefits," *Commercial Appeal* (Memphis, TN), September 17, 2014.

3268 Ibid.

3269 Bill Dries, "Council Broods over 'Key Members'," *Memphis Daily News,* October 10-16, 2014.

3270 Ibid.

3271 Ibid.

3272 Daniel Connolly, "Workers to bear riskier pension," *Commercial Appeal* (Memphis, TN), December 3, 2014; Daniel Connolly, "'Betrayal' confusion themes of pension talks," *Commercial Appeal,* December 17, 2014.

3273 Daniel Connolly, "Council backs pension alternative," *Commercial Appeal* (Memphis, TN), October 22, 2014.

3274 Daniel Connolly, "Council members can stay in old plan," *Commercial Appeal* (Memphis, TN), December 23, 2014.

3275 Ibid.

3276 Editorial, "Pension deal is not ideal, but is a step forward," *Commercial Appeal* (Memphis, TN), February 22, 2015.

3277 Daniel Connolly, "Workers to bear riskier pension," *Commercial Appeal* (Memphis, TN), December 3, 2014; George Brown, Stephanie Scurlock, "City of Memphis employees suing over pension," *WREG News Channel 3* (Memphis, TN), November 11, 2015.

3278 Editorial, "Behind budget smiles, big fiscal issues remain," *Commercial Appeal* (Memphis, TN), June 12, 2016; Ryan Poe, "Public safety, paving, pensions guide budget," *Commercial Appeal* (Memphis, TN), April 26, 2016.

3279 Kyle Veazey, "Chumney among names for state Senate seat," *Commercial Appeal* (Memphis, TN), September 3, 2014.

3280 Ibid.

3281 Peggy Burch, "Sara Kyle gets nod from Democrats," *Commercial Appeal* (Memphis, TN), September 9, 2014.

3282 Kyle Veazey, "No shortage of mayoral hopefuls in wings to challenge Wharton," *Commercial Appeal* (Memphis, TN), September 26, 2014.

3283 Ibid.

3284 Ibid.; Kyle Veazey, "Road to City Hall goes through Poplar 'A' list," *Commercial Appeal* (Memphis, TN), October 31, 2014.

3285 Daniel Connolly and Maria Ines Zamudio, "Memphis' thin blue line gets thinner," *Commercial Appeal* (Memphis, TN), November 9, 2014.

3286 Kevin McKenzie, "'Long way to go'," *Commercial Appeal* (Memphis, TN), November 9, 2014; Viewpoint, "Shift in strategies could help grow minority firms," *Commercial Appeal* (Memphis, TN), June 15, 2014.

3287 Otis Sanford, columnist, "Wharton recovers at end of tough year," *Commercial Appeal* (Memphis, TN), December 21, 2014.

3288 Chris Davis, "Fly on the Wall 1330,"*Memphis Flyer,* August 21, 2014.

3289 Editorial, "Spike in rates of violent crimes leaves questions," *Commercial Appeal* (Memphis, TN), August 26, 2014.

3290 Ibid.; Yolanda James, "A Thousand Words," *Commercial Appeal* (Memphis, TN), October 5, 2014.

3291 Fredrick Harris, "A Moment or a Movement?" *Commercial Appeal* (Memphis, TN), September 7, 2014.

3292 Editorial, "Citizens want immediate action on mobs," *Commercial Appeal* (Memphis, TN), October 5, 2014.

3293 Ibid.; Yolanda James and Jody Callahan, "Second teen mob investigated," *Commercial Appeal* (Memphis, TN), September 30, 2014.

3294 Louis Goggans, "Memphis Gang Problem," *Memphis Flyer,* September 18-24, 2014.

3295 Daniel Connolly, "Agenda: Prevent youth crime," *Commercial Appeal* (Memphis, TN), November 26, 2014.

3296 Viewpoint, "Curbing supply of illegal guns can reduce violence," *Commercial Appeal* (Memphis, TN), March 16, 2014.

3297 Otis Sanford, columnist, "Adult mob fails to see rehab needs of juveniles," *Commercial Appeal* (Memphis, TN), November 2, 2014.

3298 Katie Fretland and Timberly Moore, "Violent crime rises in city and county, report shows," *Commercial Appeal* (Memphis, TN), August 23, 2014; AC Wharton, Special to Viewpoint, "Battle against crime can't be lost," *Commercial Appeal,* October 12, 2014.

3299 Viewpoint, "New, solid ideas needed to curb youth violence," *Commercial Appeal* (Memphis, TN), September 14, 2014.

3300 Viewpoint, "The time is right for dash cameras," *Commercial Appeal* (Memphis, TN), August 27, 2014; Daniel Connolly, "Police dash cameras coming," *Commercial Appeal,* August 23, 2014; Daniel Connolly, staff reporter Yolanda Jones contributed, Viewpoint, "More eyes on police, public," *Commercial Appeal,* September 26, 2014.

3301 Editorial, "Violent crime countywide continues rising," *Commercial Appeal* (Memphis, TN), September 20, 2014.

3302 Ibid.

3303 Wayne Risher, "City's image under cloud," *Commercial Appeal* (Memphis, TN), September 14, 2014.

3304 Randy Keller, Letter to Editor, "Recipe for disaster," *Commercial Appeal* (Memphis, TN), September 9, 2014.

3305 Viewpoint, "Image issue is more about how we see ourselves," *Commercial Appeal* (Memphis, TN), September 16, 2014.

3306 Ibid.

3307 Jackson Baker, "Lowery's Breakfast Boner," *Memphis Flyer,* January 8-14, 2015; Kyle Veazey, "Lighting the fuse," *Commercial Appeal* (Memphis, TN), January 2, 2015.

3308 Jackson Baker, "Lowery's Breakfast Boner," *Memphis Flyer,* January 8-14, 2015.

3309 Ibid.; Kyle Veazey, "Breakfast praise is an awkward start to Memphis mayor's race," *Commercial Appeal* (Memphis, TN), January 2, 2015.

3310 Ibid.; Ibid.

3311 Editorial, "Mayor's call for raises was beyond reason," *Commercial Appeal* (Memphis, TN), January 3, 2015.

3312 Editorial, "EDGE review would be good for PILOT process," *Commercial Appeal* (Memphis, TN), November 29, 2015.

3313 Ibid.

3314 AC Wharton, Special to the CA, "King holiday continues to call us to action," *Commercial Appeal* (Memphis, TN), January 11, 2015.

3315 Kyle Veazey, "Strickland joins mayor's race, ready for a fight," *Commercial Appeal* (Memphis, TN), January 16, 2015.

3316 Ibid.; Kyle Veazey, "What's next for mayoral sprint?" *Commercial Appeal* (Memphis, TN), January 16, 2015.

3317 Kyle Veazey, "Strickland joins mayor's race, ready for a fight," *Commercial Appeal* (Memphis, TN), January 16, 2015.

3318 Kyle Veazey, "What's next for mayoral sprint?" *Commercial Appeal* (Memphis, TN), January 16, 2015.

3319 Ibid.

3320 Bianca Phillips, "Memphis Shelby County Crime Commission Hires Harold Collins," *Memphis Flyer,* September 8, 2016.

3321 Editorial, "Employee raises not the best use of county funds," *Commercial Appeal* (Memphis, TN), January 15, 2015.

3322 Ibid.

3323 Ryan Poe, "Mayor takes tax hike off the table," *Commercial Appeal* (Memphis, TN), February 8, 2015; Editorial, "Refinancing plan is a reminder of city's fiscal woes," *Commercial Appeal,* February 21, 2015.

3324 Ryan Poe, "Mayor takes tax hike off the table," *Commercial Appeal* (Memphis, TN), February 8, 2015.

3325 Ibid.

3326 Editorial, "Refinancing plan is a reminder of city's fiscal woes," *Commercial Appeal* (Memphis, TN), February 21, 2015.

3327 Ibid.; Ryan Poe "City will restructure large debt to plug budget holes," *Commercial Appeal* (Memphis, TN), March 18, 2015.

3328 Ryan Poe, "City will restructure large debt to plug budget holes," *Commercial Appeal* (Memphis, TN), March 18, 2015.

3329 Editorial, "Refinancing plan is a reminder of city's fiscal woes," *Commercial Appeal* (Memphis, TN), February 21, 2015.

3330 Ryan Poe, staff reporters Yolanda Jones & David Waters contributed, "Man found dead in cold," *Commercial Appeal* (Memphis, TN) February 19, 2015.

3331 Katie Fretland, "Potholes season keeping city busy," *Commercial Appeal* (Memphis, TN), February 25, 2015.

3332 Kyle Veazey and Ryan Poe, "Shake-up in works for Wharton cabinet," *Commercial Appeal* (Memphis, TN), March 3, 2015.

3333 Ibid.

3334 Ibid.; Richard Locker and Ryan Poe, "Mayor's hiring of Sammons on hold," *Commercial Appeal* (Memphis, TN), March 10, 2015.

3335 Wayne Risher, "Sammons may need one more briefcase," *Commercial Appeal* (Memphis, TN), March 7, 2015.

3336 Ibid.

3337 Ibid.

3338 Kyle Veazey, "Shake up in works for Wharton cabinet," *Commercial Appeal* (Memphis, TN), March 3, 2015.

3339 Kyle Veazey and Wayne Risher, "Mayor bats back CAO critics," *Commercial Appeal* (Memphis, TN), March 12, 2015.

3340 Ibid.

3341 Les Smith, "The Natural," *Memphis Flyer,* March 12-18, 2015.

3342 Ibid.

3343 Ibid.

3344 Ibid.

3345 Ryan Poe, "Sammons taking post as city CAO," *Commercial Appeal* (Memphis, TN), March 31, 2015.

3346 Ibid.

3347 Ibid.

3348 Ibid.

3349 Ibid.

3350 Ryan Poe and Kyle Veazey, "Council likely to approve new CAO," *Commercial Appeal* (Memphis, TN), April 1, 2015.

3351 Ibid.

3352 Jackson Baker, "The Beat Goes ON," *Memphis Flyer,* April 9-15, 2015.

3353 Kyle Veazey, "Collins' hat in crowded ring for job at City Hall," *Commercial Appeal* (Memphis, TN), April 9, 2015.

3354 Ibid.

3355 Matthew Daly, "At least 101 women will serve in new Congress; one is just 30," *Commercial Appeal* (Memphis, TN), November 6, 2014.

3356 Kyle Veazey, "Minorities, Democrats in short supply at legislature," *Commercial Appeal* (Memphis, TN), January 9, 2015.

3357 Ibid.

3358 Jackson Baker, "Healthcare Showdown in Nashville!" *Memphis Flyer,* January 29-February 4, 2015.

3359 Robert Arail, "Viewpoint," *Commercial Appeal* (Memphis, TN), April 5, 2015.

3360 Ibid.

3361 Ibid.

3362 Kyle Veazey, "Giving in 1Q tops $300k," *Commercial Appeal* (Memphis, TN), April 13, 2015.

3363 Ken Thomas and Lisa Lerer, "Clinton back in running for White House," *Commercial Appeal* (Memphis, TN) April 13, 2015.

3364 Editorial, "De-annexation bill laden with damage for municipalities," *Commercial Appeal* (Memphis, TN), April 16, 2015.

3365 Ibid.

3366 Thomas Bailey Jr. and Ryan Poe, "Gaining steam," *Commercial Appeal* (Memphis, TN), April 18, 2015.

3367 Marc Perrusquia and Grant Smith, "Our Financial Mess," *Commercial Appeal* (Memphis, TN), April 19, 2015.

3368 Ibid.

3369 Ibid.

3370 Ibid.; Marc Perrusquia and Grant Smith, "Our Debt," *Commercial Appeal* (Memphis, TN), April 20, 2015.

3371 Marc Perrusquia and Grant Smith, "Our Financial Mess," *Commercial Appeal* (Memphis, TN), April 19, 2015.

3372 Marc Perrusquia, "Our Debt," *Commercial Appeal* (Memphis, TN), April 20, 2015.

3373 Ibid.

3374 Ibid.; Marc Perrusquia, "Our Financial Mess," *Commercial Appeal* (Memphis, TN), April 19, 2015.

3375 Editorial, "It's time to shape Memphis' future," *Commercial Appeal* (Memphis, TN), April 28, 2015.

3376 Ibid.

3377 Marc Perrusquia and Grant Smith, "Our Financial Mess," *Commercial Appeal* (Memphis, TN), April 19, 2015.

3378 Ibid.

3379 Ibid.

3380 Ibid.

3381 Marc Perrusquia, "You had a lot of people voting with their feet," *Commercial Appeal* (Memphis, TN), April 19, 2015.

3382 John Branston, "12 Years On," *Memphis Flyer,* September 11, 2003.

3383 Marc Perrusquia, "You had a lot of people voting with their feet," *Commercial Appeal* (Memphis, TN), April 19, 2015.

3384 Ibid.

3385 Ibid.

3386 "An Issue that Roars," *Memphis Business Journal,* March 10, 2002.

3387 Marc Perrusquia, "We created disposable communities," *Commercial Appeal* (Memphis, TN), April 19, 2015.

3388 Ibid.

3389 Ibid.

3390 Ibid.

3391 Ibid.

3392 Marc Perrusquia, "Our Debt," *Commercial Appeal* (Memphis, TN), April 20, 2015.

3393 Ibid.

3394 Ibid.

3395 Ibid.

3396 Ibid.

3397 Ibid.

3398 Marc Perrusquia and Daniel Connolly, "The Big Picture: Pensions," *Commercial Appeal* (Memphis, TN), April 21, 2015.

3399 Ibid.

3400 Ibid.

3401 Ibid.

3402 Ibid.

3403 Ibid.

3404 Ibid.

3405 Jamel Major, "Council amendment would close loophole in city's pension plan," *WMC Action News 5* (Memphis, TN), 2009.

3406 Ryan Poe, "Wharton seeks hike in spending," *Commercial Appeal* (Memphis, TN), April 22, 2015.

3407 Ibid.

3408 Beth Warren, "The Big Picture: MPD Spending," *Commercial Appeal* (Memphis, TN), April 23, 2015.

3409 Ibid.

3410 Bill Dries, "Wharton and Strickland Roll Out Anti-Crime Platforms," *Memphis Daily News*, September 11-17, 2015.

3411 Kyle Veazey, "The Pain Ahead," *Commercial Appeal* (Memphis, TN), April 26, 2015.

3412 Jackson Baker, "A Two-Man Mayor's Race?" *Memphis Flyer*, July 2-8, 2015.

3413 Jordan Danelz, Letter to Editor, "What They Said," *Memphis Flyer*, July 9-15, 2015.

3414 Ibid.

3415 Bianca Phillips, "In Her Shoes," *Memphis Flyer*, June 25-July 1, 2015.

3416 Ibid.

3417 Ibid.

3418 Jackson Baker, "Whalum Goes for Super-District Council Seat, Not Mayor," *Memphis Flyer*, July 15, 2015.

3419 Wayne Carter, "Mike Williams endorsed by several, but not all unions," *WREG News Channel 3* (Memphis, TN), August 20, 2015.

3420 Jackson Baker, "Four-Handed Race, Four-Handed Debate," *Memphis Flyer*, August 20, 2015.

3421 Kyle Veazey, "Numbers don't lie: Anyone could win," *Commercial Appeal* (Memphis, TN), August 8, 2015.

3422 Ibid.

3423 *WREG News Channel 3*, (Memphis, TN), September 17, 2009, 10pm.

3424 Jackson Baker, "Cohen Credited with Influence on Iran Deal, Endorses AC Wharton," *Memphis Flyer*, September 10, 2015.

3425 CA Poll, August 8, 2015.

3426 Jackson Baker, "Coattails—and More," *Memphis Flyer*, September 10-16, 2015; Bill Dries, "Poll Shows Wharton With Slim Lead in Mayor's Race," *Memphis Daily News*, September 11-17, 2015; Jackson Baker, "Close, But No Cigars," *Memphis Flyer*, September 17-23, 2015.

3427 Jackson Baker, "Coattails—and More," *Memphis Flyer*, September 10-16, 2015.

3428 Bianca Phillips, "Carter Malone and Taser International cancel controversial contract," *Memphis Flyer*, October 1, 2015.

3429 Ibid.; Lee Eric Smith, "Deidre Malone Speaks!" *Tri-State Defender* (Memphis, TN), October 15-21, 2015.

3430 Lee Eric Smith, "Deidre Malone Speaks!" *Tri-State Defender* (Memphis TN), October 15-21, 2015.

3431 Ryan Poe, "Mayoral Candidates campaign on radio," *Commercial Appeal* (Memphis, TN), October 7, 2015.

3432 Ibid.

3433 Bill Dries, "Collins: Conduct media mayoral debates even if Herenton, Strickland are no-shows,"*Daily Memphian*, September 6, 2019.

3434 Lee Eric Smith, "Deidre Malone Speaks!" *Tri-State Defender* (Memphis, TN), October 15-21, 2015.

3435 Ibid.

3436 Ibid.

3437 TSD Newsroom, "The way forward: A message from the board of directors of TSD's parent company," *Tri-State Defender* (Memphis, TN), December 19, 2017.

3438 Don Wade, "Memphis CFO Brian Collins 'Constantly at 50,000 Feet'," *Daily News* (Memphis, TN), January 28, 2016; Don Wade, "New Memphis COO Doug

McGowen Knows Importance of Carrying Out Orders," *Daily News,* January 14, 2016.

3439 John Branston, "Memphis Has An ED Problem," *Memphis Magazine,* October 16, 2015.

3440 Ibid.

3441 Ibid.

3442 Ibid.

3443 Ibid.

3444 Ibid.

3445 Ibid.; "Strickland thumps Wharton in Memphis mayoral race," *Tennessee Journal,* October 9, 2015.

3446 Bernal E. Smith, II, "The 2015 Memphis Municipal Election in seven lessons," *Tri-State Defender* (Memphis, TN), October 15-21, 2015.

3447 Ibid.

3448 Ibid.

3449 Joseph A. Weinberg, Special to Viewpoint, "How can we trust the accuracy of recent vote counts?" *Commercial Appeal* (Memphis, TN), November 29, 2015.

3450 Ibid.

3451 Ibid.

3452 Ibid.

3453 Bill Dries, "Shelby County Election Commission Changes Preparations Following Tabulation Issues," *Memphis Daily News,* October 27, 2015.

3454 Ibid.

3455 *Wanda Halbert v. Richard Holden, Administrator of Elections, etal,* No. CH-15-1448, Shelby County Chancery Court, (2015).

3456 *Shelby County Election Process Final Report,* January 7, 2013, pg. 5.

3457 Ibid., pg. 5.

3458 Ibid. pg. 7.

3459 "Trust But Verify," "Increasing Voter Confidence in Election Results," *Tennessee Advisory Committee on Intergovernmental Relations, Staff Report 2007,* Appendix A," Concerns Regarding Shelby County Diebold Gems Central Tabulator Administration in the August 3, 2006 Primary Election," pg. 75.

3460 Ibid., pg. 75.

3461 Ibid., pg. 75.

3462 Ibid., pg. 75.

3463 Ibid., pg. 75.

3464 Ibid., pg. 75.

3465 Ibid., pgs. 75-76.

3466 Ibid., pg. 76.

3467 *Voting on Thin Ice Report* (2017).

3468 Ibid.

3469 Bernal E. Smith, II, "The 2015 Memphis Municipal Election in seven lessons," *Tri-State Defender* (Memphis, TN), October 15-21, 2015.

3470 Ibid.

3471 Steve Steffens, "Madame Mayor?" *Memphis Flyer,* September 17-23, 2015.

3472 Ibid.

3473 Ibid.

3474 Ibid.

3475 Linda A. Moore, "City, county short on female leaders," *Commercial Appeal* (Memphis, TN), November 29, 2015.

3476 Ibid.

3477 Ibid.

3478 Ibid.

3479 Ibid.

3480 Ibid.

3481 Ibid.

3482 Ibid.

3483 Ibid.

3484 Ibid.

3485 Karanja A. Ajanaku, "Candidate Clinton campaigns at Lemoyne-Owen," *Tri-State Defender* (Memphis, TN), November 26-December 2, 2015.

3486 Ibid.

3487 Tom Charlier, "Mayor wants to de-annex two more areas," *Commercial Appeal* (Memphis, TN), July 10, 2018.

3488 Jamie Munks, "Memphis city council de-annexes two more areas on eastern edge," *Commercial Appeal* (Memphis, TN), October 16, 2018.

3489 Yolanda Jones and Ryan Poe, "Most qualified," *Commercial Appeal* (Memphis, TN), August 9, 2016.

3490 "Memphis hits 161 homicides so far this year, mayor says the count is more than statistic," *WREG News Channel 3* (Memphis, TN), September 15, 2016.

3491 Ryan Poe, "Has Strickland hired enough women? 5 of 17 hires criticized as 'long ways from equity'" *Commercial Appeal* (Memphis, TN), December 19, 2015.

3492 Ryan Poe, "City Council approves 13 Strickland appointments," *Commercial Appeal* (Memphis, TN), January 6, 2016.

3493 Maya Smith, "Strickland's Team," *Memphis Magazine,* September 3, 2018.

3494 Editorial, "Strickland kept diversity pledge," *Commercial Appeal* (Memphis, TN), December 20, 2015.

3495 Jamel Major, "Council amendment would close loophole in city's pension plan," *WMC Action News 5* (Memphis, TN), 2009.

3496 Andrew Douglas, "Ken Moody: On the Record," *WMC Action News 5* (Memphis, TN), July 28, 2009.

3497 Ryan Poe, "Communications office will handle public records," *Commercial Appeal* (Memphis, TN), December 9, 2015.

3498 Carol Chumney, "City's new media policy restrains free speech," *Commercial Appeal* (Memphis, TN), August 14, 2016.

3499 Jackson Baker, "A Brunch with Mayor-Elect Jim Strickland," *Memphis Magazine,* December 7, 2015.

3500 "Decommissioned," *Commercial Appeal* (Memphis, TN), January 1, 2016; Michelle Corbet, "Strickland paying C-Suite $815,000, cutting Music Commission, 10 jobs," *Memphis Business Journal,* December 24, 2015.

3501 *Lucille Catron, et. al v. City of Memphis, et. al,* No. 2:16-cv-02661-JDT-dkv, ECF 50 (January 6, 2017).

3502 Daniel Connolly, "Shootings, stampede cited as fee gets OK," *Commercial Appeal* (Memphis, TN), May 9, 2019.

3503 Ibid.

3504 Bill Dries, "Paying Beale Street Security Costs Raises Lease Questions," *Memphis Daily News* (October 3, 2017).

3505 "*Beale Street Blues,*" W.C. Handy (1917).

3506 Tom Charlier, "Nearly $100 million Fairgrounds complex planned," *Commercial Appeal* (Memphis, TN), July 11, 2018.

3507 Ibid.

3508 Tonyaa Weathersbee, "Will Fairgrounds be a boom to Orange Mound," *Commercial Appeal* (Memphis, TN), July 13, 2018.

3509 "Graceland on the Move," *Celebretainment,* April 10, 2019.

3510 Ibid.

3511 Meagan Nicols, "Elvis Presley Enterprises' owner looks to fund Memphis mayoral candidate," *Memphis Business Journal,* November 8, 2018.

3512 Samuel Hardiman, "Tennessee Supreme Court to hear Elvis Presley Enterprises appeal in lawsuit against Grizzlies," *Commercial Appeal* (Memphis, TN), July 31, 2020; *Elvis Presley Enterprises, Inc. v. City of Memphis, etal,* No. W2019-00299-COA-R3-CV (Tenn. App. 2019).

3513 Eryn Taylor, "Where was Mayor Strickland during protests?" *WREG News Channel 3* (Memphis, TN), July 11, 2016.

3514 Jody Callahan, Katie Freeland contributed, "Marchers shut down I-40 bridge at Memphis during Black Lives Matter rally," *Commercial Appeal* (Memphis, TN), July 11, 2016.

3515 "Rallings praised for handling of BLM protest; Strickland criticized," *WMC Action News 5* (Memphis, TN), July 11, 2016.

3516 Kristen Leigh, "Crowd clashes with Memphis mayor at Black Lives Matter meeting," *Fox 13 Memphis News* (Memphis, TN), July 11, 2016.

3517 Tonyaa Weathersbee, "Some of that $200,000 to guard the mayor could fix real issues," *Commercial Appeal* (Memphis, TN), June 27, 2018.

3518 Ibid.

3519 Daniel Connolly, "ACLU 'blacklist' lawsuit against city of Memphis approaches trial," *Commercial Appeal* (Memphis, TN), July 15, 2018.

3520 Ibid.

3521 Ibid.

3522 *ACLU of Tennessee, Inc. v. City of Memphis,* No. 2:17-cv-2120-JPM-egb, ECF 151, (W.D. Tenn. October 26, 2018.), "*Opinion and Order.*"

3523 Danielle Allen, "Memphis murder rate appears to be highest in decades," *WKRN. com* (Memphis, TN), April 16, 2017.

3524 Karanja A. Ajanaku, "What Dr. Herenton said: Declaration, backlash, and next step? Mayor's prayer breakfast has a lot of talk;

will action follow?" *Tri-State Defender* (Memphis, TN), January 5, 2017.

3525 Bill Dries, "Strickland, Herenton seek Larger, More Focused Volunteerism Efforts," *Memphis Daily News,* January 4, 2017.

3526 Tonyaa Weathersbee, "Angela Rye's speech wasn't an attack. It was a wake-up call," *Commercial Appeal* (Memphis, TN), March 6, 2018.

3527 Wendi C. Thomas, "The meeting with Memphis activists that fueled Angela Rye's fire," *MLK50.com,* February 24, 2018.

3528 Ibid.

3529 Jessica Holley, Kendall Downing and Janice Broach, "Willie Herenton will run for Memphis Mayor in 2019," *WMC Action News 5* (Memphis, TN), April 5, 2018; Ryan Poe, "Herenton to run for mayor of Memphis," *Commercial Appeal,* April 6, 2018.

3530 Jennifer Pignolet, "Two schools run by former Memphis mayor Willie Herenton to close," *Commercial Appeal* (Memphis, TN), April 19, 2018.

3531 Ibid.

3532 Ryan Poe, "The 9:01: Strickland sacks Inland and Collierville preps for The Purge: Deer Edition," *Commercial Appeal* (Memphis, TN), July 20, 2018.

3533 Ibid.

3534 Ryan Poe, "Herenton to run for mayor of Memphis," *Commercial Appeal* (Memphis, TN), April 6, 2018.

3535 Ibid.

3536 Jessica Holley, Kendall Downing and Janice Broach, "Willie Herenton will run for Memphis Mayor in 2019," *WMC Action News 5* (Memphis, TN), April 5, 2018.

3537 Yolanda Jones, "FBI: Memphis ranks as 3rd most violent big city in U.S.," *Daily Memphian,* October 9, 2018; "Mayor-elect talks crime prevention, Toney Armstrong's future," *WMC Action News 5* (Memphis, TN), October 22, 2015; Kelsey Ott and Eryn Taylor, "Collins, Strickland, Wharton advocate for better Memphis in debate," *WREG News Channel 3* (Memphis, TN), September 15, 2015. Although the City-County's mayoral appointed Crime Commission announced crime down in the

first half of 2018, property crimes increased in the same time-period. Bill Dries, "Violent Crime Drops by Crime Commission Numbers, Property Crimes Up," *Daily News* (Memphis, TN), July 20, 2018.

3538 Ted Evanoff, "Memphis: High crime, high taxes, too few police," *Commercial Appeal* (Memphis, TN), August 13, 2017.

3539 Brandon Richard, "FBI Data: Overall violent crime down in Memphis, but homicides, assaults up," *WMC Action News 5,* (Memphis, TN), October 5, 2019.

3540 Yolanda Jones, "FBI: Memphis ranks as 3rd most violent big city in U.S.," *Daily Memphian,* October 9, 2018.

3541 "Herenton: 'Very serious' about 2019 mayor bid," *WMC Action News 5* (Memphis, TN), July 19, 2018.

3542 https://www.facebook.com/groups/ MEMPHISPOTHOLES/

3543 Ted Evanoff, "Richard Smith is a sign of the changing of the guard," *Commercial Appeal* (Memphis, TN), May 6, 2018; Ted Evanoff, "Smith says EDGE overhaul can spur Memphis economy," *Commercial Appeal,* April 29, 2018.

3544 Ted Evanoff, "Evanoff: Looking at Lee Harris' populist vision from a pragmatist's viewpoint," *Commercial Appeal* (Memphis, TN), August 19, 2018.

3545 Tonyaa Weathersbee, "Angela Rye's speech wasn't an attack. It was a wake-up call," *Commercial Appeal* (Memphis, TN), March 6, 2018.

3546 Jacob Steimer, "Disrupt then Unify: Behind Richard Smith's strategy to push and pull Memphis forward," *Memphis Business Journal,* January 3, 2020.

3547 Tonyaa Weathersbee, "Weathersbee: Deep poverty and other problems plague Memphis. It should expect to be called out on it," *Commercial Appeal* (Memphis, TN), February 27, 2018.

3548 Ibid.

3549 Ted Evanoff, "'Memphis has lost focus', says Council chairman," *Commercial Appeal* (Memphis, TN), May 13, 2018; Ted Evanoff, "Smith says EDGE overhaul can spur Memphis economy," *Commercial Appeal,* April 29, 2018.

3550 Ted Evanoff, "The tale of 2 cities," *Commercial Appeal* (Memphis, TN), May 20, 2018; Ted Evanoff, "Smith says EDGE overhaul can spur Memphis economy," *Commercial Appeal*, April 29, 2018.

3551 Ted Evanoff, "The tale of 2 cities," *Commercial Appeal* (Memphis, TN), May 20, 2018.

3552 Ted Evanoff, "Smith says EDGE overhaul can spur Memphis economy," *Commercial Appeal* (Memphis, TN), April 29, 2018.

3553 Ibid.

3554 Joe Kent, Guest columnist, "Memphis economy needs a better EDGE plan in place," *Commercial Appeal* (Memphis, TN), June 9, 2018.

3555 Ibid.

3556 Tonyaa Weathersbee, "How to stop people from leaving Memphis," *Commercial Appeal* (Memphis, TN), July 9, 2018.

3557 Ibid.

3558 https://www.weforum.org/agenda/2018/02/these-are-the-best-countries-and-cities-for-attracting-and-developing-talent/ ; https://www.pwc.com/gx/en/about/diversity/international womensday/the-female-millennial.html

3559 https://www.newsweek.com/are-millennials-putting-end-gender-differences-715922

3560 Daniel Connolly, "Memphis People's Convention endorses Sawyer for mayor," *Commercial Appeal* (Memphis, TN), June 10, 2019.

3561 Tonyaa Weathersbee, "Strickland shouldn't shun People's Convention," *Commercial Appeal* (Memphis, TN), June 2, 2019.

3562 Ibid.

3563 Micaela A. Watts, "People's Convention 2019: What you need to know," *Commercial Appeal* (Memphis, TN), June 2, 2019.

3564 Ibid.

3565 Kody Leibowitz, "Did Mayor Jim Strickland accomplish his short-term goal for hiring more police officers?" *Fox 13 Memphis News,* Updated October 1, 2019.

3566 Ibid.

3567 Yolanda Jones, "City's violent crime rate continues decline but homicide count rises," *Daily Memphian,* January 17, 2020.

3568 Strickland for mayor website, 2019.

3569 Bill Dries, "Strickland, Herenton go after each other in mayor's race," *Daily Memphian,* July 30, 2019.

3570 Ibid.

3571 Editorial, "Memphis mayoral election Endorsement—The CA backs Strickland in race," *Commercial Appeal* (Memphis, TN), September 22, 2019.

3572 Ibid.

3573 Ibid.

3574 Samuel Hardiman, "After review, City of Memphis finds more errors, additional spend in MWBE data," *Memphis Business Journal,* May 6, 2019; Katherine Burgess, "MWBE: City of Memphis used faulty data to tout growth in spending with minority-women-owned businesses," *Commercial Appeal* (Memphis, TN), March 14, 2019.

3575 Editorial Board, "Memphis Mayoral Election Endorsement- the CA backs Strickland in race," *Commercial Appeal* (Memphis, TN), September 22, 2019.

3576 Ibid.

3577 Ibid.

3578 David Royer, "Memphis' magazine pulls issue, apologizes after cover art controversy," *WREG News Channel 3,* (Memphis, TN), September 1, 2019.

3579 Ibid.

3580 Ibid.

3581 Ibid.

3582 Editorial Board, "Memphis Mayoral Election Endorsement- the CA backs Strickland in race," *Commercial Appeal* (Memphis, TN), September 22, 2019.

3583 "2019 Memphis mayoral election," *Wikipedia.*

3584 Ibid.

3585 Ibid.

3586 Ibid.

3587 Ibid.

3588 Luke Jones, "Take 'em down 901 activist takes aim at mayor on anniversary of statue removals," *WREG News Channel 3,* (Memphis, TN), December 20, 2018.

3589 Bill Dries, "Strickland administration pushes for police force of 2,800, end of bid to kill residency referendum," *Daily Memphian,* July 31, 2020.

3590 Ibid.

3591 Bill Dries, "Residency issue removed from November ballot, goal of 2,800 police force delayed," *Daily Memphian,* August 5, 2020.

3592 Corinne S. Kennedy, "After a dip in violent crime early in the year, murder, aggravated assault increase during COVID-19," *Commercial Appeal* (Memphis, TN), July 17, 2020.

3593 Stacy Jacobson, "Memphis reports 323 homicides so far in 2020, a record," *WREG News Channel 3* (Memphis, TN), December 21, 2020; Yolanda Jones, "Memphis hits homicide record as officers grapple with rise," *Daily Memphian,* September 20, 2020.

3594 Samuel Hardiman, "'Memphis to restore firefighter and police benefits cut in 2014. It will cost hundreds of millions," *Commercial Appeal* (Memphis, TN), November 1, 2020.

3595 Yolanda Jones and Bill Dries, "Memphis names first female police chief," *Daily Memphian*, April 19, 2021.

3596 Jordan Robertson and David Kocieniewski, "The Computer Voting Revolution is Already Crappy, Buggy, and Obsolete," *Bloomberg Businessweek,* September 29, 2016.

3597 Facts in this section are set forth in the *Voting on Thin Ice Report* (and exhibits), as well as in the *Shelby Advocates for Valid Elections, etal v. Hargett, etal,* No. 19-1399, U.S. Supreme Court, June 9, 2020, *"Petition for Writ of Certiorari"* (hereinafter *"Petition")."*

3598 *Petition*, pg. 16, ECF 104, 1256, No. 205.

3599 Ibid., No. 206.

3600 *Petition*, pg. 7, ECF 104, 1244, No. 166.

3601 Ibid.

3602 Ibid.

3603 Sam Lubell, "To Register Doubts, Press Here," *New York Times,* May 15, 2003.

3604 *Shelby Advocates for Valid Elections, etal v. Hargett, etal,* No. 2:18-cv-02706-TLR-dkv, ECF 1. (W.D. Tenn). An original plaintiff, Yahweh was dropped as a plaintiff, but continued his life-long advocacy for election reforms.

3605 Report of the Select Committee on Intelligence United States Senate on Russian Active Measures Campaigns and Interference in the 2016 U.S. Election, pg. 8, 12, July 25, 2019.

3606 Ibid. , pg. 10.

3607 Ibid., pg. 36.

3608 Ibid., pg. 37

3609 Ibid., pg. 37.

3610 Ibid., pg. 41.

3611 Ibid., pg. 41.

3612 Ibid.

3613 Ibid., pg. 42, U.

3614 Ibid.

3615 Ibid.

3616 Ibid., pg. 40-41.

3617 Ibid., pg. 42.

3618 Ibid.

3619 Ibid., pg. 59.

3620 Ibid., pg. 59.

3621 Minority View of Senator Wyden, pg. 2, July 29, 2019.

3622 Ibid., pgs 2-3.

3623 Ibid. ,pgs. 4-5.

3624 Ibid., pg. 4.

3625 Ibid., pg. 5.

3626 Ibid., pg. 5.

3627 Ibid., pg. 5.

3628 *SAVE, etal v. Hargett,* No. 2:18-cv-02706-TLP-dkv, (W.D. Tenn. September 13, 2019.)

3629 Amici Curiae Brief filed by 13 Election Officials, No. 19-6142, No. 26 (Sixth Circuit), (November 7, 2019); Amicus Brief filed by National Election Defense Coalition, U.S. Technology Policy Committee of Association for Computing Machinery, No. 19-6142, No. 30 (Sixth Circuit) (November 8, 2019).

3630 Ibid.

3631 *SAVE, etal v. Hargett,* 947 F. 3d 977 (6th Cir. 2020).

3632 *SAVE, etal v. Hargett,* No. 19-1399 (U.S. Supreme Court June 9, 2020).

3633 Brief of Amici Curiae of Individual Election Security Experts, No. 19-1399 (July 22, 2020). A special thanks to Susan Greenhalgh with Free the Speech People.

3634 *Curling v. Kemp,* No. 17-cv-02989-AT, ECF 579, (N.D. Ga.), *"Order,"* pg. 152.

3635 *SAVE, etal v. Hargett,* 947 F. 3d 977 (6th Cir. 2020).

3636 *Curling v. Kemp,* 334 F. Supp. 3d 1303, 1310 (N.D. Ga. 2018).

3637 Ibid.

3638 Ibid.

3639 Tenn. Code Ann. 2-20-101.

3640 *Stewart v. Blackwell,* 473 F. 3d 692 (6th Cir. 2007).

3641 *SAVE, etal v. Hargett,* 947 F. 3d 977 (6th Cir. 2020).

3642 Ibid.

3643 *Tenn. Rep. Party v. SEC,* 863 F. 3d 507, 517 (6th Cir. 2017).

3644 There have been queens and empresses who have been successful leaders of many countries over the years in our world history, including in England, Egypt, Georgia, Spain, Russia, and Japan; female Prime Ministers of India, Israel, Pakistan, United Kingdom, China, Portugal, Norway, Finland, Belgium, Denmark; Chancellor of Germany; and even presidents, such as those of Argentina, Iceland, Philippines, Ireland, Liberia, Bolivia, Moldova, Kosovo, Greece, Slovakia, Ethiopia, and South Korea. In fact over seventy countries have had a woman leader at one time or the other. Even "Wisdom" in the Bible is feminine.

3645 Joey Garrison, "Special report: Inside the final 34 days before Megan Barry resigned," *Tennessean,* (Nashville, TN), April 7, 2018.

3646 David Plazas, "Editorial board endorses Megan Barry for Nashville mayor," *Tennessean* (Nashville, TN), July 12, 2015.

3647 Editorial, "Shelby County election's good pink wave," *Commercial Appeal* (Memphis, TN), August 4, 2018.

3648 Ibid.

3649 Ibid.

3650 Lee Harris, "Promotion without Progress," Book Review, *Univ. of Mem. L. Review,* Vol. 48, No. 2 (Winter 2017).

3651 Otis Sanford, *From Boss Crump to King Willie, How Race Changed Memphis Politics* (Knoxville U.T. Press 2017).

3652 Otis Sanford, "Sanford: Tennessee has a man problem in politics, public policy," *Daily Memphian,* February 20, 2020.

3653 Ibid.

3654 Ibid.

3655 Otis Sanford, "Biden's bet on Harris is backed by the numbers," *Daily Memphian,* August 12, 2020.

3656 Natalie Allison, "Proportion of women in TN legislature low," *Commercial Appeal* (Memphis, TN), December 7, 2020.

3657 Ibid.

3658 Ibid.

About the Author

Carol Chumney graduated from White Station High School in 1979 and was a National Merit Semi-Finalist, Editor of the *Scroll* student newspaper, and President of Astra service club. She earned her B.A. in History with Honors and Economics, *magna cum laude*, from the University of Memphis as a Presidential Scholar in 1983. She was elected President of the University of Memphis Student Government Association. Chumney received her Juris Doctorate from the University of Memphis Cecil C. Humphreys School of Law as a Herff Law Scholar in 1986. She was Editor-in-Chief of the University of Memphis Law Review. Upon graduation, she clerked for Judge Harry Wellford on the Sixth Circuit Court of Appeals. She also served as President of the Memphis Federal Bar Association in 1991.

Carol Chumney earned a partnership at Glankler Brown law firm where she practiced for 16 years. She also was an elected Tennessee State Representative for 13 years, including serving as House Majority Whip and Chair of the House Children & Family Affairs Committee. Chumney was elected and served for 4 years on the Memphis City Council, and chaired the Public Safety & Homeland Security, O & M Budget, MLGW, Public Service & Neighborhood and Healthcare committees. Her law firm Carol Chumney Law PLLC has litigated cases in federal and state courts.

Chumney was previously appointed to serve on the Tennessee Supreme Court Commissions on foster care, and on gender fairness. She served as an Adjunct professor in the University of Memphis Department of Political Science in 2008. She has sat as a special judge in the Shelby County General Sessions civil and criminal courts. She was appointed by the Shelby County Mayor to serve as a Deputy Divorce Referee in 2018. She was recently counsel for the election security lawsuit, *Shelby Advocates for Valid Elections, et al v. Hargett, etal,* 947 F. 3d 977 (6th Cir. 2020), cert. denied, S.Ct. 2020 WL 5882333 (2020).

Dear Reader:

Thank you for reading The Arena: One Woman's Story!

I would appreciate your honest feedback. Please email me at *carol@carolchumneylaw.com*, subscribe to my blog available on *www.carolchumney.com*, and leave a review online!

And thanks again to so many who have helped me fight the battles for truth and justice over the years! While some have departed this life already, their contributions are truly remembered. There are many who generously gave their time, money and support. It means so much that you believe in me! Thank you all from the bottom of my heart!

And a special thanks to my mother who was my uncompensated campaign treasurer, my father who worked the polls for me, my sisters, Mary and Gail, and so many other supportive family members, including grandparents, uncles, aunts, in-laws, nieces, nephews, and cousins!

Carol Chumney

CPSIA information can be obtained
at www.ICGtesting.com
Printed in the USA
JSHW050917181121
20562JS00001B/2

9 781735 342825